UNDERSTANDING WHITE COLLAR CRIME

D0861566

UNDERSTANDING WHITE COLLAR CRIME

Third Edition

J. Kelly Strader
Professor of Law
Southwestern Law School

 LexisNexis

ISBN: 978-1-4224-9604-6

Library of Congress Cataloging-in-Publication Data

Strader, J. Kelly.
    Understanding white collar crime / J. Kelly Strader. -- 3rd ed.
        p. cm.
    Includes index.
    ISBN 978-1-4224-9604-6
    1. White collar crimes--United States. I. Title.
        KF9350.S77 2011
        345.73'0268--dc23

2011036921

NOTE TO USERS

To ensure that you are using the latest materials available in this area, please be sure to periodically check the LexisNexis Law School web site for downloadable updates and supplements at www.lexisnexis.com/lawschool.

Editorial Offices
121 Chanlon Rd., New Providence, NJ 07974 (908) 464-6800
201 Mission St., San Francisco, CA 94105-1831 (415) 908-3200
www.lexisnexis.com

MATTHEW◆BENDER

Dedication

For Hal

Preface

Overview of the Text

This book is primarily intended for students in White Collar Crime, Federal Criminal Law, and Corporate Crime classes. The text should also prove useful to practitioners, judges, law clerks, and scholars seeking an introduction to and an overview of the law in this area.

The bulk of this text provides a substantive overview of the principal federal white collar crimes. The book also covers the basic principles of criminal law and criminal procedure necessary to an understanding of white collar crime, and includes chapters on the process of white collar criminal investigations and prosecutions. Finally, the book covers remedies and penalties, including sentencing and forfeitures.

White collar crime is primarily based upon a complex set of statutes. This book provides the texts of the relevant statutes, along with analyses of the statutes' elements and requirements. Because many of these statutes are open to varying interpretations, the book also extensively discusses the main cases interpreting the statutes, including a large number of United States Supreme Court cases. Finally, the book discusses the significant policy issues that arise in white collar investigations and prosecutions, such as enforcement barriers and prosecutorial discretion.

Because of the complexity of the subject, a text such as this necessarily condenses a great deal of information. In addition, readers should note that this area of the law is changing rapidly. For a more extensive discussion of any particular subject, the reader may wish to refer to such sources as *White Collar Crime: Business and Regulatory Offenses* (Otto Obermaier & Robert Morvillo, eds.) (updated annually), and the *Annual Survey of White Collar Crime*, published by the American Criminal Law Review. These sources are also referred to throughout this text.

A Special Request

Any book of this length is bound to contain errors. Those errors are entirely my responsibility, and I would like to know about all of them. I welcome any comments you may have. Please do not hesitate to call ((213) 738-6753), e-mail (kstrader@swlaw.edu), or write (Southwestern Law School, 3050 Wilshire Boulevard, Los Angeles, CA 90010).

Acknowledgments

This book would not have been possible without the generous support of the Southwestern Law School Faculty Development Program. In addition, a number of my colleagues — Catherine Carpenter, Mark Cammack, Eileen Gauna, Warren Grimes, and Karen Smith — gave generously of their time and read various of the book's chapters. I am forever in their debt. I have also received enormous help from my many research assistants. Too many pitched in to name them all, but thanks to Steven Bercovitch, Elizabeth Hall, Matthew Newman, Whitney Nonnette, and, especially, research assistant extraordinaire Christopher DeClue. And thanks to Southwestern Faculty Support Supervisor Angelique Porter and the members of the Faculty Support staff for all their help. Thanks to my mentors at Morvillo, Abramowitz, Grand, Iason, Anello, and Bohrer for inspiring me to undertake this career. Finally, thanks to all of you who have used this book and have given me such helpful feedback over the years. I am very grateful.

On a personal note, I would like to thank my partner, Hal, our children, Eleanor and Sam, and their moms, Helen and Marian, for all their love and support.

TABLE OF CONTENTS

TABLE OF CONTENTS

TABLE OF CONTENTS

TABLE OF CONTENTS

TABLE OF CONTENTS

TABLE OF CONTENTS

TABLE OF CONTENTS

TABLE OF CONTENTS

TABLE OF CONTENTS

TABLE OF CONTENTS

TABLE OF CONTENTS

TABLE OF CONTENTS

TABLE OF CONTENTS

TABLE OF CONTENTS

TABLE OF CONTENTS

TABLE OF CONTENTS

TABLE OF CONTENTS

Chapter 1

INTRODUCTION TO WHITE COLLAR CRIME

§ 1.01 THE DEFINITION OF "WHITE COLLAR CRIME"

Criminologist and sociologist Edwin Sutherland first popularized the term "white collar crime" in 1939. He defined a white collar crime as one "committed by a person of respectability and high social status in the course of his occupation." Sutherland also included crimes committed by corporations and other legal entities within his definition.[1]

Sutherland's study of white collar crime was prompted by the view that criminology had incorrectly focused on social and economic determinants of crime, such as family background and level of wealth. According to Sutherland's view, crime is committed by persons with widely divergent socio-economic backgrounds at all levels of society. In particular, according to Sutherland, crime is often committed by persons operating through large and powerful organizations. White collar crime, Sutherland concluded, has a greatly-underestimated impact upon our society.

Sutherland's definition is now somewhat outdated for students of criminal law. As white collar crime began to capture the attention of prosecutors and the public in the latter part of the twentieth century,[2] the term came to have definitions quite different from the one Sutherland used. Indeed, studies have shown that crimes we generally consider "white collar," such as securities fraud and tax fraud, are committed not just by persons of "high social status" but by people of divergent backgrounds.[3] Thus, the term "white collar crime" is a misnomer. Nonetheless, it continues in widespread use. This is probably so because "white collar crime"

---

[1] Edwin H. Sutherland, White Collar Crime: The Uncut Version 7 (1985). Sutherland used the term in a 1939 speech, entitled "The White-Collar Criminal," that he gave to a joint meeting of the American Sociological Society and the American Economic Association. For a further discussion of the definition of "white collar crime," see Stuart P. Green, *The Concept of White Collar Crime in Law and Legal Theory*, 8 Buff. Crim. L. Rev. 1 (2004); J. Kelly Strader, *The Judicial Politics of White Collar Crime*, 50 Hastings L. J. 1199, 1204–14 (1999).

[2] *See* William J. Genego, *The New Adversary*, 54 Brook. L. Rev. 781, 787 (1988) ("In the mid-1970s federal prosecutors became increasingly interested in white collar offenses."); Peter J. Henning, *Testing the Limits of Investigating and Prosecuting White Collar Crime: How Far Will the Courts Allow Prosecutors to Go?*, 54 U. Pitt. L. Rev. 405, 408 (1993) ("Beginning in the mid-1970s . . . the federal government began targeting white collar crime as a high-priority prosecutorial area.").

[3] *See* John Braithwaite, *Crime and the Average American*, 27 Law & Soc'y Rev. 215, 216–24 (1993) (reviewing David Weisburd et al., Crimes of the Middle Classes: White-Collar Offenders in the Federal Courts (1991) ("white collar" defendants are much like non-white collar defendants)).

provides a convenient moniker for distinguishing such crime in the public mind from "common" or "street" crime.

As an alternative to the socio-economic focus, many definitions of "white collar crime" instead are based on the manner in which the crime is committed. In 1981, the United States Department of Justice described white collar crime as

> [n]onviolent crime for financial gain committed by means of deception by persons whose occupational status is entrepreneurial, professional or semi-professional and utilizing their special occupational skills and opportunities; also, nonviolent crime for financial gain utilizing deception and committed by anyone having special technical and professional knowledge of business and government, irrespective of the person's occupation.[4]

This definition focuses on the use of deception as the criminal means. The defendant, however, still must be at least "semi-professional" or have "special technical and professional knowledge." Thus, in some ways, this definition is still too narrow. Not all defendants in white collar cases have professional or semi-professional status, nor do they necessarily possess special skills. A defendant in a tax fraud or government benefits case, for example, might have neither of these characteristics.

Perhaps a better way to look at white collar crime is to focus on the ways that practitioners and judges distinguish white collar crime from common or street crime. A "white collar" prosecutor or defense attorney, for example, would more likely define "white collar crime" as crime that does *not*:

(a)   necessarily involve force against a person or property;

(b)   directly relate to the possession, sale, or distribution of narcotics;

(c)   directly relate to organized crime activities;

(d)   directly relate to national policy-driven crimes such as immigration and civil rights; or

(e)   directly involve "vice crimes."

It is important to note that it is not always possible to tell whether an offense is a "white collar" offense simply by looking at the statute. Sometimes the criminal statute itself will render almost all crimes charged under that statute "white collar" by definition. For example, charges brought under the securities fraud and antitrust criminal statutes are generally "white collar" crimes. On the other hand, under some criminal statutes charges can be brought for both white collar and non-white collar offenses depending on the nature of the defendant's conduct. For example, conspiracy, extortion, and obstruction of justice charges are brought in both white collar and non-white collar cases.

The most common and notable white collar crimes are covered in the chapters that follow. These include crimes committed both in corporate and governmental settings, and crimes committed by individuals.

---

[4] Bureau of Justice Statistics, United States Department of Justice, Dictionary of Criminal Justice Data Terminology 215 (2d ed. 1981).

In the context of the debate about white collar criminalization, it is significant that not all court cases relating to white collar crime are criminal cases. As discussed more fully below, some statutes, such as the securities laws, the environmental laws, and the federal racketeering ("RICO") statute, provide for both civil and criminal liability. In most instances, the statutory interpretations that courts provide in the civil cases will also control in criminal cases brought under those statutes. Therefore, an understanding of the leading civil cases interpreting those statutes is important in determining potential criminal liability.

White collar criminal offenses are, of course, defined by both state and federal law. This text will focus on federal law, and make comparisons to state law where helpful. This coverage is representative of the range of federal — and equivalent state — white collar criminal statutes, but cannot be comprehensive given the hundreds of such statutes in existence.

§ 1.02 RECURRING ISSUES IN WHITE COLLAR INVESTIGATIONS AND PROSECUTIONS

[A] The Harm Caused by White Collar Crime

Prosecutors have powerful reasons to target white collar criminals. Most important, white collar crime causes huge financial losses to federal, state, and local governments, to private organizations, and to individuals. As early as 1988, the United States Supreme Court characterized white collar crime as "one of the most serious problems confronting law enforcement authorities."[5]

Recurring high profile white collar crimes are an ongoing reality. In recent decades, major corporations and financial institutions have failed due to fraudulent activities, resulting in widespread harm to our economy.[6] Major political figures have been charged with engaging in corrupt activities.[7] And high profile public figures have been accused of insider trading and other fraudulent activities.[8]

---

[5] Braswell v. United States, 487 U.S. 99, 115 (1988).

[6] For example, the 1990s the savings and loan scandals caused major harm. *See, e.g.*, United States v. BCCI Holdings (Lux.), S.A., 961 F. Supp. 287 (D.D.C. 1997). In the early 20th century, major companies, such as Enron, WorldCom, HealthSouth, Adelphia, and many others, failed at least in part because of fraudulent activities. *See, e.g.*, United States v. Arthur Andersen, LLP, 374 F.3d 281 (5th Cir. 2004). Largely in response to these scandals, Congress enacted the Sarbanes-Oxley Act, which was signed into law in July 2002. Provisions of the Act relevant to white collar crime are discussed in the materials below.

[7] These include, for example, the former governor of Illinois, the former Chief of Staff of the Vice President of the United States, and many others. *See, e.g.*, Douglas Belkin & David Kesmodel, *Illinois Outs Governor*, Wall St. J., Jan. 29, 2009, at A1; United States v. Libby, 432 F. Supp. 2d 26 (D.D.C. 2006).

[8] In the 1980s, fraud prosecutions were brought against Wall Street investor Ivan Boesky and "junk bond" king Michael Milken. *See* United States v. Milken, 759 F. Supp. 109 (S.D.N.Y. 1990); FMC Corp. v. Boesky, 852 F.2d 981, 982 n.1 (7th Cir. 1988). In more recent years, investment banker Bernard Madoff pled guilty and was sentenced to 150 years in prison in connection with a scheme that defrauded investors of billions of dollars. *See* Diana B. Henriques, *Claims Total Over 15,400 in Fraud by Madoff*, N.Y. Times, July 10, 2009, at B3. The co-founder of the Galleon group hedge fund was convicted in connection with a massive insider trading scheme, said to be the largest such scheme since Boesky's

Further, white collar criminals are using technology to commit sophisticated crimes in areas such as computer fraud and related financial crimes. These are just examples of the effects of white collar crime. Thousands of white collar crimes are committed each year, causing untold harm.

On the other hand, with many white collar crimes, both the identity of the victim and the nature and amount of the harm may be difficult to ascertain. For example, the Supreme Court has recognized that the over-enforcement of some white collar offenses may do more harm than good by inhibiting beneficial commercial activities.[9] The uncertain nature of the harm caused by many white collar offenses is another way in which these offenses are different from common crime cases, in which the identity of the victim and the nature and extent of the harm are usually readily apparent.

[B] Difficulties in Enforcing White Collar Statutes

One reason white collar crime remains widespread is that it is often very difficult to detect. Unlike street and common property crimes, white collar crimes are usually committed in the privacy of an office or home; usually there is no eyewitness, and only occasionally is there a "smoking gun." Instead, the government's proof is more likely to depend upon circumstantial evidence culled from a complex paper trail.

Moreover, the government's ability to identify white collar crimes is sometimes hampered by lack of resources and expertise. Particularly with respect to financial crimes committed by methods such as computer fraud and money laundering, prosecutors may require technical assistance from government entities other than the Department of Justice. Finally, the sheer scope of many white collar crimes places severe burdens on many United States Attorneys' offices. Investigations of complex white collar matters often last for years, and ensuing trials can easily last weeks or months. Further, the burden on federal resources has increased as the federal government has expanded its white collar efforts in recent decades to areas previously covered primarily by state and local law enforcement.

---

scheme. *See* Peter Lattman & Azam Ahmed, *Hardball Tactics Against Insider Trading: Prosecutors Hope Verdict Will Be a Deterrent to Others*, N.Y. Times, May 12, 2011, at B1. And celebrity white collar defendants, include actor Wesley Snipes and businesswoman and media figure Martha Stewart, were convicted of white collar crimes. *See* Rachel Lee Harris, *Snipes's Appeal Denied*, N.Y. Times, July 19, 2010, at C2; United States v. Stewart, 305 F. Supp. 2d 368 (S.D.N.Y. 2004). A number of other corporate executives have received lengthy prison sentences, some of them effective life sentences. For example, 80-year-old John Rigas, Adelphia's founder and former CEO, received a 15-year sentence; 64-year-old Bernard Ebbers, former WorldCom CEO, received a 25-year sentence. *See* Jane Sasseen & David Polek, *White-Collar Crime: Who Does Time?*, Bus. Wk., Feb. 6, 2006, at 60.

[9] United States v. United States Gypsum Co., 438 U.S. 422, 441 (1978). *See* Green, *supra* note 1, at 33.

§ 1.03   ISSUES OF FEDERALISM IN WHITE COLLAR PROSECUTIONS

[A]   Federal and State Overlap

Criminal law in the United States is primarily adopted and enforced at the state level; fewer than one in twenty criminal cases is brought at the federal level. Although most state cases involve street crimes, a large number are white collar cases. Indeed, most states have adopted a wide range of white collar criminal statutes, many of which parallel their federal counterparts.

In many instances, then, white collar criminal activity can be prosecuted at the state level, the federal level, or both.[10] Under the doctrine of dual sovereignty, the state government and the federal government may prosecute the same conduct, assuming that state or federal law provisions do not bar successive prosecutions in the particular instance. As a matter of policy, the Department of Justice will bring a federal action following a state action only in special circumstances. For example, a federal action may be initiated when there is a substantial federal interest in a second prosecution.[11]

The largest and most complex white collar cases, however, are usually brought at the federal level. This occurs for at least two reasons. First, many such cases involve wide-ranging activities that spread across state lines and that are, therefore, appropriate for federal prosecution. Second, many of the cases involve highly complex criminal schemes the investigation and prosecution of which require resources that most state law enforcement agencies simply do not possess.

Complementing the federal government's ability to fight white collar crime are the many specialized administrative divisions that investigate, and sometimes bring, the cases. For example, the Securities and Exchange Commission ("SEC"), which cannot itself bring a criminal case, possesses highly sophisticated resources for identifying and investigating instances of securities fraud. Where the fraud is believed to be criminal, the SEC can refer the matter to the United States Department of Justice for prosecution. In addition to or instead of a criminal case, the SEC can initiate a civil action, as can a private party. Similarly, the Internal Revenue Service and Customs Agency provide expertise and resources for investigating sophisticated money laundering schemes and other financial crimes. Thus, the federal government possesses significant resources that often enable it to investigate and prosecute complex white collar cases more effectively than state governments.

---

[10] Issues of successive prosecutions are discussed *infra* § 1.04.

[11] The United States Attorneys' Manual, *Dual and Successive Prosecution* 9-2.031 (2000) provides:

> This policy precludes the initiation or continuation of a federal prosecution, following a prior state or federal prosecution based on substantially the same act(s) or transaction(s) unless three substantive prerequisites are satisfied: first, the matter must involve a substantial federal interest; second, the prior prosecution must have left that interest demonstrably unvindicated; and third, applying the same test that is applicable to all federal prosecutions, the government must believe that the defendant's conduct constitutes a federal offense, and that the admissible evidence probably will be sufficient to obtain and sustain a conviction by an unbiased trier of fact.

[B] Federal Jurisdiction

A federal case cannot be brought in the absence of a constitutional basis for federal jurisdiction. Jurisdiction for most federal white collar crimes is based upon the Commerce Clause, which provides that Congress may "regulate Commerce with Foreign Nations, and among the several states, and with the Indian Tribes."[12] The United States Supreme Court has voided non-white collar federal statutes for lack of a jurisdictional basis. The Court found that the prohibited activities did not meet the requirement of "substantially affect[ing] interstate commerce."[13] White collar statutes and cases brought under those statutes, however, generally meet the interstate commerce requirement.[14] Other sources of federal jurisdiction include the postal power,[15] and the taxing power.[16]

[C] The Debate Concerning the Federalization of Crimes

White collar crime raises issues concerning the "overfederalization" of crime, a trend that has been the subject of substantial critical commentary.[17] Former Chief Justice William Rehnquist, for example, called upon Congress to restrict new federal criminal laws to five limited categories of "clearly defined and justified national interests."[18] And the American Bar Association Task Force on the Federalization of Criminal Law noted that "the Congressional appetite for new crimes regardless of their merit is not only misguided and ineffectual, but has serious adverse consequences, some of which have already occurred and some of which can be confidently predicted."[19]

Nonetheless, in a trend that began in the 1970s and 1980s and continues today, Congress has adopted laws, such as the federal racketeering ("RICO") and money-laundering statutes, criminalizing a broad range of activities that have traditionally

---

[12] U.S. Const., Art. I, § 8, cl. 3.

[13] See United States v. Lopez, 514 U.S. 549 (1995) (invalidating the Gun-Free School Zones Act of 1990 because of absence of effect on interstate commerce); United States v. Morrison, 529 U.S. 598 (2000) (holding that the Violence Against Women Act of 1994 was not a valid exercise of Congress's authority under the Commerce Clause because gender-motivated crimes of violence are not economic activity). But see Gonzales v. Raich, 545 U.S. 1 (2005) (rejecting argument that the Controlled Substances Act ("CSA") of 1970, as applied to personal medical marijuana use, was not a valid exercise of Congress's commerce authority because the production of marijuana, even for personal medical consumption, has a substantial effect on the national market for marijuana).

[14] See, e.g., United States v. Robertson, 514 U.S. 669 (1995). In Robertson, the Supreme Court overturned an appeals court decision that had invalidated a federal racketeering conviction on the ground that the criminal acts had not substantially affected interstate commerce, and reinstated the conviction.

[15] See Chapter 4, Mail and Wire Fraud, infra, for a discussion of the mail fraud statute.

[16] See Chapter 13, Tax Crimes, infra, for a discussion of the tax fraud statutes.

[17] See, e.g., Sara Sun Beale, The Many Faces of Overcriminalization: From Morals and Mattress Tags to Overfederalization, 54 Am. Univ. L. Rev. 747 (2005); Samuel W. Buell, The Upside of Overbreadth, 83 N.Y.U. L. Rev. 1491, 1497–98 (2008); Sanford H. Kadish, The Folly of Overfederalization, 46 Hastings L.J. 1247 (1995); Erik Luna, The Overcriminalization Phenomenon, 54 Am. U. L. Rev. 703 (2005); Stephen F. Smith, Proportionality and Federalization, 91 Va. L. Rev. 879 (2005).

[18] William H. Rehnquist, The 1998 Year-End Report of the Federal Judiciary, Jan. 1999, at 3.

[19] Report of the ABA Task Force on the Federalization of Criminal Law 1-2 (1998).

been the subject of state law. For example, a federal RICO case can be based not only upon such federal crimes as mail fraud, securities fraud, and bank fraud, but also upon the commission of state law crimes such as bribery and extortion.[20] Arguably, some federal statutes used in white collar cases reach activities that would more appropriately be handled at the state level. As discussed below, federal prosecutors have, for example, used the mail and wire fraud statutes in both ordinary fraud[21] and local political corruption[22] cases.

§ 1.04   PARALLEL CIVIL AND ADMINISTRATIVE PROCEEDINGS

Under statutes that provide for both civil and criminal penalties, the white collar defendant may face successive or concurrent proceedings. For many reasons, including the increased criminalization of regulatory matters, multiple proceedings in white collar cases have become ever more common.[23]

Parallel proceedings may be brought in a number of areas, including health care fraud, environmental crime, and securities fraud. In some areas, such as securities fraud, the government (in this instance, the Securities and Exchange Commission) or a private plaintiff may bring a civil action. As a general matter, the substantive legal rules in criminal cases also apply to civil cases; the reverse is also true.

The government has many reasons to institute civil or administrative proceedings in addition to or instead of criminal proceedings. These reasons include the ability to recoup money, to obtain injunctive relief, or to protect the public from further harm. The United States Attorneys' Manual now sets forth methods for coordinating criminal, civil, and administrative proceedings.[24]

The possibility of parallel proceedings raises important issues in two areas. First, prosecutors have much discretion in deciding whether to leave matters to civil and/or administrative proceedings, or whether to bring criminal charges. Second, multiple proceedings raise important tactical issues for both sides. A prosecutor, for example, may be unfavorably disposed to a civil proceeding that occurs prior to or concurrently with a criminal case. During the civil case, defense counsel may be able to learn the identity and gain the testimony of government witnesses.[25] Pre-trial and trial examination of government witnesses by defense counsel provides the defense with the prosecution's evidence well in advance of the criminal trial,

---

[20] *See* 18 U.S.C. § 1961(1). For an overview of the RICO statute's applicability to white collar cases, see Paul Vizcarrondo, Jr., *Racketeer Influenced and Corrupt Organizations (RICO)*, in White Collar Crime: Business and Regulatory Offenses §§ 11.01 *et seq.* (Otto G. Obermaier & Robert G. Morvillo eds., 2011).

[21] *See, e.g.*, United States v. Maze, 414 U.S. 395 (1974).

[22] *See, e.g.*, McNally v. United States, 483 U.S. 350 (1987).

[23] *See* Jeffrey T. Green, *The Thin Line Between Civil and Criminal Proceedings*, 9 No. 3 Bus. Crimes Bull. 1 (April 2002). These issues are discussed in more detail in Chapter 20, Civil Actions, Civil Penalties, and Parallel Proceedings, *infra*.

[24] U.S. Dep't of Justice, U.S. Attorneys' Manual, Ch. 1-12.

[25] Note that pre-trial depositions of witnesses are available to the defense in civil cases but not in criminal cases.

evidence that would not otherwise be available to the defense. Further, that testimony could be used to impeach the government witnesses at the criminal trial should the testimony be inconsistent.

Parallel proceedings also raise difficult issues for the defendant. For example, a defendant in a civil case will face the difficult choice of deciding to testify, thereby waiving the Fifth Amendment privilege against self-incrimination, or not to testify, and thereby allowing that failure to be used in favor of the government in the civil case.[26]

§ 1.05　ISSUES OF PROSECUTORIAL DISCRETION IN WHITE COLLAR CRIME

Perhaps more than in any other area of the criminal law, prosecutors in white collar matters have enormous discretion in deciding whether to bring a criminal case, and in deciding what charges to bring if they do decide to seek an indictment. This is true for several reasons. First, as noted above, in some circumstances civil and/or administrative penalties may be available. In that instance, the criminal prosecutor must decide whether civil and/or administrative remedies are sufficient in the context of the particular defendant's actions. If so, then the prosecutor might decide that criminal charges are unwarranted.

Second, where parallel state and federal criminal proceedings can be brought, a prosecutor must decide whether additional criminal punishment for the same conduct is appropriate. A state prosecutor may decide to bring a parallel proceeding if there is no statutory or case law prohibiting such a proceeding. In addition, some federal statutes prohibit a prosecution where the defendant has been tried to a verdict in state court. Also, the prosecutorial agency may have policies governing the issue. For example, the United States Department of Justice has a policy against a successive federal prosecution unless it is necessary to vindicate a substantial federal interest.

Finally, and most importantly, the nature of white collar statutes often cedes vast discretion to prosecutors. Many of these statutes are at once broad and vague.[27] This problem sometimes arises because many white collar crimes encompass economic regulations that some believe are best left to civil enforcement. Indeed, the United States Supreme Court has noted the difficulty in distinguishing criminal acts from those that fall within the "gray zone of socially acceptable and economically justifiable business conduct."[28] The phenomenon of extending the criminal law to areas for which it may not be suited is referred to as "overcriminalization."

---

[26] In a civil proceeding, the jury is permitted to draw an adverse inference from a defendant's invocation of the Fifth Amendment privilege against self-incrimination. Of course, no such use may be made in a criminal case. For issues relating to parallel proceedings, see Chapter 20, Civil Actions, Civil Penalties, and Parallel Proceedings, *infra.*

[27] *See, e.g.*, Skilling v. United States, 130 S. Ct. 2896 (2010) (limiting honest services statute to avoid holding the statute unconstitutionally vague) (discussed *infra*, § 4.05); H.J. Inc. v. Northwestern Bell Telephone Co., 492 U.S. 229, 255–56 (1989) (Scalia, J., concurring) (inviting a vagueness challenge to the federal racketeering statute) (discussed *infra* § 16.06[D][1]).

[28] *United States Gypsum Co.*, 438 U.S. at 441.

Because many white collar statutes are broad and vague, the task of defining the particular crime falls in the first instance to prosecutors, and ultimately to the courts.[29] Particularly during the 1980s, prosecutors began to read white collar statutes quite broadly, and the courts were required to attempt to set the boundaries of criminal liability.[30] As discussed more fully below in connection with the particular white collar crimes, students of white collar crime must remain aware of the often uncertain boundary of criminal liability under these statutes.[31]

§ 1.06   WHITE COLLAR CRIME AND THE GENERAL CRIMINAL LAW

White collar crimes are governed by the general principles of criminal law. Thus, with some exceptions, to gain a white collar conviction the government must prove (1) the required mental state, or *mens rea*, (2) the required physical component, or *actus reus* (generally either the defendant's *conduct*, such as entering into a conspiracy, or a *result* of the defendant's actions, such as causing damage to a protected computer), and (3) where the crime requires a result, that the defendant's acts *caused* the result. Some crimes also require proof of an attendant circumstance (for example, under the principal computer crimes statutes, that the affected computer was a "protected computer" as defined by the statute). Finally, general principles of liability for the acts of others ("vicarious liability") apply in white collar cases, as do certain principles relating to "inchoate," or incomplete, crimes.

[A]   Mens Rea

With the narrow exception of strict liability crimes discussed in Chapter 2, Corporate and Individual Liability, there is a presumption that the elements of any federal crime will include a mens rea requirement. Determining both the level of mens rea required, and whether that level of mens rea has been proven, are the central issues in white collar cases far more frequently than they are in common

---

[29] In theory, under the rule of lenity, courts are required to interpret an ambiguous criminal statute in the manner favorable to the defendant. As shown in cases discussed throughout this book, however, in practice the doctrine as currently applied does not produce consistent outcomes. For a critical examination of the rule of lenity, see Zachary Price, *The Rule of Lenity as a Rule of Structure*, 72 Fordham L. Rev. 885 (2004).

[30] *See* John C. Coffee, *Does "Unlawful" Mean "Criminal"? Reflections on the Disappearing Tort/Crime Distinction in American Law*, 71 B.U. L. Rev. 193, 198 (1991) ("The federal law of 'white collar' crime now seems to be judge-made to an unprecedented degree, with courts deciding on a case-by-case, retrospective basis whether conduct falls within often vaguely defined legislative prohibitions.").

[31] On May 19, 2010, Attorney General Holder issued a memorandum providing federal prosecutors with more flexibility in making charging decisions and sentencing recommendations than prosecutors had under the previous memorandum issued by former Attorney General John Ashcroft. The latter directed prosecutors to charge the most serious readily provable offense. The Holder Memorandum not only instructs prosecutors to "ordinarily charge 'the most serious offense that is consistent with the nature of the defendant's conduct, and that is likely to result in a sustainable conviction,'" but also requires prosecutors to consider the requirements of justice in the individual case. *See* Eric Tirschwell, *Holder Memorandum Presents New Opportunities for Defense Advocacy*, N.Y. L.J., June 16, 2010, at 4, col. 1.

crime cases. Indeed, with many white collar offenses, the mens rea finding will often distinguish criminal conduct from entirely lawful conduct. For example, giving a public official money with the intent that the official perform a quid pro quo in return amounts to the crime of bribery, while giving a public official money as a legitimate campaign contribution is no crime at all.[32] This section highlights these mens rea issues. More in-depth discussions of these principles are provided in connection with the individual crimes discussed in the chapters that follow.

As noted above, white collar cases often turn upon the factual determination of the defendant's mens rea at the time the defendant committed the actus reus of the crime.[33] In *United States v. United States Gypsum Co.*,[34] a criminal antitrust case, the United States Supreme Court reviewed the possible levels of mens rea. Relying upon the Model Penal Code, the Court noted that "the Code enumerates four possible levels of intent — purpose, knowledge, recklessness and negligence."[35]

These four types of mens rea are arranged from the most to the least difficult to prove.[36] "Purpose" requires a finding that the defendant had the conscious objective to commit the act or consciously desired the result proscribed by the crime. "Knowledge" requires a finding that the defendant knew the act or result would almost certainly occur. "Recklessness" requires a finding that the defendant was aware of a substantial and unjustifiable risk that the act or result would occur. Each of these types of mens rea is subjective, requiring that the fact finder conclude that the defendant personally possessed the required state of mind. The fourth level of mens rea — "negligence" — is an objective test judged by the reasonable person standard. "Negligence" requires a finding that the defendant should have known that the act or result would occur.

Finally, in some limited areas generally known as public welfare offenses, the particular statute may eliminate the general requirement that mens rea be proven in order to obtain a criminal conviction. Such offenses are deemed "strict liability" offenses.[37]

---

[32] *See* Green, *supra* note 1, at 33 ("white collar offenses frequently . . . make proof of mens rea so important that conduct performed without it not only fails to expose the actor to criminal liability, but may not be regarded as wrongful at all.").

[33] For further, in-depth discussion of these issues, see Joshua Dressler, Understanding Criminal Law §§ 10.01–07 (5th ed. 2009).

[34] 438 U.S. 422 (1978). In this case, the Court used the term "intent" as a synonym for mens rea. This use of the word "intent" can be confusing because "intent" — particularly in the case of "specific intent" — is also used to describe a *particular level* of mens rea. Indeed, courts in general are notoriously imprecise when using mens rea terminology. In many cases, it may be easier to determine the required level of mens rea by looking at the substantive definition the court uses rather than the label it employs.

[35] *Id.* at 444, *citing* the Model Penal Code ("MPC"). The American Law Institute adopted the MPC in 1962. The model code has been enormously influential, substantially affecting the revisions of the penal codes of 34 states. *See* Dressler, *supra* note 38, § 3.03.

[36] Model Penal Code § 2.02.

[37] Such offenses are discussed below in Chapter 2, Corporate and Individual Liability, *infra*, and Chapter 7, Environmental Crimes, *infra*.

[1]   Purpose, Knowledge, and Willful Blindness

The most litigated levels of mens rea in white collar criminal cases involve the concepts of "purpose" and "knowledge." For example, in *Gypsum*, the Court held that mens rea is an element that must be proven in a criminal antitrust case. The Court further found that the required level of mens rea, in cases where anticompetitive effects have been shown, is *knowledge* that the defendant's actions would have such effects.[38] In a footnote, the Court also implied that *purpose* to engage in actions with an anticompetitive effect would be required in cases where such an effect could not be proven.[39]

Another issue arises in connection with the meaning of the term "knowledge." In some limited areas, the Supreme Court has held that the government must prove that the defendant knew that the alleged acts violated the law.[40] This issue also arises under the terms "willfulness" and "specific intent," discussed below.

Finally, "knowledge" can be shown by proof that the defendant was willfully blind, that is, that the defendant deliberately avoided learning the truth.[41] This rule is also termed the "deliberate ignorance," "conscious avoidance," or the "ostrich" rule.[42] The United States Supreme Court has described the willful blindness doctrine thus:

> [T]he Courts of Appeals . . . all appear to agree on two basic requirements [for willful blindness]: (1) the defendant must subjectively believe that there is a high probability that a fact exists and (2) the defendant must take deliberate actions to avoid learning of that fact. We think these requirements give willful blindness an appropriately limited scope that surpasses recklessness and negligence. Under this formulation, a willfully blind defendant is one who takes deliberate actions to avoid confirming a high probability of wrongdoing and who can almost be said to have actually known the critical facts. By contrast, a reckless defendant is one who merely knows of a substantial and unjustified risk of such wrongdoing, see Model Penal Code § 2.02(2)(c), and a negligent defendant is one who should have known of a similar risk but, in fact, did not, see § 2.02(2)(d).[43]

---

[38]   438 U.S. at 444.

[39]   *Id.* at 444 & n.21. The trial judge had instructed the jury that it could *presume* mens rea if an anticompetitive effect were established. Because the jury was not required to *find* proof of mens rea, the defendant's conviction was reversed. *Id.*

[40]   *See* Liparota v. United States, 471 U.S. 419, 433 (1985). *See also* Richard M. Cooper, *Defining "Knowingly" in Federal Criminal Statutes: A Primer*, 9 No. 1 Bus. Crimes Bull. 1 (Feb. 2002).

[41]   In the most often-cited case articulating this rule, the Ninth Circuit in *United States v. Jewell* held that "'knowingly' in criminal statutes is not limited to positive knowledge, but includes the state of mind of one who does not possess positive knowledge only because he consciously avoided it. United States v. Jewell, 532 F.2d 697, 702 (9th Cir. 1976). A jury instruction noting that "knowledge" can be proven by showing conscious avoidance has often been termed a "*Jewell* instruction."

[42]   The Model Penal Code adopts the willful blindness rule in § 2.02(7) ("When knowledge of the existence of a particular fact is an element of an offense, such knowledge is established if a person is aware of a high probability of its existence, unless he actually believes that it does not exist."). For an application of the willful blindness rule to the law of conspiracy, see *infra* § 3.06[C].

[43]   Global-Tech Appliances, Inc. v. SEB S.A., 131 S. Ct. 2060 (2011) (citations omitted).

As seen in the materials below, willful blindness is a concept that is often relevant to proof of the knowledge element in white collar offenses.

[2] Willfulness

Another mens rea issue that often arises in white collar cases concerns the definition of the word "willfully." Many white collar statutes require proof that the defendant acted "willfully." As discussed in various contexts below, the term is interpreted to mean many different things, including recklessness, knowledge, and purpose.

Indeed, the United States Supreme Court has found that "willfulness" may, in certain circumstances, require the government to prove that the defendant knew of and intended to violate the law. Sometimes termed "specific intent," this high proof requirement is limited to particular areas of the law, such as tax fraud. In *Cheek v. United States*,[44] for example, the Court abandoned the traditional doctrine that "ignorance of the law is no excuse" and imposed an intent to violate the law requirement in connection with tax fraud offenses. As the Court explained, "[t]his special treatment of criminal tax offenses is largely due to the complexity of the tax laws."[45]

[3] Recklessness and Negligence

Either by statutory authority or under case law, some white collar convictions may be based upon recklessness.[46] This means that the government need not show that the defendant intended or even knew that the harm would occur, but merely was aware of the risk. In some limited areas such as certain environmental crimes, a conviction may be based upon mere negligence.[47]

[4] Strict Liability

In some limited cases, known as "public welfare offenses," a defendant may be liable for a white collar crime absent any showing of mens rea. As discussed in the next chapter,[48] the Supreme Court has rejected constitutional challenges to these laws. The Court's decisions are largely based upon a policy determination that it is within Congress's powers to dispense with the mens rea requirement where laws (such as food and drug laws) seek to prevent significant physical harm to the public.

---

[44] 498 U.S. 192 (1991).

[45] *Id.* at 200. The Court has rendered similar holdings in other areas of white collar crime. *See, e.g.,* Ratzlaf v. United States, 510 U.S. 135 (1994) (requiring knowledge that defendant's activity violated law concerning currency transaction structuring); Liparota v. United States, 471 U.S. 419 (1985) (requiring knowledge that defendant's activity violated laws or regulations governing food stamps). *Cf.* Bryan v. United States, 524 U.S. 184 (1998) (distinguishing *Cheek* and *Ratzlaf* and holding that conviction for willfully dealing in firearms without a federal license does not require proof that the defendant knew of the federal licensing requirement). Note that the MPC's position is that "[a] requirement that an offense be committed willfully is satisfied if a person acts knowingly." § 2.02(8) & com. 10.

[46] *See* Chapter 5, Securities Fraud, *infra*, and Chapter 7, Environmental Crimes, *infra*.

[47] *See* § 7.01[C], *infra*.

[48] Corporate and Individual Liability, *infra* § 2.02.

[B] Vicarious Liability

As in other areas of criminal law, a white collar defendant may be liable for someone else's crime. For example, under the law of conspiracy, co-conspirators may be liable for each other's criminal acts under special rules relating to conspiracies.[49] Also, the general federal aiding and abetting statute, § 2 of the federal criminal code,[50] applies in white collar cases. That section punishes as a principal in the crime any person who "aids, abets, counsels, commands, induces or procures" the commission of a crime by another. Aiding and abetting liability generally requires the government to prove both the act of aiding and abetting, and mens rea as to (a) the act of aiding and abetting, and (b) the goal that the object crime be achieved. The general rule, as articulated in MPC § 2.06, requires proof that the defendant had the purpose to aid and abet the principal, and also had the same level of mens rea that would be required to convict the principal of the object crime.[51]

[C] Inchoate Crimes

Many white collar offenses are "inchoate," that is, the defendant may be criminally liable even though the criminal objective is never achieved. Classic inchoate crimes include both conspiracy and attempts to commit crimes.

The law of conspiracy is discussed in detail in Chapter Three below. For present purposes, it is sufficient to note that the crime of conspiracy is complete once the defendant has entered into an agreement with one or more persons to commit an object crime or crimes. The actus reus is the act of agreeing to enter into the conspiracy and, under some statutes, an "overt act" towards the criminal objective. Liability for the crime of conspiracy may arise very early on in a criminal venture, long before the goal is achieved.

With respect to attempts, in most states an "attempt" to commit a crime is itself rendered a crime, assuming the required mens rea and actus reus are present.[52] There is no general federal law of attempt. Certain statutory provisions do provide for liability for attempts, however. First, in the Sarbanes-Oxley Act of 2002, Congress enacted an attempt and conspiracy statute, codified at § 1349 of Title 18, the federal criminal code. The statute provides that "[a]ny person who attempts or conspires to commit any offense under this chapter shall be subject to the same penalties as those prescribed for the offense, the commission of which was the object of the attempt or conspiracy." Thus, for certain fraud offenses set forth in that chapter of the criminal code, attempts will be punished in the same manner as the completed offenses.

Second, many white collar statutes themselves provide inchoate liability. Often, this liability arises even before the defendant has committed an "attempt" under the general common law. There are many examples of white collar statutes that

---

[49] See Conspiracy, *infra* § 3.03[D].

[50] 18 U.S.C. § 2.

[51] See Dressler, *supra* note 33, § 30.05.

[52] See Dressler, *supra* note 33, §§ 27.05–06.

provide for inchoate liability. For instance, an "'endeavor" to obstruct justice is sufficient under the principal federal obstruction of justice statutes.[53] The crime of tax evasion reaches "[a]ny person who willfully attempts in any manner to evade or defeat any tax imposed by this title or the payment thereof."[54] Also, note that fraud offenses, including those under the mail and wire fraud statutes,[55] and the various securities fraud statutes,[56] are complete irrespective of whether the defendant succeeds in defrauding the victim.

§ 1.07 APPLICATION OF CRIMINAL PROCEDURE PRINCIPLES TO WHITE COLLAR CRIME

Federal constitutional criminal procedure principles apply to all the crimes discussed below. Principally, the cases raise issues under the Fifth Amendment's Self-Incrimination Clause and under the Fourth Amendment's prohibition against unreasonable government searches and seizures. As a general matter, these issues are discussed as they arise in the chapters that follow; the exception is Chapter 19's discussion of self-incrimination issues.

As to the Fifth Amendment, Chapter 19 (the Fifth Amendment Right Against Compelled Self-Incrimination) supplements discussions of the various Fifth Amendment issues that arise in the other chapters below. In particular, Self-Incrimination Clause issues arise in connection with environmental crimes, securities fraud, obstruction of justice, perjury, and false statements.

As to the Fourth Amendment, the United States Constitution prohibits the government from conducting "unreasonable searches and seizures."[57] Most of the evidence in white collar cases is not obtained by searches and seizures, but rather by voluntary responses to grand jury subpoenas. Occasionally, however, a search and seizure issue may arise in a white collar case. When search warrants are used, searches and seizures pursuant to those warrants are subject to objection on reasonableness grounds. These issues are discussed below in connection with environmental crimes (§ 7.06[C]), computer crimes (§ 6.05[A]), and grand jury subpoenas (§ 17.04).

---

[53] *See* 18 U.S.C. § 1503, discussed in Chapter 12, Obstruction of Justice, *infra.*

[54] 26 U.S.C. § 7201, discussed in Chapter 13, Tax Crimes, *infra.*

[55] 18 U.S.C. §§ 1341, 1343, discussed in Chapter 4, Mail and Wire Fraud, *infra.*

[56] Discussed in Chapter 5, Securities Fraud, *infra.*

[57] Fourth Amendment doctrine is both vast and complex, and readers should refer to criminal procedure sources for a more in-depth discussion. *See, e.g.,* 1 Joshua Dressler & Alan C. Michaels, Understanding Criminal Procedure (5th ed. 2010).

Chapter 2

CORPORATE AND INDIVIDUAL LIABILITY

§ 2.01 INTRODUCTION

When a crime involves an artificial entity such as a corporation, the government may choose to indict (a) the entity itself, and/or (b) the individual wrongdoers.[1] In some cases, the government may also charge the corporate manager(s) responsible for the area in which wrongdoing occurred.

In recent years, the government has increasingly tended to charge artificial entities in white collar cases.[2] Corporations are by far the most frequently named entities, but courts have also allowed prosecutions of other entities, including partnerships.[3]

Recall that criminal liability is generally premised upon a physical component (actus reus) and mental component (mens rea). Thus, it may seem odd in a criminal case to charge, convict, and sentence an abstract entity like a corporation that literally cannot possess a mental state. Partly because of this conceptual difficulty, the historical development of corporate criminal liability has been lengthy and controversial.

This chapter outlines the basic doctrines of corporate criminal liability. In addition, the chapter discusses the individual liability of those employees and other agents who act on behalf of corporate and other legal entities.

§ 2.02 THE DEVELOPMENT OF CORPORATE CRIMINAL LIABILITY

During the nineteenth century, courts in England and the United States increasingly began to impose corporate criminal liability for "strict liability" crimes. Because these cases did not require proof of mens rea, these courts avoided the

---

[1] Harry First, *General Principles Governing the Criminal Liability of Corporations, Their Employees and Officers, in* White Collar Crime: Business and Regulatory Offenses §§ 5.01–05 (Otto Obermaier & Robert Morvillo, eds. 2011); Elizabeth A. Plimpton & Danielle Walsh, *Corporate Criminal Liability,* 47 Am. Crim. L. Rev. 331 (2010). The United States Department of Justice has issued guidelines for prosecuting corporate fraud. *See* Principles of Federal Prosecution of Business Organizations, U.S. ATTORNEYS' MANUAL § 9-28.000, *available at* http://www.justice.gov/opa/documents/corp-charging-guidelines.pdf.

[2] Particular issues arise with respect to corporate liability for the crime of conspiracy. *See* Chapter 3, Conspiracy, *infra,* § 3.05[A][2].

[3] *See, e.g.,* United States v. A & P Trucking Co., 358 U.S. 121 (1958).

conceptual difficulty of attributing a mental state to an abstract entity.[4] Near the turn of the century, however, the issue of corporate liability became more pressing as Congress began to implement a system of economic regulations designed to curb corporate abuses. The Sherman Antitrust Act of 1890 specifically included corporate criminal liability and, later, other statutes did likewise.[5]

In 1909, the Supreme Court in *New York Central & Hudson River Railroad v. United States*[6] approved the broad use of criminal sanctions against corporations. In *New York Central*, the railroad company and an employee were convicted of violating the Elkins Act, which regulated the rates that common carriers charged for transporting property. The statute explicitly imposed corporate criminal liability for acts done by a corporate agent:

> A]nything done or omitted . . . by a corporation common carrier . . . which, if done or omitted . . . by any director or officer [or other agent] thereof . . . would constitute a misdemeanor under . . . this Act shall also be held to be a misdemeanor committed by such corporation. . . .

> In construing and enforcing the provisions of this section, the act, omission, or failure of any officer, agent, or other person acting for or employed by any common carrier acting within the scope of his employment shall in every case be also deemed to be the act, omission, or failure of such carrier as well as that of the person.[7]

On appeal, the corporation argued that its conviction violated the Fifth Amendment's Due Process Clause on two grounds. First, the company argued that the conviction improperly punished innocent shareholders. Second, the company asserted that its conviction violated the presumption of innocence because there was no evidence that the company's board of directors had authorized the illegal acts.[8]

The Supreme Court unanimously rejected these arguments, and approved the concept of corporate criminal liability. In reaching its decision, the Court focused on the dominant role of corporations in the United States' economy. The Court reasoned that "to give [corporations] immunity from all punishment because of the old and exploded doctrine that a corporation cannot commit a crime would virtually take away the only means of effectually controlling the subject-matter [of the Elkins Act] and correcting the abuses aimed at."[9]

To reach its result, the Court in *New York Central* expressly extended the tort doctrine of respondeat superior to criminal cases. Under this doctrine, which is

---

[4] *See* First, *supra* note 1, § 5.02.

[5] *See* First, *supra* note 1, § 5.02. In 1978, the Supreme Court held that antitrust violations under the Sherman Act are not strict liability offenses. *See* United States v. United States Gypsum Co., 438 U.S. 422, 435 (1978).

[6] 212 U.S. 481 (1909).

[7] *Id.* at 491–492, *quoting* the Elkins Act, Ch. 708, 32 Stat. 847 (1903), *repealed by* Interstate Commerce Act of 1978, Pub. L. No. 95-473, § 4(a)-(b), 92 Stat. 1337, 1467.

[8] 212 U.S. at 492.

[9] *Id.* at 496.

discussed in more detail below, a corporate agent's acts may be imputed to the corporation itself.[10]

§ 2.03   STANDARDS FOR IMPUTING LIABILITY TO CORPORATIONS

[A]   Respondeat Superior

[1]   Application in the Federal System

The doctrine of respondeat superior now forms the basis of corporate criminal liability throughout the federal system. This standard applies to federal criminal statutes, whether or not they expressly impose liability on corporations.[11] The only exception occurs when the language or legislative context of a statute makes clear that Congress did not intend that the statute apply to corporations.[12] As discussed below, the doctrine of respondeat superior is controversial. Many commentators describe the doctrine as overly broad and unfair to corporations.[13]

[2]   Elements of Respondeat Superior

In its simplest terms, respondeat superior imposes liability on corporations for acts committed by corporate agents acting (1) on behalf of the corporation, (2) to benefit the corporation, and (3) within the scope of the agent's authority.[14] The latter requirement is met when an agent is acting under actual or apparent authority, and is very easy to prove.[15] The first two requirements, however, are often contested, and are discussed in more detail below.[16]

[3]   Agents Whose Liability May Be Imputed to the Corporation

Respondeat superior imposes liability for the acts of all corporate agents, including employees and independent contractors, even when those agents operate at the lowest levels of responsibility.[17] Because inconsistent verdicts generally do not require reversal under federal law, corporate liability may also be imposed even when the agent upon whose wrongdoing corporate liability rests has been acquit-

---

[10] *Id.* at 493, *citing* Lakeshore & M.S.R. Co. v. Prentice, 147 U.S. 101 (1893). *See infra* § 2.03[A].

[11] *See* First, *supra* note 1, §§ 5.02–03.

[12] *See id.*

[13] *See infra* § 2.03[D].

[14] The first two requirements are often merged together; some courts have, however, articulated each as a separate element. *See infra* § 3.05.

[15] Apparent authority exists when a third party would conclude that an agent's acts are authorized because of the agent's position with the corporation and the agent's conduct in general. *See* First, *supra* note 1, § 5.03[1].

[16] *See infra* § 3.05.

[17] *See* First, *supra* note 1, §§ 5.02–03.

ted.[18]

[4] Liability of Successor and Non-Existent Corporations

Courts have also held that successor corporations can be held liable for actions committed by agents of predecessor corporations. Furthermore, a corporation can be indicted for a crime even if it is a "dead" corporation that has ceased to exist.[19]

Both of these issues arose in *United States v. Central National Bank.*[20] In that case, the Alamo Bank merged with Central National Bank, and Central National Bank thereafter ceased to exist. Both banks were later indicted for violations of the currency transaction reporting laws allegedly committed by agents of Central National Bank. The defendants moved to dismiss the indictment on the grounds that (1) Central National Bank could not be liable because it was a "dead" corporation, and (2) Alamo Bank could not be liable for crimes committed by Central National. The trial court denied the motion. First, with respect to Central National Bank, the court found that the applicable Texas statutes specifically provided that merged banks and corporations continue to exist in their new incarnations. Second, with respect to Alamo Bank, the court found that successor corporations are liable for the acts of predecessor corporations.

[B] Model Penal Code

State courts are not bound to follow the doctrine of respondeat superior, and some states have adopted other bases for corporate criminal liability. Most importantly, a number of states use the standards set forth in the Model Penal Code ("MPC"). The MPC sets forth a corporate liability standard that is somewhat more restrictive than the respondeat superior test.

MPC Section 2.07(1) provides that a corporation may be convicted of a crime where:

(a)   the offense is a violation[21] or the offense is defined by a statute other than the Code in which a legislative purpose to impose liability on corporations plainly appears and the conduct is performed by an agent of the corporation acting on behalf of the corporation within the scope of his office or employment . . . ; or

(b)   the offense consists of an omission to discharge a specific duty of affirmative performance imposed on corporations by law; or

(c)   the commission of the offense was authorized, requested, commanded,

---

[18] For a fuller discussion of this issue under conspiracy law, see *infra* § 3.08. *See generally* First, *supra* note 1, § 5.04[1], and cases cited therein.

[19] *See, e.g.*, Melrose Distillers, Inc. v. United States, 359 U.S. 271, 272–73 (1959) (antitrust case against dead corporation may proceed if state law permits).

[20] 705 F. Supp. 336, 337–39 (S.D. Tex. 1988), *aff'd sub nom.* United States v. Alamo Bank, 880 F.2d 828 (5th Cir. 1989).

[21] A "violation" under the MPC is a minor offense that does not constitute a crime. *See* MPC § 1.04(5) (Official Draft and Revised Comments 1980).

performed or recklessly tolerated by the board of directors or by a high managerial agent acting on behalf of the corporation within the scope of his office or employment.

Further, the MPC provides a "due diligence" defense in all non-strict liability cases brought under § 2.07(1)(a). Under § 2.07(5), the defense applies "if the defendant proves by a preponderance of the evidence that the high managerial agent having supervisory responsibility over the subject matter of the offense employed due diligence to prevent its commission." The defense is not available, however, where the legislature has demonstrated its intent that such a defense not be sanctioned in the state.

[C]   Comparing Respondeat Superior and § 2.07

As is apparent from the foregoing, MPC § 2.07 provides a more restrictive test for corporate liability than does respondeat superior. First, § 2.07(1)(a) applies to criminal cases where MPC general interpretive principles apply but where the specific criminal offense is not itself defined under the MPC. In such a case, there must be a clear legislative intent to impose liability on corporations under the applicable statute. Such clear legislative intent is not an element of respondeat superior.

Second, in cases to which § 2.07(1)(c) applies, the government must show that the agent's act was approved of or "recklessly tolerated" by high-level management. Respondeat superior imposes no such requirement.

In both of these ways, and through the use of a limited due diligence defense, the MPC narrows the scope of corporate criminal liability compared to respondeat superior. As shown below, some courts have declined to adopt the MPC approach to corporate liability precisely for this reason.

[D]   The Debate Over over Corporate Criminal Liability

Many commentators argue that corporate criminal liability, particularly under respondeat superior, is overly broad and even counter-productive in terms of deterrence.[22] Principally, the argument focuses on the absence of any requirement that the corporation itself have possessed a mens rea — generally a prerequisite for criminal liability in English and American law. Further, these critics argue that it is not appropriate to apply standards developed in the civil law torts context to criminal matters. For example, the tort doctrine developed as an economic method for shifting costs, a rationale not applicable to criminal law.[23]

---

[22] Much has been written on this issue. *See, e.g.*, Assaf Hamdani & Alon Klement, *Corporate Crime and Deterrence*, 61 Stan. L. Rev. 271, 274 (2008) (arguing that "subjecting business entities to criminal liability carrying severe collateral consequences might, in fact, undermine deterrence"). In addition, simply filing criminal charges against a business entity can amount to a "corporate death penalty," as was notably the case with Arthur Andersen LLP. That "big five" accounting firm was charged with obstruction of justice in the Enron scandal and later went out of business. This case is discussed *infra*, § 12.06.

[23] *See* First, *supra* note 1, § 5.03[3].

Federal courts have rejected these arguments, and have imposed corporate liability based upon the following arguments. First, such liability is necessary to ensure that corporations adequately supervise their agents and employees. Second, corporate liability encourages corporations to develop general policies to deter wrongdoing. Third, corporate liability appropriately places responsibility on the entity that benefits from the wrongdoing rather than solely upon the individual wrongdoer.[24]

§ 2.04 ISSUES ARISING UNDER THE MODEL PENAL CODE

[A] Legislative Intent to Impose Liability

As noted above, the MPC raises certain issues that do not arise in respondeat superior cases. For example, to impose corporate liability for crimes not defined by the MPC itself, § 2.07(1)(a) requires the government to show that "a legislative purpose to impose liability on corporations [for that crime] plainly appears." This will generally not be difficult to prove.

For example, in *State v. Shepard Construction Company*,[25] the corporation was indicted under a state antitrust law. The defendant argued that it could not be found guilty under the statute because the statute only authorized a penalty of imprisonment, a penalty that cannot be imposed on a corporation. The Supreme Court of Georgia rejected the argument, noting that (1) the statute provided that a "person" could be convicted, (2) the statute defined the term "person" to include corporations, and (3) the law provided that a fine could be imposed.[26] The dissent disagreed, finding that there was insufficient evidence of legislative intent to support the imposition of corporate liability.[27]

[B] Approval by High Managerial Agent

In cases to which MPC § 2.07(1)(c) applies, the government must show that "the commission of the offense was authorized, requested, commanded, performed or recklessly tolerated by the board of directors or by a high managerial agent." Section 2.07(4)(c) defines "high managerial agent" as "an officer of a corporation or an unincorporated association, or, in the case of a partnership, a partner, or any other agent of a corporation or association having duties of such responsibility that his conduct may fairly be assumed to represent the policy of the corporation or association."

The definition of "high managerial agent" does not always yield predictable results. In *State v. Chapman Dodge Center*,[28] the Louisiana Supreme Court used a

---

[24] *See id.* at § 5.3(B), and authorities cited therein.

[25] 281 S.E.2d 151 (Ga.), *cert. denied*, 454 U.S. 1055 (1981).

[26] *Id.* at 156.

[27] *Id.* at 157 (Smith, J., dissenting).

[28] 428 So. 2d 413, 417–20 (La. 1983).

narrow reading of the term, and found that a car dealership's general manager was not a "high managerial agent." In that case, the general manager committed ongoing auto license fee fraud. The car dealership was a subsidiary of a closely-held corporation run by a single owner/officer. The owner/officer did not live in Louisiana, and had no knowledge of the general manager's activities. Thus, the court found, the manager's intent could not be imputed to the corporation. The majority reached this conclusion even though the car dealership was having financial difficulties — a fact presumably known to the owner — that had led the manager to commit the fraud. The dissent argued that the company could be liable under MPC § 2.07(1)(c) because the acts were committed by the general manager, who was in charge of the dealership's day-to-day operations.[29]

The court in *State v. Christy Pontiac-GMC, Inc.*[30] reached the opposite result based upon facts that showed that high-level management was aware of the wrongdoing. In that case, a car dealership was convicted of charges relating to two thefts of manufacturer rebates that should have been paid to customers. The evidence showed that the rebate applications were forged by Hesli, a salesman and fleet manager. On appeal, the corporation argued that there was insufficient evidence that the transactions were "authorized, tolerated, or ratified by corporate management." The Minnesota Supreme Court rejected the argument, noting that Hesli was a mid-level manager who had the authority to sign and process the rebate applications. Further, the benefit from the fraud went to the corporation. Finally, a corporate officer signed one of the rebate applications, and the president was aware of the dispute over the other application.

Entities other than corporations may also be liable under the MPC standard. In *People v. Lessof & Berger*,[31] a law partnership moved to dismiss insurance fraud and related charges. The charges were based solely on the acts of one partner. The court denied the motion to dismiss, noting that the criminal statutes authorized charges against a "person," defined to include a "partnership." The court also concluded that a law partner is the equivalent of a "high managerial agent" whose acts can be attributed to a corporation. Finally, the court found that public policy supported this result both because the law firm itself allegedly benefited from the fraud and because the public has strong interest in "regulating the ethics of the legal profession."[32]

§ 2.05   ACTING ON BEHALF OF THE CORPORATION

For an agent's acts to be imputed to the corporation, both the MPC and respondeat superior require that the agent have been acting "on behalf of the corporation." Although some similar issues arise under both approaches, they differ in the extent to which an agent's actions can be imputed to the corporation.

---

[29] *Id.* at 420 (Lemmon, J., dissenting).

[30] 354 N.W.2d 17 (Minn. 1984).

[31] 608 N.Y.S.2d 54 (N.Y. Sup. Ct. 1994).

[32] *Id.* at 55.

[A] Model Penal Code vs. Respondeat Superior

In states where clear standards for corporate liability have not been established, courts have considered the respective merits of respondeat superior and MPC § 2.07. In *Commonwealth v. Beneficial Finance*,[33] the Massachusetts Supreme Court declined to adopt the Model Penal Code approach and adhered to respondeat superior principles. The defendants in *Beneficial Finance* included "small loan" companies. Agents of the companies had bribed public officials to ensure that the companies could charge the highest possible interest rates. In its instructions on corporate liability, the trial court told the jury to apply a standard similar to the common law respondeat superior standard.[34]

On appeal, the defendant corporations argued that the MPC standards for corporate liability should apply. Under this approach, they argued, the trial court erred when it failed to require that the jury find that high-level management had approved of or recklessly tolerated the bribery scheme.

The Massachusetts Supreme Court rejected the defendants' argument. Initially, the court noted that the jury probably could have found the defendant liable even under the MPC standard. Nonetheless, the court rejected the MPC's requirement of high managerial approval. The court stated that the MPC standard was too lenient because "[e]vidence of such authorization or ratification is too easily susceptible of concealment."[35]

The court also found that a requirement of high managerial approval would prompt large organizations to attempt to avoid potential liability. Thus, corporations could delegate decision making to lower-level employees and otherwise attempt to conceal management's role in wrongdoing.

[B] Corporate Compliance Programs and Actions Contrary to Corporate Policy

Courts applying respondeat superior have held that a corporation can be liable for an agent's acts that are performed on the corporation's behalf, even where those acts are contrary to explicit corporate policy.[36] Further, this is true even where the defendant has in place a "corporate compliance" program, that is, a

---

[33] 275 N.E.2d 33 (Mass. 1971), *cert. denied*, 407 U.S. 914 (1972).

[34] The trial judge instructed the jury that:

The Commonwealth must prove that the individual for whose conduct it seeks to charge the corporation criminally was placed in a position by the corporation where he had enough power, duty, responsibility and authority to act for and in behalf of the corporation to handle the particular business or operation or project of the corporation in which he was engaged at the time that he committed the criminal act, with power of decision as to what he would or would not do while acting for the corporation, and that he was acting for and in behalf of the corporation in the accomplishment of that particular business or operation or project, and that he committed a criminal act while so acting.

Id. at 34.

[35] *Id.* at 36.

[36] *See generally* Kathleen F. Brickey, 1 Corporate Criminal Liability: A Treatise on the Criminal Liability of Corporations, Their Officers and Agents § 3.08 (1992 & Supp. 2001).

program that the corporation has adopted to ensure that its agents and employees comply with the law.[37]

For example, in *Dollar Steamship Co. v. United States*,[38] the Ninth Circuit affirmed the conviction of a corporation under the Refuse Act based upon an employee's act of throwing refuse from a ship into the Honolulu harbor. At trial, the company showed that its employees were advised of its policy against such dumping, that the ship's officers had no knowledge of the dumping, and that the company had taken reasonable steps to prevent the dumping. The court nonetheless affirmed the conviction. The court found that the statute explicitly imposed strict liability on individuals and corporations for engaging in the prohibited acts, and that the exercise of due care was not a defense under the statute.

Similarly, in *United States v. Hilton Hotels Corp.*,[39] the defendant corporation was convicted of violating the Sherman Act's criminal antitrust provisions despite contrary corporate policy. In that case, an agent of the corporation had participated in a plan that violated the Sherman Act. Under the plan, the agent acted to benefit suppliers who contributed to a local hotel organization, and acted to punish those suppliers who did not contribute. The agent's actions were contrary to corporate policy, and defied the instructions of hotel management not to participate in the scheme. The agent testified that he ignored the instructions because he held a personal grudge against a supplier's representative.

On appeal, Hilton argued that the trial court erred when instructing the jury that "[a] corporation is responsible for acts and statements of its agents, done or made within the scope of their employment, even though their conduct may be contrary to their actual instructions or contrary to the corporation's stated policies."[40] The Ninth Circuit upheld the conviction, finding that the judge's instruction was in accord with the Sherman Act's design to deter proscribed anti-competitive activity in the broadest possible way. Such activity often occurs when large, complex organizations institute policy decisions over time to maximize profits. Thus, it is appropriate to punish the corporation because the corporation, rather than its employees, profits from the illegal activity, and because it is often difficult to identify the particular agent who engaged in the activity.[41] The existence of corporate policy forbidding the agent's acts in this case, and the instructions of local management to the same end, therefore were not a defense.

---

[37] In a case to which MPC § 2.07(1)(c) applies, this result would require specific proof that high management had approved of or recklessly tolerated the activity. In a non-strict liability case brought under MPC § 2.07(1)(a), the company could assert a "due diligence" defense. Most federal courts have declined to allow such a defense. *See, e.g.*, United States v. Hilton Hotels Corp., 467 F.2d 1000 (9th Cir. 1972), *cert. denied sub nom.* 409 U.S. 1125 (1973).

[38] 101 F.2d 638 (9th Cir. 1939).

[39] 467 F.2d 1000 (9th Cir. 1972).

[40] *Id.* at 1004.

[41] *Id.* at 1006.

[C] Actions Not Taken "For the Benefit" of the Corporation

Many courts applying respondeat superior require that an agent's acts be "for the benefit" of the corporation. This requirement is met so long as the agent intended in part to benefit the corporation. The presence of additional motives, such as an agent's intent to gain personally from the illegal acts, will not relieve the corporation of responsibility. Further, an actual benefit is not required; it is the agent's intent, not the result, that governs.[42]

The decision in *United States v. Automated Medical Laboratories*,[43] demonstrates the breadth of respondeat superior liability. In that case, the defendant corporation, its subsidiary, and three employees were charged with conspiracy and with making false statements to the federal government under 18 U.S.C. § 1001. The government alleged that the defendants falsified books and records to conceal the subsidiary's repeated violations of federal regulations. On appeal from its conviction, the corporation argued that (1) the government failed to prove that it intended to violate § 1001, and that (2) the government failed to prove that the corporation's agents acted within the scope of their employment and for the benefit of the corporation under respondeat superior. The court rejected the first argument, finding that proof of criminal intent is not required under respondeat superior. The court also rejected the second argument. The court held that, even if the agents were acting contrary to corporate policy, they were still acting within the scope of their employment. Further, the agents were acting to benefit the corporation because their actions were intended, at least in part, to prevent the government from learning of the regulatory violations and thus to benefit their employer.

Can a corporation be liable for acts that are actually harmful to the corporation? As shown by the following two decisions, the result is likely to depend on the facts of the particular case. In *Standard Oil Company v. United States*,[44] the corporate defendants were convicted of knowingly violating laws regulating oil production. The convictions were based upon employees' actions that were designed to benefit a third party rather than the corporations. Further, the employees' actions actually harmed the corporations because the employees both stole oil from their employers and caused the corporations to pay for oil they did not receive. The Fifth Circuit reversed the convictions, finding that the employees' actions were not done to benefit the corporations and could not be imputed to the corporations.

In *Steere Tank Lines v. United States*,[45] however, the same court later found that a company could be found guilty where truck drivers falsified their records to earn more money solely to benefit themselves.

Because knowledge and willfulness were elements of the offense, the appeals court found that the trial court had erred when it failed to require that corporate

---

[42] *See generally* Elizabeth A. Plimpton & Danielle Walsh, *Corporate Criminal Liability*, 47 Am. Crim. L. Rev. 331, 336–37 (2010); First, *supra* note 1, § 5.03[1], and cases cited therein.

[43] 770 F.2d 399, 406–07 (4th Cir. 1985).

[44] 307 F.2d 120 (5th Cir. 1962).

[45] 330 F.2d 719 (5th Cir. 1964).

agents other than the drivers knew of the illegal activity. Nonetheless, the court affirmed the convictions. The court reasoned that, because there was evidence that conditions at the company fostered the drivers' illegal practice, and that management knew of the practice, there was sufficient evidence of the company's intent. Thus, the error in the jury instructions was harmless.

§ 2.06   CORPORATE MENS REA

[A]   Managerial Approval of Criminal Conduct

As discussed above, corporate criminal liability originally arose in the context of strict liability offenses, for which proof of mens rea is not required. Employing the doctrine of respondeat superior, decisions such as *Hudson River Railroad* later extended corporate liability to crimes requiring proof of criminal intent. In these cases, proof of corporate mens rea is generally premised upon the mens rea possessed by the agent who committed the wrongdoing. Under a strict application of respondeat superior, that is the only proof of mens rea that is required. Thus, the government need not show that the corporate management itself possessed any mens rea.[46]

Federal courts, however, have not consistently applied the doctrine of respondeat superior in this regard. In particular, where the crime charged requires a showing of knowledge or willfulness, some federal courts look for proof in addition to that possessed by the agent/wrongdoer.[47] These courts require some evidence that corporate management knew of or acquiesced in the agent's wrongdoing. Presumably, these courts are concerned about the harshness of imposing criminal liability on a corporation based solely upon an agent's intent. These courts state that they are applying respondeat superior principles, but in fact are requiring something more.[48] By looking for evidence of corporate criminal intent, these courts are approaching the MPC standard for corporate liability, which requires proof that high-level management either approved or recklessly tolerated the wrongdoing.[49]

[B]   Collective Knowledge

One way that a court may find proof of corporate mens rea is through a showing of "collective knowledge." Under this doctrine, all the knowledge of the individual corporate agents is collected together, and then attributed to the organization.[50] The doctrine of collective knowledge may be necessary for conviction where no individual corporate agent possessed the mens rea necessary for the crime.

---

[46] *See* First, *supra* note 1, § 5.03[1].

[47] *See* Brickey, *supra* note 36, § 4.04.

[48] *See* First, *supra* note 1, § 5.03[3], and cases cited therein.

[49] *See supra* § 2.03[B].

[50] *See* First, *supra* note 1, § 5.03[3][b], and cases cited therein.

The leading case on collective knowledge is *United States v. Bank of New England*.[51] The Bank of New England was charged with violating the currency transaction reporting ("CTR") laws, which required the bank to submit to the government CTRs for all cash transactions over $10,000 by a single customer.[52] A customer had come to the bank thirty-one times to obtain checks from different accounts. He then cashed the checks in amounts between $5,000 and $9,000, for a total of more than $10,000 a day. Because the customer's total cash transactions on given days totaled more than $10,000, the bank was required to file CTRs, but failed to do so.

At trial, the government was required to prove that the bank knowingly and willfully violated the CTR laws. As to the knowledge requirement, the trial judge instructed the jury on the concept of collective knowledge:

> [Y]ou have to look at the bank as an institution. As such, its knowledge is the sum of the knowledge of all of the employees. That is, the bank's knowledge is the totality of what all of the employees know within the scope of their employment. So, if Employee A knows one facet of the currency reporting requirement, B knows another facet of it, and C a third facet of it, the bank knows them all.[53]

The judge then instructed the jury as to how it should apply the concept of collective knowledge to the facts of the case:

> [I]f you find that an employee within the scope of his employment knew that CTRs had to be filed, even if multiple checks are used, the bank is deemed to know it. *The bank is also deemed to know it if each of several employees knew a part of that requirement and the sum of what the separate employees knew amounted to knowledge that such a requirement existed.*[54]

On appeal from the bank's conviction, the First Circuit first found that the collective knowledge instruction was appropriate. To hold otherwise, the court concluded, would mean that corporations could avoid criminal liability by compartmentalizing the knowledge of different corporate departments so that no single agent had the requisite knowledge.[55] Applying the law to the facts, the court found sufficient evidence of collective knowledge: the head bank tellers knew of the customer's transactions and of the CTR reporting requirements, and a bank manager knew that cash transactions in a single day had to be aggregated for reporting purposes.[56]

Finally, the defendant argued that the trial court erred in its jury instruction on willfulness. The trial court had told the jury that it could find the bank acted willfully, with "specific intent" to disobey the law, based on proof that individual employees possessed the requisite intent or that the bank exhibited "flagrant

---

[51] 821 F.2d 844 (1st Cir.), *cert. denied*, 484 U.S. 943 (1987).

[52] For a discussion of the currency transaction reporting laws, see Chapter 14, *infra*.

[53] 821 F.2d at 855.

[54] *Id.* (emphasis added).

[55] *Id.* at 856.

[56] *Id.* at 857.

organizational indifference" to the wrongdoing. The appeals court held that this was an appropriate instruction, and further found that there was sufficient evidence of such organizational indifference.[57] Note that not all courts accept the collective knowledge doctrine, however.[58]

§ 2.07   LIABILITY OF CORPORATE OFFICERS AND AGENTS

[A]   Scope of Individual Wrongdoers' Liability

Courts applying federal law have consistently held that corporate officers, employees, and agents may be held criminally liable for their own actions. This is so even when the individual was acting solely on behalf of the corporation at the time of the wrongdoing.[59] That the defendant was merely "following orders" generally will not be a defense.

Of course, to prove that such an individual is liable, the government must prove all the elements of the crime beyond a reasonable doubt. With the exception discussed in the next section, part of the government's proof will be that the individual defendant possessed the mens rea necessary for conviction of the specific crime.[60]

Likewise, under MPC § 2.07(6), an individual officer or agent is liable for an action taken as a corporate representative "to the same extent as if it were performed in his own name or behalf."

---

[57] *Id.*

[58] For example, the Massachusetts Supreme Court has rejected the college knowledge doctrine. *See* Commonwealth v. Life Care Ctrs. of Am., Inc., 926 N.E.2d 206, 212 (Mass. 2010) ("We conclude, consistent with our existing case law, that a corporation acts with a given mental state in a criminal context only if at least one employee who acts (or fails to act) possesses the requisite mental state at the time of the act (or failure to act)".). In private securities litigation cases, federal courts are split as to the viability of the "collective scienter" theory. *See* Glazer Capital Mgmt., LP v. Magistri, 549 F.3d 736, 743–44 (9th Cir. 2008) (describing circuit split and listing cases). *See generally* Ashley S. Kircher, *Corporate Criminal Liability versus Corporate Securities Fraud Liability: Analyzing the Divergence in Standards of Culpability*, 46 Am. Crim. L. Rev. 157, 160–67 (2009).

[59] *See, e.g.*, United States v. Wise, 370 U.S. 405, 416 (1962) (reversing dismissal of indictment of corporate officer and finding that the officer could be individually liable under the Sherman Act even for acts taken on behalf of a corporation). *See generally* First, *supra* note 1, § 5.04[1]. Additionally, corporate directors may be civilly liable for failing to maintain appropriate corporate compliance programs. *See In re* Caremark Int'l, 698 A.2d 959, 969–70 (Del. Ch. 1996) (directors must ensure that effective compliance programs are in place and may be "liable for losses caused by non-compliance with applicable legal standards"). *Accord* Stone v. Ritter, 911 A.2d 362, 370 (Del. 2006) ("Where directors fail to act in the face of a known duty to act, thereby demonstrating a conscious disregard for their responsibilities, they breach their duty of loyalty by failing to discharge that fiduciary obligation in good faith.").

[60] *See, e.g.*, United States v. United States Gypsum Co., 438 U.S. 422, 436–437 (1978) (holding that, in order to convict a defendant of criminal charges under the Sherman Act, the government must prove that each defendant acted with the requisite mens rea; that is, knowledge); United States v. Brown, 151 F.3d 476, 486–87 (6th Cir. 1998) (reversing conviction for aiding and abetting violation of false statements statute because the government failed to prove either that the defendant acted with the intent that a false statement be made or that she assisted in making the false statement).

[B] Strict Liability of Management for Subordinates' Acts

A general principle of criminal law is that the punishment should match the defendant's culpability. In the vast majority of criminal cases, culpability is measured by the level of the defendant's criminal intent. In some limited contexts, however, an individual may be convicted absent any showing of mens rea. That is, the government need not prove that the defendant (1) intended to violate the law, (2) knowingly engaged in the unlawful activity or caused the proscribed result, or (3) recklessly or negligently committed the illegal acts or caused the proscribed result. Such crimes are "strict liability" crimes, and were originally approved by the Supreme Court in the context of the liability of corporate executives.

The Supreme Court originally confronted the concept of strict liability in its 1943 decision in *United States v. Dotterweich*.[61] Dotterweich was the president and general manager of a pharmaceutical company. The company had engaged in interstate shipments of adulterated and misbranded products. At the trial of Dotterweich and the company, Dotterweich was convicted of violating the federal Food, Drug, and Cosmetic Act.[62] The Supreme Court upheld the conviction. First, the Court found that Dotterweich was a "person" who could be liable under the Act.[63] Second, the Court held that Dotterweich could be convicted absent any showing that he knew of the illegal activity. Rather, the Court stated that the conviction could be sustained under the responsible corporate officer doctrine, based upon evidence that Dotterweich had a "responsible share in the furtherance of the transaction."[64]

In reaching this result, the Court emphasized the threat to the public welfare created by the violation. This threat, the Court said, justified Congress's imposition of liability without any proof that the defendant knew of the wrongdoing:

> The purposes of this legislation thus touch phases of the lives and health of people which, in the circumstances of modern industrialism, are largely beyond self-protection . . . . Such legislation dispenses with the conventional requirement for criminal conduct — awareness of some wrongdoing.

---

[61] 320 U.S. 277 (1943).

[62] The statute prohibited "[t]he introduction or delivery for introduction into interstate commerce of any drug that is adulterated or misbranded."

[63] 320 U.S. at 281 ("[21 U.S.C. § 201(e)] specifically defines 'person' to include 'corporation.' . . . But the only way in which a corporation can act is through the individuals who act on its behalf").

[64] 320 U.S. at 284. The "responsible corporate officer" theory of liability may arise in many areas, and the doctrine's meaning may vary according to the context. For example, defendants have been charged as "responsible corporate officers" in environmental crimes prosecutions. In the environmental area, however, the doctrine imposes liability on persons whose responsibilities included the relevant corporate activities *and* who possessed the mens rea required by the statute. *See, e.g.*, United States v. MacDonald & Watson Waste Oil Co., 933 F.2d 35, 55 (1st Cir. 1991) (reversing conviction where jury instruction had failed to require that the jury find the mens rea required by the statute), discussed *infra*, § 7.02[b]. Under the strict liability version of the doctrine, no proof of mens rea is required. *See also* United States v. Jorgensen, 144 F.3d 550, 560 (8th Cir. 1998) (defendant corporate officers could be guilty under fraudulent food mislabeling statute if they (a) possessed the intent to defraud required by the statute and (b) either personally participated in the fraud or stood in a "responsible [corporate] relationship" regarding the mislabeling).

In the interest of the larger good it puts the burden of acting at hazard upon a person otherwise innocent but standing in responsible relation to a public danger.[65]

The majority stated that only individuals responsible for the matter have the power to prevent the violations in the first instance. Thus, to obtain a conviction, the government need only show that the defendant had the authority to prevent the violation and did not prevent or correct the violation.[66]

Four justices dissented, arguing that such strict liability was inappropriate. The dissent concluded that "in the absence of clear statutory authorization it is inconsistent with established canons of criminal law to rest liability on an act in which the accused did not participate and of which he had no personal knowledge."[67]

In 1975, the Court again confronted the issue of strict liability in *United States v. Park*.[68] Park was the president and chief operating officer of a national retail food chain. Once again, the individual defendant and the company were charged with shipping adulterated products in violation of the Federal Food, Drug, and Cosmetic Act. After the company pleaded guilty, Park was convicted of five counts and sentenced to a $50 fine on each count.

On appeal, Park objected to the jury charge, which allowed conviction based on a finding that Park "held a position of authority and responsibility in the business . . . , even though he may not have participated personally [in the violations]."[69] The appeals court agreed with Park's argument, finding that the jury should have been required to find both that Park engaged in some "wrongful action" exhibited by, for example, "gross negligence or inattention."[70]

The Supreme Court reversed and reinstated the conviction. The Court noted that, where congressional intent is clear, *Dotterweich* allows for strict liability in the context of public welfare offenses in order to deter the violations in the first instance. The only requirement for such liability is proof that the individual defendant was responsible for the matter. Three justices dissented, arguing that at a minimum the government should have been required to prove negligence; that is, that the defendant breached a standard of due care.[71]

In a 2003 case, *Meyer v. Holley*,[72] the United States Supreme Court again confronted the issue of an individual's strict liability for the acts of employees. The

----

[65] 320 U.S. at 280–81. *See* United States v. International Minerals & Chemical Corp., 402 U.S. 558, 564–65 (1971) (lower mens rea requirement appropriate under statutes regulating "dangerous or deleterious devices or products or obnoxious waste materials"). *See also* Staples v. United States, 511 U.S. 600 (1994) (declining to extend public welfare rationale to statute regulating the possession of machineguns).

[66] *Id.* at 282.

[67] *Id.* at 286 (Murphy, J., dissenting).

[68] 421 U.S. 658 (1975).

[69] *Id.* at 666.

[70] *Id.* (quoting United States v. Dotterweich, 320 U.S. 277, 281 (1943)).

[71] *Id.* at 678–79 (Stewart, J., dissenting).

[72] 537 U.S. 280 (2003).

defendant, Meyer, was the sole shareholder and president of a real estate corporation. The plaintiffs, an interracial married couple, sued Meyer under the Fair Housing Act on the theory that Meyer was personally liable for the discriminatory action of an employee. The district court dismissed the action, finding that the Fair Housing Act does not impose vicarious personal liability. On appeal, the Ninth Circuit reversed, holding that a defendant can be held to be vicariously liable under the Fair Housing Act where the defendant had "control" over, or "authority to control," the employee's actions.[73]

The Supreme Court reversed, finding that the "right to control," standing alone, does not provide the basis under traditional agency principles for imposition of vicarious liability on an individual defendant. The Court distinguished the issue in *Holley* from the issues presented in *Dotterweich* and *Park*. Those cases, the Court noted, were brought under statutes that expressly provided for strict personal liability. Congress, however, had made no such provision in the Fair Housing Act. In addition, the Court noted that the Department of Housing and Urban Development, the federal agency that administers the Act, had determined that ordinary vicarious liability rules apply under the Act.[74]

Although a tort action, the *Meyer* decision affirms the principle that corporate managers generally will not be personally liable for the acts of employees absent explicit congressional intent to impose such liability. In the absence of such intent, the corporation may be strictly liable under the doctrine of respondeat superior, but the corporate officers and directors will not be.

When does a person qualify as a responsible corporate officer? The court confronted this issue in *United States v. Ming Hong*.[75] In that case, the defendant acquired a corporation that operated a wastewater treatment facility. The defendant avoided any formal association with the corporation, and was not identified as an officer of the company. The government showed at trial, however, that the defendant controlled the company's finances and otherwise played a substantial role in company operations. Defendant and the corporation's general manager installed a waste treatment facility that they knew was inadequate, leading to the discharge of untreated waste water in violation of federal law. Based upon his status as a responsible corporate officer, the defendant was convicted of violating federal environmental laws.

On appeal, Hong argued that the government failed to prove that he was a responsible corporate officer because (a) he was not a formally designated corporate officer and (b) in any event, there was insufficient evidence that he exerted sufficient control over the corporation to be held responsible for the improper discharges. The Fourth Circuit rejected both arguments. The court stated that the government was not required to prove that Hong was a formally designated corporate officer. Instead, the issue was whether the defendant's relationship to the corporation rendered it appropriate to hold him criminally liable for failing to prevent the

---

[73] *Id.* at 286.

[74] *Id.* at 287.

[75] 242 F.3d 528 (4th Cir. 2001).

violations. Because the defendant substantially controlled corporate operations, the proof was sufficient.

The responsible corporate officer doctrine remains an important component of white collar criminal practice. In some areas, including prosecutions of pharmaceutical and medical device companies for misbranding and other criminal violations, the government has made wide-spread use of the doctrine.[76]

---

[76] *See* Michael A. Rogoff, et al., A Perfect Storm: Prosecutors' Increasing Focus on Individual Liability in the Drug and Device Sectors and the Responsible Corporate Officer Doctrine, 5 White Collar Crime Rep. 862 (BNA), Dec. 3, 2010.

Chapter 3

CONSPIRACY

§ 3.01 INTRODUCTION

[A] Nature of Conspiracy Charges

Because of their complexity, white collar crimes are often effected through schemes that involve multiple actors. If there is evidence that two or more persons have agreed to commit a crime, the government may be able to charge those persons with the crime of conspiracy. Such a charge gives the government significant substantive and tactical advantages both before and during trial.[1] Prosecutors will therefore include a conspiracy count wherever possible, and it is one of the most frequently charged federal crimes.[2]

Conspiracy starkly illustrates the policy tension — between effective enforcement of difficult-to-detect crimes and the rights of criminal defendants — that runs through much of white collar criminalization. First, as is often true with crimes charged in the white collar context,[3] the boundaries of conspiracy are inherently uncertain. As Justice Jackson wrote, conspiracy is "so vague that it almost defies definition."[4] Second, because of this vagueness and expansiveness, the government can often use conspiracy both to criminalize conduct that otherwise would not be subject to prosecution and to gain increased penalties for minor crimes.[5]

Finally, given the amorphous nature of the crime, conspiracy provides prosecutors with an enormous amount of discretion in deciding whether to bring a criminal case. For these reasons, and because of the tremendous strategic and tactical advantages it provides the government, conspiracy is a controversial crime.[6]

---

[1] *See infra* § 3.03.

[2] Thus, Judge Learned Hand famously referred to conspiracy as "that darling of the modern prosecutor's nursery." Harrison v. United States, 7 F.2d 259, 263 (2d Cir. 1925).

[3] *See, e.g.,* Chapter 16, RICO, *infra.*

[4] Krulewitch v. United States, 336 U.S. 440, 446 (1949) (Jackson, J., concurring).

[5] *See, e.g.,* United States v. Tuohey, 867 F.2d 534 (9th Cir. 1989) (defendant convicted of felony under defraud clause even though the object offense was only a civil offense that could not give rise to felony conviction).

[6] *See Krulewitch,* 336 U.S. at 445–46 (Jackson, J., concurring); Mark F. Pomerantz & Otto G. Obermaier, *Defending Charges of Conspiracy, in* White Collar Crime: Business and Regulatory Offenses § 4.01 (Otto Obermaier & Robert Morvillo, eds. 2011); Phillip E. Johnson, *The Unnecessary Crime of Conspiracy,* 61 Cal. L. Rev. 1137 (1973).

Although states generally include conspiracy provisions within their penal codes, the substantive law of conspiracy has primarily been developed through the federal case law discussed here. This chapter presents an overview of the federal law of conspiracy, including the elements of the crime and the major issues that often arise in conspiracy cases.

[B] Policy Bases

Conspiracy, like the crime of attempt, is an inchoate, or incomplete, crime. Thus, as with attempt, a defendant can be charged with and convicted of the inchoate crime even though the criminal objective is never accomplished. The crime of conspiracy is complete as soon as two or more people agree to commit a crime and, where required, one of those people commits an overt act in furtherance of the conspiracy. Unlike the crime of attempt, conspiracy requires no "substantial step" towards or "dangerous proximity" to the criminal end. Conspiracy is thus an unusual crime because liability may accrue long before any criminal harm is directly threatened. Nevertheless, allowing the charge of conspiracy may serve to protect society in at least two ways. First, the defendant can be arrested long before the criminal scheme comes to fruition and harm may occur.[7] Second, courts have noted that group criminality is especially dangerous because of the support that co-conspirators provide for each other and because of the ongoing momentum of such criminal groupings.[8] According to this perception, the dangers to individual rights inherent in the vague crime of conspiracy are outweighed by the criminal harms against which the crime of conspiracy protects.[9] Not all commentators agree that criminal groupings are particularly dangerous, and in fact some reach the contrary conclusion.[10]

§ 3.02 THE FEDERAL CONSPIRACY STATUTES

[A] Types of Federal Conspiracy Statutes

Federal law provides numerous sources for a conspiracy charge. First, and most important, § 371 of the federal criminal code is the *general* federal conspiracy statute. This section makes it a crime to conspire to commit any federal criminal offense or to defraud the United States government.[11] Second, some separate statutory provisions make it a crime to conspire to commit crimes of a particular *category*, such as narcotics offenses.[12] Third, some criminal statutes themselves

---

[7] *See* United States v. Feola, 420 U.S. 671, 694 (1975).

[8] *See id.*; Iannelli v. United States, 420 U.S. 770, 778–79 (1975).

[9] *See* Pomerantz & Obermaier, *supra* note 6, § 4.01.

[10] Some argue that the involvement of multiple actors increases the chances that the criminal scheme will be aborted before the goal is achieved. *See* Joshua Dressler, Understanding Criminal Law § 29.02[B] (5th ed. 2009), *citing* Abraham S. Goldstein, *Conspiracy to Defraud the United States*, 68 Yale L.J. 405, 414 (1959).

[11] 18 U.S.C. § 371. This statute is discussed in detail *infra* §§ 3.02, 3.05.

[12] These statutes appear both in the federal criminal code, Title 18 [*see, e.g.*, 18 U.S.C. § 241 (conspiracy against citizens' rights)], and elsewhere in federal statutes [*see, e.g.*, 21 U.S.C. § 846

include conspiracy provisions applicable only to that one *particular crime*, such as the federal racketeering statute.[13]

[B] The Elements of the General Conspiracy Statute — § 371

Under both common law and modern federal conspiracy statutes, conspiracy is defined by two basic elements: (1) the agreement between or among two or more persons to commit an object crime or crimes; and (2) the required mental state. Some modern statutes also require that the government prove an "overt act" in furtherance of the conspiracy.

Section 371 provides the basis for the vast majority of conspiracy charges in white collar cases. That statute makes it a crime for "two or more persons to conspire either to commit any offense against the United States, or to defraud the United States, or any agency thereof in any manner or for any purpose."[14] As discussed more fully below,[15] the statute also requires the commission of an overt act in furtherance of the conspiracy.

Under § 371, the government must show that:

1. An agreement existed -

   (a) to commit an offense against the United States, *and/or*

   (b) to defraud the United States;

2. Two or more persons were parties to that agreement (the "plurality" requirement);

3. The defendant intended -

   (a) to enter into the agreement, *and*

   (b) that the object offense(s) or fraud come to pass; *and*

4. A co-conspirator committed an "overt act" in furtherance of the offense.

The maximum statutory sentence under § 371 is five years. The actual sentence will vary according to the United States Sentencing Guidelines' recommended sentence, and the sentencing judge's discretionary application of the advisory Guidelines, in the particular case.[16] With conspiracy convictions, the sentences are tied to those for the substantive offenses, and thus will vary considerably from case to case.

(conspiracies to commit controlled substance offenses); 15 U.S.C. §§ 1, 2 (antitrust conspiracies)].

[13] 18 U.S.C. § 1962(d), discussed in Chapter 16, RICO, *infra.*

[14] 18 U.S.C. § 371.

[15] *See infra* § 3.02[C].

[16] *See* Chapter 21, Sentencing, *infra.*

[C] The Overt Act

At a minimum, the vast majority of crimes have both a mental component (mens rea)[17] and physical component (actus reus). The common law of conspiracy treated the agreement itself as the sole necessary actus reus of the crime.[18] The "agreement" is a meeting of the minds. Thus, deeming the agreement to be the actus reus of conspiracy is to engage in something of a legal fiction. This fiction renders conspiracy a unique crime to the extent that proof of a physical act or omission, as those terms are generally perceived, is not required. As commentators have noted, this aspect of the law of conspiracy increases the likelihood that the innocent will be ensnared by this crime, for there often is little objective proof of guilt.[19]

At least in part to overcome this criticism, many modern conspiracy statutes, including the general federal conspiracy statute,[20] further require that the government prove, as an element of its case, an "overt act" in furtherance of the conspiracy. Other federal conspiracy statutes do not include an overt act requirement,[21] however, and the Supreme Court has held that it will not impose such a requirement in the absence of clear congressional intent.[22]

An "overt act" is any act, or failure to act,[23] by any co-conspirator during and in furtherance of the conspiracy. The overt act itself need not be unlawful, so long as it contributes to the illegal end. Significantly, the government can meet this requirement with evidence that is far less than that required to demonstrate the actus reus of an attempt crime. Seemingly minor actions, such as meetings and phone calls, can qualify as overt acts. The overt act requirement is thus very easy to meet, and failure to prove an overt act rarely provides the ground for an acquittal in a conspiracy case.[24] Nonetheless, the overt act does provide some evidence that corroborates the existence of the agreement and the threat that the criminal combination poses to society.[25]

---

[17] Strict liability crimes are the exception to this rule. *See* Chapter 2, Corporate and Individual Liability, *supra*, § 2.07[B]; United States v. Bailey, 444 U.S. 394, 404 n.4 (1980).

[18] *See* United States v. Shabani, 513 U.S. 10, 16 (1994). *See generally* Dressler, *supra* note 10, § 29.04[E].

[19] *See* United States v. Dimeck, 24 F.3d 1239, 1248 (10th Cir. 1994); United States v. Thomas, 8 F.3d 1552, 1556 (11th Cir. 1993); United States v. Gaviria, 740 F.2d 174, 184 (2d Cir. 1984).

[20] 18 U.S.C. § 371.

[21] *See, e.g.*, 18 U.S.C. § 1962(d) (RICO); 15 U.S.C. §§ 1, 2 (antitrust).

[22] *See, e.g.*, Whitfield v. United States, 543 U.S. 209, 214–16 (2005) (interpreting the money laundering conspiracy statute, 18 U.S.C. § 1956(h)); United States v. Shabani, 513 U.S. 10, 14 (1994) (interpreting the federal drug conspiracy statute, 21 U.S.C. § 846).

[23] A failure to act will suffice when there is a duty to act.

[24] *See* Pomerantz & Obermaier, *supra* note 6, § 4.02[4], p. 4-24 ("The overt act requirement has seldom increased the prosecutor's difficulty in securing a conviction for conspiracy, and the ease with which prosecutors may meet the requirement has made its effect minimal.").

[25] *See Developments in the Law — Criminal Conspiracy*, 72 Harv. L. Rev. 922, 948 (1959); Chavez v. United States, 275 F.2d 813, 817 (9th Cir. 1960) ("an overt act is an outward act done in pursuance of the crime and in manifestation of an intent or design, looking toward the accomplishment of the crime").

The overt act is attributable to all co-conspirators who are members at the time the act is committed or who join later.[26] Thus, an overt act by any co-conspirator satisfies that element; the government need not show that each co-conspirator committed such an act.

The overt act requirement reflects some of the procedural advantages for the government inherent in conspiracy charges. As noted below,[27] venue lies in any federal district in which any overt act has been committed.[28] Also, the commission of an overt act will serve to show that the conspiracy has not ended and that the statute of limitations has not begun to run.[29]

[D]　The Unlawful Object

The common law of conspiracy included agreements to commit a crime or any other "unlawful" act. This rule created the anomalous consequence that the agreement itself would be a crime even where the commission of the object offense would be "unlawful" (for example, a tort) but not criminal. This anomaly, combined with the vague definition of the object offense, has rendered this aspect of common law conspiracy subject to substantial criticism.[30]

The first clause of § 371, on its face, also criminalizes both civil and criminal offenses by including "any offense against the United States," although the scope of liability is narrower than common law conspiracy by the reference to United States law. The language "offense against the United States" refers to offenses defined under federal law; the United States need not itself be the target of the offense. Thus, for example, a fraud scheme criminalized under federal law would qualify under this clause even where the intended victim is a private party unrelated to the federal government.

As discussed more fully below,[31] under the "defraud" clause of § 371, conspiracy can also be charged whenever the defendants have conspired to deprive the federal government of money or property, or to subvert the federal government's functioning or deprive it of information.[32]

As also noted below, courts generally allow one conspiracy charge to be based both on the theory that the defendant conspired to commit an offense against the United States and on the theory that the defendant conspired to defraud the United States. This is in accord with the general rule that the government may

---

[26] *See* Salinas v. United States, 522 U.S. 52, 64 (1997); United States v. Rabinowich, 238 U.S. 78, 86 (1915); Bannon v. United States, 156 U.S. 464, 468 (1895); Kaplan v. United States, 7 F.2d 594, 596 (2d Cir.), *cert. denied*, 269 U.S. 582 (1925).

[27] *See infra* § 3.03[B].

[28] *See* Hyde v. United States, 225 U.S. 347 (1912); Finley v. United States, 271 F.2d 777 (5th Cir. 1959), *cert. denied*, 362 U.S. 979 (1960).

[29] *See* Grunewald v. United States, 353 U.S. 391, 396–97 (1957).

[30] *See* Dressler, *supra* note 10 § 29.04[C].

[31] *See* § 3.05, *infra.*

[32] *See, e.g.*, Haas v. Henkel, 216 U.S. 462, 479 (1910) (finding that a conspiracy count does not have to allege a pecuniary loss to the United States; the statute includes "any conspiracy for the purpose of impairing, obstructing, or defeating the lawful function of any department of the government").

pursue a single criminal charge under alternative but consistent theories.[33] Under this approach, a jury could convict the defendant under either or both theories, but the defendant would only be subject to penalty for a single conspiracy count.[34]

§ 3.03 THE ADVANTAGE OF A CONSPIRACY CHARGE

[A] Joinder

For a number of reasons, a conspiracy charge under federal law provides the prosecutor with a uniquely potent weapon.

A conspiracy charge allows the government to prosecute at a single trial all defendants alleged to have been parties to the conspiracy. Under Rule 8(b) of the Federal Rules of Criminal Procedure, defendants may be joined if the government sufficiently alleges that they participated in "the same act or transaction or in the same series of acts or transactions." As discussed below,[35] if a case actually involves multiple conspiracies rather than a single conspiracy, then it is improper to try all the defendants at the same trial. Bringing defendants together in a single trial can substantially increase the chances of conviction, particularly of those defendants whose roles may have been minor or peripheral.[36]

[B] Venue

Under federal law, the government may bring a conspiracy case in any federal district in which the conspiratorial agreement was reached or in any district in which any co-conspirator committed any act in furtherance of the conspiracy.[37] Procedurally, it is to the prosecutor's advantage to bring a case in a district that is the most convenient to the government and its witnesses. Of course, such a venue may just happen to be far from the residence of a defendant and the defendant's witnesses. Conspiracy gives prosecutors enormous discretion in this regard.

[C] Evidence

As discussed more fully below,[38] a conspiracy charge brings substantial evidentiary advantages to the government. First, including a conspiracy charge may greatly expand the scope of relevant evidence because all acts done by any co-conspirator in furtherance of the conspiracy are potentially relevant. Second, the rule that hearsay statements are inadmissible is greatly weakened in conspiracy

---

[33] *See, e.g.,* United States v. Huebner, 48 F.3d 376, 381 (9th Cir. 1994); United States v. Hauck, 980 F.2d 611, 615 (10th Cir. 1992); United States v. Bilzerian, 926 F.2d 1285, 1301 (2d Cir.), *cert. denied,* 503 U.S. 813 (1991).

[34] *See id.*

[35] *See infra* § 3.08.

[36] *See infra* § 3.08[B].

[37] *See* Hyde v. United States, 225 U.S. 347, 367 (1912); Pomerantz & Obermaier, *supra* note 6, § 4.02[5].

[38] *See infra* §§ 3.07, 3.08.

cases. Under the Federal Rules of Evidence, statements made by a co-conspirator during the course and in furtherance of the conspiracy are admissible even if such evidence would normally be inadmissible as hearsay.[39]

[D] Vicarious Liability — The *Pinkerton* Rule

A conspiracy charge may substantially increase the scope of a defendant's potential liability. Under general conspiracy law, the defendant may be found guilty both of the conspiracy and of the object crime(s) of the conspiracy. In addition, under *Pinkerton*, the defendant may *also* be found guilty of substantive offenses that were committed by other co-conspirators but that were not included within the object offense(s) of the original conspiracy.[40]

[E] Multiple Punishments

The crime of conspiracy under federal law is different from the crime of attempt in one significant respect. Conspiracy, unlike attempt, does not merge with the object crime.[41] Where the criminal scheme has been completed, therefore, a defendant can be convicted of and sentenced for both the crime of conspiracy and the object crime or crimes; the Supreme Court has held that this result does not violate the Double Jeopardy Clause.[42]

Again, this result may be seen as unfair to defendants, and indeed the Model Penal Code and many states reject the imposition of liability for both the crime of conspiracy and the object offenses.[43]

[F] Statute of Limitations

Bringing a conspiracy charge may also extend the limitations period in a particular case. Under federal law, a conspiracy charge must be brought within five years of the offense.[44] Because conspiracy is an ongoing crime, it is likely to extend over a period of time. Courts have held that the limitations period for conspiracy does not begin to run until all members of the conspiracy abandon the criminal scheme or its goals are achieved.[45] Even if the limitations period has run for some substantive offenses, *all* members of a conspiracy may therefore be liable for *conspiracy* so long as an overt act was committed by *one* of them within five years of the indictment.[46] Finally, overt acts that occurred outside the five-year

---

[39] *See infra* § 3.07[B].

[40] *See* § 3.09, *infra.*

[41] *See* Pinkerton v. United States, 328 U.S. 640, 643–44 (1946).

[42] *See* United States v. Felix, 503 U.S. 378 (1992). The actual sentence will depend upon the trial's judge's application of the advisory sentencing.

[43] *See* Model Penal Code § 1.07(1)(b).

[44] 18 U.S.C. § 3282. Specific conspiracy statutes may provide for a different limitations period. For example, in tax conspiracy cases the statute of limitations is six years. *See* 26 U.S.C.A. § 6531.

[45] *See* Fiswick v. United States, 329 U.S. 211, 216 (1946).

[46] *See* Grunewald v. United States, 353 U.S. 391, 396–97 (1957). *Cf.* United States v. Hayter Oil Co., 51 F.3d 1265, 1271 (6th Cir. 1995) (holding that because price fixing itself is a crime, the government need

limitations period may nonetheless be included within the proof of the conspiracy count so long as at least one of those acts occurred within that time.[47] If, however, a conspiracy has ended and all the overt acts have been completed, then the limitations period will begin to run.

It is not always clear when an act is an "overt act" that may fairly be included within the conspiracy. For example, in *United States v. Nazzaro*,[48] the defendant was convicted of conspiracy to commit mail fraud based upon a scheme to fraudulently obtain a civil service promotion. On appeal, the First Circuit found that the promotion itself was properly alleged as an overt act because it was a discrete event indicating that the conspiracy was continuing. The court further concluded, however, that the defendant's receipt of salary in his new job did not meet the requirement of an "overt act" because it was not sufficiently part of the conspiracy. Thus, the salary payments did not suspend the running of the limitations period.

§ 3.04 THE AGREEMENT

The essence of conspiracy — the actus reus in traditional common law terms — is the agreement itself. Thus, conspiracy is an unusual crime because the criminal act is primarily mental, somewhat belying the usual notion that we do not punish for "thoughts alone." As noted above, the law has taken this step because of the perceived dangers inherent in criminal groupings.

The agreement determines both the parties to the conspiracy and the scope of the object crimes. As one court stated, "[n]obody is liable in conspiracy except for the fair import of the concerted purpose or agreement as he understands it; if later comers change that, he is not liable for the change; his liability is limited to the common purposes while he remains in it."[49]

As an initial matter, under federal law there must be two or more parties to the agreement. This prerequisite is sometimes referred to as the "plurality" requirement. The federal law relating to the plurality requirement is commonly termed the "bilateral" approach to conspiracies. Under the bilateral approach, at least two parties must both enter into an agreement and actually intend for the object crime or crimes to occur.[50] The Model Penal Code, on the other hand, allows for a defendant to be convicted based upon that defendant's intent alone, irrespective of whether others intended for the object crime(s) to occur. This approach, termed the "unilateral" approach to conspiracies, attempts to match punishment with the

---

only establish that this agreement existed during the statutory period). As noted *infra* § 3.12, the limitations period as to a particular defendant will begin to run at the time the defendant withdraws from the conspiracy.

[47] *See* Pomerantz & Obermaier, *supra* note 6, § 4.01[11].

[48] 889 F.2d 1158 (1st Cir. 1989).

[49] United States v. Peoni, 100 F.2d 401, 403 (2d Cir. 1938).

[50] This is the approach followed under federal law and under the law of many states. *See* State v. Pacheco, 882 P.2d 183 (Wash. 1994) (determining that the state follows the federal law "bilateral" approach).

individual's culpable state of mind.[51] Under the bilateral approach, a single individual who entered into an agreement to commit a crime with an undercover police officer would not be guilty of conspiracy. That individual would be guilty under the unilateral approach, however.

An individual conspirator may be tried, convicted, and sentenced for the crime even if some or all of the defendant's co-conspirators are not brought to trial.[52] Thus, it is not necessary that all co-conspirators be charged, or convicted, or even known to the government for an individual to be found guilty of the crime. Indeed, indictments often refer to "unknown and unindicted co-conspirators." So long as the government can prove beyond a reasonable doubt that a co-conspirator existed, the plurality requirement is met.

[A] Government Agents as Co-Conspirators

Also, at least two parties must have intended both (1) to enter into the conspiracy, and (2) that the object crime or crimes be committed. Thus, an agreement between a defendant and a government undercover agent, who never intended that the criminal scheme be carried out, does not meet the plurality requirement under federal law.[53] In that instance, there are not at least two people who intend to agree that an object offense be committed.

[B] Plurality in the Corporate Context

The plurality requirement raises particular issues in the corporate context, both with respect to corporate and individual liability. As to a corporation's liability for conspiracy, the following general principles apply:

(1) Courts hold that two or more corporations are capable of conspiring with one another. Note, however, that one court held that the plurality requirement is defeated if the corporations act through the same agent.[54]

(2) Some courts have held that a corporate entity can itself conspire with individuals associated with that entity so long as at least two corporate agents participate.[55] There are two significant exceptions to this rule: (a) in the antitrust context, a corporation is generally not capable of conspiring

---

[51] *See* Model Penal Code § 5.03(1) commentary.

[52] A separate issue arises when one co-conspirator is convicted but all other co-conspirators are acquitted. *See infra* § 3.10.

[53] *See, e.g.*, United States v. Nelson, 66 F.3d 1036, 1044 (9th Cir. 1995); United States v. Schmidt, 947 F.2d 362, 367 (9th Cir. 1991); United States v. Barboa, 777 F.2d 1420, 1422 (10th Cir. 1985). *Cf.* Miller v. State, 955 P.2d 892, 897 (Wyo. 1998) (noting that the modern trend in state courts is to rule that a conspiracy count is viable even when one of the participants is a government agent).

[54] *See* United States v. Santa Rita Store Co., 113 P. 620, 621 (N.M. 1911) (finding that while two corporations can conspire, the agreement cannot be accomplished through one agent).

[55] *See, e.g.*, United States v. Hughes Aircraft Co., 20 F.3d 974, 978–79 (9th Cir.), *cert. denied*, 513 U.S. 987 (1994); United States v. Peters, 732 F.2d 1004, 1008 (1st Cir. 1984); United States v. Hartley, 678 F.2d 961, 972 (11th Cir. 1982). *See generally* 1 Kathleen F. Brickey, Corporate Criminal Liability: A Treatise on the Criminal Liability of Corporations, Their Officers, and Agents § 6.23 at 272–73 (2d ed. 1992).

with its own agents and subsidiaries;[56] and (b) where the alleged conspiracy is between a corporation and a sole stockholder who completely controls the corporation, the plurality requirement may not be met because the dangers of group criminality are not present.[57]

(3) Under respondeat superior, a corporation can be liable for a conspiracy entered into by its agents.[58]

As to individuals' liability, courts have held that a group of individuals may be guilty of conspiracy even though they are all associated with the same corporation.[59]

[C] Wharton's Rule

The plurality agreement may not be met in the unusual circumstance where the crime, by its very nature, requires the participation of multiple actors. Under the so-called Wharton's Rule, conspiracy cannot be charged for crimes in this category. For example, adultery and bigamy are by definition crimes that cannot occur unless at least two (adultery) or more (bigamy) persons are involved.[60]

Under federal law, however, Wharton's Rule is a presumption that will rarely be applied. In *United States v. Iannelli*,[61] the Supreme Court held that, where Congress has deemed certain activity to be criminal, that activity will provide the basis for a conspiracy charge absent clear evidence that Congress intended that no conspiracy charge should lie. Thus, the Court sustained a conspiracy conviction under a gambling statute. One of the elements of this statute was the participation of five or more persons. Although a multiplicity of actors was required for the object crime, it was unlike classic Wharton's Rule offenses in that it "appear[ed] likely to pose the distinct kinds of threats to society that the law of conspiracy seeks to avert."[62]

§ 3.05   THE "OFFENSE" CLAUSE AND THE "DEFRAUD" CLAUSE

It is important to note that § 371 contains clauses creating two types of offenses: conspiracies to violate federal law and conspiracies to defraud the United States. The former offense is punished as a felony where the object crime was a felony, and

---

[56] *See, e.g.*, Copperweld Corp. v. Independence Tube Corp., 467 U.S. 752, 769–71 (1984). The antitrust laws seek to prohibit threats posed by agreements between entities with separate economic interests. Thus, in the antitrust context, the plurality requirement is not met by an agreement (1) among officers or employees of a single corporation, (2) among such persons and the corporation itself, or (3) between a corporation and one of its divisions or wholly-owned subsidiaries. *See id.*

[57] *See* United States v. Stevens, 909 F.2d 431, 431–32 (11th Cir. 1990), *citing* United States v. Hartley, 678 F.2d 961, 970 (11th Cir. 1982).

[58] *Id.* at 433.

[59] *See* United States v. S & Vee Cartage Co., 704 F.2d 914, 920 (6th Cir.), *cert. denied*, 464 U.S. 935 (1983); United States v. Hartley, 678 F.2d 961, 972 (11th Cir. 1982).

[60] *See* Dressler, *supra* note 10, § 29.09[C][1].

[61] 420 U.S. 770, 785 (1975).

[62] *Id.* at 783.

as a misdemeanor where the object crime was a misdemeanor.[63] Conspiracies to defraud the United States are punished as felonies.[64]

[A] The "Offense" Clause

The first clause of § 371 (the "offense" clause) is often used in white collar cases, and creates liability wherever the defendant has agreed with one or more people to violate other federal laws.[65] An agreement to commit securities fraud or mail fraud, for example, would constitute the crime of conspiracy under the first clause of § 371. Moreover, on its face the statute includes agreements to commit object offenses that themselves would be only punished civilly.[66] Finally, under the federal law of conspiracy, impossibility is not a defense. Thus, a conspiracy charge can stand even where it would be impossible for the co-conspirators to commit the object offense.[67]

Issues sometimes arise as to what constitutes an "offense" against the United States. Courts generally construe the term broadly. For example, in *United States v. Arch Trading Co.*,[68] the defendant company had entered into a contract with an Iraqi-owned entity. After Iraq invaded Kuwait in 1990, the President issued an order broadly forbidding United States companies from engaging in business dealings with Iraq. In violation of the order, Arch Trading attempted to carry out its obligations under the contract. The company was convicted under the offense clause based upon its participation in a conspiracy to violate the executive order. On appeal, Arch Trading argued that an executive order does not create an "offense" against the United States, and therefore it could only have been charged and convicted under the defraud clause. The Fourth Circuit rejected the argument. The court held that where, as in this case, Congress authorized the executive order and criminal sanctions for violations of the order, such violations do constitute offenses against the United States.

---

[63] *See* 18 U.S.C. § 371.

[64] *See* United States v. Tuohey, 867 F.2d 534 (9th Cir. 1989).

[65] The "offense" clause may encompass not only violations of formally-enacted statutes, but also violations of executive orders issued pursuant to congressional authorization. *See* United States v. Arch Trading Co., 987 F.2d 1087, 1091–92 (4th Cir. 1993).

[66] *See, e.g.*, United States v. Hutto, 256 U.S. 524, 529 (1921) (§ 372 is violated by conspiring to commit an "offense," even if the offense is not punishable by criminal prosecution); United States v. Tuohey, 867 F.2d 534, 536 (9th Cir. 1989) (noting that a civil law violation is sufficient for the purposes of § 371).

[67] *See, e.g.*, United States v. Jimenez Recio, 537 U.S. 270, 274 (2003) (defendants guilty of conspiracy even though they could not complete object crime of narcotics sale because federal agents had seized the narcotics); United States v. Wallach, 935 F.2d 445, 470–71 (2d Cir. 1991) (defendants guilty of conspiracy to pay federal official even though the payee never became a federal official).

[68] 987 F.2d 1087 (4th Cir. 1993).

[B]   The "Defraud" Clause

[1]   Breadth of the Defraud Clause

The second prong of § 371 (the "defraud" clause) criminalizes conspiracies to defraud the United States. This clause encompasses both (1) schemes to deprive the United States of money or property (such as taxes) and (2) schemes to obstruct or interfere with government functioning or to deprive the government of information.[69] This clause does not require proof that the defendants intended to engage in conduct constituting a separate federal "offense," but the scheme must involve a misrepresentation, trick, or deceit.[70]

The defraud clause is used in a wide variety of circumstances in which the conspirators have attempted to impede the government's functioning. In *United States v. Furkin*,[71] for example, the government charged Furkin with conspiring to "defraud the United States 'by impairing, obstructing and defeating the lawful function of the Internal Revenue Service . . . to ascertain, compute, assess and collect income taxes,' in violation of 18 U.S.C. § 371.'"[72] This theory is known as a "*Klein* conspiracy."[73] Furkin appealed his conviction, arguing that there was insufficient evidence that his co-conspirator was involved in the conspiracy and that therefore the plurality requirement was not met. The appeals court rejected the argument, finding evidence that the co-conspirator undertook actions — such as concealing income from the government — supporting his knowing participation in the scheme.[74]

[2]   The Federal Government as Victim

Some courts hold that the defraud clause requires proof that the defendant have intended that the federal government itself be defrauded. In *United States v. Licciardi*,[75] for example, the defendant was charged in connection with a fraudulent scheme to sell misidentified grapes to wineries. The prosecution also alleged that the defendant intended to defraud the United States because the wines would be mislabeled, thereby obstructing the government agency that had jurisdiction over such labeling. The Ninth Circuit reversed the conspiracy conviction on the ground that, although the defendant clearly intended to defraud the wineries, there was no evidence that he intended to defraud the United States.[76]

---

[69] *See, e.g.*, United States v. Bilzerian, 926 F.2d 1285, 1302 (2d Cir.), *cert. denied*, 502 U.S. 813 (1991) (finding that failure to comply with record-keeping statutes and regulations amounts to interference with a government function under the defraud clause). Such a charge does not require that the government have lost money or property. *See generally* Pomerantz & Obermaier, *supra* note 6, § 4.02[2].

[70] *See* Hammerschmidt v. United States, 265 U.S. 182, 188 (1924); United States v. Southland Corp., 760 F.2d 1366, 1382 (2d Cir.), *cert. denied*, 474 U.S. 825 (1985).

[71]   119 F.3d 1276 (7th Cir. 1997).

[72]   *Id.* at 1279.

[73]   *Id., citing* United States v. Klein, 247 F.2d 908 (2d Cir. 1957), *cert. denied*, 355 U.S. 924 (1958).

[74]   *Furkin*, 119 F.3d at 1280).

[75]   30 F.3d 1127 (9th Cir. 1994).

[76]   *Id.* at 1131–35.

The defraud clause does, however, encompass schemes that affect the United States only indirectly. In *United States v. Hay*,[77] the United States made foreign aid loans, which loans remained subject to United States government supervision. The defendants were convicted under the defraud clause for conspiring to misuse the loan funds. The Tenth Circuit affirmed the convictions, noting that the "United States has a fundamental interest in the manner in which projects receiving its aid are conducted."[78]

On the other hand, in *Tanner v. United States*,[79] the Supreme Court held that a scheme to defraud a private corporation that had merely received government aid did not constitute a scheme to defraud the United States where the aid did not remain subject to government supervision.

[C]   Relationship Between the Offense Clause and the Defraud Clause

Courts generally provide the government with a great deal of flexibility in crafting charges under § 371. Thus, the government can bring a single § 371 conspiracy count alleging that the defendant violated both the offense and defraud clauses.[80]

Most federal circuit courts hold that the two prongs of § 371 create alternate theories that form the basis of a single offense. A defendant thus could not be convicted and punished for two separate charges, based on a single conspiracy, under the two clauses of § 371. In *United States v. Rigas*,[81] for example, the defendants were principals of Adelphia Communications Corporation. The defendants were twice charged under § 371 in connection with the collapse of that company. First, the defendants were charged and convicted in a New York federal court under the *offense clause* for conspiring to commit various fraud offenses relating to Adelphia's collapse. Later, the defendants were charged in a Pennsylvania federal court under the *defraud clause* with conspiring to defraud the United States by evading taxes on monies they had received in connection with their Adelphia fraud scheme. Based upon the plain language of the statute, the court found that § 371 creates a single offense with two possible alternative underlying theories. Accordingly, if the second prosecution was based upon the same conspiratorial agreement as the first, then it would violate the Double Jeopardy Clause for the defendants to be twice convicted and punished for that same conspiracy.[82] A minority of courts do allow the government to charge two

---

[77] 527 F.2d 990 (10th Cir. 1975), *cert. denied*, 425 U.S. 935 (1976).

[78] *Id.* at 998.

[79] 483 U.S. 107 (1987).

[80] *See, e.g.*, United States v. Bilzerian, 926 F.2d 1285, 1301–02 (2d Cir.), *cert. denied*, 502 U.S. 813 (1991).

[81] 605 F.3d 194 (3d Cir. 2010) (en banc).

[82] The Third Circuit stated that it was "inclined to agree" that the government had twice charged the defendants for the same offense. 605 F.3d at 214. Nonetheless, the court remanded the case for an evidentiary hearing on the double jeopardy issue under a totality of the circumstances test. The court stated that this test includes consideration of (1) whether there was a common goal among the

separate crimes, one under each clause, arising out of a single conspiracy.[83]

Courts are also flexible in allowing the government to choose its theory. Thus, courts generally allow the government to proceed under the defraud clause even where the defendant's conduct would have constituted an "offense" under § 371.[84] Conversely, courts allow the government to use the offense clause even where the facts would support a charge under the defraud clause. In *Arch Trading*,[85] for example, the defendant argued that the government must use the defraud clause if the facts support that theory. The court rejected the argument, holding that where the facts support a charge under either clause, the government may choose which theory to use.

Occasionally, a court will restrict the government's ability to charge under either clause. In *United States v. Minarik*,[86] for example, the Sixth Circuit held that the government must proceed under the offense clause rather than the defraud clause where there is evidence that the defendant violated a specific federal statute. Subsequent Sixth Circuit cases, however, have severely limited *Minarik*'s import. Those cases explain that the result in *Minarik* was based upon the prejudice to the defendant because of the way the conspiracy charge was framed.[87]

§ 3.06   REQUIRED MENTAL STATE

In most white collar criminal cases, the government's proof of the criminal mental state, or mens rea, is likely to be key to the jury's determination of guilt or innocence. This is particularly true in conspiracy cases, where proof of the conspiratorial agreement itself will rest on evidence of the co-conspirators' intent.

Courts have stated that conspiracy is a "specific intent" crime.[88] Further, in a conspiracy case, the government must prove that the defendant possessed two levels of mens rea: (1) the intent to agree; and (2) the intent that the object

---

co-conspirators, (2) whether there was a common, continuous scheme among the co-conspirators, and (3) the overlap of the co-conspirators participation in the scheme. Other relevant factors include (a) the location of the conspiracies, (b) temporal overlap of the conspiracies, (c) overlap of personnel, (d) the overlap of overt acts charged, and (e) the similarity in roles played by the defendants. *Id.* at 213.

[83] *See* United States v. Ervasti, 201 F.3d 1029, 1039–40 (8th Cir. 2000) (holding that each clause creates a separate offense and allowing two charges based upon a single agreement, but acknowledging that other circuits disagree). *See also Rigas*, 605 F.3d at 200–11 (describing circuit split and listing cases). For further discussion of when a statute creates separate offenses for purposes of the Double Jeopardy Clause, see Chapter 10, False Statements, *infra*, § 10.08.

[84] *See* United States v. Harmas, 974 F.2d 1262, 1266 (11th Cir. 1992); Dennis v. United States, 384 U.S. 855, 863–64 (1966).

[85] 987 F.2d 1087 (4th Cir. 1993).

[86] 875 F.2d 1186 (6th Cir. 1989).

[87] *See, e.g.,* United States v. Kraig, 99 F.3d 1361, 1366–67 (6th Cir. 1996). *See also Arch Trading*, 987 F.2d at 1092 ("*Minarik* did not hold that the two clauses of § 371 are mutually exclusive, but only that in the case then before the court confusion prejudicial to the defendant had arisen from the government's choice of proceeding under the 'defraud' clause.").

[88] *See* United States v. Bailey, 444 U.S. 394, 405 (1980). This general rule is subject to a qualification discussed in § 3.06[C], *infra*.

offense(s) be committed.[89] Recall that conspiracy and the object offense(s) are separate crimes, with distinct elements. Thus, specific intent is required for a conspiracy conviction, even in cases where the object crime could be proven based upon a lower level of mens rea, such as knowledge or recklessness.[90]

[A] Specific Intent

The general rule is that the government must prove both that the defendant (1) specifically intended to enter into the conspiratorial agreement, and (2) specifically intended that the object offense(s) be committed. Although the government must show that the defendant intended that the criminal objective be achieved, most courts hold that the government need not prove that the defendant specifically intended to violate the law. It is enough that the government prove that the defendant intended to agree and intended that the illegal act or acts be committed.[91]

Definitions of the term "specific intent" are notoriously imprecise.[92] In the most common formulation in the conspiracy context, proof of specific intent requires, in the language of the Model Penal Code, proof that the defendant acted "purposely" — that is, that the defendant "consciously desire[d]" to achieve the criminal result.[93] This high level of mens rea is appropriate with such inchoate crimes as attempt and conspiracy because the criminal harm has not come to pass, and society has an interest in assuring that only the guilty are punished.[94]

The government need not prove, however, that the defendant specifically intended that all the object crimes be committed, nor need the government prove that the defendant knew all the details of the object crimes. It is sufficient if the defendant knew of the general nature of the scheme and intended that some object offense or offenses be committed. For example, in *United States v. Stavroulakis*,[95] the court affirmed the conviction for conspiracy to commit money laundering where the defendant believed that the money to be laundered came from gambling and not from narcotics sales; it was sufficient that the defendant intended to commit acts that fell within the statute. Also, the government need not prove that the defendant knew the identities of all the alleged co-conspirators, so long as the

---

[89] United States v. United States Gypsum Co., 438 U.S. 422, 444 n.20 (1978).

[90] *See* Dressler, *supra* note 10, § 29.05[A] at 434.

[91] *See* United States v. Blair, 54 F.3d 639, 642–43 (10th Cir.), *cert. denied*, 516 U.S. 883 (1995) ("There can be no doubt . . . that conspiracy is a specific intent crime. . . . Specific intent crimes do not, as a rule, necessitate a showing the defendant intentionally violated a known legal duty. . . . 18 U.S.C. § 371 offers no textual support for the proposition that to be guilty of conspiracy a defendant in effect must have known that his conduct violated federal law.").

[92] *See* Dressler, *supra* note 10, § 10.06.

[93] United States v. United States Gypsum Co., 438 U.S. 422, 445 (1978), *quoting* Wayne R. LaFave & Austin W. Scott, Criminal Law § 6.5(g)(4), at 564–65 (2d ed. 1986). *See* Dressler, *supra* note 10, § 10.07[B][1].

[94] *See* Bailey, 444 U.S. at 405 (with inchoate offenses, "a heightened mental state separates criminality itself from otherwise innocuous behavior"); Dressler, *supra* note 10, § 29.05[B].

[95] 952 F.2d 686, 691 (2d Cir.), *cert. denied*, 504 U.S. 926 (1992).

defendant was generally aware of the co-conspirators' existence.[96]

Proof of specific intent to agree and proof of specific intent to effect the object crime(s) are often two sides of the same coin. Thus, in most cases, proof of intent to effect the object crime will also constitute proof of intent to enter into a conspiracy.

There is one typical case where there is a distinction between the intent to agree and the intent that the criminal objective be achieved — an undercover "sting" operation. Imagine, for example, a bribery sting targeting a corrupt legislator. A person is guilty of paying a bribe when that person pays off a public official with the understanding that the public official will perform an official act in return (the "quid pro quo"). In this scenario, the undercover government agent may agree, and intend to agree, with the legislator to pay the official an illegal bribe in return for a favor. Although the agent intends to enter into an agreement, the agent does *not* intend that the government official actually perform the quid pro quo. In fact, the undercover agent probably intends to arrest the targeted official before the target can do the official "favor." Because the undercover agent does not have the mens rea to complete the object crime, there is no conspiracy under the bilateral approach to conspiracy followed by federal courts.[97]

[B] "Knowledge" vs. "Specific Intent"

Two issues arise concerning knowledge and specific intent in conspiracy cases. First, is proof of specific intent always required, or may proof of knowledge suffice? Second, even assuming proof of specific intent is required, what is the burden on the government in making that showing?

As to the first issue, the federal cases use the imprecise term "specific intent." There is some confusion in the case law over whether it is sufficient that the defendant acted with mere "knowledge" of the scheme's illegality, or whether the defendant must have acted with purpose.[98] A defendant acts "knowingly" when the defendant "is aware that it is practically certain that his conduct will cause [the criminal] result."[99]

Because of the vague nature of the offense, courts should require proof that the defendant acted with purpose.[100] In one illustrative case, the court reversed a conspiracy conviction where the government had proven that the defendant sold an ingredient merely *knowing* that the ingredient would be used to manufacture illegal whiskey.[101] As the Second Circuit stated in that case, "[i]t is not enough that

---

[96] *See* Blumenthal v. United States, 332 U.S. 539, 558 (1947).

[97] *See* § 3.04[A], *supra.*

[98] For example, one court held that a corporate official could be liable for conspiracy where he had knowledge of a subordinate's participation in a conspiracy and did nothing to prevent the conspiracy from going forward. United States v. Misle Bus. & Equip., 967 F.2d 1227, 1236 (8th Cir. 1992). *See generally* Dressler, *supra* note 10, § 29.05[B].

[99] Model Penal Code § 2.02(2)(b)(ii).

[100] *See* United States v. Dimeck, 24 F.3d 1239, 1248 (10th Cir. 1994) (holding that "mere knowledge of illegal activity, even in conjunction with participation in a small part of the conspiracy" is not sufficient to establish that the participant knowingly joined the conspiracy).

[101] United States v. Falcone,109 F.2d 579, 581 (2d Cir.), *aff'd*, 311 U.S. 205 (1940).

[the defendant] does not forego a normally lawful activity, of the fruits of which he knows that others will make an unlawful use; he must in some sense promote their venture himself, make it his own, have a stake in its outcome."[102] The court went on to note that the requirement of such heightened proof is essential to protect against unfairness: "The distinction [between mere knowledge and purpose] is especially important today when so many prosecutors seek to sweep within the dragnet of conspiracy all those who have been associated in any degree whatever with the main offenders."[103] Just three years later, however, the Supreme Court affirmed a conspiracy conviction in similar, although arguably distinguishable, circumstances.[104] Thus, the case law remains somewhat muddled.

As to the second issue — the level of the required proof for specific intent — the cases show that distinguishing proof of "knowledge" from proof of "purpose" is not easy. One court gave the following example: "Selling a camera to a spy [with mere knowledge of the camera's illegal use] does not make one a traitor — but selling camera and film, developing the prints, enlarging the detail in the critical areas, and collecting half of the payment for the secret information [*i.e.*, acting with the purpose that the crime be committed] would surely land one in prison."[105] Courts continue to struggle to establish the level of proof necessary to show purpose to engage in a conspiracy.

[C] Conscious Avoidance

At a minimum, the government should be required to prove both that the defendant knew of the illegal nature of the scheme and had the purpose to achieve the criminal objectives. If a person agrees to enter into a scheme, but deliberately avoids learning of the illegal nature of the scheme, is that person guilty of conspiracy? Most courts hold in the affirmative.[106] In *United States v. Svoboda*,[107] defendant Robles appealed his securities fraud conviction. At trial, the government alleged that Robles and his co-conspirator Svoboda illegally traded securities based upon secret information that Svoboda had stolen from his employer and had given to Robles. In defense, Robles claimed that he did not know that Svoboda had obtained the information illegally and therefore did not know of the alleged conspiracy's illegal objectives. At the government's request, the trial judge instructed the jury that it could find the requisite knowledge if it found that Robles

---

[102] 109 F.2d at 581.

[103] *Id.*

[104] Direct Sales Co. v. United States, 319 U.S. 703 (1943) (finding a sufficient showing of intent where the defendant sold an ingredient knowing it would be used to manufacture illegal drugs). One commentator argued that *Direct Sales* differed from *Falcone* in that the sale in *Direct Sales* could only be used for illegal purposes, given the nature and quantity of the ingredient sold, but that the same could not be said about *Falcone*. *See* Sara N. Welling et al., Federal Criminal Law and Related Actions § 2.14[C] at 75–76 (1998 & Supp. 1999). *See also* United States v. Blankenship, 970 F.2d 283 (7th Cir. 1992) (finding an insufficient showing of intent where the defendant leased property for a short period knowing it would be used for an illegal drug laboratory).

[105] *Blankenship*, 970 F.2d at 286.

[106] *See, e.g.*, United States v. Lanza, 790 F.2d 1015, 1023–24 (2d Cir. 1986). For a discussion of "willful blindness" as meeting the mens rea requirement of "knowledge," see *supra*, § 1.06[A][1].

[107] 347 F.3d 471 (2d Cir. 2003).

had deliberately avoided acquiring knowledge of the information's source.

On appeal, Robles argued that a conscious avoidance instruction is improper in a conspiracy case, particularly when there are only two alleged co-conspirators. According to this argument, the plurality requirement is not met unless the government proves that both co-conspirators had actual knowledge of the conspiracy's illegal objectives. The Second Circuit rejected the argument. The court held that, where the facts support such an instruction, a conscious avoidance instruction is proper as to the knowledge prong of a conspiracy case.[108]

[D] Mens Rea and Federal Jurisdiction

It is important to distinguish between the mens rea as to the agreement and the object crimes, on the one hand, and the jurisdictional elements of the crime on the other. In *United States v. Feola*,[109] the Supreme Court held that the defendant need not have acted with specific intent as to the jurisdictional element of the object crime. In that case, the defendants were drug dealers charged with conspiring to assault a federal officer. The defendants agreed to attack the victim, who they believed was a drug buyer but who was actually an undercover federal agent. The defendants argued that, because they did not know the victim was a federal agent, they could not have acted with the specific intent or purpose to assault a *federal* officer.

The Supreme Court rejected the defendants' argument, and held that it was sufficient that the defendants intended to achieve the desired criminal result, the physical harm to the victim. The Court noted that the victim's status as a federal officer was not a substantive element of the crime but merely a circumstance element that provided federal jurisdiction. As to that jurisdictional element, the defendants were strictly liable, *i.e.*, the government was not required to prove any mental state.[110]

§ 3.07 PROOF OF GUILT IN A CONSPIRACY CASE

[A] Level of Required Proof

Of the elements discussed above, the most difficult to prove is usually the meeting of the co-conspirators' minds. In showing the existence of the agreement, and the defendant's mental state concerning the agreement and the object crimes, the government will rarely have direct, concrete evidence; co-conspirators usually

---

[108] *Id.* at 479. Robles relied upon an earlier Second Circuit decision, United States v. Reyes, 302 F.3d 48 (2d Cir. 2002). In *Svoboda*, the court found that the *Reyes* language upon which Robles relied was dictum, and in any event the language "simply means that just as actual knowledge of the illegal purpose of a conspiracy is insufficient to prove a defendant's joinder in a conspiracy, so conscious avoidance of such knowledge is also insufficient. There must be further proof that the defendant joined in the illegal agreement with the intent of helping it succeed in its criminal purpose." 347 F.3d at 479.

[109] 420 U.S. 671 (1975).

[110] *Id.* at 696.

know better than to reduce their agreement to writing.[111] Thus, courts grant the government substantial latitude in relying on circumstantial evidence.

Courts rarely reverse conspiracy convictions based upon the insufficiency of the evidence. Facts from which a jury could reasonably infer a defendant's participation, even in the face of the defendant's denial, will usually support a conviction. In *United States v. Brown*,[112] for example, the appellant was an associate with a law firm that assisted two clients in a bankruptcy fraud scheme. Although Brown was a subordinate attorney acting at a superior's direction, the court found that his extensive participation in handling the case — attending meetings where wrongdoing was discussed, destroying records, and failing to produce documents — entitled the jury to infer that he agreed to enter into the illegal scheme.

[B]   Co-Conspirators' Exception to the Hearsay Rule

One of the most important tactical advantages that a conspiracy charge affords prosecutors is the admissibility of certain "hearsay" evidence that would be excluded absent such a charge. Hearsay is an out-of-court statement offered for its truth. For example, a prosecutor would call a witness, who would testify that a third person (the "declarant") said, "I saw the defendant commit the crime." The prosecutor would offer the statement for its truth, *i.e.*, to show that the defendant committed the crime. Because such statements are considered unreliable (there is no way to know whether the declarant actually saw the defendant commit the crime), and because the defense has no opportunity to cross-examine the declarant, hearsay statements are generally excluded from admission at trial under the rules of evidence.

Under Rule 801(d)(2)(E) of the Federal Rules of Evidence, the "co-conspirator's exception, an out-of-court statement offered for its truth, is deemed not to be hearsay and is admissible. Under the rule, the party offering the statement must show that it was "made by the co-conspirator of a party during the course of and in furtherance of the conspiracy."

This exception is generally justified on two grounds. First, a party's own statement offered at trial against that party would be deemed non-hearsay and thus admissible as a party admission under Rule 801(d)(2)(A). Because co-conspirators are considered to have been acting as each other's agents, the co-conspirator's statement is in effect a party's statement offered against the party. Second, because conspiracies can rarely be proven by direct evidence, the exception provides the government with an additional route to prove that the crime was committed.

Admitting an alleged co-conspirator statement creates a procedural problem. The prosecution will proffer the statement during the trial, before the jury has

---

[111] *See* Goode v. United States, 58 F.2d 105, 107 (8th Cir. 1932) (conspiracy is rarely susceptible to proof by direct evidence). For an example of the rare case where the agreement was reduced to writing, see United States v. Hay, 527 F.2d 990 (10th Cir. 1975), *cert. denied*, 425 U.S. 935 (1976).

[112] 943 F.2d 1246 (10th Cir. 1991).

determined whether or not a conspiracy existed. In most circuits, the trial judge will admit the statement subject to a defense motion to strike at the end of the government's case on the ground the government failed to adduce sufficient evidence that the conspiracy existed and that the out-of-court declarant and the defendant were parties to the conspiracy. Some courts require a preliminary showing, outside the presence of the jury, that the conspiracy existed before the co-conspirator statement can be introduced.[113] Under the United States Supreme Court's decision in *Bourjaily v. United States*,[114] the court may use the co-conspirator's declaration in determining whether the government has made a sufficient showing. Furthermore, under these principles, the government may invoke the co-conspirators' exception even where the defendant has not been charged with conspiracy.[115]

There are limitations on the admission of co-conspirators' statements, however. Specifically, the statement must have been made by a co-conspirator of the defendant during the course of and in furtherance of the conspiracy. Thus, in *Krulewitch v. United States*, the United States Supreme Court held that a co-conspirator's statement may not be introduced against a defendant if the statement was made after the conspiracy has ended.[116] In that case, the criminal scheme had been completed, and the co-conspirators arrested, before the statement was made; thus, the conspiracy was over, and the hearsay exception did not apply. Nor does the exception apply if the statement was made *after* the defendant had withdrawn from the conspiracy.[117] Most courts do allow a co-conspirator's statement to be introduced where the statement was made *before* the defendant joined the conspiracy, however. Those courts reason that a co-conspirator adopts the statements by joining the conspiracy.[118]

§ 3.08 THE BREADTH OF THE AGREEMENT

[A] Overview

One of the most significant issues arising in a typical conspiracy case concerns the breadth of the conspiracy. Recall that the very term "conspiracy" refers not to a group of individuals but to an agreement to an illegal end.[119] Determining the scope of the agreement is essential for assessing who can appropriately be brought

---

[113] *See* Pomerantz & Obermaier, *supra* note 6, at § 4.02[10].

[114] 483 U.S. 171 (1987). Three Justices dissented, arguing that it was unfair to the defendant to allow the conspiracy to be shown by evidence not wholly independent of the declarant's hearsay statements. Although the Supreme Court did not reach the issue, most courts also require *some* evidence, apart from the co-conspirator's statement, showing that the conspiracy existed. *See, e.g.*, United States v. Lindemann, 85 F.3d 1232, 1239 n.4 (7th Cir. 1996); United States v. Silverman, 861 F.2d 571 (9th Cir. 1988). For an argument in support of this requirement, see Pomerantz & Obermaier, *supra* note 6, § 4.02[10].

[115] *See* United States v. Rinaldi, 393 F.2d 97, 99 (2d Cir.), *cert. denied*, 393 U.S. 913 (1968).

[116] 336 U.S. 440, 444 (1949).

[117] The requirements for withdrawal are discussed *infra* § 3.12.

[118] *See, e.g.*, United States v. Holder, 652 F.2d 449, 451 (5th Cir. 1981).

[119] *See supra* § 3.04.

in as a defendant in the conspiracy case. This issue manifests itself as two overlapping sub-issues. First, for a defendant to be properly joined in a conspiracy case, the facts must show that the defendant was a party to the agreement charged. Second, if the facts do not show a single conspiracy, but rather two or more distinct conspiracies, then the defense has several arguments for an acquittal at trial or a reversal after appeal.

Resolution of these issues is often determined by the same factual analysis, which focuses on the breadth of the agreement itself. Thus, in many ways, the procedural determination of whether a defendant is properly joined in a conspiracy trial mirrors the substantive issues of whether the government has proven both that the alleged agreement existed and that the defendant had the requisite mens rea to be found guilty of entering into that agreement.[120]

[B] Advantages of a Single Trial

Whether a defendant is included in a conspiracy case, or is tried separately, can be very important. For example, in a conspiracy case with multiple defendants, it will often be true that the government's case will be much stronger against some defendants than others. If there is a single trial, however, the natural tendency will be for the jury to assess the defendants' guilt collectively and to convict those against whom there is relatively weak evidence.[121]

Correspondingly, all the advantages to the government in a conspiracy case — including choice of venue, liability for others' acts, attribution of overt acts to all defendants, and the application of the co-conspirators' exception to the hearsay rule — will of course only apply if a defendant is tried as part of a conspiracy case.[122] Further, it is usually easier and more efficient for the government to try one large case rather than two or more small ones; witnesses need testify at only one trial, and other logistical burdens are reduced by a single trial.

[C] Single Conspiracy vs. Multiple Conspiracies

[1] Joinder Issues

Recall the basic principle that the scope of a conspiracy is determined by the agreement itself. Unless a particular defendant is party to the overarching agreement charged in the indictment, that defendant cannot properly be tried with other alleged co-conspirators. This result is compelled both by the due process requirement of a fair trial[123] and by the Federal Rules of Criminal Procedure. Under Rule 8(b), a defendant can only be joined with one or more codefendants in

---

[120] *See* Pomerantz & Obermaier, *supra* note 6, § 4.02[7], p. 4-30.

[121] *See Krulewich*, 336 U.S. at 454 (Jackson, J., concurring) ("A co-defendant in a conspiracy trial occupies an uneasy seat. There generally will be evidence of wrongdoing by somebody. It is difficult for the individual to make his own case stand on its merits in the minds of jurors who are ready to believe that birds of a feather are flocked together.").

[122] *See* United States v. Morrow, 39 F.3d 1228, 1235 (1st Cir.1994), *cert. denied*, 514 U.S. 1010 (1995).

[123] *See* United States v. Lane, 474 U.S. 438, 446 n.8 (1986) (misjoinder may violate due process right to a fair trial where the prejudice is sufficient).

a single trial if they participated in "the same act or transaction or in the same series of acts or transactions constituting an offense or offenses." In a conspiracy case, a defendant who was not part of the single scheme either must be severed from the case and granted a separate trial or the conspiracy count must be dismissed (and presumably will be re-filed naming the appropriate parties). The defendant can raise the joinder issue in a pre-trial motion to dismiss the indictment, on motions during and at the conclusion of trial,[124] and on appeal.

Alternatively, even if joinder is proper under Rule 8(b), a trial judge may grant a defendant a separate trial under Rule 14's discretionary severance provision in order to assure the defendant a fair trial.[125] Such severance might be granted as to defendant A, for example, where evidence admissible only as to defendants B and C is highly inflammatory or prejudicial, and where a judge's instruction that the jury not consider the evidence as to defendant A would likely be ineffective.

The issue of whether a defendant is properly joined in a case will often turn upon whether the facts charged demonstrate one single conspiracy or, instead, two or more discrete conspiracies. This issue arises frequently in conspiracy cases. Assume, for example, that A and B agree to stage an automobile accident, and to mail an insurance claim form to complete their fraud. Further assume that B and C agree to falsely report that a car is stolen, and to mail a fraudulent claim form to recover the insurance proceeds. At a minimum, there are two separate conspiracies — one between A and B, and another between B and C. But can all three properly be joined in a single trial for conspiracy to commit mail fraud?

The answer depends upon whether each defendant intended to enter into a scheme broader than the single scheme to which that defendant was a party. Although each defendant need not specifically agree to each illegal act, at a minimum a defendant must understand the essential nature of the scheme in order for that defendant to be properly joined in a single conspiracy trial. Assuming that the government has *alleged* sufficient facts to show a single conspiracy, but that the evidence may be *interpreted* to support the finding of *either* a single conspiracy or multiple conspiracies, then the issue goes to the jury. If the jury finds that the defendant was not a member of the single conspiracy charged, then it must acquit.[126]

The leading case applying this rule is *Kotteakos v. United States.*[127] In that case, Brown acted as a real estate broker for eight or more groups of defendants who had fraudulently obtained loans from the Federal Housing Administration. Although each group acted through Brown, there was no evidence that any group had any connection with any other group. The government had characterized the conspiracy as a "wheel," with Brown as the hub and his customers as spokes. As the Supreme Court stated, however, in order for there to be a single conspiracy the individual spokes must be connected by a single "rim" — the overarching agreement that ties

---

[124] *See* Fed. R. Crim. P. 29(a) (motion to acquit at the end of the government's case); Fed. R. Crim. P. 29(b) (motion for acquittal notwithstanding the verdict).

[125] *See* Developments in the Law, *supra* note 25, at 982.

[126] *See* Pomerantz & Obermaier, *supra* note 6, § 4.02[8], at 4-35.

[127] 328 U.S. 750 (1946).

together all the co-conspirators.[128] Thus, there were eight or more separate conspiracies, and not the single conspiracy charged in the indictment.

If the defendants have reason to know of a broader scheme, however, then a single conspiracy is properly charged. In *Blumenthal v. United States*,[129] for example, the Supreme Court found that the defendant was part of one conspiracy to sell whiskey at illegal prices. The scheme involved a wholesaler, two distributors, and two salespeople. The latter argued that they had no dealings with the wholesaler, and were not part of a single conspiracy involving the wholesaler. The Court found, however, that even though the salespeople may not have known the wholesaler's identity, they did know that they were selling portions of one large lot of whiskey and thus knew of the broader scheme.[130]

In this sense, the facts in *Blumthental* showed not a "wheel" conspiracy, but a "chain" with three links: the wholesaler (link one), the distributors (link two), and the salespeople (link three). The finding of a single conspiracy reflects the mens rea requirement for membership in a conspiracy, which requires only that a defendant know of the co-conspirators' existence. Thus, even though the individual salespeople (link three) may not have known the identity, or even of the existence, of the wholesaler (link one), they must have known that they were part of a broader scheme to sell one large lot of whisky that necessarily involved a supplier (link one) in addition to the distributors (link two).[131]

Courts often struggle to establish a standard for determining whether a single conspiracy existed. In *United States v. Morrow*,[132] for example, the court articulated the "governing principle" thus:

> [A]t a minimum, a conspirator must have knowledge or foresight of the conspiracy's multiplicity of objectives before that defendant is convicted of a multiple-crime conspiracy. Conviction . . . remains possible even if the conspiracy is open-ended (e.g., a conspiracy to rob banks) and the specifics of the future crimes (e.g., which banks) is [sic] undetermined or at least unknown to the defendant. But if a defendant agrees with others simply to commit a single crime (e.g., to rob one bank) and has no knowledge or foresight of the conspiracy's broader scope, that defendant is a member only of the narrower, one-crime conspiracy.

Applying this approach, the *Morrow* court found that the government had proven one conspiracy involving A and B, another involving A, B, and C, and a third involving A, B, and D. Because C and D were not aware of, and therefore not members of, the broader criminal scheme, there was insufficient evidence to convict

---

[128] *Id.* at 754–55.

[129] 332 U.S. 539 (1947).

[130] *Id.* at 559.

[131] *See* Dressler, *supra* note 10, § 29.07[C][3], [D][4]. Not all conspiracies neatly fall into the "wheel" or "chain" categories; some will evince characteristics of each type. *See id.* at 414, *citing* United States v. Bruno, 105 F.2d 921 (2d Cir.), *rev'd on other grounds*, 308 U.S. 287 (1939).

[132] 39 F.3d 1228, 1234 (1st Cir. 1994).

them of a single conspiracy.[133]

More often, however, courts do find evidence sufficient to support a single conspiracy. In *United States v. Gatling*,[134] for example, defendants Walker and Gatling were convicted of conspiracy to commit bribery with respect to federally-funded housing subsidies. The government alleged that the defendants engaged in a single conspiracy to commit bribes involving subsidies to ineligible residents in both Chicago and Washington, D.C. On appeal, Walker argued that the evidence established two separate conspiracies, one involving Chicago residents and one involving D.C. residents. The appeals court disagreed, and affirmed the conviction. The court found that the two schemes were similar in operation, and that the schemes overlapped in terms of timing and participants; Walker and Gatling were the principal figures in both schemes.[135]

[2] The Showing of Prejudice

Even if the defense succeeds in convincing an appellate court that the government failed to prove a single conspiracy, a reversal is not necessarily required. Rather, the defense also has the burden of proving that the error resulted in substantial prejudice.[136] In *Kotteakos*, for example, the Supreme Court found prejudicial error and reversed the conviction. In that case, the government conceded that there was a "variance" between the evidence at trial, which showed multiple conspiracies, and the indictment, which charged but a single conspiracy.[137] The government argued that the variance had not prejudiced the defendants. The Court rejected the government's argument on two grounds. First, the jury could have considered evidence as to some defendants that was irrelevant to other defendants because they were not all part of the same conspiracy. Second, the jury could have imputed overt acts of any alleged co-conspirator to all the defendants, even though the defendants were not all part of a single conspiracy.[138] The Court concluded by noting that "[g]uilt with us remains individual and personal," and that mass conspiracy trials pose a particular danger to this principle.[139]

More often, however, an appeals court will find that a defendant has failed to prove that substantial prejudice resulted from a variance between the charges and the proof.[140] In *Morrow*, for example, the appeals court affirmed the conviction in

---

[133] Large conspiracies based upon loose connections among defendants are frequently charged in narcotics cases, and courts generally sustain such charges. *See, e.g.*, United States v. Briscoe, 896 F.2d 1476 (7th Cir. 1990); United States v. Vanwort, 887 F.2d 375 (2d Cir. 1989), *cert. denied*, 495 U.S. 910 (1990).

[134] 96 F.3d 1511 (D.C. Cir. 1996).

[135] *Id.* at 1520.

[136] *See* Benjamin M. Dooling & Marissa A. Lalli, *Federal Criminal Conspiracy*, 47 Am. Crim. L. Rev. 561, 575–76 (2010).

[137] 328 U.S. at 771.

[138] *Id.* at 772.

[139] *Id.*

[140] *See* William H. Theis, *The Double Jeopardy Defense and Multiple Prosecutions for Conspiracy*, 49 SMU L. Rev. 269, 287 (1996) (referring to the *Kotteakos* holding as "a perennial beacon of false hope for the criminal defense bar").

a case where the government charged a single conspiracy but the evidence showed multiple conspiracies. Even though the proof at trial varied from the crime charged, the defendants failed to show that the variance prejudiced them. First, despite the variance, the defendants knew the essential nature of the charges against them.[141] Second, even though some hearsay evidence was improperly admitted under the co-conspirators' rule, the defendants were not prejudiced by this error because there was strong proof that each participated in an illegal scheme.[142]

[3] Double Jeopardy Issues

There are cases where, instead of arguing that there were multiple conspiracies, it will be to the defendants' advantage to argue that there was one overarching conspiracy. If a defendant is charged in one court for conspiracy X, and in another court for conspiracy Y, then the defendant will likely assert that X and Y were not discrete conspiracies but were actually parts of a single conspiracy. Thus, conviction and consecutive sentencing for both conspiracy X and Y would violate the Double Jeopardy Clause's prohibition against multiple punishments for the same act.[143] It would not violate double jeopardy, however, to punish the defendant for two counts of conspiracy based upon one agreement where there are *separate conspiracy statutes* that apply to the defendant's conduct. For example, in *Albernaz v. United States*,[144] the Supreme Court held that the defendant could receive separate sentences for violations of separate conspiracy statutes (conspiracy to import marijuana, and conspiracy to distribute marijuana) that arose out of the same criminal scheme.

The *Albernaz* scenario should be distinguished from an agreement that violates only one conspiracy statute but that has multiple object crimes. As the Supreme Court held in *United States v. Braverman*,[145] one agreement to commit multiple offenses can only give rise to one count under the general conspiracy statute.

§ 3.09 VICARIOUS LIABILITY — THE *PINKERTON* DOCTRINE

[A] The *Pinkerton* Decision

The United States Supreme Court spelled out the scope of the special co-conspirators' vicarious liability rule in *Pinkerton v. United States*.[146] In that case, the defendant, Daniel, entered into a conspiracy with his brother to commit tax fraud. The brother committed tax fraud on a number of occasions when Daniel was

---

[141] 39 F.3d at 1235.

[142] *Id.* at 1236.

[143] *See, e.g.*, United States v. Smith, 82 F.3d 1261 (3d Cir. 1996) (rejecting the argument that there was one single conspiracy).

[144] 450 U.S. 333, 338 (1981).

[145] 317 U.S. 49, 53 (1942).

[146] 328 U.S. 640 (1946).

actually in jail and did not participate in or even know of the offenses.[147] Nonetheless, the Court upheld Daniel's conviction on the substantive offenses committed by his brother under the theory that co-conspirators are responsible for each other's acts.

Under the *Pinkerton* rule, a defendant may be vicariously liable for a substantive offense that another member of the conspiracy committed if

(1)   the defendant was a party to that conspiracy;[148]

(2)   the offense was "within the scope of the unlawful project"

(3)   the offense was "in furtherance of" the conspiracy; and

(4)   the defendant could have "reasonably foreseen" the offense as a "necessary or natural consequence of the unlawful agreement."[149]

Generally, *Pinkerton* liability arises where the substantive crime either falls directly within the conspiracy's primary goals[150] or helps achieve those goals.[151]

[B]   The Policy Debate

Because a co-conspirator may be liable for acts that the defendant *should* have foreseen, the effect of this rule is to impose liability for substantive offenses as to which the defendant was merely negligent. The standard of proof is therefore lower than it would be if the defendant were charged with aiding and abetting the substantive offense. Aiding and abetting liability requires proof that the defendant possessed the same mental state that would be required for the completed offense. Under the facts of *Pinkerton*, for example, had Daniel been charged with *aiding and abetting* his brother's tax fraud, then the government would have had to prove that Daniel possessed the specific intent to defraud required for conviction of that crime. But because Daniel was charged under a *conspiracy* theory, the government merely had to prove that Daniel could have reasonably foreseen the brother's commission of tax fraud.[152] This reduced mens rea standard for vicarious liability

---

[147]   *See Id.* at 648 (Rutledge, J., dissenting).

[148]   Although some cases have stated to the contrary, *see* Welling et al., *supra* note 36, § 4.5 n. 14, the defendant should not be held liable for substantive offenses committed after the defendant has withdrawn from the conspiracy. *See infra* § 3.12.

[149]   *Pinkerton*, 328 U.S. at 647–48. *See generally* Welling et al., *supra* note 104, § 4.5; Dressler, *supra* note 10, § 30.08[B].

[150]   *See, e.g.*, United States v. Tilton, 610 F.2d 302, 309 (5th Cir. 1980) (liability for mail fraud based upon conspiracy to commit mail fraud).

[151]   *See* cases cited in United States v. Alvarez, 755 F.2d 830, 850 n.24 (11th Cir. 1985), *cert. denied*, 474 U.S. 905 (1987).

[152]   For an expansive application of the *Pinkerton* doctrine in a non-white collar case, see United States v. Alvarez, 755 F.2d 830, 850 (11th Cir. 1985) (conceding perhaps "an unprecedented application of *Pinkerton*," the court affirmed the second-degree murder convictions of defendants in a drug conspiracy case who were uninvolved in and had no knowledge of the circumstances leading to the homicides). *But see* United States v. Cherry, 217 F.3d 811, 817 (10th Cir. 2000) (declining to expand *Pinkerton* liability to include reasonably foreseeable but originally unintended substantive crimes).

is another ground upon which the federal law of conspiracy is criticized as unfair to defendants.[153]

[C] Application to White Collar Crimes

It is not rare in white collar cases for defendants to be convicted of charges under *Pinkerton*. For example, in *United States v. Tilton*,[154] the defendant was convicted of conspiracy and of object offenses including mail fraud. Tilton managed projects for Sea-Land Inc. In exchange for selecting companies to perform work for Sea-Land, he received bribes. Tilton was convicted of mail fraud based upon other persons' mailing of invoices that were inflated to cover the bribe amounts. On appeal, he argued that the mail fraud convictions should be reversed because he did not personally engage in and did not know about the mailings. The court rejected the argument, and affirmed the mail fraud convictions under *Pinkerton*. The mailings of the inflated invoices furthered the conspiracy, and were a natural and foreseeable consequence of the kickback scheme.[155]

§ 3.10 INCONSISTENT VERDICTS

Often in white collar cases a defendant will argue that the conviction must be reversed on the ground that the jury reached verdicts that appear inconsistent. The argument is that, in such a circumstance, the jury must have speculated instead of reaching a conclusion based upon the reasonable doubt standard.[156] Conspiracy is particularly ripe for such arguments, because by its nature the crime requires that at least two people have entered into the agreement. But what if one co-conspirator is convicted and the other (or others) acquitted? Does that mean the jury must have made a mistake, and that the conviction must be reversed?

Most courts say not. Although the Supreme Court has not addressed the issue in a conspiracy case, in *United States v. Powell*[157] the Court held that inconsistent verdicts in general do not require reversal. In that case, the defendant was acquitted of narcotics charges but convicted of using a telephone to commit those very crimes. The Court reasoned that an acquittal in such a case does not necessarily mean that the jury found the defendant innocent of the charge. For example, the jury may have simply decided to exercise leniency with respect to a particular charge.

A majority of circuit courts have applied the *Powell* reasoning to conspiracy cases and have declined to reverse the conviction of a conspirator whose co-conspirators were acquitted. For example, in *United States v. Valles-Vallencia*,[158] the Ninth

---

[153] Thus, the Model Penal Code rejects *Pinkerton* liability. *See* Model Penal Code § 2.06 commentary.

[154] 610 F.2d 302 (5th Cir. 1980).

[155] *Id.* at 309.

[156] *See, e.g.*, United States v. Valles-Valencia, 811 F.2d 1232 (9th Cir.), *amended by* 823 F.2d 381 (9th Cir. 1987).

[157] 469 U.S. 57 (1984).

[158] 811 F.2d 1232 (9th Cir. 1986). The initial opinion noted that there were two circumstances when acquittal of co-conspirators did not require reversal: (1) when the government presents substantial

Circuit initially dismissed a conspiracy conviction because the jury had acquitted the co-conspirators. On rehearing, however, the court applied the *Powell* reasoning and affirmed the conviction. The Ninth Circuit continued to follow this rule in *United States v. Hughes Aircraft Co.*,[159] where it upheld the corporate defendant's conspiracy conviction even though the individual through whom the company acted was acquitted. Although most courts have followed the Ninth Circuit's approach,[160] there is language in some circuit opinions indicating that consistent verdicts may be required in conspiracy cases based upon the bilateral nature of the crime.[161]

§ 3.11 DURATION

For several reasons, it will be important in many cases to determine when the conspiracy began and/or when it ended. First, the statute of limitations begins to run at the time a conspiracy ends. Second, the *Pinkerton* vicarious liability doctrine only applies to crimes committed by co-conspirators while the conspiracy is in existence. Third, the co-conspirator exception to the hearsay rule will only apply to statements made during the conspiracy.[162]

Determining when a conspiracy began is usually not difficult. The crime of conspiracy is based upon the agreement among the co-conspirators. Therefore, a conspiracy began when the agreement was formed and, where the law requires, when an overt act was committed.

It is often more difficult, however, to determine when a conspiracy ended. Under *Krulewitch*,[163] a conspiracy ends when the criminal activities have been completed and the scheme is over. That was clearly the case in *Krulewitch* because the co-conspirators had completed their scheme and had been arrested. Under this reasoning, a conspiracy also ends if all the co-conspirators discontinue their participation in the conspiracy and abandon the scheme.

But what if it becomes impossible for the co-conspirators to achieve their objectives? Can a conspiracy continue even after the point when the object crimes cannot be achieved? That was the issue in *United States v. Jimenez Recio.*[164] In that case, government agents stopped a truck and its two occupants and seized narcotics they found in the truck. The agents then arranged with the occupants to go forward

---

evidence that the defendant conspired with unindicted or unnamed co-conspirators; and (2) when the judgment as to the defendant is not based upon the merits, as with a hung jury. *Id.* at 1239.

[159] 20 F.3d 974 (9th Cir. 1994).

[160] *See, e.g.*, Robertson v. Klem, 580 F.3d 159 (3d Cir. 2009); United States v. Loe, 248 F.3d 449 (5th Cir. 2001). *See generally* Dooling & Lalli, *supra* note 136, 492–93, and cases cited therein.

[161] *See, e.g.*, United States v. Howard, 966 F.2d 1362, 1364 (10th Cir. 1992); United States v. Levario, 877 F.2d 1483, 1486 (10th Cir. 1989). Note that *Powell* involved inconsistent verdicts as to crimes allegedly committed by a single defendant. Some have argued that the *Powell* reasoning does not apply to conspiracy cases, in which there are inconsistent verdicts as to different defendants. *See* United States v. Andrews, 850 F.2d 1557, 1570 (11th Cir. 1988) (en banc) (Clark, J., dissenting).

[162] *See* Krulewitch v. United States, 336 U.S. 440, 442–43 (1949) (the hearsay exception does not apply where statement was made after the conspiracy ended).

[163] *Id.*

[164] 537 U.S. 270 (2003).

with the occupants' scheme to hand over the drugs to other parties. When two other parties took possession of the drugs, the agents arrested them. Those two parties were convicted of conspiracy to distribute narcotics.

On appeal to the Ninth Circuit, the two defendants argued that the conspiracy had terminated when the government seized the drugs. Because there was insufficient evidence that the defendants had joined the conspiracy prior to the seizure of the drugs, their convictions could not stand. The defendants relied upon the Ninth Circuit's decision in *United States v. Cruz*,[165] which held that a conspiracy terminates when "there is affirmative evidence of the abandonment, withdrawal, disavowal or defeat of the object of the conspiracy."[166] According to this argument, because the government had "defeat[ed] the object of the conspiracy" by seizing the drugs, the conspiracy had already ended by the time the defendants were arrested. The Ninth Circuit agreed and reversed the conspiracy convictions.

On appeal, the Supreme Court rejected the rule articulated in *Cruz* and reinstated the convictions. The Court found that "[a] conspiracy does not automatically terminate simply because the government, unbeknownst to some of the conspirators, has 'defeat[ed]' the conspiracy's 'object.' "[167] In finding that impossibility is not a defense to a conspiracy charge, the Court focused on the dangers of group criminality that underlie the crime of conspiracy.[168]

§ 3.12 WITHDRAWAL

Even when a conspiracy is ongoing, a co-conspirator may withdraw from the conspiracy. Although one is guilty of the crime of conspiracy upon commission of the requisite elements, a co-conspirator's withdrawal from a conspiracy can have substantial consequences for that person.[169] First, the statute of limitations will begin to run as to that co-conspirator upon withdrawal.[170] Second, most courts hold that a co-conspirator who has withdrawn from a conspiracy may not be held vicariously liable under the *Pinkerton* doctrine for the crimes committed by co-conspirators after the defendant withdrew from the conspiracy.[171] Finally, co-conspirator statements made after withdrawal are not admissible as to that defendant.[172]

---

[165] 127 F.3d 791 (9th Cir. 1997), *abrogated by* United States v. Jimenez Recio, 537 U.S. 270 (2003).

[166] 537 U.S. at 272.

[167] *Id.* at 274.

[168] *Cf.* United States v. Wallach, 935 F.2d 445, 470–71 (2d Cir. 1991) (impossibility of completion of object offense is not a defense to conspiracy charge).

[169] *See* United States v. Gonzalez, 797 F.2d 915, 916 (10th Cir. 1986); Roger Spaeder & Gary Weinfeld, *Effective Withdrawal from a Business Conspiracy*, 9-SPG Crim. Justice 8-9 (1994).

[170] *See* United States v. Steele, 685 F.2d 793 (3d Cir.), *cert. denied*, 459 U.S. 908 (1982); United States v. Read, 658 F.2d 1225, 1232–33 (7th Cir. 1981).

[171] *See* Dooling & Lalli, *supra* note 136;; Spaeder & Weinfeld, *supra* note 169, at 8-9.

[172] *See* United States v. Patel, 879 F.2d 292, 293 (7th Cir. 1989), *cert. denied*, 494 U.S. 1016 (1990).

The Supreme Court set forth the general requirements for withdrawal in *United States v. United States Gypsum Co.*[173] As the Court stated, simply ceasing to participate in the conspiracy is not sufficient: "Affirmative acts inconsistent with the object of the conspiracy and communicated in a manner reasonably calculated to reach co-conspirators have generally been regarded as sufficient to establish withdrawal or abandonment."[174]

One way that a defendant may withdraw from a conspiracy is to resign or retire from the business through which the conspiracy was conducted.[175] In *United States v. Steele,*[176] for example, the court found that the defendant had effectively withdrawn from a corporate conspiracy to bribe public officials. In that case, there was no evidence that the defendant continued to participate in the conspiracy after he resigned from the corporation.[177] The court found that the defendant had made a prima facie showing of withdrawal, and that the government had failed to rebut the showing.

If the defendant continues to receive benefits from or otherwise participate in the illegal scheme, however, a claim of withdrawal will not be effective. In *United States v. Eisen,*[178] for example, persons associated with a personal injury law firm were convicted of conspiring to fix cases. Two defendants, an investigator and an attorney, argued that they had withdrawn from the conspiracy when they discontinued their work for the firm. The court rejected the argument. Even after he left the firm the investigator continued to work for the firm on an ad hoc basis; the attorney continued to participate in fees earned on cases he had tried while at the firm.[179] Thus, the defendants had not effectively withdrawn from the conspiracy.

---

[173] 438 U.S. 422, 464–65 (1978).

[174] *Id.*

[175] *See* Spaeder & Weinfeld, *supra* note 169, at 11.

[176] 685 F.2d 793 (3d Cir.), *cert. denied,* 459 U.S. 908 (1982).

[177] 685 F.2d at 803–04.

[178] 974 F.2d 246 (2d Cir. 1992), *cert. denied,* 507 U.S. 1029 (1993). *See also* United States v. Lowell, 649 F.2d 950, 958 (3d Cir. 1981) (after defendant terminated his employment he participated in the conspiracy by warning co-conspirators of the government investigation).

[179] *Id.*

Chapter 4

MAIL FRAUD, WIRE FRAUD, AND RELATED OFFENSES

§ 4.01 BREADTH OF THE MAIL AND WIRE FRAUD STATUTES

[A] The Statutes' Appeal to Prosecutors

Like the conspiracy statute discussed in the previous chapter, the mail and wire fraud statutes[1] are broad-ranging laws used in a large number and variety of federal white collar prosecutions. In an oft-quoted passage, one former federal prosecutor referred to these statutes as "our Stradivarius, our Colt 45, our Louisville Slugger, our Cuisinart — our true love . . . . [W]e always come home to the virtues of [the mail fraud statute], with its simplicity, adaptability, and comfortable familiarity."[2] Other commentators, however, have suggested a more cynical view of these statutes, suggesting that "[i]n effect, mail and wire fraud have long provided prosecutors with a means by which to salvage a modest, but dubious, victory from investigations that essentially proved unfruitful. The desirability of such an escape route is open to question."[3]

Whatever the merits of the mail and wire fraud statutes, an understanding of these statutes is critical in the study of white collar crime. There are several reasons why federal white collar cases so often include mail and/or wire fraud charges. First, the statutes are relatively simple and easy to use. In basic terms, the statutes only require that the government prove a scheme to defraud using the United States mails, a private courier, or interstate wires. Prosecutors have thus used the statutes in cases ranging from ordinary fraud cases to political corruption cases and complex securities fraud cases. As commentators have noted, the statutory phrase "scheme to defraud" has "provided more expansive interpretations from prosecutors and judges than probably any other phrase in the federal criminal law. . . . [The] refusal by the courts to delimit the scope of the mail and wire fraud statutes with objective criteria helps explain both [their]

---

[1] 18 U.S.C. §§ 1341, 1343.

[2] Jed Rakoff, *The Federal Mail Fraud Statute (Part I)*, 18 Duq. L. Rev. 771, 771 (1980). Mr. Rakoff is now a United States Judge for the Southern District of New York.

[3] John C. Coffee, Jr. & Charles K. Whitebread, *The Federalization of Fraud: Mail and Wire Fraud Statutes, in* White Collar Crime: Business and Regulatory Offenses § 9.05 (Otto Obermaier & Robert Morvillo, eds. 2011).

unique versatility and [their] popularity with prosecutors."[4] Second, mail and wire fraud may form the basis for much more serious offenses under the RICO[5] and money laundering statutes.[6] Third, the statutes may be used instead of, or in addition to, other statutes that are directed to particular types of conduct, such as the securities fraud and bank fraud statutes. This is true even where there may be barriers to convicting the defendant under the more specific fraud statutes.[7]

Largely because of the statutes' breadth, mail and wire fraud are more likely than most other statutes to raise complex issues of prosecutorial discretion.[8] Perhaps most importantly, the statutes allow federal prosecutors to bring cases that normally would fall to state and local law enforcement, such as small-scale consumer fraud and state and local political corruption. Also, by reaching breaches of fiduciary duties owed by, for example, employees to their employers, the statutes raise both issues of federalism and of criminalization of matters traditionally left to civil law. Further, because these statutes overlap with other statutes and present the potential for a large number of counts (one count for each use of the mail or wires), they give prosecutors broad discretion in determining both the type and number of charges brought.[9] Finally, as with many other white collar statutes, the boundaries of the mail and wire fraud statutes are vague, providing prosecutors with the opportunity to extend the statutes' coverage.[10]

[B] Courts' Interpretations of the Statutes

For all these reasons, the use of the mail and wire fraud statutes has grown expansively over the last several decades. Perhaps as a result, the United States Supreme Court and other courts have — with mixed degrees of success — attempted to establish some limitations on the statutes' application. This chapter

---

[4] *Id.* at § 9.01 & n.4. For critiques of the use of the federal mail and wire fraud statutes in state and local political corruption cases, see Sara Sun Beale, *Comparing the Scope of the Federal Government's Authority to Prosecute Federal Corruption and State and Local Corruption: Some Surprising Conclusions and a Proposal*, 51 Hastings L.J. 699 (2000).

[5] 18 U.S.C. §§ 1961 *et seq.*, discussed in Chapter 16, RICO, *infra.*

[6] 18 U.S.C. §§ 1956–57, discussed in Chapter 15, Money Laundering, *infra.*

[7] *See* Wendy Gerwick Couture, *White Collar Crime's Gray Area: The Anomaly of Criminalizing Conduct Not Civilly Actionable*, 72 Alb. L. Rev. 1, 5-12 (2009) (describing circumstances in which the government may successfully charge mail/wire fraud for the underlying crime of securities fraud, even in circumstances in which a charge under the securities fraud statutes may not be viable).

[8] *See* Coffee & Whitebread, *supra* note 3, §§ 9.01, 9.05.

[9] The United States Sentencing Guidelines impose sentences based upon a specific set of criteria that the sentencing court will use, thus in some circumstances lessening the sentence imposed when the defendant has been convicted of multiple counts. *See* Chapter 21, Sentencing, *infra*, for a discussion of the Guidelines.

[10] In United States v. Handakas, 286 F.3d 92, 107–08 (2d Cir. 2002), the court found the mail and wire fraud statutes were unconstitutionally vague as applied, noting that "[a]n indefinite criminal statute creates opportunity for the misuse of government power." In United States v. Rybicki, 354 F.3d 124, 144 (2d Cir. 2003), however, the Second Circuit abrogated the *Handakas* holding without reaching the merits of the constitutional issue. In Skilling v. United States, 130 S. Ct. 2896 (2010), discussed *infra*, § 4.05[B], the United States Supreme Court addressed the constitutional issue. In that case, the Court narrowly interpreted the "honest services" theory of mail and wire fraud in order to avoid deciding whether the honest services statute is unconstitutionally vague.

provides an overview of the statutes, and of judicial interpretation of their elements. When reading the cases, it is important to note that judicial interpretation of one statute also generally applies to the other.[11] The only exception to this general rule relates to the jurisdictional element of each crime — the use of the mails or wires. Otherwise, where this chapter mentions interpretations of either the mail or wire fraud statute, the assumption is that the interpretation also applies to the other statute.

§ 4.02 STATUTORY OVERVIEW

[A] Sections 1341 and 1343

The mail and wire fraud statutes are, on their face at least, remarkably simple. Section 1341, entitled "Frauds and swindles," punishes:

> Whoever, having devised or intending to devise any scheme or artifice to defraud, or for obtaining money or property by means of false or fraudulent pretenses, representations, or promises, . . . for the purpose of executing such scheme or artifice or attempting so to do, places in any post office or authorized depository for mail matter, any matter or thing whatever to be sent or delivered by the Postal Service, or deposits or causes to be deposited any matter or thing whatever to be sent or delivered by any private or commercial interstate carrier, or takes or receives therefrom, any such matter or thing, or knowingly causes to be delivered by mail or such carrier according to the direction thereon, or at the place at which it is directed to be delivered by the person to whom it is addressed, any such matter or thing . . .

Section 1343, entitled "Fraud by wire, radio, or television," punishes:

> Whoever, having devised or intending to devise any scheme or artifice to defraud, or for obtaining money or property by means of false or fraudulent pretenses, representations, or promises, transmits or causes to be transmitted by means of wire, radio, or television communication in interstate or foreign commerce, any writings, signs, signals, pictures, or sounds for the purpose of executing such scheme or artifice . . .

The punishment for a violation of the mail and wire fraud statutes includes a fine, imprisonment, or both. Section 903 of the Sarbanes-Oxley Act increased the maximum sentence from five to twenty years. If the violation affects a financial institution, the maximum penalty is a $1,000,000 fine, imprisonment for not more than 30 years, or both. As is always the case with federal crimes, the actual sentence imposed will depend upon the trial court's application of the advisory United States Sentencing Guidelines to the case.[12]

---

[11] *See, e.g.*, United States v. Morelli, 169 F.3d 798, 806 n.9 (3d Cir.), *cert. denied*, 528 U.S. 820 (1999) ("As we have noted, the wire fraud and mail fraud statutes differ only in form, not in substance, and cases . . . interpreting one govern the other as well.").

[12] *See* Chapter 21, Sentencing, *infra*.

[B] The Elements

The mail and wire fraud statutes have produced a great deal of judicial interpretation, much of it by the United States Supreme Court. According to the statutes and the cases interpreting them, in a mail or wire fraud case the government must prove that:

1. The defendant engaged in a "scheme to defraud";

2. The scheme involved material misstatements or omissions;

3. The defendant acted with the specific intent (or purpose) to defraud;

4. The scheme resulted, or would result upon completion, in the loss of money, property, or honest services; and

5. The United States mail, a private courier, or interstate or international wires -

     (a) were used "in furtherance" of the scheme to defraud, and

     (b) the defendant used, or caused the use, of the United States mail, a private courier service, or interstate or international wires.

[C] The Inchoate Nature of Mail and Wire Fraud

Mail and wire fraud are inchoate crimes that are complete once all the elements occur, regardless of whether the fraud reaches fruition. In other words, the government need *not* prove that the scheme to defraud succeeded. Thus, the government is not required to show that the intended victim was deprived of money, property, or the right to honest services.

[D] Federal Jurisdiction

[1] Jurisdictional Bases

The use of the mails and wires provides the basis for federal jurisdiction in prosecutions under §§ 1341 and 1343. Under the mail fraud statute, any use of the federal mails — intrastate or interstate — provides federal jurisdiction under the postal power that the constitution provides to the government.[13] With respect to use of a private courier service such as United Parcel Service or Federal Express, lower federal courts have held that such use qualifies under the Commerce Clause whenever the service has interstate operations.[14]

---

[13] U.S. Const. Art. I, § 8.

[14] *See* United States v. Photogrammetric Data Serv., 259 F.3d 229, 248 (4th Cir. 2001) ("The unambiguous language of current § 1341 criminalizes all mailings in furtherance of a fraudulent scheme if the mailings are placed with either the United States Postal Service or with other private or commercial mail delivery services which operate interstate, regardless of whether any particular mailing actually crosses state lines."), *overruled on other grounds by* Crawford v. Washington, 541 U.S. 36, 62–64 (2004). *See also* Elizabeth Wagner Pittman, *Mail and Wire Fraud*, 47 Am. Crim. L. Rev. 797, 801 & n.25 (2010).

The wire fraud statute relies solely upon the Commerce Clause,[15] and wires must be used in *inter* state or foreign commerce to provide federal jurisdiction. As discussed below,[16] the mail or wire need not itself contain a fraudulent deception, so long as the use of the mail/wires is in furtherance of the fraudulent scheme.

When wire fraud is the charge, must the government prove that the defendant knew or should have known that the wire actually would travel across state lines? For example, assume a defendant sends an email to another city in the same state. Unbeknownst to the defendant, the email is routed by phone lines through a neighboring state before arriving at the intended destination. Assume that the defendant neither knew nor reasonably should have known of the interstate nature of the transmission. The general rule under federal law is that the government need not prove that the defendant possessed any particular mens rea in connection with a purely jurisdictional element of a crime.[17] Most lower federal courts have applied this principle to the wire fraud statute.[18] Thus, in the above hypothetical, the jurisdictional element would be met.

Finally, most courts have upheld wire fraud convictions even where a government agent instigated the interstate use of the wires. For example, in *United States v. Wallace*,[19] the Second Circuit stated that government-instigated use of a jurisdictional element will suffice so long as a defendant engaged in a "voluntary, affirmative act" connected to the jurisdictional element.

In that case, the defendant argued that the government "manufactured" federal jurisdiction because the only link between defendant's crime and the jurisdictional basis (a federally-insured bank) was introduced into the case by the FBI. The Second Circuit rejected the argument, noting that the government proved that the defendant intentionally attempted to defraud that bank knowing that it was a federally-insured institution. Although some decisions indicate that "manufactured jurisdiction" will not suffice, the trend is to uphold such cases.[20]

---

[15] U.S. Const. Art I, § 8.

[16] *See infra* § 4.04[A][1].

[17] *See, e.g.*, United States v. Feola, 420 U.S. 671, 684 (1975) (the government need not prove that the defendant had knowledge of a fact — in this case, that the intended victim was a federal officer — that provides the basis for federal jurisdiction).

[18] *See, e.g.*, United States v. Lindemann, 85 F.3d 1232, 1241–42 (7th Cir.), *cert. denied*, 519 U.S. 966 (1996); United States v. Bryant, 766 F.2d 370, 375 (8th Cir. 1985), *cert. denied*, 474 U.S. 1054 (1986). This is a different issue from whether the defendant could have reasonably foreseen the use of the wires for purposes of (1) establishing vicarious liability for wire fraud under the law of conspiracy (*see* § 3.03[D]), or (2) showing that the defendant "caused" the use of the wires (*see* § 4.04[B], *infra*).

[19] 85 F.3d 1063 (2d Cir. 1996).

[20] *See* United States v. Peters, 952 F.2d 960, 963–64 (7th Cir.), *cert. denied*, 503 U.S. 911 (1992) (rejecting claim of manufactured jurisdiction). *But see* United States v. Archer, 486 F.2d 670, 682 (2d Cir. 1973). In *Archer*, federal agents intentionally induced targets of a sting operation to place interstate calls. The court dismissed the case, brought under the Travel Act, on the grounds of "manufactured federal jurisdiction." Later cases have limited the *Archer* holding to cases where the defendant appears to have been entrapped. *See* Coffee & Whitebread, *supra* note 3, § 9.02][2].

[2]   Federalism Issues

As noted above, the federalization of crimes generally left to state and local law enforcement raises serious issues. For example, the federal mail fraud statute has been used in purely local, run-of-the mill fraud schemes, including fraud in the sale of used cars[21] and land tracks.[22]

The statute has also been used to prosecute breaches of various state law fiduciary duties. In *Carpenter v. United States*,[23] a Wall Street Journal reporter misused the Journal's confidential business information to profit from a stock fraud scheme involving use of the mails. The defendant's actions violated explicit company policy requiring that employees maintain the secrecy of confidential information. The Court affirmed the defendant's conviction, finding that the reporter's acts violated his duty to his employer and were therefore sufficient to support a mail fraud charge. The *Carpenter* decision has been criticized for providing a dangerously expansive reading of the federal mail and wire fraud statutes.[24]

§ 4.03   THE SCHEME TO DEFRAUD

[A]   Intent to Defraud

The mail and wire fraud statutes do not define the required "scheme to defraud," and there is little legislative history on the issue. Courts therefore have struggled to provide a precise definition of the term. In general, the defendant must have engaged in a deception or deceit — a false or misleading statement or omission intended to trick the victim.[25]

[1]   The *Durland* Decision

The Supreme Court first interpreted an earlier version of the mail fraud statute in its 1896 decision in *Durland v. United States*.[26] The government alleged that the defendants had used the mail to sell bonds on which they never intended to make payments. The defendants argued that this did not amount to fraud because, at that time, the common law crime of obtaining property by false pretenses only applied when a defendant had misrepresented *past* or *present* facts. Here, the defendants had instead merely lied about their intent to make payments *in the future*.

The Court rejected the argument that the statute was limited by the common law definition of false pretenses. In its analysis, the Supreme Court assumed that the defendants acted with an intent to defraud. The Court further found that the

---

[21] Schmuck v. United States, 489 U.S. 705 (1989).

[22] Lustiger v. United States, 386 F.2d 132 (9th Cir. 1967), *cert. denied*, 390 U.S. 951 (1968).

[23] 484 U.S. 19 (1987). For further discussion of this case, see Chapter 5, Securities Fraud, *infra* § 5.06[D][1].

[24] *See* John C. Coffee Jr., *Hush!: The Criminal Status of Confidential Information after* McNally *and* Carpenter *and the Enduring Problem of Overcriminalization*, 26 Am. Crim. L. Rev. 121 (1988).

[25] *See* Coffee & Whitehead, *supra* note 3, § 9.02[1].

[26] 161 U.S. 306 (1896).

statutory language "any scheme or artifice to defraud" was broader than the common law of false pretenses. The Court concluded that the statute "includes everything designed to defraud by representations as to the past or present, or suggestions and promises as to the future. The significant fact is the intent and purpose."[27] Because such intent was present, the convictions were affirmed.

The *Durland* decision foreshadowed much of the debate over the mail and wire fraud statutes that has followed. By expanding the federal fraud statute beyond existing common law crimes, the Court ensured that the government would have a broad anti-fraud weapon that would overlap with and even expand upon state fraud statutes.

[2] Deception Relating to the Economic Bargain

There are limits on mail fraud prosecutions, however. In the context of business transactions, courts have found that the defendant must have intended that the deception go to the substance of the bargain between the defendant and the intended victim. The economic substance requirement means that mere "puffing" will not support a mail or wire fraud charge.[28] Take a car salesperson who tells a customer, "This is the world's greatest car." Even if the car turns out to be a mediocre product, the salesperson has simply engaged in hyperbole and has committed no fraud. But if the salesperson says, "This car has never been wrecked and runs fine," when the car had been in a serious crash and barely operates, then the misstatement goes to the economic bargain itself.

Further, assume that an office supply salesperson speaks with a potential customer's receptionist. The salesperson falsely says, "I'm a friend of the president of the company, and I'd like to speak with the purchasing agent." After accurately describing the cost and quality of the products to the purchasing agent, the salesperson sells the supplies to the company by using the mail or wires. Does this amount to fraud? In *United States v. Regent Office Supply*,[29] the Second Circuit framed the issue as whether "solicitation of a purchase by means of false representations not directed to the quality, adequacy or price of goods to be sold, or otherwise to the nature of the bargain, constitute[s] a 'scheme to defraud.' "[30] The court held that such a solicitation does not amount to mail fraud.

[3] Literally True and Misleading Statements

On the other hand, literally true statements designed to deceive a party concerning the essential economic bargain *will* support mail fraud charges. In *Lustiger v. United States*,[31] the defendant was convicted of mail fraud based upon Arizona property sales. As part of the marketing campaign, Lustiger mailed to potential buyers advertising materials containing misleading representations con-

---

[27] *Id.* at 313.

[28] "Puffing" is the expression of an exaggerated opinion — as opposed to a factual misrepresentation — with the intent to sell a good or service. Black's Law Dictionary (9th ed. 2009).

[29] 421 F.2d 1174 (2d Cir. 1970).

[30] *Id.* at 1179.

[31] 386 F.2d 132 (9th Cir. 1967), *cert. denied*, 390 U.S. 951 (1968).

cerning the availability of water for recreational and home use. On appeal from his conviction, the defendant argued that there was insufficient proof that the representations — including statements, photographs, and maps — were false or misleading.

The Ninth Circuit disagreed, finding that "[w]hile the statements in the advertising materials may not have been literally false, taken as a whole they were fraudulently misleading and deceptive."[32] For example, although the materials accurately said that a large recreational lake was only five miles from the property, the materials did not say that the actual driving distance was from fifteen to forty miles on roads not generally useable by passenger cars. The court found substantial evidence that the materials contained numerous statements that were either false or deceptive, and that went beyond mere sales "puffing." The court concluded, "If a scheme is devised with the intent to defraud, and the mails are used in executing the scheme, the fact that there is no misrepresentation of a single existing fact is immaterial."[33]

[4] Omissions and Concealment

Material acts of omission or concealment can give rise to mail or wire fraud charges. For example, in *United States v. Siegel*,[34] the defendants engaged in a scheme to misuse proceeds from the sales of their employer's products. The Second Circuit affirmed the convictions, finding that the government had proven that the defendants used some of the proceeds for personal gain. Thus, the defendants breached their fiduciary duties to the corporation and its shareholders by failing to reveal their scheme to the company and its auditors. This omission satisfied the deception element of the wire fraud statute.[35]

The finding of an intent to defraud is the key, and all deceptions may not amount to fraud. Thus, when a corporate employee encouraged a corporate agent to mislead the company, the agent was not guilty of mail fraud. This situation arose in *United States v. D'Amato*.[36] In that case, the defendant had been hired by Gardner, who was an employee of Unisys, a defense contractor. The defendant was an attorney who was also the brother of a sitting United States senator. The senator sat on the Senate Appropriations Committee, which funded government defense programs.

The government claimed that the defendant, with Gardner's help, had defrauded Unisys in two ways.[37] First, in his bills to the company, the defendant created the misleading impression that he was being paid to perform legal services for the company rather than the lobbying services he actually performed. According to the

---

[32] *Id.* at 136.

[33] *Id.* at 138.

[34] 717 F.2d 9 (2d Cir. 1983).

[35] Significantly, both the majority, 717 F.2d at 23, and the dissent, *id.* at 23 (Winters, J., dissenting), recognized the potential for federal over-criminalization and abuse in federal fraud cases that are merely based on breaches of fiduciary duties. For further discussion of this issue, see the discussion of the *Carpenter* case, *supra* § 4.02[D][2].

[36] 39 F.3d 1249 (2d Cir. 1994).

[37] The mailings were of bills and invoices to the company.

government, this scheme defrauded Unisys by depriving it of the "right to control" how its funds would be used. Second, the defendant was under a contract to write reports for Unysis. At Gardner's direction, however, the defendant never wrote the reports. The government believed this scheme constituted "false pretenses."

On appeal from his mail fraud convictions, the defendant argued that the government had failed to prove that he had intended to cause economic harm to Unisys. The Second Circuit agreed. As to the right to control theory, there was no evidence that the misleading bills were intended to cause economic harm to the company. As to the false pretenses theory, there was no such proof because Gardner, a Unisys employee, had told the defendant that he was not required to write the reports.

[5] Good Faith and Reliance on Counsel Defenses

Mail fraud requires proof of a specific intent to defraud. Thus, a finding that the defendant acted in good faith — *i.e.*, acted with good will and without intent to harm — will provide a complete defense to the charge.[38] A specific type of good faith defense is that the defendant acted in honest reliance on counsel. If the fact-finder determines that the defendant fully disclosed the material facts to the attorney, and honestly relied upon the attorney's advice in an attempt to conform with the law, then a good faith defense has been shown.[39]

[B] Materiality

[1] The *Neder* Decision

Under the Supreme Court's decision in *Neder v. United States*,[40] the mail and wire fraud statutes require that the scheme to defraud involve a *material* deception. In that case, the defendant was charged with multiple counts of mail and wire fraud based upon fraudulent bank loans applications. The defendant argued on appeal that the trial judge committed reversible error by failing to require that the jury find that the defendant's misstatements were material to the transactions. The Supreme Court unanimously agreed. Conceding that the statutes on their face do not contain such a requirement, the Court nonetheless found that Congress incorporated the common law definition of "defraud," which includes a "misrepresentation or concealment of material fact."[41] The Court went on, however, to affirm

---

[38] *See* Coffee & Whitehead, *supra* note 3, at § 9.04[1].

[39] *See id.*; United States v. Walters, 913 F.2d 388, 392 (7th Cir. 1990) (reversible error for trial court to fail to instruct jury that reliance on counsel is a defense) (decision discussed *infra* § 4.04[A][1]).

[40] 527 U.S. 1 (1999).

[41] *Id.* at 3. In defining materiality, the Court cited the Restatement of Torts: "[A] matter is material if: '(a) a reasonable man would attach importance to its existence or nonexistence in determining his choice of action in the transaction in question; or (b) the maker of the representation knows or has reason to know that its recipient regards or is likely to regard the matter as important in determining his choice of action, although a reasonable man would not so regard it.' Restatement (Second) of Torts § 538 (1977)." *Id.* at 22 n.5.

the conviction on the ground that the jury instruction error did not affect the verdict and was therefore harmless.[42]

[2] The "Reasonable Reliance" Issue

Some circuits courts have suggested that, in order for a deception to be material, it must have been one upon which a reasonable person would have relied.[43] These courts reasoned that, without such a requirement, even the most implausible deception would fall within the statute.[44] Thus, the statutes' reach would be unduly expansive.

For example, in *United States v. Brown*,[45] the defendants were accused of defrauding home buyers by selling homes at above-market prices. The alleged misrepresentations included statements that the investments were safe, that rental income would exceed mortgage payments, and that the homes could be sold for a profit after a year. The Eleventh Circuit reversed the convictions, holding that a reasonable person would not have relied on these misrepresentations. Market information was freely available to potential buyers, and a reasonable person thus would not have been deceived. The court expressed concern that a contrary holding would intrude into ordinary business dealings and result in over-criminalization.

In a later en banc decision, however, the Eleventh Circuit overturned *Brown* and aligned itself with the circuits that hold that mail fraud exists even if the person relying upon the deception is unusually gullible.[46] The Seventh Circuit adopted a middle approach in *United States v. Coffman*.[47] In that case, the defendants claimed on appeal that there was insufficient evidence of intent to defraud because the intended victim would never have fallen for their far-fetched scheme. In rejecting the argument, Judge Posner opined that the "reasonable reliance" requirement is simply a way of drawing the distinction, discussed above, between mere "puffing" and fraudulent behavior. Moreover, he noted, the victim's level of gullibility may be relevant to prove the defendant's intent to deceive; the greater the victim's vulnerability, the more likely it is that the defendant made a highly implausible deceptive statement with the intent to defraud. The court concluded that "there is

---

[42] *Id.* at 25. Neder was also charged under the bank fraud statute, 18 U.S.C. § 1344, which is modeled upon the mail and wire fraud statutes. The Court found that the bank fraud statute also includes a materiality requirement. *Id.* at 4. As the *Neder* decision makes clear, the government need not show reliance as part of a mail fraud case. *Id.* at 24.

[43] Some circuits disagree. *See generally* United States v. Brown, 79 F.3d 1550, 1557 (11th Cir. 1996) (describing the circuit court split and citing cases).

[44] Some courts following that general approach would find the deception to be material if there were an existing relationship between the parties that imposed a duty upon the defendant to deal fairly with the alleged victim. *See* Emery v. American General Finance, 71 F.3d 1343, 1346–47 (7th Cir. 1995) (civil RICO action based upon the predicate acts of mail fraud).

[45] 79 F.3d 1550 (11th Cir. 1996).

[46] United States v. Svete, 556 F.3d 1157, 1166 (11th Cir. 2009) (en banc). *See, e.g.*, United States v. Maxwell, 920 F.2d 1028, 1036 (D.C. Cir. 1990); United States v. Brien, 617 F.2d 299, 311–12 (1st Cir.), *cert. denied*, 446 U.S. 919 (1980). *See also* United States v. Falkowitz, 214 F. Supp. 2d 365, 376–77 (S.D.N.Y. 2002) ("recent case law in other circuits reflects that the majority of appellate courts addressing the issue decline to introduce the civil, justifiable reliance principle into the criminal fraud context").

[47] *See* United States v. Coffman, 94 F.3d 330 (7th Cir. 1996), *cert. denied*, 520 U.S. 1165 (1997).

a difference between lies so small that they are discounted in advance, as part of the language of business, and so are harmless, and lies so large that the sophisticated see through them."

§ 4.04   THE USE OF THE MAILS AND WIRES

The mail and wire fraud statutes require that the use of the mail or wire be for the "purpose of executing [the] scheme or artifice" to defraud. The courts have long attempted to define those uses of the mail/wires that are sufficiently connected to the fraud scheme to support federal charges. A related issue is whether the defendant "caused" the mailing or the use of wires.

[A]   The "In Furtherance" Requirement

A mailing that is far removed from the fraud may not support a mail fraud charge. Courts have also held, however, that mailings need not be essential to the fraudulent scheme and indeed may even be incidental to the scheme. The courts have had difficulty in defining the line between a mailing that is in furtherance of the scheme and one that is not.

[1]   The *Schmuck* Rule

In 1989, in *United States v. Schmuck*,[48] the United States Supreme Court attempted to provide some guidance to lower courts on this issue, and in the process articulated a broad view of the "in furtherance" requirement. Mr. Schmuck was in the business of selling used cars to dealers, who would then resell the cars to retail customers. Unbeknownst to the dealers or the customers, for fifteen years Schmuck had rolled back the odometers on the cars he sold, enabling him to charge more for the cars than they were worth.

As part of the retail sales transactions, dealers mailed change of title forms to the state. On appeal, the defendant argued that this use of the mail was not sufficiently connected to the deception itself to support mail fraud charges. Because each mailing occurred after the sale and was not part of the deception, he asserted that the mailings were not done "for the purpose of executing the scheme."

In a five-to-four decision, the Court upheld the conviction. The Court stated that, "[t]o be a part of the execution of the fraud . . . the use of the mails need not be an essential element of the scheme. It is sufficient for the mailing to be 'incident to an essential part of the scheme.' "[49] The Court found that the mailings were part of the fraudulent scheme. Without the mailings, the dealers could not have transferred title to the buyers. Had the dealers been unable to transfer title, the ongoing scheme could not have continued. As the Court explained, "a failure in this passage of title would have jeopardized Schmuck's relationship of trust and goodwill with the retail dealers upon whose unwitting cooperation his scheme depended."[50]

---

[48] 489 U.S. 705 (1989).

[49] *Id.* at 710–11, *quoting* Badders v. United States, 240 U.S. 391, 394 (1916).

[50] 489 U.S. at 714.

In an opinion written by Justice Scalia, the dissent sharply criticized the majority's holding and reasoning.[51] The dissenters argued that the title registration mailings were not a part of the defendant's scheme and therefore did not meet the "in furtherance" requirement. As the dissent stated, "it is mail fraud, not mail and fraud, that incurs liability. This federal statute is not violated by a fraudulent scheme in which, at some point, a mailing happens to occur — nor even by one in which a mailing predictably and necessarily occurs. The mailing must be in furtherance of the fraud."[52]

The *Schmuck* dissent relied upon three earlier cases, each distinguished by the majority, that the dissent believed should have controlled. In *Kann v. United States*,[53] the defendants cashed fraudulently-obtained checks knowing that the checks would be mailed for collection. The Supreme Court reversed the mail fraud conviction. The Court found that, at the time of the mailings, the defendants' plan "had reached fruition" and that the mailings were therefore "immaterial . . . to any consummation of the scheme."[54] Similarly, in *United States v. Maze*,[55] the defendant committed credit card fraud, and the merchants who accepted the card mailed bills for payment to the credit card issuer. Once again the Court found that such mailings were not in furtherance of the underlying fraud. Finally, in *Parr v. United States*,[56] public school district officials embezzled tax funds from the school district for several years, resulting in the mailing of tax bills and payments each year. The Court in *Parr* reversed the convictions even though the mailings were necessary for the ongoing fraud scheme to continue. This was the mail fraud theory that the *Schmuck* court used to affirm the conviction in the case before it, while at the same stating that its holding was consistent with *Parr*.[57]

Upon a careful reading of the *Schmuck* majority and dissent, one conclusion is clear — that the legal standard for determining whether the use of the mails and wires was in furtherance of the scheme is less than precise. As seen below, courts continue to struggle to differentiate between the sorts of facts presented in *Kann*, *Maze*, and *Parr* and those presented in *Schmuck*. It is probably safe to say, however, that most mailings necessary to the continuation of an ongoing scheme will be sufficient.[58]

Even the use of mails and wires in support of ongoing schemes may fail, however, if the mails/wires are too far removed from the defendant's plan. For example, in

---

[51] *Id.* at 722 (Scalia, J., dissenting). In yet another unusual criminal case alignment, Justice Scalia's dissent was joined by Justices Brennan, Marshall, and O'Connor.

[52] *Id.* at 723.

[53] 323 U.S. 88 (1944).

[54] *Id.* at 94.

[55] 414 U.S. 395 (1974).

[56] 363 U.S. 370, 388–92 (1960).

[57] 489 U.S. at 712, *citing Parr*, 363 U.S. at 388–92.

[58] Most circuits recognize a required mailings exception to this general rule. *See* United States v. Lake, 472 F.3d 1247, 1256 (10th Cir. 2007) ("Most other circuits to address the issue have interpreted *Parr* to hold that 'mailings of documents which are required by law to be mailed, and which are not themselves false and fraudulent, cannot be regarded as mailed for the purpose of executing a fraudulent scheme.' ").

United States v. Walters,[59] the defendant secretly contracted with college football players to act as their professional football agent after their graduation. Walters would benefit by obtaining a percentage of the players' professional incomes. The scheme therefore required that the students complete their collegiate careers, which required that they be eligible to play college football under National Collegiate Athletic Association (NCAA) rules. According to the plan, the players would later negotiate professional contracts. Sports attorneys at a major law firm advised Walters that his plan would violate NCAA rules by making the players ineligible, but was not illegal.

The government's theory was that Walters had fraudulently caused the universities to pay scholarship funds to athletes who, unbeknownst to the schools, were actually ineligible to play college football under NCAA rules because they had signed with an agent and received compensation. The universities required the athletes to complete forms verifying their eligibility, and then used the mails to send forms to various athletic conferences. Applying the *Schmuck* test, the court observed:

> Did the evidence establish that Walters conceived a scheme in which mailings played a role? We think not . . . . [D]eceit was an ingredient of the plan. We may assume that Walters knew that the universities would ask athletes to verify that they were eligible to compete as amateurs. But what role do the mails play? . . . Forms verifying eligibility do not help the plan succeed; instead they create a risk that it will be discovered if a student should tell the truth . . . . For all Walters cared, the forms could sit forever in cartons. Movement to someplace else was irrelevant . . . . A college's mailing to its conference has less to do with the plot's success than the mailings that transferred title in *Schmuck.*[60]

The court conceded that the issue was a close one, and that the controlling cases supported both the government's and the defendant's positions.[61] Thus, the court declined to reverse the conviction under *Schmuck,* but reversed on alternate grounds.

[2] The "Lulling" Rule

There is a particular rule where use of the mail/wires was designed to "lull" the victim into a false sense of security. In such cases, mail/wire fraud charges may be brought even though the scheme had previously reached fruition. In the leading case of *United States v. Lane,*[62] the Supreme Court affirmed a conviction in such a

---

[59] 997 F.2d 1219 (7th Cir. 1993).

[60] *Id.* at 1222.

[61] Expressing doubt that the *Schmuck* test was satisfied, the court nonetheless assumed that the government's proof on this issue was sufficient. Instead, the court reversed the conviction on the grounds that the defendant had not "caused" the mailings." *Id.* at 1227 (The government's theory was that "the use of the mails was integral to the profits Walters hoped to reap, even though Walters would have been delighted had the colleges neither asked any questions of the athletes nor put the answers in the mail. Let us take this as sufficient under *Schmuck* (although we have our doubts)"). *See infra* § 4.04[B].

[62] 474 U.S. 438 (1986).

circumstance. Lane had arranged to have buildings burned for which Lane had obtained fire insurance. After Lane received his final payments from his fire insurance company, he mailed a form to the company listing expenses he had claimed and attaching false invoices for the expenses.

The Supreme Court found that this mailing was in furtherance of the scheme. This was true even though Lane had already engaged in the primary deception and had obtained his money. As the Court stated, "Mailings occurring after receipt of the goods obtained by fraud are within the statute if they 'were designed to lull the victims into a false sense of security, postpone their ultimate complaint to the authorities, and therefore make the apprehension of the defendants less likely than if no mailings had taken place.' "[63]

Similarly, in *United States v. Sampson*,[64] the defendants called prospective customers offering to help the customers obtain loans and sell businesses. Customers made payments for services the defendants never intended to provide. After the payments were received, the defendants sent the customers letters designed to assure them that the defendants intended to perform the promised services. The Supreme Court held that, even though the defendants had already received the benefits of their fraud, the letters to customers were in furtherance of the fraudulent scheme because they were sent "for the purpose of lulling [the customers] by assurances that the promised services would be performed."[65]

Even if a court does not cite the "lulling" cases, it may find a post-fraud mailing to be sufficient under those cases' reasoning. In *United States v. McDougal*,[66] for example, the defendants were convicted of, among other charges, mail fraud. The mail fraud charge was based upon the mailing of a false Small Business Administration (SBA) loan application form. At trial, the government showed that the defendants used the SBA money for personal expenses, not for business expenses as stated on the form. On appeal, the defense argued that the mailing of the SBA form was not in furtherance of the fraud because the mailing occurred after the defendants received the loan funds. The court rejected the argument, finding that the mailing of the form was a necessary step in enabling the defendants to use the funds; if the form had not been mailed, the SBA would likely have investigated and uncovered the fraud.

Although a "lulling" theory can be helpful to the government in many contexts, the theory should not be read too broadly. As some courts have noted, a lulling theory will only work where the communication is specifically designed to delay or cover-up detection of the fraud. Further, some courts have held that the communication must be directed to the intended victim of the fraud scheme. For example,

---

[63] *Id.* at 451, *citing* United States v. Maze, 414 U.S. at 403.

[64] 371 U.S. 75 (1962).

[65] *Id.* at 81.

[66] 137 F.3d 547 (8th Cir. 1998). This was yet another politically-charged case; the defendants in that case were James and Susan McDougal, who lived in Arkansas and were closely associated with President Bill Clinton.

in *United States v. Strong*,[67] the defendants purported to buy cars with buyers' drafts that the defendants never intended to honor. After taking possession of the cars, defendants used forged documents to apply for titles from the state department of transportation ("DOT"). Defendants used the titles to sell the cars to innocent purchasers. In processing the title applications, local DOT offices routinely mailed the applications to DOT headquarters for record-keeping purposes. The court found that these mailings were not in furtherance of the scheme because the scheme was over when the defendant sold the cars to the innocent buyers. Nor did the mailings fall within the lulling rule because the victims — the parties from whom the defendants bought the cars and the persons to whom the defendants sold the cars — were not deceived or "lulled" by the mailings to state DOT headquarters. Contrast this result with those in *Lane* and *Sampson*, where the mailings were specifically directed to the victims of the schemes.

[B] The "Causation" Requirement

In addition to requiring proof that the use of the mail was in furtherance of the fraud, courts have also required proof that the defendant "caused" the mailing.[68] The causation requirement is usually proven by showing the defendant knew or should have reasonably foreseen that the mail would be used as part of the scheme.[69] Although these issues often are discussed separately, in practice the "in furtherance" and "causation" requirements frequently overlap.

The Supreme Court dealt with the causation issue in *Pereira v. United States*.[70] In that case, the defendants engaged in a scheme to defraud a wealthy widow through Pereira's marriage to her. Pereira and an accomplice misled the victim concerning Pereira's financial and professional status in a successful effort to obtain money from the victim. As the basis for the mail fraud, the government relied upon a check, written on a California bank account, that the victim endorsed to Pereira. He deposited the check in a Texas bank, which then mailed it to California for collection.

The defendant argued that there was insufficient proof that he had "caused" the check to be mailed. The Court disagreed, holding that "[w]here one does an act with knowledge that the use of the mails will follow in the ordinary course of business, or where such use can reasonably be foreseen, even though not actually intended, then he 'causes' the mails to be used."[71] Because it was common knowledge that checks are sent to the banks on which they are drawn, Pereira knew or should have known that the Texas bank would mail the check to the California bank.

---

[67] 371 F.3d 225, 230–32 (5th Cir. 2004). *See also infra* § 4.05[A] (discussion of the "money or property" requirement).

[68] *Schmuck*, 489 U.S. at 714.

[69] *Id.*

[70] 347 U.S. 1 (1954).

[71] *Id.* at 8–9. The Court also assumed, without analyzing the issue, that the mailing was in furtherance of the fraud. *Id.*

On the other hand, in the *Walters*[72] case discussed above, the Seventh Circuit found that the defendant had not caused the universities to mail the athletes' eligibility forms to the NCAA. The court found no evidence that Walters even knew that the forms existed, much less that they would be mailed. Further, a respected law firm retained by Walters advised him that his scheme would violate NCAA rules but not the law; how could Walters have foreseen that the mails would be used when his expert advisors had not? Providing a cautionary note as to the mail fraud statute, the court concluded:

> In the end, the prosecutor insists that the large size and interstate nature of the NCAA demonstrate that something would be dropped into the mails. To put this only slightly differently, the prosecutor submits that all frauds involving big organizations necessarily are mail frauds, because big organizations habitually mail things. No evidence put before the jury supports such a claim, and it is hardly appropriate for judicial notice in a criminal case . . . . That statute has been expanded considerably by judicial interpretation, but it does not make a federal crime of every deceit. The prosecutor must prove that the use of the mails was foreseeable, rather than calling on judicial intuition to repair a rickety case.[73]

In sum, the government must prove both that the mailing was in furtherance of the fraud and that the defendant caused the mailing. In the substantial majority of cases, the government is able to adduce such proof. Courts do express concern about the elasticity of the mail fraud statute, however, and will not uphold convictions where the relationship between the fraud and the use of mails is particularly tenuous.

§ 4.05 DEPRIVATION OF MONEY, PROPERTY, OR HONEST SERVICES

In *McNally v. United States*,[74] the Supreme Court rejected long-prevailing law and held a mail fraud prosecution must include proof that the defendant intended to cause some loss of money or property. That case and its progeny, however, have failed to provide a clear definition of "money or property." And Congress has further complicated matters by enacting a statute stating that a mail fraud case can be based upon an intended deprivation of "honest services." Defining this term has likewise proven to be an elusive task for courts.

[A] The "Money or Property" Requirement

[1] The *McNally* Decision

Before the *McNally* decision, courts had consistently read the mail fraud statute to encompass many different types of schemes. Sometimes, these schemes were not designed to lead to the loss of money or property. Most significantly, federal

---

[72] 997 F.2d 1219, discussed *supra* § 4.04[A][1].

[73] 997 F.2d at 1223–24.

[74] 483 U.S. 350 (1987).

prosecutors used the mail fraud statute to prosecute state and local political corruption.[75] These cases were brought on the theory that the public officials had defrauded their constituents of the officials' duty to provide the public with honest services.

In *McNally*, the Court rejected prevailing law and held that a mere deprivation of "good and honest services" does not violate the mail fraud statute. In that case, a Kentucky state official was involved in a kickback scheme under which the defendants arranged for the state to select a specific insurance carrier. In exchange, the defendants received payments from the carrier designed to benefit those involved in the scheme. At the trial, the government did not allege that the state of Kentucky or its citizens lost any money as a result of this scheme, presumably because the company charged fair rates and provided the services contracted for. Rather, the government argued that the defendants' actions deprived the state and its citizens of the state officials' honest services.

The *McNally* majority rejected this theory and reversed the convictions. First, the Court focused on the statutory language, which criminalizes "any scheme or artifice to defraud, or for obtaining money or property by means of false or fraudulent pretenses." Although the statute describes both schemes to defraud and false pretenses schemes, the Court held that the statute should not be read to apply the money or property requirement solely to false pretenses schemes. The Court reasoned that Congress had added the false pretenses clause in order to codify *Durland*, which held that mail fraud reaches future fraud schemes; Congress did not otherwise modify the definition of the crime. Second, the Court found that, based upon the legislative history and on the common law of fraud, any mail or wire fraud scheme must be designed to deprive the victim of money or property.

[2] Intangible Property Rights

[a] Secret Business Information

In *McNally*, the Court stated that the "mail fraud statute clearly protects property rights, but does not refer to the *intangible* right of the citizenry to good government."[76] Although the statute does not encompass the intangible right to honest government, the Court subsequently held that the term "property" does include intangible *property* rights.

The leading case is *United States v. Carpenter*.[77] There, a Wall Street Journal reporter wrote a regular financial column. When published, the column's contents had the potential to affect prices of stocks discussed in the column. Prior to the

---

[75] *See, e.g.*, United States v. Mandel, 862 F.2d 1067 (4th Cir. 1988), *cert. denied*, 491 U.S. 906 (1989); United States v. Silvano, 812 F.2d 754 (1st Cir. 1987); United States v. Margiotta, 688 F.2d 108, 112–13 (2d Cir. 1982). The government continues to use the mail and wire fraud statutes in political corruption cases. For example, in one highly publicized case, the government charged Rod Blagojevich, former governor of Illinois, with wire fraud and other crimes. *See* Emma Graves Fitzsimmons, *Blagojevich Could Face Fewer Charges*, N.Y. Times, Feb. 24, 2011, at A19.

[76] 483 U.S. at 356 (emphasis added).

[77] 484 U.S. 19 (1987). This case is also discussed in Chapter 5, Securities Fraud, *infra* § 5.06[D][1].

column's publication, the reporter and his co-conspirators traded securities of companies to be discussed in the column. After the columns were published and mailed to subscribers, the defendants traded in those stock, making profits. Although the reporter had not taken tangible property from the newspaper, he did act in violation of his employer's policies and did use information — the columns' contents — to his benefit.

The Court rejected the defendants' argument that the Wall Street Journal was not deprived of property. It found that the paper was deprived of the rights to keep the information confidential, and to have exclusive use of the information prior to its publication. The reporter violated his duty to keep this information private, and to act for the benefit of his employer. The information had value to the Journal because the Journal's reputation would suffer if it were known that its reporters wrote stories that provided them with personal benefits. Such proof was sufficient for a mail fraud conviction.

The *Carpenter* decision is controversial. Professor Coffee, for example, has argued that *Carpenter* extends the federal mail fraud statute to mere state law breaches of fiduciary duties owed by employees to employers. Professor Coffee concludes that this result is:

> (a) historically unsound, (b) inconsistent with most statutory law dealing with the subject of trade secrets, and (c) capable of trivializing the Court's decision only months earlier in *McNally v. United States*, which clearly sought to cut back on the amoeba-like growth of the mail and wire fraud statutes. More important than all these considerations, however, is the fact that *Carpenter*'s logic has the potential to alter significantly the relationship between employers and employees across the landscape of American business life.[78]

Whether or not this conclusion is correct, it is at least clear that *Carpenter* is another step in the extension of federal criminal law into realms traditionally handled by state law. *Carpenter* was in essence a securities fraud case based on insider trading. Because the Court did not reach a conclusion as to the defendants' liability for securities fraud, it apparently viewed the mail fraud statute as an appropriate alternative for punishing the wrongdoing.

The decision in *United States v. Alsugair*[79] provides an interesting application of the mail fraud statute using a theory somewhat similar to that in *Carpenter*. In *Alsugair*, the defendant was charged with mail fraud based upon a scheme to have an imposter take the Test of English as a Foreign Language (TOEFL) administered by the Educational Testing Service (ETS). In granting the defendant's motion to dismiss in part and denying the motion in part, the court found that ETS's administration and scoring services were not "property" under the statute, but that

---

[78] John C. Coffee Jr., *Hush!: The Criminal Status of Confidential Information after* McNally *and* Carpenter *and the Enduring Problem of Overcriminalization*, 26 Am. Crim. L. Rev. 121, 122–23 (1988).

[79] 256 F. Supp. 2d 306 (D.N.J. 2003). *See also* United States v. Hedaithy, 392 F.3d 580, 593–604 (3d Cir. 2004) (the court affirmed convictions based upon similar schemes; the court relied upon *Carpenter* and found that ETS had a property interest in its confidential business information and tangible score results).

ETS did have a property interest in its goodwill and trademark.

[b]   Licenses and Permits

After *McNally* and *Carpenter*, courts struggled to determine whether licenses and permits are another type of "intangible" property that fall within the mail fraud statute.[80] The Supreme Court resolved this issue in *Cleveland v. United States*.[81] In that case, Cleveland and others mailed an application for a state license permitting them to operate video poker machines. The government alleged that Cleveland had legal and financial difficulties that disqualified him from owning a gambling business. Therefore, the defendants made false statements in the applications concerning the true ownership of the business.

The Court reversed Cleveland's mail fraud convictions, unanimously holding that unissued permits or licenses are not "property" under § 1341. Even if a license may become property owned by the recipient after the license is issued, the Court reasoned, it is not property of the state or local authority that has the power to issue the license or permit. The Court found that such a license is regulatory in nature, and that neither the fee paid for the license nor the state's right to revoke the license amounted to a "property" interest. Otherwise, the Court said, the mail fraud statute would be extended into areas traditionally controlled by state and local authorities.

[c]   The Right to Control Property Interests

Prosecutors have employed a broad definition of "property" in attempts to avoid *McNally*. One such theory is that mail fraud occurs when the defendant fails to reveal information to the victim that might have affected the victim's ability to control how the victim's money or property was used.

In *United States v. Evans*,[82] for example, the government alleged that the defendants defrauded the United States government by arranging sales of American-made weapons to Iran. United States law prohibits such sales. As part of the scheme, the defendants allegedly used the mail to deceive the United States into believing that the true destination of the arms was a country other than Iran. The Second Circuit held that this scheme did not involve a loss of money or property and did not support mail fraud charges. The court rejected the prosecution's argument — dubbed the "alienation" theory — that the government's right to veto sales of U.S.-made or licensed weapons by one foreign government to another is a property right for wire and mail fraud purposes. The government did not allege that it ever owned the weapons, or that it had a right to own the weapons in the future. Its only right was to restrict the weapons' destination, which was akin to a regulation but was not a property right.

The government has successfully used a "right to control" theory in other

---

[80] Cleveland v. United States, 531 U.S. 12, 18 (2000) (listing cases).

[81] *Id.* at 15. For a later case applying *Cleveland*, see United States v. Antico, 275 F.3d 245, 267 (3d Cir. 2001).

[82] 844 F.2d 36 (2d Cir. 1988).

contexts. For example, in *United States v. Catalfo*,[83] the court held that, because a commodities fraud scheme prevented the victim commodities firm from controlling its risk of loss, the scheme fell within the wire fraud statute. The court rejected the defendant's argument that this was merely an intangible right, and held that depriving the firm of its ability to control its business risks satisfied *McNally's* money or property requirement. Similarly, in *United States v. Gray*,[84] the court held that an insurance company has a right to control to whom the benefits of an insurance policy would be paid. This right to control the payment of benefits sufficed under *McNally*. This was so even assuming that the company would have paid the benefits to *someone* and that the company therefore was not financially harmed by paying the benefits to the defendant.

Another variation of the right to control theory arose in *United States v. Hawkey*.[85] In that case, the defendant was a sheriff convicted of mail fraud based upon the misuse of public funds. Acting on behalf of public agencies, the defendant arranged with a concert promoter to hold annual concerts to benefit local youth programs. The promoter solicited money to support the concerts. Supporters mailed checks to the promoter, which in turn mailed statements and invoices to the supporters. Two bank accounts were set up to handle these funds, including funds received for advertising the concert and payments for concert tickets. Defendant converted most of these funds for personal use. On appeal, the defendant argued that no one lost any property because the businesses received their advertising and the attendees received their tickets; thus, there was no scheme to defraud. The court disagreed; those parties intended that their funds assist the local youth programs, not benefit the defendant.

Prosecutors have thus become more creative in using the right to control theory. The theory appears to have a good chance of success where the intended victim had an interest in the property at issue. This was the case with the risk of financial loss in *Catalfo*, the payment of insurance benefits in *Gray*, and the payments in *Hawkey*, but was not the case in *Evans*, where the government never owned the weapons at issue.

[3] Property Interests of Foreign Governments

It is difficult to determine whether the Supreme Court will continue to read the mail and wire fraud statutes narrowly, as in *McNally* and *Cleveland*, or broadly, as in *Carpenter* and in the 2005 decision of *Pasquantino v. United States*.[86] In the latter case, the Court held five-to-four that the mail and wire fraud statutes apply where the victim is a foreign government. In that case, the majority concluded that Canada's right to collect taxes on imported liquor is "property" under the wire fraud

---

[83] 64 F.3d 1070, 1076–77 (7th Cir. 1995), *cert. denied*, 517 U.S. 1192 (1996). *See also* United States v. Wallach, 935 F.2d 445, 462–63 (2d Cir. 1991) (upholding convictions based upon the theory that the defendants deprived a corporation's shareholders of the "right to control" how the corporation's money was spent).

[84] 405 F.3d 227, 234 (4th Cir. 2005). For examples of other cases upholding the right to control theory, see *id.* and the cases cited therein.

[85] 148 F.3d 920 (8th Cir. 1998).

[86] 544 U.S. 349 (2005).

statute. The Court distinguished *Cleveland*, stating that Canada's right to tax revenue was a "straightforward 'economic' interest."[87] The Court also rejected the defendants' argument that this result violates the common law "revenue rule," which generally bars United States courts from enforcing the tax laws of foreign countries. The Court stated that, at the time the wire fraud statute was adopted, no case had "held or clearly implied that the revenue rule barred the United States from prosecuting a fraudulent scheme to evade foreign taxes."[88]

[4] The "Convergence" Requirement

In *McNally*, the Supreme Court arguably implied that, in a mail fraud case, the intended victim of the fraudulent scheme must also be the subject of the deception. As the Court stated: "Insofar as the sparse legislative history reveals anything, it indicates that the original impetus behind the mail fraud statute was to protect the people from schemes to deprive them of *their* money or property."[89] Similarly, in *Cleveland*,[90] the Court stated, "[w]e conclude that § 1341 requires the object of the fraud to be *'property'* in the victim's hands." Some courts have termed this as a "convergence" requirement.[91]

A number of courts have required that the deceived party also be the intended victim of the fraud. For example, in *Corcoran v. American Plan Corp.*,[92] the New York State Insurance Commissioner brought a civil RICO action, with mail fraud as the predicate act.[93] The Commissioner alleged that the defendants schemed to steal money from two insurance companies. The alleged deceptions, however, were made to the Commissioner through false reports mailed to the state authorities. Because the deceived party — the Insurance Commissioner — was not the intended victim of the fraud, the Second Circuit dismissed the case.

Similarly, in *United States v. Walters*,[94] the forms mailed to the NCAA deceived the NCAA into believing that the student athletes were eligible to play college football. Yet, the government alleged that the universities themselves were the victims of the fraud because they paid scholarship funds to ineligible athletes. This scheme, the court found, did not amount to mail fraud; the scheme did not envision that the parties deceived by the mailings — the athletic conferences — be deprived of money or property in any way.[95] Other courts have rejected this approach,

---

[87] *Id.* at 357.

[88] *Id.* at 360. The dissent argued that "the Court has ascribed an exorbitant scope to the wire fraud statute." *Id.* at 373 (Ginsburg, J., dissenting).

[89] 483 U.S. at 356 (emphasis added).

[90] 531 U.S. at 26.

[91] *See, e.g.,* United States v. Sawyer, 85 F.3d 713, 734 n.18 (1st Cir. 1996).

[92] 886 F.2d 16 (2d Cir. 1989).

[93] *See* Chapter 16, RICO, *infra*.

[94] 997 F.2d 1219, discussed *supra* § 4.04[A][1].

[95] *Accord* United States v. Lew, 875 F.2d 219, 221 (9th Cir. 1989). In that case, the defendant was an attorney who made *false statements to the federal government* to gain benefits for his clients. The government alleged that the *clients were defrauded* of the fees they paid the attorney. The Ninth Circuit reversed the conviction because there was no evidence that Lew had deceived his clients of money or

however, and have affirmed mail fraud convictions when the deceived party was not the intended victim. For example, the court in *United States v. Christopher*,[96] disagreed with the result in *Corcoran*, stating that "[i]f, for example, the role of a government regulator is to protect the monetary interests of others, a scheme to mislead the regulator in order to get at the protected funds will affect 'property rights' as required in *McNally*."[97]

A similar issue arises where the scheme does not envision that the defendant receive the benefits from the fraud. For example, in *Walters* the universities were victimized when they paid scholarship money to student athletes who were not eligible for those scholarships; Walters did not receive any money or property from the universities. The court found that this was not sufficient for a mail fraud conviction.[98] Other courts have disagreed, holding that the government need not prove that the scheme envisioned that the defendant actually obtain money or property from the victim.[99]

In *Bridge v. Phoenix Bond & Indemnity Co.*,[100] the United States Supreme Court apparently assumed, without directly deciding, that convergence is not required. In *Bridge*, a civil RICO case based on mail fraud predicate acts, the defendants made false statements in mailings to persons who owned property against which the local government had placed tax liens. The mailings of the notices were required by state law. The defendants hoped to purchase the tax liens through a bidding process and later sell the properties for profit if the owners did not pay off the liens. The defendants schemed to rig the bidding process to obtain opportunities to buy the liens, thus depriving other potential bidders of the chance to profit from buying the liens and reselling the properties. The Court found that the plaintiffs had sufficiently alleged mail fraud based on these facts, even though the deceived party (the local government) was not among the alleged victims (the

---

property. The court stated that "[McNally] made it clear that the intent must be to obtain money or property from the one who is deceived" *See also Gray*, 405 F.3d at 234 ("[i]t is essential to a conviction under these statutes that the victim of the alleged fraud actually have an interest in the money or property obtained by the defendant").

[96] 142 F.3d 46, 53–54 (1st Cir. 1998).

[97] *Cf.* Ideal Steel Supply Corp. v. Anza, 373 F.3d 251 (2d Cir. 2004) (in a civil RICO case with mail fraud as the predicate act, court questioned whether *Evans* and *Corcoran* relied on the convergence principle); *In re* Lupron Marketing and Sales Practices Litigation, 295 F. Supp. 2d 148, 168 (D. Mass. 2003) (in a civil RICO case, court stated that "[n]othing in the mail and wire fraud statutes requires that the party deprived of money or property be the same party who is actually deceived").

[98] 997 F.2d at 1224. Other lower federal courts have similarly required that the defendant intend to profit from the fraud. *See, e.g.*, United States v. Alsugair, 256 F. Supp. 2d 306 (D.N.J. 2003), and cases cited therein.

[99] *See* United States v. Hedaithy, 392 F.3d 580, 602 (3d Cir. 2004) (The defendants argue that "any violation of the mail fraud statute must involve a scheme for obtaining the victim's property. We do not read *McNally* or *Cleveland* as providing any such requirement.").

[100] 128 S. Ct. 2131, 2138 (2008). The specific issue in the case was whether first-party reliance is an element of a civil RICO case. The Court held that it is not, without ever terming the issue one of "convergence" for mail/wire fraud purposes: "[W]e hold that a plaintiff asserting a RICO claim predicated on mail fraud need not show . . . that it relied on the defendant's alleged misrepresentation." *Id. See* § 16.07, *infra*, for a discussion of issues arising in civil RICO cases.

other potential bidders) of the scheme.[101] It is unclear whether the *Bridge* decision overturns earlier circuit court cases requiring convergence.[102]

[B]   Section 1346 and the Deprivation of "Honest Services"

A mail or wire fraud scheme must be designed to deprive a victim of money, property, or honest services. Honest services fraud cases have been brought against both public officials and private persons. As discussed in this section, the "honest services" theory has produced a great deal of confusing and conflicting case law. In 2010, in *Skilling v. United States*,[103] the United States Supreme Court attempted to clarify the scope of honest services fraud. This section traces the background of honest services fraud, the conflicting case law concerning that fraud, and the Court's *Skilling* decision. The section concludes with a discussion of questions that remain concerning honest services fraud in the wake of the *Skilling* decision.

[1]   The Adoption and Interpretation of § 1346

Recall that, in 1988, the Supreme Court held in *McNally* that a mail fraud case must include proof that the defendant's scheme involved a loss of money or property, and that a public official's mere failure to provide "honest services" to the government and the public does not suffice. The following year, Congress adopted a law that appears at § 1346 of the federal criminal code and that was intended to overrule *McNally*.[104] This section provides:

---

[101] Because this was a civil case seeking damages on behalf of the other potential bidders, the case did not raise the issue whether the local government may have been injured by the bid-rigging scheme by, for example, increasing the price of successful bids. If this were true, then any convergence requirement would have been met.

[102] One way to reconcile *Bridge* with those earlier cases may be to view *Bridge* in light of the "scheme to defraud" requirement. Assume, for example, that a person acting with the intent to defraud makes a material, false statement made to a third party who is not the intended victim of the fraud scheme. Further assume that a mailing that satisfies the *Schmuck* rule was made in furtherance of that scheme. Although the third party — the deceived party — would not be deprived of money, property, or honest services if the scheme succeeded, the misstatement would be part of the scheme to defraud if it were directly related to the intended injury to the scheme's victim. In *Bridge*, for example, the misstatements to the local government would produce the intended injury to the victims by depriving the other potential bidders of their opportunity to profit from the bidding. In *Walters*, on the other hand, the misstatements to the athletic conferences did not directly lead the universities to pay the scholarship money to the athletes.

[103] 130 S. Ct. 2896 (2010).

[104] Section 1346 did not operate to overturn *McNally* completely. Although one Congressperson did state that the law "restores the mail [and wire] fraud provision[s] to where [they were] before the *McNally* decision," 134 Cong. Rec. H33296 (daily ed. Oct. 21, 1988) (statement of Rep. Conyers), the Supreme Court determined that § 1346 did not have that effect. In *Cleveland*, the Court held that fraudulent schemes to obtain licenses and permits do not fall under the mail fraud statute. As the Court stated in that case, § 1346 covers "only the intangible right of honest services even though federal courts, relying on *McNally*, had dismissed, for want of monetary loss to any victim, prosecutions under § 1341 for diverse forms of public corruption, including licensing fraud." 531 U.S. 12, 20 (2000). Thus, under *Cleveland*, where the government alleged a scheme to deprive the victim of property, *McNally* operated to limit the scope of covered property interests.

> For purposes of this Chapter, the term "scheme or artifice to defraud" includes a scheme or artifice to deprive another of the intangible right of honest services.

Section 1346 was adopted as part of an unrelated bill, and there is little legislative history to guide the courts when interpreting the statute.

This statute produced a wealth of cases struggling to define its scope. As the Supreme Court noted in *Skilling*, "[c]ourts have disagreed about whether § 1346 prosecutions must be based on a violation of state law,[105] whether a defendant must contemplate that the victim suffer economic harm,[106] and whether the defendant must act in pursuit of private gain."[107] In addition, some circuits decided to incorporate pre-§ 1346 law when interpreting the statute, while others declined to do so.[108] This state of affairs resulted in substantial confusion, from which no clear definition of "honest services" emerged.

[2]   The *Skilling* Decision

In *Skilling*, the Supreme Court limited the scope of "honest services" fraud under § 1346 in an effort to clear up the substantial confusion over the statute's reach. Jeffrey Skilling was the former CEO of Enron. The collapse of that corporation in 2001 led to one of the largest bankruptcies in United States history. Skilling and others were charged in connection with Enron's collapse, and Skilling was convicted of conspiracy, mail fraud under the honest services theory, and securities fraud.

On appeal, the Supreme Court reversed Skilling's honest services fraud conviction. In order to avoid striking down the entire statute as unconstitutionally vague, the Court relied upon the honest services case law to discern limitations on the scope of § 1346. The Court stated:

> The 'vast majority' of the honest-services cases involved offenders who, in violation of a fiduciary duty, participated in bribery or kickback schemes. Indeed, the *McNally* case itself, which spurred Congress to enact § 1346, presented a paradigmatic kickback fact pattern. Congress' reversal of

---

[105] *Skilling*, 130 S. Ct. at 2928 n.36 (*"compare, e.g.,* United States v. Brumley, 116 F.3d 728, 734–735 (5th Cir. 1997) (en banc), *with, e.g.,* United States v. Weyhrauch, 548 F.3d 1237, 1245–1246 (9th Cir. 2008), *vacated and remanded*, 130 S. Ct. 2971 (2010)").

[106] *Id.* (*"compare, e.g.,* United States v. Sun-Diamond Growers, 138 F.3d 961, 973 (D.C. Cir. 1998), *with, e.g.,* United States v. Black, 530 F.3d 596, 600–602 (7th Cir. 2008), *vacated and remanded*, 130 S. Ct. 2963 (2010)").

[107] *Id.* (*"compare, e.g.,* United States v. Bloom, 149 F.3d 649, 655 (7th Cir. 1998), *with, e.g.,* United States v. Panarella, 277 F.3d 678, 692 (3d Cir. 2002)"). In his *Skilling* concurring opinion, Justice Scalia went into much greater depth in describing the various uncertainties and ambiguities in the honest services fraud cases. *See id.* at 136–39 (Scalia, J., concurring in the judgment).

[108] In United States v. Handakas, 286 F.3d 92, 103 (2d Cir. 2002), *abrogated in part by* United States v. Rybicki, 354 F.3d 124 (2d Cir. 2003) (en banc), a Second Circuit panel reviewed the circuits' approaches to this issue and found that pre-*McNally* cases were not relevant to interpretations of § 1346. In *Rybicki*, the Second Circuit sitting en banc overruled *Handakas* on this point and employed pre-*McNally* law when interpreting the statute. 354 F.3d at 143. *Skilling* resolved this dispute by directly relying upon pre-*McNally* case law in its decision. 130 S. Ct. at 2933–34.

McNally and reinstatement of the honest-services doctrine, we conclude, can and should be salvaged by confining its scope to the core pre-*McNally* applications . . . .

In view of this history, there is no doubt that Congress intended § 1346 to reach *at least* bribes and kickbacks. Reading the statute to proscribe a wider range of offensive conduct, we acknowledge, would raise the due process concerns underlying the vagueness doctrine. To preserve the statute without transgressing constitutional limitations, we now hold that § 1346 criminalizes *only* the bribe-and-kickback core of the pre-*McNally* case law.[109]

Justice Scalia, in a concurring opinion joined by Justices Thomas and Kennedy, argued that § 1346 should have been stricken in its entirety as unconstitutionally vague. He concluded that, "in transforming the prohibition of 'honest-services fraud' into a prohibition of 'bribery and kick-backs' [the majority] is wielding a power we long ago abjured: the power to define new federal crimes."[110]

[3] Questions Post-*Skilling*

Many commentators have observed that the *Skilling* decision leaves open many questions concerning the scope of § 1346.[111] One question that the courts will confront post-*Skilling* is whether the government must prove that the defendant owed a fiduciary duty or its equivalent to the intended victim.[112] In *Skilling*, the Court relied upon the "leading" decision in *Rybicki* when delineating the scope of honest services fraud.[113] As the *Rybicki* dissent noted, however, there a number of open questions concerning the scope of honest services fraud:

1.   What is the *duty* that must be breached to violate § 1346? The majority holds that it is the duty owed by an employee to an employer, or by "a person in a relationship that gives rise to a duty of loyalty comparable to that owed by employees to employers" (whatever that means). Some circuits only allow prosecutions for breach of an employee's duty to an employer. Other circuits require the breach of a fiduciary duty.

2.   Is the source of that duty state or federal law? The majority does not say, and other circuits are split.[114]

---

[109] *Skilling*, 130 S. Ct. at 2930–31.

[110] *Id.* at 2935 (Scalia, J., concurring in the judgment).

[111] Justice Scalia raised several of these issues in his *Skilling* concurrence. *See Skilling*, 130 S. Ct. at 2938–39 (Scalia, J., concurring in the judgment). *See also* Sara Sun Beale, *An Honest Services Debate*, 8 Ohio St. J. Crim. L. 251 (2010) (describing uncertainties post-*Skilling*).

[112] The Court in *Skilling* appeared to signal that it did not expect such issues to arise under its limited definition of honest services.130 S. Ct. at 2931 n.41 (citations omitted). The Court stated that issues concerning whether a fiduciary duty is required have been "rare in bribe and kickback cases. The existence of a fiduciary relationship, under any definition of that term, usually [has been] beyond dispute; examples include public official-public, employee-employer, and union official-union members."

[113] *Id.* at 2939 (citing United States v. Rybicki, 354 F.3d 124, 137–38 (2003) (en banc)).

[114] *Rybicki*, 354 F.3d at 163 (Jacobs, J., dissenting).

These questions continue to arise even after *Skilling*. In *United States v. Milovanovic*,[115] for example, the defendants were indicted in connection with a bribery scheme concerning a state's issuance of commercial driver's licenses. One defendant was employed by a company that the state hired to provide translating services. In exchange for bribes, that defendant schemed to assist applicants to obtain licenses through various misrepresentations. The district court dismissed the honest services charges on the grounds that the government had failed to allege a breach of fiduciary duty. In reversing, the Ninth Circuit held that a breach of a fiduciary duty is not required. Instead, the court held that the government need only allege "a legally enforceable right to have another provide honest services."[116] The dissent argued that, "[w]ithout some kind of limiting principle, honest services wire fraud could potentially make relatively innocuous conduct subject to criminal sanctions."[117] In this light, the *Skilling* decision has not resolved the many open questions regarding the scope of honest services fraud. In the years ahead, courts will confront many questions. Among these:

- Must the defendant owe a fiduciary duty to the victim of the honest services fraud scheme?[118]

- If so, what is the source of that duty?[119]

- Does the statute cover only public officials or also private persons? If it applies to both, are the standards the same?

- What are the definitions of "bribes" and "kickbacks?" What is the source of those definitions?

- Must the bribe or kickback violate state law? State criminal law?

- In the case of a private party, must the bribe or kickback scheme be designed to harm the victim(s)? If so, how is that harm defined? Is economic harm required, or would some sort of other harm suffice?[120]

- In a case involving non-disclosed self-dealing, could the government successfully allege that the defendant intended to deprive the victim of some sort of intangible property right instead of a right to honest services?[121]

---

[115]   627 F.3d 405 (9th Cir. 2010).

[116]   *Id.* at 412 (citing *United States v. Rybicki*, 354 F.3d 124, 155 (2d Cir.2003) (Raggi, J., concurring)).

[117]   *Id.* at 414 (Fernandez, J., dissenting) (quoting United States v. Kincaid-Chauncey, 556 F.3d 923, 940 (9th Cir.2009)).

[118]   *See* United States v. Milovanovic, 627 F.3d 405 (9th Cir. 2010) (holding that no fiduciary duty is required). The dissent strongly disagreed. *Id.* at 413 (Fernandez, J., dissenting).

[119]   In United States v. Milovanovic, 627 F.3d 405 (9th Cir. 2010).

[120]   This issue was before the Court in United States v. Black, 530 F.3d 596, 600–602 (7th Cir. 2008), *vacated and remanded*, 130 S. Ct. 2963 (2010)").

[121]   *See* Dane C. Ball, *Repacking* Skilling-*Barred Fraud Theories: A Form of Damage Control that Goes Too Far*, 5 White Collar Crim. Rep. 741 (2010).

§ 4.06　RELATED STATUTES AND CRIMES

The mail and wire fraud statutes are all-encompassing provisions that criminalize fraudulent use of the mails and wires. In a number of areas, Congress has adopted statutory schemes specifically aimed at particular types of fraud. This section discusses four such statutory schemes. Recall that mail and/or wire fraud charges will generally be available to prosecutors instead of or in addition to the charges discussed below.

[A]　Bank Fraud

The bank fraud statute, 18 U.S.C. § 1344, provides:

> Whoever knowingly executes, or attempts to execute, a scheme or artifice
>
> —
>
> (1)　to defraud a financial institution; or
>
> (2)　to obtain any of the moneys, funds, credits, assets, securities, or other property owned by, or under the custody or control of, a financial institution, by means of false or fraudulent pretenses, representations, or promises;
>
> shall be fined not more than $1,000,000 or imprisoned not more than 30 years, or both.

Under this statute the defendant's scheme must be designed to defraud a financial institution. Otherwise, courts generally define the "scheme to defraud" under § 1344 as they do under the mail and wire fraud statutes.[122]

Bank fraud charges are commonly brought in connection with financial fraud schemes. For example, in *United States v. Doke*,[123] the defendants were charged with conspiracy, bank fraud, and false statements to a financial institution. The charges arose out of a real estate loan that the bank made to defendant Bass. The loan application documents failed to disclose Doke's participation in the transaction. Because banking regulations limit loans to bank insiders, and because Doke was in fact a bank insider, regulators would have barred the full loan had they been aware of Doke's involvement in the transaction. After the loan was made, the borrower failed to make payments, the bank foreclosed on the property, and the bank ultimately failed.

The defendants argued on appeal that the evidence was not sufficient to convict under § 1344 because the bank knew of Bass's credit-worthiness, knew the purpose of the loan, and knew what collateral would secure the loan. The court affirmed the conviction, finding that concealing Doke's involvement did amount to fraud because it placed the bank in violation of banking regulations. Such proof was sufficient even if the bank was not misled as to the economic substance of the loan transaction.

---

[122] *See supra* § 4.03. For an analysis of the statute's reach, see United States v. Reaume, 338 F.3d 577 (6th Cir. 2003).

[123] 171 F.3d 240 (5th Cir. 1999).

As in other areas, such as securities fraud, bank fraud charges may be brought in tandem with mail or wire fraud charges. Indeed, the defendant in a mail or wire fraud case faces special hurdles where the fraud affected a financial institution. The mail and wire fraud statutes provide for an increased sentence, and for extension of the statute of limitations period from five years to ten years, in such cases. In *United States v. Bouyea*,[124] the court analyzed the meaning of this provision of the mail and wire fraud statute. The defendants were convicted of wire fraud and bank fraud. The wire fraud count alleged that defendants defrauded a corporation of money or property, and that this fraud affected the corporation's parent corporation, a financial institution. After finding sufficient evidence of fraudulent intent, the Second Circuit turned to the issue whether the evidence was sufficient to show that the scheme "affected a financial institution." Such evidence was essential because the indictment was filed six years after the fraud took place. The court found that, although the defrauded entity was not a financial institution, the fraud had a financial impact on the victim's parent corporation, which did qualify as a financial institution under the statute.

[B] Bankruptcy Fraud

The principal bankruptcy fraud statutes are contained in §§ 151–157 of the federal criminal code.[125] Section 152 is the most often-used provision, and criminalizes concealing assets, making false statements, and using bribery and extortion in bankruptcy proceedings. Other important provisions include § 153, which criminalizes embezzlement by bankruptcy trustees and their agents, and § 155, which criminalizes wrongdoing by a bankruptcy petition preparer.

Finally, § 157 is an all-encompassing provision that is patterned after the mail fraud statute. That section criminalizes fraud in connection with filing a bankruptcy petition or related document, or making a "false or fraudulent representation, claim, or promise" in a bankruptcy proceeding. As in other areas, general criminal statutes, such as the federal conspiracy statute and the mail fraud statute, remain applicable in bankruptcy cases.

[C] Health Care Fraud

Health care fraud, committed by providers and consumers of health care services and others, is increasingly the subject of criminal prosecution.[126] Although most prosecutions are based upon such traditional criminal law statutes such as mail and wire fraud, Congress has enacted specific statutes addressed to this issue. Most significantly, § 1320a-7b(a) of Title 42 of the federal code[127] criminalizes false statements made to the federal government for the purpose of obtaining, inflating,

---

[124] 152 F.3d 192 (2d Cir. 1998).

[125] 18 U.S.C. §§ 151–157.

[126] Stephen A. Warnke et al., *Health Care Fraud and Abuse, in* White Collar Crime: Business and Regulatory Offenses §§ 19.01–05 (Otto Obermaier & Robert Morvillo, eds. 2011). For an example of a complex health care fraud prosecution, see Siddiqi v. United States, 98 F.3d 1427 (2d Cir. 1996) (prosecution for mail fraud, theft of government property, and false claims).

[127] 42 U.S.C. § 1320a-7b(a).

keeping, or qualifying for benefits under a federal health care program.

[D] False Government Claims and Procurement Fraud

In addition to charges under the general mail and wire fraud statutes, fraud against the United States can be charged under a number of statutes specifically directed to that conduct. For example, § 287 of the federal criminal code criminalizes the making of a false claim to the federal government knowing the claim to be false, fictitious, or fraudulent. A companion statute, § 286, criminalizes entering into a conspiracy to make false claims.[128] Another statute, 18 U.S.C. § 1031(a), criminalizes "major fraud" against the United States. Together with the general false statements statute, 18 U.S.C. § 1001,[129] these statutes are used to punish fraud committed upon the government itself.

[1] False Claims

Section 287 targets knowingly making false claims to the federal government to obtain money or property. The statute overlaps considerably with the major fraud statute, the mail and wire fraud statutes, and the false statement statute. Section 287 provides:

> Whoever makes or presents to any person or officer in the civil, military, or naval service of the United States, or to any department or agency thereof, any claim upon or against the United States, or any department or agency thereof, knowing such claim to be false, fictitious, or fraudulent, shall be imprisoned not more than five years and shall be subject to a fine in the amount provided in this title.

Under the false claims statute, the government must prove that the defendant:

1.   Made or presented a claim to the United States government; and

2.   Knew that the claim was false, fictitious, or fraudulent.

One issue that arises under the statute is the requisite level of intent. Courts have generally declined defendants' invitations to impose a heightened mens rea requirement. In *United States v. Maher*,[130] for example, the defendant had entered into a number of contracts with the government. When billing the government under the contracts, the defendant made false statements. He argued that he lacked the intent to defraud because he made the false statements for legitimate business purposes and attempted to ensure that the government was billed the correct amount. The court rejected the argument, noting that the statute criminalizes claims that are false, fictitious, *or* fraudulent. Because the defendant knew the

---

[128] Private parties may also initiate actions under the false claims statutes. *See* Chapter 20, Civil Actions, Civil Penalties, and Parallel Proceedings, *infra*, § 20.07.

[129] Section 1001 is discussed in detail in Chapter 10, False Statements, *infra*. In some respects, the false statements statute, 18 U.S.C. § 1001, is broader than the false claims statute because § 1001 does not require that (a) the statement be made to obtain money or property or (b) the statement be presented to the government. On the other hand, materiality is an element of § 1001 but not of § 287. *See* United States v. Irwin, 654 F.2d 671 (10th Cir. 1981).

[130] 582 F.2d 842 (4th Cir. 1978).

statements were false, the mens rea requirement was met even if the defendant did not intend to deprive the government of money or property. And in *United States v. Irwin*,[131] the Tenth Circuit held that proof of willfulness is not required but that knowledge suffices.

[2] Procurement Fraud

The Major Fraud Act of 1988, codified at 18 U.S.C. § 1031(a), provides:

(a)   Whoever knowingly executes, or attempts to execute, any scheme or artifice with the intent -

    (1)   to defraud the United States; or

    (2)   to obtain money or property by means of false or fraudulent pretenses, representations, or promises,

in any procurement of property or services as a prime contractor with the United States or as a subcontractor or supplier on a contract in which there is a prime contract with the United States, if the value of the contract, subcontract, or any constituent part thereof, for such property or services is $1,000,000 or more shall . . . be fined not more than $1,000,000, or imprisoned not more than 10 years, or both.

Under this statute, the government must prove that the defendant:

1.   Acted knowingly and intentionally;

2.   Executed or attempted a scheme -

    (a)   to defraud the United States; or

    (b)   to obtain money or property by means of false or fraudulent pretenses, representations, or promises; and

3.   Acted in any procurement of property or services as a prime contractor with the United States, or as a subcontractor or supplier on a contract in which there is a prime contract with the United States; and

4.   The value of the contract or subcontract was $1,000,000 or more.

Courts have held that, although each act in furtherance of a scheme does not necessarily constitute a separate offense, multiple counts may be brought when there are multiple "executions" of a single scheme.[132] The determination of whether there are multiple "executions" is highly fact-intensive, and depends upon whether, for example, the claims were made in discrete instances over a period of time.

The issue of whether the value of the contract or subcontract met the statutory amount is a major contested issue under this statute. The Fourth Circuit addressed this question in *United States v. Brooks*.[133] In that case, the defendants were

---

[131] 654 F.2d 671 (10th Cir. 1981).

[132] United States v. Reitmeyer, 356 F.3d 1313, 1317 (10th Cir. 2004), *citing* United States v. Sain, 141 F.3d 463, 473 (3d Cir.), *cert. denied*, 525 U.S. 908 (1998).

[133] 111 F.3d 365 (4th Cir. 1997).

subcontractors of the United States Navy. The defendants entered into contracts to provide less than $55,000 in goods to the two principal contractors. Each of the principal contractors had contracts with the government worth more than $1 million. The defendants misrepresented the quality of the goods that they provided under the contracts. On appeal from their § 1031(a) convictions, the defendants argued that the statutory threshold amount was not met. The court rejected the argument on two grounds. First, the statutory language makes clear that the statute covers any "contract, subcontract, or any constituent part thereof, for such property or services is $1,000,000 or more."[134] Because the total contractual amount was more than $1 million, the threshold was met. Second, the court found that this result comported with the statute's purpose because defects even in minor parts of military equipment can cause substantial harm.[135]

---

[134] *Id.* at 368–69.

[135] *Id.* at 369.

Chapter 5

SECURITIES FRAUD

§ 5.01 INTRODUCTION

Perhaps no area of white collar crime has so captured the public's attention as the major securities fraud scandals of recent decades, including high-profile Wall Street insider trading scandals[1] and massive corporate financial fraud schemes.[2] The fortunes made and the lives affected by the insider trading and corporate fraud schemes came to symbolize for many a corrupt aspect of American corporate culture. These events also led law-makers and prosecutors to focus their efforts on white collar crime enforcement.

Securities fraud also raises the law enforcement issues that typically confront the government when it attempts to enforce white collar criminal statutes. Fraud in the purchase or sale of securities may cause substantial injury to individual victims. Further, as discussed in more detail below, such fraud may also threaten the integrity of the securities markets. The challenge for the government is to identify and seek punishment of those who engage in securities fraud, which, by its very nature, is conducted in secret and is difficult to detect.

In many ways, issues of statutory vagueness and prosecutorial discretion surrounding the enforcement of the securities laws highlight broader issues about the way white collar criminal statutes are written, interpreted, and enforced. First, the government typically has broad discretion in deciding whether to pursue administrative, civil, and/or criminal remedies in a securities fraud case. Indeed, the distinction between potential civil and criminal liability, and the potential for overlap between the two, are difficult issues under the securities laws.[3] Second, securities laws violations may be charged as violations of other statutes, such as mail/wire

---

[1] Highly publicized, large-scale insider trading schemes led to the convictions of Raj Rajaratnam, the founder of the hedge fund firm Galleon Group, in 2011, and Wall Street guru Ivan Boesky and "junk bond king" Michael Milken in the 1980s. *See* Peter Lattman & Azam Ahmed, *Hardball Tactics Against Insider Trading: Prosecutors Hope Verdict Will Be a Deterrent to Others*, N.Y. Times, May 12, 2011, at B1. In another high-profile case, media figure Martha Stewart was convicted in 2004 of attempting to cover-up her alleged insider trading scheme. *See* § 5.04[C][2], *infra*.

[2] These fraud schemes led to the demise of such major companies as Enron, WorldCom, HealthSouth, Adelphia, and many others. *See, e.g.*, United States v. Ebbers, 458 F.3d 110 (2d Cir. 2006); United States v. Arthur Andersen, LLP, 374 F.3d 281 (5th Cir. 2004).

[3] *See* Julian W. Friedman, Nathaniel Z. Marmur & Charles A. Stillman, *Securities Fraud, in* White Collar Crime: Business and Regulatory Offenses Volume 2, § 12.01[1], at 12-2 (Otto Obermaier & Robert Morvillo, eds., 2011). Indeed, in some cases, it may be easier to bring a criminal securities fraud case than a civil securities fraud case. *See* Wendy Gerwick Couture, *White Collar Crime's Gray Area: The Anomaly of Criminalizing Conduct Not Civilly Actionable*, 72 Alb. L. Rev. 1, 5–12 (2009).

fraud and conspiracy. Prosecutors therefore have broad discretion in deciding how many charges to bring based upon a single criminal act.[4] Third, the boundaries of many aspects of securities fraud, such as insider trading, are notoriously vague. Thus, prosecutors have the discretion to apply, or not to apply, the securities laws to "gray area" activities that have not previously been found to be illegal.

§ 5.02 STATUTORY OVERVIEW AND DEFINITIONS

[A] Introduction

As noted above, federal securities laws violations are potentially subject to administrative, civil, and criminal sanctions. These proceedings can be pursued simultaneously or consecutively, and raise special issues relating both to strategy and Fifth Amendment rights.[5]

The Securities and Exchange Commission (the "SEC" or the "Commission") is the government agency principally responsible for administering and enforcing the federal securities laws. The SEC's Division of Enforcement may institute administrative proceedings and/or bring civil cases in federal court (denominated "Securities and Exchange Commission v. _____"). In addition, private parties may initiate civil law suits under the federal securities laws. If the SEC determines that a defendant may have acted willfully, it may also refer a matter to the United States Department of Justice for criminal prosecution (denominated "United States v. _____"). Because the statutory issues decided in civil cases govern those issues in criminal cases, the important civil securities fraud cases are discussed in this chapter.

Of course, there must be federal jurisdiction in any federal civil or criminal securities fraud case. This requirement is easily met, as securities transactions invariably involve interstate commerce.

It should also be noted that each state has its own set of securities laws, known as "blue sky laws."[6] While there is overlap between the state and federal laws, most major securities fraud cases are brought on the federal level.[7]

---

[4] *See* Chapter 4, Mail and Wire Fraud, *supra* § 4.01[A]. Indeed, the government may bring mail/wire fraud charges based upon securities fraud in circumstances in which criminal securities fraud charges might not be viable. *See* Couture, *supra* note 3, at 5–12.

[5] *See supra* § 5.01, and *infra* § 5.06.

[6] *See* Palmer T. Heenan et al., *Securities Fraud*, 47 Am. Crim. L. Rev. 1015, 1017 n.8 (2010) ("the term 'blue sky' refers to the practice of land salesmen who were so fraudulent that they would 'sell building lots in the blue sky in fee simple' ") (citing Jonathan R. Macey & Geoffrey P. Miller, *Origin of the Blue Sky Laws*, 70 Tex. L. Rev. 347, 359 n.59 (1991)).

[7] Significantly, states have become increasingly aggressive in enforcing their own securities statutes, a development that has caused conflict between state and federal officials. *See* Robert G. Morvillo & Robert J. Anello, *Securities Investigations and Prosecutions under the Martin Act*, N.Y.L.J., April 1, 2003, at 3.

[B]   The 1933 and 1934 Acts

[1]   The Statutory Scheme

The two main securities laws[8] were enacted in the wake of the stock market crash of 1929. These statutes were intended to provide substantial governmental oversight to the securities industry, and to provide both civil and criminal remedies.

The Securities Act of 1933 (the "Securities Act" or the "1933 Act"), broadly speaking, regulates a company's original *registration* and *issuance* of securities by requiring full disclosure of information to potential investors. This statute applies to what is generally referred to as the "primary" or "new-issue" securities market.

The Securities Exchange Act of 1934 (the "Exchange Act" or the "1934 Act") generally seeks to regulate *trading* in the securities markets. This statute applies to what is generally referred to as the "secondary" or "trading" market.

[2]   The Definition of "Security"

In order for the defendant to be subject to civil or criminal sanctions for securities fraud, the alleged activity must have involved a "security."[9] In general, the term includes both equity instruments such as "stocks," which give the stockholder an ownership interest in the issuing company, and "bonds," debt instruments that serve as loans that the bond holders make to the companies. The courts have generally construed the term "security" broadly in order to extend the securities laws' protections.[10]

[3]   Secondary Liability

The potential for aiding and abetting liability in securities fraud cases depends upon the context. First, defendants have been held criminally liable under the federal aiding and abetting statute[11] for primary violations of the securities laws committed by others. Second, in *Central Bank of Denver v. First Interstate Bank of Denver*,[12] the Supreme Court held that there is no aiding and abetting liability in *civil* actions brought by private *litigants* under the 1934 Act's antifraud provision. Third, the Private Securities Litigation Reform Act of 1995[13] allows the *SEC* to institute actions for injunctive relief or monetary damages against those who aid and abet violations of the securities laws.

---

[8] Securities Act of 1933, 15 U.S.C. §§ 77a–77aa; Securities Exchange Act of 1934, 15 U.S.C. §§ 78a–78ll.

[9] *See* Section 2(1) of the Securities Act, 15 U.S.C. § 77b(1); Section 3(a)(10) of the Exchange Act, 15 U.S.C. § 78c(a)(10). An "investment contract" may also qualify as a security if it meets the test set forth in SEC v. W.J. Howey Co., 328 U.S. 293, 298–99 (1946). *See* Heenan et al., *supra* note 6, at 1033–34.

[10] *See generally* Marc I. Steinberg, Understanding Securities Laws (5th ed. 2009).

[11] 18 U.S.C. § 2. *See* Friedman, Marmur & Stillman, *supra* note 3, § 12.02.

[12] 511 U.S. 164 (1994).

[13] Pub. L. No. 104-67, 109 Stat. 737 (1995).

§ 5.03 CIVIL ENFORCEMENT OF THE SECURITIES LAWS

[A] The Statutory Provisions

The 1933 and 1934 Acts contain both express and implied civil remedies. The issues arising in civil cases often apply to criminal cases. Thus, a basic overview of civil enforcement is necessary to understand the context of criminal enforcement of the securities laws.

Of the express civil remedies in the securities laws, several are of particular significance:

- Section 11 of the 1933 Act[14] provides a remedy for damages resulting from material misstatements or omissions in certain documents filed with the SEC or distributed to potential investors. This provision imposes strict liability on certain categories of defendants.[15]

- Section 12(1) of the 1933 Act[16] provides corresponding remedies for failure to file a "registration statement" where such a statement is required in connection with the issuance of securities.

- Section 12(2) of the 1933 Act[17] imposes liability for all misrepresentations and omissions in connection with an offer or sale of securities if the plaintiff can show that the defendant at least acted negligently.

- In the trading context, Section 9 of the 1934 Act[18] provides a civil remedy for stated "manipulative devices," such as trading solely for the purpose of affecting the stock price, in which the defendant "willfully" engaged.

In addition to these and other *express* remedies that exist on the face of the statutes, courts have found *implied* civil remedies under both the 1933 and 1934 Acts. Most significantly, courts have determined that under the 1934 Act's general antifraud provision, Section 10b[19] and SEC Rule 10b-5[20] thereunder, plaintiffs may bring civil actions.

[B] The Elements

A defendant may be civilly liable under Section 10b where:

---

[14] 15 U.S.C. §§ 77a–aa.

[15] 15 U.S.C. § 77k(a).

[16] 15 U.S.C. § 77l(1).

[17] 15 U.S.C. § 77l(2).

[18] 15 U.S.C. § 78i.

[19] 15 U.S.C. § 78j(b).

[20] 17 C.F.R. § 240.10b-5. The SEC has the power to issue regulations under the securities statutes that more fully spell out the statutes' requirements. Rule 10b-5 is the most important such regulation for present purposes. It provides that it is unlawful for any person "[t]o make any untrue statement of a material fact or to omit to state a material fact necessary in order to make the statements made . . . not misleading . . . in connection with the purchase or sale of a security."

1. The defendant engaged in a fraudulent scheme, or made a material misstatement or omission;

2. The act or omission occurred in connection with the purchase or sale of a security;

3. The defendant's act or omission was the proximate cause of damages to the plaintiff;[21]

4. The plaintiff reasonably relied on the defendant's act or omission; and

5. The defendant acted with the intent to defraud, or "scienter."

The Supreme Court has not set forth a specific test for determining "scienter." Therefore, confusion abounds among the courts as to the term's meaning.[22] Some courts have held that a showing of recklessness is sufficient.[23]

§ 5.04 CRIMINAL ENFORCEMENT OF THE SECURITIES LAWS

[A] The Statutory Scheme

A number of federal statutes provide criminal penalties for securities fraud. Section 24 of the 1933 Act[24] and Section 32(a) of the 1934 Act,[25] for example, provide that "willful" violations of the statutes, and of the rules and regulations adopted under the statutes, are subject to criminal sanctions.

---

[21] Causation is an oft-litigated issue in civil securities fraud cases. For example, in one case, the plaintiff-investor alleged that the stock price was inflated due to the defendant's fraud, and that this inflation damaged the investor. The Supreme Court held that this was an insufficient allegation of causation, stating that "an inflated purchase price will not itself constitute or proximately cause the relevant economic loss." Dura Pharmaceuticals v. Broudo, 544 U.S. 336, 342 (2005). For a further discussion of causation in civil securities fraud cases, see Michael J. Kaufman, *At A a Loss: Congress, The the Supreme Court And and Causation Under The the Federal Securities Laws*, 2 N.Y.U. J. L. & Bus. 1 (2005).

[22] *See* William H. Kuehnle, *On Scienter, Knowledge, and Recklessness Under the Federal Securities Laws*, 34 Hou. L. Rev. 121, 122 (1997) ("The state of mind required to commit fraud under section 10b . . . and, in particular, whether recklessness can be a basis for liability has long been a subject of uncertainty").

[23] *See, e.g.*, Ziemba v. Cascade International, Inc., 256 F.3d 1194, 1202 (11th Cir. 2001) ("a showing of severe recklessness satisfies the scienter requirement"). *See also* Robert A. Prentice, *The Future of Corporate Disclosure: The Internet, Securities Fraud, and Rule 10B-5*, 47 Emory L.J. 1, 49 & n.218 (1988). In 1995, Congress passed the Private Litigation Securities Reform Act (PLSRA), 15 U.S.C.A. § 78u-5, which requires a showing of actual knowledge, as opposed to mere recklessness, for private actions relating to "forward-looking" statements. For a discussion of the meaning of recklessness, see *infra* § 5.04[B][2]. The PLSRA also provides a "safe-harbor" that limits liability for "forward looking" statements in private actions, but not in actions brought by the SEC. *See* Heenan et al., *supra* note 6, at 1066.

[24] 15 U.S.C. § 77x.

[25] 15 U.S.C. § 78ff.

Most criminal cases are brought under the "catch-all" anti-fraud provisions of Section 17(a) of the 1933 Act[26] and Section 10b of the 1934 Act and Rule 10b-5 thereunder.[27] As seen in the materials in this chapter, securities fraud prosecutions under these catch-all provisions are brought in a wide variety of contexts. Such prosecutions range from the "insider trading" cases that are the focus of this chapter to cases based upon falsehoods in documents issued to shareholders and potential shareholders. In addition, and as discussed more fully elsewhere in this book, securities fraud prosecutions often involve additional charges under the conspiracy and mail/wire fraud statutes, and under the "cover-up" statutes involving false statements, perjury, and obstruction of justice.

[B] The Elements

Most of the cases discussed in this chapter were brought under Section 10b and Rule 10b-5. To obtain a conviction under these provisions, the government must prove that:

1. The defendant

    (a) engaged in a fraudulent scheme, or

    (b) made a material misstatement, or

    (c) omitted material information to one to whom the defendant owed a duty;

2. The scheme, misstatement, or omission occurred in connection with the purchase or sale of a security; and

3. The defendant acted "willfully."

The meanings of such key terms as "material" and "willfully" are discussed below.

[C] The "Willfulness" Requirement

[1] Definition

As noted above, only "willful" violations of the securities laws render the defendant subject to criminal sanctions. Not surprisingly, the courts have been inconsistent in defining "willful" behavior.

In general terms, it is at least clear that the government must prove beyond a reasonable doubt that the defendant deliberately and intentionally committed the prohibited act. Proof of mere negligence will not meet the willfulness require-ment.[28] The government need not prove a specific intent to violate the law,[29] but it

---

[26] 15 U.S.C. § 77q(a).

[27] 15 U.S.C. § 78j. *See generally* Steinberg, *supra* note 10, at 181–214.

[28] *See* Ernst & Ernst v. Hochfelder, 425 U.S. 185 (1976).

[29] *See* United States v. O'Hagan, 139 F.3d 641, 647 (8th Cir. 1998) ("willfulness" in the securities fraud context does not require proof of an intentional violation of a known legal duty).

must prove an improper, fraudulent intent.[30] In *United States v. Tarallo*,[31] for example, the Ninth Circuit rejected the defendant's argument that the government should have been required to prove that he specifically intended to violate the law. The court reasoned that the "no knowledge" proviso — providing that a defendant who can show lack of knowledge of the relevant rule or regulation will not be subject to imprisonment — would be pointless if a defendant could avoid conviction when the government failed to prove an intent to violate the law.[32]

One unsettled issue in defining "willfulness" is whether knowledge of wrongdoing is required, or whether recklessness will suffice. The United States Supreme Court has not yet addressed the issue whether recklessness is sufficient. The term "recklessness" connotes an act committed when a defendant may not actually know of the act's fraudulent nature, but has reason to be suspicious.[33] Some lower courts have held that a defendant may be found to have acted willfully where the defendant acted with reckless indifference to the truth.[34]

One notable case applying the recklessness standard is *United States v. Weiner.*[35] In that case, the defendants included auditors of a company that inflated the value of its stock by publishing false financial information. On appeal from their securities fraud convictions, the auditors argued that the trial court had erred in instructing the jury that "willfulness" includes reckless indifference to the truth. The Ninth Circuit held that the instruction was appropriate. The court went on to find sufficient evidence of intent based upon (1) the auditors' failure to use accepted accounting techniques, (2) the pervasive scope of the fraud, and (3) the long period of time during which the fraud went undetected. From these facts, the jury could have properly inferred that, even if the auditors did not have actual knowledge of the illegality, they were at least reckless as to the wrongdoing. This recklessness standard is very close to the "willful blindness" or "constructive knowledge" standards that courts have applied in order to meet the knowledge requirement in other contexts.

[2] The Level of Proof

As in other areas of white collar criminal law, the mens rea requirement is often the most hotly contested issue in a securities fraud case. Willfulness can be proven by both direct and circumstantial evidence. The required level of proof for the willfulness element was the key issue in one high profile securities fraud prosecution.

---

[30] *Ernst & Ernst*, 425 U.S. at 1934 n.12.

[31] 380 F.3d 1174 (9th Cir. 2004).

[32] *Id.* at 1188.

[33] *See generally* Kuehnle, *supra* note 22, at 190–94.

[34] *E.g.*, United States v. Weiner, 578 F.2d 757 (9th Cir. 1978). Most circuits have held that recklessness suffices, though they disagree as to the definition of the term. *See* Kuehnle, *supra* note 22, 134–35; Heenan *et al.*, *supra* note 6, 1024.

[35] 578 F.2d 757 (9th Cir.), *cert. denied*, 439 U.S. 981 (1978). *See also* United States v. Tarallo, 380 F.3d 1174, 1189 (9th Cir. 2004) (holding that a securities fraud conviction may be based upon proof of recklessness).

In *United States v. Stewart*, the government charged Martha Stewart with securities fraud in connection with the purchase and sale of Martha Stewart Living Omnimedia (MSLO) securities.[36] At the time of the alleged fraud, Stewart was under investigation for her trading in ImClone stock. The government's theory centered on three public statements Stewart made about her reasons for selling the ImClone stock when she did. According to the government, Stewart lied in those statements with the intent to bolster the price of MSLO stock, thus defrauding investors who might have sold their stock if they had not been persuaded that Stewart had acted properly.

At the end of the government's case, the trial court dismissed the securities fraud count. The court held that no reasonable juror could find beyond a reasonable doubt that the defendant had lied for the purpose of influencing the market for MSLO stock. The court rejected the government's argument that Stewart's intent could be inferred by evidence of her financial stake in MSLO and by her understanding that her reputation would affect the price of MSLO's stock. The Court found that this evidence, although consistent with Stewart's guilt, was insufficient to establish her guilt beyond a reasonable doubt.[37] The Stewart case is indicative of the substantial burden that the government faces on the mens rea element of securities fraud.

Where, however, a jury has found willfulness beyond a reasonable doubt, the defendant then bears a heavy burden of overturning a conviction based upon insufficient evidence. For example, in *United States v. O'Hagan*,[38] discussed more fully below,[39] the defendant was an attorney who bought stock in companies that his law firm's client was attempting to acquire. On appeal, the Eighth Circuit found sufficient evidence that O'Hagan knowingly breached fiduciary duties that he owed both to the firm and to the firm's client, thus supporting the jury's finding of willfulness.

Similarly, in *Tarallo*,[40] the Ninth Circuit rejected the defendant's argument that there was insufficient evidence that he knowingly engaged in fraud. In that case, the defendant participated in a fraudulent telemarketing scheme soliciting securities investments. On appeal from his securities fraud conviction, the court found sufficient evidence that the defendant knew that the investors' funds were not kept in "trust" as promised but rather were used to benefit the defendant and others. Because the defendant knew that he was paid with funds that were supposed to be held in trust, the jury could have concluded that he knew of the fraudulent nature of the scheme.[41]

---

[36] 305 F. Supp. 2d 368 (S.D.N.Y. 2004).

[37] *Id.* at 377–78. Stewart was convicted of conspiracy, false statements, and obstruction of justice. She was sentenced to five months imprisonment and five months of home detention, the lowest possible sentence under the Federal Sentencing Guidelines. *See* Kara Scannell & James Bandler, *Stewart Sentence Boosts Prospects of Her Company*, Wall St. J., July 19, 2004, at C1.

[38] 139 F.3d 641 (8th Cir. 1998).

[39] *See* § 5.07[D][1], *infra.*

[40] 380 F.3d 1174.

[41] *Id.* at 1182.

Many high profile securities fraud prosecutions have been based on attempts to "cook the books" to inflate corporate earnings and stock prices. In one such case, *United States v. Ebbers*,[42] the defendant was the CEO of WorldCom, Inc., a large telecommunications company that filed for bankruptcy after the fraudulent accounting practices were revealed. On appeal from his convictions for securities fraud and for making false filings with the SEC, Ebbers argued that the government should have been required to prove that WorldCom's accounting practices violated Generally Accepted Accounting Principles (GAAP).[43] The Second Circuit rejected the argument, finding that an intent to defraud may exist even when the defendant has complied with GAAP. Although potentially relevant to a good faith defense, such compliance does not negate an intent to defraud "in a case such as the present one, where the evidence showed that accounting methods known to be misleading . . . were used for the express purpose of intentionally misstating WorldCom's financial condition and artificially inflating its stock price."[44]

In another notable case, *United States v. Goyal*,[45] the government relied upon the defendant's alleged failure to follow GAAP in attempting to prove its case. In *Goyal*, the government charged the defendant with securities fraud and with making materially false statements to auditors. With respect to the securities fraud counts, the court found that the government had failed to prove that the alleged deception was material.[46] With respect to the lying to the auditors counts,[47] the court found that the government failed to prove that the defendant's representations were materially false or misleading, and that the defendant knew that the statements were materially false or misleading.[48] In this case, the government rather than the defense relied upon GAAP, but the court found that even if the company violated GAAP, the government had failed to prove that the defendant knew of the violation.

Both *Ebbers* and *Goyal* demonstrate the technical nature of alleged securities fraud schemes based upon highly complex accounting practices. Where there is clear intent to defraud, as in *Ebbers*, compliance with GAAP may not be sufficient to save the defendant from conviction. Without such clear evidence of fraudulent intent, however, arguable non-compliance with GAAP will not alone be sufficient to support conviction.

---

[42] 458 F.3d 110 (2d Cir. 2006).

[43] These are the official standards set forth by the American Institute of Certified Public Accountants. *Id.* at 130.

[44] *Id.* at 126.

[45] 629 F.3d 912 (9th Cir. 2010).

[46] *See* § 5.09, *infra*, for a discussion of materiality.

[47] These charges were brought under 15 U.S.C. § 78m(b)(2) and Rule 13b2-2 thereunder. 629 F.3d at 916 n.6.

[48] 629 F.3d at 917–22. The concurring opinion strongly criticized the government for bringing a criminal case on these facts. *See id.* at 922 ("This is just one of a string of recent cases in which courts have found that federal prosecutors overreached by trying to stretch criminal law beyond its proper bounds.") (Kozinski, J., concurring).

[3] The "Good Faith" Defense and Reliance on Counsel

A defendant may rebut a willfulness showing with a "good faith" defense. This defense asserts that the defendant did not have the improper or fraudulent intent required for conviction. The government must prove beyond a reasonable doubt that the defendant did not act in good faith.[49]

A defendant may establish good faith by showing that the defendant relied upon the advice of counsel. To assert such reliance successfully, the defendant must meet certain specific requirements, including full disclosure to counsel of facts needed for counsel to render an opinion.[50]

In one significant holding on the reliance-on-counsel issue, *United States v. Bilzerian*,[51] the defendant sought to testify that he relied upon the advice of counsel and that he believed that his actions were lawful. He also sought a ruling from the trial court that such testimony on the willfulness issue would not constitute a waiver of the attorney-client privilege. The trial judge denied the motion. The Second Circuit affirmed, holding that:

> [T]he attorney-client privilege cannot at once be used as a shield and a sword. A defendant may not use the privilege to prejudice his opponent's case or to disclose some selected communications for self-serving purposes. Thus, the privilege may implicitly be waived when defendant asserts a claim that in fairness requires examination of protected communications . . . . This waiver principle is applicable here for Bilzerian's testimony that he thought his actions were legal would have put his knowledge of the law and the basis for his understanding of what the law required in issue. His conversations with counsel regarding the legality of his schemes would have been directly relevant in determining the extent of his knowledge and, as a result, his intent.[52]

Bilzerian had, in effect, requested an advisory ruling from the trial court before a factual context had been laid. Therefore, the trial judge was within his discretion in refusing the request.

[D] The "No Knowledge" Proviso

Section 32(a) of the 1934 Act contains a "no knowledge proviso" under which a defendant may not be sentenced to prison if "he proves that he had no knowledge of [the applicable] rule or regulation."[53] The burden of proof is on the defendant to make this showing. If the defendant shows no knowledge of the provision, then the

---

[49] *See, e.g.*, United States v. Gross, 961 F.2d 1097, 1100 (3d Cir. 1992).

[50] *See generally* Heenan *et al.*, *supra* note 6, at 1061. For a discussion of a reliance-on-counsel defense in the context of stock parking, see § 5.07[A], *infra*.

[51] 926 F.2d 1285 (2d Cir. 1991).

[52] *Id.* at 1292.

[53] 15 U.S.C. § 78ff. This section applies to false or misleading statements made in filings made under the Act.

finding of liability stands but the defendant may not be sentenced to prison.[54]

One issue is whether "no knowledge" means that the defendant lacked knowledge of the particular laws or regulations that the defendant violated. In *United States v. Lilly*,[55] for example, the defendants pled guilty to a charge that they manipulated stock prices.[56] At sentencing, the defendants attempted to rely on the "no knowledge" proviso, arguing that they did not know that their activities were prohibited by the provision to which they pleaded. The court rejected the argument on the ground that the defendants knew they were violating the law, even if they "did not happen to know that [their activity] was in violation of a particular rule or regulation."

The court further ruled that, even if the no knowledge proviso did apply to the case, the defendants had not met their burden of proof. First, they admitted they knew securities fraud was illegal, and, second, they admitted they knew their conduct was fraudulent. Thus, they were aware of the rule proscribing their activity.[57]

§ 5.05 THE SARBANES-OXLEY ACT OF 2002

The Sarbanes-Oxley Act of 2002 created a new crime, entitled "Securities Fraud." This crime is not codified in the securities laws, but rather at § 1348 of Title 18, the federal criminal code. The statute provides:

Whoever knowingly executes, or attempts to execute, a scheme or artifice -

(1) to defraud any person in connection with any security of an issuer with a class of securities registered under section 12 of the Securities Exchange Act of 1934 (15 U.S.C. § 78l) or that is required to file reports under section 15(d) of the Securities Exchange Act of 1934 (15 U.S.C. § 78o(d)); or

(2) to obtain, by means of false or fraudulent pretenses, representations, or promises, any money or property in connection with the purchase or sale of any security of an issuer with a class of securities registered under section 12 of the Securities Exchange Act of 1934 (15 U.S.C. § 78l) or that is required to file reports under section 15(d) of the Securities Exchange Act of 1934 (15 U.S.C. § 78o(d));

shall be fined under this title, or imprisoned not more than 25 years, or both.

The mens rea required under the statute is knowledge, as compared with the

---

[54] 15 U.S.C. § 78ff(a).

[55] 291 F. Supp. 989 (S.D. Tex. 1968).

[56] Generally, "market manipulation" occurs when a purchase or sale is designed solely to affect the market price of the securities, and is not based upon a legitimate investment purpose.

[57] United States v. Lilley, 291 F. Supp. at 993–94.

willfulness requirement of the securities fraud statutes. The section seems to duplicate the general fraud coverage of the mail and wire fraud statutes, though without those statutes' jurisdictional requirements. To date, this section has been little-used.

§ 5.06 THE CIVIL/CRIMINAL OVERLAP

As noted above, the SEC has primary responsibility for enforcing the securities laws, but cannot itself institute criminal cases. The SEC's mandate, however, includes bringing to the attention of the United States Department of Justice matters for which criminal charges may be appropriate.[58] The SEC has broad discretion to make such referrals.

Further, civil SEC actions and federal criminal actions may proceed simultaneously, placing the defendant in a difficult position. For example, if a defendant in a civil action declines to testify, the trier of fact may draw an inference against the defendant. If the defendant does testify in the civil action, however, then the defendant has waived the Fifth Amendment right to remain silent, and that testimony may be used in the criminal trial. This aspect of securities law enforcement has produced much criticism.[59]

§ 5.07 INSIDER TRADING

[A] Introduction

Insider trading is perhaps the quintessential white collar crime. In the popular image, the crime entails persons of wealth and power abusing their positions at the expense of ordinary stockholders and investors.[60] In scandals involving such notables as Ivan Boesky, Michael Milken, and Martha Stewart,[61] insider trading captured the popular imagination like no other white collar crime.

Insider trading involves the purchase or sale of securities based on material, nonpublic information. In most cases, the accused bought securities prior to a planned "extraordinary corporate transaction" such as a merger, tender offer, or proxy contest, and sold those securities after the transaction was made public and

---

[58] 15 U.S.C. § 78u(d).

[59] *See* Friedman, Marmur & Stillman, *supra* note 3, § 12.05 at 12-40-41.

[60] David Weisburd *et al.*, Crimes of the Middle Classes: White-Collar Offenders in the Federal Courts 28 (1991). For an overview of the law relating to insider trading, see Steinberg, *supra* note 10, at 267–86.

[61] For two highly contrasting views of the Wall Street investigations of the 1980s, and particularly the investigation focusing on Michael Milken, see Jesse Kornbluth, Highly Confident (1992); and James B. Stewart, Den of Thieves (1991). Although originally under investigation for insider trading, Martha Stewart ultimately was not criminally charged on that theory. She was, however, accused of insider trading in a civil suit brought by the SEC. For an analysis of the Stewart investigation and prosecution, see Ellen S. Podgor, *Jose Padilla and Martha Stewart: Who Should Be Charged with Criminal Conduct?*, 109 Penn. St. L. Rev. 1059, 1068–69 (2005) (noting that Stewart was originally under investigation for insider trading but was not criminally charged with that crime).

the stock price had risen.[62] In others, the defendant bought or sold based upon yet-to-be-released information, such as financial projections, the public dissemination of which affected the price.

Congress responded to the perceived insider trading abuses, and in 1984 enacted the Insider Trading Sanctions Act. The Act allows the SEC to seek fines in federal court cases of up to "three times the profit gained or loss avoided."[63] In 1988, Congress passed the Insider Trading and Securities Fraud Enforcement Act, which increased the maximum sentence from five to ten years, and the maximum fines for individuals from $100,000 to $1 million and for corporations from $500,000 to $2.5 million. The Act also created "controlling person" liability for persons who control others who engage in insider trading.[64] Finally, under the Sarbanes-Oxley Act of 2002, Congress again raised the maximum penalties for certain securities violations. Maximum prison time was increased to twenty years; maximum fines were increased to $5 million for individuals and $25 million for corporations. As always, the actual sentences imposed will depend upon the trial court's application of the Federal Sentencing Guidelines to the facts of the case.[65]

[B]   Policy Bases

The perceived harm from insider trading is to the investing public, which assumes that it is operating on a playing field that is level for all potential investors. In an early seminal case, *In re Cady, Roberts & Co.*,[66] the SEC asserted the policy view that now underlies insider trading law. In that case, the Commission ruled that an "insider" — one who obtains material, nonpublic information because of a special position with or relationship to the issuing company — violates Section 10b and Rule 10b-5 if the insider trades on the information without first disclosing it. The SEC reasoned that it was inherently unfair to let such a person take advantage of information intended to benefit only the company and its shareholders. A person who possesses material, nonpublic information must therefore either disclose that information, or refrain from trading.[67]

---

[62] A tender offer is an offer to buy all of a company's stock at a certain price, which generally includes a substantial premium over the then-prevailing market price. A proxy contest involves a shareholder vote, via "proxies," for such corporate decisions as the election of a board of directors.

[63] Pub. L. No. 98-376, § 2, 98 Stat. 1264, 1264 (1984).

[64] Pub. L. No. 100-704, §§ 3-4, 102 Stat. 4677, 4677-4678 (1988). The Act's legislative history quotes the following statement that Wall Street entrepreneur Ivan Boesky made to a group of business students in 1985: "Greed is all right, by the way. I want you to know that. I think greed is healthy. You can be greedy and still feel good about yourself." *See* Stewart, *supra* note 69, at 223. Under investigation for insider trading, Mr. Boesky later pled guilty to a felony, was sentenced to three years in prison, and was banned from the securities industry for life. *See* FMC Corp. v. Boesky, 852 F.2d 981, 982 n.1 (7th Cir. 1988).

[65] *See* Chapter 21, Sentencing, *infra.*

[66] 40 S.E.C. 907 (1961). Another basis for the *Cady, Roberts* holding, that the insider breached a duty to the market at large, was rejected by the Supreme Court in Chiarella v. United States, 445 U.S. 222, 229-30 (1980).

[67] *In re Cady, Roberts & Co.*, 40 S.E.C. at 911-12.

The Supreme Court recently articulated the perceived dangers from insider trading. In a decision broadly construing the government's ability to prosecute insider trading, the Court stated that "an animating purpose of the Exchange Act [is] to insure honest securities markets and thereby promote investor confidence."[68]

Some commentators argue, however, that insider trading actually benefits the market. Under this view, trading based upon nonpublic information causes stock prices to change based upon information not otherwise revealed to the public, thus rendering the markets more efficient.[69] Nonetheless, the SEC's view has prevailed, and insider trading is now a broadly-criminalized act.

[C] Insider Trading Defined

[1] Insider Trading Theories

Insider trading is just one type of securities fraud, but it is the theory used in many high-profile cases. Most insider trading prosecutions are brought under the general antifraud provisions of the 1934 Act, Section 10b and Rule 10b-5.[70] Those provisions, and the regulations promulgated under them, do not provide a comprehensive definition of "insider trading." That task has therefore largely been left to the courts.

Two different, and sometimes overlapping, theories of insider trading have developed:

1. *The "traditional" or "classical" theory.* This theory applies to persons who take secret information from a company and then trade in that company's stock in violation of a *direct duty to that company and its shareholders.* There are two types of defendants under this theory:

    (a) *"Insider" defendants.* Such defendants include corporate officers, directors, and others who owe a direct fiduciary duty both to the company and to the company's shareholders; and

    (b) *"Temporary" or "quasi"-insider defendants.* Such defendants include lawyers, accountants, and others who work for a company on a temporary basis and thereby acquire a temporary duty to the company and its shareholders.[71]

---

[68] United States v. O'Hagan, 521 U.S. 642, 658 (1997).

[69] *See* Richard W. Painter *et al.,* Don't Ask, Just Tell: Insider Trading After *United States v. O'Hagan,* 84 Va. L. Rev. 153, 168 n.57 (1998). *Cf.* Dirks v. SEC, 463 U.S. 646, 658 (1983) (noting the role of market analysts in bringing information to the market and helping the market function more effectively).

[70] *See infra* § 5.05[e]. Insider trading in connection with tender offers may also be charged under Rule 14e-3. 17 C.F.R. § 14-3(3). Such a charge does not require a showing of a breach of fiduciary duty. *See infra* § 5.07[F].

[71] *See* Dirks v. SEC, 463 U.S. 646, 655 n.14 (1983) ("[U]nder certain circumstances, such as where corporate information is revealed legitimately to an underwriter, accountant, lawyer, or consultant working for the corporation, these outsiders may become fiduciaries of the shareholders . . . . For such a duty to be imposed, however, the corporation must expect the outsider to keep the disclosed non-public

2. *The "misappropriation" theory.* This theory applies to trading by one who takes information in violation of a fiduciary duty, as an employee owes to an employer.

As noted above, these two theories overlap. Thus, any person liable under the traditional theory is also liable under the misappropriation theory. The reverse is not true, however; many misappropriators are not liable under the traditional theory because they owe no duty to the company the stock of which was traded.

In assessing which theory applies in a particular situation, it is essential to determine (a) the entity or person to whom the defendant owed a duty, (b) the company the stock of which was traded; and (c) the harm that flowed from the trading. It is very useful, when considering any insider trading case, to diagram the relationships among all the corporate and individual participants.

[2] Elements of Insider Trading

Based upon the above theories, we can glean the following about a principal actor's insider trading liability ("tippee" liability and aiding and abetting liability are discussed below). In an insider trading case against a principal actor, the government must prove that:

1. The defendant bought or sold securities;

2. The defendant -

   (a) was an insider of the company the securities of which were traded;

   (b) was a temporary insider of the company the securities of which were traded; and/or

   (c) was a misappropriator of information from a person or entity to whom the defendant owed a fiduciary duty;[72]

3. The defendant knowingly possessed material, nonpublic information; and

4. The defendant acted willfully.

[D] The Evolution of the Misappropriation Theory

Trading based upon material, nonpublic information under the "traditional" theory is squarely covered by *Cady, Roberts* and its progeny. The rules governing such trading are fairly well-established and non-controversial. Charging insider trading based upon the "misappropriation" theory, however, goes beyond the traditional theory. The misappropriation theory also renders the term "insider trading" a misnomer because it encompasses much more than trading by those with a duty to the issuing company and its shareholders.

---

information confidential, and the relationship at least must imply such a duty.").

[72] This duty requirement does not apply to insider trading prosecutions under the tender offer rules. *See* § 5.07[F], *infra.*

[1]   The Supreme Court Cases

In 1980, the United States Supreme Court for the first time addressed criminal securities fraud liability for insider trading. The decision in *Chiarella v. United States*[73] established the basic requirement that, under the Section 10b and Rule 10b-5 antifraud provisions, insider trading liability must be premised upon a breach of duty.

In *Chiarella*, the defendant was a commercial printing company employee. The printing company prepared materials for clients to use when making tender offer bids for "target" companies. The defendant bought stock in the target companies before the bids were made public, and sold afterwards,[74] making a profit of more than $30,000 over fourteen months.[75]

At trial, the defendant was convicted of securities fraud based on the theory that he traded based upon material, nonpublic information and was therefore under a duty either to disclose that information or refrain from trading on it.[76] The Second Circuit affirmed on two grounds. First, the defendant was liable as a "market insider." Under this theory, in order to prevent an unfair advantage, *anyone* who possesses material, nonpublic information is under a duty to disclose or refrain from trading. Second, the defendant was liable because he had "misappropriated" the information from the printing company in breach of his fiduciary duties to his employer.

The United States Supreme Court reversed. First, the Court rejected the "market insider" theory of liability. Applying common law fraud principles, the Court concluded that: "When an allegation of fraud is based upon nondisclosure, there can be no fraud absent a duty to speak."[77] The Court further found:

> No duty could arise from [defendant's] relationship with the sellers of the target company's securities, for petitioner had no prior dealings with them. He was not their agent, he was not a fiduciary, he was not a person in whom the sellers had placed their trust and confidence. He was, in fact, a complete stranger who dealt with the sellers only through impersonal market transactions.[78]

Second, the majority declined to apply the misappropriation theory because it had not been presented to the jury.[79] The majority thus voted to reverse Chiarella's conviction.

In his dissent, Chief Justice Burger argued that the conviction could stand on a broad version of the "misappropriation" theory.[80] Under this theory, the defendant

---

[73] 445 U.S. 222 (1980).

[74] *Id.* at 224.

[75] *Id.*

[76] *See In re* Cady, Roberts & Co., 40 S.E.C. 907, 911 (1961).

[77] *Chiarella*, 445 U.S. at 235.

[78] *Id.* at 232–33.

[79] *Id.* at 237 n.21.

[80] *Id.* at 240–41 (Burger, C.J., dissenting).

could be liable because he breached his fiduciary duties to the printing company by stealing the secret information from the company in violation of its policies.[81] Thus, the fraud was not on the sellers of the target companies' stocks, but upon the employer, as the "significant relationship for purposes of the misappropriation theory [exists] between the misappropriator and the person to whom he owes an obligation of confidentiality."[82]

The misappropriation theory was at issue in *Carpenter v. United States*.[83] In *Carpenter*, a Wall Street Journal reporter wrote a regular column that had the potential to affect the stock prices of companies discussed in the column. Prior to the column's publication, the reporter and his confederates schemed to buy stock in companies to be discussed in the columns. They sold after the columns were published, making profits on the sales. The Second Circuit affirmed the use of the misappropriation theory based upon the reporter's theft of information from and breach of fiduciary duty to his employer.[84] The Supreme Court split four-to-four on the issue, and thus did not decide whether the misappropriation theory was a viable basis for securities fraud liability.[85]

It is important to note that *Carpenter* is different from all the other insider trading cases discussed here. In *Carpenter*, unlike the other cases, the information did not come from someone connected to the company the stock of which was being bought or sold. Rather, as noted in the Second Circuit dissent, the information that the reporter used was publicly-available information that the reporter had gathered. Indeed, because it could not violate a duty to itself, the Wall Street Journal could have lawfully traded on the information.[86] Whether fraud on an employer, as opposed to fraud on a market participant, should give rise to federal securities law liability remains a source of controversy.[87]

The Second Circuit's acceptance of the misappropriation theory in *Carpenter* reflected one side of a circuit split on this issue.[88] In 1997, the Supreme Court resolved the issue in *United States v. O'Hagan*; on a six-to-three vote, the Court approved the misappropriation theory.[89] In that case, the defendant was a law firm

---

[81] *Id.* at 243–45 (Burger, C.J., dissenting). The Chief Justice argued that either the jury had been properly instructed on this issue, or that the failure to instruct was harmless error.

[82] *See, e.g.,* United States v. Willis, 737 F. Supp. 269 (S.D.N.Y. 1990); United States v. Willis, 778 F. Supp. 205, 208–09 (S.D.N.Y. 1991).

[83] 484 U.S. 19 (1987).

[84] *Id.* at 23–24.

[85] *Id.* at 24. The Court affirmed Carpenter's conviction under the mail fraud statute.

[86] *See* United States v. Carpenter, 791 F.2d 1024, 1037 (2d Cir. 1986) (Miner, J., dissenting in part).

[87] *See id.* at 1028–30.

[88] For decisions applying the misappropriation theory, see United States v. Newman, 664 F.2d 12 (2d Cir. 1981); SEC v. Cherif, 933 F.2d 403 (7th Cir. 1991). For cases rejecting the theory, see United States v. Bryan, 58 F.3d 933 (4th Cir. 1995); United States v. O'Hagan, 92 F.3d 612 (8th Cir. 1996), *rev'd*, 521 U.S. 642 (1997).

[89] 521 U.S. 642 (1997). The other two issues in the case involved whether the SEC exceeded its rule-making authority and, on alternate grounds, O'Hagan's attack on the mail fraud convictions. The Court ruled the SEC did not exceed its rule-making authority, did not address O'Hagan's other arguments, and remanded to the Eighth Circuit. *Id.* at 667–68, 678.

partner who bought stock in companies that his firm's client was attempting to acquire. According to the *O'Hagan* majority, the "deception" in this case was the misappropriator's theft and fraud upon the law firm, which possessed the secret information.

The majority found the misappropriation theory necessary to ensure investors that misappropriators were not taking unfair advantage of material, nonpublic information.[90] The Court did not, however, delineate the boundaries of the required fiduciary duty. Accordingly, the misappropriation basis of liability remains a vague and controversial basis for insider trading liability.[91]

[2]   The Boundaries of Fiduciary Duties

[a]   Pre-*O'Haganagan* Case Law

Courts have applied the misappropriation theory in a variety of contexts. In *United States v. Newman*,[92] for example, two employees of an investment firm stole information concerning clients' plans for launching takeover bids for other companies. The employees passed the information to confederates, who bought the target companies' stocks. The Second Circuit reversed the trial court's dismissal of the case, holding that the government had adequately alleged a basis for insider trading liability — that the employees breached a duty to their employer and its clients, and that their confederates aided and abetted the employees in securities fraud.

Because they depend upon the common law of fiduciary duties, the boundaries of the misappropriation theory are vague. It is not clear what types of duties will suffice to support an insider trading conviction. For example, in *SEC v. Willis*,[93] the court found that a psychiatrist and his broker who traded on secret information that a patient revealed to the psychiatrist had committed securities fraud based upon the psychiatrist's breach of duty to his patient. And in *SEC v. Materia*,[94] the Second Circuit affirmed a finding of liability based upon the misappropriation theory on facts very similar to those in *Chiarella*.

In one widely-cited case decided before *O'Hagan*, however, the Second Circuit reversed a conviction on the grounds that the government had not proven the

---

[90] *Id.* at 653.

[91] *Compare* David M. Brodsky & Daniel J. Kramer, *A Critique of the Misappropriation Theory of Insider Trading*, 20 Cardozo L. Rev. 41, 80 (1998) ("By injecting unclear notions of unfairness into the federal securities laws, the misappropriation theory fails to provide a clear or rational standard."), *and* Steve Thel, *Statutory Findings and Insider Trading Regulation*, 50 Vand. L. Rev. 1091, 1120–21 (1997) (noting that the boundaries of the theory are unclear), *with* Christopher J. Bebel, *A Detailed Analysis of United States v. O'Hagan: Onward Through the Evolution of the Federal Securities Laws*, 59 La. L. Rev. 1, 61 (1998) ("[p]rinciples articulated in the opinion . . . will fuel efforts to attack misconduct arising in the financial sector"), *and* Elliot J. Weiss, *United States v. O'Hagan: Pragmatism Returns to the Law of Insider Trading*, 23 J. Corp. L. 395, 423–24 (1998) (the theory is necessary and appropriate).

[92] 664 F.2d 12 (2d Cir. 1981).

[93] 825 F. Supp. 617 (S.D.N.Y. 1993).

[94] 745 F.2d 197 (2d Cir. 1984).

necessary breach of duty. In *United States v. Chestman*,[95] a corporate insider gave material, nonpublic information concerning the sale of the company to his sister so that she could make the necessary financial arrangements.[96] The sister gave the information to her daughter, who in turn gave it to her husband. At each step, the recipient was told that the information was confidential. The husband gave the information to his broker, who traded on it.

The court reversed the broker's Section 10b conviction, which was based upon the husband's liability.[97] The husband was not a quasi-insider because he had no duty to the company; nor was he liable as a misappropriator, for the same reason; the husband's relationships with his wife and his wife's family were insufficient to create a fiduciary duty.[98] Thus, the broker could not be guilty for aiding and abetting the husband, nor for participating in the breach.[99]

In some cases, as where a person has violated a fiduciary duty to an employer, liability under the misappropriation theory will be clear. In others, however, the outcome is less certain. The courts have not clearly articulated, for example, whether and when relationships such as those among family members and professionals and their clients will be sufficient.[100]

[b] The SEC's Attempt to Extend the Boundaries of Fiduciary Duties — Rule 10b5-2

In 2000, the SEC adopted Rule 10b5-2, entitled "Duties of trust or confidence in misappropriation insider trading cases."[101] This rule attempts to clarify the scope of insider trading liability based on a misappropriation theory in certain non-business relationships. The rule provides that a duty of trust and confidence exists in three circumstances:

1. When the party receiving the material nonpublic information agrees to keep it confidential.

2. When the parties involved in the communication of material nonpublic information have a history or pattern of sharing confidences, and both parties have a reasonable expectation of confidentiality.

---

[95] 947 F.2d 551 (2d Cir. 1991) (en banc), *cert. denied*, 503 U.S. 1004 (1992).

[96] Because he gave the information for a proper business purpose, the insider did not breach his duty to the company and its shareholders.

[97] *See* § 5.07[E], *infra*, for a discussion of tipper/tippee liability.

[98] In reaching this conclusion, the *Chestman* court distinguished the holding in United States v. Reed, 773 F.2d 477 (2d Cir. 1985), which found a father/son relationship sufficient to sustain a conviction. *See Chestman*, 947 F.2d at 568. The *Chestman* court stated, somewhat unpersuasively, that *Reed* was different because the father and son regularly discussed business matters. *See id.* at 569.

[99] The court did sustain Chestman's conviction under § 14e and Rule 14(e)(3) because that conviction did not require the government to show a breach of duty. *Id.* at 563. *See* § 5.05[F], *infra.*

[100] *See* SEC v. Willis, 825 F. Supp. 617 (S.D.N.Y. 1993).

[101] 17 C.F.R. § 240.10b5-2.

3.   When a person receives material nonpublic information from certain family members, including spouses, parents, children, and siblings.[102] The latter provision is an explicit attempt to undercut the *Chestman* decision. The rule provides an affirmative defense based on the facts and circumstances of the family relationship that demonstrate no reasonable expectation of confidentiality. To date, courts have relied upon Rule 10b5-2 in just a handful of cases.[103]

Is a breach of a fiduciary duty always required in a case brought under § 10b and Rule 10b-5? In *SEC v. Dorozhko*,[104] the Second Circuit held not. In that case, the Commission alleged that the defendant — a corporate outsider — hacked into a company's computer, retrieved material, nonpublic information, and traded on the information, profiting nearly $300,000 on the trading. The district court denied the SEC's request for a preliminary injunction freezing the proceeds of the trading. The court held that the SEC had failed to allege a breach of fiduciary duty, as required by *Chiarella*. On appeal, the SEC conceded that the case fell within neither the traditional nor the misappropriation theories of insider trading. The Second Circuit nonetheless reversed, holding that the fiduciary duty requirement applies only where the fraud theory is nondisclosure rather than an affirmative misrepresentation or deception. Because the SEC had alleged that the defendant had used an affirmative deception to obtain the information upon which he traded, a breach of duty was not required.[105]

[3]   The "On the Basis of" Requirement

[a]   The Circuit Split

Recall that one of the elements of insider trading is that the defendant act "*on the basis of*" material nonpublic information. The circuit courts split as to the meaning of this requirement. Some courts held that the government must prove that the defendant actually used the information when trading. Other courts held that it was sufficient that the defendant knowingly possessed the information.

Courts that adopted the knowing possession standard did so principally in order

---

[102] *See* United States v. Kim, 184 F. Supp. 2d 1006, 1014 (N.D. Cal. 2002), *citing* Selective Disclosure and Insider Trading, SEC Release Nos. 33-7787, 34-42259, and IC-24,209, 17 CFR Parts 230, 240, 243, and 249, 1999 SEC LEXIS 2696(Dec. 20, 1999).

[103] *See, e.g.*, SEC v. Kornman, 391 F. Supp. 2d 477, 489–90 (N.D. Tex. 2005) (allegations sufficient to support claim that financial advisor owed duty to companies who were considering retaining the advisor, based upon an agreement to keep information confidential).

[104] 574 F.3d 42 (2d Cir. 2009). The Fifth Circuit apparently disagrees. *See id.* at 48, *citing* Regents of the Univ. of Cal. v. Credit Suisse First Boston, 482 F.3d 372, 389 (5th Cir. 2007).

[105] *Id.* at 49. The court remanded for a determination of whether the defendant's acts amounted to deception, noting a potential distinction between affirmatively misrepresenting one's identity and "exploiting a weakness in an electronic code to gain unauthorized access." *Id.* at 51. The SEC has brought other "hacking and trading" cases. For an analysis of the issues arising in these cases, see Donna M. Nagy, *Insider Trading and the Gradual Demise of Fiduciary Principles*, 94 Iowa L. Rev. 1315, 1340–45 (2009).

to ease the government's burden of proof. In *United States v. Teicher*,[106] for example, the defendants were engaged in the business of "arbitrage." Arbitrage involves trading in the stocks of companies potentially involved in "extraordinary corporate transactions" such as mergers and tender offers. The government alleged that the defendants and their co-conspirators gave each other secret information relating to such transactions, and traded on that information.

On appeal from their insider trading convictions, two defendants argued that the trial judge should have instructed the jury that it had to find that the defendants "used" the secret information in their trading. The Second Circuit rejected the argument, finding proof that defendants *knowingly* possessed the information when they traded was sufficient.[107] The court noted that it would be hard for any trader to ignore such information, and that to require affirmative proof that the defendant "used" the information would place too great a burden on the government.

Other circuits ruled to the contrary. These courts required that the government prove that the defendant actually used the illegally-obtained information when trading. Most such rulings reasoned that the "knowing possession" standard placed too low a burden on the government and therefore was unfair to defendants.[108]

[b]   SEC Adoption of the "Knowing Possession" Standard — Rule 10b5-1

In 2000, the SEC enacted Rule 10b5-1,[109] which adopts the "knowing possession" standard. The rule states that, for insider trading purposes, a person trades "on the basis" of inside information if the person was "aware" of the information when making the purchase or sale. The rule also sets forth an affirmative defense where, in specified circumstances, the person making the purchase or sale demonstrates that before becoming aware of the information, the person had (a) entered into a binding contract to purchase or sell the security, (b) instructed another person to purchase or sell the security for the instructing person's account, or (c) adopted a written plan for trading securities. This section has been seldom-litigated.

---

[106] 987 F.2d 112 (2d Cir. 1993).

[107] *Id.* at 119–20.

[108] *E.g.*, United States v. Smith, 155 F.3d 1051, 1067 (9th Cir. 1998); SEC v. Adler, 137 F.3d 1325, 1334–36 (11th Cir. 1998). *See* John H. Sturc & Catharine W. Cummer, *Possession vs. Use for Insider Trading Liability*, 12 No. 6 Insights 3 (1998).

[109] 17 C.F.R. § 240.10b5-1.

[E]   Tippee Liability

[1]   The *Dirks* Decision

An insider trading defendant who is not an insider, a quasi-insider, or a misappropriator can be liable as a "tippee." Such a person is one who receives material, nonpublic information from a "tipper," who *is* typically an insider, quasi-insider, or misappropriator.

In *Dirks v. SEC*,[110] the Supreme Court addressed the circumstances in which a "tippee" can be liable for securities fraud. The *Dirks* decision affirms that a tippee can be liable based upon a "derivative" breach of duty — that is, a breach that derives from the tipper's breach. Thus, *Dirks* expands the law of insider trading to those who are neither insiders/temporary insiders nor misappropriators, and who have not themselves breached any duty.

The *Dirks* defendant was an investment analyst who received information from Secrist, a former employee of Equity Funding. Secrist told Dirks that Equity Funding has committed fraud by overstating its assets.[111] The employee hoped to gain Dirks's assistance in exposing the fraud.[112] After learning the information, Dirks recommended that his clients sell their stock in the company, while also facilitating the fraud's exposure.[113] Dirks did not himself trade in the company's securities.[114]

The SEC brought a civil enforcement proceeding against Dirks, on the theory that he aided and abetted his clients' trading in Equity Funding stock. The Commission found him liable on the ground that one who knowingly receives material, nonpublic information has a duty to disclose the information or refrain from trading. According to the SEC, because Dirks had not publicly disclosed the information before giving it to his clients, he had violated Section 10b.[115]

The United States Supreme Court reversed the holding that Dirks was liable. Examining Dirks' status as a "tippee" of secret information given him by a corporate insider,[116] the Court affirmed the *Chiarella* principle that equal information is not required among all traders. The Court then held that a tippee of secret information can be liable only in specified circumstances. In particular, the *tippee* cannot be liable unless the *tipper* breached a duty: "[A] tippee assumes a fiduciary duty to the shareholders of a corporation not to trade on material nonpublic

---

[110] 463 U.S. 646 (1983). Although a civil enforcement action rather than a criminal case, *Dirks* governs the law in criminal 10b-5 actions as well as in civil cases.

[111] *Id.* at 648–49.

[112] *Id.* at 649.

[113] *Id.*

[114] *Id.*

[115] *Id.* at 651 ("Where 'tippees' — regardless of their motivation or occupation — come into possession of material 'corporate information that they know is confidential and know or should know came from a corporate insider,' they must either publicly disclose that information or refrain from trading.").

[116] *Id.* at 655–56.

information *only* when [1] the insider has breached his fiduciary duty to the shareholders by disclosing the information to the tippee and [2] the tippee knows or should know that there has been a breach."[117]

The Court further held that a tipper breaches a duty only in the specific circumstance where the tipper stood to benefit personally from passing the information.[118] This benefit can be in the form of (1) the tipper's direct or indirect profits from the trading, (2) a reputational or business benefit to the tipper, or (3) the tipper's giving of a gift, which could benefit the tipper in the future as the recipient of a return gift. The tipper in *Dirks* was a whistle-blower who did not stand to gain financially or in any other way. Thus, because Secrist had breached no duty to Equity Funding, Dirks could not be liable as a tippee.[119]

[2] The Elements of Tippee Liability

Based upon the current case law and upon Rule 10b5-1, for a tippee to be liable as a principal:

1. The tipper must have been an insider, quasi-insider, or misappropriator;

2. The tipper must have been acting for personal gain (as defined in *Dirks*);

3. The tippee must have obtained material, nonpublic information from the tipper;

4. The tippee must have bought or sold securities;

5. The tippee must have *knowingly possessed* the information when making the purchase or sale; and

6. The tippee must have acted willfully (as defined below).

Of course, as in *Dirks*, a tippee can also be charged with aiding and abetting trading by others ("remote tippees"), who have further been tipped by the original tippee.

[a] Proof of Willfulness

There is a fair amount of confusion over the level of willfulness the tippee must possess as to the tipper's breach of duty. Much of this confusion has resulted from the *Dirks* opinion. In that case, the Court said that if a tippee knows or "should know" of the breach of fiduciary duty, then the tippee can be held liable.[120] This,

---

[117] *Id.* at 660 (italics and numbering added).

[118] *Id.* at 662–63 ("It is important in this type of case to focus on policing insiders and what they do . . . rather than on policing information per se and its possession.").

[119] The "should know" language, *see* text at n.107, *infra*, has produced confusion. See *infra*, notes 150–151 and accompanying text. In Ernst & Ernst v. Hochfelder, 425 U.S. 185 (1976), the Supreme Court held that negligence does not suffice in the civil context. *See generally* Friedman, Marmur & Stillman, *supra* note 3, § 12.02.

[120] 463 U.S. at 660. The Second Circuit has stated that the government must prove that the tippee had "knowledge" that the tipper has breached a duty. United States v. Falcone, 257 F.3d 226, 232 (2d Cir. 2001).

however, sounds like a negligence standard, which is not the standard that most lower courts use given that the statute itself requires a showing of "willfulness."[121]

Most courts appear to apply a knowledge requirement, while others apply a recklessness requirement. Assume insider A gives the information to tippee B. Under these approaches, B is liable if the government shows that B knew (or recklessly disregarded) facts indicating that A breached a duty.

Further, assume B then gives the information to tippee C, a "remote" tippee. Assuming the other elements of tippee liability are met, C can be held liable under this reading if C knew or recklessly disregarded facts showing that the information came as a result of some breach of duty.

[b] Eavesdropper Liability

Another question is whether the tippee can be held liable where the tipper has not given the tippee the information expressly for the purpose of facilitating trading based on inside information. For example, if a tippee overhears a conversation that the "tipper" thought was private, and then trades on the information, has the "tippee" committed insider trading? Commentators have noted that *Dirks* can be fairly read both to impose, and not to impose, liability in such circumstances.[122] The SEC has taken the position that a tippee can be liable even where the tipper did not intend to benefit the tippee. At least two decisions have applied this approach.[123]

[c] Intent to Benefit — Misappropriation Theory

Dirks was charged under the traditional theory of insider trading. Because Secrist was an insider of Equity Funding, his original breach fell within the traditional theory. Recall that one element of tippee liability under *Dirks* is that the tipper gave the information to benefit the tippee. One unsettled question is whether this element of tippee liability applies when the tipper is a misappropriator rather than an insider.

Though the courts are split, most courts have held that the government must prove, under either the traditional or misappropriation theory, that the tipper

---

[121] One commentator has suggested that the *Dirks* "should have known" language only goes to whether the tippee is to be put in the position of a fiduciary. In other words, would a reasonable person in the tippee's position have known that the tipper breached a fiduciary duty in revealing the information? Then the willfulness requirement — requiring that the defendant have known (or recklessly disregarded) facts showing the information was material and nonpublic — is to be applied to the trading. Thus, a tippee could be liable if the tippee was at least negligent as to the tipper's breach of duty, and knew or recklessly disregarded facts that the information was material and nonpublic. *See generally* Donald Langevoort, The Law of Insider Trading (1992).

[122] *See* SEC v. Falbo, 14 F. Supp. 2d 508, 526 (S.D.N.Y. 1998) (finding that if the trader/tippee believed that the information was obtained by eavesdropping, she might not have the level of scienter required for a 10b-5 violation).

[123] *See* SEC v. Switzer, 590 F. Supp. 756 (W.D. Okla. 1984) (eavesdropping tippees can be liable, but defendant not liable here because "tipper" did not breach his *Dirks* duty in the discussion which the defendant overheard); SEC v. Musella, Fed. Sec. L. Rep. § 91, 647 (S.D.N.Y. 1984).

intended to benefit by giving the information to the tippee.[124] For example, in *SEC v. Yun*,[125] defendant Yun was married to a corporate insider. Yun tipped Burch, a business colleague, with confidential information that Yun learned from her husband. The SEC charged Yun and Burch with insider trading, under the theory that Yun had misappropriated the information from her husband. The defendants were found liable.

On appeal, the defendants argued that there was insufficient evidence that Yun breached a duty to her husband or gave the information to benefit herself. The court rejected the first argument, finding evidence of a duty based upon the family relationship.[126] As to the second argument, the SEC argued that an intent to benefit is not even required in a misappropriation case because *Dirks* focused on the insider's duty to corporate shareholders. The court rejected the SEC's argument, reasoning that the rules for tippee liability should be the same under either theory.[127]

[F] Trading in Connection with a Tender Offer

As seen in cases such as *O'Hagan* and *Chestman*, the government can charge insider trading under laws other than Section 10b and Rule 10b-5. Most significantly, Section 14 of the Exchange Act and Rule 14e-3(a) prohibit trading while in possession of material nonpublic information relating to a tender offer. Recall that, in a tender offer, the offering company offers to buy all of a "target" company's stock at a specified price over the then-current market price for the stock. Because stock prices may fluctuate dramatically in such circumstances and the temptations for fraud are great, Congress and the SEC have specific provisions relating to such trading. Rule 14e-3(a) thus provides:

> If any person has taken a substantial step or steps to commence, or has commenced, a tender offer (the "offering person"), it shall constitute a fraudulent, deceptive or manipulative act or practice within the meaning of section 14e of the [Exchange] Act for any other person who is in possession of material information relating to such tender offer which information he knows or has reason to know is nonpublic and which he knows or has reason to know has been acquired directly or indirectly from:
>
> (1) The offering person,
>
> (2) The issuer of the securities sought or to be sought by such tender offer, or

---

[124] *See* SEC v. Yun, 327 F.3d 1263, 1274–75 (11th Cir. 2003), and cases cited therein.

[125] *Id.*

[126] The trades in this case took place before Rule 10b5-2 was enacted. Nonetheless, the appeals court indicated its disapproval of *Chestman*, 947 F.2d at 579. The court indicated that even before Rule 10b5-2 a duty could be created by a family relationship, at least in the civil context. *Yun*, 327 F.3d at 1272.

[127] *Id.* at 1276–79. The court went on to find sufficient evidence because Yun "expected to benefit from her tip to Burch by maintaining a good relationship between a friend and frequent partner in real estate deals." *Id.* at 1280. Nonetheless, the court reversed the finding of liability because the court failed to instruct the jury that it had to find an intent to benefit.

(3)   Any officer, director, partner or employee or any other person acting on behalf of the offering person or such issuer,

to purchase or sell or cause to be purchased or sold any of such securities . . . , unless within a reasonable time prior to any purchase or sale such information and its source are publicly disclosed by press release or otherwise.[128]

The Supreme Court interpreted this provision in *O'Hagan*.[129] As noted above,[130] in addition to his convictions under Section 10b and Rule 10b-5, O'Hagan was convicted under Section 14e and Rule 14e-3. And as seen in the text of the rule above, these provisions do not require that the information have been acquired in breach of a fiduciary duty.[131]

On appeal, O'Hagan argued that the SEC exceeded its authority when it adopted Rule 14e-3(a). Specifically, O'Hagan asserted that, because that Rule imposes liability when the defendant has not obtained the information in breach of a fiduciary duty, the Rule violates the *Chiarella* holding. The Court rejected O'Hagan's argument. The Court emphasized that O'Hagan had a fiduciary duty to his firm and its client. The Court concluded that the SEC, "to the extent relevant to this case, did not exceed its authority."[132] Thus, the Court affirmed the validity of Rule 14e-3, but only as applied to the facts of the case.[133] The scope of potential liability under these provisions therefore remains uncertain.[134]

It can be argued that, by the language quoted above, the Court implied that Rule 14e-3(a) might be invalid where there has been no breach of duty. Indeed, the Court stated that "[w]e leave for another day, when the issue requires decision, the legitimacy of Rule 14e-3(a) as applied to 'warehousing,' which the government describes as 'the practice by which bidders leak advance information of a tender offer to allies and encourage them to purchase the target company's stock before the bid is announced.' "[135]

Further, the courts are uncertain about the mens rea required for a violation of Section 14 and Rule 14e-3(a). In one case, for example, the defendant traded on material, nonpublic information relating to a tender offer. The defendant, however, did not breach a duty in obtaining the information and did not know that the information involved a tender offer.[136] The trial judge granted a judgment of acquittal, holding that proof of willfulness under these provisions requires proof

---

[128]   17 C.F.R. 240.14e-3(a).

[129]   United States v. O'Hagan, 521 U.S. 642 (1997).

[130]   *See* § 5.05[D][1], *supra.*

[131]   15 U.S.C. § 78n(e); 17 C.F.R. § 240.14e-(3)(a).

[132]   *O'Hagan*, 521 U.S. at 642.

[133]   *See* James W. Morrissey, United States v. O'Hagan: *A Results-Oriented Approach to Insider Trading Cases*, 48 DePaul L. Rev. 161, 191–92 (1998) ("This ruling leaves the extent of liability under Rule 14e-3 undecided").

[134]   *See* Thel, *supra* note 91, at 1118.

[135]   *Id.*

[136]   United States v. Cassese, 290 F. Supp. 2d 443 (S.D.N.Y. 2003), *aff'd*, 428 F.3d 92 (2d Cir. 2005).

that the defendant knew or had reason to know that the information related to a tender offer.[137] The Second Circuit affirmed on other grounds, but the dissenting judge argued that the trial court had imposed too high a willfulness burden on the government.[138] The Supreme Court has yet to address the level of willfulness required for conviction under the tender offer rules.

§ 5.08   THE "IN CONNECTION WITH" REQUIREMENT

In any criminal or civil securities fraud case, the government or private plaintiff must show that the fraud was "in connection with" a purchase or sale of a security. Courts have read this element broadly. For example, in *United States v. O'Hagan*,[139] an attorney traded on information he stole from his law firm and his law firm's client. The information involved the client's potential bid to acquire another company (the "target"). On appeal from his insider trading conviction, the defendant argued that his trade was not in connection with the fraud. Because he traded in the stock target company, and not in the stock of the law firm's client, the trading was too attenuated from the fraud upon the firm and the client. The Court rejected the argument, explaining:

> [The in connection with] element is satisfied because the fiduciary's fraud is consummated, not when the fiduciary gains the confidential information, but when, without disclosure to his principal, he uses the information to purchase or sell securities. The securities transaction and the breach of duty thus coincide. This is so even though the person or entity defrauded is not the other party to the trade, but is, instead, the source of the nonpublic information.[140]

The dissent in *O'Hagan* disagreed, stating that "[w]here the relevant element of fraud has no impact on the integrity of the subsequent transactions . . . , one can reasonably question whether the fraud was used in connection with a securities transaction."[141]

The Court again interpreted this element broadly in *SEC v. Zandford*.[142] Before the SEC initiated that action, Zandford had been convicted of wire fraud for selling his client's securities and using the proceeds for his own benefit. The SEC then filed a civil complaint against Zandford under Section 10b and Rule 10b-5. On appeal from summary judgment for the SEC, the Fourth Circuit reversed and remanded with directions to dismiss the complaint. The court reasoned that the fraud was not

---

[137] 290 F. Supp. 2d at 450–51 ("Since there is no general duty to refrain from trading on material nonpublic information, the defendant must have believed that the information related to, or most likely related to, a tender offer in order to impose criminal liability. . . . To conclude otherwise would impose absolute liability for all who trade on material nonpublic information, and this is not the law.").

[138] 428 F.3d at 109 (Raggi, J., dissenting) ("[W]illfulness required that the government prove only Cassese's awareness of the general unlawfulness of his conduct. It was not required to prove further that Cassese knew that the nonpublic information on which he traded related to a tender offer").

[139] 521 U.S. 642 (1997), discussed § 5.07[D][1], *supra*.

[140] *Id.* at 656.

[141] *Id.* at 691 (Thomas, J., dissenting).

[142] 535 U.S. 813 (2002).

in connection with the purchase or sale of a security because the sale of securities was merely incidental to the fraud upon the client. The Supreme Court unanimously reversed and remanded. The Court held that Zandford's alleged misappropriation of the proceeds constituted fraud "in connection with the purchase or sale of any security." The Court stated that "[i]t is enough that the scheme to defraud and the sale of securities coincide."[143]

§ 5.09 MATERIALITY

As seen above, the securities laws prohibit trading on the basis of "material" nonpublic information in certain circumstances. In fact, materiality is a concept that is critical to the determination of liability throughout the securities laws.

The securities laws prohibit trading with an *unfair informational advantage.* For this requirement to be met, the information must be "material." That is, the information must be sufficiently important to the investing public to cause a price movement when the information becomes available.

The United States Supreme Court has decided two cases that provide the basis for the definition of materiality. First, in *TSC Industries, Inc. v. Northway, Inc.*,[144] the Court announced the basic definition of materiality. In that case, TSC and another company, National, agreed upon a friendly merger to be effectuated through a proxy contest.[145] Plaintiff was a TSC shareholder who sued TSC and National for allegedly making false statements in proxy materials in violation of Section 14(a) of the 1934 Act. The plaintiff claimed that the defendants had failed to disclose that National had already obtained substantial control over TSC, and had misstated the favorability of the merger's terms.

Plaintiff moved for summary judgment. The trial court denied the motion, but the Seventh Circuit reversed. The appeals court held that certain omissions of fact were material as a matter of law. The court stated that a misstatement or omission is material if a reasonable investor *might* consider the omitted fact important in deciding how to vote in a proxy contest.

The Supreme Court reversed, holding that the Seventh Circuit's materiality standard set too low a threshold. In reaching this conclusion, the Court expressed its concern that the appellate court's standard would result in shareholders being deluged by an "avalanche" of trivial information. A great deal had been disclosed concerning the TSC-National merger. Therefore, the appropriate question was whether the disclosure of the *additional* information would have been material to an investor. The Court then articulated the general standard for materiality — the trier of fact must find that there is "a *substantial likelihood* that the disclosure of the omitted fact *would* have been viewed by the reasonable investor as having *significantly* altered the 'total mix' of information made available."[146] Under this

---

[143] *Id.* at 822.

[144] 426 U.S. 438 (1976).

[145] A "proxy contest" is a mechanism by which shareholders give their "proxies" to vote on corporate decisions such as election of a board of directors. *See* § 5.08[B], *supra.*

[146] *TSC Industries*, 426 U.S. at 449 (emphasis added).

test, summary judgment for the plaintiffs was not appropriate.[147]

The next important case, *Basic Inc. v. Levinson*,[148] dealt with the materiality issue in the context of pre-merger negotiations. In *Basic*, on three occasions the parties made public statements that they were not involved in merger talks, when in fact negotiations were ongoing. The district court granted summary judgment to the defendants. The court found the statements immaterial as a matter of law because the statements were not made at a time when the parties were "destined, with reasonable certainty, to [enter into] a merger agreement in principle."[149] The Sixth Circuit reversed, and rejected the "agreement-in-principle" test. The court articulated a far broader test, one that would hold *any* false denial of ongoing negotiations to be material.[150]

The Supreme Court rejected both the district court's and the appellate court's approaches to defining materiality in the context of merger negotiations. Instead, the Supreme Court applied the *TSC* standard to the merger context, and held that materiality is to be determined by assessing (1) the likelihood of the event and (2) the degree of the event's potential impact on the shareholders. As the Court stated:

> Even before this Court's decision in *TSC Industries*, the Second Circuit had explained the role of the materiality requirement of Rule 10b-5, with respect to contingent or speculative information or events, in a manner that gave that term meaning that is independent of the other provisions of the Rule. Under such circumstances, materiality "will depend at any given time upon a balancing of both the indicated probability that the event will occur and the anticipated magnitude of the event in light of the totality of the company activity."[151]

In its 2011 decision in *Matrixx Initiatives, Inc. v. Siracusano*,[152] the United States Supreme Court again rejected a bright-line materiality test. Matrixx investors sued a pharmaceutical company and three of its executives, alleging that the company had failed to disclose to investors certain reports — termed "adverse events" — that linked one of the company's products (a cold nasal remedy) with a medical risk (loss of smell). Because of the small number of the reports, the plaintiffs did not allege that the data was "statistically significant." The district court dismissed the case, holding that the plaintiffs had not sufficiently alleged facts

---

[147] For an application of the *TSC* test, see United States v. Margala, 662 F.2d 622 (9th Cir. 1981), where the defendants entered into a scheme to force investors in a company out of their stock and then to underpay them for their stock. The defendants argued that their omissions of fact in communications with stockholders were not material because the state could not have enjoined the transaction. The Ninth Circuit rejected this argument because a reasonable investor in possession of the information could have avoided the loss by selling the stock.

[148] 485 U.S. 224 (1988).

[149] *Id.* at 229.

[150] *Id.* at 230.

[151] *Id.* at 238, *quoting* SEC v. Texas Gulf Sulphur Co., 401 F.2d 833, 849 (2d Cir. 1969).

[152] 131 S. Ct. 1309 (2011).

demonstrating that the omitted information was material.[153] On appeal, the Ninth Circuit reinstated the case, and the Supreme Court affirmed. Relying on *TSC Industries* and *Basic*, the Court rejected a bright-line test for materiality that would require that the information be statistically significant: "As in *Basic*, Matrixx's categorical rule would 'artificially exclud[e]' information that 'would otherwise be considered significant to the trading decision of a reasonable investor.' "[154] In this case, the Court noted, medical experts could find that there is a causal link between the product and the adverse events. The Court concluded by cautioning that not all adverse events must be reported, but only those that a reasonable investor might consider material.[155]

The lesson from all three of these leading cases is that the materiality determination is at all times highly-fact specific. Thus, in a jury trial, the jury will usually decide the issue. Under the Court's rulings, only when the information is so obviously important, or unimportant, that a reasonable investor would, or would not, want to consider the information may the trial court rule a fact material or immaterial as a matter of law.

In insider trading cases, information generally will be considered material when its disclosure would likely result in a substantial change in the security's price. In most cases, the information will relate to a major corporate event, as in *Chiarella* (a tender offer bid). But in cases where there is only a *possibility* that the price would be affected, the inquiry is more complex. What if one company approaches another to discuss the possibility of an acquisition, which the first company will only undertake if it is done on a friendly basis? The overture itself is probably not material. But, if the subject shows any interest, is there a different result? To further complicate the scenario, is the information material if the company is seriously considering a hostile takeover bid, but learns that there are practical barriers making the deal impossible? Would a tip that the company is considering a bid be material?[156] In the case of a company's product, at what point do signs of possible defects become material? One report out of 100,000 sales is likely immaterial, but how many reports are necessary to prove materiality?

There are no easy answers to these questions. The important points are that materiality is an essential element of securities fraud, that it is an issue disputed in many securities fraud cases, and that the determination is usually quite fact-specific. In insider trading cases, factors to take into account include the actual market impact of the information, trading by the parties, and confidential handling of the information by the issuer or the issuer's agents. Apart from extraordinary corporate transactions, the types of information that courts have found to be material include business plans, projections or estimates,[157] litigation or the

---

[153] *Id.* at 1317. The district judge also found that the facts alleged did not support a finding of scienter. *Id.*

[154] *Id.* at 1319, *quoting Basic*, 485 U.S. at 236.

[155] *Id.* at 1321–22.

[156] *See* United States v. Teicher, 987 F.2d 112 (2d Cir. 1993) (finding the information to be material because the company had taken steps, including hiring a law firm, towards making a bid).

[157] United States v. Margala, 662 F.2d 622 (9th Cir. 1981).

possibility of litigation, and information that might affect the sales of important corporate products.

§ 5.10   OTHER OFFENSES

[A]   Stock Parking

One example of prosecutors' broad discretion in bringing securities fraud cases is their ability to employ theories never before used for a criminal charge. One such theory involves the "parking" of stock. Stock parking occurs when the first party, who is the true owner of the stock, arranges with a second party (the "nominal" owner) to hold the stock in the nominal owner's name. Under such an arrangement, any profits and losses that the nominal owner has are later transferred to the real owner. At a minimum, stock parking may give rise to criminal charges for keeping false books and records, which do not reflect the true stock ownership.

An owner of stock might decide to "park" it with someone else for a number of reasons. For example, margin rules limit the amount that can be borrowed to buy stock. If a stock owner has exceeded or is about to exceed that limit, the owner can temporarily "sell" (*i.e.*, park) the stock, which is no longer in the owner's portfolio and therefore does not apply towards the margin requirements. Another reason to park stock is to avoid taxes. For example, a stock owner with substantial gains in a given year might wish to "sell" some stock at a loss, with the agreement to "buy" it back later.[158] Finally, one who accumulates more than five percent of a company's stock is required to file a Form 13D with the SEC, to put investors on notice. Someone interested in secretly moving to acquire control of a company might "sell" some of the stock to avoid public filing requirements and hide its ownership.[159]

One of the first major stock parking convictions occurred in *United States v. Bilzerian*,[160] which the government brought under Section 10b, the general antifraud provisions of the 1934 Act. In that case, the court defined the term "parking" thus:

> "Parking" refers to a transaction in which a broker-dealer buys stock from a customer with the understanding that the customer will buy the stock back at a later date for the purchase price plus interest and commissions. [T]here is no market risk to the broker-dealer who is the owner of the shares in name only.[161]

Stock parking was also charged in perhaps the most famous Wall Street case of the 1980s, that against "junk bond" king Michael Milken. Milken ultimately pleaded

---

[158] *See, e.g.*, United States v. Regan, 937 F.2d 823 (2d Cir. 1991).

[159] *See, e.g.*, United States v. Bilzerian, 926 F.2d 1285 (2d Cir. 1991). For another example of a stock parking criminal prosecution based upon this theory, see United States v. Mulheren, 938 F.2d 364 (2d Cir. 1991), where the jury failed to reach a verdict on this charge.

[160] 926 F.2d 1285 (2d Cir. 1991).

[161] *Id.* at 1290.

guilty to that charge.[162]

[B]   Proxy Statements

False statements or omissions, willfully made in documents filed under the securities laws, can also give rise to criminal charges. One example of such a document is a proxy solicitation, which is sent to shareholders to allow them to vote on such matters as choosing a board of directors.

For example, in *United States v. Matthews*,[163] the government alleged that the defendant, a corporate officer, was involved in a scheme to avoid paying state taxes and to file federal tax returns that falsely described as a legal fee what was, in fact, a bribe. The government's theory was that Matthews, a candidate for the company's board of directors, committed securities fraud when he failed to disclose in the proxy materials that he was the subject of a grand jury investigation into these matters. Rule 14a-9 proscribes the use of false and misleading statements in proxy materials. Item 6 of Schedule 14A further requires that, if the information is material to the candidate's integrity, the candidate must indicate whether he or she has been convicted of a crime or named in a criminal proceeding.

In reversing the conviction, the Second Circuit held that disclosure would have meant that Matthews was confessing to an uncharged crime, and that this clearly was not required. Uncharged criminal conduct is not required to be disclosed by any SEC rule, and therefore nondisclosure cannot be the basis of a criminal securities fraud charge.[164]

The court was also concerned with the government's broad application of a regulation that did not clearly delineate the types of "qualitative" information that must be disclosed.[165]

§ 5.11   PROFESSIONALS' LIABILITY

Attorneys and other professionals who assist their clients' fraud may themselves be liable. This is especially true in the wake of corporate accounting scandals such as Enron and WorldCom, and the passage of the Sarbanes-Oxley Act.[166] In addition to liability under federal securities laws, professionals also face exposure under state securities laws.

The decision in *United States v. Natelli*,[167] illustrates the potential scope of attorney liability. In that case, the defendants were a partner and an employee of an accounting firm. The partner, and, at the partner's direction, the employee,

---

[162]   759 F. Supp. 109 (S.D.N.Y. 1990).

[163]   787 F.2d 38 (2d Cir. 1986).

[164]   *Id.* at 44 n.3. The case turned on the court's interpretation of what it means to be "named in a criminal proceeding." The court distinguished a "subject" of a grand jury investigation (one whom the grand jury has an interest in investigating) from a "target" (one whom the grand jury seeks to indict).

[165]   *Id.* at 49.

[166]   For an overview, see Marc L. Steinberg, Attorney Liability After Sarbanes-Oxley (2006).

[167]   527 F.2d 311 (2d Cir. 1975).

assisted a client in preparing false financial information that was distributed to shareholders in a proxy statement. The Second Circuit affirmed the partner's conviction, and went on to reject the employee's argument that he could not be liable because he was merely carrying out his superior's order. The court did reverse the employee's conviction, however, because, as to one of the government's allegations, there was insufficient evidence that he was reckless given that the error was "not within his sphere of responsibility."[168]

Courts have declined to find attorneys liable where the attorneys were merely passing along their clients' misrepresentations. In *Schatz v. Rosenberg*,[169] for example, the plaintiffs were persons who sold an interest in two companies. The plaintiffs sued parties involved in the purchase, and sued the law firm that assisted the purchasers, alleging securities fraud and tortuous misrepresentation. In the transaction, the purchasers misstated their financial position in documents the law firm prepared.

The trial court dismissed the counts against the law firm, and the Fourth Circuit affirmed. The appeals court noted that the law firm had no duty to disclose their clients' wrongdoing, and indeed such disclosure was prohibited by the attorney-client privilege. The law firm had no relationship with the plaintiffs, and made no affirmative statements. In this respect, the case was distinguishable from those involving statements in securities filings such as prospectuses and proxy statements.[170]

---

[168] *Id.* at 321–22.

[169] 943 F.2d 485 (4th Cir. 1991).

[170] *Id.* at 491–92. *Compare* Roberts v. Peat, Marwick, Mitchell & Co., 857 F.2d 646, 652–53 (9th Cir. 1988) (lawyers not responsible for failure to disclose information to investors), *with In re* Rospatch Securities Litigation, 640 Fed. Sec. L. Rep. § 96, 939 (W.D. Mich. 1992) (applying Sixth Circuit law rejecting the holding in *Schatz v. Rosenberg*, and denying summary judgment in favor of defendant attorneys).

Chapter 6

COMPUTER CRIME

§ 6.01 INTRODUCTION

Computer crime has increased and will increase commensurate with the rapid growth in internet use.[1] Such crime occurs for many reasons, ranging from national security infiltration to industrial espionage, financial theft, and personal spite.[2] As commercial transactions increasingly become electronically-based, most types of white collar crime will involve computers to some extent. This chapter provides an overview of the primary federal statutes currently used to prosecute computer crimes and the related constitutional and enforcement issues that arise in these cases.

§ 6.02 CHALLENGES TO LAW ENFORCEMENT

For several reasons, computer crime has long proven difficult to identify and prosecute.[3] First, these crimes are particularly hard to uncover. Computer crime victims may not be sure whether a breach has occurred, or to what extent an intruder has taken valuable information.[4] Second, victims of computer crimes often do not report them. Corporate victims, for example, may wish to avoid the attendant negative publicity. Finally, the dramatic increases in computer crimes require the government to devote ever-more human resources, and to provide increasingly sophisticated technical training. For all these reasons, government efforts so far have been insufficient to meet the challenge.

Law enforcement has begun to emphasize more effective efforts to battle computer crime,[5] and time will tell whether their efforts have been effective. In addition, Congress has taken important first steps with its enactment and revisions of the most important computer crime statute, which is now entitled the Computer

---

[1] Fernando M. Pinguelo & Bradford W. Muller, *Virtual Crimes, Real Damages: A Primer Oon Cybercrimes Iin Tthe United States and Efforts to Combat Cybercriminals*, 16 Va. J.L. & Tech. 116 (2011).

[2] William H. Jordan, Debra Bernstein & Michael Zweiback, *Computer Crime, in* White Collar Crime: Business and Regulatory Offenses § 21.01 (Otto Obermaier & Robert Morvillo, eds. 2011).

[3] *See id.* § 21.02[2] (describing the government's efforts to increase its ability to effectively prosecute computer crimes).

[4] *See* Pinguelo & Muller, *supra* note 1, at 609.

[5] *See, e.g,* Jordan et al, *supra* note 2, § 21.02; *FBI Chief Mueller Emphasizes Need Ffor Global Collaboration to Fight Cybercrime*, 74 U.S.L.W. 2511 (Feb. 28, 2006).

Fraud and Abuse Act ("CFAA").[6] The next section provides an overview of this statute.

§ 6.03 THE COMPUTER FRAUD AND ABUSE ACT

The CFAA was originally enacted in 1984 as the "Counterfeit Access Device and Computer Fraud and Abuse Act."[7] This statute focused on protecting computers and electronically-stored information. In 1986, the statute was substantially revised and given its current title. Subsequent amendments have broadened the statute's reach, and the CFAA now sets forth a number of distinct offenses. Care should be taken to identify the elements of each offense, particularly the levels of the applicable mens rea. The punishment under each section is graded according to the level of culpability, as measured by the required mens rea, and/or the damage caused by the defendant's actions.

[A] The Statutory Provisions

[1] Section (a)(1) — Knowing and Willful Theft Involving National Security

This section criminalizes the theft and conveyance of protected government information. The crime requires that the defendant have committed two acts: (1) accessing a computer without authorization or in excess of authorization; *and* (2) conveying or attempting to convey the information obtained to a person not entitled to receive it.

Further, the section requires that the defendant have acted with three levels of mens rea.[8] First, the defendant must have acted *with the belief* that the information could be used to injure the United States or to benefit another country. Second, the defendant must have "*knowingly*" accessed a computer, either without authorization or by exceeding authorized access. Finally, the defendant must have "*willfully*"

---

[6] 18 U.S.C. § 1030. As in other white collar crime areas, states have enacted their own computer crime statutes. In fact, all states now have statutes addressing this problem. *See* Jessica L. McCurdy, *Computer Crimes*, 47 Am. Crim. L. Rev. 287, 299–300 (2010).

[7] Pub. L. No. 98-473, 2101(a), 98 Stat. 2190 (1984). For an argument that the CFAA must be narrowly interpreted in order to avoid be found unconstitutionally vague, see Orin S. Kerr, *Vagueness Challenges to the Computer Fraud and Abuse Act*, 94 Minn. L. Rev. 1561 (2010).

[8] 18 U.S.C. § 1030(a)(1) provides:

(a) Whoever -

(1) having knowingly accessed a computer without authorization or exceeding authorized access, and by means of such conduct having obtained information that has been determined by the United States Government pursuant to an Executive order or statute to require protection against unauthorized disclosure for reasons of national defense or foreign relations, or any restricted data, as defined in paragraph y of section 11 of the Atomic Energy Act of 1954, with reason to believe that such information so obtained could be used to the injury of the United States, or to the advantage of any foreign nation willfully communicates, delivers, transmits, or causes to be communicated, delivered, or transmitted, or attempts to communicate, deliver, transmit or cause to be communicated, delivered, or transmitted the same to any person not entitled to receive it, or willfully retains the same and fails to deliver it to the officer or employee of the United States entitled to receive it.

revealed or attempted to reveal the information to a person not entitled to receive it. The punishment for violations of this section includes a fine and prison term of up to ten years, or twenty years if the defendant has previously violated § 1030.[9]

[2] Section (a)(2) — Intentional Theft of Protected Information

This section requires that the defendant have obtained certain information *"intentionally"* Again, the government must prove two acts: (1) accessing a computer without authorization or accessing a computer by exceeding authorized access, *and* (2) thereby obtaining (a) certain financial information as defined by the statute, (b) government agency information, *or* (c) information from a "protected" computer[10] involving interstate commerce.[11] The term "protected computer" is very broad, and includes all federal government and financial institution computers, and all computers used in interstate or foreign commerce. The punishment for this section includes a fine and a one-year prison term, or a ten-year term if the defendant has previously been convicted of violating § 1030.[12]

[3] Section (a)(3) — Intentional Gaining of Access to Government Information

This section criminalizes *intentionally* gaining improper access to nonpublic federal government information where the access affects the use of the computer.[13] The crime requires that the government prove:

---

[9] 18 U.S.C. §§ 3571, 1030(c)(1)(A), 1030(c)(1)(B).

[10] 18 U.S.C. § 1030(e)(2) provides:

[T]he term "protected computer" means a computer -

(A) exclusively for the use of a financial institution or the United States Government, or, in the case of a computer not exclusively for such use, used by or for a financial institution or the United States Government and the conduct constituting the offense affects that use by or for the financial institution or the Government; or

(B) which is used in interstate or foreign commerce or communication, including a computer located in the United States that is used in a manner that affects interstate or foreign commerce or communication in the United States.

[11] 18 U.S.C. § 1030(a)(2) provides:

(a) Whoever -

(2) intentionally accesses a computer without authorization or exceeds authorized access, and thereby obtains -

(A) information contained in a financial record of a financial institution, or of a card issuer as defined in section 1602(n) of title 15, or contained in a file of a consumer reporting agency on a consumer, as such terms are defined in the Fair Credit Reporting Act (15 U.S.C. 1681 et seq.);

(B) information from any department or agency of the United States; or

(C) information from any protected computer if the conduct involved an interstate or foreign communication.

[12] 18 U.S.C. § 3571. When certain circumstances, such as financial motive, are present, the one-year minimum increases to five years. 18. U.S.C. § 1030(c)(2)(B)(i).

[13] 18 U.S.C. § 1030(a)(3) provides:

(a) Whoever -

(1) mens rea (intent to gain access); (2) the act of gaining access; and (3) the result of an effect on the computer's use. The punishment includes a fine, and a prison term of not more than a year, or not more than ten years if the defendant has previously been convicted of violating § 1030.[14]

The punishment as a misdemeanor reflects the lack of a mens rea requirement as to the result (effect on the computer).

[4] Section (a)(4) — Fraud Through a Protected Computer

This section requires two levels of mens rea: the defendant must have (1) *known* that the defendant gained access to a protected computer without authorization or by exceeding authorized access; and (2) acted with *intent to defraud*. Further, the government must prove that the defendant committed three acts. The defendant must have: (1) *gained access* to a protected computer without authorization or by exceeding authorized access; (2) *used* this conduct to further the fraud, and (3) *obtained* a "thing of value." The "thing of value" is defined to include the use of the computer only where the value of that use is at least $5,000 within a year.[15] The punishment for violations of this section includes a fine, and a prison term of not more than five years, or ten years if the defendant has previously been convicted of violating § 1030.[16]

[5] Section (a)(5)(A)(i) — Intentionally Causing Damage Through a Computer Transmission

This section criminalizes a *knowing* computer transmission that results in *intentional* damage, without authorization, to a protected computer.[17] This section has a two-tiered mens rea requirement: (1) the defendant must *knowingly* cause a transmission; and (2) the defendant must *intend* to cause damage as a result. The government must also prove both an act (the transmission) and a result (damage) to achieve a conviction under this section. The punishment for violations of this section includes a fine, and a prison term of not more than five years, or ten years

---

(3) intentionally, without authorization to access any nonpublic computer of a department or agency of the United States, accesses such a computer of that department or agency that is exclusively for the use of the Government of the United States or, in the case of a computer not exclusively for such use, is used by or for the Government of the United States and such conduct affects that use by or for the Government of the United States.

[14] 18 U.S.C. §§ 3571, 1030(c)(2)(A).

[15] Whoever -

(4) knowingly and with intent to defraud, accesses a protected computer without authorization, or exceeds authorized access, and by means of such conduct furthers the intended fraud and obtains anything of value, unless the object of the fraud and the thing obtained consists only of the use of the computer and the value of such use is not more than $5,000 in any 1-year period.

[16] 18 U.S.C. §§ 3571, 1030(c)(3)(A).

[17] Whoever -

(5)(A) knowingly causes the transmission of a program, information, code, or command, and as a result of such conduct, intentionally causes damage without authorization, to a protected computer.

if the defendant has previously been convicted of violating § 1030.[18]

[6]　Section (a)(5)(A)(ii) — Recklessly Causing Damage Through Unauthorized Access

This section criminalizes *intentionally* accessing a protected computer, without authorization, and *recklessly* causing damage as a result.[19] Again, there is a two-tiered mens rea requirement. The government also must prove both an act (accessing the computer) and a result (damage) to obtain a conviction. The punishment for violations of this section includes a fine, and a prison term of not more than five years, or ten years if the defendant has previously been convicted of violating § 1030.[20]

[7]　Section (a)(5)(A)(iii) — Causing Damage Through Unauthorized Access

This section criminalizes *intentionally* accessing a protected computer, without authorization, thereby causing damage.[21] The only required mens rea is the intent to access the computer. As with the previous section, the government also must prove both an act (accessing the computer) and a result (damage) to obtain a conviction.

This offense is punished as a misdemeanor, with a fine and a maximum penalty of one year if the defendant has not previously been convicted of violating § 1030.[22] This lower level of punishment comports with a mens rea requirement that is lower than in some other sections. Although the government must show mens rea (intent) as to the act (accessing the computer), it is not required to prove any level of mens rea as to the result of the act (*i.e.*, damage). Thus, as to the result of causing damage, the statute imposes strict liability.

[8]　Subsection (a)(6) — Fraudulent Trafficking in Passwords

This section criminalizes trafficking in information, such as passwords, that provides access to computers. The defendant must have acted *knowingly* and with the *intent to defraud*, and the trafficking must have affected interstate commerce or a federal computer.[23] The fraud need not be complete in order for the defendant to

---

[18]　18 U.S.C. §§ 3571, 1030(c)(3)(B).

[19]　Whoever -

(5)(A)(ii) intentionally accesses a protected computer without authorization, and as a result of such conduct, recklessly causes damage.

[20]　18 U.S.C. §§ 3571, 1030(c)(4)(B).

[21]　Whoever -

(A)(iii) intentionally accesses a protected computer without authorization, and as a result of such conduct, causes damage.

[22]　18 U.S.C. §§ 3571, 1030(c)(2)(A), 1030(c)(3)(B).

[23]　Whoever -

(6) knowingly and with intent to defraud traffics (as defined in section 1029) in any password

be liable. This offense is punished as a misdemeanor, with a fine and a maximum penalty of one year if the defendant has not previously been convicted of violating § 1030.[24]

[9] Subsection (a)(7) — Extortion

This section criminalizes the *intentional* extortion of anything of value from any legal entity by threatening to damage a protected computer.[25] The mens rea is intent to extort; the actus reus is the threat to cause damage. Also, the jurisdictional element requires that the threat be transmitted in interstate or foreign commerce. The punishment for violations of this section includes a fine, and a prison term of not more than five years, or ten years if the defendant has previously been convicted of violating § 1030.[26]

[B] The Sentencing Scheme

Congress has graded the punishment under each of the foregoing sections according to the level of mens rea the defendant possessed and the degree of harm the defendant caused. Thus, sentences under § 1030 range from: up to ten years under subsection (a)(1) (theft of computer information generally related to espionage); up to five years under subsections (a)(4) (intent to defraud), (a)(5)(A)(i)-(ii) (intentionally and recklessly causing damage), and (a)(7) (extortion), and up to one year under subsections (a)(2) (theft of information), (a)(3) (gaining access to information), (a)(5)(A)(iii) (causing damage), and (a)(6) (trafficking in passwords). The statute provides for increases in maximum sentences in certain circumstances, such as repeat offenses.[27] In addition, the USA Patriot Act of 2001 extended the definition of a prior offense to include those convictions under state law that involved unauthorized access to a computer.[28] As always, the actual sentence in a given case will depend upon the application of the United States Sentencing Guidelines to the case.[29]

---

or similar information through which a computer may be accessed without authorization, if -

(A) such trafficking affects interstate or foreign commerce; or

(B) such computer is used by or for the Government of the United States.

[24] 18 U.S.C. §§ 3571, 1030(c)(2)(A).

[25] Whoever -

(7) With intent to extort from any person any money or other thing of value, transmits in interstate or foreign commerce any communication containing any threat to cause damage to a protected computer.

[26] 18 U.S.C. §§ 3571, 1030(c)(3)(A).

[27] 18 U.S.C. §§ 1030(c)(2), 1030(c)(3)(B).

[28] USA Patriot Act of 2001, Pub. L. No.107-56, § 814(c)(1)(B). *See* McCurdy et al., *supra* note 6, at 230–31.

[29] *See* Chapter 21, Sentencing, *infra.*

§ 6.04　PROSECUTING COMPUTER CRIME

Most computer crime prosecutions to date have been brought under the CFAA and/or under the wire fraud statute. As discussed below, both statutes pose difficulties for prosecutors.

[A]　Issues in Cases Brought Under the CFAA

[1]　Determining the Required Mens Rea

As with other white collar statutes, the mens rea provisions of § 1030 are often the key to prosecutions under the statute. In perhaps the most notorious "hacker" case to date, *United States v. Morris*,[30] the Second Circuit interpreted the mens rea provisions of an earlier version of § 1030.

The *Morris* defendant was a Cornell graduate student in computer science who was authorized to use university computers. Morris developed a type of program, commonly known as a "worm" or "virus," designed to infiltrate computer networks through the Internet.[31] The program was designed to detect weaknesses in network security systems without being detected and without interfering with the computers' use. Once released, the program caused extensive, unintended disruptions to computer systems around the country. Although the program did not damage computer hardware or software, the labor costs required to restore the computers' functioning, according to some estimates, amounted to millions of dollars.[32]

Under the version of the CFAA in force at that time, Morris was charged with "intentionally access[ing] a Federal interest computer[33] without authorization, and by means of one or more instances of such conduct . . . prevent[ing] authorized use of any such computer or information, and thereby . . . caus[ing] loss to one or more others of a value aggregating $1,000 or more during any one year period."[34] The statute thus required proof of four elements: (1) the act of gaining access; (2) the result of preventing use; (3) the additional result of loss; and (4) the mens rea of intent.

It was clear both that Morris intentionally gained access to the affected computers, and that the computers were "federal interest computers" under the terms of the statute. It was also obvious that Morris did not intend to cause the damage that resulted from the virus. Therefore, the key issue was whether the government should have been required to prove that Morris intended to prevent use and cause loss. The district court interpreted the statute to require only that the government prove, as to mens rea, that the defendant intentionally gained access to the computer; the court did not require the government also to prove that the

---

[30]　928 F.2d 504 (2d Cir. 1991).

[31]　*Id.* at 505.

[32]　John K. Marky & James F. Boyle, *New Crimes of the Information Age*, Metropolitan Corporate Counsel, Feb. 2000 at 12.

[33]　The new version of the statute replaces the term "federal interest computer" with the broader term "protected computer." 18 U.S.C. § 1030(e)(2). *See* note 11, *supra.*

[34]　928 F.2d at 506, *citing* the then-current version of 18 U.S.C. § 1030(a)(5)(A).

defendant intended to cause the resulting damage.

On appeal, Morris argued that the government should have been required to show intent both with respect to the act (access) and result (preventing use and causing loss) elements of the crime. The Second Circuit rejected Morris's argument. After reviewing the legislative history, the court concluded that Congress had focused on the intentional *accessing* of computers without authorization. This interpretation was reinforced by comparison to other sections of the statute, which did contain mens rea language before each of the elements. This comparison showed that Congress specified mens rea when it intended for it be proven, and omitted mens rea language when such a showing was not required. More importantly, an earlier version of the statute repeated the intent requirement before the accessing element and the remaining elements, while the revised version did not do so.[35]

Morris also argued that there was insufficient evidence that he gained access to federal interest computers without authorization, and that at most he exceeded authorized access. The Second Circuit rejected the argument, primarily because Morris' program was designed to gain access to computers other than the one for which Morris had authority.[36]

In a later case, *United States v. Sablan*,[37] the court confronted a similar issue. The defendant was a former bank employee who entered the bank after hours and logged onto the computer system using her old password. She then changed several files and deleted some others, causing financial loss to the bank. On appeal from her conviction under § 1030(a)(5), the defendant argued that the statute requires two separate showings of mens rea: (1) the intent to access a federal interest computer; and (2) the intent to cause loss. The government argued that only the former is required, and the Ninth Circuit agreed based upon the statutory language and legislative history.

[2] Determining the "Thing of Value"

In another major computer crime prosecution, *United States v. Czubinski*,[38] the defendant gained access to confidential federal government information. The defendant was an Internal Revenue Service employee whose duties mainly involved answering taxpayers' questions concerning their returns. The defendant was authorized to use his Boston computer to gain access to IRS computer systems to retrieve information from the computer database in West Virginia. Acting outside the scope of his official duties, and in violation of IRS policy, Czubinski retrieved information about various individuals for personal reasons.[39] The evidence did not

---

[35] *Id.* at 508.

[36] *Id.* at 510–11.

[37] 92 F.3d 865 (9th Cir. 1996).

[38] 106 F.3d 1069 (1st Cir. 1997).

[39] Czubinski used his position in the IRS to access information regarding tax returns, including those of two individuals involved in a political campaign, a District Attorney who had prosecuted his father in an unrelated offense, a Boston Housing Authority Police Officer who was involved in an organization with Czubinski's brother, and others, in order to build dossiers on people involved in the white supremacist movement and for other personal reasons. *Id.* at 1072.

show, however, that Czubinski used the information in any way, or that he disclosed it to any third parties.[40]

The defendant was charged and convicted under both the wire fraud statute[41] and § 1030(a)(4) of the CFAA.[42] At the time Czubinski was prosecuted, § 1030(a)(4) punished one who "knowingly and with intent to defraud, accesse[d] a Federal interest computer without authorization, or exceed[ed] authorized access, and by means of such conduct further[ed] the intended fraud and obtain[ed] anything of value, unless the object of the fraud and the thing obtained consist[ed] only of the use of the computer."[43]

The First Circuit reversed the conviction, finding that the government had not shown that the defendant obtained "anything of value" in connection with a fraudulent scheme.[44] Because the government failed to show "that Czubinski intended anything more than to satisfy idle curiosity,"[45] this element of the crime was not present.

The result will be different when a defendant uses confidential government information to further an illegal scheme. In *United States v. Rice*, for example, the defendant was an IRS agent who used secret government information to assist a friend avoid the forfeiture of property obtained with narcotic trafficking proceeds. The defendant was convicted of, among other crimes, violating § 1030(a)(3) of the CFAA, which, at that time, prohibited the unlawful access of a federal computer when "such conduct affect[ed] the use of the Government's operation of such computer." Rice used his IRS position to access the IRS's database in order to find out what the IRS knew about his friend's activities, thus violating § 1030(a)(3).[46]

In addition, the current version of the CFAA, § 1030(a)(2)(b), contains a misdemeanor provision criminalizing "intentionally access[ing] a computer without authorization or exceed[ing] authorized access, and thereby obtain[ing] . . . information from any department or agency of the United States." Defendants have been convicted under this provision for obtaining information for personal use even in the absence of financial gain or illegal motivation.[47]

---

[40] *Id.* at 1072.

[41] 18 U.S.C. § 1343.

[42] 18 U.S.C. § 1030(a)(4).

[43] 106 F.3d at 1078. The current version of the statute, *supra* note 16, provides that the "thing of value" may be the computer time alone if it amounts to more than $5,000 within any one-year period.

[44] For a discussion of this aspect of the crimes of mail and wire fraud, see Chapter 4, Mail and Wire Fraud, *supra*, § 4.05[B][3][a].

[45] *Id.* at 1078.

[46] 961 F.2d 211 (4th Cir. 1992). *See also* United States v. John, 597 F.3d 263 (5th Cir. 2010) (CFAA criminalizes access, otherwise authorized, where the defendant intended to use the information obtained in criminal activity).

[47] *See* United States v. Rodriguez, 628 F.3d 1258 (11th Cir. 2010) (affirming conviction of Social Security Administration employee for using office computers to obtain personal information about friends and relatives in violation of agency policy).

[3]   Determining Covered Losses

Under many provisions of the CFAA, liability will attach only when the defendant's actions cause the requisite damage. When examining whether this element has been met, issues of both statutory interpretation and factual sufficiency often arise. For example, in *United States v. Middleton*,[48] the defendant gained unauthorized access to his former employer's computer system, and changed passwords and deleted databases. The government charged him under § 1030(a)(5)(A)(i), which criminalizes "knowingly caus[ing] the transmission of a program, information, code, or command, and as a result of such conduct, intentionally caus[ing] damage without authorization, to a protected computer." The statute defines "damage" as "any impairment to the integrity or availability of data, a program, a system, or information, that causes loss aggregating at least $5,000 in value during any 1-year period to one or more individuals."[49]

On appeal, the defendant argued that Congress did not intend that the phrase "one or more individuals" include corporations. The court rejected the argument, finding that the plain language of the statute and the legislative history indicated that Congress intended that corporations be protected by the statute.[50] In addition, the defendant argued that there was insufficient evidence that the victim had suffered $5,000 in damages. The court found sufficient evidence, based upon the value of the employee hours needed to correct the problems and upon the costs of hiring an outside consultant and obtaining new software.

[B]   Issues in Wire Fraud Prosecutions of Computer Crime

As discussed more fully in Chapter 4, the mail and wire fraud statutes generally require the government to prove that the defendant intended to deprive the victim of money or property or of the right to "honest services."[51] This requirement has proven problematic in some computer crime prosecutions. In *Czubinski*, for example, the court reversed the wire fraud conviction because the government had failed to prove that the IRS had been deprived of either property or of the defendant's honest services.[52]

In other instances, the potential breadth of the wire fraud statutes as applied to computer crimes has led courts to narrow the wire fraud statute's application in such cases. For example, in *United States v. LaMacchia*,[53] the defendant was a student who used his college computer network to make free copies of copyrighted computer software available for uploading. The government charged the defendant with wire fraud on the theory that the scheme damaged the copyright holders.[54]

---

[48]   231 F.3d 1207 (9th Cir. 2000).

[49]   18 U.S.C. § 1030(e)(8)(A).

[50]   231 F.3d at 1211–12.

[51]   *See* Chapter 4, Mail and Wire Fraud, *supra*, § 4.05.

[52]   For a discussion of this aspect of the case, see § 4.05, Mail and Wire Fraud, *supra*, § 4.05[B][3][a].

[53]   871 F. Supp. 535 (D. Mass. 1994).

[54]   The court noted that the defendant could not have been charged under the then-existing felony provision of the copyright laws, 18 U.S.C. § 2319 (1988), because the government could not make the

The district court dismissed the case under the reasoning of *Dowling v. United States*.[55] In *Dowling*, the Supreme Court held that the National Stolen Property Act was not an appropriate vehicle for criminalizing the interstate transportation of pirated sound recordings. The Court found that this activity did not involve the type of "property" covered by that Act.[56] The court in *LaMacchia* found that the same reasoning applied, and that LaMacchia's scheme did not involve a deprivation of "property" as that term is defined in the wire fraud statute. The court further opined that to allow such a prosecution would potentially criminalize "the myriad of home computer users who succumb to the temptation to copy even a single software program for private use."[57]

[C] Other Applicable Statutes

As seen above, many cases involving the use of computers to commit wrongdoing are brought under statutes in addition to or instead of § 1030. For example, the Copyright Act,[58] the Digital Millennium Copyright Act,[59] the Economic Espionage Act,[60] the mail and wire fraud statutes,[61] interstate transportation of property obtained by fraud,[62] and conspiracy[63] may all be used to prosecute computer crimes. In addition, all states have adopted statutes geared towards computer crime.[64]

---

required showing that the defendant acted for the "purpose of commercial advantage or private financial gain" as required under 17 U.S.C. § 506(a). *See LaMacchia*, 871 F. Supp. at 539. As the court noted in United States. v. Rothberg, 222 F. Supp. 2d 1009, 1018 (N.D. Ill. 2002), the Congress amended 17 U.S.C. § 506 in 1997 in response to *LaMacchia*. The amended section makes it a crime to infringe a copyright willfully by reproducing copies of copyrighted works worth more than $1,000, eliminating the requirement of proof of financial motivation.

[55] 473 U.S. 207 (1985).

[56] Article I, § 8, cl. 8 of the United States Constitution grants Congress the exclusive power to regulate copyrights. The Court in *Dowling* was therefore unwilling to extend protection for copyrighted materials under statutes that were not specifically designed to provide such protection. 473 U.S. at 216–17.

[57] 871 F. Supp. at 544.

[58] 17 U.S.C. § 506. Congress has also revised the penalty provisions of the Copyright Act, 18 U.S.C. § 2319, to include felony sanctions for copyright infringements, including those relating to computers. Computer facilitated copyright violations are sometimes charged under the wire fraud statute. *See, e.g.,* United States v. LaMacchia, 871 F. Supp. 535 (1994), discussed *supra* § 6.04[B].

[59] 17 U.S.C. § 1204. Congress enacted this statute in 1998 as a response to issues raised by copyright infringements over the Internet. For an overview of the statute, *see* Teddy C. Kim, Taming the Electronic Frontier: Software Copyright Protection in the Wake of *United States v. LaMacchia*, 80 Minn. L. Rev. 1255 (1996).

[60] 18 U.S.C. §§ 1831; 1832. This statute was passed in 1996. For an overview, see Gerald J. Mossinghoff, J. Derek Mason & David A. Oblon, *Economic Espionage Act: A Prosecution Update*, 80 J. Pat. & Trademark Off. Soc'y 360 (1998).

[61] 18 U.S.C. §§ 1341; 1343. The mail and wire fraud statutes have not always proven to be effective vehicles for prosecution of computer crimes. *See, e.g.,* United States v. LaMacchia, 871 F. Supp. 535 (1994), discussed *supra,* § 6.04[B]; United States v. Czubinski, 106 F.3d 1069 (1997), discussed *supra,* § 6.04[B].

[62] 18 U.S.C. § 2314.

[63] 18 U.S.C. § 371.

[64] *See* McCurdy, et al., *supra* note 6, at 267.

In *United States v. Martin*,[65] for example, the government charged computer crime under several statutes. In that case the defendant had been sending electronic mail messages from his office in California to a "pen-pal" in Maine. In these messages, the defendant outlined a scheme to use trade secrets, marketing plans, and other confidential information from the company he was working for in order to start his own competing business. The First Circuit upheld the defendant's convictions under the mail and wire fraud statutes, the conspiracy statute, and the Economic Espionage Act.[66]

§ 6.05   INTERNATIONAL COMPUTER CRIME

Many white collar crimes, particularly financial crimes such as money laundering and currency transaction reporting crimes,[67] occur across international borders. Computer crimes also can involve a wide variety of international activities, creating enforcement obstacles and raising complex legal issues.

A key issue in such cases is whether a court within the United States has jurisdiction over the alleged criminal activity. In one case, *United States v. Ivanov*,[68] the victim, Online Information Bureau, Inc. (OIB), was a Connecticut corporation. OIB collected and maintained financial data from credit card companies and other institutions. While in Russia, Ivanov hacked into the OIB computer system and gained the ability to access OIB's data. Ivanov then revealed to OIB that he gained this access and attempted to extort money from OIB. The government charged him with, among other crimes, multiple violations of the CFAA.

Ivanov moved to dismiss the charges, arguing that the court lacked subject matter jurisdiction because he was in Russia when the offenses were committed. The court denied the motion, for two reasons. First, Ivanov's actions were intended to and did affect a victim within the United States. Second, Congress clearly intended that the statutes apply to actions undertaken outside the United States when the impact was within the United States.

§ 6.06   CONSTITUTIONAL AND STATUTORY CONSTRAINTS

Computer crime investigations raise unique problems. First, these cases may involve issues that arise out of constitutional constraints on government action. Second, these cases may also raise issues under statutes passed to protect individual privacy.

---

[65]   228 F.3d 1 (1st Cir. 2000).

[66]   *Id.*

[67]   *See* Chapter 14, Currency Transaction Reporting Crimes; Chapter 15, Money Laundering, *infra.*

[68]   175 F. Supp. 2d 367 (D. Conn. 2001).

[A] Search and Seizure Issues

The Fourth Amendment to the United States Constitution prohibits unreasonable searches and seizures.[69] In addition, Congress has passed laws designed to protect the privacy of electronic information.[70] Investigators must take care not to violate either constitutional or legislative limitations when investigating computer crimes.[71]

Among other requirements, the Fourth Amendment requires that search warrants particularly describe the place to be searched and the items to be seized.[72] This requirement may be particularly difficult when investigating computer crimes. First, it may prove difficult to describe the precise "location" of information sent via the Internet. Second, it may also be difficult to locate relevant computer files without also looking at unrelated files and thereby violating the computer owner's privacy interests. Thus, the issuance and execution of search warrants relating to information contained in computers raise complex Fourth Amendment issues.[73]

In the latter respect, Congress has adopted a number of statutes in response to concerns that individual privacy interests may be undermined by access to confidential computer information.[74] Government investigators must take care not to run afoul of these statutes when seeking electronically-stored information. This issue arose in *Steve Jackson Games, Inc. v. United States Secret Service.*[75] In that case, the plaintiff was a publishing company that sued the government for damages arising out of the execution of a search warrant. The government had searched the plaintiff's facilities under the mistaken belief that the plaintiff had illegally

---

[69] For an overview of Fourth Amendment issues relating to computer crimes, see McCurdy, et al., *supra* note 6, at 261–66; Michael Adler, Cyberspace, General Searches, and Digital Contraband: *The Fourth Amendment and the Net-Wide Search*, 105 Yale L.J. 1093 (1996).

[70] *See infra*, note 74.

[71] The Justice Department has issued guidelines for searching and seizing computer hardware and data. Computer Crime and Intellectual Property Section (CCIPS) of the Criminal Division of the U.S. Department of Justice http://usdoj.gov/criminal/cybercrime/searching.html. The site notes the changes to federal statutes governing the searching and seizing of computers and the gathering of electronic evidence since the passage of the Patriot Act.

[72] *See* Andresen v. Maryland, 427 U.S. 463 (1976) (finding a broad subpoena for business records to be sufficiently particular under a sliding scale test that allows the government flexibility according to the difficulty in listing in advance all relevant items to be seized).

[73] *Compare, e.g.*, United States v. Adjani, 452 F.3d 1140, 1147–52 (9th Cir. 2006) (finding that search warrant for electronic data satisfied the specificity requirements and that e-mails seized during search were within the scope of the warrant), *and* United States v. Campos, 221 F.3d 1143 (10th Cir. 2000) (upholding search pursuant to warrant based on probable cause to seize particular pornographic computer files when the search uncovered similar files not specified in the warrant), *with* United States v. Carey, 172 F.3d 1268 (10th Cir. 1999) (invalidating search for computer files containing pornography undertaken pursuant to a search warrant for files relating to narcotics trafficking).

[74] These include the Electronic Communications Privacy Act, 18 U.S.C. §§ 2510–2521; the Privacy Protection Act, 42 U.S.C. §§ 2000aa *et seq.*; and the Stored Wire and Electronic Communications and Transnational Records Act, 18 U.S.C. §§ 2701 *et seq.* For example, 18 U.S.C. § 2703, Required Disclosure of Customer Communications or Records, covers information contained in email and other electronic communications, and requires warrants in certain circumstances.

[75] 816 F. Supp. 432 (W.D. Tex. 1993), *aff'd*, 36 F.3d 457 (4th Cir. 1994).

distributed another company's proprietary information via the Internet. The government seized numerous materials that were vital to the operation of the plaintiff's business, and kept the materials for four months. During this time, government agents read confidential e-mail messages, some of which were deleted. The court found that the government's actions violated the Privacy Protection Act[76] and the Wire and Electronic Communications and Interception of Oral Communications Act,[77] and awarded the plaintiff damages.

Government searches of electronically stored information continue to raise constitutional issues. In *United States v. Comprehensive Drug Testing*,[78] for example, a federal grand jury was investigating the use of steroids by major league baseball players. Pursuant to warrant, the government searched the records of the company that conducted drug testing of the players. When executing the warrant, the government agents seized many more records than those listed in the warrant. The Ninth Circuit, sitting *en banc*, upheld the district court's order to return the records not described in the warrant.[79]

[B] First Amendment Issues

The First Amendment has proven relevant to computer crimes in two ways. First, the government's efforts to criminalize pornography on the Internet have run afoul of free speech concerns. In *Reno v. American Civil Liberties Union*,[80] the Supreme Court invalidated the Communications Decency Act of 1996. The

---

[76] 42 U.S.C. § 2000aa (1988) *et seq.*

[77] 18 U.S.C. § 2701 (1988) *et seq.* The court found, however, that the stored e-mail at issue was not covered by the Federal Wiretap Act, 18 U.S.C. § 2510 (1988) *et seq.*

[78] 579 F.3d 989 (9th Cir. 2009), *revised and superseded*, 621 F.3d 1162 (9th Cir. 2010).

[79] In its original decision, the court announced general guidelines for searches of electronically stored information. The court later modified its opinion and omitted the mandatory guidelines. Instead, the guidelines are set forth as advisory guidelines in a concurring opinion. 621 F.3d at 1179–80 (Kozinski, J., concurring). The concurring opinion stated:

1. Magistrate judges should insist that the government waive reliance upon the plain view doctrine in digital evidence cases.
2. Segregation and redaction of electronic data must be done either by specialized personnel or an independent third party. If the segregation is to be done by government computer personnel, the government must agree in the warrant application that the computer personnel will not disclose to the investigators any information other than that which is the target of the warrant.
3. Warrants and subpoenas must disclose the actual risks of destruction of information as well as prior efforts to seize that information in other judicial fora.
4. The government's search protocol must be designed to uncover only the information for which it has probable cause, and only that information may be examined by the case agents.
5. The government must destroy or, if the recipient may lawfully possess it, return non-responsive data, keeping the issuing magistrate informed about when it has done so and what it has kept.

Id. at 1180 (citations omitted). Two other circuit courts, however, have approved of the application of the plain-view doctrine to searches of personal computers. *See* United States v. Williams, 592 F.3d 511 (4th Cir. 2010); United States v. Mann, 592 F.3d 779 (7th Cir. 2010). *See generally* Elkan Abramowitz & Barry A. Bohrer, *Search and Seizure of Digital Evidence: Evolving Standards*, N.Y.L.J., Mar. 1, 2011, at p. 3, col. 1.

[80] 521 U.S. 844 (1997).

Court found the Act unacceptably vague because it attempted to regulate speech based on its content, and because it invoked criminal penalties to enforce this regulation.

Second, free speech issues may also arise in civil suits brought under the provisions of the CFAA that allow for private rights of action. So long as a party is acting purely as a private agent, however, First Amendment limitations on government actions will not apply.[81]

§ 6.07 CIVIL ACTIONS

As in many other areas of white collar crime, such as securities fraud and RICO, some computer crime statutes provide for civil causes of action. The statutes provide plaintiffs with potentially powerful weapons in combating computer fraud and abuse.[82] Civil cases have been brought in a variety of contexts.[83]

[A] Suits by Internet Service Providers

Internet service providers are obvious targets of computer crimes, and can use the CFAA's civil provisions to fight back. For example, in *America Online, Inc. v. LCGM, Inc.*,[84] the plaintiff, AOL, sought damages based upon alleged violations of then-existing versions of two sections of the CFAA, § 1030(a)(2)(c) (Exceeding Authorized Access) and § 1030(a)(5)(c) (Impairing Computer Facilities). The complaint alleged that defendants violated AOL's terms of service and sent unauthorized and unsolicited bulk e-mail advertisements ("spam") to AOL customers. AOL further alleged that defendants' actions injured AOL by (1) consuming capacity on AOL's computers, (2) causing AOL to incur technical costs, (3) impairing the functioning of AOL's e-mail system, (4) forcing AOL to upgrade its computer networks, (5) damaging AOL's goodwill with its members, and (6) causing AOL to lose customers and revenue.

The trial court denied AOL's summary judgment motion, concluding that a trial was required to determine damages. The court also found, however, that the defendants had violated both sections of the CFAA. The court therefore granted injunctive relief preventing the defendants from further distributing unsolicited bulk e-mail messages to AOL members, from using their AOL accounts to send and distribute e-mail messages, and from using the AOL network for the purpose of harvesting the addresses of AOL members.

---

[81] *See, e.g.,* Cyber Promotions, Inc. v. America Online, Inc., 948 F. Supp. 436 (E.D. Pa. 1996) (AOL may block e-mail from Cyber Promotions because AOL is not a state actor and is not constrained by the First Amendment).

[82] *See* 18 U.S.C. § 1030(g). Some state computer crime statutes likewise provide for civil causes of action. *See* McCurdy, et al., *supra* note 6, at 270 n.364 (listing statutes).

[83] *See* McCurdy, et al., *supra* note 6, at 228 n.33 (listing cases).

[84] 46 F. Supp. 2d 444 (E.D. Va. 1998).

[B]   Suits by Private Individuals

Large damage amounts can result when pursuing a private cause of action under § 1030 because of the broad statutory language. In *Shaw v. Toshiba America Information Systems, Inc.*,[85] for example, the plaintiffs brought the first class action under § 1030(g)[86] for monetary and injunctive relief. In *Shaw*, the defendant corporations sold computers that contained defective floppy disk controllers. Because of the defect, information contained on the plaintiffs' computers was damaged or destroyed. The defendants argued that the CFAA should not apply because the statute is directed to hacking and not to the sale of defective computer equipment. The court disagreed, finding that the statute is not limited to damages from hacking. Thus, the court determined that the $2.1 billion settlement agreement was fair, just, and reasonable.

After the *Shaw* decision, Congress amended § 1030(g) in order to limit manufacturers' liability. The amendment provides that "[n]o action may be brought under this subsection for the negligent design or manufacture of computer hardware, computer software, or firmware."[87]

Statutes other than the CFAA also provide private causes of action. Suits under these statutes will often involve complex issues of statutory interpretation. Such issues arose in *Konop v. Hawaiian Airlines, Inc.*[88] Konop was a pilot for Hawaiian Airlines, Inc., who sued the airline under the Wiretap Act[89] and Stored Communications Act.[90] Konop had created and maintained a password-protected website for use by employees to post complaints concerning the airline. Hawaiian Airline's president gained access to the website by obtaining permission from two registered users to use their user names and passwords. Konop alleged that the airline violated the statutes when its president accessed Konop's computer.

The trial court granted summary judgment to the airline on both claims. On appeal, the court upheld the trial court's grant of summary judgment on the Wiretap Act claim. For the Wiretap Act to be violated, a person has to intercept the

---

[85] 91 F. Supp. 2d 942 (E.D. Texas 2000).

[86] At the time of this case, this statute provided: "Any person who suffers damage or loss by reason of a violation of this statute may maintain a civil action against the violator to obtain compensatory damages and injunctive relief or other equitable relief."

[87] Pub. L. 107-56, § 814(e) (Oct. 26, 2001). The statute now provides:

(g) Any person who suffers damage or loss by reason of a violation of this section may maintain a civil action against the violator to obtain compensatory damages and injunctive relief or other equitable relief. A civil action for a violation of this section may be brought only if the conduct involves 1 of the factors set forth in clause (i), (ii), (iii), (iv), or (v) of subsection (a)(5)(B). Damages for a violation involving only conduct described in subsection (a)(5)(B)(i) are limited to economic damages. No action may be brought under this subsection unless such action is begun within 2 years of the date of the act complained of or the date of the discovery of the damage. No action may be brought under this subsection for the negligent design or manufacture of computer hardware, computer software, or firmware.

Section 1010(a)(5)(B)(i) covers "loss to 1 or more persons during any 1-year period . . . aggregating at least $5,000 in value" that results from violations of § 1030(a)(5)(A)(i), (ii), or (iii).

[88] 302 F.3d 868 (9th Cir. 2002).

[89] 18 U.S.C. §§ 2510, 2522.

[90] 18 U.S.C. §§ 2701–2711.

communication while it is in transmission. The information on Konop's site was stored, and not transmitted. Therefore, Hawaiian could not have "intercepted" the information within the meaning of the statute.

The appeals court, however, reinstated the plaintiff's claim under the Stored Communication's Act. The trial court had found the defendant exempt from liability under § 2701(c)(2), which allows a person to authorize a third party to access the electronic communication if the person is a user of the service. The appeals court held that there was a question of fact as to whether the registered users from whom the defendant obtained access were indeed "users" within the definition of the statute.

Chapter 7

ENVIRONMENTAL CRIMES

§ 7.01 INTRODUCTION

During the last several decades, environmental issues have risen to the forefront of public awareness. From specific instances of pollution, such as the Exxon Valdez oil tanker spill and the Deepwater Horizon offshore oil platform explosion and spill,[1] to general concerns over global warming and destruction of the ozone layer,[2] environmental policy attracted a new level of public interest. Correspondingly, during these decades, Congress enacted more comprehensive environmental laws, along with stiffer criminal penalties for violating those laws.[3] This chapter examines several of the most important environmental crime statutes, including those relating to hazardous waste,[4] water pollution,[5] and air pollution.[6]

---

[1] In 1989 the Exxon Valdez oil tanker ran aground off the coast of Alaska, spilling 232,000 barrels of oil. The accident resulted in thousands of wildlife casualties and over two billion dollars in cleanup costs. The defendants paid one billion dollars in civil and criminal damages and penalties. For current information relating to this catastrophe, see Exxon Valdez Oil Spill Trustee Council, http://www.evostc.state.ak.us/. In 2010, an explosion on the Deepwater Horizon offshore oil platform in the Gulf of Mexico killed eleven workers and produced the largest marine oil spill in history. *See* Robert Force et al., *Deepwater Horizon: Removal Costs, Civil Damages, Crimes, Civil Penalties, and State Remedies iIn Oil Spill Cases*, 85 Tul. L. Rev. 889 (2011); Peter Jan Honigsberg, Comment, *Conflict of Interest That Led Tto Tthe Gulf Oil Disaster*, 41 Envtl. L. Rep. News & Analysis 10414 (2011). For an overview of applicable criminal laws, see Andrew H. Costinett et al., *Environmental Crimes*, 47 Am. Crim. L. Rev. 441 (2010).

[2] Global warming and the depletion of the ozone layer are linked to the increased use of chloroflourocarbons (CFCs). Most studies link ozone depletion to a rise in Ultraviolet B levels resulting in deleterious effects on plants and aquatic ecosystems and in a rise in global temperatures. *See generally* Steven Ferrey, *The Failure of International Global Warning Regulation to Promote Needed Renewable Energy*, 37 B.C. Envtl. Aff. L. Rev. 67 (2010); Katherine A. Guarino, *The Power of One: Citizen Suits in the Fight Against Global Warming*, 38 B.C. Envtl. Aff. L. Rev. 125 (2011); Bradford C. Mank, *Standing and Global Warming: Is Injury to All Injury to None?*, 35 Envtl L. 1 (2005).

[3] The number of criminal prosecutions for violation of these statutes has varied. Such prosecutions increased dramatically during the 1980s and 1990s, but decreased during the first decade of the 21st century. *See* David R. Berz & Peter D. Isakoff, *Environmental Crimes, in* White Collar Crime: Business and Regulatory Offenses § 14.01 (Otto Obermaier & Robert Morvillo, eds. 2011).

[4] *See* the Resource Conservation Recovery Act (RCRA), 42 U.S.C. §§ 6901–87 and the Comprehensive Environmental Response, Compensation, and Liability Act (CERCLA), 42 U.S.C. §§ 9601–75, discussed *infra* § 7.03.

[5] *See* the Clean Water Act, 33 U.S.C. §§ 1251 *et seq.* and the Refuse Act, 33 U.S.C. §§ 407, 411, discussed *infra* § 7.04.

[6] *See* the Clean Air Act, 42 U.S.C. §§ 7401–91, discussed *infra* § 7.05.

These laws touch on themes found throughout white collar crime. As in other areas, environmental laws may be enforced through administrative, civil, and criminal proceedings, thus blurring the distinction between civil and criminal liability. Further, these laws often do not precisely define the scope of potential criminal liability,[7] and thus raise significant vagueness concerns. The statutes' ambiguities also grant the government substantial discretion in bringing criminal charges. In particular, a prosecutor has wide latitude in deciding whether: (a) a particular environmental crime statute applies to a defendant's conduct; (b) a defendant should be subject to civil and/or criminal proceedings; and (c) a defendant should be charged under other criminal statutes, such as the conspiracy, false statements, or mail/wire fraud statutes, in addition to environmental law charges.[8]

On the other hand, over the years many have argued that environmental regulation has been *under*-criminalized — that the government has not been sufficiently aggressive in prosecuting alleged polluters.[9] Certainly, it is undisputable that environmental pollution has the potential to cause great physical and economic harm. Once again, we can see the tension between the need to protect society against harm — in this instance a quite tangible harm — and the need to enact clearly drafted laws that provide effective notice of potential criminal liability.

Although there are dozens of laws relating to environmental regulation, this chapter focuses on five principal statutes covering hazardous waste, water pollution, and air pollution.[10] With respect to hazardous waste, the Resource Conservation Recovery Act (RCRA)[11] criminalizes acts relating to the transport, storage, and disposal of hazardous waste. The Comprehensive Environmental Response, Compensation, and Liability Act (CERCLA)[12] requires notification of the release of hazardous substances and allows the EPA to require record keeping, and criminalizes violations of these laws and regulations. With respect to water pollution, the Clean Water Act (CWA)[13] and the Refuse Act[14] provide specific criminal penalties. Finally, the Clean Air Act (CAA)[15] provides corresponding penalties for actions relating to air pollution. In addition, states and localities have enacted extensive environmental laws and regulations that may give rise to criminal liability.

---

[7] *See* Joshua D. Yount, *Comment, The Rule of Lenity and Environmental Crime*, 1997 U. Chi. Legal F. 607, 609 (1997) ("the notorious ambiguity of environmental statutes leaves significant discretion to courts, prosecutors, and bureaucrats to resolve textual uncertainty").

[8] RICO has also been used in environmental prosecutions, with mail/wire fraud as the predicate acts. *See id.* at 613–15; Brendan Rielly, *Using RICO to Fight Environmental Crime: The Case for Listing Violations of RCRA as Predicate Offenses for RICO*, 70 Notre Dame L. Rev. 651 (1995).

[9] *See* Jane F. Barrett, *"Green Collar" Criminals: Why Should They Receive Special Treatment?*, 8 Md. J. Contemp. L. Issues 107 (1996-97); Barbara H. Doerr, *Comment, Prosecuting Corporate Polluters: The Sparing Use of Criminal Sanctions*, 62 U. Det. L. Rev. 659 (1985); Margaret K. Minister, *Federal Facilities and the Deterrence Failure of Environmental Laws: The Case for Criminal Prosecution of Federal Employees*, 18 Harv. Envtl. L. Rev. 137 (1994).

[10] For an overview of the statutory scheme, see Oliveira, *supra* note 1.

[11] 42 U.S.C. §§ 6901–87.

[12] 42 U.S.C. §§ 9601–75.

[13] 33 U.S.C. §§ 1251–1387.

[14] 33 U.S.C. §§ 407, 411.

[15] 42 U.S.C. §§ 7401–71.

§ 7.02   COMMON ISSUES IN ENVIRONMENTAL PROSECUTIONS

The criminal enforcement of the various environmental statutes raises a number of common issues. These issues are discussed in more detail in the sections below. When reviewing the case law under the statutes, it will be helpful to keep several overarching concepts in mind.

[A]   Corporate Liability

More than in most other areas of white collar crime, environmental laws often result in criminal liability for corporate actors. Such liability is explicitly stated on the face of the applicable statutes. These laws impose liability on specified "persons," a term defined to include corporations and other entities in addition to individuals.[16] Thus, if a corporate agent violates criminal environmental law provisions, and is acting within the scope of employment and for the corporation's benefit, the corporation may be liable under respondeat superior.[17]

[B]   Individual Liability and the Responsible Corporate Officer Doctrine

Within the scope of "persons" who may be liable for environmental crimes are individual officers, directors, and employees.[18] Such liability may arise even where the individual's actions give rise to entity liability under respondeat superior. Numerous individuals have been prosecuted under the environmental laws, perhaps due to the perception that corporate liability alone does not produce sufficient deterrence.[19]

Of special significance in the environmental area is the "responsible corporate officer doctrine." Under this doctrine, those corporate managers who are responsible for an area of corporate activity and who otherwise possess the mens rea required by the statute may be liable for a violation. Such liability may be imposed instead of, or in addition to, the liability of the person who actually committed the act constituting the violation.[20]

The responsible corporate officer doctrine as applied in the environmental area sometimes has a different meaning than it does under the *strict liability* statutes

---

[16] *See* Oliveira, *supra* note 1, at 353–54.

[17] *See* Chapter 2, Corporate and Individual Liability, *supra* § 2.03[A].

[18] *See, e.g.*, 33 U.S.C. § 1362(5) ("The term "person" means an individual, corporation, partnership, association, State, municipality, commission, or political subdivision of a State, or any interstate body").

[19] *See* Minister, *supra* note 9, at 141–45.

[20] *See generally* Peter C. White, *Environmental Justice Since Hammurabi: From Assigning Risk "Eye for an Eye" to Modern-Day Application of the Responsible Corporate Officer Doctrine*, 29 Wm. & Mary Envtl. L. & Pol'y Rev. 633 (2005); Jeremy D. Heep, *Comment, Adapting the Responsible Corporate Officer Doctrine in Light of* United States v. MacDonald & Watson Waste Oil Co., 78 Minn. L. Rev. 699 (1994); Barry M. Hartman & Charles A. DeMonaco, *The Present Use of the Responsible Corporate Officer Doctrine in the Criminal Enforcement of Environmental Laws*, 23 Envtl. L. Rep. 10145 (March 1993).

that the United States Supreme Court approved in *United States v. Dotterweich*[21] and *United States v. Park*.[22] The term "strict liability" means that a defendant may be found guilty of a crime even when that individual possesses no mens rea.

In the environmental area, the "responsible corporate officer doctrine" works to impose liability on persons whose responsibilities include the relevant corporate activities, but generally does so only where those persons possessed the mens rea required by the statute.[23] As discussed in the next section, these crimes generally require that the defendant have acted with knowledge or, in some cases, negligence.

As is true in other areas, a "responsible" corporate officer is one who possesses supervisory responsibilities for the matter in question. Courts tend to be flexible when interpreting this term. In *United States v. Ming Hong*,[24] for example, the defendant was the owner of a wastewater treatment facility. He was convicted and sentenced for 13 violations under the CWA based on the company's discharge of untreated wastewater. On appeal, the defendant argued that the government failed to prove that he was a responsible corporate officer because he was not an officer of the company and did not exercise the necessary control over its operations. The court rejected the argument, finding that he controlled the company's finances and played a substantial role in operating the company, including the system that produced the discharge.[25] His actual responsibilities, rather than his formal title, determined the outcome.

[C] Mental State

Liability in most felony environmental law prosecutions turns on whether the defendant possessed the requisite mens rea.[26] Most of the statutes discussed here require proof that the defendant acted with "knowledge,"[27] although some only require negligence.[28] As in other areas, knowledge generally means that the defendant knew of the action that gave rise to liability, not that the defendant knew the action violated a specific law; thus "mistake of law" is generally not a defense.

---

[21] 320 U.S. 277 (1943).

[22] 421 U.S. 658 (1975). These cases are discussed in Chapter 2, Corporate and Individual Liability, *supra*, at § 2.07[B].

[23] *See, e.g.*, United States v. MacDonald & Watson Waste Oil Co., 933 F.2d 35, 55 (1st Cir. 1991) (reversing conviction under RCRA where jury instruction had failed to require that the jury find the necessary mens rea).

[24] 242 F.3d 528 (4th Cir. 2001).

[25] *Id.* at 531–32.

[26] Note that not all such felony provisions require proof of mens rea. Under the Migratory Bird Treaty Act, for example, courts have split as to whether the strict liability provisions violate due process. *Compare* United States v. Wulff, 758 F.2d 1121, 1125 (6th Cir. 1985) (requiring some proof of scienter), *with* United States v. Engler, 806 F.2d 425, 431 (3d Cir. 1986) (absence of scienter requirement does not violate due process).

[27] *E.g.*, 42 U.S.C. § 6928(d)(2).

[28] *E.g.*, 33 U.S.C. § 1319(c)(1).

Courts have been less than precise in defining the boundaries of "knowledge." Most courts have held, however, that "willful blindness" will satisfy the knowledge requirement.[29] One frequently litigated issue is whether the knowledge requirement applies to all, or only some, of the elements of the particular statute.

[D] Overlap of Civil and Criminal Liability

Defendants may be subject to both civil and criminal proceedings at both the state and federal levels.[30] As elsewhere, parallel proceedings raise issues concerning a defendant's assertion of the Fifth Amendment right not to testify.[31] Such proceedings also raise tactical issues for the government, which may seek a stay of a civil case in order not to jeopardize an ongoing criminal investigation.[32] Finally, as in areas such as securities law,[33] some environmental statutes also allow suits to be brought by private parties. One significant issue in these cases is what type of circumstances must be present to grant private plaintiffs standing to sue. For example, in *Friends of the Earth, Inc. v. Laidlaw*, the Supreme Court found that petitioners had standing to bring a CWA suit over respondent's discharges.[34] Petitioners alleged that they intended to use the affected area, and that the discharges affected their aesthetic and recreational values.[35] The Court held that civil penalties in such circumstances would have a deterrent effect that made it likely that the penalties would redress the petitioners' injuries. Therefore, the petitioners had standing.[36]

§ 7.03 HAZARDOUS WASTE — THE RESOURCE CONSERVATION AND RECOVERY ACT (RCRA) AND COMPREHENSIVE ENVIRONMENTAL RESPONSE, COMPENSATION, AND LIABILITY ACT (CERCLA)

[A] The Statutory Provisions

The RCRA establishes what is commonly referred to as "cradle-to-grave" EPA regulation of hazardous waste from production to treatment, transportation, and storage.[37] This regulation is primarily effected through extensive record-keeping and handling requirements. These include a system of (a) "manifests," which are

---

[29] *See, e.g.*, United States v. Buckley, 934 F.2d 84, 88 (6th Cir. 1991) (proof that defendant "closed his eyes to obvious facts or failed to investigate when aware of facts which demanded investigation" sufficient to show "knowledge" for Clean Air Act conviction).

[30] *See, e.g.*, United States v. Louisville Edible Oil Products, 926 F.2d 584 (6th Cir.), *cert. denied*, 502 U.S. 859 (1991). *See generally* Oliveira, *supra* note 1, at 350–51.

[31] *See* Chapter 5, Securities Fraud, *supra*.

[32] *See* § 7.06[B], *infra*.

[33] *See* Chapter 5, Securities Fraud, *supra*.

[34] 528 U.S. 167 (2000).

[35] *Id.* at. 183–84.

[36] *Id.*

[37] *See* Oliveira, *supra* note 1, at 404–11.

documents prepared by hazardous waste generators, and (b) permits, which must be obtained by those who deal with hazardous wastes.

CERCLA, which is also known as Superfund, is designed primarily to cover regulation of hazardous waste sites. The Act regulates the clean-up of such sites, and criminalizes the failure to notify the government when certain hazardous substances are released into the environment.[38]

[B] Knowing Violations

[1] Applicability of the Responsible Corporate Officer Doctrine

As noted above, the strict liability scheme for "responsible corporate officers" does not apply to those environmental laws that require proof of mens rea. Most frequently, the required mens rea is knowledge, which the jury must find beyond a reasonable doubt.

In *United States v. MacDonald & Watson Waste Oil Co.*,[39] the court analyzed the level of mens rea that the government must prove under the RCRA. In that case, the individual defendant was charged with transporting hazardous waste to, and disposing of hazardous waste at, a facility that operated without the required permit. A series of events led to the criminal charges. First, a company produced a hazardous chemical that leaked from a storage tank and contaminated the surrounding soil. The contaminated soil constituted hazardous *solid* waste. Second, that company in turn hired a consulting firm to assist in removing the soil. Third, the consulting firm hired MacDonald & Watson to dispose of the waste. Fourth, MacDonald & Watson leased a disposal facility from Narragansett Improvement Co. ("NIC"). The permit for the NIC facility only allowed the disposal of *liquid* hazardous waste and *soils contaminated with nonhazardous waste.* Because the waste at issue was *solid hazardous* waste, it did not fall within the permit. MacDonald & Watson employees arranged for the hazardous soil to be disposed of at the facility, without reporting the release.

Among those charged and convicted based upon this series of events was Eugene K. D'Allesandro, the president and manager of MacDonald & Watson. D'Allesandro was found individually liable for knowingly transporting and disposing of the waste.

The First Circuit reversed D'Allesandro's conviction based upon faulty jury instructions relating to mens rea. The trial judge had instructed the jury that it could find the defendant guilty under the responsible corporate officer doctrine if it found that he (a) was an officer with direct responsibility for the illegal activities and (b) "must have known or believed that the illegal activity of the type alleged occurred."[40]

---

[38] *See id.* at 399–403.

[39] 933 F.2d 35 (1st Cir. 1991).

[40] *Id.* at 50–51.

The government conceded that it had no direct evidence that D'Allesandro actually knew of the specific illegal activity alleged in the case. Under the trial judge's instruction, however, the jury could have convicted if it merely found that the defendant "believed that the illegal activity *of the type alleged occurred.*" Because the jury was not specifically required to find that the defendant knew of the particular transportation and disposal that formed the basis for the charges against him, the appeals court reversed the conviction.[41]

[2] Knowledge of Permit Status

Another issue is whether the requirement of proof that the defendant acted knowingly applies to all the elements of the crime charged. For example, in *United States v. Johnson & Towers*,[42] the defendant corporation and two managers were convicted of violating RCRA § 6928(d)(2)(A). The government alleged that the defendants disposed of hazardous chemical wastes without a permit. Section 6928(d)(2) imposes liability on:

Any person who -

knowingly treats, stores, or disposes of any hazardous waste identified or listed under this subchapter -

(A) without a permit under this subchapter . . . or

(B) in *knowing* violation of any material condition or requirement of such permit; or

(C) in *knowing* violation of any material condition or requirement of any applicable interim status regulations or standards . . . .[43]

The Third Circuit reversed the conviction under Subsection A. Initially, the court concluded that the defendants were "persons" who could be liable under the Act. It further held, however, that the conviction could not stand because the trial court had failed to require that the jury find that the defendants knew that there was no permit. The court acknowledged that Subsection A on its face does not require proof of such knowledge. Because knowledge is required under Subsections B and C, however, the court inferred that such a requirement also applies to Subsection A. The court reached this conclusion on alternate grounds: either (a) the initial knowledge requirement in the prefatory language relating to treatment, storage, and disposal applies to Subsection A; or (b) Congress's omission of the knowledge language from Subsection A was inadvertent.[44]

Other courts have declined to read a knowledge requirement into Subsection A. These courts have reached this conclusion based upon the plain language of the statute. For example, in *United States v. Hoflin*,[45] the Ninth Circuit noted that Congress explicitly omitted the knowledge element for Subsection A while including

---

[41] *Id. Accord,* United States v. White, 766 F. Supp. 873 (E.D. Wash. 1991).

[42] 741 F.2d 662 (3d Cir. 1984), *cert. denied,* 469 U.S. 1208 (1985).

[43] 42 U.S.C. § 6928(d)(2) (emphasis added).

[44] 741 F.2d 662.

[45] 880 F.2d 1033, 1037 (9th Cir. 1989), *cert. denied,* 493 U.S. 1083 (1990).

that element for Subsection B. The court also found that this reading comports with the statute's policy goal of placing upon those who handle hazardous waste the burden of providing the EPA with information about that waste.[46]

A different issue arises under the section of the RCRA that deals with the *transport*, as opposed to the *treatment, storage, or disposal* (as in *Johnson & Towers*) of hazardous waste. The Eleventh Circuit confronted the transport issue in *United States v. Hayes International Corp.*,[47] which arose under § 6928(d)(1). That section imposes criminal liability on "[a]ny person who (1) *knowingly transports* or causes to be transported any hazardous waste identified or listed under this subchapter to a facility which does not have a permit under this subchapter."[48] Hayes International had generated hazardous wastes. L.H. Beasely, the employee responsible for arranging disposal, contracted with another company, Performance Advantage Inc. ("Performance") to perform this task. When the waste was later discovered buried or dumped at illegal disposal sites, Beasely and Hayes International were charged with and convicted of violating the statute.

The trial court granted the defendants' motions for judgments of acquittal notwithstanding the verdicts, and the government appealed. The defendants argued that the government (a) was required to prove that they knew Performance did not have the required permit, and (b) failed to prove such knowledge. As to the first point, the appeals court agreed that the government was required to prove such knowledge, reasoning that this interpretation of the statute comported with Congress's intent to criminalize wrongful conduct. Otherwise, a defendant who was misled by another company as to its permit status could be convicted.[49] The court reinstated the conviction, however, because the record revealed sufficient circumstantial evidence upon which the jury could have concluded that the defendants had the requisite knowledge.[50]

[3] Knowledge of the Nature of the Waste

Courts treat the issue of knowledge of *permit status* differently from knowledge of the *nature of the waste*. As to the latter, courts hold that the government need *not* prove that the defendant knew either that the EPA considered the waste to be hazardous, or that the waste was a particular substance. Instead, the government must only show the defendant knew that the substance was potentially harmful to

---

[46] *See id.* Other circuits have agreed, and have rejected the *Johnson & Towers* holding. *See* United States v. Wagner, 29 F.3d 264, 266 (7th Cir. 1994); United States v. Dean, 969 F.2d 187, 191 (6th Cir. 1992); United States v. Dee, 912 F.2d 741, 745 (4th Cir. 1990); United States v. Hayes International, 786 F.2d 1499, 1502–05 (11th Cir. 1986).

[47] 786 F.2d 1499 (11th Cir. 1986).

[48] 42 U.S.C. § 6928(d)(1) (emphasis added).

[49] *Hayes International*, 786 F.2d at 1504. *Accord,* United States v. Speach, 968 F.2d 795, 796–97 (9th Cir. 1992) (subsection (d)(1) is aimed at those who deliver wastes for treatment and disposal, as opposed to subsection (d)(2), which is aimed at those who themselves treat, store, or dispose of the waste; the latter group should have the burden of providing the necessary information, but the former group could be misled by the recipient).

[50] *See Hayes International*, 786 F.2d at 1500.

the environment.[51] This is in accord with the general principle, applicable to most white collar crimes, that mistake of law is not a defense. Thus, the government is required to prove only that the defendant knew of the conduct constituting the offense, not that the conduct violated the applicable law or regulation.[52]

[C] Knowing Endangerment

The RCRA contains a "knowing endangerment" provision. Section 6928(e) provides punishment for "any person who knowingly transports, treats, stores, disposes of, or exports any hazardous waste identified or listed under [the RCRA] or in violation of [RCRA's criminal provisions] who knows at that time that he thereby places another person in imminent danger of death or serious bodily injury."[53] Section 6928(f)(6) defines "serious bodily injury" as that which involves substantial risk of death, unconsciousness, extreme physical pain, protracted and obvious disfigurement, or protracted loss or impairment of bodily or mental function.[54]

The first appellate decision to interpret these provisions was *United States v. Protex Industries.*[55] In that case, the defendant corporation operated a facility that recycled drums that had contained toxic chemicals. Among other crimes, the indictment charged that Protex knowingly placed three employees in imminent danger of death or serious bodily injury because of its violations of the RCRA. In particular, the government showed that safety provisions did not protect the employees from the dangers of their work, and that the employees were at risk of "solvent poisoning."

On appeal, the defense argued that (a) the trial court's reading of "serious bodily injury" rendered the statute unconstitutionally vague, and (b) the risk of future injuries (including cancer) was not sufficient to constitute "serious bodily injury."[56] As to the first argument, the Tenth Circuit found that the defendants were on notice that their behavior fell within the statute's proscriptions. As to the second, the court responded harshly, noting that the argument "demonstrates a callousness toward the severe physical effect" of the employees' working conditions.[57] The court went on to find that the potential dangers posed by the exposure were more than sufficient to fall within the statute.

---

[51] *See* United States v. Kelley Technical Coatings, Inc., 157 F.3d 432, 440 (6th Cir. 1998); United States v. Goldsmith, 978 F.2d 643, 645–46 (11th Cir. 1992); United States v. Baytank (Houston), Inc., 934 F.2d 599, 612 (5th Cir. 1991); *Hoflin*, 880 F.2d at 1039.

[52] *See, e.g.*, United States v. Laughlin, 10 F.3d 961, 965 (2d Cir. 1993) (government need not prove that the waste has been specifically identified or listed under the RCRA); *Hoflin*, 880 F.2d at 1038 (government need not prove that the defendant knew a permit was lacking).

[53] 42 U.S.C. § 6928(e). The CWA, 33 U.S.C. § 1319(c)(3)(A), contains a similar provision. *See* United States v. Borowski, 977 F.2d 27 (1st Cir. 1992), discussed *infra* § 7.04.

[54] 42 U.S.C. § 6928(f)(6).

[55] 874 F.2d 740 (10th Cir. 1989).

[56] *Id.* at 743–44.

[57] *Id.* at 743.

[D] Individual Liability

As seen above, individuals may be liable under RCRA and CERCLA when they violate the applicable statute with the necessary mens rea. As to the required mental state, evaluation of individual liability entails two steps. First, courts must interpret the statute to determine the requisite mens rea. Second, the fact-finder must evaluate whether the facts support the necessary showing.[58]

Specific statutory violations may also require that other elements be met. For example, Chapter 103 of CERCLA[59] imposes criminal liability on anyone who is "in charge of a facility" that engages in certain releases of hazardous substances and who fails to report a release to the responsible federal agency.[60]

The issue of who is "in charge" of a facility arose in *United States v. Carr*.[61] In that case, the defendant was a civilian maintenance supervisor at a military installation. The defendant had directed workers to dispose of waste improperly, and had failed to report the release. On appeal from his conviction, the defendant argued that he could not be liable because he was only a low-level employee who was not "in charge" of the facility. The Second Circuit rejected the argument. Initially, the court acknowledged that the statute did not define the category of those "in charge" of a facility. Looking then to the underlying purpose of the statute, the court found that CERCLA's reporting requirements are central to the government's hazardous waste control efforts. To effect that purpose, the statute's reporting requirements should be extended to those who are responsible for dealing with such wastes and who are in a "position to detect, prevent, and abate a release of hazardous substances."[62] Because the defendant was in such a position, he could be liable.[63]

Thus, any individual who meets the statutory requirements may be liable. Many of these requirements are quite technical, and require courts to interpret the statute's terms. For example, in *United States v. Fiorillo*,[64] the manufacturer of industrial cleaning products entered into a contract with two disposal companies. The companies improperly disposed of most of the cleaning products, storing them at a facility that lacked the required permit. The defendants were two individuals affiliated with the disposal companies. The defendants were convicted under the RCRA provision applicable to one who "knowingly transports or causes to be

---

[58] *See, e.g.*, United States v. MacDonald & Watson, 933 F.2d 35 (1st Cir. 1991).

[59] 42 U.S.C. § 9603(b)(3).

[60] The term "release" is read quite broadly. For example, in United States v. Freter, 31 F.3d 783, 788 (9th Cir. 1994), the court found that the defendant "released" a hazardous substance when he abandoned sealed drums containing the substance on a property from which he had been evicted.

[61] 880 F.2d 1550 (2d Cir. 1989).

[62] *Id.* at 1554.

[63] *See* Apex Oil Co. v. United States, 530 F.2d 1291, 1294 (8th Cir. 1976), where a similar issue arose under the Water Pollution Control Act (now the Clean Water Act, discussed *infra* § 7.04.). In that case, the corporate defendant argued that it was not a person "in charge" under the Act and could therefore not be held liable. The court rejected the argument based upon the statute's plain language and the statute's purpose of prompting timely reporting of water pollution.

[64] 186 F.3d 1136 (9th Cir. 1999).

transported any hazardous waste . . . to a facility which does not have a permit."[65] On appeal, they argued that the "causes to be transported" provision only applies to those who generate hazardous waste for transport by others. The court generally agreed, but affirmed their convictions. The court found that, because the defendants took responsibility for the waste and transported it to the warehouse where it was stored, they caused the transportation to occur.[66]

[E]   Corporate Parent Liability

In a civil case, *United States v. Bestfoods*,[67] the Supreme Court addressed the CERCLA liability of a corporate parent for its subsidiary's acts. In that case, the United States sought costs for the cleanup of industrial waste generated by the defendant corporation's defunct subsidiary. First, the Court held that, where the corporate veil can be pierced, the parent can be held derivatively liable for its subsidiary's acts.[68] Second, the Court found the parent may also be directly liable where it acted as a facility's "operator or owner" under the terms of CERCLA.[69]

§ 7.04   WATER POLLUTION — THE CLEAN WATER ACT (CWA) AND THE THE REFUSE ACT

[A]   Statutory Scheme

The two water pollution statutes covered in this section raise many issues that parallel those in the previous section, including statutory construction issues relating to mens rea. It is useful to both compare and contrast the hazardous waste statutes discussed above and the water pollution statutes covered in this section.

The CWA, formerly known as the Federal Water Pollution Control Act (FWPCA), is part of the major environmental statutory scheme enacted during the latter part of the 20th century. The CWA regulates pollutant discharges into navigable waters and sets water quality standards for those waters. As in other areas, the CWA regulations operate largely through a system of permits issued by the EPA and by states. The Act provides civil and criminal penalties. The Act grades punishment according to the level of mens rea (knowledge or negligence) the defendant possessed.[70]

The Rivers and Harbors Act (the "Refuse Act") is of much older provenance, having been enacted in 1899 to regulate navigation of waterways. The Act is relevant to antipollution efforts because it prohibits a vessel or onshore site from

---

[65]   42 U.S.C. § 6928(d)(1).

[66]   *Id.* at 1151–52.

[67]   524 U.S. 51 (1998).

[68]   *Id.* at 55. The Court declined to decide whether state law or federal common law should apply to this determination. *Id.* at 64 n.9.

[69]   *Id.* at 55, *citing* 42 U.S.C. § 9601(20)(A)(ii). The Court did not extend its holding to the criminal context.

[70]   *See* 33 U.S.C. § 1319(c)(1)–(4) (knowing violations are felonies; negligent violations are misdemeanors).

discharging "refuse matter of any kind," subject to limited exceptions.[71] In 1966, the Supreme Court defined "refuse" as "all foreign substances and pollutants" set forth in the applicable statutes and regulations.[72]

Most criminal prosecutions for water pollution are brought under the CWA. The typical CWA defendant is charged with having: (a) discharged, (b) a pollutant, (c) from a point source, (d) into navigable waters.[73] As discussed below, the government must prove each of these elements, plus the required mental state. Courts have held that individuals are "persons" who may be held criminally liable under the CWA.[74]

[B] Discharge from a Point Source Under the CWA

The CWA governs discharges from particular, identifiable sources, such as factory outfall pipes; other types of discharges, such as agricultural runoffs over wide areas, are not covered because they are difficult to control and trace.[75] The precise definition of "discharge from a point source" was before the Second Circuit in *United States v. Plaza Health Lab, Inc.*[76] In that case, a blood-testing facility official transported blood vials in his personal car. He unloaded the vials and placed them on the bank of the Hudson River in a location below the high water line. As the river waters rose, they swept the vials into the river. The vials later washed onto a beach, where they were discovered by school children on a field trip. Although no one was injured, a number of the vials were found to be contaminated with the hepatitis-B virus.[77] At trial, the defendant was convicted of knowingly discharging pollutants from a point source without a permit.[78]

On appeal, the court assessed each element of the crime. First, the blood vials met the definition of a "pollutant."[79] Second, the river was a navigable waterway.[80] The case therefore turned on whether there was a "discharge" from a "point source." The defendant argued that no "discharge" occurred. The statute defines the term as "any addition of any pollutant to navigable waters from any point

---

[71] *See* 33 U.S.C. § 407.

[72] United States v. Standard Oil Co., 384 U.S. 224, 230 (1966).

[73] *See generally* Oliveira, *supra* note 1, at 377–86. The term "navigable waters" has been broadly construed to include storm drainage systems that empty into navigable waters. *See* United States v. Eidson, 108 F.3d 1336, 1341–43 (11th Cir. 1997).

[74] *See* United States v. Brittain, 931 F.2d 1413 (10th Cir. 1991).

[75] *See Eidson*, 108 F.3d at 1339; Oregon Natural Desert Association v. Dombeck, 172 F.3d 1092, 1094 (9th Cir. 1998).

[76] 3 F.3d 643 (2d Cir. 1993).

[77] *Id.* at 644.

[78] *Id.* at 643 (*see* 33 U.S.C. §§ 1311, 1319(c)(2)).

[79] 33 U.S.C. § 1362(6) defines "pollutant" to include "dredged spoil, solid waste, incinerator residue, sewage, garbage, sewage sludge, munitions, chemical wastes, *biological material*, radioactive materials, heat, wrecked or discarded equipment, rock, sand, cellar dirt and industrial, municipal and agricultural waste *discharged* into water." (Emphasis added.)

[80] *Plaza Health*, 3 F.3d at 645.

source."[81] A "point source" is in turn defined to include "any discernable, confined and discrete conveyance."[82]

The trial judge had instructed the jury that the definition of a "point source" could include a human being (the defendant). The defendant argued that this definition did not conform to the statute, and the appellate court agreed. In reaching this conclusion, the court relied on the statute's lengthy definition of "point source," which does not include individuals. The court also stated that this reading comports with the purpose of the CWA, which "generally [only] targets industrial and municipal sources of pollutants."[83]

The dissent vigorously disagreed, arguing that the discharge fell within the statute's intended reach because the discharge came from an identifiable, controllable source.[84] The majority's interpretation narrowly construes the statutory language in circumstances where the defendant's conduct was obviously despicable. In this context, it is interesting to compare *Plaza Health* with cases in areas such as securities fraud and mail fraud, where courts have more broadly construed statutes as applied to conduct that is, arguably, less obviously culpable.[85] Line -drawing problems are abundant in white collar crime, far more than in common crime cases. Students of these cases might attempt to ascertain the underlying reasons why courts reach the results they do in these cases.[86]

[C]   Discharge Under the Refuse Act

As noted above, the Refuse Act prohibits a vessel or an onshore facility from discharging "refuse matter" into navigable waterways.[87] The Supreme Court has broadly construed the term "refuse" to include all foreign substances, whether the substance has some commercial value, or whether it is simply discarded material lacking in value.[88]

Each act of discharging refuse gives rise to a separate count under the Refuse Act. Courts have differed, however, in defining an "act" of discharge. In *United*

---

[81] *Id., quoting* 33 U.S.C. § 1362(12).

[82] 3 F.3d at 645, *quoting* 33 U.S.C. § 1362(14). Examples of "point sources" are "any pipe, ditch, channel, tunnel, conduit, well, discrete fissure, container, rolling stock, concentrated animal feeding operation, or vessel or other floating craft from which pollutants are or may be discharged. This term does not include agricultural stormwater discharges and return flows from irrigated agriculture." *Id.*

[83] 3 F.3d at 646.

[84] *Id.* at 650–56 (Oaks, J., dissenting).

[85] *See, e.g.,* United States v. O'Hagan, 521 U.S. 642 (1997) (affirming insider trading conviction under court-adopted theory not appearing in the statute); United States v. Carpenter, 484 U.S. 19 (1987) (affirming mail fraud conviction for violation of fiduciary duty to employer).

[86] It may be that the results in white collar criminal cases often appear inconsistent because the types of "harm" produced in such cases can be very different from the more obvious types of harm produced in common crime cases. *See* J. Kelly Strader, *The Judicial Politics of White Collar Crime*, 50 Hastings L.J. 1199, 1263–67 (1999).

[87] "It shall be not lawful to . . . discharge, or deposit . . . any refuse matter of any kind or description." 33 U.S.C. § 407.

[88] United States v. Standard Oil Co., 384 U.S. 224, 226–27 (1966) (rejecting the argument that gasoline, because it has commercial value, is not "refuse").

States v. Allied Chemical Corp.,[89] for example, the government brought 456 counts under the Refuse Act, one count for each day the defendant discharged pollutants that washed into the James River. In support of a motion to dismiss the charges, the defendant argued that the indictment was "multiplicitous," that is, that it charged a single crime in more than one count.[90] The trial court denied the motion. The court agreed with other courts in rejecting an approach that all discharges within a 24-hour period could only constitute a single "act" of discharge. The court found that the length of time alone did not determine an "act" each interruption and renewal of the discharge would give rise to a separate count. Thus, only upon proof at trial could the court determine the appropriate number of counts.[91]

[D] Required Mental State Under the CWA and the Refuse Act

Under the CWA, a defendant may be convicted based upon a mens rea of knowledge or negligence, depending upon the statutory provision.[92] The Supreme Court has not established the required mens rea under the Refuse Act. Lower courts have treated the Refuse Act as a public welfare offense for which strict liability is appropriate.[93]

[1] Negligent Acts Under the CWA

Courts have rejected challenges to the CWA's imposition of criminal liability based upon negligence. In *United States v. Hanousek*,[94] for example, the defendant failed to use customary care when supervising work on an oil pipeline. The pipeline was later damaged, and discharged oil into an adjacent river. The government charged the defendant for negligent actions under criminal provisions of the CWA, and he was convicted.[95] On appeal, the Ninth Circuit affirmed. The court held that, under the statute's plain language, a defendant can be convicted under the CWA for acting with ordinary negligence. The court further held that, because the CWA is a public welfare statute, this result did not violate the defendant's rights under the Due Process Clause.[96]

---

[89] 420 F. Supp. 122 (E.D. Va. 1976).

[90] *Id.* at 123. Multiplicitous counts implicate the Double Jeopardy Clause, and are forbidden by Rule 7C of the Federal Rules of Criminal Procedure.

[91] *Allied Chemical*, 420 F. Supp. at 124.

[92] *See* Oliveira, *supra* note 1, at 385.

[93] *See id.* at 393.

[94] 176 F.3d 1116 (9th Cir. 1999), *cert. denied*, 528 U.S. 1102 (2000).

[95] 33 U.S.C. §§ 1319(c)(1)(A) & 1321(b)(3). *See* 176 F.3d at 1119.

[96] 176 F.3d at 1119–21.

[2] Mistake of Law Under the CWA

As with the RCRA, prosecutions under the CWA raise issues concerning the definition of "knowledge" under the statute. Under § 1311(a) of the CWA,[97] it is a violation to discharge pollutants into navigable waters without the required permit. Under § 1319(c)(2), it is a felony to "*knowingly* violate § 1311 . . . , or any permit condition."[98]

These provisions were at issue in *United States v. Weitzenhoff.*[99] In *Weitzenhoff*, sewage treatment plant officials violated the governing permit when discharging waste into the ocean. The officials arranged for the discharge to be done in a way that avoided detection by state and federal authorities. In addition, one official instructed another employee to assist in covering up the discharges. Two defendants were each convicted of six counts of violating the CWA.[100]

On appeal, the defendants acknowledged that they authorized the discharges, but argued that the district judge erred in declining to instruct the jury that the government was required to prove that the defendants *knew* their conduct was *unlawful.*[101] The trial court had rejected the defendants' proposed instruction requiring the jury to acquit if it found that the defendants believed that the terms of the applicable permit allowed the discharges.

Examining the legislative history, the Ninth Circuit rejected the defendants' argument. The court found that the term "knowingly" encompasses knowledge of the unlawful act, not knowledge of the law. The court stated, "[b]ecause they speak in terms of 'causing' a violation, the congressional explanations . . . strongly suggest that criminal sanctions are to be imposed on an individual who knowingly engages in conduct that results in a permit violation, regardless of whether the polluter is cognizant of the requirements or even the existence of the permit."[102] Courts have reached similar conclusions under both the RCRA[103] and the CAA.[104]

---

[97] 33 U.S.C. § 1311(a).

[98] 33 U.S.C. § 1319(c)(2) (emphasis added).

[99] 35 F.3d 1275, 1281–82 (9th Cir. 1993).

[100] Under 33 U.S.C. § 1311(a) it is a violation to discharge pollutants into navigable waters without the required permit. Under § 1319(c)(2), it is a felony to "*knowingly* violate § 1311 . . . , or any permit condition." *Id.* (emphasis added).

[101] *Weitzenhoff*, 35 F.3d at 1279.

[102] *Id.* at 1283–84. *Accord*, United States v. Sinskey, 119 F.3d 712, 715–17 (8th Cir. 1997); United States v. Hopkins, 53 F.3d 533, 538–39 (2d Cir. 1995).

[103] *See* United States v. Wagner, 29 F.3d 264, 266 (7th Cir. 1994), and cases cited therein.

[104] *See infra* note 154 (discussion of *Buckley*).

[3] Mistake of Fact Under the CWA

A different issue arises when a defendant argues lack of knowledge of one of the factual prerequisites for conviction. In *United States v. Ahmad*,[105] for example, the defendant was the owner of a gasoline station that had released the contents of a storage tank. The tank's contents, which included both water and gasoline, were pumped into the street and entered the sewage system.[106] Based on these facts, the defendant was charged with knowingly discharging a pollutant and with knowingly operating a "source" (the station) in violation of applicable regulations.

Ahmad 's primary defense at trial was that he believed the released fluid was merely water. The trial court instructed the jury, however, that proof of "knowledge" of the *discharge* meant proof that the defendant knew that the discharge itself occurred. Thus, the court only required the government to prove that the defendant knew *of the discharge*, not that he knew what *substance* (*i.e.*, the gasoline) was being discharged.[107]

On appeal, the defendant argued that the trial court erred in not requiring the government to prove that the defendant actually knew the discharged fluid contained a "pollutant" (the gasoline). The Fifth Circuit agreed with the defendant and reversed the conviction. The court found that the term "knowingly" in § 1319 modifies each substantive element of the offense, including the discharge of a pollutant.[108]

There is thus an important, if sometimes subtle, distinction between (a) knowledge that a particular substance (for example, gasoline as opposed to water) is being discharged, and (b) knowledge that the discharge of the particular substance violates the law. Lack of knowledge in the first example is a mistake of fact that generally will be a defense; lack of knowledge in the latter instance is a mistake of law that generally will not be a defense. By allowing mistake as to a factual element to be a defense, courts protect defendants against prosecutions for accidental discharges. Furthermore, by not allowing mistake of law as a defense, courts conform with the general rule that ignorance of the law is no excuse.[109]

[4] Strict Liability Under the Refuse Act

Courts have interpreted the Refuse Act's misdemeanor provisions to impose strict liability on those who violate the Act.[110] In *United States v. White Fuel Corporation*,[111] for example, the defendant corporation acted promptly and "dili-

---

[105] 101 F.3d 386 (5th Cir. 1996). For a discussion of mens rea issues in environmental prosecutions, see Andrew J. Turner, *Mens Rea in Environmental Crime Prosecutions: Ignorantia Juris and the White Collar Criminal*, 23 Colum. J. Envtl. L. 217 (1998).

[106] *Id.* at 387.

[107] *Id.* at 389.

[108] *Id.* at 389–90.

[109] *See, e.g.*, United States v. Wilson, 133 F.3d 251, 260–62 (4th Cir. 1997); United States v. Sinskey, 119 F.3d 712, 715–16 (8th Cir. 1997).

[110] *See, e.g.*, United States v. White Fuel Corporation, 498 F.2d 619, 622 (1st Cir. 1974).

[111] *See id.*

gently" in response to reports that oil was leaking from its facility into the Boston harbor. Despite the defendant's corrective measures, oil continued to leak into the harbor. The trial court imposed liability under the Refuse Act, finding that the defendant's mental state was irrelevant.

On appeal, White Fuel argued that the government should be required to show that it at least acted negligently. The First Circuit disagreed. First, the court reasoned that Congress had not added such an element to the statute, in contrast to the mens rea requirement added to the then-newly-enacted CWA amendments.[112] Second, the court found that the Refuse Act is designed to deter all discharges, and that imposing a mens rea requirement would undermine this intent.[113] In this respect, the court treated an offense under the Refuse Act as a public welfare offense, the purpose of which is met by strict liability.[114]

[5] Applicability of the Responsible Corporate Officer Doctrine

Courts have also had occasion to apply the responsible corporate officer doctrine under the CWA. In *United States v. Iverson*,[115] for example, the defendant was a corporate executive who was convicted under the CWA in connection with the illegal discharge of the company's wastewater into the local sewer system. On appeal, the defendant argued that the trial court erred in instructing the jury that he could be found liable as a responsible corporate officer. The court instructed the jury that it could convict the defendant if it found beyond a reasonable doubt "(1) [t]hat the defendant had knowledge of the fact that pollutants were being discharged to the sewer system by [company] employees; (2) [t]hat the defendant had the authority and capacity to prevent the discharge of pollutants to the sewer system; and (3) [t]hat the defendant failed to prevent the on-going discharge of pollutants to the sewer system.[116] According to the defendant, the jury should also have been required to find that the defendant "in fact exercis[ed] control over the activity causing the discharge or [had] an express corporate duty to oversee the activity."[117]

The court rejected the argument. Although the CWA does not define "responsible corporate officer," the court noted that Congress was aware of previous judicial decisions broadly defining that term and that Congress approved of those decisions.[118] The court thus concluded that, "[u]nder the CWA, a person is a 'responsible corporate officer' if the person has authority to exercise control over the corporation's activity that is causing the discharges. There is no requirement that the officer

---

[112] *Id.* at 622–23.

[113] *Id.* at 623.

[114] State environmental law statutes may contain similar strict liability provisions. *See, e.g.,* Pennsylvania v. CSX Transportation, Inc., 653 A.2d 1327 (Pa. 1995) (imposition of strict liability does not violate due process).

[115] 162 F.3d 1015 (9th Cir. 1998).

[116] *Id.* at 1022.

[117] *Id.*

[118] *Id.* at 1025, *citing* United States v. Park, 421 U.S. 658 (1975) and United States v. Dotterweich, 320 U.S. 277 (1943). *See* § 2.07[B], *supra*, for a discussion of *Park* and *Dotterwich*.

in fact exercise such authority or that the corporation expressly vest a duty in the officer to oversee the activity."[119] Because the evidence supported a finding that the defendant was a responsible corporate officer under this definition, the court affirmed the conviction.

[E] The CWA Permit Requirement

As in other areas of environmental law, water pollution is monitored and controlled largely through a permit system. The Third Circuit's decision in *United States v. Frezzo Brothers, Inc.*,[120] affirmed the first criminal conviction for a violation of the FWPCA (now the CWA) permit provisions. In that case, a corporation and certain of its officers were charged in connection with a mushroom farming operation. The operation produced pollutants that ran into a waterway. The defendants were convicted both of willfully and negligently discharging the pollutants without the proper permits.[121]

On appeal, the defendants argued that they could not be convicted under the FWPCA because there were no specific regulations governing their industry. The Third Circuit rejected this argument, noting that "the basic policy of the Act is to halt uncontrolled discharges of pollutants." Thus, specific regulations need not be in place in order for the government to criminally enforce actions in violation of this broad policy.[122] The permit requirement seeks to control such pollution, and the EPA cannot be expected to have anticipated or promulgated regulations with respect to all possible types of discharges.[123]

[F] Knowing Endangerment

As under the RCRA,[124] the CWA criminalizes knowing endangerment of persons when the defendant violates certain provisions of the statute. Under CWA § 1319(c)(3), it is a crime knowingly to violate standards for industrial waste discharges in public treatment facilities and thereby knowingly place someone in imminent danger of death or serious bodily injury.

In *United States v. Borowski*,[125] the First Circuit held that this provision only applies to persons at downstream locations, and not to employees who are threatened with endangerment at the facility from which the harmful substance is discharged. The court reasoned that the plant workers were endangered on the job, and that this danger existed whether or not the substances were *discharged.*

---

[119] 162 F.3d at 1025.

[120] 602 F.2d 1123 (3d Cir. 1979), *cert. denied*, 444 U.S. 1074 (1980).

[121] *Id.* at 1125. Note that the willfulness provision has been replaced by a knowledge requirement in the current statute.

[122] *Id.* at 1128.

[123] *See id. See also* Sierra Club v. Cedar Point Oil Co., 73 F.3d 546, 558–65 (5th Cir. 1996) (citizens' suit may be brought even where EPA has not established applicable effluent limitation or permit for "pollutant").

[124] *See supra* § 7.03[C].

[125] 977 F.2d 27 (1st Cir. 1992).

The CWA statutory scheme is designed to cover release of pollutants into the environment, not workplace conditions; the RCRA, but not the CWA, explicitly deals with the latter situation.[126] This result also conforms with the rule of lenity, which requires that ambiguous criminal statutes be interpreted in favor of the defendant.[127]

§ 7.05   AIR POLLUTION — THE CLEAN AIR ACT (CAA)

[A]   Overview of the CAA

The Clean Air Act promotes the establishment of air quality standards and regulation of air pollution sources.[128] The Act delegates to the states the responsibility for creating and implementing programs that meet these requirements.[129] The primary crime under the statute is the emission of a hazardous pollutant in violation of an "emission standard."[130] The Act does not define the term "emission." It does, however, define the term "hazardous air pollutant" by providing an extensive list of air pollutants.[131]

Amendments to the CAA have both established stricter antipollution standards and increased the penalties for and scope of violations of the Act.[132] It is a felony knowingly to violate certain provisions of the Act, knowingly to endanger persons when otherwise violating the Act, and knowingly to make false statements under the Act. The Act also contains a negligent endangerment provision.

[B]   Definition of "Knowledge"

As the foregoing shows, most criminal violations under the CAA require proof that the defendant acted "knowingly."[133] As in other areas, courts must determine whether this term requires knowledge of the law, or knowledge of the acts constituting the violation. In *United States v. Buckley*,[134] the Sixth Circuit followed courts interpreting other environmental statutes and found that knowledge of the law is not required. The court held that the government must prove that the defendant knew "only of the emissions themselves, not knowledge of the statute or of the hazards that emissions pose."[135]

---

[126] *Id.* at 31.

[127] *Id.* at 31–32.

[128] *See* 42 U.S.C. § 7401(b).

[129] *Id.* § 7407(a).

[130] *Id.* § 7412(d).

[131] *See* 42 U.S.C. § 7412(a)(6), (b)(1).

[132] Clean Air Act Amendments of 1990, 42 U.S.C. § 7413.

[133] 42 U.S.C. § 7413.

[134] 934 F.2d 84, 88 (6th Cir. 1991).

[135] *Id.* at 88. Other courts have agreed. *See* United States v. Ho, 311 F.3d 589, 605 (5th Cir. 2002), *cert. denied*, 539 U.S. 913 (2003); United States v. Dipentino, 242 F.3d 1090, 1096–97 (9th Cir. 2001).

Appeals courts generally allow juries to make the mens rea determination. In *United States v. Dipentino*,[136] for example, the president of a company, along with an employee, were convicted under the CAA.[137] The company was hired to supervise the removal of asbestos from a building prior to its demolition, and violated the CAA in doing so. On appeal, the defendants argued that the trial court constructively amended the indictment by instructing the jury that it could convict based upon the defendants' failure to place the asbestos-containing waste material at an appropriate waste disposal site. The court agreed; the indictment charged the defendants under the theory that they had left the debris on surfaces where it was allowed to dry, not under the theory upon which they were convicted.[138] The constructive amendment violated the defendants' Fifth Amendment right to be notified of the charges against them.

The employee then argued that there was insufficient evidence to remand for a new trial. He asserted that the government could not prove that he was an owner/operator as required by the statute, or that he knowingly was responsible for leaving the debris on the floor. The court rejected the argument, finding that he had the requisite "significant or substantial or real control and supervision" over the project.[139] The court also found sufficient evidence that he had knowingly violated the work practice standards because he had seen the asbestos debris on the floor.[140] The court therefore remanded for a new trial.

[C] Judicial Review

The primary crime under the CAA is the violation of an "emission standard." In order to ensure effective enforcement, the CAA by its terms precludes a court in a criminal case from reviewing the validity of the particular emission standard at issue.[141]

The United States Supreme Court interpreted this CAA provision in *Adamo Wrecking Co. v. United States*.[142] In that case, the defendant was charged with violating an emission standard by releasing asbestos during a building demolition. The trial court granted the defendant's motion to dismiss on the ground that the applicable regulation was not an "emission standard."[143] The appeals court reversed, holding that the statute precluded the defendant from arguing that the regulation was not an emission standard.[144]

On appeal, the Supreme Court reinstated the dismissal. Addressing the procedural point of whether the defendant could raise the issue, the Court held

---

[136] 242 F.3d 1090 (9th Cir. 2001).

[137] 42 U.S.C. §§ 7412(f)(4) and (h), 7413(c)(1).

[138] 242 F.3d at 1095.

[139] *Id.* at 1096.

[140] *Id.*

[141] *See* 42 U.S.C. § 7607.

[142] 434 U.S. 275 (1978).

[143] *Id.* at 277–78.

[144] *Id.* at 278.

that the CAA provision prohibiting the challenge of an emission standard did not apply to the determination, in the first instance, of whether the provision at issue actually is an "emission standard." Thus, a trial court could address the defendant's argument. The Court noted, however, that a trial court does *not* have the power to assess either the *merits* of the regulation or the *procedures* that led to its adoption.[145]

Turning to the defendant's substantive argument that the regulation at issue was not an emissions standard, the Court agreed. It held that the standard was a "work product standard" rather than an "emission standard." A work product standard is used when an emission standard is not feasible, such as a requirement prohibiting the release of all asbestos during a building demolition. Because the defendant was not alleged to have violated an "emission standard" upon which criminal liability would be based, the indictment was properly dismissed.[146]

[D] Double Jeopardy Issues

As in other areas of white collar crime, CAA prosecutions may raise issues under the Double Jeopardy Clause. That clause proscribes multiple punishments for the same offense. In particular, the issue may arise in connection with prosecutions of the same conduct (a) under parallel state and federal laws, (b) under different federal laws, and (c) under civil and criminal provisions of the same federal law.[147]

The first two of these issues arose in *United States v. Louisville Edible Oil Products, Inc.*[148] In that case, the federal government charged the defendants under both the CAA and CERCLA for knowingly emitting asbestos during the demolition and renovation of two facilities. A local environmental enforcement agency had previously fined Louisville Edible a total of $174,000 in connection with the emissions. The defendants moved to dismiss on the grounds that (a) the CAA and CERCLA charges amounted to multiple prosecution for the same conduct, and (b) the fines were punitive and therefore constituted previous punishment for the same conduct that formed the basis of the federal charges.

On appeal, the Sixth Circuit rejected both of the defendant's arguments. First, the defendants could be prosecuted under both CAA and CERCLA because they are separate offenses for which the government must prove different elements.[149] Second, the Court rejected the defendant's argument that imposition of the local fines constituted punishment that triggered the Double Jeopardy Clause. In an earlier case, the United States Supreme Court had found that federal civil fines

---

[145] *Id.* at 284–85.

[146] *Id.* at 286–87. Also, EPA-issued regulations must be sufficiently clear to provide fair notice to potential defendants. *See, e.g.*, United States v. Hoechst Celanese Corp., 128 F.3d 216 (4th Cir. 1997) (assessing whether regulations provided fair notice).

[147] *See* Oliveira, *supra* note 1, at 350–51, 360.

[148] 926 F.2d 584 (6th Cir. 1991), *cert. denied*, 502 U.S. 859 (1991).

[149] *Id.* at 588. *See* Blockburger v. United States, 284 U.S. 299 (1932) (Court announced the test, which states that two offenses are the same for double jeopardy purposes unless each statutory provision requires proof of an element the other does not).

imposed by the government after a federal criminal conviction for the same conduct were so severe as to constitute double punishment.[150] In *Louisville Edible*, however, the fines were imposed by the state. Under the dual sovereignty doctrine, both the state/local and federal governments are entitled to enforce their own laws as to same conduct.[151] The court also rejected the defendants' argument that the local agency was acting as "tool" for federal authorities. Thus, the Double Jeopardy Clause was not violated.[152]

§ 7.06 ENFORCEMENT ISSUES

[A] Enforcement Bodies

Criminal investigation and enforcement of the environmental laws are shared by the Environmental Protection Agency's Office of Criminal Enforcement and the Department of Justice's Environmental Crimes Unit. The EPA refers matters to the Department of Justice for possible criminal prosecution.[153] As noted above, the statutes and regulations provide for overlapping administrative, civil, and criminal proceedings. In addition, state and local authorities also often investigate and prosecute environmental crimes.

[B] Parallel Proceedings

As in other areas, the possibility for simultaneous civil/criminal and/or state/federal proceedings against a defendant raises particular concerns.[154] For example, a defendant in parallel civil and criminal proceedings may seek temporarily to halt, or "stay" one of the proceedings. The defendant thus seeks to avoid the choice between (a) testifying in the civil case and waiving the Fifth Amendment right to remain silent even for the purpose of the criminal case, or (b) not testifying and having an adverse inference drawn against the defendant at the civil trial.

Courts generally reject defendants' efforts to stay proceedings that parallel either (a) federal civil proceedings, or (b) civil or criminal proceedings in other

---

[150] The defendants relied upon United States v. Halper, 490 U.S. 435 (1989). The Supreme Court has since disavowed the double jeopardy analysis used in *Halper. See* Hudson v. United States, 522 U.S. 93 (1997), discussed in Chapter 20, Civil Actions, Civil Remedies, and Parallel Proceedings, *infra*, § 20.06.

[151] 926 F.2d at 587–88.

[152] *Id.* at 587.

[153] *See* Berz & Isakoff, *supra* note 3, at § 14.01. The EPA's Office of Criminal Enforcement has specified criteria for use in determining whether a case should be pursued criminally; these focus on the harm to the environment and the culpability of the conduct. *See id.* at § 14.03A.

[154] Issues concerning stays may also involve actions in quite different arenas. In *In re* Commonwealth Oil Refining, 805 F.2d 1175 (5th Cir. 1986), *cert. denied*, 483 U.S. 1005 (1987), the company filed a petition under Chapter 11 of the Bankruptcy Code, which provides for an automatic stay of claims against the debtor. After the filing, the EPA brought an action to compel compliance with environmental laws. The court declined to stay the EPA action, finding that such a stay would not further the purposes of the Bankruptcy Code's stay provisions, which are designed to give the debtor a "breathing spell," and that a stay of the EPA action could produce environmental harm. *Id.* at 1182.

jurisdictions.[155] For example, in *In re Grand Jury Proceedings (U.S. Steel-Clairton Works)*,[156] the appeals court reversed an order that had stayed a federal grand jury investigation pending resolution of state court civil contempt proceeding. The court found that the stay would improperly interfere with the grand jury's function in investigating possible environmental crimes.[157]

[C] Fourth Amendment Issues

As discussed elsewhere,[158] white collar prosecutions generally do not raise the broad scope of search and seizure issues that arise in common crime cases.[159] Occasionally, however, the courts do confront such issues in white collar cases. For example, in *Dow Chemical v. United States*,[160] the defendant challenged the EPA's aerial photographing of the defendant's facilities, arguing that the photography constituted a "search" without a warrant as required by the Fourth Amendment.

The Supreme Court rejected the defendant's argument, holding that the surveillance and photography were not a "search." The Court stated that the EPA's action was similar to the observation of an "open field."[161] Because the EPA surveillance occurred in navigable airspace and used ordinary photography equipment, the defendant could not have reasonably expected that the areas observed would remain private.[162] Therefore, no search occurred, no warrant was required, and the action did not violate the Fourth Amendment.[163]

---

[155] *See* Chapter 20, Civil Actions, Civil Remedies, and Parallel Proceedings, *infra*, § 20.05[D]. *See generally*, Randy S. Eckers, Note, *Unjust Justice in Parallel Proceedings: Preventing Circumvention of Criminal Discovery Rules*, 27 Hofstra L. Rev. 109, 111 n.20 (1998) ("There is no general federal constitutional, statutory, or common law rule barring the simultaneous prosecution of separate civil and criminal actions by different federal agencies against the same defendant involving the same transactions.").

A different issue arises when a private environmental action parallels a federal criminal proceeding. In Barry Farm Resident Council, Inc. v. United States Department of the Navy, 45 E.R.C. (BNA) 1599 (D.D.C. 1997), the government sought to stay such a civil case against it, arguing that the civil case would interfere with an ongoing federal criminal investigation. Balancing the parties' interests, the court found that the plaintiffs had already endured substantial delays. The court also rejected as premature the government's argument that, because witnesses would assert their right to remain silent in light of the criminal investigation, its defense of the civil case would be compromised.

[156] 525 F.2d 151 (3d Cir. 1975).

[157] *Id.* at 155–56. For an extended discussion of this case, see Chapter 20, Civil Actions, Civil Remedies, and Parallel Proceedings, *infra*, § 20.05[D].

[158] *See* Chapter 1, Introduction, *supra*, at § 1.07.

[159] *See* Strader, *supra* note 101.

[160] 476 U.S. 227 (1986).

[161] *Id.* at 235–36, *citing* Oliver v. United States, 466 U.S. 170 (1984) (the government does not need a warrant to observe an "open field" that is beyond a person's home or the area immediately surrounding the home because the observation is not a "search").

[162] 476 U.S. at 238–39.

[163] The defendant also argued that the EPA exceeded its authority in conducting the search. The Court rejected the argument, based upon the statute's plain language. *Id.* at 233–34 (citing 42 U.S.C. § 7414(a)(2)(A)). Similarly, in Boliden Metech, Inc. v. United States, 695 F. Supp. 77 (D.R.I. 1988), the defendant argued that the EPA did not have the authority to obtain a warrant from a federal judicial officer under the Toxic Substance Control Act. The court rejected the argument, finding that Congress's

---

intent and the purpose of the statute allowed such warrants so that the EPA could effectively carry out its functions. *Id.* at 79–80.

Chapter 8

BRIBERY AND GRATUITIES

§ 8.01 INTRODUCTION

Along with the federal extortion law,[1] the federal bribery statutes provide prosecutors with the primary means for targeting government corruption.[2] Over the last twenty years, the Supreme Court has broadly interpreted both the bribery and extortion statutes so as to provide substantially expanded federal jurisdiction over crimes involving state and local political corruption. The expansion of federal power over matters traditionally reserved to state and local law enforcement has been the subject of considerable controversy.[3] This expansion provides federal prosecutors with substantial discretion when deciding whether to assume control over such cases.

There are many federal bribery statutes, but by far the most important is contained in § 201 of the federal criminal code.[4] This statute criminalizes both the receipt of bribes and gratuities by, and the giving of bribes and gratuities to, federal public officials. Unlike the crime of extortion, in which the payer is an innocent victim, with bribery and gratuities both the payer and payee can be charged and convicted.[5] In addition, § 666 of the federal criminal code[6] is an increasingly important section that criminalizes giving and receiving bribes in connection with

---

[1] 18 U.S.C. § 1951(a), discussed in Chapter 9, Extortion, *infra* § 9.07[B] (noting the overlap between the crimes of bribery and extortion under color of official right).

[2] Many other statutes are also used in government corruption cases, such as the mail/wire fraud statutes and the false statements statute. *See* Chapter 4, Mail and Wire Fraud, *supra*, and Chapter 10, False Statements, *infra*.

[3] Indeed, the late Chief Justice Rehnquist spoke directly to this issue. *See Chief Justice Criticizes Trend Toward Federalization of Crime*, 66 U.S.L.W. 2722 (May 26, 1998). For critical commentary, see Sara Sun Beale, *Too Many and Yet Too Few: New Principles to Define the Proper Limits for Federal Criminal Jurisdiction*, 46 Hastings L.J. 979 (1995); Kathleen Brickey, *Criminal Mischief: The Federalization of American Criminal Law*, 46 Hastings L.J. 1135 (1995); Steven D. Clymer, *Unequal Justice: The Federalization of Criminal Law*, 70 S. Cal. L. Rev. 643 (1997); Sanford H. Kadish, *The Folly of Overfederalization*, 46 Hastings L.J. 1247 (1995).

[4] 18 U.S.C. § 201. For examples of other federal bribery statutes, see generally 18 U.S.C. §§ 201 *et seq.* Note that § 201 also criminalizes the bribery of witnesses. This chapter focuses on bribery involving public officials.

[5] *See* Chapter 9, Extortion, *infra*, § 9.07[B], for a comparison of bribery and extortion. Another important bribery statute was enacted by the Foreign Corrupt Practices Act ("FCPA"), Pub. L. No. 95-213, §§ 101–104, 91 Stat. 1494 (1977), *codified as amended at* 15 U.S.C. §§ 78m(b), 78dd-1, 78ff(a) & (c). These provisions, *inter alia*, criminalize bribes paid by United States companies and their agents to foreign officials. For a detailed discussion of the FCPA, see Otto G. Obermaier, Timothy E. Hoeffner & Amy S. Kline, *The Foreign Corrupt Practices Act*, *in* White Collar Crime: Business and Regulatory Offenses §§ 16.01–05 (Otto Obermaier & Robert Morvillo, eds. 2011).

federal programs. This chapter provides a detailed discussion of § 201's bribery and gratuities provisions, and also provides an overview of federal program bribery under § 666. Finally, the chapter provides a brief overview of the anti-bribery provisions of the Foreign Corrupt Practices Act.[7]

§ 8.02 SECTION 201 — STATUTORY OVERVIEW

Section 201 sets forth the distinct crimes of bribery and gratuity, and defines the terms used in those offenses.[8]

[A] Bribery

The crime of bribery, as set forth in § 201(b), provides that one who:

1.　directly or indirectly, corruptly gives, offers or promises anything of value to any public official or person who has been selected to be a public official, or offers or promises any public official or any person who has been selected to be a public official to give anything of value to any other person or entity, with intent -

　　a.　to influence any official act; or

　　b.　to influence such public official or person who has been selected to be a public official to commit or aid in committing, or collude in, or allow, any fraud, or make opportunity for the commission of any fraud, on the United States; or

　　c.　to induce such public official or such person who has been selected to be a public official to do or omit to do any act in violation of the lawful duty of such official or person;

2.　being a public official or person selected to be a public official, directly or indirectly, corruptly demands, seeks, receives, accepts, or agrees to receive or accept anything of value personally or for any other person or entity, in return for:

　　a.　being influenced in the performance of any official act;

　　b.　being influenced to commit or aid in committing, or to collude in, or allow, any fraud, or make opportunity for the commission of any fraud, on the United States; or

　　c.　being induced to do or omit to do any act in violation of the official duty of such official or person;

---

[6]　18 U.S.C. § 666.

[7]　Pub. L. No. 95-213, §§ 101–104, 91 Stat. 1494 (1977), *codified as amended at* 15 U.S.C.S. §§ 78m(b), 78dd-1, 78ff(a) & (c).

[8]　Omitted portions of § 201 criminalize bribery and gratuities in connection with federal witnesses.

* * *

shall be fined under this title or not more than three times the monetary equivalent of the thing of value, whichever is greater, or imprisoned for not more than fifteen years, or both, and may be disqualified from holding any office of honor, trust, or profit under the United States.

[B] Gratuity

The crime of gratuity, as set forth in § 201(c), provides that one who:

1. otherwise than as provided by law for the proper discharge of official duty -

    a. directly or indirectly gives, offers, or promises anything of value to any public official, former public official, or person selected to be a public official, for or because of any official act performed or to be performed by such public official, former public official, or person selected to be a public official; or

    b. being a public official, former public official, or person selected to be a public official, otherwise than as provided by law for the proper discharge of official duty, directly or indirectly demands, seeks, receives, accepts, or agrees to receive or accept anything of value personally for or because of any official act performed or to be performed by such official or person;

* * *

shall be fined under this title or imprisoned for not more than two years, or both.

[C] Statutory Definitions

Section 201(a) defines the terms used in the bribery and gratuity provisions:

1. the term "public official" means Member of Congress, Delegate, or Resident Commissioner, either before or after such official has qualified, or an officer or employee or person acting for or on behalf of the United States, or any department, agency or branch of Government thereof, including the District of Columbia, in any official function, under or by authority of any such department, agency, or branch of Government, or a juror;

2. the term "person who has been selected to be a public official" means any person who has been nominated or appointed to be a public official, or has been officially informed that such person will be so nominated or appointed; and

3. the term "official act" means any decision or action on any question, matter, cause, suit, proceeding or controversy, which may at any time be pending, or which may by law be brought before any public official, in such official's official capacity, or in such official's place of trust or profit.

Each of these definitions has been the subject of judicial interpretation, and is discussed in more detail below.

§ 8.03 ELEMENTS OF BRIBERY AND GRATUITY UNDER § 201

[A] Bribery

The elements of the crime of *giving or offering to give* a bribe are:

1. The defendant gave or offered to give something of value;

2. The recipient or offeree was (or was selected to be) a federal public official;

3. The defendant acted with corrupt intent; and

4. The defendant's scheme was designed to -

    (a) influence the public official in an official act,

    (b) influence the public official to commit a fraud on the United States, or

    (c) induce the public official to act in violation of a lawful duty.

The elements of the crime of *receiving or agreeing to receive* a bribe are:

1. The defendant received or agreed to receive something of value;

2. The defendant was (or was selected to be) a federal public official;

3. The defendant acted with corrupt intent; and

4. The scheme was designed to -

    (a) influence the defendant in an official act.,

    (b) **influence the defendant to commit a fraud on the United States, or**

    (c) induce the defendant to act in violation of a lawful duty.

In one sense, bribery is an inchoate crime; it is complete when the payment is either offered or requested, even if the criminal objective is never achieved. Thus, in a bribery case, the payment need not actually influence the public official so long as it was offered or requested with the necessary intent.

[B] Gratuity

The elements of the crime of *giving or offering to give* an illegal gratuity are:

1. The defendant gave or offered to give something of value;

2. The recipient or offeree was (or was selected to be) a federal public official; and

3. The defendant intended that the thing of value be given as compensation for an official act already performed or to be performed otherwise than as provided by law for the proper discharge of the defendant's official duty.

The elements of the crime of *receiving or agreeing to receive* an illegal gratuity are:

1. The defendant received or agreed to receive something of value;

2. The defendant was (or was selected to be) a federal public official; and

3. The defendant received or agreed to receive the thing of value as compensation for an official act already performed or to be performed, otherwise than as provided by law for the proper discharge of the defendant's official duty.

[C] Sentencing

Because a gratuity involves merely giving a gift, while bribery involves using "corrupt" influence on an official act, gratuity is punished much less severely than bribery. Currently, gratuity is punished by up to two years in prison, bribery by up to fifteen years in prison. Of course, the actual sentence will depend upon the application of the Federal Sentencing Guidelines, and upon the trial court's application of those guidelines, to the particular case.[9]

[D] Comparison of Bribery and Gratuity

[1] Intent and Quid Pro Quo

The party's intent provides the key distinction between bribery and gratuity. The essence of the crime of bribery is the intent that the public official be influenced in a particular way in connection with a particular official act. In essence, the briber says, "I'll give you this money as a *quid pro quo, i.e.,* I will give you this, and in exchange you agree to do that particular act." The crime of gratuity, on the other hand, requires no *quid pro quo.* Instead, the crime only requires that the payment be intended as compensation for an official act; it does not require an intent to influence or be influenced in a particular way. The criminalization of gratuities is thus premised on the appearance of improper influence, without requiring proof of an intent to corrupt a particular government action.[10]

---

[9] 18 U.S.C. §§ 201(b) & (c). *See* Chapter 21, Sentencing, *infra.*

[10] In United States v. Sun-Diamond Growers, 526 U.S. 398 (1999), the Supreme Court succinctly delineated the difference between the intent to commit bribery and the intent to pay or receive an illegal gratuity:

> Bribery requires intent "to influence" an official act or "to be influenced" in an official act, while illegal gratuity requires only that the gratuity be given or accepted "for or because of" an official act. In other words, for bribery there must be a *quid pro quo* — a specific intent to give or receive something of value in exchange for an official act. An illegal gratuity, on the other hand, may constitute merely a reward for some future act that the public official will take (and may already have determined to take), or for a past act that he has already taken. The punishments prescribed for the two offenses reflect their relative seriousness.

Id. at 404–05.

The distinction between the intent to give or receive a bribe and the intent to give or receive an illegal gratuity is fuzzy. In fact, courts generally hold that gratuity is a lesser-included offense of bribery,[11] and the government often includes a gratuity charge in a bribery case. As in other areas of the criminal law (*e.g.*, the distinction between murder and manslaughter), the issue must be determined by the jury. This leaves the jury to decide whether a defendant's intent amounted to bribery, gratuity, or neither.

[2] Intent and Timing

One clear distinction between the two crimes relates to timing. If a defendant formulates an intent to give the payment knowing that the public official has *already* performed or decided to perform the official act, then only a gratuity charge is appropriate. In that circumstance, the defendant could not intend that the public official be influenced in connection with that act because the decision has already been made. As one court stated, "[b]ribery is entirely future-oriented, while gratuities can be either forward or backward looking. In other words, whereas bribery involves the present giving, promise, or demand of something in return for some action in the future, an unlawful gratuity can [relate to past, present, or future actions]."[12] It is the timing of the formulation of intent to pay that is key, not the timing of the payment itself. One could, for example, agree to pay a bribe before an official act occurs, but actually make the payment after the act.

How do we distinguish bribery and gratuity in the situation where one pays a public official *before* an official action is undertaken? In this situation, one approach would be to define a gratuity as a gift given with the expectation that the public official will be more likely to act in a specific way in connection with a specific official act.[13] Thus, a mere expectation — as opposed to an agreement — would give rise to a gratuity charge but not a bribery charge. Whether the party acted with a mere expectation, or whether the party believed that there was a specific agreement, would be a jury question.

Another approach would hold that a gratuity in the context of a future action is simply a reward for an action the public official has *already* decided to undertake. If the official has not yet made a decision, then only a bribery charge is appropriate.[14] Courts are split as to which approach is the better one.[15]

---

[11] *See, e.g.*, Valdes v. United States, 475 F.3d 1319 (D.C. Cir. 2007) (en banc); United States v. Alfisi, 308 F.3d 144, 152 (2d Cir. 2002).

[12] United States v. Schaffer, 183 F.3d 833, 841 (D.C. Cir. 1999). *See* United States v. Campbell, 684 F.2d 141, 148 (D.C. Cir. 1982).

[13] *See* Charles B. Klein, *What Exactly is Is an Unlawful Gratuity After* United States v. Sun-Diamond Growers?, 68 Geo. Wash. L. Rev. 116, 122 (1999).

[14] *See id.*, and cases cited therein.

[15] *See id.*

§ 8.04   DEFINITION OF "SOMETHING OF VALUE" UNDER § 201

The government must show that a defendant in a bribery or gratuity case offered to give or receive "something of value." Courts have broadly interpreted this term. For example, in *United States v. Williams*,[16] the Second Circuit found that "value" is measured by the defendant's subjective view, not by an objective measure. That case grew out of the widely-publicized "Abscam" government sting operation. As part of the sting, a United States Senator received stock in exchange for using his official influence to secure government contracts. Although the stock was worthless, the defendant's belief that it had value evidenced his corrupt intent to be influenced in his official capacity.

Similarly, in *United States v. Gorman*,[17] the defendant was a government official convicted under the gratuity statute. The conviction was based upon the defendant's receipt of a loan and of a promise of future employment. On appeal, he argued that these things had no value because he fully repaid the loan with interest, and any salary received in the course of the employment would be in return for his services. The Sixth Circuit upheld the conviction, finding that the defendant's financial position at the time he received the loan would have prevented him from receiving such a loan from a financial institution, and that the promised employment was at a substantially higher salary than his government position. Therefore, these items had "value" to the defendant.[18]

§ 8.05   DEFINITION OF FEDERAL "PUBLIC OFFICIALS" UNDER § 201

Under the bribery and gratuity statutes, the intended recipient of the "thing of value" must be a federal public official. Any federal officer or employee will generally qualify.[19] Whether a defendant qualifies as a public official is more likely to be an issue where the defendant is not officially employed by the United States government.

[A]   Employees of Entities Other than the Federal Government

The Supreme Court defined the term "public official" in *Dixson v. United States*.[20] In that case, the city of Peoria received federal housing block grants. The city then turned over a portion of those funds to a private not-for-profit corporation charged with administering those funds. The defendants were employees of the corporation, and were convicted of receiving bribes under § 201.

---

[16]   705 F.2d 603, 622–23 (2d Cir.), *cert. denied*, 464 U.S. 1007 (1983).

[17]   807 F.2d 1299, 1304–05 (6th Cir. 1986), *cert. denied*, 484 U.S. 815 (1987).

[18]   *Id.* at 1305. *See also* United States v. Biaggi, 909 F.2d 662, 684 (2d Cir. 1990) (promise of future employment may qualify as a thing of value if in exchange for specific official act).

[19]   *See* 18 U.S.C. § 201(a)(1).

[20]   465 U.S. 482 (1984).

On appeal, the defendants argued that the conviction could not be sustained because they were employees of a private corporation and were not federal "public officials." In a five-to-four decision, the Court rejected their argument, finding that Congress intended that the term "public official" be broadly interpreted. The majority framed the issue as whether the defendants "occupie[d] a position of public trust with official federal responsibilities."[21] The Court answered in the affirmative: "[T]hese . . . officials hold precisely the sort of positions of national public trust that Congress intended to cover . . . . The Federal Government has a strong and legitimate interest in prosecuting petitioners for their misuse of Government funds."[22] The dissent found that the majority's broad reading of the statute was justified neither by the statute's language nor by congressional intent.[23]

The *Dixson* test for defining the term "public official" — "whether the person occupies a position of public trust with official federal responsibilities" — hardly provides a bright line rule. As one commentator has noted, the *Dixson* defendants were two steps removed from the federal government — the City of Peoria was not part of the federal government, nor was the private corporation for whom the defendants worked.[24] Thus, the *Dixson* test provides a standard that is often difficult to apply. The decision also presents vexing issues of federal intrusion into local corruption.

To date, lower courts applying *Dixson* have found that private actors and state and local employees are federal "public officials" if they have any responsibilities relating to federal matters.[25] Examples of persons found to be federal "public officials" under the *Dixson* test include a state deputy sheriff with authority over federal and state prisoners in a county jail,[26] a director of a city housing authority funded with both state and federal money,[27] and a low-level corporate employee responsible for determining eligibility for federally-subsidized housing.[28]

---

[21] *Id.* at 496. The majority relied upon Congress's approval of the result in *United States v. Levine*, 129 F.2d 745 (2d Cir. 1942), where the defendant worked for a locally-administered federal program, but was not a federal employee. *Id.* at 747.

[22] 465 U.S. at 500–01. Justice Marshall, generally a pro-defendants' rights justice, wrote the pro-government majority opinion.

[23] *Id.* at 501. Justice O'Connor wrote the dissent, which was joined by Justices Brennan, Rehnquist, and Stevens, an unusual criminal dissent alignment. The dissent rejected the majority's interpretation of the *Levine* decision, noting that "[t]he individual involved in *Levine* was an employee of a person appointed by the Federal Government to carry out a federally defined regulatory task. As an employee of an agent of the United States, he was obviously acting for the United States. An employee of a grantee or subgrantee of the United States [as in *Dixson*] is in a quite different position." *Id.* at 503 (O'Connor, J., dissenting). Students of the *Dixson* opinion might query whether the dissent indeed has a valid point.

[24] *See* Kenneth R. Feinberg, *The Federal Law of Bribery and Extortion: Expanding Liability, in* White Collar Crime: Business and Regulatory Offenses § 3.04[1] (Otto Obermaier & Robert Morvillo, eds. 2011).

[25] *See* Stephanie E. Lapidus & Mariya Mogilevich, *Public Corruption*, 47 Am. Crim. L. Rev. 915, 921–22 (2010).

[26] United States v. Velazquez, 847 F.2d 140, 142 (4th Cir. 1988).

[27] United States v. Strissel, 920 F.2d 1162, 1165–66 (4th Cir. 1990).

[28] United States v. Hang, 75 F.3d 1275, 1279–80 (8th Cir. 1996).

[B]   Participants in the Legislative Process

Courts have not hesitated to apply the bribery statute to members of Congress and to others, such as lobbyists, who participate in the legislative process. For example, in *United States v. Anderson*,[29] the government alleged that a lobbyist made payments to United States Senator Daniel Brewster in return for Brewster's agreement to vote in a manner favorable to the lobbyist's employer. The jury convicted Anderson, the lobbyist, of bribery, and convicted the Senator of receiving an illegal gratuity. On appeal, Anderson argued that the trial judge should have instructed the jury that lobbying efforts are not corrupt, and that lobbyists are paid to try to influence legislators. The District of Columbia Circuit rejected the argument on the ground that the proposed instructions could have misled the jury into believing that lobbying activities can never violate the bribery statute. Here, because there was sufficient evidence that the defendant made the payments intending to influence the Senator's actions, there was sufficient evidence to convict.[30]

In a related case, *United States v. Brewster*,[31] the Supreme Court reinstated Senator Brewster's bribery and gratuity indictment over his objection that he was immunized from such prosecution under the United States Constitution's Speech and Debate Clause. That clause provides: "[F]or any Speech or Debate in either House [of Congress, Senators or Representatives] shall not be questioned in any other place." The Court found that the clause only protects "legislative acts," which it defined as "those things generally said or done in the House or the Senate in the performance of official duties," as well as the motivation for those acts.[32]

The clause was not, the Court found, intended to provide blanket immunity for all acts in which a legislator might engage. Taking a bribe or receiving a gratuity does not constitute a legislative act, and proof of those crimes in this case did not require the government to rely upon a particular legislative act or the motivation for that act. In other words, in its case the government could not rely on "any showing of how [the Senator] acted, voted, or decided."[33] So long as the government proved that the Senator agreed to receive the payment with the necessary corrupt intent, then it could meet its burden without any inquiry into how the Senator actually voted or his motivation for that vote.

§ 8.06   DEFINITION OF "OFFICIAL ACT" UNDER § 201

In a bribery case, the government must show that the bribing party intended to influence a public official in an "official act." Likewise, in a gratuity case, the government must show that the payment was intended as compensation for an "official act." Section 201(a) defines an "official act" as "any decision or action on any

---

[29] 509 F.2d 312 (D.C. Cir. 1974).

[30] *Compare* United States v. Helstoski, 442 U.S. 477, 488–89 (1979) (the Speech and Debate Clause prohibits the government in a bribery or gratuities case from using evidence of a legislative act).

[31] 408 U.S. 501 (1972).

[32] *Id.* at 512.

[33] *Id.* at 527.

question, matter, cause, suit, proceeding or controversy, which may at any time be pending, or which may by law be brought before any public official, in such official's official capacity, or in such official's place of trust or profit." Determining whether there is an official act requires an assessment both of the parties' intent and of the scope of the public official's duties.

[A] The Parties' Intent

One key to determining the "official act" element is the *intent* behind the illegal scheme — not the actual performance of the "official act." Thus, it is sufficient if the bribing party believed that the public official would be influenced in an official act, even if the public official never intended to be so influenced and never undertook the official act. And if the public official understands that the bribing party has that belief, then the public official is likewise culpable.

The Seventh Circuit applied these principles when affirming the bribery conviction in *United States v. Arroyo.*[34] In that case, the defendant was a United States Small Business Administration loan officer who solicited a cash payment from a loan applicant in return for a loan approval. At the time he solicited the payment, Arroyo had already approved the loan, and thus could not actually be influenced in his decision.

On appeal, the defendant argued that he could not be convicted of bribery because he could not actually be influenced in his official act, given that he had already undertaken the act when he solicited the alleged bribe. The Seventh Circuit rejected the argument. The key point, the court noted, is the defendant's understanding of "what the payer believes he is paying for."[35] Arroyo understood that the bribe payer (the loan applicant) believed that Arroyo would be influenced in his official decision; that is all the statute demands.[36]

Thus, a defendant may be convicted of giving or receiving a bribe even if the public official had no intention of being influenced, or in fact could not be influenced, in an official act.[37]

[B] The Scope of the Public Official's Duties

Courts have interpreted the term "official act" to include acts that were not formally within the public official's duties. So long as the public official had the power to influence a pending official matter, the official act element is met. For example, in *United States v. Parker,*[38] the defendant was employed by the United States Social Security Administration. In exchange for money, she helped applicants obtain benefits to which they were not entitled. On appeal, the defendant argued that the payments were not made for official acts because her official duties did not encompass the authority to grant or deny the benefits. The

---

[34] 581 F.2d 649 (7th Cir. 1978), *cert. denied,* 439 U.S. 1069 (1979).

[35] *Id.* at 655.

[36] *Id.*

[37] *See generally* Lapidus, et al., *supra* note 25, at 923.

[38] 133 F.3d 322 (5th Cir. 1998).

court rejected the argument. The court concluded that "the term 'official act' encompasses use of governmental computer systems to fraudulently create documents for the benefit of the [public official] for compensation, even when the [public official's] scope of authority does not formally encompass the act."[39]

On the other hand, if the matter does not involve some kind of official determination, then the official act element will not be met. If a public official receives something of value in a purely private venture, for example, there is no "official act." In *United States v. Muntain*,[40] the defendant was an employee of the United States Department of Housing and Urban Development ("HUD") who had labor relations responsibilities. He was convicted under the gratuity statute for his part in a private scheme to sell group automobile insurance policies to labor unions. Muntain used his HUD contacts to further this scheme, and in return received certain things of value.

The District of Columbia Circuit reversed the conviction. The court held that the private insurance scheme did not involve "any question, matter, cause, suit, proceeding or controversy which by law might have been brought before Muntain in his official capacity."[41] The court noted that the essence of § 201 is "the corruption of official decisions through the misuse of influence in governmental decision-making," a concern not raised by Muntain's conduct.[42]

The court also reversed the conviction in *Valdes v. United States*.[43] *In Valdes*, an undercover agent paid the defendant, a District of Columbia police detective, as a reward for the defendant's search of a police database. In a split decision, the *en banc* D.C. Circuit reversed the gratuities conviction. Citing *Muntain*, the court held that the official act element was not met. All the defendant did was to disclose the information; his actions did not involve, in the language of the statute, "any decision or action . . . which may at any time be pending." The dissent argued that the defendant's actions fell within the scope of his official duties, and that the actions therefore qualified as "official acts."[44] A concurring opinion emphasized that Valdes had originally been charged with bribery but was convicted instead of the lesser-included offense of gratuities. A bribery conviction could have been affirmed under the theory that the bribe was paid to induce the defendant to act in

---

[39] *Id.* at 326. A court may find a federal "official act" even if the conduct of the federal official was directed to state or local officials. For example, in United States v. Biaggi, 853 F.2d 89, 98–99 (2d Cir. 1988), a company that was doing business with a city was having financial difficulties. In return for a bribe, a congressperson wrote the city's mayor a letter on congressional stationery urging that the city take action favorable to the company. The court deemed such an action to be an "official act."

[40] 610 F.2d 964 (D.C. 1979). The gratuity statute at issue in *Muntain*, 18 U.S.C. § 201(g), has since been recodified at 18 U.S.C. § 201(c).

[41] 610 F.2d at 967.

[42] *Id.* at 968. The court did label Muntain's conduct otherwise "reprehensible," presumably because he used government contacts to further his own financial goals while still federally employed. The court was concerned about the apparent impropriety of a government official engaging in such activities on taxpayers' time.

[43] 475 F.3d 1319 (D.C. Cir. 2007) (en banc).

[44] *Id.* at 1333 (Garland, J., dissenting).

violation of his "official duty" under § 201(b)(2)(C).[45]

In *Muntain* and *Valdes*, the D.C. Circuit read the official act element quite narrowly. The Second Circuit in *Parker*, however, took a more expansive approach. The decisions can be read as consistent — only in *Parker* did the defendant actually undertake to make a federal "decision," that is, to award the social security benefits. Nonetheless, the decisions do not provide clear guidelines for determining when an official act is present. The United States Supreme Court has yet to provide a more specific definition of the term "official act."

§ 8.07 DEFINITION OF CRIMINAL INTENT UNDER § 201

[A] Bribery

In proving bribery, the government must show that the bribe giver or receiver acted "corruptly." As is generally the case in white collar crime, there is rarely direct evidence of corrupt intent. Typically, the government must prove corrupt intent through circumstantial evidence.

To a large extent, the corrupt intent requirement is met simply by showing that the payment was given or received with the understanding that it was designed to influence an "official act."[46] Courts often describe this as a *"quid pro quo"* requirement; the parties must have specifically intended that the payment be given in exchange for influence over an official act.[47] Again, the government is not required to show that the bribe achieved the desired result. In that regard, bribery is an inchoate, or incomplete, crime.

As discussed more fully in connection with the crime of extortion,[48] troublesome issues arise when the government's case requires that it prove corrupt intent in connection with the payment of campaign contributions. Here, the trier of fact must distinguish between a legitimate campaign contribution, which is made with the mere hope or expectation that the public official will act in the way that the donor desires, and illegal bribery, which is made with the specific understanding that the public official will be influenced in a particular way in connection with a specific official act.[49]

Significantly, it is quite possible for parties to a bribery or gratuity scheme to have different intents. For example, in *Anderson*,[50] the corporate lobbyist and the United States Senator were both charged with bribery and gratuity in connection

---

[45] *Id.* at 1330 (Kavanaugh, J., concurring).

[46] *See supra* § 8.06.

[47] *See* Lapidus, et al., *supra* note 25, at 923.

[48] *See infra* § 9.07[C].

[49] *See* United States v. Tomblin, 46 F.3d 1369, 1379 (5th Cir. 1995) ("a jury instruction must adequately distinguish between the lawful intent associated with making a campaign contribution and the unlawful intent associated with bribery"). *Cf.* Biaggi, 909 F.2d 662, 683 (a payment having both lawful and unlawful purposes may be found to constitute a bribe because "[a] valid purpose that partially motivates a transaction does not insulate participants in an unlawful transaction from criminal liability").

[50] 509 F.2d at 316.

with payments the lobbyist made to the Senator. The jury convicted Anderson of bribery, but acquitted Brewster of that charge and instead convicted him of unlawfully receiving gratuities.

On appeal, Anderson argued that these verdicts were fatally inconsistent and required reversal of his conviction. Noting that inconsistent verdicts do not automatically require reversal, the court found that in any event the verdicts were not inconsistent. As the Court stated, "[t]he payment and the receipt of a bribe are not interdependent offenses, for obviously the donor's intent may differ completely from the donee's. Thus, the donor may be convicted of giving a bribe despite the fact that the recipient had no intention of altering his official activities, or even lacked the power to do so."[51] The key is the parties' understanding, which may differ on the facts of a particular case.

One interesting issue arises where the public official effectively coerces the payment of the bribe. For example, in *United States v. Alfisi*,[52] the defendant worked for a produce wholesaler. The government charged Alfisi with bribery based upon payments he had made to a federal food inspector. Alfisi's defense was that the inspector had extorted the payments, which Alfisi made to ensure that the inspector would simply do his job properly.

On appeal, Alfisi asserted that the jury should have been required to find that he intended to induce some *quid pro quo* beyond the inspector's mere performance of his ordinary duties. The majority rejected the argument, and affirmed the conviction. The majority found that the defendant's conduct fell within the literal language of the statute, and held that to exclude the conduct would create a loophole whenever a person has paid a public official in exchange for favorable treatment.[53] The dissent sharply disagreed, arguing that "a payment made in the course of a shakedown where the public official demands payment as a *quid pro quo* for proper execution of his duty is *not* a bribe."[54] Both arguments carry some weight, but the majority may be correct that a coercion exclusion would open the door to an array of defenses that Congress may not have intended.

[B] Gratuity

The gratuity statute on its face requires that the alleged illegal payment be made "for or because of any official act performed or to be performed by such public official." Prior to the Supreme Court's decision in *United States v. Sun-Diamond Growers*,[55] some courts had interpreted the statute to criminalize *any* payment made to a public official because of the official's general ability to engage in official acts.

---

[51] *Id.* at 332.

[52] 308 F.3d 144 (2d Cir. 2002).

[53] *Id.* at 150–52.

[54] *Id.* at 155 (Sack, J., dissenting) (emphasis in original).

[55] 526 U.S. 398 (1999).

In *Sun-Diamond Growers*,[56] the Supreme Court unanimously rejected this broad reading of the intent element of the gratuity statute. Sun-Diamond was a trade association that engaged in marketing and lobbying on behalf of its members. The government charged Sun-Diamond with paying illegal gratuities to former Secretary of Agriculture Michael Espy. At the time of the payments, two matters of importance to Sun-Diamond members were pending before Secretary Espy.[57] The government did not, however, allege or prove that there was a specific connection between these particular official matters and the things of value given to Espy.[58]

In reversing the conviction, the Court focused on the statutory requirement that the thing of value be given to a public official "for or because of any official act performed or to be performed by such public official." Based on this language, a conviction cannot rest on proof that the defendant merely gave something of value in order to create goodwill and to possibly affect future official acts.[59] Moreover, the government's proposed interpretation would lead to absurd results, by criminalizing all token gifts made to public officials but not linked to specific official acts. Finally, the Court noted that Congress has banned all gifts in other contexts, and contrasted the language of those statutes with that of the gratuity statute. Thus, to obtain a gratuity conviction, the government must show that the party intended to make the payment for specific official acts.

Courts grant the government broad leeway in proving intent to pay or receive an illegal gratuity. For example, in *United States v. Campbell*,[60] the government's theory was that the defendant, a judge, gave lenient treatment on traffic tickets to a company that later provided him with free moving services. The defendant argued on appeal that, because he actually paid $60 for the move and offered to reimburse other expenses, there was insufficient evidence that he intended to receive the moving services as payment for lenient treatment. The court rejected the argument, finding that the jury could have concluded the $60 was merely a tip, and that Campbell accepted the gift knowing that it was intended as compensation for his past acts.

---

[56] *Id.*

[57] *Id.* at 401. The alleged "things of value" were "tickets to the 1993 U.S. Open Tennis Tournament (worth $2,295), luggage ($2,427), meals ($665), and a framed print and crystal bowl ($524)."

[58] *Id.* at 403. The trial judge told the jury that "[t]he government need not prove that the alleged gratuity was linked to a specific or identifiable official act or any act at all."

[59] *Id.* at 405–06.

[60] 684 F.2d 141 (D.C. Cir. 1982).

§ 8.08   FEDERAL PROGRAM BRIBERY

[A]   Statutory Overview

Section 666 of the criminal code was enacted to extend the reach of bribery prosecutions, where federal money is involved, beyond federal public officials.[61] Although the statute covers activities that § 201 does not reach, the two sections substantially overlap given *Dixson's* expansive definition of the term "federal official."[62]

The key portion of § 666 applies to:

(a)   Whoever, if the circumstance described in subsection (b) of this section exists -

     (1)   being an agent of an organization, or of a State, local, or Indian tribal government, or any agency thereof -

           * * *

     (B)   corruptly solicits or demands for the benefit of any person, or accepts or agrees to accept, anything of value from any person, intending to be influenced or rewarded in connection with any business, transaction, or series of transactions of such organization, government, or agency involving anything of value of $5,000 or more; or

     (2)   corruptly gives, offers, or agrees to give anything of value to any person, with intent to influence or reward an agent of an organization or of a State, local or Indian tribal government, or any agency thereof, in connection with any business, transaction, or series of transactions of such organization, government, or agency involving anything of value of $5,000 or more; shall be fined under this title, imprisoned not more than 10 years, or both.

(b)   The circumstance referred to in subsection (a) of this section is that the organization, government, or agency receives, in any one year period, benefits in excess of $10,000 under a Federal program involving a grant, contract, subsidy, loan, guarantee, insurance, or other form of Federal assistance.

(c)   This section does not apply to bona fide salary, wages, fees, or other compensation paid, or expenses paid or reimbursed, in the usual course of business.

[B]   Elements of § 666

In a prosecution under § 666(a)(1)–(2), the government must prove that:

1.   The defendant solicited or received, or offered or gave, a thing of value;

---

[61] 18 U.S.C. § 666.

[62] *See supra* § 8.05[A].

2. The thing of value was solicited or received, or offered or given, in order to benefit an agent of an organization, or of a state, local, or Indian tribal government, or any agency thereof;

3. The thing of value was given in connection with any business, transaction, or series of transactions of an organization, or of a state, local, or Indian tribal government, or any agency thereof, involving anything of value of $5,000 or more;

4. The defendant acted corruptly; and

5. The entity for which the defendant acted as an agent received more than $10,000 a year in federal assistance.

[C] Scope of § 666

Section 666 has only come into wide use relatively recently. As seen by the cases in this section, courts are just beginning to define the statute's boundaries.

[1] The Connection Between the Bribe and Federal Funds

In *Salinas v. United States*,[63] the Supreme Court addressed the issue whether, in a § 666 case, the government is required to prove that the bribes affected federal funds by, for example, diverting or misappropriating them. Salinas was a local sheriff's deputy at a county prison that also held federal prisoners, a service for which the federal government paid the county well in excess of $10,000 per year. A prisoner paid bribes to Salinas in return for "contact visits" with the prisoner's girlfriend.

The Court affirmed the conviction, holding that the government was not required to prove that the bribes affected federal funds. The Court noted that the statute prohibits bribery in connection with "any business, transaction, or series of transactions . . . ;" on its face, the statute does not require that the bribe divert, misappropriate, or otherwise directly affect federal funds. Furthermore, when enacting the statute, Congress clearly intended to cover bribery involving state and local officials employed by federally-funded agencies.[64]

In *Salinas*, the Court explicitly left open the question whether § 666 "requires some other kind of connection between a bribe and the expenditure of federal funds."[65] Some lower courts held that the government must show a connection between the bribe and a risk to the integrity or operation of a federally-funded program, while others held that no such connection was required.[66]

---

[63] 522 U.S. 52 (1997). Another aspect of this case is discussed in the Chapter 16, RICO, *infra*, § 16.03[D].

[64] *Id.* at 56–58.

[65] *Id.* at 59.

[66] Because the bribe in *Salinas* threatened the integrity and operation of the federally-funded prison, the Supreme Court found that it met any such requirement on the facts of the case, but did not determine whether such a requirement is generally mandated. *See* 522 U.S. at 61. *Compare, e.g.*, United States v. Zwick, 199 F.3d 672, 687 (3d Cir. 1999) (§ 666 requires government to prove defendant's conduct affected

The United States Supreme Court resolved this conflict in *Sabri v. United States*.[67] Sabri was a real estate developer who offered three bribes to a Minneapolis city councilperson. Minneapolis received more than $10,000 a year in federal funds, and Sabri was charged under § 666. The Court rejected Sabri's argument that Congress lacked the authority to criminalize bribes not directly tied to federal funds. The Court found that the Spending Clause of the United States Constitution[68] authorizes Congress to appropriate federal moneys to promote the general welfare, and that the Necessary and Proper Clause[69] allows Congress to adopt measures to ensure that the federal moneys are not ill-spent because of bribes. The Court noted that not all bribes of government officials covered by § 666(b) will be directly traceable to federal funds, which are fungible and can be moved among accounts. The Court concluded that Congress has the power "to promote the general welfare . . . and see to it that taxpayer dollars [are] not frittered away in graft."[70]

[2]　Bribes and Gratuities

It is not clear whether § 666 is limited to bribes, or also encompasses gratuities. On the one hand, the term "corruptly" seems to suggest that § 666 is limited to bribes. In *United States v. Thompson*,[71] for example, the Seventh Circuit stated that the section only covers clearly corrupt acts, such as bribery.[72]Several courts, however, have held that § 666 also reaches gratuities.[73]

Similarly, the courts of appeal are split as to whether the government must allege and prove a *quid pro quo* under §§ 666(a)(1)(B) and (a)(2). For example, in *United States v. McNair*,[74] the Eleventh Circuit aligned itself with those circuits holding that no such proof is required. The court relied upon the plain language of §§ 666(a)(1)(B) and (a)(2), which neither mention a *quid pro quo* nor contain such language as "in exchange for" or "in return for" a specific official act. To hold otherwise, the court said, "would permit a person to pay a significant sum to [a covered agent] intending the payment to produce a future, as yet unidentified favor without violating § 666."[75]

---

a federal interest), *with* United States v. Dakota, 188 F.3d 663, 668 (6th Cir. 1999) (finding no such requirement).

[67]　541 U.S. 600 (2004).

[68]　Art. I, § 8, cl. 1.

[69]　Art. I, § 8, cl. 18.

[70]　124 S. Ct. at 1946.

[71]　484 F.3d 877 (7th Cir. 2007).

[72]　*Id.* at 881 (§ 666 is limited to "theft, extortion, bribery, and similarly corrupt acts.). *See* § 8.08[C][5], *infra.*

[73]　*Compare* United States v. Bonito, 57 F.3d 167, 171 (2d Cir. 1995) (§ 666 encompasses gratuities), *and* United States v. Crozier, 987 F.2d 893, 899–900 (2d Cir. 1993) (same), *with* United States v. Jennings, 160 F.3d 1006, 1015 n.4 (4th Cir. 1998) (positing an argument that gratuities are not prohibited by § 666, but declining to decide the issue), *and* United States v. Jackowe, 651 F. Supp. 1035, 1036 (S.D.N.Y. 1987) (§ 666 does not encompass gratuities).

[74]　605 F.3d 1152 (11th Cir. 2010).

[75]　*Id.* at 1188. *Accord* United States v. Abbey, 560 F.3d 513, 520 (6th Cir. 2009) (holding that proof of

Another question is whether the *Sun-Diamond Growers* requirement that the benefit to the public official be in connection with a specific official act applies to cases brought under § 666 based on a bribery theory. In *United States v. Ganim*,[76] the Second Circuit held not. The court focused on the language in the gratuities statute, which refers to giving benefits to a public official "for or because of *any official act* performed or to be performed." Section 666, however, contains no such language. Thus, a bribe under that section occurs whenever the official accepted the benefit generally in exchange for a promise to perform official acts for the giver in the future.

[3]　The Meaning of Federal "Benefits"

In *Fischer v. United States*,[77] the Supreme Court held that a health care provider participating in the Medicare program received "benefits" within the meaning of § 666. The Court reached this result even though the direct benefits are paid to the individual who is covered by Medicare, and not to the health care provider. The Court found that the bribes at issue qualified under § 666 because they threatened Medicare's integrity and raised the risk that organizations participating in Medicare will lack the resources needed to provide the requisite level and quality of care. The Court said that whether a benefits program will qualify under § 666 depends on the facts of each case.[78]

[4]　The Meaning of "Agent"

In *Salinas*, *Sabri*, and *Fischer*, the Supreme Court broadly interpreted the reach of § 666. Some federal circuit courts, however, have limited the statute's reach by narrowly interpreting the term "agent." Under the statute, the government must show that a bribed party was an "agent" of a private organization or of a state, local, or tribal government or agency that received more than $10,000 a year in federal benefits. Under the statute, an "agent" is a "person authorized to act on behalf of another person or a government and, in the case of an organization or government, [the term "agent"] includes a servant or employee, and a partner, director, officer, manager, and representative." In *United States v. Langston*,[79] the defendant worked for a state agency but the government charged him as an agent of the state itself. To determine whether the defendant was an agent of the state, the Fifth Circuit said, "[w]e must necessarily scrutinize that which purports to create the employment relationship with the agency to determine if the employee is authorized to act on the principal entity's behalf."[80] Because the defendant was not authorized to act on behalf of the state under state law, the court found that he was not a state

---

a *quid pro quo* is sufficient but not necessary under § 666(a)(1)(B) or (a)(2)); United States v. Gee, 432 F.3d 713, 714–15 (7th Cir. 2005) (holding that a *quid pro quo* is not required under § 666(a)(1)(B) and that payment for the official's "influence" is sufficient). *But see* United States v. Jennings, 160 F.3d 1006, 1014 (4th Cir.1998) (holding that the "corrupt intent" element in § 666 requires a *quid pro quo*).

[76]　510 F.3d 134, 134 (2d Cir. 2007).

[77]　529 U.S. 667 (2000).

[78]　*Id.* at 681–82.

[79]　590 F.3d 1226 (11th Cir. 2009).

[80]　*Id.* at 1234.

"agent" under § 666 even though he was paid by a state commission with state money.[81] The court thus reversed the defendant's convictions under counts alleging that he acted as a state agent.

In *United States v. Lupton*,[82] on the other hand, the court broadly construed the term "agent." In that case, the defendant was a real estate broker who acted as an independent contractor for the state. Even though the contract stated that the defendant was not an "agent" of the state, the Seventh Circuit found that in substance the defendant did act as the state's agent because, in the words of the statute, he was "authorized to act on behalf" of the state. Acting as a facilitator for a sale and lease-back arrangement for a state building, the defendant took kickbacks from a prospective buyer who was bidding for the property. Because the defendant in fact acted as the state's agent in the transaction, he fell within the statute.[83]

[5] The Meaning of "Misapplies"

Among other acts, § 666 criminalizes "intentionally misapply[ying]" $5,000 or more of property. In *United States v. Thompson*,[84] the defendant was a state official who manipulated a state contract bidding process so that a contract would be awarded to a politically connected travel agency. The government charged the defendant with violating § 666 by depriving another bidder of the contract. The government's theory was that this benefited the defendant because the raise she received was in part based on her actions involving the contract award. The Seventh Circuit reversed the conviction, reasoning that § 666 essentially criminalizes bribery. The court concluded that the section should be limited to "theft, extortion, bribery, and similarly corrupt acts."[85]

§ 8.09   THE FOREIGN CORRUPT PRACTICES ACT

Another important bribery statute was enacted by the Foreign Corrupt Practices Act ("FCPA").[86] The anti-bribery provisions of the FCRA criminalize bribes paid to foreign officials by United States companies, and foreign companies listed on a United States stock exchange, and their agents.[87] Specifically, the statute

---

[81] *Id. See also* United States v. Whitfield, 590 F.3d 325 (5th Cir. 2009) (assuming that judges were "agents" of a state agency, to the extent that they performed functions that involved agency funds, their decisions as presiding judges in two lawsuits were not made "in connection with any business, transaction, or series of transactions" of the agency under § 666).

[82] 620 F.3d 790 (7th Cir. 2010).

[83] *Id.* at 801–02.

[84] 484 F.3d 877 (7th Cir. 2007).

[85] *Id.* at 881.

[86] Pub. L. No. 95-213, §§ 101–104, 91 Stat. 1494 (1977), *codified as amended at* 15 U.S.C. §§ 78m(b), 78dd-1, 78ff(a) & (c).

[87] For a detailed discussion of the FCPA, see Otto G. Obermaier, Timothy E. Hoeffner, & Amy S. Kline, *The Foreign Corrupt Practices Act*, in White Collar Crime: Business and Regulatory Offenses §§ 16.01–05 (Otto Obermaier & Robert Morvillo, eds. 2011). *See also* Rollo C. Baker, *Foreign Corrupt Practices Act*, 47 Am. Crim. L. Rev. 647 (2010); Mike Koehler, *The Facade of FCPA Enforcement*, 41 Geo.

prohibits (a) corruptly paying, offering to pay, promising to pay, or authorizing the payment of money, a gift, or anything of value, (b) to a foreign official, (c) in order to obtain or retain business.[88] This statute has played an increasingly important role in national and international anti-corruption efforts.

Many of the provisions of the FCPA are subject to judicial interpretation. In *United States v. Kay*,[89] for example, the defendants were charged under the FCPA based upon payments to foreign officials designed to avoid customs duties and sales taxes. The district court dismissed the charges, holding that such payments were not made in order to obtain or retain business. The Fifth Circuit reversed and reinstated the charges, holding that the FCPA is not limited to bribes that directly lead to the award or renewal of contracts.[90] The court held that the government should be allowed to prove the precise manner in which the payments, by leading to tax savings, were designed to assist in obtaining or retaining business.[91]

J. Int'l L. 907 (2010); Amy Deen Westbrook, *Enthusiastic Enforcement, Informal Legislation: The Unruly Expansion of the Foreign Corrupt Practices Act*, 45 Ga. L. Rev. 489 (2011).

[88] *See id.*

[89] 359 F.3d 738 (5th Cir. 2004).

[90] *Id.* at 755.

[91] *Id.* at 756. The defendants were later convicted of the charges. *See* United States v. Kay, 513 F.3d 432 (5th Cir. 2007).

Chapter 9

EXTORTION

§ 9.01 INTRODUCTION

Along with bribery, gratuities, and mail and wire fraud, the crime of extortion is one of the government's most important weapons in fighting public corruption. The principal federal extortion statute is known as the Hobbs Act.[1] This statute specifies two distinct types of extortion. First, extortion can be committed through use of force, violence, or fear. Extortion by use of fear can be further divided between (a) exploiting fear of *physical* harm, and (b) exploiting fear of *economic* harm. Extortion using physical force or physical threats is not a "white collar crime," but extortion by using economic threats certainly can be.[2]

Second, extortion can be committed "under color of official right." This occurs when a public official uses the power of a public office to obtain payment from a victim. Unlike the federal crimes of bribery and gratuity, the federal crime of extortion under color of official right is not limited to *federal* public officials. The Hobbs Act therefore can be used in state and local corruption cases. Because the Supreme Court has broadly interpreted the Hobbs Act in recent years, the statute raises complex issues of federal intrusion into matters traditionally reserved for state and local law enforcement.[3]

In theory, the crime of extortion is principally distinguished from the crimes of bribery and gratuity by the culpability of the parties. With bribery and gratuity, both the payer and the payee may be criminally liable because each has voluntarily acted in a way that potentially corrupts the governmental system. In extortion cases, however, the defendant has used some form of coercion to obtain payment from the payer, who is an innocent victim. Thus, in a federal extortion case, the person receiving the payment is the culpable party; the person making the payment is generally not criminally liable.[4] In many instances, however, extortion may be

---

[1] 18 U.S.C. § 1951. The Hobbs Act also creates a federal robbery offense.

[2] As noted in the definition of "white collar crime" set forth in Chapter 1, *supra*, in some circumstances we can determine whether a crime is "white collar" based upon how the crime is committed rather than upon how the crime is defined by statute. Thus, under the Hobbs Act, crimes of extortion may sometimes be "white collar," as when "under color of official right" or by use or threat of economic harm, see U.S. Sentencing Guidelines Manual § 2C1.1, and sometimes not, as when committed by use or threat of physical force, see U.S. Sentencing Guidelines Manual § 2B3.2.

[3] *See* Kenneth R. Feinberg, *The Federal Law of Bribery and Extortion: Expanding Liability, in* White Collar Crime: Business and Regulatory Offenses § 3.01 (Otto Obermaier & Robert Morvillo, eds. 2011).

[4] *Cf.* Model Penal Code § 240.1 (1962) (victim of extortion may be liable for bribery).

difficult to distinguish from bribery.[5]

This chapter reviews the Hobbs Act in detail, and also discusses issues that frequently arise in prosecutions under the Hobbs Act. Finally, the chapter briefly discusses the Travel Act,[6] which provides the government with another tool for fighting extortionate activities.

§ 9.02 STATUTORY OVERVIEW

[A] Statutory Background and Definitions

The Hobbs Act was enacted in 1946 to combat robbery and extortion in interstate commerce.[7] An earlier version of the law was contained in the Anti-Racketeering Act of 1934. The 1946 law was intended to extend the earlier law to extortionate labor activities, which had previously been excluded from the statute's reach.

Section (a) of the Hobbs Act states that "[w]hoever in any way or degree obstructs, delays, or affects commerce . . . by robbery or extortion or attempts or conspires so to do" shall be punished under the Act. Section (b) sets forth the two theories of extortion, and defines the crime as "the obtaining of property from another, with his consent, induced by wrongful use of actual or threatened force, violence, or fear, *or* under color of official right."

The "white collar" theories of extortion — (a) by the use of fear or threats of economic harm, and (b) extortion under color of official right — are distinct theories under the statute. The theories are not mutually exclusive, however, and may overlap. Indeed, the government has, in some cases, charged extortion by both theories based upon a single set of facts.[8]

[B] Elements of Extortion

The crime of extortion, as applied to white collar prosecutions, requires proof of the following elements:

1. The defendant's acts affected interstate commerce;

2. The defendant obtained, or attempted or conspired to obtain, another person's property to which the defendant was not entitled;

---

[5] For a comparison of the two crimes, see generally James Lindgren, *The Theory, History, and Practice of the Bribery-Extortion Distinction*, 141 U. Pa. L. Rev. 1695, 1695 (1993) (hereinafter *Theory, History, and Practice*); James Lindgren, *The Elusive Distinction Between Bribery and Extortion: From the Common Law to the Hobbs Act*, 35 U.C.L.A. L. Rev. 815 (1988) (hereinafter *Elusive Distinction*).

[6] 18 U.S.C. § 1952.

[7] For an overview of the legislative history of the Hobbs Act, see Steven C. Yarbrough, *The Hobbs Act in the Nineties: Confusion or Clarification of the Quid Pro Quo Standard in Extortion Cases Involving Public Officials*, 31 Tulsa L.J. 781, 783–84 (1996).

[8] *See, e.g.*, United States v. Garcia, 907 F. 2d 380 (2d Cir. 1990).

3. The property was obtained, or would have been obtained, with the other person's consent;[9]

4. The defendant acted with the required mens rea; and

5. The property was obtained, or would have been obtained, by:

    (a)   the wrongful use of fear; and/or

    (b)   under color of official right.

Under 18 U.S.C. § 1951, extortion is punished by up to 20 years in prison. As discussed in Chapter 21, Sentencing, the sentence imposed in a particular case will depend upon the application of the Federal Sentencing Guidelines, and upon the trial court's application of the Guidelines, to that case.

[C] Extortion as an Inchoate Crime

Under the plain language of the statute, the crime of extortion encompasses the inchoate conduct of conspiring or attempting to commit extortion. Because there is no general attempt statute under federal law, the crime of attempted extortion exists only because the statute itself contains this provision.[10] On the other hand, conspiring to commit extortion could be charged under the extortion statute or under § 371, the general federal conspiracy statute.[11]

§ 9.03   EFFECT ON INTERSTATE COMMERCE

Because the crime of extortion is not limited to federal public officials, it depends upon the interstate commerce element for federal jurisdiction. In practice, this element rarely provides a barrier to an extortion prosecution. The statute itself says that it is sufficient if the defendant obstructed, delayed, or affected commerce "in any way or degree."[12] Courts have consistently held that minor, or "de minimis," effects on commerce will suffice.[13] This broad interpretation of the Hobbs Act's jurisdictional element has continued even in the wake of the Supreme Court's efforts to restrict federal jurisdiction in other areas.[14]

Courts have used creative methods to find bases for federal jurisdiction in Hobbs Act prosecutions. For example, some courts have developed a "depletion of assets" theory. Under this theory, extortion of any interstate business will be found to affect

---

[9] It is this element that historically has distinguished the crime of extortion from the crime of robbery. *See* Peter Megargee Brown & Richard S. Peer, *The Anti-Racketeering Act: Labor and Management Weapon Against Labor Racketeering*, 32 N.Y.U. L. Rev. 965, 972 (1957).

[10] For another example of federal statutory attempt provisions, see the obstruction of justice statutes, 18 U.S.C. §§ 1503, 1505, which punish "endeavors" to obstruct. *See* Chapter 12, Obstruction of Justice, *infra*.

[11] *See* Chapter 3, Conspiracy, *supra*.

[12] 18 U.S.C. § 1951(a).

[13] *See* Feinberg, *supra* note 3, § 3.03[1] at 3-24 & n.66.

[14] *See* United States v. Lopez, 514 U.S. 549 (1995) (invalidating the Gun Free School Zones Act under the Commerce Clause). For a critique of the broad application of the Hobbs Act to local matters, see United States v. Hickman, 179 F.3d 230, 231 (5th Cir. 1999) (en banc) (Higginbotham, J., dissenting).

commerce if the extortion depletes the victim's assets.[15] In *United States v. Stillo*,[16] for example, the defendant was a judge who had accepted payments in return for fixing cases. In one instance, a defense attorney approached the judge in connection with an FBI sting operation, and asked the judge to fix the case. The judge agreed, and was charged with extortion.

The Seventh Circuit upheld the judge's Hobbs Act conviction. The court found that interstate commerce was implicated both because the payment would have depleted the lawyer's firm's assets, and because the firm purchased supplies in interstate commerce. Under such an analysis, it is apparent that almost any extortionate activity will support federal jurisdiction.

§ 9.04   OBTAINING PROPERTY FROM ANOTHER

As part of an extortion case, the government must show that the defendant obtained, or attempted or conspired to obtain, property from another. As with the interstate commerce element, courts have generally read the property element quite broadly.[17]

The United States Supreme Court, however, has imposed one significant requirement with respect to the property element. In *Scheidler v. Nat'l Org. for Women*[18] (referred to here as *"Scheidler II"*)[19] the Court held that the alleged extortion must be designed not only to injure the victim but also to benefit the defendant. In that case, the Court overruled earlier decisions that had allowed the Hobbs Act to be used against defendants who were not acting to obtain money or property. In *Scheidler II*, abortion supporters sued abortion opponents under RICO, alleging that the defendants' tactics constituted the RICO predicate of extortion under the Hobbs Act. The jury found the defendants liable. On appeal, the Supreme Court held that, because the abortion opponents had not been acting to "obtain" property, they could not be guilty of extortion.[20] The Court reiterated that the Hobbs Act requires that property "be obtained from another" and that "merely interfering with or depriving someone of property" does not meet that requirement.[21] Because the abortion opponents had not attempted to obtain property from the plaintiffs, the elements of extortion were not present.[22]

---

[15] *See* Feinberg, *supra* note 3, § 3.03[1].

[16] 57 F.3d 553 (7th Cir. 1995). *Accord,* United States v. Rabbitt, 583 F.2d 1014, 1023 (8th Cir. 1978).

[17] *See* Andrews & Hirose, *supra* note 13, at 494–95.

[18] 537 U.S. 393 (2003).

[19] In an earlier decision in the same litigation, the Court addressed an issue relating to the RICO statute. *See* Nat'l Org. for Women v. Scheidler, 510 U.S. 249 (1994) (*"Scheidler I"*), discussed in Chapter 16, RICO, § 16.04[C], *infra.*

[20] *Id.* at 405.

[21] *Id.*

[22] For a later decision applying *Scheidler,* see United States v. McFall, 558 F.3d 951, 957 (9th Cir. 2009) (threat to competitor in bidding process did not suffice under *Scheidler* because "decreasing a competitor's chance of winning a contract, standing alone, does not amount to *obtaining* a transferable asset for oneself").

Finally, in its third decision in this case,[23] the Court unanimously rejected the plaintiffs' attempt to use an alternative extortion theory to support the result at trial. Under this theory, the jury's finding of Hobbs Act violations could rest on four instances of physical violence or threats that were unrelated to robbery or extortion. The Court rejected the argument, holding that physical violence that is unrelated to robbery or extortion does not fall within the Hobbs Act.

Courts have held that "property" interests under the Hobbs Act include both tangible and intangible property interests. In *United States v. Gotti*,[24] for example, the defendants deprived labor union members of their statutory rights to free speech and democratic participation in the affairs of their union. The Second Circuit affirmed the convictions, rejecting the defendants' argument that *Scheidler II* limits extortion to tangible property interests.[25]

§ 9.05 THE REQUIRED MENS REA

The Hobbs Act on its face specifies no particular mens rea. As in other areas, courts generally agree that no mens rea is required as to the jurisdictional element — that is, the government is not required to prove that the defendant intended to affect commerce in any way.[26]

Otherwise, courts are split on mens rea. Some require that the government show that the defendant specifically intended to achieve the desired result, while others only require the government to show that the defendant generally intended to commit the acts proscribed by the statute.[27]

As a practical matter, most courts hold that, where the theory is use of force or fear, proof that the defendant purposefully or knowingly used force, induced fear, or exploited the victim's fear, is sufficient. Where the theory is that the defendant acted under color of official right, the government similarly must show that the defendant purposefully or knowingly used an official position to obtain property. As the Supreme Court stated in *Evans v. United States*,[28] in an extortion under color of official right case, the government must show that "a public official has obtained a payment to which he was not entitled, knowing that the payment was made in return for official acts."

§ 9.06 EXTORTION BY THE USE OF FEAR

As noted above, extortion by fear does not require the government to show that the victim had a fear of physical harm, but may be based solely on proof that the defendant feared economic harm. The government must further show that the

---

[23] Scheidler v. Nat'l Org. for Women, 547 U.S. 9 (2006).

[24] 459 F.3d 296 (2d Cir. 2006).

[25] *Id.* at 322–23 (citing United States v. Tropiano, 418 F.2d 1069 (2d Cir.1969)).

[26] *See, e.g.*, United States v. Wiseman, 172 F.3d 1196, 1214 (10th Cir. 1999).

[27] *See* Jeremy N. Gayed, *"Corruptly": Why Corrupt State of Mind Is an Essential Element for Hobbs Act Extortion under Color of Official Right*, 78 Notre Dame L. Rev. 1731 (2003).

[28] 504 U.S. 255, 268 (1992). *See generally* Andrews & Hirose, *supra* note 13, at 496–99.

defendant intended to take advantage of the victim's fear. The prosecution need not, however, show that the defendant created or attempted to create the fear.[29]

Whether the government has offered sufficient proof of "fear" is a frequently litigated issue in white collar cases. Perhaps the most often-cited case on this issue is *United States v. Capo*.[30] In *Capo*, the defendants were involved in a job-selling scheme at an Eastman Kodak plant. The plant had an immediate need for a large number of new employees. Prospective employees paid the defendants, who used their influence to ensure that these applicants received jobs. The defendants were tried and convicted of extortion based upon the theory that they had placed the job applicants in fear of economic harm. According to the government's theory, the defendants induced fear by threatening to withhold their assistance unless the job applicants made the required payments.

Sitting *en banc*, the Second Circuit reversed the convictions. The court found that there was insufficient evidence that the alleged victims had acted out of fear.[31] Initially, the court held that a determination of whether there was fear of economic loss must be viewed from the victim's perspective. Then, the court set forth the widely-used test for determining whether the alleged victim acted out of fear. Specifically, the government must show that the victim both actually and reasonably believed "first, that the defendant had the power to harm the victim, and second, that the defendant would exploit that power to the victim's detriment."[32]

Applying this test to the facts, the court found that the job applicants were not victims who acted out of fear. Rather, the applicants were willing participants in the plan. Because the applicants were seeking to obtain an economic benefit, and were not being confronted with the threat of economic loss, the activity constituted bribery rather than extortion. The court further noted that extending the Hobbs Act into matters traditionally covered by state law bribery statutes would contravene established principles of federalism.[33]

The *Capo* decision is often cited for the proposition that, where a payer seeks to obtain an economic benefit rather than to avoid an economic loss, the activity constitutes bribery rather than extortion. In *Capo*, the job applicants had no fear that the defendants would deprive them of something to which they were entitled if the applicants did not make the payments. Therefore, the defendants did not commit extortion.

In *United States v. Garcia*,[34] the Second Circuit used the *Capo* holding to reverse an extortion conviction in a major political corruption scandal. The *Garcia* case involved a scheme by Wedtech, a defense contracting firm, to gain government

---

[29] *See, e.g.*, United States v. Abelis, 146 F.3d 73, 82 (2d Cir. 1998) (the "defendant need only attempt to exploit a fear to be guilty of attempted extortion; he need not attempt to create it"). *See generally* Feinberg, *supra* note 3, § 3.03[1].

[30] 817 F.2d 947 (2d Cir. 1987) (*en banc*).

[31] *Id.* at 952. An earlier panel had affirmed the conviction. *See* United States v. Capo, 791 F.2d 1054 (2d Cir. 1986), *rev'd*, 817 F.2d 947 (2d Cir. 1987) (*en banc*).

[32] 817 F.2d at 951.

[33] *Id.* at 954–55.

[34] 907 F.2d 380 (2d Cir. 1990).

business through illegal payments. The government alleged two extortionate events involving Congressman Robert Garcia, his wife Jane Garcia, and Wedtech official Robert Moreno. First, over dinner with Moreno, the Congressman suggested that he use his influence to obtain contracts for Wedtech, and suggested that Wedtech make payments to Mrs. Garcia for consulting work. The court found that this arrangement did not amount to extortion because Moreno did not have "the mindset of a victim of economic extortion' rather, it is the thinking of a shrewd, unethical businessman who senses and seeks to capitalize on a money-making opportunity . . . . By paying the Garcias, Wedtech was purchasing an advocate, not buying off a thug."[35] Second, Garcia requested a loan from Moreno. Again, the court found that, in making the payment, Moreno acted not out of fear but out of a calculated determination to gain the Congressman's favor.

The decisions in *Capo* and *Garcia* suggest that offers to provide preferential treatment — the jobs in *Capo*, the contracts in *Garcia* — do not amount to extortion by fear of economic harm. On the other hand, a threat to withhold access to a level playing field may constitute extortion. In *United States v. Collins*,[36] for example, the governor's husband and Kentucky state officials solicited investments from out-of-state banks. Subsequently, the banks were awarded state business. The defendants argued that the banks were merely given preferential treatment, and that threatening to withhold such treatment did not amount to extortion. The Sixth Circuit disagreed, finding that failure to make the investments would have deprived the banks of an opportunity to compete on a fair basis for the state business.[37]

The distinction between *Garcia* and *Collins* is subtle but important. In *Garcia*, Wedtech had a right to *compete* for contracts in a fair process, but had no right to be *awarded* contracts; Wedtech could have fairly competed for government contracts whether or not Congressman Garcia provided his assistance. What Wedtech sought was preferential treatment in the process, and fear of being denied such treatment was not extortion. By contrast, the *Collins* court suggested, the out-of-state banks could not have even competed for business with the state of Kentucky had they not made the investments with the defendants. As the court stated, "without the payments [the banks] could lose the opportunity to compete for government contracts on a level playing field, an opportunity to which they were legally entitled."[38] The banks were not seeking preferential treatment, but merely an opportunity to compete.

Thus, the courts seem to distinguish between requiring a payment to obtain preferential treatment, which is not extortion by use of fear, and requiring a payment to obtain fair treatment, which is not extortion by use of fear, and requiring a payment to obtain fair treatment, which is. This distinction may be less than perfect' providing an opportunity to compete where none existed, as in *Collins*, is arguably a form of "preferential" treatment. Nevertheless, the distinction

---

[35] *Id.* at 383–84.

[36] 78 F.3d 1021 (6th Cir. 1996).

[37] *Id.* at 1030.

[38] *Id.*

continues to be followed by courts attempting to determine the scope of extortion by fear of economic harm.[39]

§ 9.07 EXTORTION UNDER COLOR OF OFFICIAL RIGHT

Many white collar extortion prosecutions in political corruption cases include charges of extortion under color of official right. In essence, this theory charges that the defendant has used, or attempted or conspired to use, the power of his or her official position to extract something of value from the alleged victim. Unlike prosecutions under the federal bribery and gratuities statute, which are limited to federal public officials, extortion cases may be brought against state and local officials. Generally, the courts have broadly construed the concept of "public official," granting the Hobbs Act wide application in matters of federal, state, and local government corruption.[40]

When using the color of official right theory, the government need not show that the victim acted out of fear. As explained in more detail below, a defendant who has committed extortion under color of official right has probably also received a bribe. If the defendant is a federal public official, then the defendant may be charged and convicted of both federal offenses if the elements are proven.

[A] "Inducement" in Extortion Under Color of Official Right

In *Evans v. United States*,[41] the Supreme Court resolved a split among the circuits as to the "inducement" requirement. Prior to *Evans*, some lower federal courts had held that, to be guilty of extortion, a public official must have affirmatively induced the victim to give the official something of value. Other courts rejected the inducement requirement, holding that extortion can be proven even where the extorted party initiated the transaction.[42] In *Evans*, the Supreme Court sided with those courts that had rejected the inducement requirement. Evans was an elected county official in Georgia, and was targeted in an FBI investigation of corruption in county zoning decisions. An undercover FBI agent sought Evans's help in a zoning matter, and gave Evans $7,000 in cash and a campaign contribution check of $1,000. The defendant reported the check, but not the cash, on election and tax forms. The defendant was convicted of extortion.

On appeal, the defendant argued that he could not be guilty of extortion under color of official right because he had not affirmatively induced the payment. In an opinion by Justice Stevens, a majority of the Supreme Court affirmed the conviction.[43] Initially, the Court held that the word "induced" in the Hobbs Act definition of extortion does not, as a matter of statutory interpretation, apply to

---

[39] *See* Lindgren, *Theory, History, and Practice, supra* note 5, at 1698–1700.

[40] *See generally* Peter J. Henning, *Federalism and the Federal Prosecution of State and Local Corruption*, 92 Ky. L.J. 75 (2004).

[41] 504 U.S. 255 (1992).

[42] *Id.* at 257.

[43] Five justices joined in Parts I, II, and III of the opinion. *See Evans*, 504 U.S. at 255.

extortion under color of official right cases. Section 1951(b) defines "extortion" as "the obtaining of property from another, with his consent, *induced* by wrongful use of actual or threatened force, violence, or fear, or under color of official right." According to the majority, the word "induced" only applies to the force/fear prong of the offense, and does not apply to the color of official right prong.[44] Alternatively, the Court found that even if the word "induced" applies to such cases, inducement was shown under the facts of the case.

The Court reasoned that, under the common law treatment of extortion, the government need only show that "a public official has obtained a payment to which he was not entitled, knowing that the payment was made in return for official acts."[45] In reviewing the facts, the Court found that Evans understood that the payments were intended to influence his actions — "although petitioner did not initiate the transaction, his acceptance of the bribe constituted an implicit promise to use his official position to serve the interests of the bribegiver."[46] According to the Court, such proof was sufficient, and the government was not required to show that the defendant affirmatively induced the payments.

Justice Thomas wrote the dissent, in which he was joined by Chief Justice Rehnquist and Justice Scalia. The dissent initially disagreed with the majority's interpretation of the statutory language and the common law of extortion. Next, Justice Thomas employed harsh rhetoric to criticize the majority decision on policy grounds.[47] First, Justice Thomas attacked the decision as "repugnant . . . to the basic tenets of criminal justice reflected in the rule of lenity."[48] Second, Justice Thomas accused the majority opinion of violating basic principles of federalism by expanding federal authority over state and local matters. Finally, the dissent stated that, by expanding the definition of extortion under color of official right, the majority had opened the door to abuse of prosecutorial discretion.[49]

[B] The Distinction Between Bribery and Extortion Under Color of Official Right

The essence of the *Evans* dissent's criticism was that the majority had failed to distinguish between the crimes of bribery and extortion under color of official right. As the dissent stated, "[b]y stretching the bounds of extortion to make it encompass bribery, the Court today blurs the traditional distinction between the crimes."[50] With the *Evans* holding, a federal public official who receives a bribe in

---

[44] 504 U.S. at 265.

[45] *Id.* at 268. In its analysis, the Court relied heavily upon the work of Professor James Lindgren (Lindgren, *Elusive Distinction, supra* note 5). *See* 504 U.S. at 258–64.

[46] 504 U.S. at 257.

[47] Justice Thomas's language is unusually harsh, all the more so given that he is a "law-and-order" justice writing a pro-defense opinion. For a fuller discussion of this aspect of *Evans*, see J. Kelly Strader, *The Judicial Politics of White Collar Crime*, 50 Hastings L.J. 1199, 1239–41, 1260 (1999).

[48] *Id.* at 290 (Thomas, J., dissenting). This rule requires that ambiguous criminal statutes be read in favor of the defendant. *Id.* at 292.

[49] *Id.* at 295, *citing* Morrison v. Olson, 487 U.S. 654, 727–32 (1988).

[50] *Id.* at 284. Professor Lindgren questioned whether there is any such "traditional distinction," *see*

a transaction initiated by another person may be liable for both extortion under color of official right and bribery.[51] (Evans, of course, was not charged with federal bribery because he was not a *federal* public official.) Thus, it will be unavailing for a public official to argue in a color of official right case that bribery, rather than extortion, is the appropriate charge.

Given the overlap between bribery and extortion under color of official right, what has happened to the bribery/extortion distinction based upon the status of the payer as a "victim"? This distinction seems to not apply to color of official right cases. Thus, courts have held that the payee in such a case can be liable for bribery and extortion, while the payer can be liable only for bribery.[52] On the other hand, the payer in a case of extortion by *fear* is truly a victim, and should not be considered criminally culpable.

[C]   Distinguishing "Extortion" from Legitimate Campaign Fundraising

Courts are often vexed when attempting to draw the line between extortion under color of official right and legitimate campaign fundraising. The Supreme Court directly confronted this issue in *McCormick v. United States*,[53] which was decided one year before *Evans*. McCormick had been a West Virginia state legislator in a region that had a shortage of medical doctors. The state had for several years allowed foreign medical school graduates to practice in the region under temporary permits, a program that McCormick strongly supported. After discussions with a lobbyist for the foreign doctors, many of whom had repeatedly failed the state licensing exam, McCormick agreed to sponsor a bill to grant these doctors permanent licenses. During his reelection campaign, McCormick told the lobbyist that his campaign was expensive, that he had paid considerable sums out of his own pocket, and that he had not heard anything from the foreign doctors. McCormick later received four cash payments from the doctors that he did not report as campaign contributions or as taxable income. McCormick successfully sponsored passage of legislation permitting experienced doctors to be permanently licensed. Thereafter, he received another cash payment from the doctors.

On appeal from his Hobbs Act conviction, McCormick argued that receipt of a campaign contribution could not constitute extortion under color of official right absent an explicit quid pro quo. The Supreme Court agreed, stating that receipt of campaign contributions may constitute extortion only where (1) the payments were induced by the use of force, violence, or fear, or (2) the payments were made under color of official right, *i.e.*, "in return for an *explicit promise or undertaking* by the

---

Lindgren, *Theory, History, and Practice, supra* note 5, at 1721–31, but did not directly address Justice Thomas's policy concerns.

[51] 504 U.S. at 268 (citations omitted). *See* Lindgren, Elusive Distinction, *supra* note 5, at 1697; Thomas A. Secrest, *Criminal Law: Bribery Equals Extortion: The Supreme Court Refuses to Make Inducement a Necessary Element of Extortion "Under Color of Official Right" under the Hobbs Act, 18 U.S.C. § 1951:* Evans v. United States, 19 U. Dayton L. Rev. 251, 279 (1993).

[52] *See* Feinberg, *supra* note 3, at § 3.02 and cases cited therein.

[53] 500 U.S. 257 (1991).

official to perform or not to perform an official act."[54] Because the trial judge had failed to instruct the jury that it must find evidence of such an explicit promise, the conviction could not stand.

Underlying the *McCormick* decision was the Court's concern that a broad application of the Hobbs Act could interfere with legitimate campaign fundraising. As the Court said,

> Money is constantly being solicited on behalf of candidates, who run on platforms and who claim support on the basis of their views and what they intend to do or have done. [T]o hold that legislators commit the federal crime of extortion when they act for the benefit of constituents or support legislation furthering the interests of some of their constituents, shortly before or after campaign contributions are solicited and received from those beneficiaries, is an unrealistic assessment of what Congress could have meant by making it a crime to obtain property from another, with his consent, "under color of official right." To hold otherwise would open to prosecution not only conduct that has long been thought to be well within the law but also conduct that in a very real sense is unavoidable so long as election campaigns are financed by private contributions or expenditures, as they have been from the beginning of the Nation.[55]

The meaning of the quid pro quo requirement is unclear, however, in the wake of the *Evans* decision.

[D] The Quid Pro Quo Requirement

[1] Does the Quid Pro Quo Requirement Apply Outside the Campaign Contribution Context?

The *McCormick* quid pro quo requirement arose because the Court was concerned about drawing a clear distinction between legitimate campaign contributions and illegitimate extortionate demands.[56] In that case, the Court did not address the issue whether a quid pro quo showing is required in *all* color of official right extortion cases, or only in those cases involving campaign contributions.[57] In *Evans*, another case that arose in the campaign contribution context, the Court did not clarify this issue.[58] Although the courts are split, most courts appear to have concluded that the government must show a quid pro quo in all color of official right prosecutions.[59]

---

[54] *Id.* at 273 (emphasis added).

[55] *Id.* at 272.

[56] *Id.*

[57] *Id.* at 274 n.10.

[58] In his concurring opinion, Justice Kennedy stated that the requirement does in fact apply to all color of official right extortion prosecutions. 504 U.S. at 278 (Kennedy, J., concurring).

[59] *See* Feinberg, *supra* note 3, at § 3.03[1], and cases cited therein.

[2] Is an Explicit Quid Pro Quo Required, or Is an Implicit Quid Pro Quo Sufficient?

The decisions in *McCormick* and *Evans* arguably set forth inconsistent standards for determining whether the quid pro quo requirement is met. On the one hand, *McCormick* clearly requires "an explicit" promise by the public official to undertake an official act in exchange for the payment.[60] On the other hand, the *Evans* majority stated that the quid pro quo requirement is met whenever the jury finds that "a public official has obtained a payment to which he was not entitled, knowing that the payment was made in return for official acts."[61] In his concurring opinion in *Evans*, Justice Kennedy stated that the government must prove only an implicit quid pro quo. In his view, the "official and the payer need not state the quid pro quo in express terms, for otherwise the law's effect could be frustrated by knowing winks and nods."[62]

Lower courts are struggling over the apparent inconsistency between the two opinions, and the result is something of a muddle.[63] One approach is to apply the *McCormick explicit* quid pro quo requirement to *campaign contribution* cases, but the *Evans implicit* quid pro quo requirement to *non-campaign contribution* cases. Another approach concludes that *Evans* modified the *McCormick* rule, and that proof of an *implicit* quid pro quo suffices in *all* color of official right extortion cases. The latter approach would make prosecutions easier in the campaign contribution context. That approach does not, however, take into account the concerns of the *McCormick* majority that politicians routinely raise money from people who expect, as politicians well understand, that the campaign contributions will influence the politicians' actions.

---

[60] 500 U.S. at 273. For a full discussion of this inconsistency, see Yarbrough, *supra* note 7, at 794–96.

[61] 504 U.S. at 257. Professor Lindgren has aptly described the *Evans* test as a "watered-down version of the [*McCormick*] quid pro quo requirement." Lindgren, *Theory, History, and Practice*, *supra* note 5, at 1733.

Three members of the *Evans* majority, including the author of the opinion, Justice Stevens, along with Justices Blackmun and O'Connor, had dissented in *McCormick*. One might reasonably conclude that these three members of the *Evans* majority read *McCormick* so narrowly as to undo the earlier decision, with which they disagreed. This perspective, however, does not explain the position of Justice White, who wrote the *McCormick* decision and also joined in the *Evans* majority.

[62] 504 U.S. at 274 (Kennedy, J., concurring). For a decision applying this approach, see United States v. Antico, 275 F.3d 245, 258 (3d Cir. 2001). *See also* United States v. Blandford, 33 F.3d 685, 696 (6th Cir. 1994) (interpreting *Evans* as holding "that the *quid pro quo* of *McCormick* is satisfied by something short of a formalized and thoroughly articulated contractual arrangement (*i.e.*, merely knowing the payment was made in return for official acts is enough.)").

[63] *See* David Mills & Robert Weisberg, *Corrupting the Harm Requirement in White Collar Crime*, 60 Stan. L. Rev. 1371 (2008); Jeremy N. Gayed, *"Corruptly:": Why Corrupt State of Mind Is an Essential Element for Hobbs Act Extortion Under Color of Official Right*, 78 Notre Dame L. Rev. 1731 (2003); Yarbrough, *supra* note 7, at 796–811, and cases cited therein.

§ 9.08   THE TRAVEL ACT

The Travel Act provides another important avenue for reaching political corruption cases.[64] Passed in 1961 as a method for fighting organized crime, this statute criminalizes activities in interstate and foreign commerce when those activities also constitute violations of state and federal bribery and extortion statutes. The statutory penalties under the Travel Act include imprisonment of not more than five years, or imprisonment of not more than 20 years in cases of violence, plus a fine.[65] As always, the actual sentence will depend upon the trial court's application of the United States Sentencing Guidelines to the case.

This statute prohibits, among other things, traveling in interstate or foreign commerce, or using the mail or interstate or foreign commerce, with the intent to further certain unlawful activity. Such activity is defined to include both federal bribery and extortion, and bribery and extortion under the laws of the state where the acts were committed. The elements of a Travel Act prosecution are:

1. The defendant engaged in interstate or foreign travel, or acted in interstate or foreign commerce, or used the mail;

2. The defendant acted with the intent to commit an act, including bribery and extortion, proscribed by the statute; and

3. The defendant performed or attempted to perform any act in furtherance of activities proscribed by the statute.

In line with its holdings involving the bribery and extortion statutes, the Supreme Court has acted to expand the reach of the Travel Act. In *Perrin v. United States*,[66] the defendants argued that the alleged bribery in the case did not fall within the meaning of the term as used in the Travel Act. The Court rejected the argument, finding that Congress intended, when enacting the statute, to expand federal jurisdiction into matters traditionally reserved for state law enforcement. So long as a jurisdictional basis was present, the Court said, such a broad statutory reach was permissible.[67]

---

[64] 18 U.S.C. § 1952. *See generally* Barry Breen, *The Travel Act*, 24 Am. Crim. L. Rev. 125 (1986); Feinberg, *supra* note 3, § 3.04[3].

[65] 18 U.S.C. § 1952.

[66] 444 U.S. 37 (1979).

[67] Some commentators have viewed *Perrin* as inconsistent with the Court's earlier decision in Rewis v. United States, 401 U.S. 808, 812 (1971), which held that the Travel Act's interstate commerce requirement should be strictly applied in light of "sensitive federal-state relations." As a result, lower courts have exhibited confusion over the reach of the Travel Act. *See* Feinberg, *supra* note 3, § 3.04[3], and cases cited therein.

Chapter 10

FALSE STATEMENTS

§ 10.01 INTRODUCTION

In general terms, the federal false statements statute, contained in § 1001 of the criminal code,[1] applies to *unsworn* statements made to the government. Prosecutors use the statute in a broad variety of contexts. Two of these contexts are particularly important in the federal criminal law and white collar crime arenas.

First, as with the other "cover-up" crimes of perjury, false declarations, and obstruction of justice,[2] the false statement statute may be used to prosecute an individual who has attempted to hide earlier illegal activities. A false statements charge may therefore be brought instead of, or in addition to, charges relating to the matters originally under investigation. As with perjury and obstruction of justice charges, bringing a false statement charge as part of a broader criminal indictment has the tactical advantage of questioning the defendant's credibility by merely asserting the charge.

Second, § 1001 is often used in government fraud cases. In its broadest terms, the statute applies to any fraudulent or deceptive statement that meets the statutory elements and that may affect the functioning of the government in matters ranging from federal employment to the enforcement of federal regulations.[3] For example, a person may be charged under the statute for making a false statement while attempting to obtain money from the government, or while resisting a claim for money brought by the government. Section 1001 serves many of the same functions as the federal fraud statutes that apply to specific types of conduct.[4] It also covers many of the same acts as those covered under the defraud clause of the general federal conspiracy statute, 18 U.S.C. § 371.

---

[1] 18 U.S.C. § 1001. In addition to the general false statements statute, federal law criminalizes the making of false statements in specific contexts. *See, e.g.*, 18 U.S.C. § 545 (making a false statement in application for federally backed loan); 15 U.S.C. § 50 (making a false statement under the Federal Trade Commission Act).

[2] *See* Chapters 11 & 12, *infra*. For an overview of these crimes, see Stuart P. Green, *Uncovering the Cover-Up Crimes*, 42 Am. Crim. L. Rev. 9 (2005).

[3] *See generally* Brendan Gallagher & Stacey N. Kime, *False Statements and False Claims*, 47 Am. Crim. L. Rev. 527, 527–29 (2010) (listing cases brought in a variety of contexts under § 1001).

[4] *See, e.g.*, 18 U.S.C. § 287 (criminalizing false claims made to the government).

§ 10.02   STATUTORY OVERVIEW

The predecessor to the current false statements statute was originally enacted in the nineteenth century. In 1948, Congress divided the statute, separating the general false claims statute (18 U.S.C. § 287) from the general false statements statute (18 U.S.C. § 1001).[5]

In the 1996 False Statements Accountability Act, Congress amended § 1001 to cover statements involving *material* matters "within the jurisdiction of the executive, legislative, or judicial branch" of the federal government.[6] The current statute criminalizes the act of "knowingly and willfully" engaging in one of three types of conduct:[7]

1.   Falsifying, concealing, or covering up a material fact by any trick, scheme, or device;

2.   Making any materially false, fictitious, or fraudulent statement, or representation; or

3.   Making or using any false writing or document knowing it to contain any materially false, fictitious, or fraudulent statement or entry.

The statute generally excludes statements made by parties or their attorneys in judicial proceedings,[8] and also limits to some extent the statute's application to statements made in congressional matters.[9]

Most false statements charges arise under the second of the above theories. Under that theory, courts have generally required the government to prove that:

1.   The defendant made a statement;

2.   The statement was false or fraudulent;

3.   The statement was material;

4.   The defendant acted knowingly and willfully; and

5.   The defendant made the statement within the jurisdiction of the executive,

---

[5] Brogan v. United States, 522 U.S. 398, 413 (1998). The false claims statute is discussed in Chapter 4, Mail and Wire Fraud, *supra*, § 4.06[D].

[6] The earlier version of the statute applied to "any matter within the jurisdiction of any department or agency of the United States . . . ." *See infra* § 10.07. *See generally* Michael Gomez, Comment, *Re-Examining the False Statements Accountability Act*, 37 Hous. L. Rev. 515 (2000).

[7] Section 1001(a) provides:

 Except as otherwise provided in this section, whoever, in any matter within the jurisdiction of the executive, legislative, or judicial branch of the Government of the United States, knowingly and willfully

  (1) falsifies, conceals, or covers up by any trick, scheme, or device a material fact;

  (2) makes any materially false, fictitious, or fraudulent statement or representation; or

  (3) makes or uses any false writing or document knowing the same to contain any materially false, fictitious, or fraudulent statement or entry.

 shall be fined under this title or imprisoned not more than 5 years, or both.

[8] 18 U.S.C. § 1001(b).

[9] 18 U.S.C. § 1001(c).

legislative, or judicial branch of the federal government.[10]

The statute provides for a fine and a sentence of not more than five years. The actual sentence will depend upon the sentencing court's application of the Federal Sentencing Guidelines. As discussed in Chapter 21, Sentencing, under the Federal Sentencing Guidelines, a false statements charge may be "grouped" with related crimes for sentencing purposes.

§ 10.03 THE MEANING OF "STATEMENT"

[A] The Scope of § 1001

The statute covers a broad range of "statements." Statements can be written or oral, sworn or unsworn. Further, volunteered statements are covered by the statute, as are those required by law. In addition, silence can qualify under § 1001 under some circumstances.

[1] Silence

Silence may also be covered under § 1001 in some instances. In false statements cases based upon silence, most courts seem to require proof either that the defendant had a duty to speak, or that the silence was affirmatively misleading.[11] For example, in *United States v. Safavian*,[12] the defendant was a federal employee who had sought an ethics opinion concerning the propriety of a trip that a lobbyist had offered to the defendant. The government charged the defendant with two counts under § 1001(a)(1), which criminalizes "knowingly and willfully falsif[ying], conceal[ing], or cover[ing] up by any trick, scheme, or device a material fact." The underlying theory was that the defendant, when seeking the ethics opinion, had failed to disclose the details of the proposed trip. On appeal, the D.C. Circuit reversed the convictions. The court held that the defendant's voluntary decision to obtain an advisory ethics opinion did not alone create a duty to disclose all relevant facts.[13]

Courts have found a duty to disclose in other circumstances. For example, in *United States v. Moore*,[14] the Seventh Circuit found that a duty to disclose existed when a HUD form contract incorporated a conflict of interest regulation requiring

---

[10] *See* United States v. Lutz, 154 F.3d 581, 587 (6th Cir. 1998) (case brought under earlier version of § 1001).

[11] *See, e.g.*, United States v. Irwin, 654 F.2d 671 (10th Cir. 1981) (government must prove that defendant had a duty to disclose facts at the time the defendant allegedly concealed them).

[12] 528 F.3d 957 (D.C. Cir. 2008).

[13] *Id.* at 964–65. For similar holdings, see United States v. Curran, 20 F.3d 560, 566 (3d Cir. 1994) (holding defendant had no duty to disclose source of campaign contributions where duty was instead imposed on the campaign treasurer); United States v. Crop Growers Corp., 954 F. Supp. 335, 348 (D.D.C. 1997) ("to the extent that any duty to disclose is predicated on professional standards not codified in any statute or regulation, there can be no criminal liability").

[14] 446 F.3d 671, 671 (7th Cir. 2006).

disclosure of conflicts. Similarly, in *United States v. Kingston*,[15] the Tenth Circuit held that the defendant had a duty to disclose where the government form that the defendant completed required a disclosure of information that the defendant omitted. In these cases, unlike *Safavian*, there were specific provisions that required disclosure.

[2] Implied Statements

The definition of "statement" is not limitless, however. For example, in *Williams v. United States*,[16] the Supreme Court held five-to-four that a check drawn on an account with insufficient funds does not assert a fact. Therefore, such a check cannot be deemed "false" under 18 U.S.C. § 1014, which criminalizes knowingly making a false statement for the purpose of influencing a federally insured bank. The dissent strongly disagreed, arguing that "[i]t defies common sense and everyday practice to maintain, as the majority does, that a check carries with it no representation as to the drawer's account balance."[17]

In a similar case, *United States v. Blankenship*,[18] the Eleventh Circuit held that a contract is not a factual assertion. Therefore, the court held, the contract itself could not form the basis for a false statements conviction even where the parties never intended to perform their contractual obligations.

[B] The "Exculpatory 'No' " Doctrine

Prior to the Supreme Court's 1998 decision in *Brogan v. United States*,[19] a majority of the federal circuit courts held statements that merely denied wrongdoing in response to an incriminating question — an "exculpatory 'no' " response — generally could not be the basis for a false statements prosecution.[20] These courts reasoned that such statements either did not fall within the statute's focus on statements designed to disrupt government functioning, or ran afoul of the Fifth Amendment's prohibition against forced self-incrimination.[21]

In *Brogan*, the Court rejected the reasoning of the majority of circuit courts, and held that there is no "exculpatory 'no' " defense to a false statements

---

[15] 971 F.2d 481, 489 (10th Cir. 1992).

[16] 458 U.S. 279, 284 (1982). *See infra*, § 10.04, for a further discussion of this issue. In response to *Williams*, Congress passed the bank fraud statute, 18 U.S.C. § 1344, which was designed to criminalize a broad range of fraudulent activities, including check-kiting. *See* Jeffrey N. Starkey et al., *Financial Institutions Fraud*, 42 Am. Crim. L. Rev. 497, 499 (2005).

[17] Williams, 458 U.S. at 291 (White, J., dissenting).

[18] 382 F.3d 1110, 1135 (11th Cir. 2004).

[19] 522 U.S. 398 (1998).

[20] *See, e.g.*, Paternostro v. United States, 311 F.2d 298 (5th Cir. 1962) (an "'exculpatory no' answer without any affirmative, aggressive or overt misstatement on the part of the defendant does not come within the scope of the statute"). *See generally* Gallagher & Kime, *supra* note 3, at 538–40, and cases cited therein.

[21] *See, e.g.*, Unites States v. Cogdell, 844 F.2d 179, 183 (4th Cir. 1988); United States v. Equihua-Juarez, 851 F.2d 1222, 1227 n.10 (9th Cir. 1988); United States v. Lambert, 501 F.2d 943, 946 n.4 (5th Cir. 1974).

prosecution. Justice Scalia's opinion for the seven-member majority found that a false statement can indeed adversely affect government functioning because it assists in hiding the truth. Thus, an "exculpatory 'no' " falls within the statute's design. Moreover, because a person being questioned by a government agent can simply decline to answer, Justice Scalia found that the Fifth Amendment did not require an "exculpatory 'no' " defense.[22]

Two justices dissented in *Brogan*, and two others concurred only in the judgment while expressing serious misgivings about the outcome. In a concurring opinion joined by Justice Souter, Justice Ginsburg agreed with the majority that an "exculpatory 'no' " falls within § 1001's literal language.[23] She went on to emphasize, however, "the extraordinary authority Congress, perhaps unwittingly, has conferred on prosecutors to manufacture crimes." Justice Ginsburg noted that, in *Brogan* and similar cases, the government had put the suspect in a position where the suspect would be inclined to deny wrongdoing. Justice Ginsburg further noted "how far removed the 'exculpatory no' is from the problems Congress initially sought to address when it proscribed falsehoods designed to elicit a benefit from the Government or to hinder Government operations."[24] In dissent, Justices Stevens and Breyer emphasized their view that Congress did not intend for an "exculpatory 'no' " to provide a sufficient basis for a false statements prosecution.[25]

In acknowledgment of the potential unfairness of "exculpatory 'no' " prosecutions, the United States Attorney's Manual discourages § 1001 prosecutions in most such situations.[26] These guidelines, however, do not have the force of law, and would not serve as a basis for dismissal of a false statements charge based upon an "exculpatory 'no.' "

[C]   The Judicial Proceeding Exception

As noted above, § 1001(b) generally exempts statements made by parties or their attorneys in judicial proceedings from prosecution under § 1001. It is not always clear, however, what statements fall within this exemption. For example, the courts of appeal have split over whether a false statement made to a probation officer who is preparing a pre-sentencing report in advance of the defendant's sentencing falls within the exemption.[27]

---

[22] *Id.* at 402–04.

[23] *Id.* at 409–11 (Ginsburg, J., concurring).

[24] *Id.* at 408–09.

[25] *Id.* at 419–20.

[26] *See* U.S. Atty's Manual § 9-42.160 — False Statements to a Federal Criminal Investigator ("It is the Department's policy not to charge a § 1001 violation in situations in which a suspect, during an investigation, merely denies guilt in response to questioning by the government."). The manual further provides that "[t]his policy is to be narrowly construed, however; affirmative, discursive and voluntary statements to Federal criminal investigators would not fall within the policy." *Id. See generally* Gallagher & Kime, *supra* note 3, at 538–40.

[27] *Compare* United States v. Manning, 526 F.3d 611, 619–21 (10th Cir. 2008) (holding that, because probation officer did not act as mere conduit to the judge but performed an independent function, defendant's false statements fell within § 1001), *with* United States v. Horvath, 492 F.3d 1075 (9th Cir. 2007), *reh'g en banc denied*, 522 F.3d 904 (9th Cir. 2008) (holding that statement made to probation

§ 10.04   FALSITY AND CONCEALMENT

[A]   Implied Falsity and Concealment

The government can prove falsity by showing either (1) that the defendant made an untrue statement or (2) that the defendant concealed a material fact. As to the first theory, at least one court has held that an expressly false statement is not required, and that a conviction may rest upon an implied falsity.[28]

When the government uses the theory that the defendant concealed a material fact, it must prove that the defendant engaged in an affirmative act of non-disclosure by means of a trick, scheme, or device. Courts disagree as to whether, under a concealment theory, the government must prove that a specific statute — other than § 1001 — imposed on the defendant a duty to disclose the concealed information.[29]

[B]   Literally True or Ambiguous Statements

There are a number of circumstances in which falsity may be a contested issue. As in the perjury context,[30] a literally true statement will not suffice. For example, in *United States v. Hixon*,[31] the court reversed the defendant's false statement conviction. In that case, the alleged false statement — that defendant was not self-employed while receiving disability compensation — was literally true because the defendant was in fact employed by a corporation that he owned and thus was not self-employed. Also, where a statement is subject to two plausible interpretations, the burden is on the government to show that the defendant's intended interpretation was the false one.

Similarly, in *United States v. Safavian*,[32] the trial judge excluded expert testimony as to the meaning of the defendant's alleged false statement. The D.C. Circuit held that this was reversible error. The defendant's asserted meaning of the statement, if accepted by the jury, would have been literally true and therefore would not have supported a false statements conviction.

---

officer concerning a matter that the law required to be included in the pre-sentence report fell within the judicial proceeding exception). *See also* United States v. McNeil, 362 F.3d 570, 573 (9th Cir. 2004) (holding that, because district court's inquiry into defendant's financial status to determine whether he qualified for court-appointed counsel was a "judicial proceeding," defendant could not be prosecuted for making false statements in affidavit submitted in support of request for appointment of counsel).

[28]   United States v. Brown, 151 F.3d 476, 485 (6th Cir. 1998).

[29]   Gallagher & Kime, *supra* note 3, at nn. 52–54, and cases cited therein; Norman Abrams & Sara Sun Beale, Federal Criminal Law and Its Enforcement 591 (3d ed. 2000).

[30]   *See* Chapter 11, Perjury, *infra*, § 11.03[C][1].

[31]   987 F.2d 1261, 1265–68 (6th Cir. 1993). *See* James Nesland, *Perjury and False Declarations, in* White Collar Crime: Business and Regulatory Offenses § 10.02[2][b] (Otto Obermaier & Robert Morvillo, eds. 2011), and cases cited therein.

[32]   528 F.3d 957, 966–67 (D.C. Cir. 2008).

[C] Statements Concerning Future Actions

Defendants have argued that a statement of an intent to undertake or not undertake a future action cannot be false at the time the statement was made. Courts have generally rejected this argument.

In the highly publicized prosecution of criminal defense attorney Lynne Stewart, for example, the government alleged that the defendant made a false statement when she agreed to abide by certain government regulations regarding her representation of an alleged terrorist. Stewart later violated the regulations, and the government charged her with having made a false statement. The trial court rejected Stewart's motion to dismiss the § 1001 charge. The court held that false promises of future actions can support such a charge.[33]

Similarly, in *United States v. Shah*,[34] the defendant promised not to disclose bids in a competitive bidding solicitation, but later disclosed the bids. On appeal, the defendant argued that promises as to future actions are not false at the time they are made and that later actions contrary to the promise do not support a conviction. The court disagreed. The court noted that the defendant intended, at the time he made the promise, not to keep it. This intent rendered the statement false at the time it was made. As the court stated, "a promise to perform is not only a prediction, but is generally also a representation of present intent. Promises and representations are simply not mutually exclusive. The plain terms of the statute can therefore be said to cover representations of present intent."[35]

[D] Documents

As discussed above, certain documents may not qualify as "false statements." In *Williams v. United States*,[36] the Supreme Court held five-to-four that depositing a check written on a bank account with insufficient funds did not constitute making a false statement under 18 U.S.C. § 1014. That statute criminalizes knowingly making a false statement for the purpose of influencing a federally insured bank. The majority reasoned "a check is not a factual assertion at all, and therefore cannot be characterized as 'true' or 'false.' "[37] The dissent disagreed, arguing that the checks implied that there were sufficient funds in the account to cover the checks.[38]

And in *United States v. Blankenship*,[39] the Eleventh Circuit held that a contract is not a factual assertion. This was true even though the contract was a sham that the parties never intended to perform. As the court stated, "[l]ike a check, a contract is not a factual assertion, and therefore cannot be characterized as 'true'

---

[33] United States v. Sattar, 272 F. Supp. 2d 348, 377 (S.D.N.Y. 2003).

[34] 44 F.3d 285, 296 (5th Cir. 1995).

[35] *Id.*

[36] 458 U.S. 279 (1982). *See supra*, § 10.03[A].

[37] 458 U.S. at 284.

[38] *Id.* at 291 (White, J., dissenting).

[39] 382 F.3d 1110, 1135 (11th Cir. 2004).

or 'false.' Just as a check is not 'false' simply because neither the drawer nor the drawee intends that the drawee cash it, a contract is not false simply because neither party intends to enforce it."[40]

Note that there were strong dissents in both *Williams* and *Blankenship*. Thus, issues concerning whether certain documents may constitute false statements are far from settled.

§ 10.05 MATERIALITY

It is now clear that materiality is an element of a false statements case. Further, the materiality issue must be submitted to the jury. In the False Statements Accountability Act of 1996,[41] Congress amended the false statements statute expressly to make materiality an element of every case brought under the statute. Earlier, in *United States v. Gaudin*,[42] the parties stipulated that materiality was an element, and the Supreme Court did not reach the threshold issue of whether materiality was an element under the previous version of the statute. Assuming that materiality was an element, the Court held that the issue is a mixed question of law and fact that must be decided by the trier of fact.[43] Presumably, a judge's failure to instruct the jury on materiality would not automatically require reversal of a conviction, but instead would be subject to harmless error analysis.[44]

The Supreme Court has described a "material" statement as one having "a natural tendency to influence, or [be] capable of influencing, the decision of the decision-making body to which it was addressed."[45] Because of the breadth of this definition, courts seldom reverse false statements convictions for failure to prove materiality. Under the above standard, the government is not required to prove that the statement actually influenced or deceived the government body or agent, just that the statement had the capacity to do so. Accordingly, false statements to a government investigator may be material even if the investigator knew that the statements were false and thus was not deceived. In such situations, the false statements nonetheless may impede the investigation by preventing the investigator from discovering the facts.[46]

---

[40] *Id.*

[41] False Statements Accountability Act of 1996 § 2, codified at 18 U.S.C. § 1001.

[42] 515 U.S. 506 (1995).

[43] *Id.* at 511–14. *Cf.* United States v. Wells, 519 U.S. 482 (1997) (materiality not an element in case brought under 18 U.S.C. § 1014, which criminalizes false statements made to federally insured financial institution).

[44] *See* Neder v. United States, 527 U.S. 1, 8 (1999) (failure to instruct jury on materiality in federal mail fraud, wire fraud, and bank fraud prosecution does not necessarily require reversal but is subject to harmless error analysis).

[45] *Gaudin*, 515 U.S. at 509, *quoting* Kungys v. United States, 485 U.S. 759, 770 (1988).

[46] *See* United States v. LeMaster, 54 F.3d 1224, 1230–31 (6th Cir. 1995).

§ 10.06   THE REQUIRED MENS REA

The false statements statute requires proof that the defendant acted knowingly and willfully. Most litigation under this provision has turned upon the meaning of "knowledge." This issue has arisen both in the context of knowledge of facts giving rise to federal jurisdiction, and knowledge of the statement's falsity. Further, some cases discuss whether the defendant acted "willfully" or with the intent to deceive.

[A]   Knowledge of Falsity

The government must prove that the defendant knew the statement was false at the time it was made. As in other contexts, knowledge can be proven either by evidence of actual knowledge or by evidence that the defendant intentionally or recklessly avoided learning whether the statement was true or false.[47]

[B]   Knowledge of Facts Giving Rise to Federal Jurisdiction

The government is not required to show knowledge as to the jurisdictional element. That is, the government need not prove that the defendant knew that the statement fell within a matter of federal jurisdiction. The Supreme Court addressed this issue in *United States v. Yermian*.[48] In that case, the defendant was convicted on three counts of violating § 1001 based upon false statements he made on a security clearance questionnaire for his employer. The employer, a private defense contractor, forwarded the questionnaire to the Department of Defense. On appeal, Yermian argued that his conviction should be reversed because "he had no actual knowledge that his false statements would be transmitted to a federal agency."[49]

In a five-to-four decision, the Supreme Court rejected Yermian's argument. Interpreting the statutory language, the Court found that Congress did not intend the terms "knowingly and willfully" to apply to the jurisdictional element of § 1001. The Court noted that "[t]he jurisdictional language appears in a phrase separate from the prohibited conduct modified by the terms 'knowingly and willfully.' "[50] Thus, the terms "knowingly and willfully" naturally relate only to the making of "false, fictitious, or fraudulent statements . . . and not the predicate circumstance that those statements are in a matter within the jurisdiction of a federal agency."[51]

In *Yermian*, the Court only held that the government need not prove *knowledge* as to federal jurisdiction. The Court did not decide whether the statute requires that the government prove some lower level of mens rea, such as negligence.[52] Circuit courts have held that no such proof is required; under these decisions, the

---

[47] *See, e.g.*, United States v. Arnous, 122 F.3d 321, 323 (6th Cir. 1997) (conscious avoidance); United States v. Darrah, 119 F.3d 1322, 1328 (8th Cir. 1997) (reckless disregard); United States v. London, 66 F.3d 1227, 1241 (1st Cir. 1995) (same).

[48] 468 U.S. 63 (1984).

[49] *Id.* at 66.

[50] *Id.* at 69.

[51] *Id.*

[52] *See id.* at 69.

statute imposes strict liability on the element of federal jurisdiction.[53]

[C] Intent to Deceive

In addition to proof of knowledge that the statement was false, the government must prove that the defendant acted with the intent to deceive. Of course, proof that the defendant knew a statement was false will be strong circumstantial evidence that the defendant intended that the statement deceive the listener. When the government's theory is that the defendant concealed a material fact, the government must show the defendant knew of the duty to disclose a material fact and intentionally failed to do so.[54]

§ 10.07 JURISDICTION

[A] Statements Made to the Federal Government

In the False Statements Accountability Act of 1996, Congress amended § 1001 to apply to "any matter within the jurisdiction of the executive, legislative, or judicial branch" of the federal government.[55] The earlier version of the statute had applied to "any matter within the jurisdiction of any department or agency of the United States." In *Hubbard v. United States*,[56] the Supreme Court interpreted "department or agency" to exclude the judicial branch.

In 1996, Congress responded to *Hubbard* by amending § 1001 to include statements made to all three branches of government. The amendment contains two limitations, however. First, to protect the rights of courtroom advocates, Congress excluded from § 1001 "statements, representations, writings or documents submitted by [a party to a judicial proceeding, or that party's counsel] to a judge or a magistrate in that proceeding."[57] Second, with respect to congressional matters, § 1001 only applies to the administrative and investigative matters that the statute specifies.[58] The statute thus excludes, for example,

---

[53] *See, e.g.*, United States v. Meuli, 8 F.3d 1481, 1484–85 (10th Cir. 1993); United States v. Leo, 941 F.2d 181, 190 (3d Cir. 1991); United States v. Green, 745 F.2d 1205, 1209 (9th Cir. 1984), *cert. denied*, 474 U.S. 925 (1985).

[54] *See, e.g.*, United States v. Hernando Ospina, 798 F.2d 1570, 1580 (11th Cir. 1986).

[55] Pub. L. No. 104-292, 110 Stat. 3459 (1996) (amending 18 U.S.C. § 1001). One court has held that the jurisdictional element must be charged in the indictment and proven at trial. United States v. Pickett, 353 F.3d 62, 66–67 (D.C. Cir. 2004). In that case, the defendant was a Capital Police officer convicted of making a false statement in connection with a "bad joke" concerning an anthrax scare at the United States Capital. Because the government had failed to allege and prove that the statement was made within federal jurisdiction, the court reversed the § 1001 conviction.

[56] 514 U.S. 695 (1995), *overruling* United States v. Bramblett, 348 U.S. 503, 509 (1955) (holding that § 1001 applies to all three branches of the federal government).

[57] 18 U.S.C. § 1001(b).

[58] 18 U.S.C. § 1001(c) excludes congressional matters other than:

> (1) administrative matters, including a claim for payment, a matter related to the procurement of property or services, personnel or employment practices, or support services, or a document required by law, rule, or regulation to be submitted to the Congress or any office or officer within the legislative branch; or

statements made to members of Congress in correspondence from constituents. This limitation reflects Congress's goal to promote effective information-gathering.[59] Thus, Congress has specified that § 1001 applies to the three branches of government.

[B] The Definition of "Jurisdiction"

Congress has not, explicitly described the circumstances in which a statement will be considered to be within the "jurisdiction" of the particular government branch. The Supreme Court broadly interpreted the term "jurisdiction" in *United States v. Rodgers*.[60] In that case, the defendant falsely told the Federal Bureau of Investigation (FBI) that his wife had been kidnapped, and falsely told the United States Secret Service that his wife was involved in a plot to kill the President. He later admitted that he made the false reports so that the agencies would locate his wife, who had voluntarily left him. The trial court dismissed the indictment on the ground that the matters in the false statements were "not matters 'within the jurisdiction' of the respective agencies, as that phrase is used in § 1001," because the statements did not relate to the agencies' power to make final or binding determinations.[61]

The Supreme Court reinstated the indictment, holding that criminal investigations by the FBI and the Secret Service are matters "within the jurisdiction" of the agencies. The Court noted that the FBI and the Secret Service both have statutorily based authority over the investigations triggered by the false reports. The Court also concluded that a broad reading of § 1001 furthers a "valid legislative interest in protecting the integrity of . . . official inquiries."[62] Finally, the Court found that the term "jurisdiction" should not be limited to the power to make final or binding determinations because such a construction would lead to the exclusion of "most . . . of the authorized activities of many 'departments' and 'agencies' of the Federal Government."[63] Such an interpretation, the Court reasoned, would defeat Congress's purpose in using such expansive language.

Although *Rodgers* arose under the earlier version of § 1001, the Court's interpretation of the term "jurisdiction" should apply to the current version of the statute. This is especially so because Congress expressly intended to expand the scope of the statute's application when enacting the 1996 amendments.

---

(2) any investigation or review, conducted pursuant to the authority of any committee, subcommittee, commission or office of the Congress.

[59] *See* House Rep. No. 104-680, 104th Cong., 2d Sess. 4 (1996).

[60] 466 U.S. 475 (1984).

[61] *Id.* at 477.

[62] *Id.* at 481–82.

[63] *Id.* at 482.

[C] Statements Made to State and Local Agencies and to Private Parties

Questions concerning the scope of "jurisdiction" also arise when the defendant's conduct is directed to state agencies, local agencies, or private parties that have some relationship with the federal government. Courts have held that § 1001 applies to such agencies and parties when federal funding, or some other connection, is sufficient to bring the agencies or parties within the ambit of the statute.[64]

Further, courts generally agree that it is not necessary that a false statement actually be submitted to the federal government. In *United States v. Lutz*,[65] the defendant operated a mortgage brokerage company that was authorized by the United States Department of Housing and Urban Development ("HUD") to originate loans. The government charged Lutz with eleven counts of making false statements in loan application documents she prepared. The Sixth Circuit upheld the convictions even though the documents were not submitted to HUD. The court found that a violation of § 1001 does not require that the false statement be made directly to, or received by, the federal department or agency. Rather, the statute only requires the false statement to have the natural tendency to influence or be capable of influencing a federal agency.[66] Similarly, courts agree that false statements made only indirectly to the federal government may give rise to federal jurisdiction.[67]

When the statement is quite removed from the federal government, the issues become more complex. For example, courts have struggled to articulate the test for determining jurisdiction when the statement was made to a state or local government and has only a tangential connection to the federal government. A number of courts have extended jurisdiction quite broadly in this context. In *United States v. Herring*,[68] the defendant lied on a state unemployment benefits application. On appeal from his § 1001 conviction, the defendant argued that, even though the state agency received federal funds to administer the program, the false statement did not give rise to federal jurisdiction because the federal government was not involved in the decision to grant the benefits, did not fund the benefits, and did not pursue investigations for false benefits claims. The court rejected the argument, finding that federal funding of and supervisory control over the program provided a sufficient nexus to the federal government.[69]

---

[64] *Compare* United States v. Candella, 487 F.2d 1223, 1226 (2d Cir. 1973) (finding federal jurisdiction), *and* United States v. Baker, 626 F.2d 512, 516 (5th Cir. 1980) (same), *with* United States v. Blankenship, 382 F.3d 1110, 1132 (11th Cir. 2004) (false statements did not fall within the federal jurisdiction), *and* Lowe v. United States, 141 F.2d 1005, 1006 (5th Cir. 1944) (same). *See* Abrams & Beale, *supra* note 29, at 584 (noting circuit split with respect to application of § 1001 to false statements made to obtain state unemployment benefits). Note that an analogous issue arises with respect to the term "federal public official" under the federal bribery statute. *See* Chapter 8, Bribery and Gratuities, *supra*, § 8.05.

[65] 154 F.3d 581 (6th Cir. 1998).

[66] *Id.* at 587–88.

[67] *See, e.g.,* United States v. Wright, 988 F.2d 1036, 1038–39 (10th Cir. 1993).

[68] 916 F.2d 1543 (11th Cir. 1990).

[69] *Id.* at 1547 ("false statements need not be presented to an agency of the United States and that

Similarly, in *United States v. Wright*,[70] the defendant submitted false reports concerning drinking water quality, and submitted the reports to the county health department. The county sent the forms to the state health department, which had authority granted by the United States Environmental Protection Agency (EPA) to enforce state drinking water standards. On appeal, the defendant argued that the federal connection was too tenuous to support § 1001 jurisdiction because there was no direct relationship between the false statements and the EPA. The court disagreed, noting that the EPA retained the authority to enforce the drinking water standards, monitored the state's enforcement of those standards, and conditioned federal funding on the state's adherence to federal regulations. The court concluded a "state agency's use of federal funds, standing alone, is generally sufficient to establish jurisdiction under § 1001."[71]

Similar issues arise when defendants make false statements in the performance of subcontracts to which the federal government is not a party. Some courts find subcontracts too far removed from the federal government to support jurisdiction. For example, in *United States v. Blankenship*,[72] a construction company contracted to provide services to a state department of transportation. The state agency received federal funds, and agreed to comply with applicable federal requirements in order to receive those funds. Subcontractors of the construction company made false statements in their contracts with the construction company, placing the state agency in violation of the federal requirements.

On appeal, the defendants argued that false statements made in the subcontracts were not within federal jurisdiction under § 1001. The majority of the court agreed, reasoning that "if § 1001 were interpreted to prohibit any false statement to any private entity whose funds, in whole or in part, happened to originate with the federal government, the results would be shocking. To start with a simple example, any employee of either [the construction company] or its subcontractors who may have padded his resume to obtain a job on the project would be guilty of a federal offense."[73] The dissent strongly disagreed, concluding that the contracts fell within federal jurisdiction under *Herring* because the state was bound to follow the federal requirements and risked losing federal funds if it failed to do so.[74]

Whether a false statement in a subcontract is within federal jurisdiction may depend on the federal government's role in enforcing the terms of the subcontract. In *United States v. Steiner Plastics Manufacturing*,[75] the federal government's

---

federal funds need not actually be used to pay a claimant for federal agency jurisdiction to exist under § 1001"). *But cf.* United States v. Holmes, 111 F.3d 463, 466 (6th Cir. 1997) ("Where, as here, the federal government neither funds the fraudulently obtained state benefit payments, nor has any authority to act upon discovering that the state program has been defrauded, false statements made to the state agency cannot be said to come 'within the jurisdiction of any department or agency of the United States' ").

[70] 988 F.2d 1036 (10th Cir. 1993).

[71] *Id.* at 1039.

[72] 382 F.3d 1110 (11th Cir. 2004).

[73] *Id.* at 1137–38.

[74] *Id.* at 1144–51 (Black, J., dissenting).

[75] 231 F.2d 149 (2d Cir. 1956).

role was sufficient to support jurisdiction. Steiner Plastics manufactured jet cockpit canopies under a contract with the Grumman Aircraft Engineering Corporation, which produced jet planes under a contract with the United States Navy. When some of the cockpits were found to be defective, the defendant switched approval stamps and serial numbers from approved canopies to the defective ones. The defendant appealed its false statement conviction, arguing that the false statements made in performance of the subcontract were not within federal jurisdiction. The court disagreed, based upon the Navy's contractual right to inspect the canopies, the canopies' shipment to the government, and the defendant's intent to deceive the government.

These cases show that courts generally read the jurisdictional element broadly, as *Rodgers* requires. At the margins, however, it is not easy to determine when jurisdiction is present. Some courts hold that any federal funding is sufficient, no matter how removed the federal government is from the local or state government operations. This approach provides for extremely broad jurisdiction, and may carry *Rodgers* too far. As a general matter, the greater the level of federal supervision over the program at issue, the more likely a court is to find that jurisdiction is present. Where the federal government's role is many steps removed from the program, as in *Blankenship*, jurisdiction may not lie.

§ 10.08   SECTION 1001 AND OTHER OFFENSES

In false statements prosecutions, as in other areas of white collar crime,[76] one instance of conduct may give rise to punishment for multiple charges so long as the punishment does not run afoul of the Double Jeopardy Clause. The guiding rule is set forth in the Supreme Court's decision in *Blockburger v. United States.*[77] Under the *Blockburger* rule, the same conduct can give rise to multiple charges so long as (1) each crime requires proof of an element that the other does not, and (2) there is no clear congressional intent to prohibit multiple charges.

This issue arose in *United States v. Woodward.*[78] There, the defendant marked "no" in response to a customs form question as to whether he or a family member was transporting over $5,000 in cash. In fact, the defendant and his wife were carrying over $20,000 in cash. Based on this conduct, the defendant was convicted and separately sentenced under both § 1001 and under the applicable currency reporting statute. Applying *Blockburger*, the Supreme Court first found that the elements of the two statutes, while overlapping, are not identical; § 1001 prohibits the failure to disclose a material fact only in instances where "the fact is 'conceal[ed] . . . by any *trick, scheme, or device.*' A person could, without employing a 'trick, scheme, or device,' simply and willfully fail to file a currency disclosure report."[79] As

---

[76] *See, e.g., infra* § 12.04 (charging perjury and obstruction of justice based upon same false testimony).

[77] 284 U.S. 299 (1932). The Supreme Court further refined the *Blockburger* test in United States v. Dixon, 509 U.S. 688 (1993). *See generally* 2 Joshua Dressler & Alan C. Michaels, Understanding Criminal Procedure ch. 14 (3d ed. 2006).

[78] 469 U.S. 105 (1985).

[79] *Id.* at 108 (emphasis in original).

to *Blockburger*'s second element, the Court found that "[t]here is no evidence in 18 U.S.C. § 1001 and [the currency reporting statute] that Congress did not intend to allow separate punishment for the two different offenses."[80] Indeed, the Court concluded, the two offenses "are directed to separate evils."[81]

Determining whether a false statement can give rise to punishment under both § 1001 and another statute depends on the application of the *Blockburger* rule to the particular statutes at issue.[82] Thus, it would violate the Double Jeopardy Clause for a defendant to be convicted and sentenced under both § 1001 and under another false statements statute with the same elements.[83] Where the elements differ, however, a defendant can be convicted and punished under both statutes. For example, in *United States v. Ramos*,[84] the defendant made false statements on a passport application. He was convicted under both § 1001 and under 18 U.S.C. § 1542, which specifically criminalizes making a false statement with the intent to secure a passport. The court rejected the defendant's double jeopardy argument, finding that each statute requires proof of an element that the other does not. Section 1001 requires proof that the false statement be of a material fact in federal jurisdiction, while § 1542 only requires proof that the false statement was made with the intent to obtain a passport.

---

[80] *Id. See generally* Missouri v. Hunter, 459 U.S. 359, 367 (1983); Albernaz v. United States, 450 U.S. 333, 340 (1981).

[81] *See Woodward*, 469 U.S. at 109, *quoting* Albernaz v. United States, 450 U.S. 333, 343 (1981).

[82] *Compare* Baker & Young, *supra* note 3, at nn.103–107 (citing cases where no *Blockburger* violation found), *with id.* at n.109 (citing cases disallowing multiple punishments under *Blockburger*).

[83] *See, e.g.*, United States v. Avelino, 967 F.2d 815 (2d Cir. 1992) (counts brought under § 1001 and 18 U.S.C. § 582, which criminalizes the making of false statements to United States Customs officials).

[84] 725 F.2d 1322, 1323 (11th Cir. 1984).

Chapter 11

PERJURY AND FALSE DECLARATIONS

§ 11.01   INTRODUCTION

In its broadest terms, the crime of perjury occurs when a person lies under oath. This rubric encompasses the general federal perjury statute,[1] the more narrowly tailored false declarations statute,[2] and the yet-narrower statutes that criminalize lying under oath in particular circumstances.[3] The general perjury statute, contained in § 1621 of the federal criminal code, is the current incarnation of a common-law based statute originally enacted in the eighteenth century.[4] The false declarations statute, contained in § 1623 of the federal criminal code, was enacted in 1970, and covers false statements in judicial and grand jury proceedings. This chapter focuses on §§ 1621 and 1623, which are used in the vast majority of federal perjury prosecutions.

As with other "cover-up" crimes, a perjury investigation or prosecution may stand on its own, as in the case of former President Bill Clinton.[5] More commonly, a perjury investigation or prosecution may grow out of a defendant's attempt to hide earlier illegal activity, as in the cases of media figure Martha Stewart, vice-presidential aid Scooter Libby, and baseball player Barry Bonds.[6] In either event,

---

[1] 18 U.S.C. § 1621.

[2] 18 U.S.C. § 1623.

[3] *See, e.g.*, 26 U.S.C. § 7206 (perjury in connection with filing a tax return). For an overview of the crimes of perjury and false declarations, see Stuart P. Green, *Perjury, in* Lying, Cheating, and Stealing: A Moral Theory of White Collar Crime (2006); James Nesland, *Perjury and False Declarations, in* White Collar Crime: Business and Regulatory Offenses §§ 10.01–03 (Otto Obermaier & Robert Morvillo, eds. 2011); William M. Sloan, *Perjury*, 47 Am. Crim. L. Rev. 889 (2010).

[4] *See* Sarah N. Welling et al., Federal Criminal Law and Related Actions § 20.1–20.2 (1998 & Supp. 2000).

[5] Clinton's alleged perjury ultimately led to the initiation of impeachment proceedings against him. *See* Stuart P. Green, *Perjury, in* Lying, Cheating, and Stealing: A Moral Theory of White Collar Crime 140, 140–47 (2006).

[6] Martha Stewart was found guilty of conspiracy to commit perjury in connection with her alleged insider trading. Peter Bacanovic, Stewart's broker and co-defendant, was found guilty of perjury. *See* United States v. Stewart, 323 F. Supp. 2d 606 (S.D.N.Y. 2004), discussed § 5.04[C][2], *supra*. Libby, under investigation for violating national security laws in connection with the CIA leak case, was convicted of perjury. United States v. Libby, 498 F. Supp. 2d 1 (D.C. Cir. 2007). Bonds, under investigation for the illegal use of steroids, was charged with perjury and obstruction. The jury convicted Bonds on the obstruction charge but was unable to reach a verdict on the perjury charges. *See* Juliet Macur, *As Bonds Appeals Verdict, Jurors Who Convicted Him Will Be Watching Closely*, N.Y. Times, May 17, 2011, at B15. For an analysis of these cases, see James B. Stewart, How False Statements Are Undermining America: From Martha Stewart to Bernie Madoff (2011).

perjury is sometimes considered difficult to prove because courts have imposed particularly strict evidentiary requirements in some cases.[7] Nonetheless, adding a perjury charge to a broader indictment provides the government with the tactical advantage of questioning the defendant's credibility at the outset of the case.

§ 11.02 THE STATUTORY PROVISIONS

[A] Introduction

This section sets forth the elements of §§ 1621 and 1623, and compares the elements under the two statutes. Initially, it is important to note the fundamental difference between the statutes. Although §§ 1621 and 1623 overlap, § 1623 *only* applies to court and grand jury proceedings. Section 1621 is much broader in application. Thus, perjury committed in a judicial or grand jury proceeding could be charged under either statute,[8] but perjury *outside the judicial or grand jury context* (as in an administrative agency proceeding, for example) could *only* be charged under § 1621.

[B] Elements of § 1621[9]

Under § 1621, the government must prove the following elements:[10]

1. The defendant testified under oath in a proceeding in which United States law provides that an oath be administered;

---

[7] *See* Robert G. Morvillo & Christopher J. Morvillo, *Untangling the Web: Defending a Perjury Case,* 33 Litigation, Winter 2007, at 8 ("perjury statutes are deliberately (and notoriously) difficult to enforce"). These evidentiary requirements are seen as necessary both to encourage witnesses to come forward and testify without an undue fear of being charged with perjury, and to prevent prosecutors from abusing their discretion in bringing a case that otherwise could simply be a "swearing contest" between two witnesses. As discussed below, Congress has reduced the proof required to obtain a conviction under § 1623. *See infra,* § 11.02[D].

[8] Although courts have allowed prosecutors discretion in choosing which statute to use, *see* United States v. Sherman, 150 F.3d 306, 312–13 (3d Cir. 1998), at least one court indicated that such discretion may be unfair. *See* United States v. Kahn, 472 F.2d 272, 283 (2d Cir.), *cert. denied,* 411 U.S. 982 (1973) ("we find not a little disturbing the prospect of the government employing § 1621 whenever a recantation exists, and § 1623 when one does not, simply to place perjury defendants in the most disadvantageous trial position").

[9] Section 1621 provides that whoever:

(1) having taken an oath before a competent tribunal, officer, or person, in any case in which a law of the United States authorizes an oath to be administered, that he will testify, declare, depose, or certify truly, or that any written testimony, declaration, deposition, or certificate by him subscribed, is true, willfully and contrary to such oath states or subscribes any material matter which he does not believe to be true; or

(2) in any declaration, certificate, verification, or statement under penalty of perjury as permitted under section 1746 of title 28, United States Code, willfully subscribes as true any material matter which he does not believe to be true; is guilty of perjury and shall, except as otherwise expressly provided by law, be fined under this title or imprisoned not more than five years, or both.

[10] *See generally* United States v. Debrow, 346 U.S. 374, 376–77 (1953).

2. The oath was administered by a person qualified by law to administer the oath;

3. The defendant made a false statement;

4. The statement was material to the proceedings; and

5. The defendant acted willfully and with knowledge of the statements falsity.

[C]   Elements of § 1623[11]

Under § 1623, the government must prove the following elements:

1. The defendant undertook an oath;

2. The oath was administered before or ancillary to a court or grand jury proceeding;

3. The defendant made a false statement or used false information;

4. The false statement or information was material to the proceeding; and

5. The defendant knew the statement or information was false.

[D]   Key Differences Between § 1621 and § 1623

Section 1623, the false declarations statute, was enacted to supplement, not replace, § 1621, the general perjury statute.[12] In particular, Congress enacted § 1623 to promote truthful testimony in court and grand jury proceedings. As explained more fully below, in some cases it is easier to prove a violation of § 1623 than it is to prove a violation of § 1621. First, under § 1623 — but not under § 1621 — the government can obtain a conviction by adducing proof of two inconsistent statements without showing which of the two statements was false.[13] Second, a conviction under § 1623 can rest solely on the testimony of a single witness; under § 1621, the government must provide additional corroborating evidence under the "two-witness" rule. On the other hand, § 1623 allows for a witness to take back, or "recant," testimony and avoid prosecution in certain circumstances; § 1621 provides

---

[11] Section 1623(a) provides:

> Whoever under oath (or in any declaration, certificate, verification, or statement under penalty of perjury as permitted under section 1746 of title 28, United States Code) in any proceeding before or ancillary to any court or grand jury of the United States knowingly makes any false material declaration or makes or uses any other information, including any book, paper, document, record, recording, or other material, knowing the same to contain any false material declaration, shall be fined under this title or imprisoned not more than five years, or both.

[12] *See* S. Rep. No. 91-617, at 109 (1969); Nesland, *supra* note 3, at § 10.01[1]. Note that the statutory sentence under each statute is the same — imprisonment of not more than five years and/or a fine for each count; the actual sentence in any case will depend upon the trial court's application of the advisory United States Sentencing Guidelines to the facts of the case. *See* Chapter 21, Sentencing, *infra.*

[13] *See, e.g.,* United States v. McAfee, 8 F.3d 1010 (5th Cir. 1993) (affirming defendant's conviction based upon inconsistent statements made in civil depositions).

no such defense.[14]

In summary, the key differences between the two statutes are:

1. Section 1623 *only* applies to *court and grand jury proceedings*; § 1621 is not so limited;[15]

2. Section 1623 allows the use of *inconsistent statements* to prove guilt, without requiring the government to prove which of the two statements was false; § 1621 contains no such provision;[16]

3. Section 1623 does away with the so-called *"two-witness rule,"* which courts have imposed under § 1621, requiring proof both by one witness and by additional corroborating evidence;[17]

4. Section 1623 provides for a limited recantation defense; § 1621 provides no such defense.[18]

Each of these differences is discussed in more detail in the sections that follow.

§ 11.03   THE ELEMENTS OF A PERJURY CASE

[A]   Oath

Under §§ 1621 and 1623, the government must prove beyond a reasonable doubt that the defendant made the alleged false statement under oath. The statutes do not, however, require any particular type of oath. In addition, § 1621 requires on its face that the person administering the oath be authorized to do so. While § 1623 contains no such explicit requirement, authorization to administer the oath is implicit in the statute.[19]

---

[14] *See* United States v. Norris, 300 U.S. 564, 573–74 (1937) (in a case decided before the enactment of the false declarations statute, the Court rejected the defendant's assertion that he should have been allowed to assert a recantation defense where he had recanted his false testimony before the end of the proceedings).

[15] *See infra*, § 11.03[B].

[16] *See infra*, § 11.03[C][3].

[17] *See infra*, § 11.03[F].

[18] *See infra*, § 11.04. There are two additional, but less significant, differences. First, § 1621 requires proof that the defendant acted knowingly and willfully; § 1623 only requires proof that the defendant acted knowingly. As a practical matter, these standards are similar. *See infra*, § 11.03[D][2]. Second, the oath requirement is somewhat more onerous under § 1621 than under § 1623, although this issue is seldom litigated. For a comparison of the two statutes, see Stuart P. Green, *Lying, Misleading, and Falsely Denying: How Moral Concepts Inform the Law of Perjury, Fraud, and False Statements*, 53 Hastings L.J. 157, 174 & n.56 (2001).

[19] *See* Nesland, *supra* note 3, § 10.01[2][a], and cases cited therein.

[B] Tribunals and Proceedings

In a prosecution under either § 1621 or § 1623, the government must show that the tribunal was authorized to conduct the proceeding.[20] As noted above, § 1623 only applies to proceedings "before or ancillary to any court or grand jury." Section 1621 applies both to court and grand jury proceedings, and to all other proceedings in which an oath is authorized under federal law, such as congressional and administrative agency proceedings.

Courts have limited the definition of proceedings "before or ancillary to any court or grand jury" under § 1623. In *Dunn v. United States*,[21] the Supreme Court interpreted the term "ancillary proceedings." In that case, Dunn testified before a grand jury and incriminated the grand jury's target, Musgrave. The grand jury subsequently indicted Musgrave. After his grand jury appearance, Dunn went to Musgrave's attorney's office and there made an oral, sworn statement denying that Musgrave had been involved in the criminal activity. Musgrave's attorney then moved to dismiss the indictment, alleging that the testimony upon which it was based was false. The trial court held an evidentiary hearing during which Dunn repeated, under oath, the statement he had made in the attorney's office. Dunn was indicted and convicted of violating § 1623 based upon the sworn statement he gave in Musgrave's attorney's office.

On appeal, Dunn argued that a sworn statement made in the informal setting of the attorney's office was not made in a proceeding "ancillary" to a court or grand jury. The Supreme Court agreed, and reversed the conviction. The Court rejected the government's contention that *any* sworn statement submitted to a court or grand jury qualifies under § 1623.[22] Relying upon the plain meaning of "proceeding" and upon the legislative history, the Court found that Congress intended that only statements made in a formal setting be prosecuted under § 1623. Such a setting would include a deposition, conducted pursuant to the applicable federal rules, in which a stenographer is present and the witness is represented by counsel.[23] It does not include a sworn statement made in the informal setting of an attorney's office, without a stenographer and opposing counsel.

[C] Falsity

[1] Literally True or Non-Responsive Answers

Any perjury charge must include proof beyond a reasonable doubt that the allegedly perjurious statement was indeed false. The leading case on the issue of falsity is *Bronston v. United States*[24] in which the United States Supreme Court held that a "literally true" but misleading statement will not suffice for a conviction.

---

[20] *Id.* at § 10.01[2][b].

[21] 442 U.S. 100 (1979).

[22] *Id.* at 107.

[23] *Id.* at 111–12.

[24] 409 U.S. 352 (1973).

In *Bronston*, the defendant's company had filed for bankruptcy protection. As part of the bankruptcy proceedings, Bronston was questioned under oath as to the company's assets:

Q: Do you have any bank accounts in Swiss banks, Mr. Bronston?

A: No, sir.

Q: Have you ever?

A: The company had an account there for about six months, in Zurich.[25]

At Bronston's perjury trial, the government proved that, prior to this testimony, Bronston had held personal Swiss bank accounts for several years. The jury convicted Bronston of perjury based upon the above testimony.

On appeal, the defendant argued that his two answers were literally true — (1) he did not, at the time of the testimony, have personal accounts in Swiss banks, and (2) the company had held Swiss bank accounts in the past. Literally true testimony, according to Bronston, could not support a perjury conviction. The government countered that his testimony was intended to mislead the questioner into believing that Bronston had *never* had personal Swiss bank accounts, and that proof of intentionally misleading and nonresponsive testimony sufficed.

The Supreme Court reversed the conviction. The Court found that § 1621 does not apply to literally true statements, and that the burden is on the questioner to clarify ambiguous or nonresponsive answers. The Court further noted that Congress would not have intended for the government to pursue a perjury prosecution in order to fix a testimonial mishap that could have been cured by a single additional question. The Court continued, "[u]nder the pressures and tensions of interrogation, it is not uncommon for the most earnest witnesses to give answers that are not entirely responsive."[26] After the above answers were given, the questioner could simply have asked, "[h]ave you ever had any personal Swiss bank accounts, Mr. Bronston?" A "no" response to this question would indeed have been perjurious.

[2] Ambiguous Questions and Answers

One aspect of the *Bronston* decision is clear — a literally true answer will not suffice for a conviction. The Court in *Bronston* declined to address, however, the issues whether a perjury conviction can rest on (a) an answer given to an *ambiguous question*, or (b) an *ambiguous answer*. Note that Bronston's answer was literally true under any interpretation of the question. Thus, the issue of an ambiguous question or answer did not arise given the Court's disposition of the case.

There are circumstances, however, in which a finding of falsity will depend on how the question or answer is interpreted. For example, a defendant might claim that a term used in the question was unclear or ambiguous. In such circumstances, some courts allow the jury to determine whether the defendant understood the questioner's meaning and intended to give false testimony. For example, in *United*

---

[25] *Id.* at 354.

[26] *Id.* at 358.

States v. Long,[27] the court affirmed a perjury conviction where the jury could have found that the defendant reasonably understood such terms as "bribe" and "kickback" used in the question.[28]

Other courts have reversed convictions, however, when they have found that the questions were genuinely ambiguous, a result that is consistent with *Bronston*. For example, in *United States v. Lattimore*,[29] the court reversed a conviction where the witness had denied being "a follower of the Communist line." The court held that a response to the question could not support a false statement conviction because the phrase used in the question was ambiguous. Similarly, when a party has given an ambiguous answer, the burden should be on the questioner to clarify the answer.[30]

[3] Inconsistent Statements

Under § 1623, but not under § 1621, the government may prove falsity by proving that the defendant made "two or more declarations, which are inconsistent to the degree that one of them is necessarily false."[31] In this situation, proof of inconsistency will suffice even if the government is unable to identify which of the statements is false. In order for the inconsistency to support a conviction, each statement must be material to the point at issue, and must have been made within the statute of limitations period.

---

[27] 534 F.2d 1097, 1100 (3d Cir. 1976). The courts are far from consistent in their approaches to this issue. *See* Nesland, *supra* note 3, § 10.01[2][g][i]–[iii], and cases cited therein.

[28] *Accord,* United States v. Thomas, 612 F.3d 1107 (9th Cir. 2010) (defendant not entitled to literal truth defense when ambiguous terms in questions and answers were open to different interpretations the meaning of which could be determined by the jury).

[29] 127 F. Supp. 405, 409–10 (D.D.C. 1955). For a more detailed discussion of this issue, see Green, *supra* note 18, at 180–82.

[30] Once again, courts are not consistent in their approaches to this issue. *See* Nesland, *supra* note 3, § 10.01[2][g][i]–[iii], and cases cited therein.

[31] Section 1623(c) provides:

An indictment or information for violation of this section alleging that, in any proceedings before or ancillary to any court or grand jury of the United States, the defendant under oath has knowingly made two or more declarations, which are inconsistent to the degree that one of them is necessarily false, need not specify which declaration is false if -

(1) each declaration was material to the point in question, and

(2) each declaration was made within the period of the statute of limitations for the offense charged under this section.

In any prosecution under this section, the falsity of a declaration set forth in the indictment or information shall be established sufficient for conviction by proof that the defendant while under oath made irreconcilably contradictory declarations material to the point in question in any proceeding before or ancillary to any court or grand jury. It shall be a defense to an indictment or information made pursuant to the first sentence of this subsection that the defendant at the time he made each declaration believed the declaration was true.

[D] Mens Rea

[1] Knowledge of Falsity

Both § 1621 and § 1623 require that the government prove beyond a reasonable doubt that the defendant knew the statement was false at the time the statement was made.[32] The knowledge requirement is not met if the defendant made an honest mistake or genuinely had a faulty recollection.[33]

[2] Willfulness

Section 1621, unlike § 1623, requires that, in addition to proof of knowledge, the government prove that the defendant acted willfully. The difference between proof of knowledge of falsity alone (under § 1623) and proof of such knowledge plus willfulness (under § 1621) is not entirely clear. Some courts have suggested that the latter requires the government to show an actual intent to deceive.[34] As a practical matter, once the government has proven that a defendant knowingly made a false statement, a jury can naturally infer that the defendant intended to deceive.

[E] Materiality

In a perjury prosecution, the government must prove beyond a reasonable doubt that the false statement was material. A material statement is one that is capable of having an effect on the tribunal or proceeding. Stated another way, a statement is material if a truthful statement would assist in the matter. The government need not show that the tribunal or proceeding was actually affected.[35]

Defendants often raise lack of materiality as a defense in perjury cases. Because "materiality" is so broadly defined, however, such arguments rarely succeed. This is particularly true in the grand jury context. The Supreme Court has consistently granted grand juries broad discretion in conducting their investigations.[36] Thus, a wide variety of statements may be material to a grand jury investigation.

Materiality is an element of the offense, and therefore must be found by the jury rather than the court. Lower courts had previously held that materiality is a question of law to be decided by the court.[37] In 1995, however, the United States Supreme Court held in *United States v. Gaudin*,[38] that in a false statements prosecution, the trier of fact must determine that the statement was material beyond a reasonable doubt.[39] In 1997, in *Johnson v. United States*,[40] the Court

---

[32] *See* United States v. DeZarn, 157 F.3d 1042, 1044 (6th Cir. 1998); Sloan, *supra* note 3, at 895.

[33] *See* Sloan, *supra* note 3, at 895.

[34] *See* United States v. Swainson, 548 F.2d 657, 662 (6th Cir. 1977).

[35] *See, e.g.,* United States v. Regan, 103 F.3d 1072, 1084–85 (2d Cir. 1997).

[36] *See, e.g.,* United States v. R. Enterprises, 498 U.S. 292 (1991) (broadly defining permissible scope of grand jury subpoena power).

[37] *See* Nesland, *supra* note 3, § 10.01[2][e].

[38] 515 U.S. 506, 522–23 (1995).

[39] *See* § 10.5, *supra.*

extended this holding to perjury prosecutions.

[F]   The "Two-Witness" Rule

In § 1621 prosecutions, courts have imposed the common-law based "two-witness" rule.[41] As the Supreme Court stated in *Hammer v. United States*,[42] the "rule in prosecutions for perjury is that the uncorroborated oath of one witness is not enough to establish the falsity of the testimony of the accused set forth in the indictment." The "two-witness" rule reflects the courts' historical reluctance to allow perjury convictions based upon the uncorroborated testimony of a single witness, and prohibits convictions based simply on a swearing contest between the defendant and the accuser. Thus, when the government's case rests upon one witness's testimony, that testimony must be supported by corroborating evidence.

Courts have set different standards for determining whether the corroborating evidence is sufficient to support a conviction. One often-applied standard requires that such evidence be inconsistent with the defendant's innocence;[43] that is, that "such evidence . . . [must] tend to substantiate that part of the testimony of the principal prosecution witness which is material in showing that the statement made by the accused under oath was false."[44]

It is important to note that the term "two-witness rule" is a misnomer. The rule requires that perjury be proven by one witness plus some corroborative evidence — including documentary and circumstantial evidence — not necessarily by two live witnesses. Also, the two-witness requirement does not apply to prosecutions under § 1623,[45] and a prosecutor has the discretion to charge under § 1623 if the other elements of that section are met.[46] In this respect, a prosecution under § 1623 is easier than a prosecution under § 1621.

Application of the two-witness rule is fact-intensive, and the outcome is likely to turn on the degree to which the corroborative evidence is incriminating. For example, in *United States v. Chestman*,[47] the Second Circuit found that the corroborative evidence did not suffice because it was consistent with the

---

[40] 520 U.S. 461, 465 (1997). *Johnson* held that materiality is an element for the jury to determine under the plain language of § 1623. The same reasoning applies to § 1621.

[41] *See, e.g.*, United States v. Menting, 166 F.3d 923, 929 (7th Cir. 1999).

[42] 271 U.S. 620, 626 (1926).

[43] *See* United States v. Weiner, 479 F.2d 923, 926 (2d Cir. 1973).

[44] *Id.* at 927–28. As the Supreme Court stated in Weiler v. United States, 323 U.S. 606, 610 (1945), a court assessing the sufficiency of the corroborative evidence must find "(1) that the evidence, if true, substantiates the testimony of a single witness who has sworn to the falsity of the alleged perjurious statement; (2) that the corroborative evidence is trustworthy."

[45] Section 1623(e) provides:

  Proof beyond a reasonable doubt under this section is sufficient for conviction. It shall not be necessary that such proof be made by any particular number of witnesses or by documentary or other type of evidence.

[46] *See* Kahn, 472 F.2d at 283.

[47] 903 F.2d 75 (2d Cir. 1990), *aff'd in part and rev'd in part on other grounds*, 947 F.2d 551 (2d Cir. 1991) *(en banc)*, *cert. denied*, 503 U.S. 1004 (1992). *Chestman* is discussed more fully in Chapter 5, Securities Fraud, *supra*, § 5.06[D][2][a].

defendant's innocence. In that case, the defendant had been under investigation for illegally trading in securities based upon inside information. Before he was criminally charged with insider trading, Chestman testified in a Securities and Exchange Commission deposition. He testified under oath that he had purchased the stock *before* he had spoken with the alleged corporate insider, Keith Loeb. Based upon this testimony, Chestman was charged under § 1621 in addition to the substantive securities fraud charges.[48]

Loeb was the government's only witness on the perjury charge. He testified that he gave Chestman inside information before Chestman purchased the securities. To corroborate Loeb's testimony, the government offered (1) a phone message indicating that Loeb had called Chestman prior to the trading, (2) Chestman's failure to record the trade in his personal notes on the day of the trade, and (3) the timing of the trade. The jury convicted Chestman of violating § 1621.

The Second Circuit reversed, finding that none of the pieces of evidence corroborated Loeb's testimony that he had spoken with Chestman prior to the securities trading. Specifically: (1) the phone message could indicate that Loeb did not reach Chestman before Chestman traded; (2) Chestman's failure to record the trade was inconsequential given that, as a stock broker, Chestman knew the trade would be documented in official records; and (3) the timing of the trade was consistent with Chestman's testimony that he traded based upon his own research.[49] This holding shows that, where the corroborative evidence is as consistent with innocence as with guilt, it may not suffice to sustain a conviction.

On the other hand, if the corroborative evidence does have a tendency to prove guilt, a court will likely find it sufficient. For example, in *United States v. Davis*,[50] the Ninth Circuit rejected a two-witness rule challenge to a perjury conviction. In that case, Davis told a government investigator that Gustafon was involved in a burglary. Davis then signed a statement implicating Gustafon. At a later grand jury appearance, however, Davis denied that he had implicated Gustafon in earlier conversations with the investigator.

The government charged Davis with seven counts of perjury based upon his grand jury testimony. The government investigator was the government's only witness in the perjury case against Davis. To corroborate the investigator's testimony, the government offered Davis's signed statement. On appeal, the Ninth Circuit found that the signed statement qualified as corroborative evidence under the two-witness rule. The court stated that corroborative evidence does not independently have to establish the guilt of the defendant,[51] and that the corroborative evidence may be circumstantial.[52] The court further rejected Davis's argument that his own acts could not provide the corroboration, concluding that

---

[48] Section 1623 was not applicable because the testimony was before an administrative agency, not a court or grand jury.

[49] 903 F.2d at 81–82.

[50] 548 F.2d 840 (9th Cir. 1977).

[51] 548 F.2d 840, 843 (9th Cir. 1977), *citing* United States v. Howard, 445 F.2d 821, 822 (9th Cir. 1971).

[52] 548 F.2d 840, 843 (9th Cir. 1977), *citing* Vuckson v. United States, 354 F.2d 918, 920 (9th Cir.), *cert. denied*, 384 U.S. 991 (1966).

"[s]ince the corroborative evidence need not be strong nor even independently sufficient in itself, it may be supplied by the defendant's own conduct."[53]

A similar issue arose in the prosecution of Peter Bacanovic, Martha Stewart's stockbroker and co-defendant.[54] Bacanovic was convicted of perjury based on statements he made during testimony before the SEC in its investigation of ImClone stock trading. Bacanovic testified that he recalled leaving a message with Stewart's assistant asking Stewart to return his call, but also testified that he did not remember saying during the conversation that the price of ImClone stock was declining. The government alleged that Bacanovic's stated lack of recollection was false, and offered as proof Stewart's assistant's testimony and an electronic message that the assistant wrote for Stewart stating that "Peter Bacanovic thinks ImClone is going to start trading downward." On appeal, the Second Circuit rejected Bacanovic's argument that the electronic message — admitted under the business records exception to the hearsay rule — did not qualify as corroborating evidence because it came from the same source (the assistant). Acknowledging that "the case presents a close question," the court found the message sufficiently corroborative.[55] The court reasoned that "[t]he assurance of accuracy and contemporaneousness that characterize a business record distinguishes that category of document from personal notations, which have been found insufficient to corroborate the author's testimony for purposes of the two-witness rule."[56]

Using *Chestman, Davis,* and *Bacanovic* as examples, it appears that corroborating evidence will meet the two-witness rule's requirements when that evidence can fairly be interpreted as inculpatory. Thus, in *Davis* the defendant's signed statement supported the witness's testimony that Davis had implicated the burglary suspect. In *Bacanovic,* the assistant's written message directly contradicted Bacanovic's testimony. On the other hand, in *Chestman* the proffered corroborating evidence was as consistent with guilt as with innocence. The prosecutors' ability and inability, respectively, to draw incriminating inferences from the corroborating evidence was determinative in each case.

§ 11.04   THE RECANTATION DEFENSE[57]

[A]   A Comparison of § 1623 and § 1621

If a defendant takes back, or "recants" false testimony, that recantation may be a complete defense in certain circumstances under the plain language of § 1623.[58] As discussed below, however, for practical reasons it is very difficult for a

---

[53] 548 F.2d 840, 843 (9th Cir. 1977). The defendant's testimony at trial provided further corroboration, as it was confusing and contradictory. *See id.* at 844.

[54] United States v. Stewart, 433 F.3d 273, 315–17 (2d Cir. 2006). Stewart's securities fraud conviction is discussed *supra,* § 5.04[C][2].

[55] 433 F.3d at 316.

[56] *Id.* at 317.

[57] Section 1623(d) provides:

Where, in the same continuous court or grand jury proceeding in which a declaration is made,

defendant to assert the § 1623 recantation defense successfully.[59] Under § 1621, recantation is not a complete defense, but a retraction may be used to show that the defendant did not intentionally make a false statement in the first instance.[60]

Does a prosecutor have the discretion to charge a defendant with perjury under § 1621 in circumstances when that defendant could successfully assert a recantation defense under § 1623? The defendant raised this issue in *United States v. Kahn*.[61] The Second Circuit did not resolve the issue, however, because it found that the defendant would have been unable to assert the defense successfully. Thus, the defendant was not prejudiced by the decision to charge under § 1621, and the court did not need to reach the issue. The court did note that it was disturbed by "the prospect of the government employing § 1621 whenever a recantation exists, and § 1623 when one does not, simply to place perjury defendants in the most disadvantageous trial position."[62]

[B] Elements of the Recantation Defense

A recantation defense will bar prosecution under § 1623 only if the defendant meets that section's requirements. Section 1623(d) provides that where:

(1)   in the *same continuous court or grand jury proceeding* in which a declaration is made,

(2)   the person making the declaration *admits such declaration to be false*, such admission shall bar prosecution under this section *if, at the time the admission is made,*

    (a)   the declaration has not *substantially affected the proceeding, or*

    (b)   it has not become manifest that such falsity has been or will be exposed.[63]

Thus, to assert the recantation defense successfully, a defendant must initially show that the recantation occurred in the same court or grand jury proceeding as the original false testimony. The defendant must also show that the recantation was a clear admission that the earlier testimony was false. An attempt by the defendant

---

the person making the declaration admits such declaration to be false, such admission shall bar prosecution under this section if, at the time the admission is made, the declaration has not substantially affected the proceeding, or it has not become manifest that such falsity has been or will be exposed.

[58]   Courts have held that this defense should be asserted prior to trial. *See* United States v. Denison, 663 F.2d 611, 618 (5th Cir. 1981); United States v. Kahn, 472 F.2d 272, 283 n.9 (2d Cir.), *cert. denied*, 411 U.S. 982 (1973) ("[S]ince § 1623(d) says that an admission of the falsity of the prior declaration '*shall bar prosecution*,' it would seem that the defense should be raised prior to trial, and disposed of then by the judge" (emphasis in original)).

[59]   *See* Nesland, note 3, § 10.01[4].

[60]   *See* Kahn, 472 F.2d at 284.

[61]   *Id.* at 283–84.

[62]   *Id.* at 283. *See also* United States v. Sherman, 150 F.3d 306, 313 (3d Cir. 1998) (a due process violation might occur if a prosecutor based a decision to charge solely on the desire to gain a tactical advantage by impairing the defendant's ability to mount an effective defense).

[63]   18 U.S.C. § 1623(d) (outline headings and italics added).

to explain earlier testimony, or to later claim faulty memory, will not suffice.[64]

The defendant must assert the recantation defense prior to trial. Otherwise, the defense is waived.[65] Courts agree that the defense is a question of law for the court to decide.[66]

[C] Must a Defendant Prove All the Elements to Prevail?

Most issues in recantation cases involve the final two elements listed above. Most important, the circuits are split as to whether the "or" in the statute means "or" or whether it means "and." Although the issue may seem nonsensical — the statute plainly says "or" — it has strong implications for the viability of the defense. If a defendant must show *both* (1) that the false testimony did not "substantially affect" the proceeding *and* (2) that the falsity had not become "manifest," then the defense will be difficult to prove.

Most circuit courts read the statute in the conjunctive, and require the defendant to show both elements. For example, in *United States v. Fornaro*,[67] the defendant was a witness at a bail hearing who testified that he lacked certain information about the bail applicant. When the prosecutor confronted Fornaro on cross-examination with prior inconsistent statements, Fornaro admitted that he had lied. The jury convicted Fornaro under § 1623 based upon his original testimony.

On appeal, Fornaro argued that he had successfully recanted his false testimony. The Second Circuit rejected the argument, holding that recantation is an effective bar to prosecution only if the false statement has not substantially affected the proceeding *and* if it has not become manifest that the falsity has been or will be exposed. The court found that "Congress did not countenance in § 1623(d) the flagrant injustice that would result if a witness is permitted to lie to a judicial tribunal and then, upon only learning that he had been discovered, grudgingly to recant in order to bar prosecution."[68] Under this reasoning, unless the "or" in § 1623(d) were read as "and," the section would encourage witnesses to lie; such witnesses would later recant only if faced with threats of exposure or prosecution. Because Fornaro only retracted his testimony after his false testimony had been exposed, he was not entitled to the recantation defense.[69]

---

[64] *See* United States v. Tobias, 863 F.2d 685, 689 (9th Cir. 1988) ("a defendant must unequivocally repudiate his prior testimony to satisfy § 1623(d)").

[65] *See* note 58, *supra.*

[66] *See, e.g.*, United States v. Fornaro, 894 F.2d 508, 511 (2d Cir. 1990).

[67] 894 F.2d 508 (2d. Cir. 1990).

[68] *Id.* at 511, *quoting* United States v. Moore, 613 F.2d 1029, 1043 (D.C. Cir. 1979), *cert. denied*, 446 U.S. 954 (1980).

[69] 894 F.2d at 511. Most other circuits have held likewise. *See, e.g.*, United States v. Moore, 613 F.2d 1029, 1042 (D.C. Cir. 1979), *cert. denied*, 446 U.S. 954 (1980) (noting that a conjunctive reading is in accord with the provisions of a New York statute upon which the federal recantation defense was modeled).

In *United States v. Smith*,[70] however, the Eighth Circuit disagreed with the other circuits that had considered the issue. The court held that a defendant can successfully assert a recantation defense by showing *either* that the proceedings had not been affected *or* that the falsity had not been exposed. In *Smith*, the defendant testified before a grand jury that was investigating a money laundering scheme. In her initial testimony, Smith said that she had used her own money for the purchase of a car, and denied that the money had come from another person. The grand jury proceedings recessed for thirty minutes, during which time Smith reviewed bank records with which the government had confronted her. She then recanted her earlier testimony and admitted that the money had come from the third person.

The government charged Smith with perjury based upon the initial testimony, and Smith moved to dismiss the charge. The trial court denied the motion. On appeal, the Eighth Circuit reversed. First, the court noted that the plain language of the statute — "or" — indicated that a defendant should prevail by proving either of the disputed conditions.[71] Second, the court found that a disjunctive reading comports with Congress's intent to promote truthful testimony by "creat[ing] an incentive for witnesses to correct false testimony early in the proceeding."[72] Finally, the rule of lenity, which requires that ambiguous criminal statutes be read in favor of the defendant, compelled this result.

The court remanded for a determination of whether Smith could meet either of the two conditions. Because such a short amount of time passed between the initial testimony and the recantation, Smith could arguably show that the proceedings had not been substantially affected.[73] Alternatively, she could argue that it had not become manifest that the falsity of her statement had been or would be exposed. The court noted that the issue was not whether the falsity was manifest to the government before the recantation, but whether imminent exposure was manifest to the witness.[74] Smith would be unlikely to prevail on this prong, however, because she changed her testimony only when confronted with the bank records.

§ 11.05   IMMUNITY

A defendant can be charged with perjury even if the allegedly perjurious testimony was given under a grant of immunity. The federal immunity statute provides:

> no testimony or other information compelled under the [immunity] order (or any information directly or indirectly derived from such testimony or

---

[70] 35 F.3d 344 (8th Cir. 1994).

[71] *Id.* at 346 ("construing the word 'or' to mean 'and' is conjunctive, and is clearly in contravention of its ordinary usage").

[72] *Id.*

[73] Courts have not established a clear standard for determining whether a proceeding has been substantially affected. *See* Nesland, *supra* note 3, § 10.01[4][b].

[74] *Smith*, 35 F.3d at 347. Other courts have held likewise. *See* Nesland, *supra* note 3, § 10[4][c].

other information) may be used against the witness in any criminal case, *except a prosecution for perjury*, giving a false statement, or otherwise failing to comply with the order.[75]

Further, in *United States v. Apfelbaum*,[76] the United States Supreme Court held that the prosecution may use a witness's truthful testimony, in addition to the allegedly false testimony, to prove that the immunized testimony was perjurious. In that case, the defendant was granted immunity to testify before a grand jury investigating a robbery. The government subsequently charged the defendant with perjury based upon his grand jury testimony. During the perjury trial, the government used truthful grand jury testimony in order to put the alleged false statements in context.

On appeal, the Supreme Court found that the immunity statute permits use of truthful immunized testimony at a subsequent perjury trial. The statute, the Court noted, does not distinguish between using truthful and untruthful testimony in a perjury case. The Court further found that the immunity statute itself provided the defendant with all the protection to which he was entitled under the Fifth Amendment. Thus, using truthful testimony against a perjury defendant does not violate the prohibition against compelled self-incrimination.

§ 11.06   VICARIOUS LIABILITY

[A]   Aiding and Abetting

A defendant may be found guilty of perjury by aiding and abetting another person's perjury. In one case, for example, the defendant had prepared a false document for an unknowing witness to use at trial.[77] The defendant was charged under the federal aiding and abetting statute[78] as a principal in the commission of perjury under § 1623.

On appeal, the Eleventh Circuit affirmed the conviction. The court found that an individual who intentionally causes an innocent person to commit perjury may be indicted as a principal for the commission of perjury; proof of aiding and abetting is sufficient for conviction. The court found that the defendant's intent that a witness give a false statement under oath, combined with the witness's taking of the oath, suffices for perjury.[79] Thus, the defendant could be convicted of perjury even if the defendant had never personally been placed under oath.

---

[75] 18 U.S.C. § 6002 (emphasis added). Other aspects of immunity are discussed in detail in Chapter 19, The Fifth Amendment Right Against Compelled Self-Incrimination, *infra*.

[76] 445 U.S. 115 (1980).

[77] United States v. Walser, 3 F.3d 380 (11th Cir. 1993).

[78] 18 U.S.C. § 2(b) ("Whoever willfully causes an act to be done which if directly performed by him or another would be an offense against the United States, is punishable as a principal").

[79] *Walser*, 3 F.3d at 389.

[B] Subornation of Perjury

Under § 1622 of the federal criminal code, a defendant may be convicted of "suborning" another person to commit perjury.[80] To prove guilt, the government must show both that the defendant knowingly persuaded another person to lie under oath, and that that person actually committed perjury under either § 1621 or § 1623.[81]

Strictly speaking, the crime of subornation does not provide for vicarious liability — it does not impose liability for an act committed by another. Rather, the statute directly punishes one who causes another to commit perjury. Subornation is similar to vicarious liability, however, because the defendant cannot be convicted unless another person has actually committed the object crime.

---

[80] 18 U.S.C. § 1622.

[81] *See* Sloan, *supra* note 3, at 893, and cases cited therein.

Chapter 12

OBSTRUCTION OF JUSTICE

§ 12.01 INTRODUCTION

The crime of obstructing justice is the third of the "cover-up" crimes. Broader than the crimes of false statements and perjury,[1] obstruction covers a range of offenses based upon acts intended to affect judicial, administrative, or legislative proceedings. As with the other cover-up crimes, an obstruction charge may stand alone or — more commonly in white collar cases — may arise out of a defendant's attempt to hide earlier illegal activity. For example, the first criminal conviction arising out of the Enron scandal was for obstruction of justice;[2] media figure Martha Stewart was convicted of obstruction and other cover-up crimes in connection with the sale of her ImClone Systems stock;[3] and baseball player Barry Bonds was convicted of obstruction of justice in connection with the major league baseball steroids scandal.[4]

In the most basic sense, obstruction charges are based upon allegations that the defendant intended improperly to interfere with official proceedings. The most common obstruction charges are based upon the acts, or attempted acts, of altering or destroying documents, offering or promoting false testimony, and threatening or influencing witnesses, jurors, and court officials. Unfortunately, as the cases discussed in this chapter show, attorneys, judges, and others involved in the legal system are charged with obstruction of justice with an unsettling degree of frequency.[5]

---

[1] See Chapter 10, False Statements, and Chapter 11, Perjury and False Declarations, *supra*.

[2] Enron's accounting firm, Arthur Anderson, L.L.P., was convicted of obstructing a Securities and Exchange Commission investigation into Enron's accounting practices. See United States v. Arthur Andersen, 374 F.3d 281 (5th Cir. 2004). The Supreme Court later reversed this conviction, finding that the jury instructions were faulty. Arthur Andersen, L.L.P. v. United States, 544 U.S. 696 (2005). See § 12.06(b), *infra*.

[3] See United States v. Stewart, 323 F. Supp. 2d 606 (S.D.N.Y. 2004), *aff'd*, 433 F.3d 273 (2d Cir. 2006). For another high-profile case, see United States v. Quattrone, 441 F.3d 153 (2d Cir. 2006) (securities fraud investigation led to charges for obstruction of justice and witness tampering), discussed *infra* § 12.03[C][2].

[4] See Juliet Macur, *As Bonds Appeals Verdict, Jurors Who Convicted Him Will Be Watching Closely*, N.Y. Times, May 17, 2011, at B15.

[5] See Justin Alexander Kasprisin, *Obstruction of Justice*, 47 Am. Crim. L. Rev. 847, 862 & n.86 (2010). Obstructive efforts also may violate an attorney's ethical duties. See *Advocates Must Heed Rules on Evidence Tampering, Dealings with Witnesses*, 88 Crim. L. Rep. 525 (BNA) (Feb. 2, 2011). An attorney may have a defense in some circumstances. See United States v. Kloess, 251 F.3d 941, 949 (11th Cir. 2001) (holding that 18 U.S.C. § 1515(c), which provides that obstruction statutes do not prohibit the provision

The federal criminal code contains a number of obstruction statutes, many of which are duplicative.[6] The principal obstruction statutes are set forth in §§ 1501–1520 of the criminal code. These statutes include §§ 1503 (obstruction of judicial proceedings), 1505 (obstruction of administrative and congressional proceedings), 1510 (bribery of witnesses), 1512 (tampering with witnesses and documents), 1513 (tampering with a witness), 1519 (destruction, alteration, or falsification of records in federal investigations and bankruptcy), and 1520 (destruction of corporate audit records).

In 2002, Congress enacted the Sarbanes-Oxley Act[7] in response to the corporate accounting scandals. This Act expanded § 1512 to include document tampering, and added §§ 1519 and 1520 to the federal criminal code. Specifically, § 1519 criminalizes the destruction, alteration, or falsification of records in federal investigations and bankruptcy proceedings. Section § 1520 criminalizes the destruction of corporate audit records. Finally, the Act amended and expanded § 1512. This chapter discusses these statutes and amendments, and compares them to the general obstruction of justice statutes, § 1503 and § 1505.

§ 12.02   A COMPARISON OF §§ 1503, 1505, 1510, AND 1512

Section 1503 is the broadest, and most commonly used, obstruction of justice statute. The statute is entitled, "Influencing or Injuring Officer or Juror Generally." The scope of the statute, however, is far broader than its title indicates. Section 1503(a) provides:

> Whoever corruptly, or by threats or force, or by any threatening letter or communication,
>
> [1]   *endeavors to influence, intimidate, or impede* any
>
> - grand or petit juror, or
> - officer in or of any court of the United States, or officer who may be serving at any examination or other proceeding before any United States magistrate judge or other committing magistrate, in the discharge of his duty, *or*
>
> [2]   *injures*
>
> - any such grand or petit juror in his person or property on account of any verdict or indictment assented to by him, or on account of his being or having been such juror, or
> - any such officer, magistrate judge, or other committing magistrate in his person or property on account of the performance of

---

of bona fide legal services in connection with or anticipation of official proceeding, sets forth an affirmative defense).

[6] For a critique of the myriad obstruction provisions in the federal criminal code, see Julie R. O'Sullivan, *The Federal Criminal "Code" Is a Disgrace: Obstruction Statutes as Case Study*, 96 J. Crim. L. & Criminology 643 (2006).

[7] Pub. L. 107-204 (2002).

his official duties, *or*

[3]   corruptly or by threats or force, or by any threatening letter or communication, *influences, obstructs, or impedes*, or *endeavors to influence, obstruct, or impede*, the due administration of justice . . . [shall be punished under the terms of the statute].[8]

In its simplest terms, § 1503 thus criminalizes: (1) endeavoring to influence a juror or court officer, (2) injuring a juror or court officer, and (3) endeavoring to interfere with the judicial system. The first and third clauses cover actions intended to affect future proceedings, while the second clause covers retaliation for earlier actions.

The third clause is all-encompassing, and is commonly referred to as the "omnibus clause." Indeed, the omnibus clause reaches conduct also covered under the first two clauses of § 1503, which are specifically directed to jurors and court officers.[9] Most obstruction charges are brought under the omnibus clause of § 1503.[10] This chapter, therefore, focuses primarily on that provision.[11]

Section 1503 only applies to federal *judicial* proceedings; § 1505 contains parallel provisions that apply only to federal *administrative and legislative* proceedings.[12] Entitled "Obstruction of Proceedings Before Departments, Agencies, and Committees," § 1505 provides:

[1]   Whoever, with intent to avoid, evade, prevent, or obstruct compliance, in whole or in part, with any civil investigative demand duly and properly made under the Antitrust Civil Process Act, willfully withholds, misrepresents, removes from any place, conceals, covers up, destroys, mutilates, alters, or by other means falsifies any documentary material, answers to written interrogatories, or oral testimony, which is the subject of such demand; or attempts to do so or solicits another to do so; or

[2]   Whoever corruptly, or by threats or force, or by any threatening letter or communication influences, obstructs, or impedes or endeavors to influence, obstruct, or impede the due and proper administration of the law under which any pending proceeding is being had before any department *or agency* of the United States, or the due and proper exercise of the power of inquiry under which any *inquiry or investigation is being had by either House, or any committee of either House or any joint committee of the Congress*

---

[8] 18 U.S.C. § 1503 (numbering, spacing, and italics added).

[9] *See* United States v. Aguilar, 515 U.S. 593, 598–99 (1995) (noting that § 1503 "serves as a catchall, prohibiting persons from endeavoring to influence, obstruct, or impede the due administration of justice. The latter clause, it can be seen, is far more general in scope than the earlier clauses of the statute").

[10] *See* Stuart P. Green, *Uncovering the Cover-Up Crimes*, 42 Am. Crim. L. Rev. 9, 18 (2005).

[11] *See* § 12.03, *infra.*

[12] Note that, unlike the principal perjury statutes, these obstruction of justice statutes do not overlap. *Cf.* 18 U.S.C. § 1621 (criminalizing perjury in general court and grand jury proceedings only); 18 U.S.C. § 1623 (criminalizing perjury in a broad range of contexts, including but not limited to court and grand jury proceedings).

. . . [shall be punished under the terms of the statute].[13]

The first clause only applies to matters under the Antitrust Civil Process Act; the second contains an "omnibus" provision similar to that contained in § 1503, and is the basis for almost all § 1505 prosecutions. Again, it is upon the "omnibus" provision that this chapter focuses.

Another important obstruction of justice provision is contained in § 1510,[14] which focuses on attempts to bribe witnesses in criminal investigations.[15] Because this section is primarily directed at the activities of organized crime and is rarely used in white collar cases, it is not discussed in detail here.

Finally, the witness tampering statute, § 1512, criminalizes a wide range of obstructive efforts. In addition, the Sarbanes-Oxley Act added a new provision to the witness tampering statute. That new provision is set forth in § 1512(c) of the federal criminal code and provides that "[w]hoever corruptly — (1) alters, destroys, mutilates, or conceals a record, document, or other object, or attempts to do so, with the intent to impair the object's integrity or availability for use in an official proceeding; or (2) otherwise obstructs, influences, or impedes any official proceeding, or attempts to do so, shall be fined under this title or imprisoned not more than 20 years, or both." This section expands the scope of § 1512 beyond witness tampering, and on its face overlaps substantially with the omnibus provisions of §§ 1503 and 1505.

§ 12.03 THE ELEMENTS OF OBSTRUCTION OF JUSTICE — THE OMNIBUS CLAUSES

Under the omnibus provision of either § 1503 or § 1505, most circuits require the government to prove that:

1. The defendant acted with "corrupt" intent;
2. The defendant endeavored to interfere with a judicial, administrative, or congressional proceeding;
3. There was a "nexus" between the endeavor and the proceeding;
4. The proceeding was actually pending at the time of the endeavor; and
5. The defendant knew that the proceeding was pending.

[A] Actus Reus — The "Endeavor"

The "endeavor" is the essence of an obstruction charge. As the term suggests, it provides for inchoate liability; a defendant need not succeed in the obstructive effort for this element to be fulfilled. An endeavor to obstruct justice, according to the Supreme Court, "must have the 'natural and probable effect' of interfering with

---

[13] 18 U.S.C. § 1505 (numbering and italics added).

[14] 18 U.S.C. § 1510.

[15] *See generally* Green, *supra* note 10, at 19 & n.39.

the due administration of justice."[16] It need not even rise to the level of an attempt.[17]

[1]   The Breadth of the "Endeavor" to Obstruct

The following sections provide examples of the types of "endeavors" that typically give rise to obstruction charges.[18] This discussion is only illustrative, and by no means describes all the possible types of endeavors.

[a]   Interfering with the Production of Documents

One of the most common circumstances giving rise to an obstruction charge involves concealing, altering, or destroying documents that pertain to judicial, administrative, or legislative proceedings. Courts have rejected arguments that such conduct does not constitute an endeavor to obstruct. In fact, destruction of documents that have not even been subpoenaed may be covered so long as the defendant had the requisite "corrupt" intent and the other elements are present.[19]

In *United States v. Faudman*[20] for example, the destruction of documents sufficed for an obstruction conviction. In that case, the defendant admitted that he altered and defaced records relevant to an ongoing grand jury investigation relating to the company for which the defendant worked. He also knew that the company had decided to cooperate with the grand jury and that the altered records were requested by the FBI. On appeal, the defendant argued that § 1503 proscribes only "threats or actual violence against persons involved in the administration of justice, and that other statutes cover the obstruction of justice by methods not enumerated in § 1503."[21] The Sixth Circuit rejected this argument, finding that the defendant's acts fell within the obstruction statute because they were intended to distort or destroy evidence being sought by the grand jury and thus to impede the administration of justice.[22]

Withholding documents can also give rise to an obstruction charge. In *United*

---

[16] United States v. Aguilar, 515 U.S. 593 (1995); United States v. Collis, 128 F.3d 313, 317–18 (6th Cir. 1997) (evidence sufficient where obstructive act has the potential to impede justice; actual obstructive effect not required).

[17] *See* Kasprisin, *supra* note 5, at 856 & n.49.

[18] The Ninth Circuit has narrowly read the omnibus clause to cover only acts, similar to those described in the first two clauses, that involve intimidation, threats, or force. *See* United States v. Aguilar, 21 F.3d 1475, 1484–87, *aff'd in part and rev'd in part on other grounds*, 515 U.S. 593 (1995). Most other courts reject this limitation and hold that force or intimidation is not an essential element of a corrupt endeavor to influence. *See* James Nesland, *Perjury and False Declarations, in* White Collar Crime: Business and Regulatory Offenses § 10.03[2] (Otto Obermaier & Robert Morvillo, eds. 2011); Kasprisin, *supra* note 5, at 857.

[19] *See* Kasprisin, *supra* note 5, at 858; Nesland, *supra* note 18, § 10.03[2] at nn. 68–69 and accompanying text; and § 12.03[C] *infra* for a discussion of the required mens rea.

[20] 640 F.2d 20 (6th Cir. 1981).

[21] *Id.* at 21–22.

[22] *Id.* at 23. *Cf.* United States v. Aguilar, 21 F.3d 1475, 1483–84, *aff'd in part and rev'd in part on other grounds*, 515 U.S. 593 (1995) (holding that the omnibus clause only covers acts similar to those described in the first two clauses, *i.e.*, those that involve intimidation, threats, or force).

States v. Lench,[23] two separate grand juries investigating possible antitrust violations issued subpoenas to a nationwide electrical contracting firm. The subpoenas requested documents pertaining to the bid-rigging activities of certain employees, including Lench. In response, Lench (1) sent the firm's attorneys a letter falsely stating that certain of the requested documents did not exist, (2) instructed another person to destroy responsive materials, and (3) withheld responsive documents. Lench was convicted of two counts of obstruction. On appeal, he argued that his acts did not constitute obstruction because the firm agreed to cooperate with the grand jury and "the return date under the subpoena was indefinitely extended by agreement between [the firm's] lawyers and the government."[24] The court rejected the argument, noting that Lench's actions "constitute at least an endeavor to conceal, if not outright concealment. Under § 1503, that is all that is necessary to obstruct justice."[25]

[b]   Giving or Encouraging False Testimony

The other most common basis for an obstruction charge involves efforts to give or to encourage others to give false testimony relating to judicial, administrative, and legislative proceedings. Again, courts generally have rejected efforts to limit the obstruction statutes' reach in such circumstances. For example, in *United States v. Griffin*,[26] the defendant testified before a grand jury investigating loan-sharking activity. During his testimony, Griffin either denied knowledge of certain facts or claimed he could not remember them. The government charged Griffin with obstruction on the theory that his testimony was false and evasive, and thus tended to obstruct the grand jury's investigation.

On appeal from his conviction, Griffin argued that § 1503 covers acts of intimidating witnesses and court officials, and does not reach perjury committed by the witness himself. The Fifth Circuit rejected this argument, stating that "[w]hether Griffin's testimony is described in the indictment as 'evasive' because he deliberately concealed knowledge or 'false' because he blocked the flow of truthful information is immaterial. In either event, the government must, and in this case did, charge in the indictment and prove at trial that the testimony had the effect of impeding justice."[27] Griffin's evasive testimony, according to the court, was no different than encouraging a witness to lie or to not testify.[28] Just as the latter effectively conceals evidence, so does the former obstruct justice by closing off avenues of inquiry to the grand jury.[29]

---

[23] 806 F.2d 1443 (9th Cir. 1986).

[24] *Id.* at 1445.

[25] *Id., citing* United States v. Washington Water Power Co., 793 F.2d 1079, 1085 (9th Cir. 1986).

[26] 589 F.2d 200 (5th Cir.), *cert. denied*, 444 U.S. 825 (1979).

[27] *Id.* at 204. *See* § 12.04, *infra*, for a discussion of whether perjury alone can give rise to an obstruction charge.

[28] 589 F.2d at 203–04. In addition to the theory used in *Griffin*, courts have sustained obstruction charges based upon encouraging witnesses to give false testimony. *See* Kasprisin, *supra* note 5, at 859, and cases cited therein. *See also* § 12.05[D], *infra*, for a discussion of the relationship between the obstruction and witness tampering statutes.

[29] 589 F.2d at 205. The court further found that the defendant's false testimony was material to the

[c]   Making False Statements to Government Agents

Prior to 1995, it was unclear whether making false statements to potential grand jury witnesses, such as government investigators, constitutes obstruction. In *United States v. Grubb*,[30] the Fourth Circuit sustained an obstruction conviction against a judge who gave false statements to FBI agents. The agents were acting on behalf of a grand jury investigating election bribery.[31] The court upheld the conviction, finding that the "evidence sufficiently supports the charge that Grubb 'corruptly endeavored to influence, obstruct, or impede' the due administration of justice by interrupting the grand jury in its pursuit of information."[32] Other courts have held to the contrary.[33]

The Supreme Court resolved this conflict in *United States v. Aguilar*,[34] a case with facts similar to those in *Grubb*. As discussed more fully below, the Court in *Aguilar* held that simply lying to a government agent who may or may not testify before a court or grand jury does not constitute an endeavor to obstruct.[35]

[d]   Encouraging a Witness to Assert the Fifth Amendment or Attorney-Client Privilege

Of course, a witness has a Fifth Amendment right to make a good faith assertion of the right not to testify and to make a good faith assertion of the attorney-client privilege. May an attorney be charged with and convicted of obstruction for urging a person to assert a privilege? Courts have found that such efforts may constitute an endeavor to obstruct justice so long as the attorney acted with corrupt intent.[36]

For example, in *United States v. Cintolo*,[37] Angiulo and his associates were under grand jury investigation in connection with their operation of a loan-sharking business. Cintolo was attorney of record for prospective grand jury witness LaFreniere. The government alleged that Cintolo was actually acting in Angiulo's interest, not in LaFreniere's interest. Cintolo advised LaFreniere to assert his right not to testify, even though LaFreniere had been granted immunity and risked being held in contempt for failing to testify. Based on these facts, the jury convicted Cintolo of obstruction. On appeal, he argued that as an attorney he had advised LaFreniere according to his client's best interests, and could not be convicted of obstruction for doing so. The First Circuit rejected this argument, finding that an obstruction charge is proper if there is proof that an attorney acted

---

proceeding because it "had the natural effect of dissuading the jury from its investigation." *Id.* at 207.

[30] 11 F.3d 426 (4th Cir. 1993).

[31] *Id.* at 438.

[32] *Id.*, *citing In re* Michael, 326 U.S. 224, 227 (1945).

[33] *See* United States v. Wood, 6 F.3d 692, 696 (10th Cir. 1993); United States v. Walasek, 527 F.2d 676, 679 (3d Cir. 1975).

[34] 515 U.S. 593 (1995).

[35] *Id.* at 600. See also *infra*, § 12.03[A][2].

[36] *See* Green, *supra* note 10, at 18 & n.36; Nesland, *supra* note 18, at § 10.03[2]; Douglas M. Tween & James D. Bailey, Over-Assertion of the Attorney-Client Privilege — *Can It Be a Crime?*, 13 No. 6 Bus. Crimes Bull. 3 (2006), and cases cited therein.

[37] 818 F.2d 980 (1st Cir.), *cert. denied*, 484 U.S. 913 (1987).

out of an improper motive in advising his client not to testify.[38] Based on the facts and inferences to be drawn, there was a sufficient basis for the jury to conclude that Cintolo was not acting in LaFreniere's interests when he counseled him to invoke his Fifth Amendment privilege. Because the grant of immunity had protected LaFreniere's Fifth Amendment rights, Cintolo had no good faith grounds for advising his client not to testify.[39]

Cases such as *Cintolo* point out the potential pitfalls that attorneys face when representing clients who are either under investigation for an alleged crime, or who have already been charged with the commission of a crime. Often, even the most circumspect attorney is faced with a conflict between doing the utmost on behalf of the client and adhering to the attorney's legal and ethical obligations. If an attorney encourages a client to give false testimony, or withhold documents, such conduct may give rise to obstruction of justice charges. It is not always clear, however, whether an attorney has crossed the line. For example, if an attorney reads a document subpoena narrowly and advises a client not to produce certain documents, has the attorney committed obstruction? Or, if an attorney advises a client to give a literally true but misleading answer, is that an "endeavor" to obstruct?[40] There are no easy answers to these questions, but students of these materials will hopefully take away a career-long adherence both to the letter and spirit of the "cover-up" crime statutes.

[e]   Threatening Jurors or Court Officers

Courts have sanctioned charges under the omnibus clause for threats made to jurors and court officers, even though that conduct is explicitly covered under other provisions of § 1503. For example, in *United States v. Bashaw*,[41] the defendant was convicted under § 1503 for making threatening statements to two jurors who had served on the jury in Bashaw's brother's trial. On appeal, the Sixth Circuit initially rejected the defendant's argument that his actions were not covered by the omnibus clause because they were explicitly proscribed by the second clause of § 1503. The court found that the omnibus clause is intended to cover all types of obstructive acts, including those explicitly covered elsewhere in § 1503.[42]

The court reversed the conviction, however, because the jurors had finished their service and were no longer acting in the discharge of their duties. As the court

---

[38] *Id.* at 992, *citing* Cole v. United States, 329 F.2d 437, 443 (9th Cir.), *cert. denied*, 377 U.S. 954 (1964) (obstruction by non-attorney for advising witness not to testify).

[39] *Cintolo*, 818 F.2d at 993–94. The court distinguished the facts of this case from those in United States v. Herron, 28 F.2d 122 (N.D. Cal. 1928), where the witness had a legitimate ground for asserting his Fifth Amendment privilege. *See* 818 F.2d at 994. For an example of another attorney charged with obstruction of justice, see United States v. Cueto, 151 F.3d 620 (7th Cir. 1998), *cert. denied*, 526 U.S. 1016 (1999). Such acts may also potentially be charged under the corrupt persuasion statute, § 1512(b). *See* § 12.06, *infra*.

[40] Note that such testimony would not constitute perjury. See the discussion of the literally true statement in perjury cases, *supra* § 11.3[C][1].

[41] 982 F.2d 168 (6th Cir. 1992).

[42] *Id.* at 171, *citing* United States v. Thomas, 916 F.2d 647, 650 n.3 (11th Cir. 1990).

stated, "there was no administration of justice for Bashaw to impede."[43] The *Bashaw* court distinguished its decision from the Eleventh Circuit's earlier decision in *United States v. Fernandez*.[44] In *Fernandez*, the defendant had threatened the prosecutor after the defendant's brother had been convicted and sentenced. Because the prosecutor would still be involved in post-trial motions and appellate proceedings, the court held that the prosecutor was acting in the discharge of his duties at the time of the threats. In *Bashaw*, however, the jurors would have no further involvement in the case.[45] The *Bashaw* court also found that the defendant's alleged "staring" at jurors during the case could not provide sufficient grounds for an obstruction conviction.[46]

An analogous issue arose with respect to a court officer in *United States v. Fulbright*.[47] In that case, the government alleged that the defendant had threatened and injured a federal bankruptcy judge, thus violating all three clauses of § 1503. The defendant argued on appeal that the judge was not acting within his official duties at the time of the defendant's acts because the acts occurred after the judge had removed himself from the defendant's case. The Ninth Circuit rejected the defendant's argument, holding that "[a]lthough he was no longer involved in the adjudication of Fulbright's case, [the judge] was still involved in adjudicating other cases, and was therefore discharging his official duties as a United States bankruptcy judge."[48]

[2]   The "Nexus" Requirement

In *United States v. Aguilar*,[49] the Supreme Court held that, in order to prove that the defendant committed an endeavor to obstruct, the government must show that there was a direct connection, or "nexus," between the defendant's act and the pending proceeding. In that case, Tham was a defendant who had been convicted of embezzling from a labor union and had filed a motion to have his conviction set aside. Aguilar was a federal judge who sat in the same district as the trial judge in Tham's case. Through intermediaries, Tham persuaded Aguilar to intercede on Tham's behalf by contacting the judge assigned to Tham's case. In connection with an FBI investigation independent of the initial criminal case against Tham, Tham's phone was tapped pursuant to court order. Aguilar learned of the wiretap. Subsequently, the FBI interviewed Aguilar in connection with the improprieties

---

[43] 982 F.2d at 172. *Compare* United States v. Taccetta, 975 F. Supp. 672, 679 (D.N.J. 1997) (upholding obstruction charge where alleged obstructive conduct directed at juror occurred both before and after the jury's verdict).

[44] 837 F.2d 1031 (11th Cir.), *cert. denied*, 488 U.S. 838 (1988).

[45] *Compare* United States v. Johnson, 605 F.2d 729 (4th Cir. 1979), *cert. denied*, 444 U.S. 1020 (1980). In *Johnson*, the court upheld the obstruction conviction of a defendant who, after appealing an earlier conviction, had attempted to induce the principal witness against him to recant. The court reasoned that the earlier case remained pending until the possibility of appeal no longer remained and there was no chance that the witness might be called to testify again at a new trial.

[46] 982 F.2d at 173.

[47] 105 F.3d 443 (9th Cir. 1997). *See infra*, § 12.03[B][1], for a more detailed discussion of *Fulbright*.

[48] 105 F.3d at 449–50.

[49] 515 U.S. 593 (1995).

revolving around the embezzlement case. During this interview, Aguilar lied about his involvement in the Tham case and about his knowledge of the wiretap. Aguilar was convicted under § 1503's omnibus clause based upon these lies.[50] The Ninth Circuit reversed, and the government appealed to the Supreme Court.

In an opinion by Chief Justice Rehnquist, the six-member majority found that merely lying to an FBI agent does not constitute obstruction. The Court reasoned that there must be a connection or "nexus" between an alleged "endeavor" to obstruct and the pending proceeding.[51] The Court explained that the alleged obstructive act "must have a relationship in time, causation, or logic with the judicial proceedings. In other words, the endeavor must have the 'natural and probable effect' of interfering with the due administration of justice."[52] The Court concluded, "We do not believe that uttering false statements to an investigating agent — and that seems to be all that was proved here — who might or might not testify before a grand jury is sufficient to make out a violation of the catchall provision of § 1503."[53] In an opinion by Justice Scalia, the dissent argued that the Court interpreted the term "endeavor" far too narrowly, "leaving a prohibition of only actual obstruction and competent attempts."[54]

The "nexus" requirement is now a much-litigated element in obstruction cases. For example, in *United States v. Jespersen*,[55] the grand jury was investigating fraudulent contract procurement practices. The defendant caused a contract to be backdated. The court found sufficient evidence of a "nexus" between the contract and the endeavor to impede the grand jury investigation. Had the grand jury believed the false information to be true, the focus of the investigation would have changed. Similarly, in *United States v. Lundwall*,[56] company officials destroyed documents requested in a pending civil class action suit. Again, the court found a "nexus" between the destruction of documents and the pending civil suit because destruction of the documents could impair the proceeding.

[3]   A Deceptive Promise to Commit an Endeavor

An interesting issue arises in the case of a deceptive promise to commit an endeavor. If someone promises to interfere with a pending proceeding, but does not intend to do so, or is not successful in doing so, is there an "endeavor" to obstruct? This issue arose in *United States v. Atkin*.[57] In that case, the defendant, Atkin, was an attorney who received $550,000 from a client who was a defendant in a criminal case. Although the client was represented by other counsel in that criminal case,

---

[50] *Id.* at 597.

[51] *Id.* at 599 ("The action taken by the accused must be with an intent to influence judicial or grand jury proceedings; it is not enough that there be an intent to influence some ancillary proceeding, such as an investigation independent of the court's or grand jury's authority").

[52] *Id.* (citations omitted).

[53] *Id.* at 600.

[54] *Id.* at 612 (Scalia, J., dissenting).

[55] 65 F.3d 993 (2d Cir. 1995).

[56] 1 F. Supp. 2d 249, 254 (S.D.N.Y. 1998).

[57] 107 F.3d 1213 (6th Cir. 1997).

Atkin promised to use the money to bribe the judge presiding over that case. However, Atkin made only one attempt to contact the judge, and no bribe was offered or paid.

Arguably, on these facts, there would appear to be no "nexus" between the conspiracy to commit bribery and the pending criminal case — no act was undertaken that could have affected that case. Nonetheless, the Sixth Circuit found sufficient evidence of an endeavor. The court reasoned that the false promise to "fix" the case could affect the proceeding by (1) lulling the defendant into abandoning the pursuit of lawful remedies, or (2) causing an investigation in the case leading to the judge's recusal.[58] It is unclear, however, whether this result fully comports with *Aguilar*'s nexus requirement; it is a stretch to conclude that Atkin's actions had the "natural and probable effect of interfering with the due administration of justice," especially when compared with the direct lie to the FBI agent in *Aguilar*.

[B] The Pending Proceeding

Under the omnibus clauses of §§ 1503 and 1505, most courts hold, the government must show that a proceeding was pending at the time of the alleged obstructive acts. Under its plain language, § 1505 applies to any "pending proceeding . . . before any department or agency of the United States" and to congressional inquiries and investigations. Thus, to prove the actus reus of an "endeavor" to obstruct justice under § 1505, the government must prove that a federal administrative proceeding or legislative inquiry or investigation was actually pending at the time of the alleged endeavor.[59] An agency proceeding is "pending" whenever an agency undertakes a formal or informal investigation pursuant to statutory authority. Thus, any authorized investigation, even without the filing of a former order of investigation or the formal commencement of a proceeding, qualifies under the statute.[60]

Most courts have applied the pending proceeding requirement to § 1503 through judicial interpretation of the statute, though some courts disagree.[61] Courts hold that, under the omnibus clause of § 1503, the government must show the existence of a federal trial or related proceeding, or a proceeding before a federal magistrate or federal grand jury.

---

[58] *Id.* at 1219.

[59] *See* Kasprisin, *supra* note 5, at 865.

[60] *See, e.g.*, United States v. Kelley, 36 F.3d 1118, 1127 (D.C. Cir. 1994) (informal interview with Inspector General qualifies as "agency proceeding").

[61] *See* Nesland, *supra* note 18, § 10.03[2][v]; Kasprisin, *supra* note 5, at 853; and cases cited therein. *See, e.g.*, United States v. Novak, 217 F.3d 566, 571–72 (8th Cir. 2000) (questioning whether a pending proceeding is required under § 1503, but not reaching the issue because a proceeding was pending in the case). Note that, under § 1503, some courts do not require that a proceeding be pending at the time a conspiracy to obstruct a proceeding is launched. *See, e.g.*, United States v. Vaghela, 169 F.3d 729, 734–35 (11th Cir. 1999).

[1]   Court Proceedings

With respect to court cases, most circuits agree that a case begins with the filing of a complaint or indictment.[62] The circuits have also generally held that a case is over when the opportunity for appeal has been exhausted.[63]

In *United States v. Fulbright*,[64] the Ninth Circuit addressed the issue of when a court proceeding is no longer pending for purposes of § 1503. Fulbright was a Montana farmer who had failed in his efforts to obtain federal bankruptcy protection against the foreclosure of his farm. Thereafter, the defendant sent the bankruptcy court a purported "warrant" that claimed to authorize the bankruptcy judge's arrest. The government indicted Fulbright for obstruction of justice under alternative factual theories, one of which was the filing of the "warrant."[65] On appeal from his conviction, the defendant argued that there was no "proceeding" pending when he filed the "warrant" because the bankruptcy case had already been dismissed. The appeals court agreed. The court found that, at the time the "warrant" was filed, the bankruptcy proceeding had concluded and the defendant's time to appeal had expired.

The *Fulbright* case provides an example of the extraordinary elasticity of the obstruction statutes, and the broad discretion that prosecutors have under the statutes. From one perspective, the defendant was little more than a disgruntled litigant expressing his frustration at the judge who sat on his case; from another, the defendant's actions entailed a real risk of harm. As the Ninth Circuit said, the case dealt with "a dangerous intersection in a free society, one at which the expression of discontent or disagreement with the actions of government can collide with legitimate efforts to deal with actions intended to threaten or impede federal officials in the carrying out of their duties."[66]

The decision in *United State v. Baum*[67] likewise addressed a pending proceeding issue. In that case, the defendant was a criminal defense attorney whose client had pleaded guilty and been sentenced to prison. The government alleged that the attorney attempted to mislead the government into believing that the client had provided substantial assistance to the government, so that the government would file a Rule 35 motion for a reduced sentence. On a motion to dismiss the § 1503 omnibus clause charge against him, the attorney argued that there was no "pending proceeding" because there was no court case involving his client. The court rejected the argument, holding that "[a]lthough [the client] had been sentenced and judgment had been entered, the sentence was not 'final' in the sense that he still had the right to file a Rule 35 motion."[68] In reaching this result, the court focused on the particular dangers for the system of justice when attorneys act corruptly.

---

[62] *See* Nesland, *supra* note 18, § 10.03[2][v].

[63] *Id. See also* United States v. Johnson, 605 F.2d 729, 731 (4th Cir. 1979), *cert. denied*, 444 U.S. 1020 (1980) (affirming conviction for endeavor to obstruct during pendency of appeal from criminal conviction).

[64] 105 F.3d 443 (9th Cir. 1997).

[65] *Id.* at 449–50.

[66] 105 F.3d at 446.

[67] 32 F. Supp. 2d 642 (S.D.N.Y. 1999).

[68] *Id.* at 648.

[2] Grand Jury Proceedings

With respect to grand juries, some circuits hold that a grand jury proceeding begins when an investigation is undertaken to obtain evidence to be presented to a grand jury at a later point; other circuits hold that the grand jury itself must initiate the investigation.[69] If the investigation is being conducted by law enforcement agents who are not acting on behalf of a grand jury, then there is no pending grand jury proceeding.[70]

Determining whether a grand jury proceeding is pending depends on the facts of the particular case. This issue arose in *United States v. Simmons*,[71] where the defendant was served with a grand jury subpoena and thereafter destroyed documents and attempted to influence potential witnesses. Appealing from a conviction on two counts of obstruction, the defendant argued that the conviction should not stand because the grand jury had neither requested the subpoena nor been advised that the subpoena had been issued. The Third Circuit rejected the argument, finding it sufficient that the grand jury had been empanelled and that the subpoena was issued to further its investigation.[72]

Courts have held, however, that the obstruction of an investigation that has only an uncertain *potential* to produce information to a grand jury will not suffice. Thus, where a potential grand jury witness lies to an FBI agent who has not been called, and who may not be called as a grand jury witness, such conduct does not qualify as an endeavor to obstruct a pending proceeding.[73]

[3] Agency and Legislative Proceedings

Under § 1505, the government must show that an agency or legislative proceeding was pending at the time of the alleged endeavor. Once again, courts broadly interpret this provision. For example, courts have found that Internal Revenue Service investigations,[74] as well as informal congressional investigations,[75] both constitute "pending proceedings."

---

[69] *See* Kasprisin, *supra* note 5, at 852. *See also* United States v. Davis, 183 F.3d 231, 241 (3d Cir. 1999), *as amended*, 197 F.3d 662 (3d Cir. 1999) (noting that most districts always have an empanelled grand jury; thus "the mere existence of a grand jury in a district does not trigger § 1503; the grand jury must have some relationship to the investigation that is obstructed").

[70] *See* Nesland, *supra* note 18, § 10.03[2][v].

[71] 591 F.2d 206 (3d Cir. 1979).

[72] *Id.* at 210.

[73] *See* United States v. Aguilar, 515 U.S. 593, 599 (1995); *Fulbright*, 105 F.3d at 450 n.4 ("'Ancillary' proceedings, such as an FBI investigation, independent of a court's or a grand jury's authority, do not satisfy § 1503's 'proceeding' requirement.") (Quoting *Aguilar*.)

[74] United States v. Hopper, 177 F.3d 824, 830–31 (9th Cir. 1999).

[75] United States v. Cisneros, 26 F. Supp. 2d 24, 39 (D.D.C. 1998). *See generally* Kasprisin, *supra* note 5, at 866.

[C] Mens Rea

Most courts hold that the omnibus clauses of both § 1503 and § 1505 impose on the government the burden of two mens rea showings — that the defendant knew of the pending proceeding, and that the defendant acted "corruptly."

[1] The Knowledge Requirement

Most circuits require the government to prove that the defendant knew of the pending proceeding, whether it was a court or grand jury proceeding under § 1503, or an administrative, agency, or a congressional proceeding under § 1505.[76] If the government's theory is that the defendant interfered with a witness at the proceeding, the government must also show that the defendant knew the victim was a witness.[77] With respect to whether a person should be deemed a "witness," courts generally hold that it is the defendant's state of mind, not the witness's state of mind, that controls. Thus, it is sufficient that the defendant had the requisite knowledge of the prospective witness's status, even if the prospective witness did not yet know that he or she might be called to testify.[78]

However, if the government's theory is that the defendant engaged in obstructive conduct toward a juror or court officer, under either the first or second clause of § 1503, then the knowledge requirement is somewhat different. On such a theory, the government must prove that the defendant knew the victim was a juror or court officer.[79]

[2] "Corrupt" Intent

Courts have varied widely in defining the term "corruptly" under § 1503. First, in what is perhaps the most onerous definition, some courts require the government to show that the defendant acted with an improper or evil motive.[80] Congress has codified this standard in obstruction cases brought under § 1505, which provides that: "[a]s used in § 1505, the term 'corruptly' means acting with an improper purpose, personally or by influencing another, including making a false or misleading statement, or withholding, concealing, altering, or destroying a document or other information."[81]

---

[76] This requirement is contained in the plain language of 18 U.S.C. § 1503, and has been applied to § 1505 through judicial interpretation. *See* Pettibone v. United States, 148 U.S. 197, 206 (1893) (interpreting predecessor statute of § 1503, and finding that "a person is not sufficiently charged with obstructing or impeding the due administration of justice in a court unless it appears that he knew or had notice that justice was being administered in such court"); United States v. Price, 951 F.2d 1028, 1031 (9th Cir. 1991).

[77] United States v. Washington Water Power Co., 793 F.2d 1079, 1084 (9th Cir. 1986), *citing* United States v. Jackson, 513 F.2d 456, 459 (D.C. Cir. 1975) (finding that, for purposes of § 1503, a witness is one who knows material facts and is expected to be called to testify as to those facts).

[78] *See* United States v. Berardi, 675 F.2d 894, 904 n.18 (7th Cir. 1982); *contra* Berra v. United States, 221 F.2d 590, 597 (8th Cir. 1955), *aff'd on other grounds*, 351 U.S. 131 (1956).

[79] *See* Nesland, *supra* note 18, § 10.03[2][iii], and cases cited therein.

[80] *See id.* at § 10.03[2][ii][A]; Kasprisin, *supra* note 5, at 855 and cases cited therein.

[81] 18 U.S.C. § 1515(b). As the court explained in United States v. Brady, 168 F.3d 574, 578 n.2 (1st Cir.

Second, other courts applying § 1503's corrupt intent requirement impose on the government the burden of proving a specific intent to obstruct justice — *i.e.*, to show that the defendant both knew of the pending proceeding and acted with the purpose to interfere with the proceeding's functioning.[82] As a practical matter, these two standards are not much different. Proof that a defendant had the specific intent to obstruct would probably also lead a jury to conclude that the defendant also had an improper motive.

Third, some courts use a "corrupt" intent standard that is easier to prove than either of the above standards. These courts will allow a conviction if a jury finds that the defendant intended to commit an action, and could have reasonably foreseen that obstruction would result from that action.[83] The latter part of this standard effectively amounts to a lower burden, one of negligence. As such, it seems too low a standard for a statute that facially contains a corrupt intent requirement.

Additionally, the *Aguilar* nexus requirement implicates the defendant's mens rea. Under that holding, the government will be unable to prove corrupt intent unless the evidence shows that the defendant knew that the obstructive efforts would affect a proceeding.[84] The government failed to prove that Aguilar knew his statements to the FBI would be relayed to the grand jury. Without direct evidence of such knowledge, the Court found that the evidence of corrupt intent was too speculative to sustain a criminal conviction.

Justices Scalia, Thomas, and Kennedy dissented, arguing that the majority's interpretation of the "endeavor" element was unjustifiably narrow.[85] Justice Scalia stated that "[t]he critical point of knowledge at issue, in my view, is not whether 'respondent knew that his false statement *would be provided* to the grand jury,' . . . but rather whether respondent knew — or indeed, even erroneously *believed* — that his false statement *might* be provided to the grand jury."[86]

One might ask why the Court, in an opinion authored by a conservative Chief Justice, seemed to go out of its way in *Aguilar* both to require a heightened level of criminal intent (actual knowledge that a proceeding would be affected) and to interpret the facts favorably to the defense. Note that the Court found that a jury could not rationally infer that the defendant, a federal judge, would understand that an FBI agent would likely testify before a federal grand jury.[87] Given that FBI

1999), this amendment was enacted "to make clear that lying or otherwise obstructing Congress was covered by § 1505, and to counter any suggestion of undue vagueness made in United States v. Poindexter, 951 F.2d 369 (D.C. Cir.1991). *See* 142 Cong. Rec. § 11605-02, § 11607-608 (1996)."

[82] *See* Kasprisin, *supra* note 5, at 855.

[83] *See id.* at 729.

[84] 515 U.S. at 599–600.

[85] *Id.* at 612 (Scalia, J., dissenting).

[86] *Id.* at 613.

[87] Early in its opinion, the Court set forth the required proof: "The action taken by the accused must be with an intent to influence judicial or grand jury proceedings." *Id.* at 599. Analyzing the facts under this standard, the Court concluded, "We think the [facts] relied upon by the Government would not enable a rational trier of fact to conclude that respondent knew that his false statement would be provided to the grand jury." *Id.* at 601.

agents typically function as the investigators for federal grand juries, this conclusion might seem implausible.

On the other hand, perhaps the majority was concerned that some limits must be placed on the concept of an "endeavor" to obstruct justice, and found this case an appropriate vehicle for doing so. As the Court explained:

> Under the dissent's theory, a man could be found guilty under § 1503 if he knew of a pending investigation and lied to his wife about his whereabouts at the time of the crime, thinking that an FBI agent might decide to interview her and that she might in turn be influenced in her statement to the agent by her husband's false account of his whereabouts. The intent to obstruct justice is indeed present, but the man's culpability is a good deal less clear from the statute than we usually require in order to impose criminal liability.[88]

In any event, in *Aguilar* the Court once again took an approach to a white collar crime issue that seemed at odds with its approach to other criminal law issues.[89]

The *Aguilar* nexus requirement thus informs the appropriate mens rea instruction that must be given in a case brought under the omnibus clauses of §§ 1503 and 1503. Indeed, in one high-profile case, *United States v. Quattrone*,[90] the Second Circuit reversed the obstruction convictions because of flawed jury instructions on this issue. Quattrone was a high-level manager of Credit Suisse First Boston Corporation ("CSFB"). In May 2000, the National Association of Securities Dealers ("NASD") began an investigation of certain CSFB business practices in connection with initial public stock offerings. In June 2000, Quattrone learned of the NASD investigation. In July 2000, he learned that the SEC was also investigating the same matters. On October 18, 2000, the SEC issued a subpoena requesting documents in connection with the investigation. That same month, a grand jury initiated an investigation; on November 21, the grand jury issued subpoenas for documents. Quattrone learned of the grand jury investigation on December 3, 2000. The next day, Quattrone sent an email to certain CSFB employees urging them to follow the CSFB's document retention policy and to destroy document under that policy.

Quattrone was charged with obstructing the grand jury and SEC investigations in violation of the omnibus clauses of §§ 1503 and 1505. On appeal, the court held that the trial judge erred in the jury instructions. On each charge, the judge instructed the jury:

> So I instruct you that if you find that either, A, the defendant directed the destruction of documents that were called for by the [the subpoena], or, B, that the defendant directed the destruction of documents that he had

---

[88] *Id.* at 602. In fact, the Court explicitly noted that "[r]ecent decisions of Courts of Appeals have likewise tended to place metes and bounds on the *very broad language* of the catchall provision." *Id.* at 599 (emphasis added).

[89] On the issue of judicial limitations on white collar crimes, see generally J. Kelly Strader, *The Judicial Politics of White Collar Crime*, 50 Hastings L.J. 1199 (1999).

[90] 441 F.3d 153 (2d Cir. 2006).

reason to believe were within the scope of the . . . investigation, then this requirement would be satisfied.[91]

The Second Circuit held that the jury instructions were reversible error. The first part of the charge violated the nexus requirement because it allowed the jury to convict without any proof that the defendant knew that the documents had been subpoenaed. Under *Aquilar*, the government must prove that the defendant knew that his actions were likely to affect the proceeding.[92] Instead, the court effectively stated that the defendant was strictly liable if he directed the destruction of the documents, irrespective of his intent at the time.

§ 12.04   THE RELATIONSHIP BETWEEN OBSTRUCTION AND PERJURY

Prosecutors have often charged defendants with obstruction based upon the defendant's commission of perjury or subornation of perjury. In some cases, the government has charged the defendant with both perjury and obstruction, each charge being solely based on the act of perjury. Such charges raise the possibility of being multiplicitous, that is, of violating the Double Jeopardy Clause by seeking to punish the defendant twice for the same conduct. Under the *Blockburger* test, however,[93] the two charges are not the same because each contains an element that the other does not.[94]

Courts disagree as to whether false testimony alone can give rise to obstruction charges. Most courts allow such charges where, as is usually the case, the government can show that the alleged perjury would likely have had an obstructive effect.[95] Similarly, an obstruction charge can be appropriate where the defendant has suborned perjury.[96]

Finally, a conspiracy that has false testimony as its object may be charged as a conspiracy to obstruct justice, whether or not the false testimony was actually given. In *United States v. Lahey*,[97] the defendant was an attorney being investigated for income tax evasion. He and his brother-in-law, Currens, were charged with obstruction based upon their agreement that Currens would falsely testify before a grand jury. The Seventh Circuit affirmed the defendants' conviction for

---

[91] *Id.* at 177 (emphasis in original).

[92] *Id.* at 178, citing *Aguilar*, 515 U.S. at 599. Given this holding, the court did not address Quattrone's argument that the second part of the instruction was also in error. Because the court also found sufficient evidence to support the convictions, it remanded for a new trial. 441 F.3d at 174–76, 180.

[93] Blockburger v. United States, 284 U.S. 299 (1932).

[94] For example, perjury requires that the defendant be under oath; obstruction does not. Obstruction requires corrupt intent; perjury does not.

[95] *See* Nesland, *supra* note 18, § 10.03[3]; Green, *supra* note 10, at 24–25. Cases in the Fourth and Sixth Circuits have rejected obstruction charges based on false testimony alone. *See* United States v. Littleton, 76 F.3d 614, 619 (4th Cir. 1996), *quoting* United States v. Grubb, 11 F.3d 426, 437 (4th Cir. 1993); United States v. Essex, 407 F.2d 214, 218 (6th Cir. 1969).

[96] *See* Nesland, *supra* note 18, § 10.03[3]. Subornation is discussed in Chapter 11, Perjury and False Declarations, *supra*, § 11.06[B].

[97] 55 F.3d 1289 (7th Cir. 1995).

conspiracy to obstruct the grand jury investigation, even though the defendants were not charged with perjury or subornation. The court noted that the government was only required to prove efforts in furtherance of the conspiracy, not that the conspiracy's objectives were actually achieved.[98]

§ 12.05 THE SARBANES-OXLEY ACT — 18 U.S.C. §§ 1519–1520

The Sarbanes-Oxley Act of 2002[99] added two new statutes to the federal criminal code.[100] Prosecutors may use these provisions in certain circumstances when pursuing obstructive activities.

[A] Section 1519 — Destruction of Records in Federal Investigations and Bankruptcy

This section, entitled "Destruction, Alteration, or Falsification of Records in Federal Investigations and Bankruptcy," provides:

> Whoever knowingly alters, destroys, mutilates, conceals, covers up, falsifies, or makes a false entry in any record, document, or tangible object with the intent to impede, obstruct, or influence the investigation or proper administration of any matter within the jurisdiction of any department or agency of the United States or any case filed under title 11 [bankruptcy], or in relation to or contemplation of any such matter or case, shall be fined under this title, imprisoned not more than 20 years, or both.

Section 1519 applies to (1) "any matter" within federal department or agency jurisdiction, and (2) bankruptcy cases. The coverage is thus broader than that of § 1505, which is limited to "pending proceeding[s]" before federal departments and agencies, but appears to overlap substantially with the expanded version of § 1512 discussed below. Also, the section contains a mens rea requirement of (1) knowledge of the obstructive acts, and (2) intent to obstruct, as compared with the corrupt intent requirement under § 1505's omnibus provision.

[B] Section 1520 — Destruction of Audit Records

In response to the corporate accounting scandals that made headlines during 2002, Congress enacted an obstruction-like statute specifically directed to corporate audits. This section, entitled "Destruction of Corporate Audit Records," provides:

> (a)
>
>   (1)   Any accountant who conducts an audit of an issuer of securities to which section 10A(a) of the Securities Exchange Act of 1934

---

[98] *Id.* at 1293. In addition, the court found sufficient evidence that the defendants conspired to obstruct justice.

[99] Pub. L. 107-204 (2002).

[100] 18 U.S.C. § 1519-20. So far, these statutes have been seldom used by prosecutors.

(15 U.S.C. 78j- 1(a)) applies, shall maintain all audit or review workpapers for a period of 5 years from the end of the fiscal period in which the audit or review was concluded.

(2) The Securities and Exchange Commission shall promulgate, within 180 days, after adequate notice and an opportunity for comment, such rules and regulations, as are reasonably necessary, relating to the retention of relevant records such as workpapers, documents that form the basis of an audit or review, memoranda, correspondence, communications, other documents, and records (including electronic records) which are created, sent, or received in connection with an audit or review and contain conclusions, opinions, analyses, or financial data relating to such an audit or review, which is conducted by any accountant who conducts an audit of an issuer of securities to which section 10A(a) of the Securities Exchange Act of 1934 (15 U.S.C. 78j-1(a)) applies. The Commission may, from time to time, amend or supplement the rules and regulations that it is required to promulgate under this section, after adequate notice and an opportunity for comment, in order to ensure that such rules and regulations adequately comport with the purposes of this section.

(b) Whoever knowingly and willfully violates subsection (a)(1), or any rule or regulation promulgated by the Securities and Exchange Commission under subsection (a)(2), shall be fined under this title, imprisoned not more than 10 years, or both.

(c) Nothing in this section shall be deemed to diminish or relieve any person of any other duty or obligation imposed by Federal or State law or regulation to maintain, or refrain from destroying, any document.

Once again, this section does not contain the corrupt intent requirement of the omnibus provisions discussed above, but rather requires that the defendant have acted "knowingly and willfully."

§ 12.06   SECTION 1512 — THE WITNESS TAMPERING STATUTE

[A]   The Statutory Provision and Elements

The Victim and Witness Protection Act of 1982[101] was enacted out of concern for the effects of witness tampering on judicial and administrative processes. Section 1512 covers tampering with a broad range of witnesses, potential witnesses, and excused witnesses.[102] In addition, § 1512 was expanded by the Sarbanes-Oxley Act

---

[101] *See* 18 U.S.C.§§ 1512–1515.

[102] *See, e.g.*, United States v. Wilson, 796 F.2d 55, 57–58 (4th Cir. 1986) (excused witnesses are covered

of 2002, [103]which added an omnibus provision, § 1512(c), to the statute.[104] The section of the statute most applicable to white collar offenses punishes:

> (b) Whoever knowingly uses intimidation, threatens, or *corruptly persuades* another person, or attempts to do so, or *engages in misleading conduct* toward another person, with intent to -
>
>> (1)   influence, delay, or prevent the testimony of any person in an official proceeding;
>>
>> (2)   cause or induce any person to -
>>
>>> (A)   withhold testimony, or withhold a record, document, or other object, from an official proceeding;
>>>
>>> (B)   alter, destroy, mutilate, or conceal an object with intent to impair the object's integrity or availability for use in an official proceeding;
>>>
>>> (C)   evade legal process summoning that person to appear as a witness, or to produce a record, document, or other object, in an official proceeding; or
>>>
>>> (D)   be absent from an official proceeding to which such person has been summoned by legal process; or
>>
>> (3)   hinder, delay, or prevent the communication to a law enforcement officer or judge of the United States of information relating to the commission or possible commission of a Federal offense or a violation of conditions of probation, supervised release, parole, or release pending judicial proceedings.[105]

It is the "corrupt persuasion" and "misleading conduct" provisions of this statute that are most applicable to white collar offenses.

As with the obstruction statutes, the defendant need not succeed in the efforts in order to be convicted of witness tampering.[106] Unlike the omnibus clauses of §§ 1503

---

under § 1512 for the duration of the judicial proceeding because of the possibility that such witnesses may be recalled to testify). *See generally* Kasprisin, *supra* note 5, at 870–71, and cases cited therein.

[103] Another section of the Act, codified at 18 U.S.C. § 1513 (Retaliating against a Witness, Victim, or an Informant), covers witness retaliation by killing or injuring the person or property of a witness, or attempting to do those acts.

[104] *See* § 1512(c) (providing that "[w]hoever corruptly — (1) alters, destroys, mutilates, or conceals a record, document, or other object, or attempts to do so, with the intent to impair the object's integrity or availability for use in an official proceeding; or (2) otherwise obstructs, influences, or impedes any official proceeding, or attempts to do so, shall be fined under this title or imprisoned not more than 20 years, or both." This section expands the scope of § 1512 beyond witness tampering, and overlaps substantially with the omnibus provisions of §§ 1503 and 1505.

[105] 18 U.S.C. § 1512(b) (emphasis added). The corrupt persuasion provision was added to the statute in 1988. For an overview of the statute, see Jeremy Freeman, *Corrupt Persuaders — Arthur Andersen and the Debate over Witness Tampering Prosecutions*, 12 No. 4 Bus. Crimes Bull. 1 (2005).

[106] *See, e.g.*, United States v. Willard, 230 F.3d 1093, 1095 (9th Cir. 2000) (holding that, under § 1512(b)(1), "[i]t is not necessary to show that the defendant actually obstructed justice or prevented a witness from testifying").

and 1505, this statute does not require that the government prove that a proceeding was pending at the time of the obstructive efforts.

[B]   Corrupt Persuasion

Under the corrupt persuasion provision, as interpreted by the courts, the government must show that the defendant:

1.   Acted knowingly and corruptly;

2.   Persuaded or attempted to persuade another person in order to -

    (a)   prevent, influence, or delay the other person's testimony or appearance,

    (b)   cause the other person to withhold, destroy, or alter documents, or

    (c)   hinder, delay, or prevent a communication to a United States official of information relating to the commission or possible commission of a federal offense or parole violation; and

3.   Acted in connection with a federal official proceeding.

Courts have struggled to define what it means "corruptly" to persuade or attempt to persuade. For example, in *United States v. Farrell*,[107] the defendant was convicted based upon his attempt to persuade a co-conspirator to assert his Fifth Amendment right-to-silence. The Third Circuit reversed the conviction, finding the term "corruptly" to be ambiguous with respect to encouraging another person to assert a constitutional right. The court thus applied the rule of lenity and stated that the statute did not encompass the defendant's conduct. Other courts have disagreed with *Farrell*'s approach. For example, the Eleventh Circuit in *United States v. Shotts*,[108] held that the term "corruptly" is not vague because it can be interpreted in accordance with the mens rea provision of § 1505.

The United States Supreme Court attempted to resolve the confusion over the required mens rea in *Arthur Andersen LLP v. United States*.[109] That case was an appeal from the first conviction arising from the Enron scandal. The Arthur Andersen accounting firm had acted as Enron's auditor, and had provided Enron with consulting services throughout Enron's rapid expansion during the 1990s. When Enron's financial performance declined during 2000 and 2001, the Securities and Exchange Commission ("SEC") opened an inquiry into Enron's accounting practices. Although the SEC investigation had not yet been publicly announced, the possibility of an investigation was reported in the press, and evidence showed that Andersen employees destroyed documents in anticipation of an investigation. In particular, employees were urged to follow Andersen's document retention policy and to destroy documents under that policy. The massive document destruction continued even after the SEC publicly announced its investigation, and did not stop until the SEC formally subpoenaed documents from Andersen. Based on the

---

[107]   126 F.3d 484, 488–90 (3d Cir. 1997). *See* Freeman, *supra* note 105, at 2.

[108]   145 F.3d 1289, 1300–01 (11th Cir. 1998).

[109]   544 U.S. 696 (2005).

document destruction, the government charged Andersen with one count of violating §§ 1512(b)(2)(A) and (B), and the jury convicted.

The Supreme Court reversed, finding that the trial judge erred when instructing the jury on the mens rea element of the offense. The statute criminalizes "knowingly . . . corruptly persuad[ing]" another person "with intent to . . . cause" that person to "withhold" documents from, or "alter" documents for use in, an "official proceeding." The issue was whether the word "knowingly" added to the government's burden of proof.

Initially, the Court stated that criminal statutes should be read narrowly to provide fair notice to potential defendants, particularly where, as here, the actus reus of "persuas[ion]" is not inherently wrongful. For example, an attorney who persuades a client to withhold documents from the government under the attorney-client privilege is not behaving in an inherently wrongful manner. Similarly, the Court noted, document retention policies are created in part to keep certain information from getting into the hands of others, are common in business, and are not necessarily wrongful.[110]

Turning to the statutory language, the Court found that under the most natural reading of the statute the term "knowingly" modifies the words "corruptly persuades." In addition, the Court noted that the term "corruptly" generally means to act in a wrongful, immoral, depraved, or evil manner; only persons conscious of wrongdoing can be said to "knowingly . . . corruptly persuad[e]." Here, the judge instructed the jury that, "even if Andersen honestly and sincerely believed that its conduct was lawful, you may find Andersen guilty." Because this would allow the jury to convict based upon conduct that the defendant did not believe to be wrongful, this instruction was in error.[111]

Finally, the Court noted that the instructions failed to require the jury to find the necessary nexus, as required by *Aguilar*. The government should have been required to prove that Andersen at least contemplated the SEC investigation when it destroyed the documents. Such proof would have provided the necessary link between the alleged obstructive acts and the proceeding.[112]

The *Andersen* decision does reign in the government's ability to use the corrupt persuasion provision. First, as previously interpreted by the lower courts, that provision could have criminalized routine document destruction under corporate document retention programs. The Court rejected that interpretation, and held that the statute could not be applied in such circumstances unless the government could prove beyond a reasonable doubt that the defendant knew that the destruction was wrongful.

Even after *Andersen*, however, courts continue to struggle to define the level of intent required for a corrupt persuasion conviction. In *United States v. Doss*,[113] for example, the defendant urged his wife to assert the marital privilege in a criminal

---

[110] *Id.* at 702–04.

[111] *Id.* at 705–07.

[112] *Id.* at 705–08.

[113] 630 F.3d 1181 (9th Cir. 2011).

investigation into the defendant's conduct. On appeal from the defendant's conviction under § 1512(b), the Ninth Circuit noted that the circuits are split over the meaning of the ambiguous term "corruptly persuades":[114] "Two of our sister circuits conclude that persuasion with an 'improper purpose' qualifies (such as self-interest in impeding an investigation), while another concludes there must be something more inherently wrongful about the persuasion (such as bribery or encouraging someone to testify falsely)."[115] Relying partly on *Andersen*, the court held that the latter was the correct interpretation, and reversed the conviction.

In *United States v. Gotti*,[116] the Second Circuit took the broader approach. In that case, the defendant suggested to a co-conspirator that the co-conspirator invoke his Fifth Amendment privilege. The Second Circuit affirmed the defendant's conviction under § 1512, holding that the defendant had a self-interested motivation in ensuring that the potential witness did not implicate the defendant. The court found that this motivation amounted to an "improper purpose" sufficient to support the conviction.

The *Andersen* decision also limits the reach of § 1512(b) in a second way. Although § 1512(b) does not contain a pending proceeding requirement, according to *Andersen* the government must show that the defendant at least contemplated that a proceeding would be pending in the future. Some courts have limited this holding to cases brought under § 1512(b)(2), the subsection at issue in *Andersen*, and have declined to extend this requirement to cases brought under § 1512(b)(3).[117] The courts reason that, although § 1512(b)(2) contains the language "an official proceeding," § 1512(b)(3) has no such language. Rather, § 1512(b)(3) requires only that the defendant intended to hinder, delay, or prevent communication to any "law enforcement officer or judge of the United States."[118]

[C] The Misleading Conduct Provision

Section 1512(b) also criminalizing "misleading conduct" undertaken with one of the purposes stated in the statute. Such a charge typically arises when one person attempts to mislead another so that the latter provides the government with false information.[119] Charges under this provision also may arise when the defendant has persuaded or attempted to persuade others to alter or destroy documents.[120]

---

[114] *Id.* at 1186, *citing* United States v. Baldridge, 559 F.3d 1126, 1142 (10th Cir. 2009).

[115] *Id.* ("*Compare* United States v. Thompson, 76 F.3d 442, 452 (2d Cir. 1996), *and* United States v. Shotts, 145 F.3d 1289, 1300–01 (11th Cir. 1998), *with* United States v. Farrell, 126 F.3d 484, 488 (3d Cir.1997).").

[116] 459 F.3d 296, 342–43 (2d Cir. 2006).

[117] *See, e.g.*, United States v. Carson, 560 F.3d 566, 582 (6th Cir. 2009) (citing cases).

[118] *Id.*

[119] For an example of such a prosecution, see United States v. Gabriel, 125 F.3d 89 (2d Cir. 1997), *abrogated by* United States v. Quattrone, 441 F.3d 153 (2d Cir. 2006). In *Gabriel*, the defendant provided a misleading document to a potential witness in a grand jury investigation into alleged fraud.

[120] *See, e.g.*, Quattrone, 441 F.3d 153 (charging the defendant under both the corrupt persuasion and misleading conduct provisions).

[D]   The Nexus Requirement

Prior to the decision in *Arthur Andersen*,[121] courts had held that *Aguilar*'s nexus requirement does not apply to the witness tampering statute.[122] In *Quattrone*,[123] the Second Circuit abrogated precedent in its own circuit and held that *Andersen* requires that the jury find the requisite nexus between the obstructive acts and the proceeding under § 1512(b). Other courts have since applied the nexus requirement to charges brought under § 1512(c)(2).[124]

[E]   The Relationship Between the Obstruction Statutes and the Witness Tampering Statute

Prior to the enactment of the Victim and Witness Protection Act,[125] obstructive acts directed at witnesses and informants, such as intimidation and threats, were plainly covered under the obstruction statutes. Congress, however, has deleted the references to witnesses in § 1503, though witness tampering still falls literally within the broad proscriptions of the omnibus clause. Congress has failed to indicate clearly whether the witness tampering statute is intended to complement, or to replace, the obstruction statutes' application to witness tampering.[126] This lack of clarity has prompted a split in the circuits as to whether witness tampering can still be prosecuted under § 1503 or instead must be prosecuted under § 1512. A majority of courts allow witness tampering to be prosecuted under either the omnibus clause of §§ 1503 and 1505 or under § 1512.[127]

---

[121] 544 U.S. 696 (2005).

[122] *See* United States v. Gabriel, 125 F.3d 89 (2d Cir. 1997), *abrogated by* United States v. Quattrone, 441 F.3d 153, 176 (2d Cir. 2006).

[123] *See id.*

[124] *See* United States v. Phillips, 583 F.3d 1261 (10th Cir. 2009); United States v. Reich, 479 F.3d 179 (2d Cir. 2007).

[125] *See* 18 U.S.C. §§ 1512–1515.

[126] *See* Nesland, *supra* note 18, § 10.03[1].

[127] *See* United States v. Lester, 749 F.2d 1288, 1292–93 (9th Cir. 1984) (upholding witness tampering charge under § 1503). *See generally* Nesland, *supra* note 21, § 10.03[1] (listing cases).

Chapter 13

TAX CRIMES

§ 13.01 INTRODUCTION

Charges under the criminal provisions of the United States tax code are brought in a wide variety of white collar prosecutions. Many such cases, such as those arising out of routine audits of tax returns, focus solely on tax violations.[1] It is also common, however, for tax charges to arise out of investigations that originally centered on other types of criminal activities. For example, a public official who receives a bribe, but does not report the payment for tax purposes, may face both bribery and tax charges. Indeed, in many instances the government may bring a tax charge instead of the charges originally contemplated because the tax crime is easier to prove. In the hypothetical bribery case, the prosecutor might determine that there is insufficient evidence to prove the mens rea required for that crime, but instead decide to use the tax laws as a vehicle for pursuing the original target of the investigation.

This chapter reviews the main statutes used in criminal tax cases. The tax code sets forth a hierarchy of tax crimes, ranging from the felony of tax evasion to the misdemeanor of failing to file a return or pay taxes. Each of these crimes is directed at a specific type of conduct. This chapter discusses the three most often used statutes — tax evasion,[2] filing of false returns,[3] and failing to file a return.[4]

Criminal tax cases raise several distinct issues. First, the Supreme Court has applied strict intent requirements to these cases. The jury's determination of the defendant's mental state is often even more crucial in criminal tax cases than in other areas of white collar crime. Second, because it is often difficult to obtain an accurate picture of a defendant's finances, tax cases raise unique problems of proof. Third, tax investigations and prosecutions are unusual in the degree to which they proceed through multiple levels of supervision. Finally, tax cases can also produce charges under provisions of the criminal laws other than the tax code.

---

[1] *See* Kathryn Keneally, Elliot Silverman, & Peter Fucci, *Criminal Tax Cases, in* White Collar Crime: Business and Regulatory Offenses § 13.01 (Otto Obermaier & Robert Morvillo, eds. 2011).

[2] 26 U.S.C. § 7201.

[3] 26 U.S.C. § 7206.

[4] 26 U.S.C. § 7203. These are the three statutes used in the vast majority of tax prosecutions. Other important tax code provisions include § 7205 (covering misstatements for tax withholding purposes), § 7212 (covering attempts to interfere with the administration of the tax laws by means of corruption, force, or threats), and § 7214 (relating to corruption of government officials). *See generally* James P. Dombach & Jennifer M. Forde, *Tax Violations*, 47 Am. Crim. L. Rev. 1089 (2010); Keneally, et al., *supra* note 1, § 13.06.

§ 13.02　TAX EVASION

[A]　Statutory Overview and Elements

The crime of tax evasion, set forth in § 7201 of the tax code, carries the most serious penalties of all the principal tax fraud crimes. The Supreme Court has described tax evasion as the "capstone of a system of sanctions which singly or in combination were calculated to induce prompt and forthright fulfillment of every duty under the income tax law and to provide a penalty suitable to every degree of delinquency."[5] A defendant may be liable for one count of tax evasion for each tax year in which the evasive activity occurred.

The evasion statute covers "[a]ny person who willfully attempts in any manner to evade or defeat any tax imposed by this title or the payment thereof."[6] To gain a conviction under this section, the government must prove that the defendant:

1. Underpaid taxes;

2. Engaged in an affirmative act of evasion; and

3. Acted willfully.[7]

The element of willfulness applies to all the tax crimes described here, and is discussed in a later section.[8] The elements of underpayment and evasion are, however, particular to the tax evasion statute.

Statutory penalties under this section include a $100,000 fine, or a $500,000 fine for a corporation, and/or imprisonment of not more than five years, together with the costs of prosecution. As with other crimes, the actual sentence imposed will depend on the operation of the United States Sentencing Guidelines, and the trial judge's application of those guidelines, in the particular case.[9]

[B]　Underpayment

The government must prove an underpayment of taxes in order to obtain a conviction for evasion. Courts are split as to whether the underpayment must be substantial, or whether even a de minimus underpayment will suffice for conviction.[10] As a matter of policy, however, minimal amounts generally will not be prosecuted.

In most cases, the government proves an underpayment by showing that the defendant failed to disclose income on the defendant's tax return. For example, the public official who obtains a bribe, but fails to include the payment as income, has understated the income.

---

[5] Spies v. United States, 317 U.S. 492, 497 (1943).

[6] 26 U.S.C. § 7201.

[7] *See* Sansone v. United States, 380 U.S. 343, 351 (1965).

[8] *See infra*, § 13.05.

[9] *See* Chapter 21, Sentencing, *infra.*

[10] *See* Dombach & Forde, *supra* note 4, at 1097; Keneally, et al., *supra* note 1, at 13.02[1][c].

Underpayments also often result from an overstatement of deductions. This can occur in many ways. One common fact pattern occurs when an individual falsely deducts personal expenses as business expenses. In the notorious case of *United States v. Helmsley*,[11] for example, the defendants undertook a major renovation of their private mansion and charged the expenses, totaling over $2 million, to various business entities they controlled. Underpayment in this case occurred both on the corporate return, because the corporation overstated its deductions, and on the individuals' returns, because the individuals omitted from income the value of expenses paid by the corporation.[12]

[C]   Affirmative Act of Evasion

As § 7201 states, it is a crime to willfully "attempt in any manner to evade or defeat any tax." The Supreme Court has noted that the "attempt," which is the actus reus of tax evasion, is not equivalent to the inchoate crime of common law "attempt." Rather, the crime of evasion is complete upon commission of any effort to evade.[13]

The Supreme Court addressed the actus reus requirement of tax evasion in *Spies v. United States*.[14] The defendant in *Spies* had sufficient income to require him to file a return and pay taxes, but did neither. Over the defendant's objection, the trial court instructed the jury that it could convict the defendant of evasion based solely on his failure to file a return and pay taxes; the jury was not required to find any affirmative act of evasion.

The Supreme Court reversed, finding that the trial judge's instruction did not take into account the offense structure of the criminal tax code. Congress has specifically defined the crime of failing to file a return or pay taxes, which is punished as a misdemeanor. Tax evasion, on the other hand, is a felony. According to the Court, it therefore makes no sense to say, as the trial judge did, that the more serious crime of evasion occurs whenever the elements of the lesser crime are met. Rather, the word "attempt" in the tax evasion statute connotes an affirmative act. The Court then gave some examples of the type of acts that the jury must be required to find:

> By way of illustration, and not by way of limitation, we would think affirmative willful attempt may be inferred from conduct such as keeping a double set of books, making false entries or alterations, or false invoices or documents, destruction of books or records, concealment of assets or covering up sources of income, handling of one's affairs to avoid making the

---

[11]   United States v. Helmsley, 941 F.2d 71, 77 (2d Cir. 1991), *cert. denied*, 502 U.S. 1091 (1992) (false business deductions included various renovations to defendants' private home, including a $2 million addition to enclose a swimming pool and install a rooftop marble dance floor, as well as purchases of four art pieces for $500,000, and installation of a $100,000 stereo system).

[12]   *See* Keneally, et al., *supra* note 1, at 13.02[1][c].

[13]   *Spies*, 317 U.S. at 498.

[14]   *Id.* at 499. Spies was prosecuted under an earlier tax evasion statute, 26 U.S.C. § 145(b).

records usual in transactions of the kind, and any conduct, the likely effect of which would be to mislead or to conceal.[15]

Any act that tends to hide income or fraudulently reduce tax liability will usually suffice to show the attempt to evade.[16] In one case, for example, the Court held that the filing of a false tax return itself constitutes an affirmative act of evasion.[17] Other courts have sustained convictions based upon any attempts to conceal income.

The evasion statute covers attempts either to (1) evade an accurate *assessment* of taxes, that is, the determination of the amount of taxes owed, or (2) evade *payment* of taxes after the amount due is determined. Most evasion cases are based upon the theory that the defendant has evaded *assessment* by understating income or overstating deductions. There are also evasion cases where the defendant has attempted to avoid *payment* even after tax liability has been determined. Such a case might be brought, for example, where a defendant has attempted to conceal assets from the government as it attempted to collect taxes owed.[18]

§ 13.03 FALSE RETURNS

Another serious felony is set forth in Internal Revenue Code § 7206, which proscribes filing or assisting in the filing of a false tax return or related document.[19] This statute is also sometimes called the "tax perjury" statute. A defendant may be liable for one count for each false return filed. This statute is designed to punish those who endeavor to mislead the government in its taxation efforts, and does not focus on the financial loss to the government. Thus, unlike a tax evasion case, the government is not required to show any tax deficiency when proving a case under § 7206.

[A] Statutory Overview and Elements

Section 7206(1) applies to the tax filer, and covers anyone who:

Willfully makes and subscribes any return, statement, or other document, which contains or is verified by a written declaration that it is made under the penalties of perjury, and which he does not believe to be true and correct as to every material matter.

Under this section, the government must prove that:

1. The defendant signed the tax return or related document;

2. The defendant signed under penalty of perjury;

---

[15] *Id.*

[16] *See, e.g.*, United States v. Eaken, 17 F.3d 203, 205–06 (7th Cir. 1994) (while the affirmative "act required for tax evasion must demonstrate something more than mere passive failure to pay income tax," the conviction was supported by sufficient evidence because of the affirmative steps taken to conceal his receipt of embezzled funds).

[17] Sansone v. United States, 380 U.S. 343, 349 (1965).

[18] *See* Dombach & Forde, *supra* note 4, at 1101–03.

[19] 26 U.S.C. § 7206.

3.   The return or related document was false;

4.   The falsity was material; and

5.   The defendant acted willfully.

Section 7206(2) applies to one who assists in the filing of a false return, and covers anyone who:

> Willfully aids or assists in, or procures, counsels, or advises the preparation or presentation under, or in connection with any matter arising under, the internal revenue laws, of a return, affidavit, claim, or other document, which is fraudulent or is false as to any material matter, whether or not such falsity or fraud is with the knowledge or consent of the person authorized or required to present such return, affidavit, claim, or document.

Under this section, the government must prove:

1.   The defendant aided or assisted in the preparation of the tax return or related document;

2.   The return or related document was false;

3.   The falsity was material; and

4.   The defendant acted willfully.

A conviction under either § 7206(1) or (2) subjects a defendant to a maximum prison term of three years, a maximum fine of $100,000 for individuals and $500,000 for organizations, and payment of the costs of prosecution. The actual sentence will vary according to the application of the United States Sentencing Guidelines.[20] Once again, the key litigated issue is often willfulness, which is discussed more fully in a later section.[21]

[B]   Tax Filer and Preparer Liability

Under § 7206(1), the government must show that the filer signed the return, and did so under penalty of perjury. Because filers routinely sign their returns, and the returns themselves state that this is under penalty of perjury, the actus reus elements for filers are usually easy to prove. Likewise, § 7206(2) broadly reaches anyone who takes any affirmative action in connection with filing the false return.[22]

A tax preparer who signs a return might be liable under either subsection. For example, in *United States v. Shortt Accountancy*,[23] the defendant was an accounting firm that had offered to create a phony tax deduction for a client. Cooperating with the IRS in its investigation of the accounting firm, the client subsequently filed a return signed by an employee of Shortt. At the direction of Shortt's chief operating officer, the employee prepared and signed the return

---

[20]   26 U.S.C. § 7206; 18 U.S.C. § 3571. *See* Chapter 21, Sentencing, *infra*, for an overview of federal sentencing.

[21]   *See infra*, § 13.05.

[22]   *See* Keneally, et al., *supra* note 1, § 13.03.

[23]   785 F.2d 1448 (9th Cir. 1986), *cert. denied*, 478 U.S. 1007 (1986).

without knowing that it claimed an improper deduction. Based upon this return and six similar returns prepared for other clients, Shortt was convicted of seven counts under § 7206(1).

On appeal, Shortt first argued that the taxpayer, not the tax preparer, is the liable party under § 7206(1) because only the taxpayer has a duty to file. The Ninth Circuit rejected the argument, finding that the statute is not limited to taxpayers. The court reasoned that this section is a tax perjury statute, and covers anyone who meets the statutory elements.[24] Second, Shortt argued that it could not possess the required intent because the person who signed the returns did not know that the deductions were improper. The court also rejected this argument, noting that to accept it would mean that "any tax return preparer could escape prosecution for perjury by arranging for an innocent employee to complete the proscribed act of subscribing a false return."[25]

[C] Falsity

As part of its case, the government must prove that the return or related document contained a false statement. Courts have held than an omission can amount to a false statement. In *Siravo v. United States*,[26] the defendant filed tax returns that correctly stated his wages. In his returns, however, he omitted income from a separate business that should have been reported on a separate "Schedule C" filed with his return. On appeal from his § 7206 conviction, the defendant argued that his returns were not false because they accurately stated the amount of his wages. The First Circuit disagreed, holding that a return must be both accurate and complete to fulfill the statute's function in helping keep track of income records. Because the defendant's returns were not complete, they properly formed the basis for his conviction.

In *Siravo*, the defendant used the correct tax form, but failed to include income that he was required to report. The court found that this amounted to a false return. Courts have held, however, that using the wrong form to file tax returns, and thereby concealing income, does not amount to filing a false return.

In *United States v. Reynolds*,[27] the defendant filed a Form 1040EZ, which asked for his "total wages, salaries and tips." The defendant reported the amount of his wages that appeared on his W-2 form, but did not report money he had fraudulently received as business expenses. Because he had a source of income other than wages, salaries, and tips, the defendant in fact should not have filed a Form 1040EZ. The defendant was convicted under § 7206(1) on the theory that his omission rendered the return false. The Seventh Circuit reversed, finding that the defendant had reported all the income that the form required, and that the form was literally correct.[28] In the alternative, the government argued that the

---

[24] *Id.* at 1454.

[25] *Id.*

[26] 377 F.2d 469 (1st Cir. 1967).

[27] 919 F.2d 435 (7th Cir. 1990).

[28] *Id.* at 437.

defendant, by filing the Form 1040EZ, impliedly stated that he had no additional income. The court noted that this theory might be viable, but refused to sustain the conviction on that basis because that theory was not charged in the indictment.[29] Either theory presumably would have been sufficient for a tax evasion charge under § 7201.[30]

[D] Materiality

The government must show that the false statement in the tax return was "material." Courts generally find that a falsity is material if it has the capacity to interfere with the government's ability to monitor and determine the tax owed.[31]

As noted above, a false statement may be material even if it does not lead to an underpayment of taxes. In *United States v. DiVarco*,[32] for example, the defendants had fully disclosed their income and paid their taxes, but had misidentified a source of their income on their tax returns. On appeal from the § 7206 convictions, the defendants argued that they could not be convicted under § 7206 because the government had not shown that they understated their income, and that they should have been charged under § 1001, the general false statement statute.[33] The Seventh Circuit rejected the argument. The court acknowledged that most misstatements of income do produce tax deficiencies, but affirmed the conviction for the simple reason that a tax deficiency is not an element under § 7206.[34] The Second Circuit reached a similar conclusion in *United States v. Greenberg*.[35] Greenberg was convicted of filing false individual and corporate tax returns. Greenberg fraudulently allocated income to his wife on their joint personal returns, and fraudulently described the corporation's payment of its owners' personal expenses as business expenses. On appeal, Greenberg argued that the false statements were not "material" because the misstatements resulted in an underpayment of only $48. The court disagreed, reasoning that "the distortions in income had potential for hindering efforts to monitor and verify tax liability of the corporation and the taxpayer."[36]

---

[29] The court in United States v. Borman, 992 F.2d 124, 126 (7th Cir. 1993), rejected this theory. In that case, the defendant filed a Form 1040A, which asks for reporting of only certain types of income. Because the defendant in fact had other sources of income, he should have filed a Form 1040. In affirming the dismissal of the indictment, the Seventh Circuit rejected the government's argument that the defendant implicitly stated he had no income requiring him to use a Form 1040. A tax evasion charge presumably would have been viable.

[30] *Reynolds*, 919 F.2d at 437.

[31] *See* Dombach & Forde, *supra* note 4, at 1119.

[32] 484 F.2d 670 (7th Cir. 1973), *cert. denied*, 415 U.S. 916 (1974).

[33] 18 U.S.C. § 1001. *See* Chapter 10, False Statements, *supra*, for a discussion of this section.

[34] "One of the . . . basic tenets running through all the cases is that the purpose behind [§ 7206] is to prosecute those who intentionally falsify their tax returns regardless of the precise ultimate effect that such falsification may have." 484 F.2d at 673, *quoting* United States v. DiVarco, 343 F. Supp. 101, 103 (N.D. Ill. 1972), *aff'd*, 484 F.2d 670 (7th Cir. 1973), *cert. denied*, 415 U.S. 916 (1974).

[35] 735 F.2d 29, 31 (2d Cir. 1984).

[36] *Id.* at 31.

Before the Supreme Court's 1995 decision in *United States v. Gaudin*,[37] most courts had held that materiality was a question of law for the judge. In *Gaudin*, however, the Court held that, in a false statements prosecution under § 1001, materiality is a mixed question of law and fact that should be determined by the jury. Although courts have split as to whether the *Gaudin* rule applies to false returns prosecutions, the prevailing view appears to be that this is a jury question.[38]

§ 13.04 FAILURE TO FILE A RETURN OR PAY TAXES — STATUTORY OVERVIEW AND ELEMENTS

Both tax evasion and false returns are felonies; the crime of failing to file a return or pay a tax, set forth in § 7203 of the Internal Revenue Code,[39] is punished as a misdemeanor. The felony offenses cover a defendant's affirmative acts that have the capacity to hinder the government's ability to keep track of matters relating to taxation. Failing to file a return or pay taxes, however, may be based solely on inaction.

Section 7203 covers:

> Any person required under this title to pay any estimated tax or tax, or required by this title or by regulations made under authority thereof to make a return, keep any records, or supply any information, who willfully fails to pay such estimated tax or tax, make such return, keep such records, or supply such information, at the time or times required by law or regulations.[40]

To obtain a conviction under this section, the government must prove that the defendant:

1. Acted willfully;

2. Failed to (a) file a required return, (b) pay a required tax, (c) keep required records, or (d) supply required information; and

3. Failed to act at the time the law specified.

A defendant convicted under this section is subject to a fine of not more than $25,000, or $100,000 for a corporation, and/or imprisoned not more than 1 year, together with the costs of prosecution. Again, the actual sentence will depend upon the application of the United States Sentencing Guidelines.

Most § 7203 cases are based upon the alleged failure to file a return.[41] Many cases brought under this section involve "tax protestors" who have consciously

---

[37] 515 U.S. 506 (1995).

[38] *See* Dombach & Forde, *supra* note 4, at 1119, and cases cited therein.

[39] 26 U.S.C. § 7203.

[40] 26 U.S.C. § 7203.

[41] *See* Keneally, et al., *supra* note 1, § 13.04.

decided not to file a return, or have filed a blank or incomplete return.[42] As with evasion and false returns, the key contested issue in failure to file cases is often willfulness.

§ 13.05   MENS REA — WILLFULNESS

As noted above, to obtain a conviction for evading taxes, filing a false return, or failing to file a return or pay taxes, the government must prove beyond a reasonable doubt that the defendant acted willfully. This is the key contested issue in many tax cases.

[A]   Definition of Willfulness

The Supreme Court has consistently held that, to prove willfulness, the government must show a "voluntary, intentional violation of a known legal duty."[43] The Court explained this standard in *United States v. Pomponio*.[44] In that case, the appeals court reversed the defendant's false returns conviction because the trial judge had failed to instruct the jury that it must find that the defendant acted with a bad purpose or evil motive. The Supreme Court reinstated the conviction, holding that willfulness means no more than "a voluntary, intentional violation of a known legal duty."[45]

In 1991, the Supreme Court reaffirmed this standard in *Cheek v. United States*.[46] Although the Court in *Cheek* used the eternally confusing term "specific intent" to describe willfulness,[47] it is more useful to view the mens rea for tax crimes as simply requiring proof that the defendant (1) intended to commit the acts charged, and (2) intended to violate the law by committing those acts.

It is the second level of willfulness — intent to violate the law — that places an unusually high burden on the government. Ordinarily, of course, "ignorance of the law is no excuse." Because the law usually assumes that everyone is on notice of what is illegal, in most cases the government need only prove mens rea as to the proscribed act and need not prove that the defendant knew or intended to violate the law.[48]

Why has the Court imposed this unusual burden in tax fraud cases? As the Court stated in *Cheek*, "[t]his special treatment of criminal tax offenses is largely due to the complexity of the tax laws."[49] The Court continued: "The proliferation of statutes and regulations has sometimes made it difficult for the average citizen to know and comprehend the extent of the duties and obligations imposed by the tax

---

[42] *See id.*

[43] United States v. Bishop, 412 U.S. 346, 360 (1973).

[44] 429 U.S. 10 (1976).

[45] *Id.* at 12.

[46] 498 U.S. 192 (1991).

[47] *Id.* at 194.

[48] *Id.* at 201.

[49] *Id.* at 200.

laws."[50] Thus, the Court concluded, Congress intended the term "willfulness" in the criminal tax code to require that the government prove the defendant knew of and intended to violate the law.

[B] Proof of Willfulness

As in other areas of the criminal law, mens rea in tax cases is a jury question that is largely proven through circumstantial evidence. On appeal, the court will read all the evidence in favor of the government. Thus, obtaining reversal on the grounds of insufficient evidence is difficult.

The decision in *United States v. Rischard*,[51] demonstrates the degree to which courts allow willfulness to be based on circumstantial evidence. Rischard was an attorney who was convicted of evading taxes and filing false returns. On appeal, the defendant argued that the government had failed at trial to introduce sufficient evidence that the defendant acted willfully. The Eighth Circuit rejected the argument, finding that the circumstantial evidence supported a finding of willfulness. In reaching this conclusion, the court relied upon the following evidence: (1) the defendant's pattern of understating his income on his tax returns over three years; (2) the defendant had a law degree; (3) the defendant had substantial professional experience, including the practice of law; (4) the defendant was able to bill clients and maintain expense records for his private practice; and (5) the defendant, when asked by an I.R.S. agent to disclose his bank accounts, failed to disclose one of the accounts.[52]

Certainly, the first and last pieces of evidence provide the basis for an inference of willfulness, but it is unclear that the other pieces of evidence add very much to that showing here. Nonetheless, attorneys are all too often defendants in tax fraud prosecutions, where their educational and professional backgrounds may lead a jury to conclude that they knew exactly what they were doing and thus intended to violate the law. Other professionals, such as accountants or stock brokers, may face similar difficulties in refuting circumstantial evidence of willfulness.

In *United States v. Guidry*,[53] the defendant was convicted of three counts of filing a false tax return. Guidry was a college graduate with a bachelor's degree in business administration. Wichita Sheet Metal hired Guidry to assist the controller of the company. Guidry then designed an embezzlement scheme that bilked the company out of $3 million, and failed to report the income on her tax returns. On appeal, she argued that the tax fraud convictions should be reversed because there was insufficient evidence of willfulness.[54] The court disagreed. Acknowledging that "willfulness cannot be inferred solely from an understatement of income," the court found that evidence of Guidry's experience in the accounting field, testimony that embezzled income is taxable income, and testimony that Guidry was in possession

---

[50] *Id.* at 199–200.

[51] 471 F.2d 105 (8th Cir. 1973).

[52] Although the defendant subsequently filed amended returns, the court discounted this evidence because the amendments were filed after the defendant learned he was under investigation. *Id.* at 108.

[53] 199 F.3d 1150 (10th Cir. 1999).

[54] *Id.* at 1156.

of Internal Revenue Service tax booklets was sufficient to support the jury's finding of willfulness.[55]

[C] Defenses

[1] Good Faith

In *Cheek*, the Supreme Court held that an honest misunderstanding of the law is a complete defense to tax fraud, even if that belief is unreasonable.[56] Cheek was a commercial airline pilot and "tax protestor" who was charged with multiple counts of failing to file returns and of tax evasion. Representing himself at trial, the defendant argued that he did not act willfully because he had, in good faith, mistakenly believed both that (1) wages are not "income" under the tax laws, and (2) the income tax is unconstitutional.[57] During deliberations, the jury twice requested that the judge clarify the standard for determining willfulness. In response, judge told the jury that "an honest but unreasonable belief is not a defense and does not negate willfulness."[58] The judge continued, "advice or research resulting in the conclusion that wages . . . are not income or that the tax laws are unconstitutional is not objectively reasonable."[59] The Seventh Circuit affirmed the conviction, and Cheek appealed to the Supreme Court.

In an opinion written by Justice White, the Supreme Court reversed the conviction and remanded for a new trial. The Court reiterated that the government must show, in a criminal tax case, that the defendant voluntarily and intentionally violated a known legal duty. The Court further reasoned that, if the defendant had an honest, good faith misunderstanding of the law, then he did not intentionally violate the law, irrespective of whether his misunderstanding was unreasonable. Thus, the trial judge had mistakenly instructed the jury on the appropriate legal standard.

The Court also went on to conclude, however, that a belief in the *unconstitutionality* of the tax code does not negate willfulness. Such a belief shows "full knowledge of the provisions at issue and a studied conclusion, however wrong, that those provisions are invalid and unenforceable."[60] A good faith misunderstanding of the law will negate intent, but a mere disagreement with the law will not.

---

[55] *Id.* at 1157–58.

[56] 498 U.S. at 203.

[57] In support, the defendant demonstrated his extensive involvement with groups that contested the legality and constitutionality of the income tax system. The government showed, on the other hand, that the defendant was aware of rulings in civil and criminal cases that rejected his views, and that a private attorney had similarly advised him. *Id.* at 195.

[58] *Id.* at 197.

[59] *Id.*

[60] *Id.* at 205. For a case holding that a defendant's disagreement with the tax laws does not negate willfulness, see United States v. Ambort, 405 F.3d 1109, 1115 (10th Cir. 2005) (defendant's assertion that certain people could claim to be "non-resident" aliens who were not subject to taxation was irrelevant to the issue of willfulness because the defendant knew this view had never been accepted).

In an opinion written by Justice Blackmun and joined by Justice Marshall, the dissent agreed with the circuit court that a mistaken belief of the law must be reasonable in order to be a defense to tax fraud. The dissent further stated that it is "incomprehensible [that] . . . any taxpayer of competent mentality can assert as his defense to charges of statutory willfulness the proposition that the wage he receives for his labor is not income."[61]

Does the *Cheek* decision really impose a substantial additional burden on the government in tax cases? It is true that a defendant's good faith belief or misunderstanding no longer need be reasonable to provide a defense. Nonetheless, as the majority itself noted in *Cheek*, "*the more unreasonable* the asserted beliefs or misunderstandings are, the more likely the jury will consider them to be nothing more than *simple disagreement* with known legal duties imposed by the tax laws and will find that the Government has carried its burden of proving knowledge."[62] Indeed, at his new trial, Cheek was convicted of the charges against him.[63]

Later cases have borne out the *Cheek* majority's prediction. In *United States v. Pensyl*,[64] for example, the defendant was convicted of three counts of tax evasion. On appeal, Pensyl argued that the district court should not have allowed the jury to consider the reasonableness of his beliefs in their deliberations on willfulness. Also, Pensyl contended that the jury instruction was confusing because it established good faith as a defense to the crime of tax evasion while simultaneously reminding the jury that ignorance of the law is not a defense to a criminal conviction.[65] The court rejected both arguments, holding that the jury instruction was not confusing and that a jury may consider the reasonableness of the defendant's belief as a factor in determining whether the good faith defense to tax evasion applies.[66]

[2] Legal Uncertainty

In *Cheek*, the law was certain — wages are indeed "income" under the Internal Revenue Code — but the defendant claimed a good faith misunderstanding of the law. A defendant may make a related argument when an aspect of the tax law is actually unclear. In that circumstance, the defendant may claim a good faith interpretation of the law that is different from the government's interpretation.

The Second Circuit confronted the issue of legal uncertainty in *United States v. Regan*.[67] In that case, Regan and other defendants were affiliated with a stock brokerage firm, Princeton-Newport Partners ("PNP").[68]

---

[61] *Id.* at 209.

[62] *Id.* at 204 (emphasis added).

[63] United States v. Cheek, 3 F.3d 1057 (7th Cir. 1993), *cert. denied*, 510 U.S. 1112 (1994) (hereinafter "*Cheek II*").

[64] 387 F.3d 456 (6th Cir. 2004).

[65] *Id.* at 457.

[66] *Id.* at 460.

[67] 937 F.2d 823 (2d Cir. 1991).

[68] *Regan*, also known as "the Princeton-Newport" case, was an extremely controversial prosecution. The case arose out of the government's investigation of Michael Milken, perhaps the most successful investment banker of the 1980s, and marked a rare use of the RICO statute in a tax fraud case. *See*

PNP had "parked" stock with — that is, temporarily sold stock to — other brokerage firms.[69] Under the guidance of defendant Regan, a managing partner of PNP and its tax expert, PNP sold the stock at a loss, deducted the losses on its taxes, and then bought the stock back later. In taking the deductions, Regan relied upon the following: (1) correspondence from his accountants, (2) a report of the Tax Section of the Association of the Bar of the City of New York, and (3) his own study of the relevant statute (I.R.C. § 1078) and a related proposed regulation.[70] Based upon the theory that these deductions were illegal, the government charged the defendants with conspiracy, securities fraud, filing false tax returns, mail fraud based upon the mailing of the tax returns, and RICO based upon the mail fraud.

At the end of the trial, the judge instructed the jury that, "[i]f the defendant signed the tax return in good faith and believed it to be true in all material matters, he has not committed a crime and must be acquitted on these counts, even if the return was incorrect."[71] The judge refused, however, specifically to instruct the jury that a good faith interpretation of Section 1078 would be a complete defense to the tax and related charges. The defendants were convicted of all charges.

The Second Circuit reversed the tax fraud and related convictions, and remanded for a new trial. Relying upon *Cheek*, the court noted that the tax laws are especially difficult to understand. The court found that, in light of the complexity of the charges in the case, "a generalized charge on good faith was insufficient to instruct the jury concerning appellants' specific good faith defense based on Section 1058. Appellants were entitled to have the trial court clearly instruct the jury, relative to appellants' theory of defense to the tax charges, that the theory, if believed, justified acquittal on those charges."[72]

The defendants in *Regan* were granted a general good faith instruction. Why, then, did the trial judge's failure to lay out the defendant's argument in more detail require reversal? A dissenting judge argued that the defendants had indeed received all to which they were entitled in the jury instruction.[73] Given the complexity of the case, however, the majority concluded that a blanket instruction did not sufficiently guide the jury in its determination of willfulness. Also, perhaps underlying the majority's opinion was its concern that the prosecutors had abused

---

Chapters 16 & 22, *infra* (RICO and Forfeitures). The case led to congressional hearings, and to the adoption of new Department of Justice Guidelines for the use of mail fraud based on tax fraud as a RICO predicate. *See* 937 F.2d at 827. For criticism of the government for bringing this case, see L. Gordon Crovitz, *How the RICO Monster Mauled Wall Street*, 65 Notre Dame L. Rev. 1050 (1990); Sherry R. Sontag, *Princeton/Newport Case: RICO Stretched Too Far?*, Nat'l L.J., Nov. 20, 1989, at 3; Marcia Chambers, *Sua Sponte*, Nat'l L.J., Feb. 10, 1992, at 15; and Sherry R. Sontag, *RICO Fades Away on Wall Street*, Nat'l L.J., Sept. 28, 1992, at 3.

[69] The *Regan* defendants were also charged with securities fraud. For a discussion of stock parking in the context of securities fraud, see Chapter 5, Securities Fraud, *supra* § 5.10[A].

[70] 937 F.2d at 825, *citing* 26 U.S.C. § 1058, and proposed regulation 1.1058-1.

[71] *Id.* at 830 (Mahoney, J., dissenting).

[72] 937 F.2d at 826–827. The defendants also argued that the trial court erred in excluding expert testimony supporting their good faith reliance on Section 1058, but the Second Circuit did not reach this issue. *Id.* at 826.

[73] *Id.* at 831 (Mahoney, J., dissenting).

their discretion in constructing a RICO case based upon tax fraud.[74]

The issue of legal uncertainty arose in a particularly unusual context in *United States v. Garber*.[75] In that case, the defendant was convicted of tax evasion for failing to report income she received from the sale of her blood, which contained a rare, medically valuable component. The *en banc* Fifth Circuit reversed the conviction on several grounds. First, the trial judge erred in refusing to allow the defendant's expert witnesses to testify as to whether the income was taxable. The court also found that it was error for the trial court to refuse to instruct the jury that the defendant's reasonable misunderstanding of the law negated willfulness. Finally, the court found that the trial judge erred in determining that the proceeds of the blood sale were taxable as a matter of law, and that the judge should have left the issue to the jury.

The Fifth Circuit decision in *Garber* is subject to criticism in two respects. First, questions of law generally are resolved by the judge, not the jury. Second, expert testimony on the law's uncertainty probably does assist the jury in deciding willfulness, absent some evidence that the defendant was aware of the uncertainty at the time of the alleged fraud.[76] Accordingly, in *United States v. Burton*,[77] the Fifth Circuit later limited the *Garber* holding to its facts.

Similarly, the Sixth Circuit in *United States v. Curtis* refused to follow *Garber*.[78] Curtis was president and sole shareholder of a business that received checks for the sale of its product. The defendant deposited some of these checks into his personal accounts, and did not report the money as income. At his tax evasion trial, the trial judge refused to allow a defense expert to testify that the law was unclear concerning the taxability of corporate payments to shareholders. The judge also declined to instruct the jury that uncertainty in the law was relevant to a finding of willfulness. On appeal, the Sixth Circuit found that neither ruling was error. Rejecting *Garber*, the Sixth Circuit held that uncertainty in the law is relevant to willfulness only when the defendant was aware of the uncertainty at the time of the alleged fraud.[79] Also, expert testimony on legal uncertainty in such a case improperly leaves to the jury a question of law that is solely for the judge.[80]

Thus, unless there is evidence that the defendant was aware of the legal uncertainty at the time of the alleged tax fraud, evidence of that uncertainty is unlikely to be admissible at trial. Where the law is genuinely unclear, however, the

---

[74] *See id.* at 827 (given the outcome of the case, "we need not become involved in the disputed issue whether federal tax violations can give rise to a RICO cause of action").

[75] 607 F.2d 92 (5th Cir. 1979) (*en banc*), *cert. denied*, 462 U.S. 1131 (1983).

[76] *See* United States v. Curtis, 782 F.2d 593, 599 (6th Cir. 1986) (rejecting the *Garber* holding that allowed "juries to find that uncertainty in the law negates willfulness even when the defendant is unaware of that uncertainty"). Also, compare *Garber* with *Regan*, 937 F.2d at 826, where there was abundant evidence that the defendants knew of the law's uncertainty at the time they claimed the controverted deductions.

[77] 737 F.2d 439, 444 (5th Cir. 1984).

[78] *See* 782 F.2d at 600 ("*Garber* [improperly] requires the jury to assume part of the judge's responsibility to rule on questions of law").

[79] *Curtis*, 782 F.2d at 599.

[80] *Id.* at 600.

defendant can argue the prosecution violates due process as a matter of law.[81]

[3] Reliance on Professional Advice

Where a taxpayer relied upon an attorney or an accountant in preparing a tax return, such reliance may be relevant to show that the defendant did not willfully commit tax fraud.[82] Because the government must show that the defendant intentionally violated a known legal duty, the defendant may assert reliance upon a professional opinion that the return conformed to the law's requirements.

To raise the defense, there must be evidence that the defendant relied in good faith on advice sought from a professional before committing the acts at issue.[83] Further, this defense will not succeed when relevant information was not fully disclosed to the professional, or when the professional was misled in some way.[84] Such failure to disclose may in fact be used by the jury as circumstantial evidence that the defendant acted willfully.[85]

If the defendant has adduced evidence of reliance on a professional, then it may be reversible error not to instruct the jury that such reliance can negate willfulness. In *Bursten v. United States*,[86] the defendant was an attorney who testified at his tax evasion trial that he had relied upon tax counsel in claiming certain losses on his return. The trial judge gave the jury a general instruction that it must find intent in order to convict, but refused the defendant's requested specific instruction that reliance on counsel is a defense.[87] The judge based this ruling on his belief that the defendant as an attorney could not assert such a defense, and that in any event the defendant's tax lawyer was "not a good tax man."[88] The Fifth Circuit found that there was sufficient evidence in the record to require a specific instruction of

---

[81] A prosecution violates due process where the alleged crime was insufficiently clear to provide the defendant with notice of what conduct was unlawful. *See Burton*, 737 F.2d at 444 ("apart from those few cases where the legal duty pointed to is so uncertain as to approach the level of vagueness, the abstract question of legal uncertainty of which a defendant was unaware is of marginal relevance"); United States v. Mallas, 762 F.2d 361 (4th Cir. 1985) (where there are "novel questions of tax liability to which governing law offers no clear guidance," the prosecution may be subject to due process challenge). *See generally* Keneally, et al., *supra* note 1, § 13.02[2][a][iii], and cases cited therein.

[82] In accordance with the general rule that "ignorance of the law is no excuse," reliance on professional advice usually is not a defense in criminal cases. Such a defense generally is valid in fraud cases, however, because it negates an intent to defraud. *See, e.g.*, United States v. Bilzerian, 926 F.2d 1285 (2d Cir. 1991) (securities fraud), discussed *supra* § 5.10[A]; United States v. Walters, 997 F.2d 1219 (7th Cir. 1993) (mail fraud), discussed *supra* § 4.04[A][1].

[83] *See Cheek II*, 3 F.3d at 1061 (rejecting Cheek's argument that he was entitled to a jury instruction on the defense of reliance on counsel).

[84] *See* Dombach & Forde, *supra* note 4, at 1121.

[85] *Id.* at 974, and cases cited therein.

[86] 395 F.2d 976 (5th Cir. 1968), *cert. denied*, 409 U.S. 843 (1972).

[87] *Id.* at 981 (the defense requested the following instruction: "If you find that the defendant had discussed this matter with competent tax counsel and that the tax return herein was prepared pursuant to that advice, then you must find that the defendant did not willfully file a false return or make a false statement, and you should bring in a verdict of not guilty.").

[88] *Id.* at 982.

reliance on counsel, and reversed the conviction.[89]

Where, however, the jury has rejected a reliance on counsel defense, an appeals court is likely to defer to that determination. For example, in *United States v. Olbres*,[90] the jury convicted the defendants of tax evasion, but the trial court granted their motion for an acquittal. The government appealed, arguing that the evidence was sufficient to prove that the defendants willfully underreported their income. The defendants contended that blind reliance on their accountant, who incorrectly prepared their tax return, precluded a finding of criminal intent.[91] The First Circuit disagreed, finding the evidence legally sufficient. The court stated that "the critical datum is not whether the defendants ordered the accountant to falsify the return, but, rather, whether the defendants knew when they signed the return that it understated their income."[92] Because the defendants had attempted to hide their income, and had understated their income in information provided to the accountant, there was sufficient evidence of willfulness.

§ 13.06 METHODS OF PROOF

As part of any criminal tax evasion case, the government must prove beyond a reasonable doubt that the defendant underpaid taxes.[93] In cases where the defendant kept incomplete or inaccurate records, such proof may be hard to come by. Because of this difficulty, courts have allowed various "methods of proof" concerning underpayment of taxes: (1) the direct or specific items method; and (2) the indirect methods based on showings of (a) net worth, (b) cash expenditures, and (c) bank deposits.[94]

[A] Direct or Specific Items Method

This is the least complicated way of proving a tax deficiency. This method only requires proof that a specific income item was not reported or that a specific deduction was improperly taken. Often, direct evidence that the defendant received some sort of illegal income, such as a bribe, forms the basis of proof in these cases.[95]

In one example, the defendant in *United States v. Black*[96] was convicted of three counts of tax evasion. The government established that the defendant wrote himself checks from the bank accounts of his two corporations to pay for personal

---

[89] *Cheek II*, 3 F.3d 1057 (7th Cir. 1993).

[90] 61 F.3d 967 (1st Cir. 1995).

[91] *Id.* at 970.

[92] *Id.* at 970–71.

[93] *See* Holland v. United States, 348 U.S. 121, 126 (1954), *reh'g denied*, 348 U.S. 932 (1955).

[94] *See* Keneally, et al., *supra* note 1, § 13.02[2][c].

[95] *Id.* at § 13.03[2]. Direct proof of unreported income or improper deductions is relatively rare in tax prosecutions. For examples of proof by the direct method, see United States v. Black, 843 F.2d 1456 (D.C. Cir. 1988) (holding the direct method applied when the defendant failed to pay taxes on money he received from corporate checks); United States v. Lawhon, 499 F.2d 352 (5th Cir. 1974).

[96] 843 F.2d 1456 (D.C. Cir. 1988).

expenditures that totaled $538,000 over three years. The government argued that every check used for his personal expenses constituted taxable income. On appeal, the defendant argued that the government had offered only indirect evidence of cash expenditures against him, which would have required that the government prove that any "increase in wealth did not come from non-taxable sources."[97] The D.C. Circuit held, however, that the government had merely used evidence of the defendant's cash expenditures to distinguish between his personal and business expenses. The court thus affirmed the conviction, reasoning that, because the government proved that the defendant received specific items of income from the checks, it did not need to disprove the possibility that the income came from non-taxable sources.

[B] Indirect Methods

In most cases, the government will prove a tax deficiency by relying upon indirect proof relating to the defendant's (1) net worth, (2) cash expenditures, or (3) bank deposits. The government may use any or all of these methods in the same case, and may also combine these methods with direct proof.[98] The government must pursue all reasonable leads that might explain unreported sources of income, such as gifts and prior savings. Where such leads prove unfruitful and the government is able to show by an indirect method that a taxpayer's income exceeded that reported to the government, the burden of proof shifts to the defendant to show that the all taxable income was reported.[99]

In *Holland v. United States*,[100] the Supreme Court sanctioned the use of the "net worth" method of proving a tax deficiency. Under this method, the government demonstrates that a defendant's total net worth increased over a tax year by an amount substantially greater than the taxpayer's reported income for the year. There may be explanations for such an increase other than unreported income, however, such as previous accumulations of cash, or the receipt of gifts or loans. Thus, the Court in *Holland* noted, the net worth method is "so fraught with danger for the innocent that the courts must closely scrutinize its use."[101] For example, the government must clearly establish opening net worth, must investigate reasonable leads as to other sources of income, and must show that any increase in net worth was due to taxable income. In this case, the Court found sufficient evidence to sustain the finding of unreported income.

Other courts have shown substantial flexibility in allowing proof of tax deficiency by the net worth method. In *United States v. Bencs*,[102] the defendant was convicted of tax evasion. Bencs operated a large marijuana selling business, and attempted to

---

[97] *Id.* at 1458. For an explanation of indirect evidence, see *infra*, § 13.06[B].

[98] *See* Dombach & Forde, *supra* note 4, at 1097. For an example of a case using multiple methods of proof, see United States v. Lacob, 416 F.2d 756 (7th Cir. 1969) (proof by both specific item method and bank deposits method).

[99] *See* Dombach & Forde, *supra* note 4, at 1097–1101.

[100] 348 U.S. 121 (1954).

[101] *Id.* at 125.

[102] 28 F.3d 555 (6th Cir. 1994).

hide the proceeds to avoid paying taxes. The government proved Bencs's tax deficiency through the net worth method. On appeal, Bencs argued that merely showing drug sales as the likely source of the income was insufficient because the government failed to negate all possible other sources of taxable income. The court disagreed, holding that, where the government proves the source of the taxable income, "it need not negate all possible nontaxable sources of alleged net worth increases, such as gifts, loans, and inheritances, when proving tax evasion through the net worth method."[103]

The "cash expenditures" method of proving a deficiency operates much like the net worth method. Under this method, the government proves that the defendant spent more money from taxable income than was reported to the I.R.S. Similarly, under the bank deposits method, the government shows that a defendant's cash expenditures plus bank deposits exceeded the reported income.[104]

The government need not prove the likely source of the defendant's unreported income. Rather, as the Supreme Court held in *United States v. Massei*,[105] it is sufficient for the government to show that the defendant had no other possible sources of income that could explain the net worth increase.

As with the net worth method, courts allow substantial leeway to the government when it uses the cash expenditures and bank deposits methods. In *United States v. Abodeely*,[106] Abodeely derived his income from several business ventures, and substantially underreported his income for two years. In showing the underpayment, the government used a combination of the cash expenditures method and the bank deposits method. The proof first established the defendant's taxable income by showing the amount of income represented by bank deposits, and then added to this amount the defendant's cash expenditures. On appeal, the court affirmed the use of these methods of proof.[107]

Similarly, in *United States v. Mounkes*,[108] the defendants were convicted of four counts of tax evasion, with the bank deposits method used to show underpayment. To determine the underpayment, the government was required to establish a cash on-hand balance for the beginning of the tax years in question. On appeal, the defendants argued that the evidence of beginning cash on-hand balances was insufficient to support a guilty verdict. The court rejected the argument. Initially, the court noted that the government is not required to determine the exact amount of cash on hand. Rather, the court is only required to determine the amount with reasonable certainty. The court then found that there was sufficient evidence; a defendant gave the government his own estimate of cash on hand, and this estimate

---

[103] *Id.* at 563.

[104] *See* Dombach & Forde, *supra* note 4, at 1097–1101.

[105] 355 U.S. 595 (1958) (per curiam).

[106] 801 F.2d 1020 (8th Cir. 1986).

[107] Other courts have consistently rejected arguments that the bank deposit method unfairly shifts the burden of proof to the defendant. *See, e.g.*, United States v. Scott, 660 F.2d 1145, 1164–65 (7th Cir. 1982); United States v. Lawhon, 499 F.2d 352, 356 (5th Cir. 1974).

[108] 204 F.3d 1024 (10th Cir. 2000).

was corroborated by the corporate balance sheets and tax returns.[109]

§ 13.07 THE PROCESS OF TAX INVESTIGATIONS AND PROSECUTIONS

Federal criminal tax investigations and prosecutions are unusual in several respects. First, many criminal tax cases begin as civil matters arising out of routine audits by I.R.S. agents. As noted above, evidence of a tax crime may also arise out of a criminal investigation into other types of criminal activities. If a civil I.R.S. investigation or another source reveals information of crime, then the matter is referred to the I.R.S.'s Criminal Investigation Division for investigation by a "Special Agent."

Second, criminal tax cases go through several levels of review and approval. When the Special Agent believes that a matter warrants prosecution, the Agent refers the matter to the I.R.S. Counsel for the region. Counsel may then decide to refer the matter to the Tax Division of the United States Department of Justice ("DOJ") in Washington for possible further investigation and prosecution.

Finally, tax prosecutions must be approved by the DOJ in Washington. With most crimes, each United States Attorney's office is solely responsible for deciding whether to seek an indictment.[110] To ensure uniformity in the complex area of tax crimes, however, the evidence in a tax investigation is reviewed by the Tax Division before a case is sent to the specific U.S. Attorney's Office for prosecution.[111]

§ 13.08 CHARGES BROUGHT IN CRIMINAL TAX CASES

Tax cases often involve charges other than those brought under the criminal provisions of Title 26, the federal tax code. One common charge is conspiracy, which is brought under § 371 of the criminal code[112] because the tax code itself contains no equivalent statute.

In the context of tax fraud, a § 371 prosecution can be based upon a conspiracy to (1) violate the criminal provisions of the tax code, and/or (2) defraud the United States in the administration of the tax system. Further, under the defraud clause, the government can allege that the defendant (a) defrauded the government out of money or property (unpaid taxes), and/or (b) defrauded the I.R.S. in its ability to function by "impeding, impairing, obstructing and defeating the lawful functions of the Department of the Treasury in the collection of the revenue; to wit, income

---

[109] *Id.* at 1028. *See also* United States v. Boulware, 384 F.3d 794, 811 (9th Cir. 2004) (under the bank deposits method, the government need not prove the exact amount of underpayment but need only prove a substantial difference between the bank deposits and the reported income).

[110] In addition to tax cases, there are other exceptions to this general rule. *See, e.g.,* Chapter 16, RICO, *infra*, § 16.01.

[111] *See* U.S. Dep't of Justice, Tax. Div., Crim. Tax Manual § 6-4.010. In some cases, the prosecutors may come from the Tax Division rather than the local U.S. Attorney's Office.

[112] 18 U.S.C. § 371; *see* Chapter 3, Conspiracy, *supra*.

taxes."[113] Under the latter theory, the prosecution need not show that the conspiracy actually succeeded, or that the government was deprived of taxes or otherwise harmed.

Other criminal statutes commonly used in tax cases include the false statements statute[114] and the false claims act.[115] Courts have also allowed the government to charge mail fraud based upon the mailing of tax returns, and even to charge RICO in such cases using the predicate act of mail fraud.[116] Although the DOJ has issued guidelines discouraging the use of mail fraud and RICO in tax cases, those guidelines do not have the force of law.

---

[113] United States v. Klein, 247 F.2d 908, 915 (2d Cir. 1957). This type of tax conspiracy is now known as a "Klein conspiracy." *See* Keneally et al., *supra* note 1, § 13.06[2]; Dombach & Forde, *supra* note 4, at 1130–32.

[114] 18 U.S.C. § 1001.

[115] 18 U.S.C. §§ 286, 287.

[116] Tax fraud itself is not a RICO predicate. For a discussion of the use of mail fraud and RICO in tax cases, see Keneally, et al., *supra* note 1, § 13.06[1], and cases cited therein. *See also supra* note 68 (discussion of the *Princeton-Newport* case).

Chapter 14

CURRENCY TRANSACTION REPORTING CRIMES

§ 14.01 INTRODUCTION

Beginning in 1970, Congress began to enact a series of currency transaction reporting laws designed to help the government track the movements of large amounts of cash. These laws work in tandem with the money laundering statutes discussed in the next chapter, and are part of the government's attempt to detect broad categories of crime that generate large amounts of cash proceeds. In the white collar arena, such crimes include tax fraud and other large-scale fraudulent activities. This chapter focuses on the principal currency transaction reporting provisions of the Bank Secrecy Act, and on related provisions of the federal tax code.[1]

As in other areas, such as environmental law and tax fraud, the currency transaction reporting statutes create liability simply *for failure to disclose* required information — information that may not necessarily reflect any underlying criminal activity.

§ 14.02 STATUTORY OVERVIEW

[A] Introduction

Federal law contains a number of specific cash transaction reporting requirements. Some of the principal laws and regulations include:

- Section 5313 of Title 31, and regulations adopted pursuant to that section, require that banks and other financial institutions file with the IRS currency transaction reports ("CTRs") of all cash transactions of more than $10,000.[2]

- Section 6050I of the Internal Revenue Code requires anyone in a trade or business to report to the IRS cash receipts of more than $10,000.[3]

---

[1] *See* 31 U.S.C. § 5311-22; 26 U.S.C. § 6050I. Section 5311 states that the purpose of the currency transaction reporting laws is to "require certain reports or records where they have a high degree of usefulness in criminal, tax, or regulatory investigations or proceedings, or in the conduct of intelligence or counterintelligence activities, including analysis, to protect against international terrorism." For an overview of these laws, see Helen Gredd & Gabriella Geanuleas, *Banking Crimes, in* White Collar Crime: Business and Regulatory Offenses § 2.01 (Otto Obermaier & Robert Morvillo, eds. 2011).

[2] 31 U.S.C. § 5313; 31 C.F.R. § 103.22.

[3] 26 U.S.C. § 6050I.

- Section § 5316 of Title 31 applies to cash movements into and out of the country, and requires the filing of a "Currency or Monetary Instrument Report" by individuals and entities who transport more than $10,000.[4]

- Section 5324 of Title 31 makes it a crime to "structure" transactions with a financial institution with the intent to violate the currency transaction reporting requirements.[5]

- Section 6050I(f) of the Internal Revenue Code prohibits the structuring of transactions to avoid the reporting requirement by anyone involved in a trade or business.[6]

- Section 5318(g) of Title 31[7] and the regulations thereunder,[8] require banks "to report any suspicious transaction relevant to a possible violation of law or regulation." Known as "Suspicious Activity Reports," these reports generally must be filed for transactions of $5,000 or more that the bank suspects involve money laundering or CTR evasion, or that are otherwise unusual for the customer involved.

[B]   Section 5313(a) — Filing of CTRs by Domestic Financial Institutions

[1]   The Statute

Section 5313(a) is at the core of the currency transaction reporting laws. The statute, which is entitled "Reports on domestic coins and currency transactions," provides:

> When a domestic financial institution is involved in a transaction for the payment, receipt, or transfer of United States coins or currency (or other monetary instruments the Secretary of the Treasury prescribes), in an amount, denomination, or amount and denomination, or under circumstances the Secretary prescribes by regulation [currently transactions in excess of $10,000], the institution and any other participant in the trans-

---

[4] 31 U.S.C. § 5316. *See also* 31 U.S.C. § 5314 (record keeping and reporting concerning foreign financial agency transactions); 31 U.S.C. § 5315 (reports on foreign currency transactions). The regulations exempt financial entities from this requirement in some circumstances. *See* 31 C.F.R. § 103.23(c)(1)–(9).

[5] The regulations exempt financial entities from this requirement in some circumstances. *See* 31 C.F.R. § 103.23(c)(1)–(9).

[6] 26 U.S.C. § 6050I(f).

[7] 31 U.S.C. § 5318(g); 12 C.F.R. § 21.11(c).

[8] 12 C.F.R. § 21.11(c). Also, in 2001, Congress passed the Uniting and Strengthening America by Providing Appropriate Tools Required to Intercept and Obstruct Terrorism Act of 2001 (the "Act"), Pub. L. 107-56. Under the Act, certain financial institutions as defined in the Bank Secrecy Act, 31 U.S.C. §§ 5312(a)(2)(A) through (X) as amended by the Act, § 352, are required to implement programs designed to prevent their institutions from being used to facilitate money laundering or the financing of terrorism.

action the Secretary may prescribe shall file a report on the transaction at the time and in the way the Secretary prescribes.[9]

When a person has willfully violated this section, the government may seek civil remedies.[10] The statute also provides for criminal liability where the defendant has acted willfully.[11] Criminal punishment includes a maximum five-year prison term, a $250,000 fine, or both. The actual sentence imposed will depend upon the application of the United States Sentencing Guidelines to the case.

[2] The Elements

To prove a violation of § 5313(a), the government must show that:

1. A "domestic financial institution" was involved in a transaction;

2. The transaction involved U.S. currency or specified monetary instruments;[12]

3. The transaction was for more than $10,000;

4. The domestic financial institution failed to file the required report; and

5. The defendant acted willfully.

The term "financial institution" is broadly defined. Section 5312(a)(2) of the Bank Secrecy Act and regulations promulgated under that section provide an extensive list of "financial institutions," ranging from banks and stock brokers to insurance companies, pawn brokers, and car dealers.[13] Most courts have also held that individual defendants who engage in the types of financial matters listed in the statutes and regulations may constitute "financial institutions."[14] Also, multiple branches of the same bank are members of the same "financial institution" for reporting purposes.[15]

[C] Section 5324(a) — Structuring and Related Crimes in Connection with Financial Institution Transactions

[1] The Statute

After passage of § 5313, Congress added § 5324(a) to close a loophole in the statute that allowed bank customers to "structure" cash transactions — that is, to avoid the reporting requirements by breaking their cash transactions into amounts of $10,000 or less.[16] Entitled "Structuring transactions to evade reporting require-

---

[9] 31 U.S.C. § 5313 (information in brackets added).

[10] 31 U.S.C. § 5321.

[11] 31 U.S.C. § 5322.

[12] 31 U.S.C. § 5312(a)(3).

[13] 31 U.S.C. § 5312(a)(2).

[14] See Gredd & Geanuleas, supra note 1, § 2.02[1][a], and cases cited therein.

[15] See United States v. Giancola, 783 F.2d 1549, 1552 (11th Cir. 1986).

[16] 31 U.S.C. § 5324(a); 31 C.F.R. 103.11(gg). For a discussion of the crime of structuring, see Sarah

ment prohibited," § 5324(a) provides:

> Domestic coin and currency transactions involving financial institutions. No person shall for the purpose of evading the reporting requirements of § 5313(a) or § 5325[17] or any regulation prescribed under any such section
>
> . . .
>
> (1)   cause or attempt to cause a domestic financial institution to fail to file a report required under § 5313(a) or 5325 or any regulation prescribed under any such section; . . .
>
> (2)   cause or attempt to cause a domestic financial institution to file a report required under § 5313(a) or 5325 or any regulation prescribed under any such section . . . that contains a material omission or misstatement of fact; or
>
> (3)   structure or assist in structuring, or attempt to structure or assist in structuring, any transaction with one or more domestic financial institutions.[18]"

All violations of § 5324 are punished criminally.[19] The penalty includes a prison term of not more than five years, a statutory fine, or both. The statute also specifies an "aggravated" sentence for "[w]hoever violates this section while violating another law of the United States or as part of a pattern of any illegal activity involving more than $100,000 in a 12-month period." In such cases, the penalty is a prison term of no more than ten years, twice the statutory fine, or both. As always, the actual sentence imposed will depend upon the application of the United States Sentencing Guidelines to the case.[20]

[2]   The Elements of § 5324(a)

To prove a violation of § 5324(a), the government must show that the defendant:

1.   Acted with the purpose of evading the CTR laws and regulations; and

2.   One of the following:

    a.   Caused or attempted to cause a domestic financial institution to fail to file a CTR;

    b.   Caused or attempted to cause a domestic financial institution to file a CTR that contained a material false statement or omission; or

    c.   Structured or attempted to structure any transaction with one or more domestic financial institutions.

N. Welling, *Smurfs, Money Laundering and the Federal Criminal Law: The Crime of Structuring Transactions*, 41 Fla. L. Rev. 287, 303–09 (1989).

[17]   31 U.S.C. § 5325 requires that financial institutions, when issuing or selling bank checks, cashier's checks, traveler's checks, or money orders of $3,000 or more, obtain identification from the buyer.

[18]   31 U.S.C. § 5324.

[19]   *See* 31 U.S.C. §§ 5324(d).

[20]   31 U.S.C. § 5324(d)(2). *See* Chapter 21, Sentencing, *infra*.

As discussed more fully below,[21] the government is required to prove that the defendant knew of the reporting laws and intended to evade them. It is not, however, required to prove that the defendant knew that structuring is a crime.

[D]   Section 6050I — Cash Transactions Reporting by Businesses

[1]   The Statute

In 1984, Congress added § 6050I to the Internal Revenue Code.[22] This section expands the cash reporting transaction requirement, which was originally limited to financial institutions, to all persons "engaged in a trade or business." Under this section, all cash transactions of over $10,000 must be reported to the IRS on Form 8300. Section 6050I provides:

(a)   Cash receipts of more than $10,000. Any person -

   (1)   who is engaged in a trade or business, and

   (2)   who, in the course of such trade or business, receives more than $10,000 in cash in 1 transaction (or 2 or more related transactions), shall make the return described in subsection (b) with respect to such transaction (or related transactions) at such time as the Secretary may by regulations prescribe.

(b)   Form and manner of returns. A return is described in this subsection if such return -

   (1)   is in such form as the Secretary may prescribe,

   (2)   contains -

      (A)   the name, address, and [tax identification number] of the person from whom the cash was received,

      (B)   the amount of cash received,

      (C)   the date and nature of the transaction, and

      (D)   such other information as the Secretary may prescribe.

Section 6050I(c) creates exceptions for filings that would duplicate information contained in CTRs filed under the Bank Secrecy Act.

A "willful" failure to file a Form 8300 is punished under § 7203 of the Internal Revenue Code; the penalty includes a prison term of not more than one year, or a statutory fine, or both. A "willful" submission of a false Form 8300 is punished under § 7206 of the Internal Revenue Code with a prison term of not more than three years, or a statutory fine, or both. Of course, the actual sentence imposed will depend upon the application of the United States Sentencing Guidelines to the case.

---

[21] *See infra*, § 14.03, for a discussion of the mens rea requirement under § 5324.

[22] 26 U.S.C. § 6050I.

Also, Section 6050I(f) prohibits the structuring of transactions to avoid the reporting requirement:

Structuring transactions to evade reporting requirements prohibited.

(1)   In general. No person shall for the purpose of evading the return requirements of this section -

    (A)   cause or attempt to cause a trade or business to fail to file a return required under this section,

    (B)   cause or attempt to cause a trade or business to file a return required under this section that contains a material omission or misstatement of fact, or

    (C)   structure or assist in structuring, or attempt to structure or assist in structuring, any transaction with one or more trades or businesses.

[2]   The Elements

To prove a failure to file a required Form 8300 under § 6050I, the government must prove all the elements of a § 7203 violation.[23] To prove the filing of a false Form 8300, the government must prove all the elements of a § 7206 violation.[24] These violations are contained in the Internal Revenue Code and are prosecuted as tax crimes. Thus, the government must prove that the defendant not only intended to violate the reporting requirements, but also that the defendant knew the conduct was illegal.[25] As noted above, the latter requirement is not an element of structuring under § 5324.

To prove the crime of structuring under § 6050I(f), the government must show that the defendant:

1.   Acted with the purpose of evading the reporting requirements;

2.   Acted "willfully," that is, with the intent to violate the law; and

3.   One of the following:

    a.   Caused or attempted to cause a trade or business to fail to file a report;

    b.   Caused or attempted to cause a trade or business to file a report that contained a material false statement or omission; or

    c.   Structured or attempted to structure any transaction with a trade or business. The regulations define the term "to structure" as engaging in one or more cash transactions for the purpose of evading the reporting requirements.[26]

---

[23] This section is discussed in the Chapter 13, Tax Crimes, *supra*, § 13.03.

[24] *See id.*

[25] *See id.*

[26] 31 C.F.R. § 103.11(gg).

[E]   Section 5316 — Transporting Monetary Instruments

[1]   The Statute

Under § 5316, a person who transports more than $10,000 into or out of the United States, or receives more than $10,000 transported into the United States, is required to file a "Currency or Monetary Instrument Report" with the federal government. The statute, entitled "Reports on exporting and importing monetary instruments," provides:

(a)   Except as provided in subsection (c) of this section, a person or an agent or bailee of the person shall file a report under subsection (b) of this section when the person, agent, or bailee knowingly —

    (1)   transports, is about to transport, or has transported, monetary instruments[27] of more than $10,000 at one time —

        (A)   from a place in the United States to or through a place outside the United States; or

        (B)   to a place in the United States from or through a place outside the United States; or

    (2)   receives monetary instruments of more than $10,000 at one time transported into the United States from or through a place outside the United States.

Section 5316(b) requires that the report contain the amount represented by the monetary instrument being transported. Section 5316(c) creates an exception for common carriers of passengers and goods under certain circumstances where the transportation of monetary instruments is unknown to them.

[2]   The Elements

To prove a violation of § 5316, the government must show that the defendant knowingly:

1.   transported or was about to transport monetary instruments of more than $ 10,000 at one time into or out of the United States, or

2.   received monetary instruments of more than $10,000 at one time transported into the United States from or through a place outside the United States

Violations of the statute may lead to both civil and criminal penalties. In addition to civil monetary penalties,[28] the property transported may be subject to civil[29] or

---

[27] "Monetary Instruments" include not only United States coins and currency, but also coins and currency of a foreign country, travelers' checks, bearer negotiable instruments, bearer investment securities, bearer securities, stock on which title is passed on delivery, and similar material; and checks, drafts, notes, money orders, and other similar instruments which are drawn on or by a foreign financial institution and are not in bearer form. 31 U.S.C. § 5312(a)(3).

[28] 31 U.S.C. § 5321(a)(2).

criminal[30] forfeiture. To establish a civil violation of the section, the government need only prove that a person knowingly was transporting over $10,000.[31] To establish a criminal violation, the government has the additional burden of proving that a person willfully failed to file a report.[32] To prove the latter, the government must show that the person (1) knowingly transported more than $10,000, and (2) acted with knowledge of the reporting requirement.

§ 14.03   MENS REA ISSUES IN CURRENCY REPORTING CASES

[A]   Knowledge of and Intent to Violate the Law

With most crimes, courts apply the general principle that "ignorance of the law is no excuse," and do not require the government to show that the defendant knew of and specifically intended to violate the law. In some areas, however, courts have imposed upon the government the additional burden of showing an intent to violate the law. In connection with tax fraud, for example, the Supreme Court interpreted the term "willfulness" in the statute to require proof of intent to violate the law, reasoning that a heightened mens rea standard is appropriate for such a complex area of the law.[33]

In *Ratzlaf v. United States*,[34] the Court confronted a similar issue in a case involving structuring under the Bank Secrecy Act. In that case, the Court reversed the conviction of a defendant who had "structured" cash transactions to avoid currency reporting requirements when paying off a gambling debt. By a five-to-four vote, the Court interpreted the term "willful" in the statute to require proof that the defendant "knew the structuring he undertook was unlawful."[35]

Subsequently, Congress removed the willfulness requirement from the structuring statute, effectively overturning *Ratzlaff*. As a result, courts have held that intent to violate the law is not an element of structuring under § 5324. Intent to violate the law is an element of structuring under § 6050I, however, because that statute is contained in the Internal Revenue Code and is governed by the *Cheek* decision.[36]

---

[29]   31 U.S.C. § 5317(c)(2).

[30]   31 U.S.C. § 5317(c)(1).

[31]   *See, e.g.*, United States v. Forty-Seven Thousand Nine Hundred Eighty Dollars, 804 F.2d 1085 (9th Cir. 1986).

[32]   31 U.S.C. § 5322.

[33]   Cheek v. United States, 498 U.S. 192 (1991).

[34]   510 U.S. 135 (1994).

[35]   *Id.* at 658.

[36]   *See* United States v. McGuire, 79 F.3d 1396, 1405 (5th Cir.), *vacated on other grounds*, 90 F.3d 107 (5th Cir.) (en banc), *opinion on rehearing*, 99 F.3d 671 (5th Cir. 1996) (en banc); United States v. Rogers, 18 F.3d 265, 267 n.4.

[B] Collective Knowledge

As discussed more fully in an earlier chapter,[37] the above mens rea elements apply to financial institutions charged with violating the reporting laws. One means of proving an institution's mens rea is through the doctrine of collective knowledge. In *United States v. Bank of New England*,[38] for example, the defendant bank was charged with violating the currency transaction reporting laws. When instructing the jury on the element of knowledge, the trial judge stated:

> [Y]ou have to look at the bank as an institution. As such, its knowledge is the sum of the knowledge of all of the employees. That is, the bank's knowledge is the totality of what all of the employees know within the scope of their employment. So, if Employee A knows one facet of the currency reporting requirement, B knows another facet of it, and C a third facet of it, the bank knows them all.[39]

On appeal, the First Circuit Court of Appeals found that this was an appropriate instruction. Otherwise, banks and other entities could avoid criminal liability when no single corporate agent had the required knowledge.[40]

[C] Proving Mens Rea

As with other white collar crimes, currency transaction reporting charges often turn on proof of mens rea. In many cases, mens rea will be demonstrated largely through circumstantial evidence. In *United States v. MacPherson*,[41] for example, the defendant made 32 deposits of $10,000 or less, totaling about $258,000, over about five months. The district court entered a judgment of acquittal on the grounds that the government had not adduced sufficient evidence of intent, and the government appealed. The Second Circuit reversed, stating that the pattern of transactions constituted circumstantial evidence sufficient to establish that the defendant knew of and intended to evade the reporting requirements. The defendant was attempting to shield his assets from a civil judgment, and there was evidence that the defendant observed a bank official filing out a CTR and therefore knew of the CTR filing requirement.

§ 14.04 ATTORNEY/CLIENT ISSUES

[A] Introduction

Section 6050I's reporting requirements apply to attorneys' fees paid in cash. The government has sought enforcement of these requirements in the face of assertions of attorney-client privilege and various constitutional provisions. Although such

---

[37] *See* Chapter 2, Corporate and Individual Liability, *supra*, § 2.06(b).

[38] 821 F.2d 844 (1st Cir.), *cert. denied*, 484 U.S. 943 (1987).

[39] 821 F.2d at 855.

[40] *Id.* at 856–57. Note that some courts have rejected the collective knowledge doctrine. *See* § 2.06[B], *supra*.

[41] 424 F.3d 183 (2d Cir. 2005).

enforcement has produced an ongoing battle between the Department of Justice and the criminal defense bar,[42] courts have generally sided with the government and have required disclosure of attorney fee and identity information.[43]

[B] Constitutional Challenges

Attorneys have raised a number of constitutional arguments when challenging § 6050I's reporting requirements, generally to no avail. For example, in *United States v. Goldberger & Dubin, P.C.*,[44] the Second Circuit rejected Fourth, Fifth, and Sixth Amendment challenges.[45] As to the latter, the court noted that a client can retain counsel and avoid the reporting requirement simply by paying other than by cash.[46]

[C] Attorney-Client Privilege

As a general matter, information relating to client identity and fees does not fall within the ambit of the attorney-client privilege. The privilege is designed to protect confidential information given to an attorney for the purpose of obtaining legal advice. Because information about client identity and fees does not usually pertain to legal advice, courts generally reason that identity and fee information does not fall within the privilege's purpose.

Courts have developed limited exceptions to this general rule. Specifically, some courts have protected identity or fee information from disclosure where such disclosure would (1) implicate the client in the very matter for which the client retained counsel (the "legal advice" exception), (2) incriminate the client by providing the last piece of evidence needed to convict the client (the "last link" exception), or (3) reveal the nature of a confidential client-attorney communication (the "confidential communication" exception).[47]

Most courts have not applied these exceptions to cases involving the filing of Form 8300. For example, in *Lefcourt v. United States*,[48] a prominent criminal defense attorney omitted his client's name from a Form 8300. The attorney argued that proof that the client possessed the cash would incriminate the client in the matter for which Lefcourt had been retained, and that this constituted a "special circumstance" in which the Second Circuit had implied that client fee information is privileged. Following its earlier holding in *Goldberger & Dubin*, the Second

---

[42] *See generally* Ellen Podgor, *Form 8300: The Demise of Law as a Profession*, 5 Geo. J. Legal Ethics 485 (1992).

[43] *See, e.g.*, United States v. Ritchie, 15 F.3d 592, 601 (6th Cir. 1994) (to consider identity and fee information privileged would "grant law firms a potential monopoly on money laundering simply because their services are personal and confidential; businesses must divulge the identity of their cash-paying clients in keeping with lawful revenue regulations and law firms should not be an exception to this rule").

[44] 935 F.2d 501 (2d Cir. 1991).

[45] *Id.* at 503.

[46] *See id.* at 504.

[47] *See, e.g.*, United States v. Sindel, 53 F.3d 874, 876–77 (8th Cir. 1995). In practice, these definitions are less than clear, and frequently overlap. *See id.* at 876 (describing the "overlapping" exceptions).

[48] 125 F.3d 79 (2d Cir. 1997).

Circuit rejected the argument, and affirmed the imposition of a civil fine. First, the court found that the law was clear in the Second Circuit that there was no "legal advice" exception to the general rule that fee information is not privileged.[49] Second, because the law was clear, Lefcourt's argument was not reasonable. Under the law, a fine is appropriate in such a circumstance.

Similarly, in *United States v. Blackman*,[50] the Ninth Circuit declined to apply the legal advice exception to client identity information. Further, because the attorney's client was not the subject of an ongoing criminal investigation, the last link exception did not apply. Finally, the attorney failed to show, under the confidential communication exception, that "'the fee-payer's identity and the fee arrangements are so intertwined with confidential communications that revealing either . . . would be tantamount to revealing a privileged communication.' "[51]

Occasionally, attorneys have successfully avoided disclosure of client identity and fee information. For example, in *United States v. Sindel*,[52] the Eighth Circuit reversed an order requiring that the attorney disclose client identity information concerning one of two clients. After reviewing the attorney's in camera testimony, the court concluded that the attorney "could not release information about the payments on behalf of [the client] without revealing the substance of a confidential communication."[53]

In another case, *United States v. Gertner*,[54] the attorneys and their law firm represented defendants in an ongoing narcotics prosecution. In filings with the IRS, the attorneys disclosed cash payments from the clients but did not reveal the clients' identities or the nature of the clients' cash payments. The IRS filed a court petition to enforce a summons compelling disclosure of the information. In the petition, the IRS asserted that it needed the information in an investigation of the law firm's tax liability. The court rejected that argument, finding that the government was actually seeking information about the clients. Thus, the court found that the "legal advice" exception applied because the court was "convinced that there is a 'strong probability' that disclosure of a large unexplained cash income could certainly be incriminating evidence in the pending narcotics prosecution."[55]

On appeal, the First Circuit affirmed the district court's order denying the government's petition, but on different grounds.[56] Initially, the appeals court

---

[49] The court labeled the exception that *Lefcourt* relied upon as the "legal advice exception," and stated that the exception "has never once been accepted in this circuit." *Id.* at 87.

[50] 72 F.3d 1418 (9th Cir. 1995).

[51] *Id.* at 1425, *quoting* Ralls v. United States, 52 F.3d 223, 225 (9th Cir. 1995).

[52] 53 F.3d 874 (8th Cir. 1995).

[53] *Id.* at 876. In the version of Form 8300 in existence at the time, the attorney was also required to disclose whether the fee payment constituted a "suspicious transaction." This question has since been deleted from Form 8300. Only "money services business[es]" are now required to report suspicious activity. *See* 31 C.F.R. § 103.20(a)(1).

[54] 873 F. Supp. 729 (D. Mass. 1995), *aff'd on other grounds*, 65 F.3d 963 (1st Cir. 1995).

[55] *Id.* at 735.

[56] United States v. Gertner, 65 F.3d 963 (1st Cir. 1995).

agreed with the district judge that the government's argument that it was seeking information concerning the law firm was a pretext, and that the summons was actually directed to the firm's clients. Because this was a "John Doe" summons directed to an unknown party, the government was required to follow specific procedures for such a summons. The government's failure to do so led the court to affirm the district court's denial of the government's petition to enforce the summons.

Chapter 15

MONEY LAUNDERING

§ 15.01 INTRODUCTION

Since their enactment in 1986, the money laundering statutes[1] have joined the Racketeer Influenced and Corrupt Organizations Act (RICO) in the federal prosecutor's arsenal of most powerful weapons.[2] In recent years, prosecutors have used the statutes with ever-increasing frequency. This has occurred for two principal reasons. First, the money laundering statutes reach a broad range of criminal activities, and can be used in a large variety of cases. Second, the sanctions for money laundering are severe.[3] Sanctions include lengthy prison terms and forfeitures of property involved in the money laundering activity.[4] For these reasons, prosecutors have a strong motivation for bringing money laundering charges. The frequent use of such charges raises the issues of prosecutorial discretion that appear throughout this book.

The money laundering statutes operate in tandem with the currency transaction reporting laws discussed in the previous chapter. Together, these laws provide the government with means to identify and criminalize the movement of money related to tax evasion and other criminal activities. As legislative history shows, Congress recognized that the movement of large sums of such money is essential to the operation of large-scale criminal activities.[5]

---

[1] 18 U.S.C. § 1956; 18 U.S.C. § 1957.

[2] *See* Elkan Abramowitz, *Money Laundering: The New RICO?*, N.Y.L.J., Sept. 1, 1992, at 3; Helen Gredd & Karl D. Cooper, *Money Laundering, in* White Collar Crime: Business and Regulatory Offenses § 2A.01 (Otto Obermaier & Robert Morvillo, eds. 2011); Emin Akopyan, *Money Laundering*, 47 Am. Crim. L. Rev. 821 (2010).

[3] The United States Sentencing Guidelines were amended in 2001 to more closely tie a money laundering sentence to that of the underlying offense. One member of the United States Sentencing Commission explained that the Commission sought this change because of its concern that the previous money laundering sentencing scheme was overly harsh. The Commission was concerned that money laundering was being used by prosecutors as a threat during plea negotiations over relatively minor underlying crimes. *White Collar Crime Institute Focuses on Recent Changes to Sentencing Guidelines*, Crim. L. Rep. 561, 561 (March 27, 2002), *citing* remarks of Judge William K. Sessions, III. The amendments also provide that the money laundering charge is now to be "grouped" with the underlying offenses, resulting in lower sentences in many cases. *See id.* at 562. In the wake of the decision United States v. Booker, 543 U.S. 220 (2005), the Sentencing Guidelines are no longer mandatory, but nonetheless remain the basis for most federal sentences. *See* Chapter 21, Sentencing, *infra*.

[4] For an overview of forfeitures under the money laundering statutes, see Chapter 22, Forfeitures, *infra*.

[5] *See* Akopyan, *supra* note 2, at 821–24.

Although these statutes were primarily intended to target money generated from the sale of illegal narcotics, the statutes extend to many types of white collar crimes.[6] Money laundering may be charged in nearly any tax fraud case in which the defendant has attempted to hide income. Money laundering may also be charged where, for example, a public official is attempting to hide the proceeds of an illegal bribery or extortion scheme. In addition, the statutes impose liability both on those who generated the "dirty" money and on those who were not involved in the original illegal activity but who later participated in the laundering in some way.[7]

This chapter reviews the two money laundering statutes, §§ 1956 and 1957 of the federal criminal code. The chapter first examines the structure of these complex statutes and discusses the statutes' elements. The chapter then examines issues that commonly arise in money laundering cases.

§ 15.02   STATUTORY OVERVIEW

The first money laundering statute, entitled "Laundering of Monetary Instruments," is contained in § 1956 of the federal criminal code. The statute principally deals with (1) financial transactions that are intended to cover up the source of the illegallyderived funds ("concealment money laundering"), and (2) financial transactions that promote the illegal activity ("promotion money laundering"). The second statute, § 1957, covers monetary transactions of criminally-derived funds in amounts over $10,000. To date, far more prosecutions have been brought under § 1956 than under § 1957.

Like the RICO statute, the money laundering statutes are structured to incorporate activities elsewhere defined as crimes under both state and federal law. Since the statutes' enactments, Congress on several occasions has substantially expanded their reach.[8]

The statutes also contain a conspiracy provision. Section 1956(h) provides: "Any person who conspires to commit any offense defined in this section or section 1957 shall be subject to the same penalties as those prescribed for the offense the commission of which was the object of the conspiracy."[9] In *Whitfield v. United States*,[10] the United States Supreme Court unanimously held that a conspiracy charge under this provision does not require proof of an overt act in furtherance of the conspiracy.[11] The Court also rejected the defendants' argument that § 1956(h)

---

[6] *See id.*

[7] *See* Gredd & Cooper, *supra* note 2, at § 2A.02

[8] *See, e.g.*, Pub. L. 109-77, 120 Stat. 242 *et seq.* (March 19, 2006); USA PATRIOT Act, Pub. L. No. 107-56, § 302, 115 Stat. 272, 296-97 (2001 P.L. 104-132, Title VII, Subtitle B, § 726, 110 Stat. 1301 (April 24, 1996); P.L. 104-191, Title II, Subtitle E, § 246, 110 Stat. 2018 (August 21, 1996).

[9] 18 U.S.C. § 1956(h).

[10] 543 U.S. 209 (2005).

[11] *Id.* at 212–14, *citing* United States v. Shabani, 513 U.S. 10 (1994) (holding that nearly identical language in the drug conspiracy statute, 21 U.S.C. § 846, does not require proof of an overt act). *See* Chapter 3, Conspiracy, *supra*, § 3.02[C], for a discussion of the overt act requirement under the general federal conspiracy statute, 18 U.S.C. § 371.

does not create a new offense but merely acts to increase the penalty for a conviction under the general federal conspiracy statute.[12] The Court found that the statutory language plainly established a new offense.[13]

Courts have found that an effect on interstate commerce is an essential element of the money laundering statutes that must be determined by the jury.[14] As in other areas, a showing of a de minimis effect on interstate commerce will suffice.

[A] Domestic Money Laundering — § 1956(a)(1) — Statutory Elements and Definitions

Section 1956(a)(1) deals with domestic money laundering activities, and comprises the heart of the statute.[15]

To prove a violation of § 1956(a)(1) the government must show that:

1. The defendant conducted or attempted to conduct[16] a financial transaction;

2. The defendant knew that the financial transaction involved the proceeds of some type of unlawful activity that constitutes a felony under state, federal, or foreign law;[17]

3. The funds in fact were proceeds from specified unlawful activity; *and*

4. Any <u>one</u> of the following:

---

[12] 18 U.S.C. § 1956(h).

[13] 543 U.S. at 215–16.

[14] *See* United States v. Ripinsky, 109 F.3d 1436, 1443, *amended*, 129 F.3d 518 (9th Cir. 1997); United States v. Aramony, 88 F.3d 1369, 1387 (4th Cir. 1996). *See also* Gredd & Cooper, *supra* note 2, § 2A.02[1], and cases cited therein.

[15] This section provides:

(a)(1) Whoever, knowing that the property involved in a financial transaction represents the proceeds of some form of unlawful activity, conducts or attempts to conduct such a financial transaction which in fact involves the proceeds of specified unlawful activity -
(A)
    (i)   with the intent to promote the carrying on of specified unlawful activity; or
    (ii) with intent to engage in conduct constituting a violation of § 7201 or 7206 of the Internal Revenue Code of 1986; or
(B)   knowing that the transaction is designed in whole or in part -
    (i)   to conceal or disguise the nature, the location, the source, the ownership, or the control of the proceeds of specified unlawful activity; or
    (ii) to avoid a transaction reporting requirement under State or Federal law
[shall be punished according to the statute]."

18 U.S.C. § 1956(a)(1). Section (a)(3) contains a substantially similar provision designed to facilitate prosecution of money laundering offenses discovered by means of government sting operations.

[16] Section 1956(c)(2) provides that "the term 'conducts' includes initiating, concluding, or participating in initiating, or concluding a transaction."

[17] Section 1956(c)(1) provides that:

the term "knowing that the property involved in a financial transaction represents the proceeds of some form of unlawful activity" means that the person knew the property involved in the transaction represented proceeds from some form, though not necessarily which form, of activity that constitutes a felony under State, Federal, or foreign law.

a. The defendant engaged in the transaction done *with the intent* to further a specified unlawful activity;

b. The defendant engaged in the transaction *with the intent* to commit tax fraud in violation of § 7201 (tax evasion) or § 7206 (false returns) of the Internal Revenue Code;

c. The defendant engaged in the transaction *knowing* that the transaction is designed in whole or in part to disguise, conceal, or hide the source of the money; *or*

d. The defendant engaged in the transaction *knowing* that the transaction is designed in whole or in part to avoid the currency transaction reporting laws.

The statute defines "financial transaction" to include a broad range of financial dealings that affect interstate or foreign commerce.[18] The definition encompasses both bank transactions and other transfers of money, property, and gifts.[19]

The "specified unlawful activit[ies]" under the statute encompass a broad range of crimes. These include the RICO predicates of the mail and wire fraud statutes,[20] financial institution fraud,[21] obstruction of justice,[22] and securities fraud,[23] as well

---

[18] Section 1956(c)(3) defines the term "transaction" to include:

a purchase, sale, loan, pledge, gift, transfer, delivery, or other disposition, and with respect to a financial institution includes a deposit, withdrawal, transfer between accounts, exchange of currency, loan, extension of credit, purchase or sale of any stock, bond, certificate of deposit, or other monetary instrument, use of a safe deposit box, or any other payment, transfer, or delivery by, through, or to a financial institution, by whatever means effected.

Section 1956(c)(4) provides the federal jurisdictional basis for § 1956 and defines the scope of covered activities:

the term "financial transaction" means (A) a transaction which in any way or degree affects interstate or foreign commerce (i) involving the movement of funds by wire or other means or (ii) involving one or more monetary instruments, or (iii) involving the transfer of title to any real property, vehicle, vessel, or aircraft, or (B) a transaction involving the use of a financial institution which is engaged in, or the activities of which affect, interstate or foreign commerce in any way or degree.

Section 1956(c)(5) defines "monetary instruments" as "(i) coin or currency of the United States or of any other country, travelers' checks, personal checks, bank checks, and money orders, or (ii) investment securities or negotiable instruments, in bearer form or otherwise in such form that title thereto passes upon delivery."

Section 1956(c)(6) incorporates the definition of "financial institution" under 31 U.S.C. § 5312(a)(2), which provides that a "financial institution" means "(A) an insured bank . . . ; (B) a commercial bank or trust company; (C) a private banker; (D) an agency or branch of a foreign bank in the United States . . . (Z) any other business designated by the Secretary whose cash transactions have a high degree of usefulness in criminal, tax, or regulatory matters."

[19] *See* Gredd & Cooper, *supra* note 2, § 2A.02[1]; Akopyan, *supra* note 2, at 836–37.

[20] 18 U.S.C. §§ 1341, 1343. *See* Chapter 4, Mail and Wire Fraud, *supra*.

[21] 18 U.S.C. § 1344.

[22] *See* 18 U.S.C. §§ 1503 (obstruction of justice), 1510 (obstruction of criminal investigations), 1511 (obstruction of State or local law enforcement), 1512 (tampering with a witness, victim, or an informant), 1513 (retaliating against a witness, victim, or an informant).

[23] 15 U.S.C. § 78ff(a).

as dozens of other crimes.[24] Although most § 1956 prosecutions involve the laundering of drug money, the statute on its face also applies to a number of white collar crimes.

Finally, the statute defines "knowing that the property involved in a financial transaction represents the proceeds of some form of unlawful activity." This element is proven by sufficient evidence that the defendant "knew the property involved in the transaction represented proceeds from some form, though not necessarily which form, of activity that constitutes a felony under State, Federal, or foreign law."[25]

The penalties for a money laundering conviction are severe, and include a fine of not more than $500,000 or twice the value of the property involved in the transaction, whichever is greater, or imprisonment for not more than twenty years, or both. Of course the actual sentence will depend upon the trial court's application of the Federal Sentencing Guidelines.[26] In addition, the money laundering statutes contain broad-ranging civil and criminal forfeiture provisions.[27]

[B]   International Money Laundering — § 1956(a)(2)

[1]   Statutory Elements and Definitions

Section 1956(a)(2) criminalizes the movement of money into or out of the United States in certain circumstances.[28] The definitions of the terms and the punishment are the same as under § 1956(a)(1).

Under § 1956(a)(2), the government must prove that:

1.   The defendant transported, transmitted, or transferred, or attempted to transport, transmit, or transfer a monetary instrument or funds;

2.   The movement or attempted movement was out of or into the United States; and

---

[24] 18 U.S.C. § 1956(c)(7).

[25] 18 U.S.C. § 1956(c)(1).

[26] *See* Chapter 21, Sentencing, *infra.*

[27] *See* Chapter 22, Forfeitures, *infra.*

[28] The statute provides:

Whoever transports, transmits, or transfers, or attempts to transport, transmit, or transfer a monetary instrument or funds from a place in the United States to or through a place outside the United States or to a place in the United States from or through a place outside the United States -
(A)   with the intent to promote the carrying on of specified unlawful activity; or
(B)   knowing that the monetary instrument or funds involved in the transportation represent the proceeds of some form of unlawful activity and knowing that such transportation, transmission, or transfer is designed in whole or in part -
　(i)   to conceal or disguise the nature, the location, the source, the ownership, or the control of the proceeds of specified unlawful activity; or
　(ii)   to avoid a transaction reporting requirement under State or Federal law,
[shall be punished according to the statute].
18 U.S.C. § 1956(a)(2).

3.   Either:

    a.   The defendant acted *with the intent* to promote a specified unlawful activity; *or*

    b.   The defendant acted *with the knowledge* that

        (i)   the monetary instrument or funds were from some form of unlawful activity, which activity constitutes a felony under state, federal, or foreign law, *and*

        (ii) the movement of funds was designed in whole or in part either to:

            (A)   conceal the source of the funds, *or*

            (B)   avoid a currency transaction reporting requirement.

[2]   Comparison of § 1956(a)(1) and § 1956(a)(2)

The main differences between the crimes of domestic money laundering under § 1956(a)(1) and international money laundering under § 1956(a)(2) include:

1.   Section 1956(a)(1) deals with transactions occurring within the United States, while § 1956(a)(2) deals with movements of funds into and out of the United States.

2.   Section 1956(a)(1) deals with broadly-defined "financial transactions," while § 1956(a)(2) deals only with transactions involving "monetary instruments."[29]

3.   Only § 1956(a)(1) encompasses an intent to commit tax fraud.

[C]   Prohibited Monetary Transactions — § 1957

Section 1957 is entitled, "Engaging in monetary transactions in property derived from specified unlawful activity."[30] Unlike § 1956, § 1957 is not geared towards attempts to hide the source of funds produced by illegal activities. Rather,

---

[29] *See* § 15.02[A], *supra*, for the definitions of these terms.

[30] Section 1957 provides:

    (a) Whoever, in any of the circumstances set forth in subsection (d), knowingly engages or attempts to engage in a monetary transaction in criminally derived property that is of a value greater than $10,000 and is derived from specified unlawful activity, shall be punished as provided in subsection (b).

* * *

    (d) The circumstances referred to in subsection (a) are -

  (1)   that the offense under this section takes place in the United States or in the special maritime and territorial jurisdiction of the United States; or

  (2)   that the offense under this section takes place outside the United States and such special jurisdiction, but the defendant is a United States person (as defined in section 3077 of this title, but excluding the class described in paragraph (2)(D) of such section).

* * *

    (f) As used in this section -

  (1)   the term "monetary transaction" means the deposit, withdrawal, transfer, or exchange, in or

§ 1957 focuses on the use of such funds within the financial system.

To obtain a conviction under § 1957, the government must prove that:

1. The defendant engaged or attempted to engage in a monetary transaction;

2. The monetary transaction was of a value greater than $10,000;

3. The transaction was derived from specified unlawful activity;

4. The transaction took place in the United States or the defendant is a "United States person"; and

5. The defendant knew that the property was criminally derived.

As shown above, where the same terms are used, the definitions of the terms in § 1957 are the same as in § 1956. Only § 1957 uses the term "monetary transaction," which includes "the deposit, withdrawal, transfer, or exchange, in or affecting interstate or foreign commerce, of funds or a monetary instrument by, through, or to a financial institution, including any transaction that would be a financial transaction under § 1956(c)(4)(B) of this title."

The penalties under § 1957 include a statutory fine or a fine of not more twice the value of the criminally-derived property involved in the transaction, whichever is greater, or imprisonment for not more than ten years, or both. Once again, the actual penalty will depend upon the application of the advisory Federal Sentencing Guidelines.[31] Like § 1956, § 1957 also includes broad-ranging civil and criminal forfeiture provisions.[32]

After § 1957's original adoption, Congress amended the section to exclude "any transaction necessary to preserve a person's right to representation as guaranteed by the Sixth Amendment to the Constitution."[33] In *United States v. Velez*,[34] the Eleventh Circuit affirmed the dismissal of § 1957 money laundering charges against a prominent criminal defense attorney. The court held that the plain meaning of the statute precludes prosecution based upon transactions used to pay attorneys' fees.[35]

---

affecting interstate or foreign commerce, of funds or a monetary instrument (as defined in § 1956(c)(5) of this title) by, through, or to a financial institution (as defined in section 1956 of this title), including any transaction that would be a financial transaction under § 1956(c)(4)(B) of this title, but such term does not include any transaction necessary to preserve a person's right to representation as guaranteed by the sixth amendment to the Constitution;

(2) the term "criminally derived property" means any property constituting, or derived from, proceeds obtained from a criminal offense; and

(3) the term "specified unlawful activity" has the meaning given that term in § 1956 of this title.

18 U.S.C. § 1957.

[31] *See* Chapter 21, Sentencing, *infra.*

[32] *See* Chapter 22, Forfeitures, *infra.*

[33] 18 U.S.C. § 1957(f)(1).

[34] 586 F.3d 875 (11th Cir. 2009).

[35] *Id.* at 877.

[D]　Comparison of § 1956(a)(1) and § 1957

Perhaps the most significant difference between § 1956(a)(1) and § 1957 is that the latter is much simpler and more straightforward. Section 1956(a)(1) requires that the government choose from among different theories, and prove two levels of intent. Section 1957 contains but one theory and one level of intent. More specifically, the technical differences between the statutes include:

	Section 1956(a)(1)	Section 1957
Mens rea	Requires proof that the defendant (i) knew the money constituted the proceeds of unlawful activity, *and* (ii) acted with further knowledge or intent as required by the specific theory.	Requires proof that the defendant "knowingly engaged . . . in a monetary transaction in criminally derived property."
Scope	Covers all "financial transactions," a broadly-defined term that includes gifts and transfers of property titles.[36]	Covers only the more narrowly-defined "monetary transactions," which are limited to transactions through financial institutions.[37]
Amount	Requires no specific dollar amount.	Requires that the transaction be of an amount greater than $10,000.

§ 15.03　PROOF OF THE DEFENDANT'S MENTAL STATE

[A]　Section 1956

Recall that § 1956 requires that the government prove two levels of mens rea: (1) knowledge that the financial transaction represented the proceeds of unlawful activity; and (2) one of four alternative theories.

[1]　First Level of Mens Rea — Knowledge that the Transaction Represented Proceeds of Unlawful Activity

Under § 1956(a)(1), the government must only prove that the defendant knew the laundered money or property came from some kind of unlawful activity; it need not prove that the defendant knew exactly what kind of unlawful activity was involved. Actual knowledge or "willful blindness" will suffice for a conviction, but negligence or recklessness will not. As the legislative history explains:

> [A] currency exchanger who participates in a transaction with a known drug dealer involving hundreds of thousands of dollars in cash and accepts

---

[36] *See* § 15.02[A], *supra.*

[37] *See id.*

a commission far above the market rate, could not escape conviction . . . simply by claiming that he did not know for sure that the currency . . . was derived from crime. On the other hand, an automobile dealer who sells a car at market rates to a person whom he merely suspects of involvement with crime, cannot be convicted . . . in the absence of a showing that he knew something more about the transaction or the circumstances surrounding it.[38]

The former scenario describes a classic case of "willful blindness" that would suffice for conviction. The latter scenario, on the other hand, merely describes a subjective suspicion that only amounts to recklessness and would not support a conviction.

In practice, however, it is not always easy to distinguish between the "willful blindness" that would support a conviction and the reckless suspicion that would not. Ultimately, assuming that there is sufficient evidence that would provide a basis for a rational juror to convict, then the issue is left to the trier of fact.

For example, in *United States v. Campbell*,[39] the trial judge found that the government had failed to prove the required mens rea, but the appeals court disagreed and reinstated the conviction. Campbell was a real estate agent. Campbell's client, Lawing, presented himself as a legitimate businessperson but was actually a drug dealer. Lawing entered into a contract to buy a house priced at $182,500. Subsequent to the initial agreement, Lawing asked the sellers to accept $60,000 in cash under the table and to lower the contract price to $122,500. The sellers agreed, and Campbell assisted in completing the transaction.[40] Lawing delivered the $60,000 in small cash bundles in a brown paper bag.

Campbell was convicted of money laundering based upon the theory that she engaged in a financial transaction designed to conceal the source of the funds. Based on Campbell's role in the transaction, the Fourth Circuit found sufficient evidence of mens rea. The court stated that the government was only required to show that Campbell actually knew or was willfully blind to the fact that Lawing's funds represented drug sale proceeds. Whether these facts proved mere suspicion or "willful blindness" was a jury question, the court concluded.[41] Reviewing the facts, the court found that the jury could have inferred that Campbell "deliberately closed her eyes" to evidence of Lawing's drug dealing, including Lawing's use of expensive sports cars, Campbell's knowledge that Lawing carried a large amount of cash in his briefcase, and Campbell's statement to a colleague that the funds "may have been drug money."[42]

---

[38] Senate Committee on the Judiciary, The Money Laundering Crimes Act of 1986, S. Rep. No. 99-433 at 10 (1986).

[39] 977 F.2d 854 (4th Cir. 1992).

[40] The transaction generated documents that contained material misstatements and that were filed with the federal government. This also led to a false statements conviction under 18 U.S.C. § 1001. *See* Chapter 10, False Statements, *supra*, for a discussion of this crime.

[41] *See* Akopyan, *supra* note 2, at 830 & nn.67–70 for other cases applying this approach.

[42] 977 F.2d at 859. Based on the same facts, the court also found sufficient evidence to convict Campbell of violating § 1957(a). *Id.* at 859–60.

Similarly, in *United States v. Corchado-Peralta*,[43] the court found sufficient circumstantial evidence that a drug-smuggler's wife was willfully blind as to the source of the family's income. The family had enormous expenditures, far exceeding the reported income, and the wife was well-educated and did the family bookkeeping. Although the court found the evidence thin, it held that the jury could have reasonably concluded that the wife was willfully blind.[44] These cases demonstrate that one who is not involved in the underlying illegal activity may nonetheless be liable for concealment money laundering in a wide range of circumstances. This is particularly so given that, as both *Campbell* and *Corchado-Peralta* show, proof of willful blindness will be sufficient to demonstrate knowledge that the money came from some form of illegal activity.

[2]   Second Level of Mens Rea — Four Possible Theories

Assuming that the government has proven the first level of mens rea — knowledge that the transaction represented proceeds of unlawful activity — it must also prove a second level of mens rea. Thus, the government must show at least one of four theories — that the defendant engaged in the financial transaction (1) with the intent to promote the unlawful activity, (2) with the intent to commit tax fraud, (3) with the knowledge that the transaction was designed to hide the source of the money, and/or (4) with the knowledge that the transaction was designed to avoid the currency transaction reporting laws.

Most reported cases deal with the third theory, "concealment" money laundering. This theory is based upon the classic money laundering activity of attempting to make "dirty" money, *i.e.*, money derived from unlawful activity, look like "clean" money. The government has also brought a substantial number of cases under the first theory — promotion of the unlawful activity — either alone or in conjunction with the third theory.

[a]   Evidence of a Design to Conceal or Disguise Dirty Money Under § 1956(a)(1)(B)(i) and 1956(a)(2)(B)(i)

Merely spending illegally-derived funds, in the absence of knowledge of a design to conceal the source of the funds, will not support a conviction under § 1956(a)(1)(B)(i) and (a)(2)(B)(i). In *United States v. Sanders*,[45] for example, the government's theory was that the defendant had attempted to hide the source of drug money by using it to buy two cars, a Volvo and a Lincoln. The Tenth Circuit reversed the conviction, finding the government had failed to prove that the defendant knew that the transaction was designed to conceal the source of the funds. With respect to the Volvo, the defendant and her husband were personally involved in the purchase, made themselves known to the salesperson, and openly used the car. Thus, there was insufficient evidence of a "design to conceal." The

---

[43] 318 F.3d 255 (1st Cir. 2003).

[44] *Id.* at 258. The court nonetheless reversed the conviction because of insufficient evidence on the second level of mens rea alleged in the case — the intent to conceal. *See* § 15.03[A][2][a], *infra*.

[45] 929 F.2d 1466 (10th Cir. 1991).

Lincoln purchase was a closer issue because the car was placed in the name of the defendant's daughter, possibly indicating a design to conceal. Nevertheless, the court found insufficient evidence with respect to that purchase as well, because once again, the defendant and her husband openly bought and used the car and the defendant's daughter was present during the transaction. In an oft-cited passage, the court stated that the government's argument was essentially that all transactions involving illegally-derived money constitute money laundering. This, the court said, would "turn the money laundering statute into a 'money spending statute.' "[46]

The court reached a similar result in *United States v. McGahee*.[47] In that case, a local housing program provided construction funds to qualifying homeowners. McGahee was a program supervisor. He approved numerous unauthorized disbursements to defendant McGuire, who owned a contracting company that did work for the program. McGuire was found guilty of nine counts of concealment money laundering. On appeal, he argued that the government had not adduced sufficient evidence to support the convictions. The government responded that McGuire wrote checks on his business account containing the illegally-derived funds. McGuire then converted the checks to cash. This, the government asserted, showed that McGuire engaged in these transactions in order to hide the source of the money. The court rejected the government's argument. As in *Sanders*, there were no indicia that the defendant engaged in these acts with the intent to conceal. Here, the defendant openly cashed the checks without using a false name or any other method of concealment.[48]

Courts have sustained convictions, however, where there was more evidence of a design to conceal. In a typical case, for example, a person takes the "dirty" money, deposits it into a bank account set up in the name of a company established for that purpose, and then withdraws the funds from that account.[49] There was a similar basis for concealment money laundering charges in *United States v. Jackson*.[50] In that case, the defendant, Davis, was a minister who also operated two crack houses. The defendant deposited some of the drug sale proceeds in two church bank accounts that also contained legitimate funds. On these accounts Davis wrote checks for various purposes, including (1) cash for personal expenses, (2) payments for beepers and mobile phones, (3) rent on his personal residence, and (4) cash for a car purchase. The government charged the defendant with four counts based on each set of checks under the theories that the drug money was laundered both to (a) promote the drug sale activity and (b) hide its source.

On appeal from his convictions, the defendant argued that the government had failed to adduce sufficient evidence as to various elements of the charges. The court rejected the arguments. Initially, the court found that the government had proven

---

[46] *Id.* at 1472.

[47] 257 F.3d 520 (6th Cir. 2001).

[48] *Id.* at 527–28. *Accord* United States v. Corchado-Peralta, 318 F.3d 255, 258–60 (1st Cir. 2003).

[49] *See* United States v. Powers, 168 F.3d 741, 748 (5th Cir. 1999) (finding sufficient evidence of concealment money laundering because of use of middleman to conceal source of funds).

[50] 935 F.2d 832 (7th Cir. 1991).

the defendant knew the illegally-derived funds were deposited in the church accounts.[51] Second, the government had shown that the funds were actually derived from the operation of a continuing criminal enterprise, a specified unlawful activity.[52] Third, under the concealment theory, there was sufficient evidence from which "[t]he jury could reasonably infer that the use of the church accounts was an attempt to hide the ownership and source of Davis' drug money while preserving his ready access to the funds in the accounts, which were as close as the church's checkbook."[53]

Finally, the court noted that the prosecution and trial judge had erred in assuming that the government was required to prove both money laundering theories — promoting the unlawful activity, and hiding the source of the funds. Noting that either alternative theory could support a conviction, the court opined that in most cases the government should choose between the theories.

The concealment theory was also proven in *United States v. Tencer*.[54] Tencer was a Louisiana-based chiropractor who was convicted of money laundering in connection with false insurance claims. Tencer placed the proceeds of the fraud in various accounts around the country and then moved the money to an account in Las Vegas. The court found sufficient evidence of intent to conceal even though the accounts were in Tencer's name. The funds were sent to locations where he did not live or work, and were moved again to a central account far from his home. Tencer also made false statements to bank employees in connection with the accounts. This, the court held, provided sufficient evidence of intent to conceal.

The defendants in *Jackson* and *Tencer* were the criminals who themselves laundered the tainted money that they had generated. It is important to note, however, that the money laundering statutes also apply to parties who are not involved in the underlying wrongdoing.[55] For example, in *United States v. Campbell*,[56] discussed above, the defendant was a real estate agent whose client was the original wrongdoer. Nonetheless, the court found sufficient evidence that Campbell actually knew or was willfully blind to the fact that the real estate transaction was designed to disguise the source of the funds. Specifically, the court found that the fraudulent nature of the transaction itself — which included a sham contract and payment of $60,000 cash under the table — showed knowledge of a design to conceal the source of the money.[57]

Equivalent issues arise under § 1956(a)(2), which criminalizes the international transportation of money derived from unlawful activities. The mens rea elements of this crime parallel those of financial transaction money laundering under § 1956(a)(2). Both statutes require proof that the defendant (1) knew that the

---

[51] *Id.* at 840. The court also held that the conviction could be sustained even though the tainted funds were mixed together with legitimate funds. For a further discussion of this issue, see *infra*, § 15.04[B][1].

[52] 935 F.2d at 841, *citing* 21 U.S.C. § 848(c).

[53] 935 F.2d at 842.

[54] 107 F.3d 1120 (5th Cir. 1997).

[55] *See* Gredd & Cooper, *supra* note 2, § 2A.02[1][c], for examples of such cases.

[56] 977 F.2d 854 (4th Cir. 1992).

[57] *Id.* at 859.

proceeds were derived from unlawful activity and (2) acted with the intent required for "promotion" or "concealment" money laundering, among other theories.

The United States Supreme Court examined the mens rea requirement under § 1956(a)(2) in *Cuellar v. United States*.[58] In that case, the defendant was driving a car from Texas to Mexico containing over $80,000 in cash proceeds of narcotics trafficking. The cash was hidden in a secret compartment under the floorboard and was bundled in plastic bags and duct tape. The defendant was convicted of transportation money laundering under a concealment theory, § 1956(a)(2)(B)(i).

On appeal, the Supreme Court unanimously reversed. The Court stated that that the design to conceal element cannot "be satisfied solely by evidence that a defendant concealed the funds during their transport. In this case, the only evidence introduced to prove this element showed that petitioner engaged in extensive efforts to conceal the funds *en route* to Mexico, and thus his conviction cannot stand."[59] What the government had failed to prove was an intent to conceal the "nature, location, source, ownership, or control of the funds."[60] Simply attempting to hide the money did not, standing alone, evince an intent to hide the fact that this was drug money.[61]

[b]   Evidence of Intent to Promote Unlawful Activity Under § 1956(a)(1)(A)(i)

As the *Campbell* court held, to prove a concealment case under § 1956(a)(1)(B)(i), the government must merely prove that the defendant acted knowingly. When using the theory that the defendant promoted unlawful activity in violation of § 1956(a)(1)(A)(i), however, the government must prove that the defendant *intended* that the illegally-derived money be used to further the activity. The following cases demonstrate that in most instances the intent element will not be difficult to prove.

The decision in *United States v. Johnson*[62] shows how broadly this theory may reach. Johnson engaged in a fraudulent scheme to buy Mexican currency at a discount and sell the currency for U.S. dollars at a profit. Investors wired money to the defendant to buy the pesos. In reality, there was no such plan, and the "profit" paid to investors came from other investors' money. The government charged the defendant with two counts of using the proceeds of the wire fraud to further the unlawful activity under § 1956(a)(1)(A)(i). The first count was based upon use of the fraud proceeds to pay off the mortgage on the defendant's home, and the second upon use of the proceeds to buy a Mercedes-Benz automobile.

The court found that there was sufficient evidence to show that the payments were made with the "intent" to further the wire fraud scheme. Specifically, the

---

[58] 553 U.S. 550 (2008).

[59] *Id.* at 553–55.

[60] *Id.* at 568–70 (Alito, J., concurring).

[61] *Compare* United States v. Warshak, 562 F. Supp. 2d 986, 991–99 (S.D. Ohio 2008) (evidence of convoluted transactions was sufficient to show knowledge of a design to conceal).

[62] 971 F.2d 562 (10th Cir. 1992).

defendant used a home office to carry out the fraud scheme, and both the house and car were used to "impress" the investors with the defendant's success. The *Johnson* decision raises the question whether all conspicuous purchases by a successful con artist may amount to money laundering.

Other courts have also broadly interpreted this provision, applying it to simply cashing or depositing checks that represent the proceeds of illegal activity. For example, in *United States v. Montoya*,[63] the defendant was a public official who was bribed by means of a check, which he then deposited. The defendant was convicted of money laundering based upon the theory that depositing the check furthered the bribery. Even though the bribery scheme was complete at the time of the deposit, the Ninth Circuit affirmed the conviction. The court reasoned that the deposit enabled the defendant to use the money with which he had been bribed.

Similarly, in *United States v. Paramo*,[64] the defendant participated in a scheme to embezzle funds by causing the I.R.S. to issue refund checks to fictitious taxpayers. The defendant was convicted based on the theory that cashing the checks promoted the unlawful activity. Even though the defendant used the money solely for personal expenses not related to the fraud scheme, the Third Circuit upheld the conviction. Cashing the checks enabled the defendant to profit from the fraud. Therefore, the court found, the activity showed an intent to "promote" the illegal scheme. A dissenting judge argued that "a person promotes a scheme only when he or she ploughs back the proceeds thereof [into] the illegal enterprise."[65]

The defendant successfully argued the latter position in *United States v. Jackson*.[66] The government alleged that the defendant/minister intended to promote his illegal drug sales by depositing the proceeds into church-related bank accounts. Specifically, the defendant used checks written on these accounts to (1) pay for wireless telephone and paging services, (2) pay his rent, and (3) obtain cash. The court found that the payments for pagers were intended to promote the illegal drug sales because the defendant's dealers used their pagers in selling drugs. There was no evidence that the defendant intended that any of the other payments be used to further the drug dealing, however, and those payments could not sustain a conviction under § 1956(a)(1)(A)(i).[67]

Similarly, in *United States v. McGahee*,[68] discussed above, the defendant embezzled money through his construction firm. Because he used his residence as his business office, the government argued, his house mortgage payments furthered the criminal activity perpetrated through his company. The court rejected the argument. It found that paying for personal goods is insufficient to

---

[63] 945 F.2d 1068 (9th Cir. 1991).

[64] 998 F.2d 1212 (3d Cir. 1993).

[65] *Id.* at 1222 (Rosenn, J., dissenting).

[66] 935 F.2d 832 (7th Cir. 1991), discussed above in § 15.03[A][2][a].

[67] *Id.* at 841. Recall, however, that the court sustained the convictions on these counts on the alternative theory that the checks were used in a scheme to conceal the source of the funds under § 1956(a)(1)(B)(i). *See id.* at 841–842.

[68] 257 F.3d 520 (6th Cir. 2001), discussed *supra*, § 15.03[A][2][a].

establish promotion money laundering. Rather, the transaction must be explicitly connected to the crime.[69]

Finally, in *United States v. Brown*,[70] the defendant was a car dealership executive convicted of money laundering in connection with various fraud schemes. For example, the defendant charged car buyers excessive title and license fees. The defendant also artificially increased the purchase prices of the cars and then repaid the purchasers the down payments as inducements to buy the cars. This practice defrauded the auto lenders by inflating the borrowers' equity interests in the cars. The defendant deposited the fraud proceeds in the car dealership's business bank account, and used funds to pay for parts, advertising, and other general business purposes. The defendant was convicted of promotion money laundering based upon the checks written for these expenditures.

On appeal, the Fifth Circuit reversed the convictions. The court stated that the government was required to prove that the defendant's expenditures were related to the promotion of his fraud schemes. Simply depositing illegally derived funds into the general business account and then writing checks for general business expenses does not satisfy the element of engaging in the transaction with the intent to promote or further the unlawful activity.[71]

These cases show that the courts are split as to the degree to which everyday expenditures of criminally-derived proceeds may support a promotion money laundering charge.

[B] Section 1957

[1] The Government's Theory

As discussed above, § 1957 operates much more simply than does § 1956. In essence, § 1957 only requires the government to show that the defendant engaged in a monetary transaction of more than $10,000 derived from specified unlawful activity, and that the defendant knew the money was derived from some form of unlawful activity. As under § 1956, defendants under § 1957 may include both the original wrongdoer and those who are paid for their products or services with criminally-derived funds.

[2] Proof of Knowledge

Once again, the government may prove knowledge by direct or circumstantial evidence of actual knowledge or willful blindness. The Department of Justice Manual provides examples of conduct suggesting sufficient evidence of willful blindness to support bringing § 1957 charges on that theory. These examples

---

[69] 257 F.3d at 527.

[70] 186 F.3d 661 (5th Cir. 1999).

[71] The court noted that a case based on the deposits of the fraud proceeds would have been more likely to succeed but that the Department of Justice disfavors such "receipt and deposit" cases because "the harm of the money laundering transaction (i.e., the deposit), is not significantly greater than that of the underlying offense." *Id.* at 669 n.12.

include acceptance of above-market commissions, use of false names to buy goods or services, use of cash in large denominations, and grossly inflated purchase or sale prices.[72]

In the *Campbell* case discussed above,[73] the government proceeded on a willful blindness theory. In that case, the real estate agent was convicted under § 1957 in addition to her conviction under § 1956. On appeal, the agent argued that her § 1957 conviction could not stand because there was insufficient proof that she knew her client's money was derived from drug sales. The court rejected the argument, finding sufficient proof from which a jury "could reasonably infer that Campbell knew of, or was willfully blind to, [her client's] true occupation."[74]

§ 15.04   PROOF THAT THE PROPERTY WAS THE PRODUCT OF CRIMINAL ACTIVITY

[A]   Issues Relating to Timing

[1]   Section 1957

Part of the government's burden under § 1957 is to show that the defendant engaged in a "monetary transaction in criminally derived property."[75] The statute defines the term "criminally derived property" as "any property constituting, or derived from, proceeds obtained from a criminal offense."[76] The statute does not specify, however, the point at which property becomes "criminally derived." This issue has produced substantial litigation.

What if, at the time of the monetary transaction, the defendant had not actually completed the crime and received the illegally-obtained funds? Courts have reversed convictions under § 1957 in such circumstances. For example, in the *Johnson* case discussed above,[77] the defendant had defrauded a number of investors who wired money to the defendant's account. The government charged Johnson with 28 counts under § 1957 based upon these wire transfers. The Tenth Circuit reversed the convictions, stating that "both the plain language of § 1957 and the legislative history behind it suggest that Congress targeted only those transactions occurring after proceeds have been obtained from the underlying unlawful activity."[78] The court found that the wire fraud was not complete and the defendant did not obtain the funds until they were actually deposited into his account. Thus, the wiring of the money by the investors occurred too early in the scheme to support the conviction.

---

[72] *See* Gredd & Cooper, *supra* note 2, § 2A.03[4], *citing* DOJ Manual § 9-105.400 at 9-2128.36.

[73] 977 F.2d at 859. *See supra*, § 15.03[A][2][a].

[74] 977 F.2d at 859. *See* United States v. Flores, 454 F.3d 149, 155–56 (3d Cir. 2006) (attorney found to have been willfully blind as to the illegal source of the client's money).

[75] 18 U.S.C. § 1957(a).

[76] 18 U.S.C. § 1957(f)(2).

[77] 971 F.2d 562, discussed *supra*, § 15.03[A][2][a].

[78] 971 F.2d at 569.

Similarly, in *United States v. Piervinanzi*,[79] the defendant engaged in a scheme to commit bank fraud and wire fraud by fraudulently transferring funds from a domestic bank to an overseas account. Based upon the wire transfer, the defendant was convicted under § 1957. On appeal, he argued that "the language of the statute only encompasses transactions in which a defendant first obtains 'criminally derived property,' and then engages in a monetary transaction with that property."[80] The Second Circuit agreed, and reversed the conviction. The court held that, because the funds transferred from the bank were not, at the time of the transfer, property derived from the wire fraud and bank fraud scheme, the transfer did not fall within the statute.

[2] Section 1956

Section 1956(a)(1) requires that the financial transaction at issue "in fact involve[] the proceeds of specified unlawful activity." *Citing Johnson*, some defendants have argued that no such "proceeds" were involved because the unlawful activity was not complete at the time of the transaction.[81] Under this argument, the underlying criminal activity must generate "proceeds" of the activity *before* the money laundering activity occurred. Some courts have accepted this argument.[82]

More frequently, however, courts have rejected such challenges to § 1956 convictions. The decision in *United States v. Allen*[83] provides an example of such a holding. In that case, defendant Cihak was a high-level bank manager who diverted funds from the bank in two ways. First, he arranged for the bank to transfer funds to consultants, who then paid kickbacks to Cihak. Second, Cihak arranged for loans to others, and then either used the loan money himself or received bribes from the borrowers. Cihak and other defendants were convicted of money laundering under § 1956(a)(1)(B)(i), based upon bank transactions that occurred in connection with the schemes.

On appeal, the defendants argued that the transactions did not constitute "proceeds." According to this argument, the wrongdoing did not occur until Cihak received the diverted funds without disclosing to the bank that he had an interest in the transactions; therefore, the transfers to the consultants and borrowers came too early in the scheme to support the § 1956 convictions. The court rejected the argument, holding that "the funds at issue in each of the transactions became the proceeds at the moment the money left the control of [the bank] and was deposited into an account of a consultant or borrower."[84] At that point, the fraud upon the bank was complete, irrespective of whether the consultants or borrowers later transferred the funds to Cihak.

---

[79] 23 F.3d 670 (2d Cir. 1994).

[80] *Id.* at 677.

[81] *See* Gredd & Cooper, *supra* note 2, § 2A.02[1][b][ii].

[82] *See id.* for an extensive discussion of this issue.

[83] 76 F.3d 1348 (5th Cir. 1996).

[84] *Id.* at 1361.

A similar issue arose under § 1956 in *United States v. Kennedy*.[85] The defendant defrauded customers in a phony investment scheme using the mails and wires. The Court held that wire and mail fraud are completed when any wiring or mailing is used in execution of a scheme; there is no requirement that the scheme be successful. The money laundering charges were sustained because the deposits that formed the basis of the charges occurred after the fraudulent use of the mail and wires. Therefore, the deposits represented the "proceeds" of specified unlawful activity as required by § 1956(a)(1).

In *United States v. Piervinanzi*,[86] discussed above, the court confronted the timing issue in connection with § 1956(a)(2)(A). That section criminalizes international money laundering used to promote the underlying illegal activity. On appeal, the defendant argued that "the overseas transmission of funds 'merges' with the underlying bank fraud, precluding independent liability under § 1956(a)(2)."[87] Relying on statutory construction, the Second Circuit disagreed. Unlike § 1956(a)(1), which requires that the money laundering involve the "proceeds" of unlawful activity, § 1956(a)(2) "contains no requirement that 'proceeds' first be generated by unlawful activity, followed by a financial transaction with those proceeds."[88] Thus, under this section, the laundering need not promote subsequent unlawful activity but rather can be simultaneous with the unlawful activity.

[B] Commingling

One of the most complex issues that arises under the money laundering statutes involves the "tracing" of "commingled" funds. Under § 1956, the government must show that the financial transaction involved the "proceeds" of the specified unlawful activity. Under § 1957, the government must show that the monetary transaction was "derived" from the unlawful activity. Has the government met its burden under either statute where the transaction potentially involved both money derived from illegal activities and money derived from legitimate activities?

[1] Cases Under § 1956

Courts have generally held that, under § 1956, the government need not "trace" illegal proceeds that have been commingled with legitimate funds.[89] For example, in the *Jackson* decision discussed more fully above,[90] the defendant argued that he could not be convicted under § 1956(a)(1) because the expenditures came from accounts that contained some funds that were not derived from specified unlawful activity. The court rejected the argument, citing both the statutory language and congressional intent. The court noted that the statute on its face only requires the government to prove that the financial transactions "involve[d]" the proceeds of the illegal activity. Thus, the statute allows for convictions "where the funds involved in

---

[85] 64 F.3d 1465 (10th Cir. 1995).

[86] 23 F.3d 670 (2d Cir. 1994).

[87] *Id.* at 679.

[88] *Id.* at 680.

[89] *See* Akopyan, *supra* note 2, at 833–35, and cases cited therein.

[90] *See* § 15.03[A][2][b], *supra*.

the transaction are derived only in part from 'specified unlawful activities.' "[91] The court also reasoned that Congress did not intend for money laundering defendants to avoid conviction simply by proving that the tainted funds were commingled with other funds.[92] Other courts have agreed with this result.[93]

[2] Cases Under § 1957

The courts are split as to whether the government must "trace" the illegally-derived funds in a § 1957 prosecution. In the *Johnson* case discussed above,[94] the court held that tracing is not required. The defendant had mixed both tainted and clean money in his bank account. Of the $5.5 million in deposits, approximately $1.2 million could not be traced to illegal activity.[95] The defendant's § 1957 conviction was based upon a $1.8 million withdrawal from the account. The government could not prove that all of the $1.8 million necessarily involved the illegally-derived funds; some of the $1.8 million may have represented legitimate funds. Nonetheless, the Tenth Circuit upheld the conviction on the ground that the government is not required to show that the money could not have possibly come from a legitimate source.[96] Otherwise, the court said, "individuals [could] avoid prosecution simply by commingling legitimate funds with proceeds of crime. This would defeat the very purpose of the money-laundering statutes."[97] Some other circuits also follow this approach.[98]

In *United States v. Rutgard*,[99] however, the Ninth Circuit rejected the above approach and reversed convictions under § 1957. Rutgard was an ophthalmologic surgeon who operated two eye care clinics that primarily served Medicare patients. At trial, the government showed that Rutgard's clinics routinely submitted fraudulent claims for Medicare payments. Rutgard's money laundering convictions were based upon two large wire transfers out of Rutgard's account.

The Ninth Circuit reversed the convictions. The court held that the government was required to trace the transferred funds to the Medicare fraud, and that it had failed to do so. The court determined that tracing is required based upon the structure and purpose of § 1957 and upon the differences between § 1956 and

---

[91] 935 F.2d at 841.

[92] *Id.* at 841.

[93] *See* Gredd & Cooper, *supra* note 2, § 2A.02[1][b][i].

[94] *See supra*, § 15.03[A][2][b].

[95] 971 F.2d at 565.

[96] *Id.* at 570.

[97] *Id.*

[98] *See* United States v. Sokolow, 81 F.3d 397, 409 (3d Cir.), *vacated on other grounds*, 91 F.3d 396 (3d Cir. 1996) (Sokolow, who committed insurance fraud and was convicted under § 1957, argued that the jury instructions were too vague and allowed for a conviction on any dollar amount. The conviction was upheld because the court reasoned that criminal proceeds do not need to be traced). *Accord* United States v. Moore, 27 F.3d 969, 976 (4th Cir. 1994) (upholding the defendant's conviction under § 1957 even though the illegally-derived funds from a fraudulent bank loan scheme were repaid; the court reasoned that illegally-derived funds need not be traced).

[99] 116 F.3d 1270 (9th Cir. 1997).

§ 1957.[100] Unlike § 1956, with its two-level mens rea requirement, § 1957 merely requires proof of knowledge that the funds were tainted. The court characterized § 1957 as a "draconian law" that criminalizes any use of criminal proceeds of over $10,000 involving a bank. Therefore, the court determined that the statute should be narrowly construed to require tracing.[101]

The court also rejected the *Johnson* reasoning that this rule would defeat the statute's purpose. First, if a defendant has attempted to commingle money to hide its source, then the government can bring a § 1956 charge. Second, if a defendant has made *deposits* of over $10,000 in illegally-derived funds, then those deposits can form the basis of a § 1957 prosecution even if the funds are commingled with legitimate funds in the account. Indeed, the court noted, the government could have successfully used the latter theory in prosecuting Rutgard under § 1957, but the government had erred when constructing its theory of the case.[102]

[C]   "Proceeds:" Net Receipts or Net Profits?

One issue that had split lower federal courts concerned the interpretation of the word "proceeds" in § 1956. Some courts had held that the term meant net receipts from the illegal activity, while others had held that the term referred to the net profits from such activities.[103] The United States Supreme Court addressed this conflict in *United States v. Santos*.[104] In that case, the Court held five-to-four that the term "proceeds" in § 1956 is ambiguous. Applying the rule of lenity, the Court held that "proceeds" means "profits," not "receipts."

After *Santos* was decided, however, Congress passed the Fraud Enforcement and Enhancement Act of 2009 (FERA). FERA amends the money laundering statutes to provide that "the term 'proceeds' means any property derived from or obtained or retained, directly or indirectly, through some form of unlawful activity, including the gross receipts of such activity."[105]

§ 15.05   THE USA PATRIOT ACT

On October 26, 2001, Congress passed the Uniting and Strengthening America by Providing Appropriate Tools Required to Intercept and Obstruct Terrorism Act of 2001 (the "Act").[106] In several ways, the Act seeks to strengthen efforts to fight international and domestic money laundering. For example, the Act expands the venue provisions of §§ 1956 and 1957; actions under those sections can be brought

---

[100] *Id.* at 1292.

[101] *Id.* at 1291.

[102] *Id.* at 1292.

[103] *Compare, e.g.,* United States v. Iacaboni, 363 F.3d 1 (1st Cir. 2004) ("proceeds" means gross income), *with* United States v. Scialabba, 282 F.3d 475 (7th Cir. 2002) ("proceeds" means net profits).

[104] 553 U.S. 507 (2008).

[105] Courts have varied widely in applying Santos to pre-FERA cases. For an overview of these cases, see Rachel Zimarowski, *Taking a Gamble: Money Laundering After* United States v. Santos, 112 W. Va. L. Rev. 1139 (2010).

[106] Pub. L. 107-56.

in "any district in which the financial or monetary transaction is conducted" or "any district where a prosecution for the underlying specified unlawful activity could be brought, if the defendant participated in the transfer of the proceeds of the specified unlawful activity from that district to the district where the financial or monetary transaction is conducted."[107]

Further, the Act requires that financial institutions implement programs designed to prevent their institutions from being used to facilitate money laundering or finance terrorism, requires certain institutions to report instances of money laundering, and requires financial institutions to act more aggressively in reporting suspicious activity and to expand their due diligence and "know your customer" programs. The Act also adds several new offenses to the list of specified unlawful activities.

---

[107] 18 U.S.C. § 1956(i)(1)(A), (B).

Chapter 16

RICO

§ 16.01 INTRODUCTION

[A] The RICO Debate

The Racketeer Influenced and Corrupt Organizations ("RICO") statute[1] is one of the most controversial laws that the government has employed to prosecute white collar crimes.[2] This is so for several reasons. First, bringing a RICO charge labels the white collar defendant as a "racketeer" — a term generally associated with organized crime family members. Second, the statute contains severe penalties,[3] including pre-trial seizure and mandatory forfeiture provisions,[4] which may significantly affect legitimate businesses.[5] Third, the statute enables the government to employ the broad-reaching mail and wire fraud statutes as the basis for a "racketeering" case. For these reasons and others discussed below, the RICO statute highlights the significant power wielded by prosecutors in deciding whether and how to charge a white collar criminal case.[6]

The controversy over RICO can be traced to the troubled history surrounding its passage. Congress enacted RICO in 1970 as part of the Organized Crime Control Act.[7] The original purpose behind the statute is the matter of some dispute. There is evidence in the legislative history that RICO was intended to

---

[1] 18 U.S.C. §§ 1961–64 (1994).

[2] One commentator has even labeled RICO as "[o]ne of the most controversial statutes in the federal criminal code." Gerald E. Lynch, RICO: *The Crime of Being a Criminal Parts I & II*, 87 Colum. L. Rev. 661, 661 (1987). The use of RICO in prosecutions relating to the 1980s Wall Street scandals produced much critical commentary and ultimately led to congressional hearings. *See* L. Gordon Crovitz, *How the RICO Monster Mauled Wall Street*, 65 Notre Dame L. Rev. 1050, 1065 (1990).

[3] Criminal penalties include imprisonment of up to twenty years ("or for life if the violation is based on a racketeering activity for which the maximum penalty includes life imprisonment"), 18 U.S.C. § 1963, and fines, 18 U.S.C. § 3571(b), (c), or up to double the profits or proceeds of a RICO offense. 18 U.S.C. § 1963(a)(3).

[4] *See generally* Chapter 22, Forfeitures, *infra*.

[5] *See* Crovitz, *supra* note 2, at 1060 (discussing United States v. Regan, 937 F.2d 823 (2d Cir. 1991), *modified*, 946 F.2d 188 (2d Cir. 1991)). As used here, a "legitimate" business is one that is not primarily a criminal endeavor. Thus, a business controlled by organized crime as a front for illegal activity is not a "legitimate" business under this definition.

[6] *See generally* Barry Tarlow, RICO: *The New Darling of the Prosecutor's Nursery*, 49 Fordham L. Rev. 165 (1980).

[7] *See* Lynch, *supra* note 2, at 664–80. In 1961, Congress enacted the Travel Act, 18 U.S.C. § 1952, which was directed at organized crime and can be seen as a forerunner of the RICO statute. *See* Perrin

address organized crime's infiltration of legitimate businesses.[8] To that end, Congress originally sought to criminalize membership in organized crime groups. Such a proscription, however, would likely have proven unconstitutional. The final version of the statute thus covers a broad array of specific forms of criminal activity that reach far beyond traditional "organized crime" activity; the statute covers repeated acts (a RICO "pattern") constituting specific crimes ("predicate acts") committed in specified ways [set forth in § 1962(a)–(d)] in connection with an identifiable entity (a RICO "enterprise").

For some commentators, Congress's original focus on organized crime shows that RICO has been stretched beyond its intended targets, and is an inappropriate vehicle for prosecuting white collar cases.[9] Others contend, however, that RICO was never intended to be limited to "organized crime" and that its use is entirely proper in white collar cases.[10]

The courts have resolved this debate in favor of a broad application of RICO. The statute has thus been applied to an array of white collar crimes including, most significantly, those based on mail and wire fraud.[11] Although the use of the RICO forfeiture provisions in white collar cases has caused controversy,[12] it is doubtful that there will be substantive limits on the RICO statute in the near future.[13] The statute's broad and imprecise language will therefore continue to prove troublesome in both civil and criminal RICO cases.

[B] Department of Justice Guidelines

Because of RICO's breadth and because the statute allows for intrusion into state criminal law enforcement, all criminal RICO cases must be approved by the Criminal Division of the Department of Justice ("DOJ") in Washington, D.C. The

---

v. United States, 444 U.S. 37 (1979) (discussing the origins of the Travel Act). The Travel Act is discussed in Chapter 9, Extortion, *supra*, § 9.08.

[8] *See* United States v. Turkette, 452 U.S. 576, 591 n.13 (1981). The government has employed RICO in a number of high-profile organized crime cases. *See, e.g.*, United States v. Bellomo, 176 F.3d 580 (2d Cir. 1999).

[9] *See* Paul Vizcarrondo, Jr., *Racketeer Influenced and Corrupt Organizations (RICO)*, *in* White Collar Crime: Business and Regulatory Offenses § 11.03 (Otto Obermaier & Robert Morvillo, eds. 2011) (citing United States v. Turkette, 452 U.S. 576, 591 (1981)).

[10] *See* G. Robert Blakey, *Foreword, Symposium: Law and the Continuing Enterprise: Perspectives on RICO*, 65 Notre Dame L. Rev. 873 (1990). *Compare* Gerard E. Lynch, *A Reply to Michael Goldsmith*, 88 Colum. L. Rev. 802, 802 (1988) ("[t]he dramatic reworking of criminal law effected by RICO was the somewhat haphazard result of a legislative process in which no member of Congress ever showed any indication of foreseeing or desiring the results actually accomplished"), *with* Michael Goldsmith, RICO and Enterprise Criminality: *A Response to Gerard E. Lynch*, 88 Colum. L. Rev. 774, 776 (1988) ("[t]he legislative history actually glitters with resolve to strike at enterprise criminality in all its forms").

[11] *See generally* Lynch, *supra* note 2.

[12] *See supra* note 5 (discussion of *Regan* case).

[13] As noted below, RICO can also be used in civil cases. There have been some limited reform efforts in the civil context. Congress took one step to limit civil RICO when it amended the statute in 1995 to require that, in a civil RICO case (but not in a criminal RICO case) under § 1964(c), securities fraud will only qualify as racketeering activity if the defendant has already been convicted of such fraud. Pub. L. No. 104-67, 109 Stat. 737 (1995), amending 18 U.S.C. § 1964(c). *See infra* § 16.06[C].

DOJ guidelines for RICO prosecutions seek to limit application of the statute by discouraging, for example, "'imaginative' prosecutions under RICO which are far afield from the congressional purpose of the RICO statute."[14] The Guidelines also seek to limit RICO's application in cases where the matter is best left to state and local law enforcement. These and other issues of prosecutorial discretion abound in RICO cases, as can be seen throughout the materials in this chapter.

[C] Civil RICO

In addition to criminal actions, RICO provides that both private parties and the government may bring civil actions. The civil and criminal cases have produced a wealth of rules, many of which are designed to limit private plaintiffs' ability to transform ordinary state law business disputes into federal RICO cases. These rules apply in civil and criminal cases, and make a RICO case potentially enormously complicated. This chapter reviews both the statute itself and the myriad of legal issues that can arise in a RICO civil or criminal case.[15]

§ 16.02   THE STRUCTURE OF THE RICO STATUTE

[A] Introduction

On its face, the RICO statute is straightforward. The statute is unusual, however, because it does not itself create any new underlying crime. Rather, RICO criminalizes repeated "predicate acts," defined to include specified existing state and federal crimes. Thus, RICO itself has no separate mens rea requirement. To gain a conviction, the government or private plaintiff[16] must only prove that the elements of the predicate acts (including, of course, the requisite mens rea) existed, and that the structural requirements of RICO are otherwise met.[17]

Another unusual feature of RICO is its express provision that the statute is to "be liberally construed to effectuate its remedial purposes."[18] This directive runs contrary to the traditional rule of lenity, which requires that courts read ambiguous criminal statutes in favor of the defendant.[19] Accordingly, and as seen in more detail below, the United States Supreme Court has consistently rejected restrictive interpretations of RICO.

---

[14] *See* U.S. Department of Justice, United States Attorneys' Manual § 9-110.200.

[15] A majority of states has enacted what are known as "little RICO" or "baby RICO" statutes, which mirror to varying degrees the federal RICO statute.

[16] This chapter primarily discusses RICO in the context of criminal prosecutions, except in § 16.07, *infra* (discussing rules relating to civil RICO). The same rules generally apply both to criminal RICO and to civil RICO cases brought by the government or by private parties.

[17] This discussion also applies to private civil RICO plaintiffs. These cases are discussed more fully *infra*, § 16.07.

[18] Pub. L. No. 91-452, § 904(a), 84 Stat. 922 (1970).

[19] *See, e.g.*, Busic v. United States, 446 U.S. 398, 406 (1980); Adamo Wrecking Co. v. United States, 434 U.S. 275, 285 (1978); United States v. Bass, 404 U.S. 336, 348 (1971).

[B]   Elements and Penalties

Courts have articulated RICO's elements in different ways, but they are the same regardless of the order in which the elements are listed or the precise language used to describe them. In any substantive RICO case under §§ 1962(a)–(c), the government must prove the following elements as set forth in § 1962:

1.   A RICO enterprise existed;

2.   The defendant(s) committed two or more predicate acts (the "racketeering activity");

3.   The commission of the predicate acts constituted a "pattern" of racketeering activity;

4.   The defendant(s):

     a.   invested in an enterprise through the pattern of racketeering activity;

     b.   acquired an interest in or maintained control over an enterprise through the pattern of racketeering activity; and/or

     c.   conducted the affairs of an enterprise through the pattern of racketeering activity; and

5.   The racketeering activity affected interstate commerce.

The following sections focus on the case law that interprets and defines the key components of RICO: the RICO theory, the enterprise, the predicate acts, and the pattern of racketeering activity.

As noted above, the repercussions of criminal or civil RICO liability are severe. In a criminal case, the defendant is subject to fines and/or imprisoned for up to twenty years, and to mandatory asset forfeiture. In addition, the defendant is subject to punishment for each of the predicate acts of which the defendant is convicted.[20]

In a civil RICO case, a successful plaintiff is entitled to recover treble damages, costs of filing the lawsuit, and reasonable attorney's fees.[21] The statute also authorizes the district court to order a wide range of equitable relief.[22]

§ 16.03   DEFINING THE RICO "THEORY"

As seen from the fourth element above, depending on the facts of the case, the government can bring a case under any or all of Subsections 1962(a), (b), or (c), which are often referred to as the "substantive" RICO theories. In addition or instead, the government may charge a defendant under Subsection (d), based upon

---

[20] 18 U.S.C. § 1963(a). As always, the actual punishment imposed will depend upon the application of the Federal Sentencing Guidelines to the case. *See* Chapter 21, Sentencing, *infra.*

[21] 18 U.S.C. § 1964(c).

[22] 18 U.S.C. § 1964(a).

the theory that the defendant conspired to violate Subsections (a), (b), and/or (c).

[A]   Subsection 1962(a)

Subsection 1962(a) prohibits any person from taking any income derived from a pattern of racketeering activity and using or investing that income in an enterprise. In the simplest terms, Subsection (a) criminalizes the use of racketeering activity to invest in an enterprise. In a typical case, a defendant uses racketeering activity to obtain money to invest in a legitimate business.

The government has used this RICO theory in many cases. In *United States v. Zang*,[23] for example, the government alleged that the defendants mislabeled low grade crude oil as high grade crude oil, and fraudulently sold the oil for a profit of approximately 7.5 million dollars. The government's theory was that the defendants used these profits to invest in a company the defendants had established, which was the "enterprise."[24] The Tenth Circuit found that these facts supported a charge under § 1962(a). Similarly, in *United States v. Robertson*,[25] the defendant was convicted of violating § 1962(a) by investing proceeds from narcotics offenses in an Alaskan gold mine, the "enterprise."

Private plaintiffs may also employ Subsection 1962(a). For example, in *Masi v. Ford City Bank and Trust Co.*,[26] the plaintiff alleged that the defendant bank was an enterprise that had defrauded the plaintiff and had reinvested the fraud proceeds in the enterprise.

[B]   Subsection 1962(b)

Subsection 1962(b) prohibits any person from acquiring or maintaining control of an enterprise through a pattern of racketeering activity. This is probably the least frequently used provision of § 1962. In a typical case under this subsection, a defendant has used the racketeering activity to infiltrate or take control of a business or other entity.

For example, the government has used this section in its attempts to ferret out organized crime's infiltration of labor organizations. In *United States v. Local 560 of the International Brotherhood of Teamsters*,[27] the government's theory under § 1962(b) was that the defendants were "members of an ongoing criminal confederation" known as "The Provenzano Group," that had acquired an interest in, and control of, Local 560 through acts of extortion and murder.[28]

---

[23] 703 F.2d 1186 (10th Cir. 1982).

[24] *Id.* at 1195.

[25] 514 U.S. 669 (1995).

[26] 779 F.2d 397 (7th Cir. 1985).

[27] 780 F.2d 267 (3rd Cir. 1985).

[28] *Id.* at 270. For other examples, see United States v. Biasucci, 786 F.2d 504, 512–513 (2d Cir. 1986), *cert. denied*, 479 U.S. 827 (1986) (acquisition through loan sharking); United States v. Jacobson, 691 F.2d 110, 112–13 (2d Cir. 1982) (acquiring property through foreclosure of security interest on usurious loan); United States v. Parness, 503 F.2d 430, 436–39 (2d Cir. 1974), *cert. denied*, 419 U.S. 1105 (1975) (acquiring property through interference with contractual note payments).

[C] Subsection 1962(c)

Subsection 1962(c) is directed to the activities of a "person" employed by or associated with any enterprise. The subsection makes it a crime for a person to conduct or participate in the enterprise's affairs through a pattern of racketeering activity. In a typical case, the defendant is charged with using a legitimate business as the vehicle for illegal activity.

Subsection (c) is the most widely-used subsection of 1962. The subsection covers a broad range of activities. Just a few examples of such activities include health care fraud[29] bankruptcy fraud,[30] securities fraud,[31] and mail/wire fraud.[32] Many of the criminal and civil RICO cases discussed throughout this chapter were brought under Subsection (c). As discussed more fully below, this subsection raises unique issues concerning the relationship between the defendant and the enterprise.[33]

[D] Subsection 1962(d)

Recall that it is a crime to conspire to commit any federal offense under the general federal conspiracy statute, 18 U.S.C. § 371.[34] In addition, a number of federal criminal statutes, including RICO, contain their own conspiracy provisions. Thus, a defendant violates RICO itself, and not only § 371, if the defendant enters into an agreement to violate any of the three substantive subsections of § 1962. Such an agreement would subject the defendant to the penalty provisions of RICO, including forfeiture, which is not available under § 371. Section 1962(d), unlike § 371, contains no overt act requirement.[35] As with other conspiracy statutes, § 1962(d) is an inchoate offense; the defendant is liable even if the underlying predicate acts are never committed.[36]

Until 1997, there was a split among the circuits concerning the reach of RICO conspiracy liability. Some courts held that, to be liable under § 1962(d), the defendant must have personally agreed to commit a predicate act or acts. Other courts held that a defendant could be liable so long as one co-conspirator — not necessarily the defendant — agreed to commit the act(s).[37] The Supreme Court resolved this conflict in *Salinas v. United States.*[38] In that case, a federal prisoner bribed local law enforcement officials to gain unauthorized prison "contact" visits with his wife or his girlfriend. Salinas, a prison deputy, was convicted under § 1962(d) for conspiracy to violate § 1962(c) based upon the predicate acts of

---

[29] *E.g.*, United HealthCare Corporation v. American Trade Insurance Co., 88 F.3d 563 (8th Cir. 1996).

[30] *E.g.*, Handeen v. Lemaire, 112 F.3d 1339 (8th Cir. 1997).

[31] *See* United States v. Regan, 937 F.2d 823 (2d Cir. 1991), *modified*, 946 F.2d 188 (2d Cir. 1991).

[32] *See id.*

[33] *See* §§ 16.04[G], 16.05, *infra.*

[34] *See* Chapter 3, Conspiracy, *supra.*

[35] *See* Salinas v. United States, 522 U.S. 52 (1997).

[36] *Id.* at 65 (citing Callanan v. United States, 364 U.S. 587, 594 (1961)).

[37] *See* Vizcarrondo, *supra* note 9, § 11.04[5].

[38] 522 U.S. 52 (1997).

bribery. The jury, however, acquitted Salinas of the substantive RICO charge under § 1962(c).

On appeal, Salinas argued that the conspiracy conviction could not stand. Because the jury had acquitted him of the substantive RICO charge, he argued, the government had failed to prove that he had personally agreed to commit the predicate acts. The Court rejected the argument. The Court noted that conspiracy liability does not generally require that all co-conspirators agree to commit or facilitate every part of the substantive offense.[39] Rather, the essence of conspiracy is that the partners agreed to the same criminal objective.[40] The Court noted that § 1962(d) broadened the coverage of conspiracy by omitting the overt act requirement, but "it did not, at the same time, work the radical change of requiring the Government to prove each conspirator agreed that he would be the one to commit two predicate acts."[41] Because there was sufficient evidence that the defendant had agreed to violate § 1962(c), the Court affirmed the conviction.[42]

§ 16.04 THE ENTERPRISE

[A] Statutory Definition

Section 1961(4) defines "enterprise" to include "any individual, partnership, corporation, association, or other legal entity, and any union or group of individuals associated-in-fact although not a legal entity."[43] Thus, a RICO enterprise is not limited to "legal entities" such as corporations and partnerships. Section 1961(4) also defines the "association-in-fact" enterprise, which can include groupings of individual persons and/or legal entities such as corporations.[44] As is clear from the foregoing, the definition of "enterprise" is both extremely broad and somewhat imprecise. It is therefore not surprising that issues concerning the enterprise element frequently arise, and that the failure to allege an "enterprise" adequately is one of the primary reasons that trial courts dismiss RICO actions.[45]

[B] Legitimate vs. Illegitimate Enterprises

Given the confusion over RICO's purpose, defendants initially argued that the statute was designed to protect organized crime's infiltration of legitimate businesses. Under this reasoning, RICO could not be applied to entities that

---

[39] *Id.* at 63 (citing United States v. Socony-Vacuum Oil Co., 310 U.S. 150, 253–54 (1940)).

[40] *Salinas* 522 U.S. at 63–64, *citing* Pinkerton v. United States, 328 U.S. 640, 646 (1946).

[41] *Id.* at 64.

[42] Most often, RICO conspiracy is charged in conjunction with one or more of the substantive RICO provisions. Occasionally, however, the government charges RICO conspiracy alone. *See, e.g.,* United States v. Jensen, 41 F.3d 946 (5th Cir. 1994) (affirming conviction for RICO conspiracy in connection with fraudulent real estate financing scheme).

[43] 18 U.S.C. § 1961(4).

[44] *See, e.g.,* Aetna Casualty Surety Co. v. P & B Autobody, 43 F.3d 1546, 1557 (1st Cir. 1994).

[45] This is particularly true of civil RICO actions. *See* Michael Goldsmith, *Resurrecting RICO: Removing Immunity for White-Collar Crime*, 41 Harv. J. on Legis. 281, 297 (2004).

engaged only in illegal acts. The Supreme Court rejected this argument in *United States v. Turkette*.[46] In that case, the government alleged that the enterprise was "a group of individuals associated-in-fact" for the purpose of engaging in various illegal activities, including narcotics trafficking, arson, mail fraud, and bribery.[47] The defense argued that RICO does not criminalize participating in an enterprise that only performs illegal acts; that is, that RICO is limited to infiltration or attempted infiltration of *legitimate businesses*.

The Supreme Court found that neither the language nor the structure of RICO supports this restrictive reading of RICO. The Court noted that the statute defines the term "enterprise" to include "any individual, partnership, corporation, association, or other legal entity, and any union or group of individuals associated in fact although not a legal entity."[48] No restrictions are placed on the associations encompassed by this definition, which thus includes any union or group of individuals associated-in-fact.

[C]   Economic Motive

Having determined in *Turkette* that a wholly illegitimate entity can be an enterprise, the Supreme Court again interpreted the enterprise element broadly in National Organization for *Women v. Scheidler*.[49] In that case, the alleged racketeering enterprise was a coalition of anti-abortion groups, the Pro-Life Action Network (PLAN). The plaintiff alleged that the defendants violated § 1962(c) by conducting the enterprise as part of a nationwide conspiracy to shut down abortion clinics.

The trial court dismissed the RICO action. The court held that a RICO enterprise under § 1962 must have a profit-generating motive, and that the plaintiff had failed to allege such a motive. The court followed the reasoning of circuit courts that had found that the term "enterprise" itself refers to a money-making venture.[50]

On appeal from the dismissal, the Supreme Court rejected the "economic motive" requirement, and reinstated the RICO claim. The language of § 1962(c) includes enterprises whose activities "affect" interstate or foreign commerce. The Court noted that the term "affect" means "to have a detrimental influence on."[51] An enterprise can have a detrimental influence on interstate or foreign commerce without having its own profit-seeking motive. The Court also found that the use of

---

[46]   452 U.S. 576 (1981). The indictment described the enterprise as "a group of individuals associated in fact for the purpose of illegally trafficking in narcotics and other dangerous drugs, committing arsons, utilizing the United States mails to defraud insurance companies, bribing and attempting to bribe local police officers, and corruptly influencing and attempting to corruptly influence the outcome of state court proceedings." *Id.* at 579.

[47]   *Id.* at 579.

[48]   18 U.S.C. § 1961(4).

[49]   510 U.S. 249 (1994).

[50]   *See* Nat'l Org. for Women v. Scheidler, 765 F. Supp. 937 (N.D. Ill. 1991), *aff'd*, 968 F.2d 612 (7th Cir. 1992), *rev'd*, 510 U.S. 249 (1994).

[51]   *Id.* at 258, *citing* Webster's Third New International Dictionary 35 (1969).

the term "enterprise" in §§ 1962(a) and (b) does not lead to the inference than an economic motive is required in Subsection (c). Under Subsection (c), the enterprise itself is the vehicle through which the unlawful pattern of racketeering activity is committed. Under Subsection (c), the enterprise is not being acquired or invested in. Thus, "it need not have a property interest that can be acquired nor an economic motive for engaging in illegal activity; it need only be an association in fact that engages in a pattern of racketeering activity."[52]

[D]   Formal Entities as Enterprises

As noted above, under the statutory definition an enterprise can include any type of existing entity. Thus, courts have found that a broad array of entities can qualify as enterprises. For example, in *United States v. Thompson*,[53] the government alleged that the "Office of the Governor" of Tennessee was the RICO enterprise. The Sixth Circuit found that this was a proper RICO allegation, although it noted the potential for the federal encroachment upon local and state governments in such a case.[54] Similarly, in *DeFalco v. Bernas*,[55] the Second Circuit found that a town government can constitute a RICO enterprise. Other examples of entity enterprises include estates created under bankruptcy laws,[56] estates created under probate laws,[57] and various state[58] and local[59] political offices and government entities.

[E]   The "Association-in-Fact" Enterprise

[1]   Interpretations of the Statutory Definition

Apart from formal enterprises, § 1961(4) provides that an enterprise may be a "group of individuals associated in fact although not a legal entity." Defining the boundaries of "association-in-fact" enterprises has proven difficult for the courts.

Association-in-fact enterprises can come in many guises. For example, courts hold that both individual persons and entities such as corporations may come together in various configurations to form an association-in-fact enterprise.[60]

---

[52] 510 U.S. at 259. At trial after remand, the jury returned a verdict for the plaintiff. On appeal, however, the Supreme Court twice ruled that the verdict could not stand because the predicate acts of extortion had not been proven. Scheidler v. Nat'l Org. for Women, 537 U.S. 393 (2003); Scheidler v. Nat'l Org. for Women, 126 S. Ct. 1264 (2006). *See* Chapter 9, Extortion, *supra*, § 9.04. These later decisions left undisturbed the original *Scheidler* holding that a RICO enterprise need not have an economic motive.

[53] 685 F.2d 993 (6th Cir. 1982) (*en banc*).

[54] *Id.* at 1000–01.

[55] 244 F.3d 286, 307–08 (2d Cir. 2001).

[56] Handeen v. Lemaire, 112 F.3d 1339 (8th Cir. 1997).

[57] Gunther v. Dinger, 547 F. Supp. 25 (S.D.N.Y. 1982).

[58] *Thompson*, 685 F.2d 993.

[59] United States v. Long, 651 F.2d 239 (4th Cir. 1981) (state legislator's office); United States v. Frumento, 563 F.2d 1083 (3d Cir. 1977) (state tax department).

[60] *See, e.g.*, United States v. Blinder, 10 F.3d 1468, 1473 (9th Cir. 1993) (a group or union composed solely of corporations or other legal entities can constitute an association-in-fact enterprise); United

Depending on the facts of a given case, a prosecutor or plaintiff may have the option to allege either a legal entity enterprise or an association-in-fact enterprise.

The decision in *United States v. London*[61] provides an example of an association-in-fact enterprise that itself includes formal entities. In that case, the defendant operated a bar that contained a check-cashing service used to launder money. The indictment alleged an association-in-fact enterprise, composed of the bar (a corporation), and the check-cashing service (a sole proprietorship). The First Circuit found that an enterprise may include not only an association of individuals, but may also be composed of legal entities. The court reasoned that the definition of "enterprise"[62] specifically enumerates various entities, but is not meant to be an exhaustive list.

Apart from finding that an association-in-fact enterprise may include both individuals and legal entities, courts have struggled to develop clear and consistent guidelines for assessing whether an enterprise has been proven. The next section deals with this issue.[63]

[2] The Proof Required for an Association-in-Fact Enterprise

In *Boyle v. United States*,[64] the United States Supreme Court in 2009 described the proof needed for an association-in-fact enterprise. The *Boyle* defendants were members of an informal group that was responsible for a series of bank thefts in a number of states over a period of years. The group had no formal organizational structure or long-term plan or agreement. On appeal, the defense argued that the trial court erred in failing to instruct the jury that it had to find proof of an enterprise "structure" separate from proof of the predicate acts. Prior to *Boyle*, the circuits split almost evenly as to whether the proof of the enterprise requires proof of some structure that is distinct from the illegal activity itself.[65]

The Supreme Court resolved this split in *Boyle*.[66] The Court sided with those circuits that did not require proof of a structure apart from the predicate acts. The Court stated:

> From the terms of RICO, it is apparent that an association-in-fact enterprise must have at least three structural features: a purpose, relationships among those associated with the enterprise, and longevity

States v. Perholtz, 842 F.2d 343, 353 (D.C. Cir. 1988) (*per curium*) (association-in-fact enterprise composed of individuals, corporations, and partnerships).

[61] 66 F.3d 1227 (1st Cir. 1995).

[62] 18 U.S.C. § 1961(4).

[63] Indeed, many RICO cases are dismissed because of the failure adequately to plead or prove the existence of such an enterprise. *See* Goldsmith, *supra* note 45, at 297.

[64] 129 S. Ct. 2237 (2009).

[65] *See* Odom v. Microsoft Corp., 486 F.3d 541, 550 (9th Cir. 2007). Five circuits held that the proof of the enterprise need not be distinct from the proof of the illegal activity. *Id.* at 550 (citing cases). Four circuits, on the other hand, held that proof of an enterprise must include more than just proof of the predicate acts. *Id.* at 549–50 (citing cases).

[66] Boyle, 129 S. Ct. at 2245.

sufficient to permit these associates to pursue the enterprise's purpose. As we succinctly put it in *Turkette*, an association-in-fact enterprise is 'a group of persons associated together for a common purpose of engaging in a course of conduct.'[67]

The Court further stated that the enterprise element does not require proof of a structure separate and apart from the racketeering activity. The Court held that the existence of an enterprise "may be inferred from the evidence showing that persons associated with the enterprise engaged in a pattern of racketeering activity. . . . We recognized in *Turkette* that the evidence used to prove the pattern of racketeering activity and the evidence establishing an enterprise 'may in particular cases coalesce.' " The Court also stated that this element could be met without specifically requiring the jury to find a "structure."[68]

In a dissent joined by Justice Breyer, Justice Stevens argued that "Congress intended the term 'enterprise' as it is used in RICO to refer only to business-like entities that have an existence apart from the predicate acts committed by their employees or associates."[69]

After *Boyle*, prosecutors will have more leeway in constructing their theories in RICO cases. No longer will the government need to allege proof of the enterprise that is separate from the underlying criminal activity. Similarly, plaintiffs in civil RICO cases may now find it easier in many cases to plead their causes of action.

[F]   Naming the Enterprise as a Defendant

As explained more fully below, courts generally allow the enterprise to be named as the defendant under §§ 1962(a) and (b), but not under § 1962(c). Courts have found that the enterprise cannot be named as a defendant in a case brought under Subsection 1962(c) because of that section's structure.[70] Subsection (c) requires that the defendant must have been "employed by or associated with" the enterprise, and must have "conduct[ed] or participat[ed] in the enterprise's affairs through a pattern of racketeering activity."[71] This language implies that a person, who was separate from the enterprise, associated with and conducted the affairs of the enterprise. Sections 1962(a) and (b), however, do not require any sort of relationship between the person and the enterprise. Subsection (a) deals with using or investing proceeds of racketeering activity in an enterprise. Subsection (b) deals

---

[67] *Id.* at 2244 (quoting Turkette, 452 U.S. at 583).

[68] *Id.*

[69] *Id.* at 2247 (Steven, J., dissenting).

[70] Vizcarrondo, *supra* note 9, § 11.04[1]. One circuit court had held to the contrary. United States v. Hartley, 678 F.2d 961 (11th Cir. 1982). The Eleventh Circuit, however, abrogated the *Hartley* ruling in United States v. Goldin Industries, 219 F.3d 1268 (11th Cir. 2000).

[71] Section 1962(c) provides: "It shall be unlawful for any person *employed by or associated with* any enterprise engaged in, or the activities of which affect, interstate or foreign commerce, to *conduct or participate*, directly or indirectly, in the conduct of such enterprise's affairs through a pattern of racketeering activity or collection of unlawful debt." (Emphasis added.) *See* Cedric Kushner Promotions v. King, 533 U.S. 158, 161 (2001), discussed *infra* § 16.04[G][2].

with acquiring or maintaining an interest in or control of an enterprise through racketeering activity.

[1]   The Enterprise as a Defendant in Cases Brought Under Subsections 1962(a) and (b)

Courts seem to agree that there is no barrier to naming the enterprise as a defendant under § 1962(a), and presumably under § 1962(b), because the statutory language under those subsections does not imply that the enterprise and defendant be separate. The court followed this reasoning in *Masi v. Ford City Bank and Trust Co.*[72] In that case, the plaintiff had opened a retirement account with the defendant bank. The plaintiff later guaranteed a loan that the bank made to Schwartz. Schwartz defaulted on the loan, and the bank withdrew funds from the plaintiff's retirement account to recover the balance on the loan. Masi sued under § 1962(a), with mail fraud as the predicate offense. Masi named the bank as both the defendant and the enterprise. The plaintiff's theory was that the bank had used the withdrawn funds to operate its own banking enterprise. The district court held that the bank could not be both the "person" and the "enterprise" under § 1962(a).

The Seventh Circuit reversed, relying upon the analysis of *Haroco, Inc. v. American National Bank and Trust Co. of Chicago.*[73] In that case, the same court had found that the "corporation-enterprise may be held liable under subsection (a) when the corporation is also a perpetrator."[74] The court reached this conclusion based upon the language of Subsection (a), which does not suggest that the defendant and the enterprise be separate.

[2]   The Enterprise as a Defendant in Cases Brought Under Subsection 1962(c)

[a]   Distinguishing the Enterprise and the Defendant

As noted above, courts hold that the enterprise cannot be named as a defendant in cases brought under § 1962(c). The court's reasoning in *Schofield v. First Commodity Corp. of Boston*[75] is illustrative. In *Schofield*, the plaintiff alleged that a broker acting on behalf of First Commodity Corp. of Boston fraudulently induced the plaintiff and her husband to invest in commodity futures. The trial court dismissed the RICO claim, holding that the corporate enterprise could not also be liable as a defendant under § 1962(c), either directly or under principles of respondeat superior.

The First Circuit affirmed. First, the court looked to the language of § 1962(c), finding that a defendant cannot be employed by or associated with itself, and that the defendant and the enterprise must be separate. Relying upon the Seventh

---

[72]   779 F.2d 397 (7th Cir. 1985).

[73]   *Masi*, 779 F.2d at 401 (citing Haroco, Inc. v. American National Bank & Trust Co., 747 F.2d 384, 399–402 (7th Cir. 1984), *aff'd*, 469 U.S. 1157 (1985)).

[74]   *Id.* at 401(citing Haroco, 747 F.2d 384, 402 (7th Cir. 1984), *aff'd*, 469 U.S. 1157 (1985)).

[75]   793 F.2d 28 (1st Cir. 1986).

Circuit's analysis in *Haroco, Inc. v. American Nat'l Bank and Trust Co. of Chicago*,[76] the court distinguished liability under § 1962(a). Under the language of that section, a relationship between the person and the enterprise is not required, as it is in § 1962(c). Thus, there need not be two separate entities under § 1962(a).[77]

The court in *Schofield* also rejected the plaintiff's argument that the corporation could be liable for the acts of its employee under § 1962(c) based upon respondeat superior.[78] The court found that the concept of vicarious liability is inconsistent with the purpose of § 1962(c) because "Congress intended to separate the enterprise from the criminal 'person' or 'persons.'"[79]

The United States Supreme Court affirmed the "person"/"enterprise" distinction in *Cedric Kushner Promotions v. King*.[80] In that case, which is discussed more fully below, the Court stated that "[w]e do not quarrel with the basic principle that to establish liability under § 1962(c) one must allege and prove the existence of two distinct entities: (1) a 'person' and (2) an 'enterprise' that is not simply the same 'person' referred to by a different name. The statute's language, read as ordinary English, suggests that principle."[81]

[b] Sole Proprietorships as Defendants

Unique issues arise when the defendant is a sole proprietorship. Can an individual who operates as a sole proprietorship be named both as a defendant and an enterprise under § 1962(c)? This issue arose in *McCullough v. Suter*.[82] The defendant in that case was Richard Suter, a sole proprietor operating under the name of the National Investment Publishing Company ("National"). Suter gave investment advice to and purchased coins for clients, including the plaintiffs in the case. The plaintiffs alleged that Suter defrauded them, and sued under § 1962(c), naming National as the enterprise.

The Seventh Circuit found that Suter could be named as the defendant and National as the enterprise even though Suter operated National as a sole proprietorship. In this case, National was properly named as an "association-in-fact" enterprise because it had employees who could associate among themselves. Thus, Suter was an individual who was distinct from the larger enterprise. The court did note that such a theory might not be viable where a sole proprietorship were truly operated by one individual without the assistance of employees.[83]

---

[76] 747 F.2d 384 (7th Cir. 1984), *aff'd on other grounds*, 469 U.S. 1157 (1985).

[77] *Schofield*, 793 F.2d at 31.

[78] For a discussion of respondeat superior, see Chapter 2, Corporate and Individual Liability, *supra*.

[79] 793 F.2d at 32.

[80] 533 U.S. 158, 161 (2001).

[81] *Id.*

[82] 757 F.2d 142 (7th Cir. 1985).

[83] Moreover, in dictum, the court stated that if an individual were working alone and "adopted the corporate form for his activity," then § 1962(c) might cover his actions because a corporation is enumerated in § 1961(4) as an enterprise. *Suter*, 757 F.2d at 144.

[c]   Corporations as Defendants

In *Cedric Kushner Promotions v. King*,[84] the Supreme Court addressed the question whether a corporation and its controlling person are distinct for purposes of § 1962(c). In that case, the plaintiff, a promoter of boxing matches, sued Don King, the president and sole shareholder of Don King Productions, a corporation. The plaintiff claimed that King had conducted the corporation's boxing-related affairs through a pattern of racketeering activity in violation of § 1962(c). The district court dismissed the case, and the appellate court affirmed. Those courts reasoned that King was an employee and agent of the corporation, acting for the corporation. Thus, the "person" (Don King) was not distinct from the "enterprise" (the corporation).

The Supreme Court reversed. The Court found that "[t]he corporate owner/employee, a natural person, is distinct from the corporation itself, a legally different entity with different rights and responsibilities due to its different legal status. And we can find nothing in the statute that requires more 'separateness' than that."[85] That King was the sole owner did not change this result, the Court noted. The Court also reasoned that this result comported with RICO's goal of punishing the use of an enterprise as a vehicle for illegal activity.[86]

[3]   Pleading Issues Arising from the Defendant/Enterprise Distinction

In civil RICO cases, plaintiffs often have a strong incentive to name a corporate enterprise as a defendant in order to obtain treble damages from the corporate "deep pocket." Thus, in cases where it is not possible to name the enterprise as a defendant under subsection (c), a plaintiff may wish to recast the case under subsections (a) and/or (b) if the facts allow this approach.

Even under § 1962(c), it may be possible to include a corporate defendant within an association-in-fact enterprise. For example, corporation A and corporation B could be named as the enterprise; or, corporation A and individuals B and C could be named as an enterprise. Assuming that the enterprise itself were sufficiently alleged, in either example corporation A could also be a named defendant under § 1962(c). Such an approach would avoid the linguistic awkwardness of naming the enterprise as a defendant; corporation A could, logically, be associated with and conduct the affairs of a broader association-in-fact of which it was a member. This is essentially the approach that the court sanctioned in *McCullough v. Suter*,[87] where the court allowed the individual defendant/sole proprietor to be named as part of the larger association-in-fact enterprise. The court held that a sole proprietorship can be an enterprise that the proprietor can be associated with, as long as that sole proprietorship has existing employees. The court also stated that,

---

[84] 533 U.S. 158 (2001).

[85] *Id.* at 163.

[86] *Id.* at 164–65

[87] 757 F.2d 142 (7th Cir. 1985). *See generally* Vizcarrondo, *supra* note 9, § 11.04[1].

in any event, the existence of employees rendered the sole proprietorship a "group of individuals associated in fact."[88]

There are limits, however, in the degree to which courts are willing to allow creative pleading of the enterprise element. For example, in order to limit the potentially expansive definition of "enterprise," some courts have held that an employer and its employees cannot constitute an enterprise.[89] Similarly, in *Fitzgerald v. Chrysler Corp.*,[90] the Seventh Circuit held that it was not appropriate to name Chrysler and various of its subsidiaries and agents as an enterprise under § 1962(c). The court concluded that naming a corporation as the person that conducted itself and its subsidiaries was far removed from RICO's purpose of ferreting criminals out of legitimate businesses.

§ 16.05   THE "OPERATION OR MANAGEMENT" TEST UNDER § 1962(C)

Under § 1962(c)'s plain language, the government must show that the defendant "conduct[ed] or participate[ed], directly or indirectly, in the conduct of such enterprise's affairs." What does it mean for a person to "conduct or participate" in the "conduct" of the enterprise's affairs? As seen below, a defendant who had only a minor or peripheral role in the enterprise may not fall within this language, and thus may not be liable under this section.

The Supreme Court addressed the meaning of this statutory language in *Reves v. Ernst & Young*,[91] which sets forth the generally applicable test. Reves alleged that the defendant, an accounting firm, conducted and participated in the affairs of the enterprise, a farmer's cooperative. The accounting firm had served as the cooperative's outside auditor. An audit had failed to disclose the cooperative's precarious financial condition. When the cooperative later filed for bankruptcy, the bankruptcy trustee successfully sued the accounting firm on behalf of the cooperative.

On appeal, the defendant accounting firm argued that there was insufficient evidence that it had "conducted" or "participated in" the affairs of the cooperative merely by engaging in an audit. The Supreme Court agreed. The Court found that, for one "to conduct or participate, directly or indirectly, in the conduct of such enterprise's affairs," one must participate in the operation or management of the enterprise itself.[92] Although to "conduct" the affairs of an enterprise indicates some degree of direction, the Court stated that the meaning of "participate" is not as

---

[88] *Id.* at 143.

[89] *See, e.g.*, Discon, Inc. v. NYNEX Corp., 93 F.3d 1055, 1063 (2d Cir. 1996); Riverwoods Chappaqua Corp. v. Marine Midland Bank, N.A., 30 F.3d 339, 343–44 (2d Cir. 1994); but *see* Haroco, Inc. v. American Nat. Bank and Trust Co., 747 F.2d 384, 402 (7th Cir. 1984), *aff'd on other grounds*, 473 U.S. 606 (1985) (wholly owned subsidiary corporation was sufficiently distinct from its parent corporation so as to be liable under RICO); Cullen v. Margiotta, 811 F.2d 698, 730 (2d Cir. 1987) (single entity can be both RICO "person" and *one* of the multiple RICO enterprise members).

[90] 116 F.3d 225 (7th Cir. 1997).

[91] 507 U.S. 170 (1993).

[92] *Id.* at 185.

clear. The Court found that, within the context of § 1962(c), Congress appears to have delineated a meaning that is "consistent with a common understanding of the word 'participate' — 'to take part in.' "[93]

Thus, the Court held that RICO liability requires that the defendant have taken some part in directing the enterprise's affairs through the "operation or management" of the enterprise.[94] Elaborating on this test, the Court stated that "[a]n enterprise is 'operated' not just by upper management but also by lower-rung participants in the enterprise who are under the direction of upper management. An enterprise also might be 'operated' or 'managed' by others 'associated with' the enterprise who exert control over it as, for example, by bribery."[95] In order for an outside party, such as an external auditor, to be liable under § 1962(c), the outsider must have "associated with" the enterprise and must also have had some part in directing its affairs. Merely auditing an enterprise's financial statements would not suffice under this test, and the accounting firm could not be liable under § 1962(c).

The *Reves* "operation or management" test limits § 1962(c) liability somewhat, but leaves unclear the precise boundaries of such liability. For example, the Court did not delineate the degree to which mid- and low-level corporate employees may be liable.[96] Nor did the Court find that outside parties, such as lawyers and accountants, could never be liable under § 1962(c).

Courts have thus struggled to establish the outer boundaries of liability under *Reves*. The issue of the liability of outside lawyers, for example, arose in *Handeen v. Lemaire*.[97] In that case, the plaintiff alleged that Lemaire and his law firm participated in a scheme to defraud Handeen of money that Lemaire owed Handeen in a bankruptcy proceeding. The plaintiff asserted a claim under § 1962(c), arguing that Lemaire and the law firm conducted the affairs of the enterprise, the bankruptcy estate, through a pattern of racketeering activity. The law firm relied upon *Reves* to argue that simply providing professional advice did not constitute "conducting" the affairs of an enterprise.

The Eighth Circuit rejected the law firm's argument, and allowed the RICO claim against the firm to proceed to trial. The court noted that the allegations, if proven, could demonstrate that "Lemaire . . . controlled his estate in name only and relied upon the firm, with its legal acuity, to take the lead in making important decisions concerning the operation of the enterprise."[98] Thus, the plaintiff could show "that the lawyers participated in the operation or management of the estate ·by assuming at least '*some* part in directing the enterprise's affairs.' "[99] The court

---

[93] *Id.* at 179, *quoting* Webster's Third New International Dictionary 1646 (1976).

[94] 507 U.S. at 179.

[95] *Id.* at 184.

[96] *See* Napoli v. United States, 45 F.3d 680, 683 (2d Cir. 1995) (finding *Reves* test met where defendants were private investigators who were given broad discretion to carry out instructions from a law firm in scheme to fix personal injury cases). This case arose from the same set of events as did United States v. Eisen, 974 F.2d 246 (2d Cir. 1992), discussed *infra*, text at note 129.

[97] 112 F.3d 1339 (8th Cir. 1997).

[98] *Id.* at 1350.

[99] *Id.* at 1350–51, *quoting* Reves v. Ernst & Young, 507 U.S. 170, 179 (1993).

stated that the enterprise as an entity must have a common or shared purpose, but each person associating with the enterprise need not stand to gain something from that purpose. "[I]t is sufficient if a RICO defendant shared in the *general* purpose and to some extent facilitated its commission."[100]

A similar issue arose in *DeFalco v. Bernas*.[101] In that case, the court found that outside persons exercised sufficient control over a town government to meet the *Reves* test. The defendants had influenced the local government's decisions regarding services provided to the town, activity that the court found sufficient. In *United States v. Cummings*,[102] on the other hand, the Seventh Circuit found that the government's evidence failed to meet the *Reves* test. In that case, the defendants engaged in a scheme to bribe low-level workers in the state's employment agency in order to get confidential information to assist defendants in their debt collection business. The court found that this did not amount to operating or managing the agency because the bribery scheme was not designed to assert control over the agency's core functions.

In sum, it remains to be seen how the *Reves* test will be applied in different contexts. The distinction between an outside auditor, as in *Reves*, and an outside counsel involved in the affairs of a bankruptcy estate, as in *Handeen*, may be evident. There will be a substantial grey area, however, in which it is unclear whether an outside lawyer or accountant, or a mid- or low-level enterprise employee, will meet the *Reves* test. As a general matter, as shown in cases such as *DeFalco* and *Handeen*, when an outside party or low-level employee has some role in directing or making decisions for the enterprise, then the *Reves* test is met. But if the outside party has no role in directing the enterprise's core affairs, as in *Cummings*, then the test is not met.

§ 16.06 THE "RACKETEERING ACTIVITY"

[A] Introduction

As noted above, RICO incorporates specified federal and state crimes as its underlying criminal activity. Proof in a substantive RICO case under §§ 1962(a)–(c) thus requires evidence that the defendant have committed at least two of the underlying crimes, or "predicate acts," as the statute terms them.

RICO does not require a defendant to have been separately convicted of the predicate acts in order for the acts to qualify as "racketeering activity."[103] Rather, the predicate acts need only be "chargeable," "indictable," or "punishable" under

---

[100] 112 F.3d at 1351. *See also* United States v. Kragness, 830 F.2d 842, 856 (8th Cir. 1987) ("Each defendant shared the common purpose alleged in the indictment, to import, receive, conceal, buy, sell, and otherwise deal in narcotic and dangerous drugs, and each to some extent carried out this purpose"); United States v. Lemm, 680 F.2d 1193, 1199 (8th Cir. 1982), *cert. denied*, 459 U.S. 1110 (1983) ("Each appellant shared . . . the purpose of setting arson fires so as to defraud one or more insurance companies, and each carried out this purpose to some extent").

[101] 244 F.3d 286, 310–12 (2d Cir. 2001).

[102] 395 F.3d 392 (7th Cir. 2005).

[103] Note that securities fraud is an exception to this rule in civil RICO cases. *See* note 126, *infra*.

the applicable state or federal statute.[104] In a case brought under the substantive RICO provisions, the government may include as predicate acts offenses that would be barred by the statute of limitations, so long as the last predicate fell within RICO's five-year statute of limitations.[105] Nor does it violate double jeopardy for the government to bring a RICO case after the defendant has been convicted or acquitted of the predicate acts in state court,[106] or convicted of the predicate acts in federal court.[107]

[B]   State Crimes

[1]   Defining the State Law Predicates

Section 1961(1) lists ten categories of state offenses that qualify as racketeering activity. These include "any act or threat involving murder, kidnapping, gambling, arson, robbery, bribery, extortion, dealing in obscene matter, or dealing in a controlled substance or listed chemical (as defined in Section 102 of the Controlled Substances Act), which is chargeable under State law and punishable by imprisonment for more than one year." Thus, if the maximum penalty for a state crime is one year or less, that crime will not qualify as a RICO predicate.

Determining whether a state crime will qualify as a RICO predicate under § 1961(1) depends not on the title of the state crime but upon its substance. For example, in *United States v. Forsythe*,[108] the defendants were charged under RICO in connection with a bail bond agency's scheme to make payments to public officials in return for referrals to the agency. The district court dismissed the case on the ground that the state bribery statute imposed a prison term not exceeding one year, and therefore the offense did not qualify as a RICO predicate.[109] The Third Circuit

---

[104] Thus, a prior prosecution or acquittal in state court of the predicate offenses will not preclude a federal RICO case based on those offenses. See United States v. Coonan, 938 F.2d 1553, 1563 (2d Cir. 1991) (acquittal of murder in state court did not prevent federal authorities from using that same offense as predicate act in RICO prosecution); United States v. Giovanelli, 945 F.2d 479 (2d Cir. 1991) (prosecution in state court for murder and attempted murder did not prevent same offenses from being charged as predicate acts in RICO action). In a criminal case, the government will have to prove beyond a reasonable doubt that the defendant committed the predicate offenses under §§ 1962(a)–(c).

[105] See, e.g., United States v. Walsh, 700 F.2d 846, 851 (2d Cir. 1983); United States v. Cody, 722 F.2d 1052, 1056 (2d Cir. 1983); United States v. Gigante, 982 F. Supp. 140, 154–55 (E.D.N.Y. 1997). Note that a different rule may apply in a RICO conspiracy case in which conspiratorial acts (but not predicate acts) took place within the limitations period. See Unites States v. Pizzonia, 577 F.3d 455, 464 (2d Cir. 2009) (holding that "while a RICO conspiracy's existence within the statute of limitations may well be proved by evidence of predicate acts occurring within the limitations period . . . that is not the only means by which the law's temporal requirement can be satisfied").

[106] The dual sovereignty doctrine allows successive prosecutions for the same conduct in state and federal court. See, e.g., United States v. Coonan, 938 F.2d 1553, 1562 (2d Cir. 1991); United States v. Kind, 194 F.3d 900, 907 (8th Cir. 1999); United States v. Williams, 104 F.3d 213, 216 (8th Cir. 1997).

[107] See, e.g., United States v. Pungitore, 910 F.2d 1084, 1107–08 (3d Cir. 1990). Presumably principles of collateral estoppel would preclude using, as a predicate act, an offense for which the defendant had been acquitted in federal court. See generally Heath v. Alabama, 474 U.S. 82 (1985), for general double jeopardy principles.

[108] 560 F.2d 1127 (3d Cir. 1977).

[109] Id. at 1136–37.

reversed. The court found that another alleged state predicate — corrupt solicitation — carried a prison term of up to two years and was in substance a state bribery statute that qualified as a RICO predicate. The court noted that Congress intended to include generic categories of state law offenses within RICO's purview.[110] Even though the predicate offense in *Forsythe* was not labeled "bribery" in the state criminal code, it qualified because in substance it was a "bribery" statute.

Courts generally agree that it is the substance of the state law crime that controls, raising the issue of how to define the scope of the listed state law predicates. This issue arose in *United States v. Garner*.[111] The defendant in that case was convicted of RICO based upon a state gratuity statute. On appeal, he argued that "gratuity," a lesser-included offense of bribery, should not qualify as a RICO predicate because "gratuity" is not listed in the RICO statute.

The court disagreed and affirmed the conviction. Initially, the court reiterated that § 1961(1)(A) describes state crime predicate acts by substance rather than by the title of the state crime. The court conceded that the state statute in *Garner* was in substance a gratuity statute, not a bribery statute, because it did not require the proof of a quid pro quo that is required for bribery under federal law. Nonetheless, the court found that the state gratuity statute qualified as state law bribery under RICO. All crimes under the federal bribery and gratuity statute, 18 U.S.C. § 201, are federal law RICO predicate acts. The court therefore reasoned that state law "bribery" should encompass all the crimes defined by § 201, including gratuity.

[2] Determining Whether the Facts Support the State Predicate Charge

In some cases, the state statute may encompass a state law predicate such as bribery, but the facts may not show that the defendant committed bribery. This issue arose in *United States v. Genova*.[112] In that case, the defendants were convicted under RICO with mail fraud and Illinois state law bribery as the predicate acts. On appeal, the defendants argued that their acts did not constitute state law bribery. One defendant, Stack, was the local public works commissioner. He was convicted of bribing public employees based upon granting of "comp time" and overtime pay for political work the employees performed. Defendant Genova was convicted of both mail fraud and of bribery, based upon his failure to disclose kickbacks that he received.

On appeal, the court found that neither of the defendant's acts constituted "bribery" under the RICO statute. First, as to Stack, compensating public employees for political work simply does not constitute bribery under Illinois law.

---

[110] *Forsythe*, 560 F.2d at 1137. This statute provided: "Whoever, directly or indirectly, by offer or promise of money, office, appointment, employment, testimonial or other thing of value, or by threats or intimidation, endeavors to influence any member of the General Assembly, State, county, election, municipal or other public officer, in the discharge, performance, or nonperformance of any act, duty or obligation pertaining to such office, is guilty of corrupt solicitation, a misdemeanor, and on conviction thereof, shall be sentenced to pay a fine not exceeding one thousand dollars ($1,000), or to undergo imprisonment not exceeding two (2) years, or both."

[111] 837 F.2d 1404 (7th Cir. 1987).

[112] 333 F.3d 750 (7th Cir. 2003).

Second, as to Genova, the mere failure to disclose kickbacks does not involve bribery; no public official has agreed to perform an act in return for a quid pro quo. In any event, the court further held, the state statute used as the RICO predicate against Genova was not a bribery statute. The court thus reversed Stack's conviction. Even after throwing out the bribery predicates, however, the court affirmed Genova's conviction based upon the remaining predicate acts of mail fraud.

[C] Federal Crimes

Section 1961(1) enumerates dozens of federal criminal statutes in its definition of "racketeering activity." Because of their breadth, the mail and wire fraud statutes[113] are the most important listed predicate acts for purposes of white collar crime. Other enumerated federal RICO predicates frequently used in white collar cases include bribery,[114] extortion,[115] financial institution fraud,[116] obstruction of justice,[117] money laundering,[118] and securities fraud,[119] among many others.

The inclusion of the mail and wire fraud statutes as RICO predicates raises significant issues concerning both RICO's broad reach and its expansive use by prosecutors. These statutes have allowed the government to base RICO cases on other federal offenses that are specifically excluded as predicate acts. In *United States v. Regan*,[120] for example, the government converted a routine tax fraud case into a RICO case, even though tax fraud is not listed as a predicate act, by using the mailing of the federal tax returns as the principal predicate act. The Department of Justice has since issued guidelines limiting the use of tax fraud, in instances when the tax return was transmitted by means of the mail or wires, as a RICO predicate under the mail and wire fraud statutes.[121] These guidelines do not act as statutory amendments, however, and RICO on its face still encompasses tax fraud committed through the use of the mail or wires.

Likewise, the government can use the federal mail and wire fraud statutes to incorporate state offenses not listed as RICO predicates. In *United States v. Eisen*,[122] for example, the defendants were associated with a personal injury law

---

[113] 18 U.S.C. §§ 1341, 1343.

[114] 18 U.S.C. § 201.

[115] 18 U.S.C. § 1951.

[116] 18 U.S.C. § 1344.

[117] *See* 18 U.S.C. §§ 1503 (obstruction of justice), 1510 (obstruction of criminal investigations), 1511 (obstruction of State or local law enforcement), 1512 (tampering with a witness, victim, or an informant), 1513 (retaliating against a witness, victim, or an informant).

[118] 18 U.S.C. §§ 1956, 1957.

[119] Section 32(a) of the Securities Exchange Act provides criminal penalties against any person who willfully violates the Act. 15 U.S.C. § 78ff(a). Congress amended RICO in 1995 to require that, in a civil RICO case (but not in a criminal RICO case) under § 1964(c), securities fraud will only qualify as racketeering activity if the defendant has already been convicted of such fraud. Pub. L. No. 104-67, 109 Stat. 737 (1995), amending 18 U.S.C. § 1964(c). Congress enacted this change in response to lobbying from the securities industry, which complained about civil RICO's use in civil securities fraud cases.

[120] 937 F.2d 823 (2d Cir. 1991), *modified*, 946 F.2d 188 (2d Cir. 1991).

[121] *See* U.S. Department of Justice, United States Attorneys' Manual § 6-4.210 (4th ed. 1997).

[122] 974 F.2d 246 (2d Cir. 1992).

firm and were convicted under RICO in connection with a wide-ranging scheme to fix cases. As predicate acts, the government included instances of mail fraud. The alleged mail fraud was based upon the use of the mail to secure false testimony in violation of state perjury law. Although § 1961(1) does not list federal or state law perjury as a predicate act, the Second Circuit upheld this use of the mail fraud statute as a RICO predicate. Nonetheless, the court recognized the potential dangers in this expansive use of the mail fraud statute to charge underlying crimes not listed as RICO predicates. Focusing on the potential for disruption in the roles of state and federal law enforcement, the court stated:

> [W]e recognize that there is some tension between the congressional decision to include federal mail fraud as a predicate offense and to exclude perjury, whether in violation of federal or state law. That tension is illustrated by this prosecution in which the fraudulent scheme consists primarily of arranging for state court witnesses to commit perjury.

> Though the tension exists, we do not believe it places the indictment in this case beyond the purview of RICO. Congress did not wish to permit instances of federal or state court perjury as such to constitute a pattern of RICO racketeering acts. Apparently, there was an understandable reluctance to use federal criminal law as a back-stop for all state court litigation. Nevertheless, where, as here, a fraudulent scheme falls within the scope of the federal mail fraud statute and the other elements of RICO are established, use of the mail fraud offense as a RICO predicate act cannot be suspended simply because perjury is part of the means for perpetrating the fraud.[123]

As elsewhere in their interpretations of RICO in criminal cases, courts may be reluctant to engage in expansive readings of mail and wire fraud as RICO predicates,[124] but have little choice given the breadth of the statute's language.[125]

[D]   The "Pattern" Requirement

One of the elements of the substantive provisions of RICO, §§ 1962(a)–(c), is that the defendant have engaged in a "pattern of racketeering activity."[126]

Subsection 1961(5) defines this element:

> "pattern of racketeering activity" requires at least two acts of racketeering activity, one of which occurred after the effective date of this chapter and

---

[123] *Id.* at 254.

[124] *See* H.J. Inc. v. Northwestern Bell Telephone Co., 492 U.S. 229 (1989).

[125] *See infra*, notes 175–176 and accompanying text. The U.S. Attorneys' Manual emphasizes the "principle that the primary responsibility for enforcing state law rests with the state concerned." U.S. Department of Justice, United States Attorneys' Manual, § 9-110.200.

[126] An individual may also violate § 1962 through "collection of an unlawful debt," which is defined at 18 U.S.C. § 1961(6), as amended by USA PATRIOT Act of 2001, Pub. L. No. 107-56, § 813, 115 Stat. 272, 382) (2001). *See* Corey P. Argust et al., *Racketeer Influenced and Corrupt Organizations*, 47 Am. Crim. L. Rev. 961, 964 & n.26 (2010).

the last of which occurred within ten years (excluding any period of imprisonment) after the commission of a prior act of racketeering activity.

As with the enterprise element, courts have struggled to provide guidelines for defining a "pattern." The rules in this respect vary among the circuits.[127] Indeed, many RICO cases, especially civil RICO cases, fail because a "pattern" has not been adequately pleaded or proven.[128]

[1] The Supreme Court's Test

The Supreme Court first addressed the pattern requirement in *Sedima, S.P.R.L. v. Imrex Co.*[129] In that case, the Court stated in a footnote that the requirement of two acts within ten years only establishes the minimum showing required for a pattern; thus, merely alleging two predicate acts within ten years may not be sufficient.[130] Citing legislative history, the Court found that, in addition to the minimum two acts, proof of a pattern must establish "relationship plus continuity" between or among the predicate acts.[131]

Not surprisingly, this definition has befuddled many judges and litigants. The Supreme Court attempted to provide further illumination in *H.J. Inc. v. Northwestern Bell Telephone Co.*[132] In that case, the plaintiff alleged that Northwestern Bell bribed public officials over a six-year period in order to influence phone rates. The complaint alleged violations of §§ 1962(a), (b), and (c), as well as RICO conspiracy under § 1962(d). The Eighth Circuit dismissed the case on the ground that the plaintiff had failed to allege a "pattern." That court determined that commission of multiple criminal acts in furtherance of a single scheme does not meet the pattern requirement. Instead, the Eighth Circuit held, a plaintiff must allege and prove *multiple illegal schemes* rather than a single illegal scheme.

The Supreme Court rejected the Eighth Circuit's restrictive interpretation of the pattern requirement. Initially, the Court noted that § 1961(5)'s language indicates that a minimum number of predicate acts (at least two) are needed to establish a pattern, but at the same time assumes something more is needed. That additional requirement is met, the Court said, through *Sedima's* "relationship plus continuity" test.[133]

The Court defined the first requirement, that there be a "relationship" among the predicate acts, in a fairly straightforward way. A "relationship" exists among the predicate acts, the Court held, if they "have the same or similar purposes, results,

---

[127] *See* Argust et al., *supra* note 126, at 970–71, for examples of the various circuits' approaches.

[128] *See* Vizcarrondo, *supra* note 9, § 11.04[4].

[129] 473 U.S. 479 (1985).

[130] *Id.* at 496 n.14.

[131] *Id.* "The legislative history supports the view that two isolated acts of racketeering activity do not constitute a pattern. As the Senate Report explained: 'The target of [RICO] is thus not sporadic activity. The infiltration of legitimate business normally requires more than one 'racketeering activity' and the threat of continuing activity to be effective. It is this factor of continuity plus relationship which combines to produce a pattern.' S. Rep. No. 91-617, p. 158 (1969)."

[132] 492 U.S. 229 (1989).

[133] *Id.* at 239.

participants, victims, or methods of commission, or otherwise are interrelated by distinguishing characteristics and are not isolated events."[134] The Court found that the defendants' alleged acts of bribery met this test.

The second requirement, that of "continuity," has proven more vexing. The Court stated that continuity can be demonstrated in either of two ways. First, continuity can be demonstrated by proving a sequence of predicate acts related to each other extending over a substantial period of time, *i.e.*, more than a "few weeks or months."[135] The Court labeled this a "closed-ended" pattern. Second, even if the racketeering activity has only occurred over a short time, continuity can be demonstrated by showing an "open-ended" pattern. Such a pattern is shown where there is an implicit or explicit threat of repetition extending into the future. The threat of continuity can likewise be shown, the Court held, by demonstrating that the predicate acts were part of an entity's regular way of doing business.[136]

Under the relationship plus continuity test, a pattern does not require an allegation or proof of multiple illegal schemes. Although the existence of multiple criminal schemes may be relevant to a finding of continuity, a single scheme may meet the "relationship plus continuity" test. The Court thus reversed the Eighth Circuit's holding in the case, because the facts revealed both relationship and continuity.

Four justices concurred. In an opinion authored by Justice Scalia, the concurring justices stated that the "relationship plus continuity" test provides little guidance to lower courts and is so vague as to violate due process.[137] In an oft-quoted passage, Justice Scalia said that "the Court counsels the lower courts: 'continuity plus relationship.' This seems to me about as helpful to the conduct of their affairs as 'life is a fountain.' "[138] Although the Supreme Court has not yet addressed a due process challenge to RICO, the *Northwestern Bell* decision provides yet another example of the imprecise boundaries of white collar criminal liability.

Lower courts have struggled to give substance to the "relationship plus continuity" test, and the approaches vary among the circuits. The best way to get a handle on this difficult concept is to review the facts and holdings of some representative cases.

[2]   Application of the Continuity Requirement

Cases dismissed because of the absence of a pattern often turn on the continuity requirement. Specifically, courts often find that there is no pattern where the illegal racketeering activity related to a single scheme that occurred over a short period of time (often defined as less than one year) and did not pose a threat of repetition.

---

[134] *Id.* at 240, *quoting* 18 U.S.C. § 3575(e), repealed by Pub. L. No. 98-473, Title II, Ch. II, § 212(a)(1), 98 Stat. 1837.

[135] 492 U.S. at 242.

[136] *Id.* at 241.

[137] *Id.* at 255–56 (Scalia, J., concurring).

[138] *Id.* at 252.

For example, in *Kehr Packages v. Fidelcor, Inc.*,[139] the Third Circuit found that there was no pattern in an alleged mail fraud scheme. In that case, the plaintiffs alleged that the defendants, a bank (Fidelity) and three of its employees, had entered into a mail fraud scheme. The scheme involved Fidelity's agreement to provide Kehr Packages, Inc. (Kehr), with financing, along with false representations that Fidelity would later lend Kehr additional working capital. The alleged goal of the mail fraud scheme was to force Kehr into bankruptcy by not providing the promised additional financing.

In a split decision, the Third Circuit affirmed the trial court's dismissal of plaintiff's claim under § 1962(c)[140] on the ground that the alleged racketeering acts did not constitute a pattern. Initially, the appeals court set forth specific factors relevant to the pattern analysis, *i.e.*, "the number of unlawful acts, the length of time over which the acts were committed, the similarity of victims, the number of perpetrators, and the character of the unlawful activity."[141] In applying these factors, the majority focused on the nature of the overall scheme rather than on the number of specific instances of mail and wire fraud.[142] The court found that the scheme entailed misrepresentations made over an eight-month period, and concluded that there was neither a closed-ended nor an open-ended pattern: "[T]he allegations here involve a short-term attempt to force a single entity into bankruptcy, and contain no additional threat of continued activity."[143]

Similarly, in *Word of Faith World Outreach Center Church Inc. v. Sawyer*,[144] the Fifth Circuit found there was no pattern because the plaintiff alleged a single, short-lived illegal scheme with no threat of repetition. In that case, *Prime Time Live*, an American Broadcasting Company television news program, broadcasted a report that criticized the fund-raising practices of Reverend Robert Tilton, a televangelist. ABC aired two subsequent broadcasts — an update of the original broadcast, and a rebroadcast of the original program. After the broadcasts, church membership and financial contributions significantly declined. The church sued ABC and individual defendants under RICO, alleging that through a pattern of racketeering acts the defendants sought to put the church out of business.

The district court dismissed the suit for failure to plead a pattern of racketeering activity, and the Fifth Circuit affirmed. The appeals court held that, where the alleged RICO predicate acts are part of a single, otherwise lawful transaction, the continuity prong of the pattern requirement has not been shown.[145] Here, the alleged predicate acts occurred when *Prime Time Live* produced and aired the broadcasts. These acts were part of a television news report, a single and lawful

---

[139] 926 F.2d 1406 (3d Cir. 1991).

[140] The court also affirmed dismissal of claims under §§ 1962(a) and (b) because the complaint did not allege a cause of action under those sections. *Id.* at 1411.

[141] *Id.* at 1412–13, *quoting* Barticheck v. Fidelity Union Bank/First National State, 832 F.2d 36, 39 (3d Cir. 1987).

[142] *Kehr Packages*, 926 F.2d at 1413.

[143] *Id.* at 1417.

[144] 90 F.3d 118 (5th Cir. 1996).

[145] *Id.* at 123.

transaction, and did not satisfy the continuity component of the pattern requirement.

Where there is a threat of repetition in the future, however, courts have found that the continuity requirement is met even where a scheme has existed only for a short time. For example, in *Libertad v. Welch*,[146] a group of individuals and organizations sued anti-abortion activists and organizations under RICO §§ 1962(c) and (d), alleging multiple acts of extortion as the predicate acts. The defendants had staged five anti-abortion demonstrations at women's health clinics in Puerto Rico between September 26, 1992 and January 8, 1993, during which they allegedly blockaded access to clinics, defaced the clinics' property, and harassed patients and staff. The trial court granted summary judgment to the defendants, holding that the plaintiffs had not alleged sufficient facts to show a pattern of racketeering activity.

The First Circuit reversed. The court acknowledged that a closed-ended pattern had not existed because of the short duration of the illegal acts.[147] The court went on to state, however, that the continuity requirement can also be met by establishing "a realistic prospect of continuity over an open-ended period yet to come."[148] The plaintiffs presented evidence that the predicate acts employed were part of the regular way the defendants conducted their activities. Thus, the allegations met the continuity prong of the pattern requirement.[149]

Courts also find that a pattern may be shown even if the racketeering activity is directed to a single victim. In *Uniroyal Goodrich Tire Co. v. Mutual Trading Corp.*,[150] Mutual Trading Corporation (MTC) engaged in an elaborate scheme to defraud plaintiff Uniroyal. For example, MTC purchased tires from Uniroyal to be resold in Saudi Arabia. MTC then requested that Uniroyal reimburse it for payments that MTC fraudulently stated it made to purchasers of defective tires. Other schemes included submission of invoices for inflated advertising costs, a fraudulent bookkeeping scheme, and fraudulent billing. Uniroyal successfully sued MTC under RICO.

On appeal, MTC argued that Uniroyal had not proven a pattern of racketeering activity because the scheme involved only a single victim. The Seventh Circuit rejected the defendant's argument. The appeals court stated that the existence of only one victim does not necessarily "preclude the existence of a pattern of racketeering activity."[151] For example, in *Liquid Air Corp. v. Rogers*,[152] the court found a pattern of racketeering activity where one victim was repeatedly injured

---

[146] 53 F.3d 428 (1st Cir. 1995).

[147] *Id.* at 445 (citing Feinstein v. Resolution Trust Corp., 942 F.2d 34, 45–46 (1st Cir. 1991)).

[148] 53 F.3d at 445, *quoting* Feinstein v. Resolution Trust Corp., 942 F.2d 34, 45 (1st Cir. 1991). This RICO theory could not survive today because the Supreme Court later held that the alleged predicate acts of extortion are not proven on these facts. *See* Scheidler v. Nat'l Org. for Women, 537 U.S. 393 (2003); Scheidler v. Nat'l Org. for Women, 126 S. Ct. 1264 (2006); discussed in Chapter 9, Extortion, *supra*, § 9.04.

[149] For a similar result, see Ikuno v. Yip, 912 F.2d 306, 309 (9th Cir. 1990) (reversing dismissal of complaint and finding that a pattern could be based upon the defendant's filing of two false annual reports because the activity threatened to continue into the future).

[150] 63 F.3d 516 (7th Cir. 1995).

[151] *Id.* at 523.

through several instances of false billing, each false billing inflicting an injury that was "separate and independent of the previous and succeeding instances of false billing."[153] "[T]he repeated infliction of economic injury upon a single victim of a single scheme is sufficient to establish a pattern of racketeering activity for purposes of civil RICO," the court stated.[154] In this case, there were numerous predicate acts spread out over several years involving several different schemes that were intended to defraud the plaintiff. Each scheme led to a distinct injury, and a "pattern" of racketeering activity was shown.

In sum, courts are likely to find that the pattern requirement is not met where the alleged predicate acts extended over a relatively short and finite period, often defined as less than one year. Where, however, the alleged predicate acts either extended over a long period of time, as in *Northwestern Bell*, or threatened to extend into the future, as in *Welch*, a court is likely to find a sufficient allegation of a pattern.

[3] Application of the Relatedness Requirement

As noted above, it is generally much easier to prove that the racketeering acts were related than it is to prove that they were continuous. Thus, most cases that fail for lack of a pattern do not turn on the relatedness requirement. There are exceptions, however. For example, in *Vild v. Visconsi*,[155] the plaintiff alleged that the defendants induced him into signing a marketing agreement for a Florida real estate venture through the predicate acts of mail fraud, wire fraud, and extortion.[156] The plaintiff's RICO claim also alleged that the defendants continued to commit wire and mail fraud by soliciting customers for the defendants' real estate venture in violation of the laws of Ohio, Indiana, and Florida.

The district court dismissed the RICO case for failure to allege a pattern, and the Sixth Circuit affirmed. The appeals court noted that under *Northwestern Bell* the relationship prong of the pattern requirement may be satisfied if the predicate acts "have the same or similar purposes, results, participants, victims, or methods of commission, or otherwise are interrelated by distinguishing characteristics and are not isolated events."[157] The court then found that plaintiff had alleged two types of predicate acts, one directed at the plaintiff and the other directed at the ultimate purchasers of the real estate. The court concluded, "Even if the predicates within each of the two types of conduct may be somehow interrelated, the two types of alleged conduct are not related within the meaning of RICO"[158] because they had "distinct and dissimilar 'purposes, results, participants, victims, or methods of

---

[152] 834 F.2d 1297 (7th Cir. 1987).

[153] *Uniroyal*, 63 F.3d at 524, *discussing* Liquid Air Corp. v. Rogers, 834 F.2d 1297, 1305 (7th Cir. 1987).

[154] *Id.*

[155] 956 F.2d 560 (6th Cir. 1992).

[156] *Id.* at 563.

[157] *Id.* at 566, *quoting* H.J. Inc. v. Northwestern Bell Telephone Co., 492 U.S. 229, 240 (1989).

[158] *Vild*, 956 F.2d at 566.

commission.' "[159] Because neither of the separate schemes, standing alone, met the continuity prong of *Northwestern Bell's* pattern test, and because the two unrelated schemes could not be combined to show continuity, the action was properly dismissed.

[4] Summary of the Pattern Requirement

The circuit courts have not provided a clear, consistent method by which to apply the *Northwestern Bell* test. This is not surprising given that test's inherent ambiguity.[160] As a general matter, to determine whether the predicate acts are related, courts examine the acts for similar purposes, participants, victims, results, and methods of commission. To determine whether continuity prong is met, for closed-ended patterns most courts will find that proof is insufficient if the racketeering activity lasted for less than one year.[161] For an open-ended pattern, courts will examine whether there appears to be a real threat of ongoing activity, as in *Libertad v. Welch.* Beyond these generalities, the pattern analysis will be very case- and fact-specific.

§ 16.07 ISSUES UNIQUE TO CIVIL RICO

Both a private party and the government may bring a civil RICO action.[162] Much of the controversy over RICO has resulted from its wide-spread use by private plaintiffs, which has been prompted at least in part by civil RICO's provision for the award of treble damages and attorneys' fees and costs to successful plaintiffs.[163] Indeed, one study found that 78 percent of all RICO cases are civil cases.[164] There is an inevitable tension between Congress's stated admonition that the statute be broadly interpreted,[165] and the desire of federal courts to prevent federal subject matter jurisdiction from being asserted via RICO in run-of-the-mill state law

---

[159] *Id., quoting* H.J. Inc. v. Northwestern Bell Telephone Co., 492 U.S. 229, 240 (1989).

[160] For an examination of the various circuits' approaches, see Argust et al., *supra* note 126, at 968–71.

[161] *See, e.g.,* Hindes v. Castle, 937 F.2d 868, 873 (3d Cir. 1991) (a closed eight-month period of mail fraud is not sufficient enough to constitute a pattern); Johnston v. Wilbourn, 760 F. Supp. 578 (S.D. Miss. 1991) (failure to prove a pattern where, over nine-month period, bank directors purchased shares of the bank from individuals in order to gain majority control of the bank but failed to disclose their plans to merge the bank with another bank; courts uniformly hold that one-year period is minimum to establish pattern). Note, however, that courts are not consistent in applying the one-year rule. *Compare* Religious Technology Center v. Wollersheim, 971 F.2d 364, 367 (9th Cir. 1992) (" pattern of activity lasting only a few months does not reflect the 'long term criminal conduct' to which RICO was intended to apply"), *with* Allwaste, Inc. v. Hecht, 65 F.3d 1523, 1528 (9th Cir. 1995) (declining to adopt the one-year bright line rule).

[162] It is unclear whether a state may bring a civil RICO action. *See* Jennifer C. Jaff, *Goliath as Victim: Can the State Bring a Civil Action Under RICO?*, 3 Quinnipiac Health L.J. 5 (1999-2000) (citing what is described as the first civil RICO action brought by a state and arguing that a state and its agencies are "persons" who may bring civil RICO actions).

[163] 18 U.S.C. § 1964. Civil RICO also provides for equitable relief, although it is unclear whether this remedy is only available in civil RICO suits brought by the government. *See* Vizcarrondo, *supra* note 9, § 11.07[2] at n.11.

[164] Pamela H. Bucy, *Private Justice*, 76 S. Cal. L. Rev. 1, 22 (2002).

[165] Pub. L. No. 91-452, § 904(a), 84 Stat. 922 (1970).

business disputes. Courts have held that the burden of proof in civil RICO cases is preponderance of the evidence,[166] instead of beyond a reasonable doubt as required in criminal cases. Nonetheless, a substantial majority of civil RICO cases are resolved in favor of the defendants prior to trial.[167]

[A]   RICO Actions Brought by Private Plaintiffs

[1]   Attempts to Limit Civil RICO: The *Sedima* Decision

Courts have taken many routes in their attempts to limit the reach of RICO in civil cases. In *Sedima, S.P.R.L. v. Imrex Co., Inc.*,[168] the Supreme Court confronted two substantial restrictions that lower courts had placed on civil RICO liability — requirements of prior convictions for RICO predicates, and of "racketeering" injury separate from the injury resulting from the predicate acts.

The *Sedima* facts presented the sort of relatively ordinary business dispute that may spawn a civil RICO case. In 1979, Sedima entered into a joint venture with Imrex Co. to provide a foreign firm with electronic components. Under the terms of the venture, Sedima obtained the orders for the parts, and Imrex obtained the parts in the United States and shipped them to the foreign firm. In its suit, Sedima alleged that Imrex had defrauded Sedima of sale proceeds by presenting inflated bills to Sedima. Sedima's complaint set forth causes of action under both §§ 1962(c) and (d), with mail and wire fraud as the predicate acts.

The trial court dismissed the action on the ground that the plaintiff had failed to allege a "RICO-type injury," defined as a showing of either a "racketeering enterprise injury" or a "competitive injury."[169] The Second Circuit affirmed, finding the complaint defective in two ways: (1) it failed to allege an injury "by reason of" a § 1962 violation; and (2) it failed to allege that the defendants had been criminally convicted either of the predicate acts or of a RICO violation.[170]

The Supreme Court rejected both grounds for dismissal, and reinstated the action. First, the Court found that the statute's plain language does not require a prior conviction. Section 1964(c) provides that "[a]ny person injured in his business or property by reason of a violation of § 1962 of this chapter may sue therefor." The Court found that the use of the word "violation" in this section indicates "a failure

---

[166] *See, e.g.*, United States v. Local 560, International Brotherhood of Teamsters, 780 F.2d 267, 279 n.12 (3d Cir. 1985). *See also* Sedima, S.P.R.L. v. Imrex Co., 473 U.S. 479, 491 (1985) (suggesting in dictum that preponderance is the appropriate burden of proof).

[167] *See* Bucy, *supra* note 174, at 22 (study of RICO cases for a two-year period showed that some 70 percent of the civil RICO cases were resolved for the defendants prior to trial). One commentator has sharply criticized federal courts' heightened pleading requirements in civil RICO cases, and has argued that these requirements have made it more difficult to use civil RICO in the corporate accounting scandal cases. *See* Michael Goldsmith, *Resurrecting RICO: Removing Immunity for White-Collar Crime*, 41 Harv. J. on Legis. 281 (2004).

[168] 473 U.S. 479 (1985).

[169] *Id.* at 484.

[170] *Id.* at 484–85.

to adhere to legal requirements"[171] and "does not imply a criminal conviction."[172] Further, the Court found that, because the civil RICO provision is partly "designed to fill prosecutorial gaps,"[173] imposition of a prior-conviction requirement would undercut the statute's purpose.

The Court also held that a rule requiring "racketeering injury" separate from the injury caused by the predicate acts alone is unsupported by the statute's language. The Court noted that "§ 1964(c) authorizes a private suit by '[a]ny person injured in his business or property by reason of a violation of § 1962.' "[174] Therefore, "[i]f the defendant engages in a pattern of racketeering activity in a manner forbidden by these provisions, and the racketeering activities injure the plaintiff in his business or property, the plaintiff has a claim under § 1964(c)."[175] Thus, a plaintiff need not plead or prove separate "racketeering" injury.

[2] Standing

The United States Supreme Court has issued a series of decisions concerning plaintiffs' standing in civil RICO cases. In *Holmes v. Securities Investor Protection Corp.*,[176] the Court in 1992 set forth the standard for establishing standing. In that case, Securities Investor Protection Corp. (SIPC) alleged that Holmes defrauded SIPC under the securities laws. SIPC is a non-profit corporation of which most securities brokers and dealers are members. In certain circumstances, SIPC is financially responsible for paying claims filed by or on behalf of customers of member broker/dealers.[177]

In its RICO claim, SIPC alleged that the defendants illegally manipulated stock prices, and that as a result member broker/dealers were unable to meet their obligations to customers. Among the injured customers were those who had not bought or sold the manipulated securities, but who were injured because of the illegal scheme's effect upon their broker/dealers. Thus, SIPC was obliged to pay claims to reimburse those customers for their losses.

The trial court entered summary judgment for the defendants. The court found that SIPC did not have standing to seek damages under RICO because (a) it was not a "purchaser-seller" of a security (as required for liability under the predicate acts of securities fraud), and (b) SIPC had not shown that its damages were proximately caused by Holmes's actions.

Without reaching the purchaser-seller issue, the Supreme Court affirmed on the second ground. The Court stated that § 1964(c)'s language provides that "[a]ny person injured in his business or property *by reason of* a violation of § 1962 of this chapter may sue therefor." The Court then rejected a broad interpretation of

---

[171] *Id.* at 489.

[172] *See* United States v. Ward, 448 U.S. 242, 249–50, *reh'g denied*, 448 U.S. 916 (1980).

[173] *Sedima*, 473 U.S. at 493.

[174] *Id.* at 495, *quoting* 18 U.S.C. § 1964(c) (1982).

[175] 473 U.S. at 495.

[176] 503 U.S. 258 (1992).

[177] *Id.* at 261–62.

standing that would encompass any party who would not have been injured "but for" the defendant's action — a requirement SIPC presumably would have met.[178] Relying upon legislative history and courts' interpretations of analogous provisions of the antitrust laws,[179] the Court said that a showing of proximate causation, rather than "but-for" causation, is required. This test, the Court noted, demands "some direct relation between the injury asserted and the injurious conduct alleged."[180] In this case, the alleged injury was too far removed from the securities fraud to sustain a RICO action.[181] Specifically, Holmes's actions did not proximately cause the damages suffered by non-purchasing customers on whose behalf SIPC sued, and SIPC had no other basis for seeking damages.[182] Many civil RICO actions turn upon whether the plaintiff is able to establish standing under the *Holmes* test.[183]

In its next important RICO standing case, the Supreme Court in 2000 held in *Beck v. Prupis* that a plaintiff may sue under the RICO conspiracy section only if the alleged injury resulted from an act that is "an act of racketeering or otherwise unlawful under the [RICO] statute."[184] Thus, a plaintiff could not recover in a case where the plaintiff alleged injury from an overt act that, while in furtherance of a RICO conspiracy, did not itself violate the statute.[185]

In *Anza v. Ideal Steel Supply Corp.*,[186] the Supreme Court in 2006 once again found that the plaintiff lacked standing. In that case, Ideal Steel brought a RICO action against Anza, a business competitor. Ideal Steel alleged that Anza committed mail and wire fraud by filing false state tax returns that failed to disclose that Anza was not requiring cash-paying customers to pay state sales tax. According to the complaint, Anza's practice allowed it to charge lower prices, thus damaging Ideal Steel, in violation of § 1962(c). The Supreme Court held that these allegations did not meet the *Holmes'* proximate cause requirement. New York State was deprived

---

[178] *Id.* at 268.

[179] Section 4 of the Clayton Act, 15 U.S.C. § 15 (1988).

[180] *Holmes*, 503 U.S. at 268.

[181] *Id.* at 271 (the harm to the plaintiff was entirely contingent on a harm sustained by the plaintiff's broker-dealers; it was only the intervening insolvency of the broker-dealers that "connects the conspirator's acts to the losses suffered by the nonpurchasing customers and general creditors").

[182] *Id.* at 271. The *Holmes* facts would not give rise to a civil RICO action today. As noted above, *supra*, note 119, Congress has amended the civil RICO statute to provide that securities fraud will not qualify as a predicate act unless the defendant has already been convicted of such fraud.

[183] *See* Goldsmith, *supra* note 45, at 288 n.41. For broad applications of the *Holmes* RICO standing rule, see Diaz v. Gates, 420 F.3d 897, 898–900 (9th Cir. 2005) (en banc) (false imprisonment that caused the victim to lose employment and employment opportunities was an injury to "business or property" sufficient to confer standing under RICO); Commer. Cleaning Servs. v. Colin Servs. Sys., 271 F.3d 374 (2d Cir. 2001) (plaintiffs, cleaning service companies, had standing to sue competitor who allegedly engaged in RICO conspiracy to hire undocumented workers thereby undercutting the plaintiffs in competitive bidding for cleaning services contracts); Mid Atl. Telecom, Inc. v. Long Distance Servs., 18 F.3d 260, 263 (4th Cir. 1994) (telecommunications company had standing to sue competitor for using fraudulent scheme to create artificially low rates).

[184] 529 U.S. 494 (2000).

[185] *Id.*

[186] 547 U.S. 451 (2006).

of tax revenue and was the party directly injured by the defendant's actions.[187]

In *Bridge v. Phoenix Bond and Indem. Co.*,[188] on the other hand, the Court in 2008 held that the plaintiffs had standing even though they were not the parties deceived by the defendants' mail fraud scheme that formed the basis of the RICO plaintiffs' RICO claims. The *Bridge* plaintiffs alleged in a civil RICO action that the defendants had rigged the bidding during a local government's auctions of valuable assets. The defendants had used the mails as part of a scheme to deceive the local government. The plaintiffs alleged that the scheme injured them by denying them the opportunity to buy the assets at the auctions.

The Supreme Court distinguished *Anza*, and held that the plaintiffs had standing. First, the plaintiffs were not required to show that they themselves had relied upon the defendants' misrepresentations; it was enough that the mails were used in furtherance of the scheme. Second, unlike *Anza*, here the plaintiffs alleged that the lost opportunity to profit from the auctions proximately caused their injuries.

In 2010, the Court returned to a narrow application of civil RICO's causation requirement in *Hemi Group LLC v. City of New York*.[189] In that case, New York City alleged that an out-of-state cigarette vendor failed to file required reports with New York State, causing the city to lose tax revenues. Writing for a four-member plurality, Chief Justice Roberts applied the *Holmes* proximate cause test and concluded that the City's injury was not a sufficiently direct product of the failure to file the reports.[190] According to Chief Justice Roberts, the fraud in not filing the required reports was committed against the state, not the city. The opinion concluded that "[w]e have never before stretched the causal chain of a RICO violation so far, and we decline to do so today."[191]

Taken together, these cases indicate that the causation requirement in civil RICO cases will limit such cases to situations where sufficiently direct harm is alleged. In *Holmes*, *Anza*, and *Hemi Group*, the losses were too attenuated from the defendants' alleged wrongdoing. In *Phoenix Bond*, on the other hand, the defendant's bid rigging scheme directly produced the competitors' losses.

[B]   Civil RICO Actions Brought by the Government

The government also has the right to bring a civil RICO suit seeking equitable relief,[192] although it is unclear whether the government can sue for damages or for disgorgement of profits.[193] The broad equitable relief provisions are designed to

---

[187] *Id.* at 458–59.

[188] 553 U.S. 639, 647 (2008).

[189] 130 S. Ct. 983 (2010).

[190] *Id.*

[191] *Id.* at 985.

[192] *See* 18 U.S.C. §§ 1964(a), (b); *Vizcarrondo, supra* note 9, § 11.07.

[193] *See, e.g.*, United States v. Philip Morris USA, Inc., 396 F.3d 1190, 1198–1202 (D.C. Cir. 2005) (split court held that government is not entitled to seek disgorgement of profits in civil RICO suit); United States v. Bonanno Organized Crime Family of La Cosa Nostra, 879 F.2d 20, 27 (2d Cir. 1989) (court held

provide the government with powerful tools to prevent the corruption of legitimate entities.[194] For example, in *United States v. Local 560*,[195] the government sought and obtained equitable relief intended to rid a labor union of organized crime influence.

§ 16.08 INTERSTATE COMMERCE

Under §§ 1962(a)–(c), any RICO case requires a showing that (a) the activities of the enterprise affected interstate commerce, *or* (b) the enterprise "engaged in . . . interstate or foreign commerce." The Supreme Court interpreted this requirement broadly in *United States v. Robertson*.[196] Robertson was charged with violating § 1962(a) by investing proceeds from narcotics offenses in the alleged enterprise, an Alaskan gold mine. The Ninth Circuit reversed the conviction on interstate commerce grounds, finding that the gold mine was essentially a local operation.[197]

The Supreme Court reinstated the conviction. Relying on the second part of the jurisdictional element, the Court found that an enterprise *engages* in interstate commerce when it directly produces, distributes, or acquires goods or services in interstate commerce. Because the gold mine purchased out-of-state equipment, solicited out-of-state workers, and shipped gold out-of-state, the interstate commerce requirement was met.[198] Thus, it is not difficult to meet the interstate commerce requirement in the vast majority of RICO cases.[199]

§ 16.09 STATUTE OF LIMITATIONS

In a criminal RICO case, the statute provides for a five-year limitations period that begins to run as of the last predicate act.[200] Although the civil RICO provisions do not contain a limitations period, the Supreme Court held in *Agency Holding Corp. v. Malley-Duff & Associates, Inc.*[201] that the four-year limitations period applicable to private antitrust actions under the Clayton Act also governs civil RICO

---

that the federal government does not have standing to bring a civil RICO action for treble damages because it is not a "person" within the meaning of § 1961(3)). *See generally* Vizcarrondo, *supra* note 9, § 11.07 (summarizing cases).

[194] *See* Russello v. United States, 464 U.S. 16, 26 (1983) ("The legislative history clearly demonstrates that the RICO statute was intended to provide new weapons of unprecedented scope for an assault upon organized crime and its economic roots").

[195] 780 F.2d 267 (3d Cir. 1985). *See also* United States v. Ianniello, 824 F.2d 203 (2d Cir. 1987).

[196] 514 U.S. 669 (1995).

[197] 15 F.3d 862, 868 (9th Cir. 1994), *rev'd*, 514 U.S. 669 (1995).

[198] *Robertson*, 514 U.S. at 671–72.

[199] This is true even though the Supreme Court has begun to limit federal authority where an "affect on" interstate commerce is the asserted jurisdictional basis. *See* United States v. Lopez, 514 U.S. 549, 558–59 (1995) (invalidating the Gun-Free School Zones Act, 18 U.S.C. § 922(q), and stating that "Congress' commerce authority includes the power to regulate those activities having a substantial relation to interstate commerce . . . ; the proper test requires an analysis of whether the regulated activity 'substantially affects' interstate commerce").

[200] *See* 18 U.S.C. § 3282.

[201] 483 U.S. 143 (1987).

actions. The circuit courts, however, have developed widely divergent approaches in determining when the civil limitations period begins to run.[202] The Supreme Court has rejected two approaches adopted by circuit courts. In *Klehr v. A.O. Smith Corp.*,[203] the Court rejected an approach that would allow the statute to begin to run upon the commission of each predicate act, finding that this approach would improperly stretch the limitations period. And in *Rotella v. Wood*,[204] the Court refused to adopt a rule that the statute would only begin to run when the plaintiff discovered, or should have discovered, both the injury and the pattern of racketeering activity, finding such an approach too lenient. The Court declined, however, to "settle upon a final rule."[205] By default, the prevailing rule in the circuit courts is that the statute begins to run when the plaintiff discovered, or should have discovered, the injury.[206]

---

[202] *See* Argust et al., *supra* note 126, at 1007–08.

[203] 521 U.S. 179 (1997).

[204] 528 U.S. 549 (2000).

[205] *Id.* at 554, n.2.

[206] *Id.* at 553; Argust et al., *supra* note 126, at 1007–08.

Chapter 17

INTERNAL INVESTIGATIONS AND COMPLIANCE PROGRAMS[1]

§ 17.01 INTRODUCTION

As noted in the earlier materials in this text,[2] in the wake of high-profile corporate accounting scandals, prosecutors continue to emphasize criminal investigations and prosecutions of corporations and other entities. Congress has also responded by enacting new laws to combat business crimes. Further, corporations and other entities may face governmental agency investigations, as well as private law suits, in addition to or instead of criminal prosecution.[3]

Thus, such entities have increasingly focused on their efforts to comply with the law. Such efforts include both developing effective compliance programs to foster adherence to the law, and launching internal investigations when there is evidence of possible wrongdoing.

This chapter focuses on such efforts, and on the difficult legal and strategic issues that they raise. The chapter builds upon the material in Chapter 2, Corporate and Individual Liability, and also provides a context for the material in Chapter 20, Civil Fines, Civil Penalties, and Parallel Proceedings.

§ 17.02 INTERNAL INVESTIGATIONS

[A] Tactical Considerations

Corporations face a number of incentives to investigate possible wrongdoing and, in some cases, to report their findings to the government. Such investigations raise important issues concerning the attorney-client privilege and the work product doctrine. Whether and how to conduct an investigation also raises a tactical question — will the corporation be better off if it declines to investigate, in the hope that any wrongdoing will go undetected? This is a risky approach, for the corporation can benefit if it cooperates fully with the government. But investigating entails risks as well, because in many cases problems will emerge that might not otherwise come to light.

---

[1] Professor Sandra D. Jordan is the co-author of this chapter.

[2] *See* Chapter 2, Corporate and Individual Liability, *supra.*

[3] *See* Chapter 20, Civil Actions, Civil Penalties, and Parallel Proceedings, *infra.*

[B] Attorney-Client Privilege and Related Issues

An evidentiary rule, the attorney-client privilege is designed to foster full communication between the client and the attorney by protecting the confidentiality of such communication. The privilege is the client's to assert. In order to do so, the person asserting the privilege must show (a) the communication related to legal advice, (b) the advice was sought from a professional legal advisor acting in that role, (c) the communication was made in confidence, and (d) the communication was by the client relating to the legal advice.[4] The privilege also extends to those, such as accountants and interpreters, retained by attorneys to assist in providing legal advice to the client.[5] Courts generally construe the privilege narrowly because the privilege restricts the information available in investigations and proceedings.[6]

In addition, the privilege will not apply if the communication was made in furtherance of an ongoing or future crime or fraud. To rely on this exception to the privilege, the government "must make a prima facie showing that (1) the client was committing or intending to commit a fraud or crime, and (2) the attorney-client communications were in furtherance of that alleged crime or fraud."[7] Communications concerning past crimes thus retain the privilege.[8]

In the context of internal investigations, legal and ethical issues arise concerning the privilege. In many instances, an attorney cannot represent the interests of both a corporation and its employees because of inherent conflicts of interest. An employee interviewed by corporate counsel may be surprised to learn later that the communication was not privileged. Counsel must therefore take care to explain exactly whom the attorney is representing.

In addition, corporations and other artificial entities do not have the right to assert the Fifth Amendment privilege.[9] Individual employees may assert that right, however. This may further hamper an attorney's ability to conduct an effective internal investigation.

---

[4] *See* United States v. Martin, 278 F.3d 988, 999 (9th Cir. 2002), *citing* 8 Wigmore, Evidence § 2292, at 554 (1961).

[5] *See, e.g.*, United States v. Kovel, 296 F.2d 918 (2d Cir. 1961) (holding that the attorney-client privilege extends to communications made by a client to an accountant retained by attorney in connection with client's obtaining legal advice from the attorney, and remanding for a determination of the circumstances under which the client's communication reached the witness).

[6] *See* Chapter 14, Currency Transaction Reporting Crimes, *supra*, § 14.04 (discussing required currency transaction reporting requirements for attorneys, and the impact of such reporting on attorney-client privilege issues).

[7] *See, e.g.*, *In re* Grand Jury Investigation, 445 F.3d 266 (3d Cir. 2006); *In re* Grand Jury Subpoena, 223 F.3d 213, 217 (3d Cir. 2000). For a case holding that the government did not meet its burden, see *In re* Sealed Case, 107 F.3d 46 (D.C. Cir. 1997) (reversing and finding that the crime-fraud exception did not apply on the facts of the case).

[8] See, e.g., *In re* Sealed Case, 107 F.3d 46 (D.C. Cir. 1997) (reversing trial court and finding the documents protected by the privilege because they related to a past crime).

[9] *See* Chapter 19, The Fifth Amendment Right Against Compelled Self-incrimination, *infra*, § 19.03[b].

When an attorney represents a corporation and interviews an employee, questions arise as to whether such an interview is protected by the privilege. The leading case is *Upjohn Co. v. United States*.[10] In that case, the government sought to obtain interview notes and other materials gathered during the company's internal investigation into possible overseas bribery. The company argued that the materials were protected by the privilege. The Court held that, in the corporate context, communications with a corporate attorney are protected when they relate to legal advice that the attorney is rendering to the company.[11] Thus, the privilege applied to this case, where the "communications at issue were made by Upjohn employees to counsel for Upjohn acting as such, at the direction of corporate superiors in order to secure legal advice from counsel."[12]

[C] The Work Product Doctrine

Closely related to the attorney-client privilege is the work product doctrine. This doctrine is designed to prevent adversaries from benefiting from an attorney's work done in anticipation of litigation. The doctrine extends to materials generated during an internal investigation, when those materials include an attorney's mental opinions and legal theories. As explained by the United States Supreme Court in *Hickman v. Taylor*,[13]

> [I]t is essential that a lawyer work with a certain degree of privacy, free from unnecessary intrusion by opposing parties and their counsel. Proper preparation of a client's case demands that [the attorney] assemble information, sift what he considers to be the relevant from the irrelevant facts, prepare his legal theories and plan his strategy without undue influence and needless interference. . . . This work is reflected, of course, in interviews, statements, memoranda, correspondence, briefs, mental impressions, personal beliefs, and countless other tangible and intangible ways — aptly . . . termed . . . the 'work product of the lawyer.' Were such materials open to opposing counsel on mere demand, much of what is now put down in writing would remain unwritten.

The work product doctrine is applied in both civil and criminal cases.[14] The doctrine is broader than the attorney-client privilege; it encompasses any documents that

---

[10] 449 U.S. 383 (1981).

[11] *Id.* at 392–93.

[12] *Id.* at 394–95.

[13] 329 U.S. 495, 510–11 (1947).

[14] Rule 26(b)(3) currently provides, in relevant part:

Ordinarily, a party may not discover documents and tangible things that are prepared in anticipation of litigation or for trial by or for another party or its representative. . . . But, subject to Rule 26(b)(4), those materials may be discovered if: (i) they are otherwise discoverable under Rule 26(b)(1); and (ii) the party shows that it has substantial need for the materials to prepare its case and cannot, without undue hardship, obtain their substantial equivalent by other means. . . . If the court orders discovery of those materials, it must protect against disclosure of the mental impressions, conclusions, opinions, or legal theories of a party's attorney or other representative concerning the litigation.

With respect to government disclosure in criminal cases, Fed. R. Crim. P. 16(a)(2) provides: "Except as

are prepared in anticipation of litigation and that contain the attorney's mental processes.

The scope of the work product doctrine is frequently the subject of litigation. One issue that arises, for example, is whether a document is protected when "it is intended to assist in the making of a business decision influenced by the likely outcome of the anticipated litigation."[15] Another issue is whether materials created for the "dual purposes" of regulatory compliance and anticipated litigation are protected by the doctrine.[16] A third issue is whether documents that a client provides to an attorney that were not created in connection with that representation fall within the doctrine.[17]

[D] Voluntary Disclosures of Documents

Both the attorney-client privilege and work product protections can be waived in certain circumstances, including instances when documents or other confidential communications are disclosed to third parties.[18] This raises serious legal and tactical issues for corporations that may be conducting internal investigations, the results of which they wish to turn over to the government in order to demonstrate their good faith and perhaps avoid civil and/or criminal charges.

This dilemma arose in the events leading up to the decision in *United States v. Bergonzi*.[19] In that case, McKesson's board of directors had authorized an internal investigation of alleged wrongdoing at the company, and retained outside counsel and accountants to assist in the investigation. The Securities and Exchange Commission and United States Attorney's Office also initiated investigations of the company. The company and the government (the SEC and the U.S. Attorney's Office) entered into confidentiality agreements. The agreements stated that the company was conducting an internal investigation and was preparing a report,

---

Rule 16(a)(1) provides otherwise, this rule does not authorize the discovery or inspection of reports, memoranda, or other internal government documents made by an attorney for the government or other government agent in connection with investigating or prosecuting the case." With respect to defense disclosure, Fed. R. Crim. P. 16(b)(2)(A) provides: "Except for scientific or medical reports, Rule 16(b)(1) does not authorize discovery or inspection of: reports, memoranda, or other documents made by the defendant, or the defendant's attorney or agent, during the case's investigation or defense."

[15] *See* United States v. Adlman, 134 F.3d 1194, 1195 (2d Cir. 1998) (holding that under the previous version of Fed. R. Civ. P. 26(b)(3) "a document created because of anticipated litigation, which tends to reveal mental impressions, conclusions, opinions or theories concerning the litigation, does not lose work-product protection merely because it is intended to assist in the making of a business decision influenced by the likely outcome of the anticipated litigation.").

[16] *See* United States v. Torf (*In re* Grand Jury Subpoena), 357 F.3d 900 (9th Cir. 2004) (holding such materials protected).

[17] *See In re* Grand Jury Subpoenas Dated March 19, 2002 and August 2, 2002 (The Mercator Corp.), 318 F.3d 379, 381 (2d Cir. 2003) (holding that parties opposing discovery failed to meet their burden to show a "real, rather than speculative, concern" that the ordered production will reveal counsel's thought processes and strategies") (citation omitted).

[18] *See, e.g., In re* Grand Jury Proceedings (Doe), 219 F.3d 175 (2d Cir. 2000) (holding that head of corporation's grand jury testimony referring to advice of counsel as validating corporation's actions did not necessarily waive corporation's attorney-client and work product privileges, and remanding for determination by the district court).

[19] 216 F.R.D. 487 (N.D. Ca. 2003).

which would be provided to the government along with back-up materials. The agreements asserted that the company had a "common interest" with the government in obtaining information contained in the report, and stated that the company was not waiving the work product protection or attorney-client privilege by providing the materials. The SEC agreed to keep the information confidential, unless disclosure was otherwise required by federal law. The agreement also stated that the U.S. Attorney's Office could use the information to prosecute the company. The SEC later advised McKesson that it intended to file charges against the company.

A grand jury subsequently returned an indictment against former McKesson executives, who then sought production of the report and back-up materials to assist in preparing their defense. McKesson objected on the grounds that the materials were protected by the attorney-client privilege and the work product doctrine. The court disagreed, and ordered the documents produced. With respect to the attorney-client privilege, the communications were disclosed to the government and therefore not made in confidence.[20]

Next, the court found that, because the report and back-up materials were prepared in anticipation of actual litigation and constituted the attorneys' mental impressions and legal analyses, the documents sought fell within the protection of the work product doctrine. Work product protection was waived, however, because McKesson disclosed the documents to adverse third parties. Although disclosure will not constitute a waiver when the parties have a common interest, that was not the case here.[21] The U.S. Attorney's Office retained the right to use the documents to bring criminal charges against the company, and the SEC had indeed indicated its intent to file civil charges. In such circumstances, the parties did not share a common interest.[22]

Similarly, in *In re Steinhardt Partners, L.P.*,[23] two companies and their principal (Steinhardt) were codefendants with several other parties in a civil class action suit. The SEC began an investigation of matters related to the suit. The SEC issued subpoenas to Steinhardt, with which he complied. Steinhardt's counsel submitted a memorandum to the SEC that addressed the facts and issues involved in the case and discussed the relevant legal theories. A notice reading "FOIA Confidential Treatment Requested" appeared on the document. There was no agreement that the SEC would maintain the confidentiality of the memorandum.

---

[20] *Id.* at 493–94.

[21] *Id.* at 495 ("The common interest privilege, frequently referred to as the joint defense privilege, applies where (1) the communication is made by separate parties in the course of a matter of common interest; (2) the communication is designed to further that effort; and (3) the privilege has not been waived. The privilege does not require a complete unity of interests among the participants, and it may apply where the parties' interests are adverse in substantial respects"). For another case analyzing the common interest privilege, see *In re* Santa Fe Int'l Corp., 272 F.3d 705 (5th Cir. 2001).

[22] *Bergonzi*, 216 F.R.D. at 497. For another waiver issue, see *In re* Grand Jury Proceedings (Doe), 219 F.3d 175 (2d Cir. 2000) (holding that a corporate officer can waive attorney-client and work-product privileges in grand jury testimony even where a corporation has refused to waive the privileges).

[23] 9 F.3d 230 (2d Cir. 1993).

During discovery in the civil case, plaintiffs requested all documents previously produced by defendants to any investigating government agency. Steinhardt declined to produce the memorandum, citing the work product doctrine. The court ordered production of the document. Once again, by voluntarily disclosing the information to an adverse party, the party asserting the doctrine had waived its protection.[24]

Finally, in *United States v. LeCroy*,[25] the defendants were employees who were charged with engaging in a scheme to defraud their employer. During the grand jury investigation, corporate counsel interviewed the employees and thereafter advised the employees to retain independent counsel. Later, counsel for the two employees and the company's outside counsel entered into a joint defense agreement. Outside counsel then conducted their own interviews with the employees. The outside counsel advised the employees that they would turn over the interview notes if the government insisted. Outside counsel first conducted interviews with the employees' counsel present, and later without the presence of the employees' counsel. The company later produced, pursuant to grand jury subpoena, notes and/or memoranda of the employees' initial interviews with internal counsel and their later interviews with the outside counsel.

The issue in the case was whether the interview materials were protected by the attorney-client privilege and/or the joint defense agreement. The court held that the employees partially waived the protections of the JDA when they were interviewed with the knowledge that the company might turn over the notes to the government. Therefore, the government could only use materials derived from interviews after the waiver.

The preceding cases illustrate the dilemma that companies and their employees face when they are under investigation. By disclosing to the government, companies face the risk that the attorney-client privilege and work product protection will have been waived.[26] In addition, employees who cooperate in an internal investigation face the risk that in some circumstances the information that they provide to corporate counsel will not be protected from disclosure to the government.[27]

---

[24] For a similar holding, see United States v. Massachusetts Inst. of Tech., 129 F.3d 681, 686 (1st Cir. 1997) (holding that university waived its privileges when it disclosed materials to government agency).

[25] 348 F. Supp. 2d 375 (E.D. Pa. 2004).

[26] *See* Thomas R. Mulroy & Eric J. Munoz, *The Internal Corporate Investigation*, 1 DePaul Bus. & Comm. L.J. 49 (2002).

[27] *See, e.g., In re* Grand Jury Subpoena (Custodian of Records, Newparent, Inc.), 274 F.3d 563 (1st Cir. 2001). For an overview of the relationship between internal corporate investigations and government civil and criminal investigations, see Jonathan N. Rosen, *In-House Counsel and the Government's War on Corporate Fraud*, 25 Crim. Just. 5 (2010).

§ 17.03   COMPLIANCE PROGRAMS

[A]   Sarbanes-Oxley Act of 2002

The Sarbanes-Oxley Act[28] was passed in the wake of the corporate and accounting scandals of 2001 and 2002. When enacting the law, Congress stated that its goal was to restore public trust in corporations. Among other provisions, the Act requires corporations to improve accounting and auditing procedures, and provides penalties for failing to do so.

[B]   Department of Justice Policies

The Department of Justice (DOJ) had previously adopted policies that penalized corporations that asserted the attorney-client privilege during criminal investigations. The DOJ deemed such assertions to be evidence of failure to cooperate. The government would consider that failure when evaluating whether to bring criminal charges against the corporation. In response to criticism, the DOJ amended these policies. Critics still contended that the DOJ was applying inappropriate pressure on corporations to waive the privilege, and congressional critics threatened to overturn the policies.[29]

In August 2008, the DOJ rescinded the earlier policies and issued the "Filip Memorandum." This memorandum prohibits federal prosecutors from considering a corporation's decision not to waive the attorney-client privilege when deciding whether to charge the corporation. Instead, "prosecutors must measure cooperation by the extent to which the organization voluntarily discloses 'relevant facts and evidence.' "[30]

[C]   Compliance Programs and Corporate Liability

An effective corporate compliance program may have a significant impact on the government's decision whether to prosecute. Such a program does not act as a legal bar to prosecution, however. For example, in *United States v. Hilton Hotels Corp.*,[31] the company was convicted of antitrust violations even though the activities violated clear corporate policy. On appeal, the Ninth Circuit held that it was appropriate for the trial judge to instruct the jury that "[a] corporation is

---

[28] Sarbanes-Oxley Act of 2002, Pub. L. No. 107-204, 116 Stat. 745 (codified as amended in scattered sections of 11, 15, 18, 28, and 29 U.S.C.).

[29] *See* Elkan Abramowitz & Barry A. Bohrer, *The Defense of Corporate America: The Year in Review,* N.Y.L.J., Jan. 2, 2007, at 6, col. 3.

[30] *See* Khizar A. Sheikh and Matthew M. Oliver, *SEC Prohibits Staff Attorneys from Seeking Privilege Waivers During Investigations,* N.Y.L.J., Feb. 9, 2009. The SEC has also adopted a similar policy. *Id.* The SEC in 2010 also announced an initiative to encourage individuals and companies to cooperate and assist in investigations. New cooperation tools include cooperation agreements, deferred prosecution agreements, and non-prosecution agreements. *See* http://www.sec.gov/news/press/2010/2010-6.htm.

[31] 467 F.2d 1000 (9th Cir. 1972), *cert. denied sub nom.* 409 U.S. 1125 (1973). *See* Chapter 2, Corporate and Individual Liability, *supra,* § 2.05[B]; Elizabeth A. Plimpton & Danielle Walsh, *Corporate Criminal Liability,* 47 Am. Crim. L. Rev. 331, 337 (2010).

responsible for acts and statements of its agents, done or made within the scope of their employment, even though their conduct may be contrary to their actual instructions or contrary to the corporation's stated policies."[32] In addition, the United States Sentencing Guidelines allow for a reduction in the sentence if the "offense occurred despite an effective program to prevent and detect violations of law."[33] The benefit is forfeited, however, if a high level employee participated in, condoned, or willfully ignored the wrongdoing.[34]

[D] Compliance Programs and Individual Liability

The failure to adopt an effective compliance program can also lead to personal liability for corporate officers and directors. In *In re Caremark Int'l Inc. Derivative Litig.*,[35] for example, the court noted that directors have an "obligation to be reasonably informed concerning the corporation," including an obligation to implement effective compliance programs.[36] Otherwise, a director may be personally liable for resulting corporate losses.[37]

---

[32] *Id.* at 1004

[33] U.S.S.G. § 8C2.5(f)(1). *See* Chapter 21, Sentencing, *infra*, § 21.05, for a discussion of organizational sentencing under the Guidelines and the Supreme Court's decision in United States v. Booker, 543 U.S. 220 (2005).

[34] U.S.S.G. § 8C2.5(f)(3).

[35] 698 A.2d 959 (Del. Ch. 1996).

[36] *Id.* at 970.

[37] The court stated that the standard was a "lack of good faith as evidenced by sustained or systematic failure of a director to exercise reasonable oversight," concluding that this standard benefits shareholders because "it makes board service by qualified persons more likely, while continuing to act as a stimulus to *good faith performance of duty* by such directors." Id. at 971 (emphasis in original). *See* Plimpton & Walsh, *supra* note 31, at 356.

Chapter 18

GRAND JURY ISSUES

§ 18.01 INTRODUCTION

Under the Fifth Amendment of the United States Constitution, a defendant has a right to be charged by a grand jury in certain cases. That provision states that "[n]o person shall be held to answer for a capital, or otherwise infamous crime, unless on a presentment or indictment of a Grand Jury." Under Rule 7(a) of the Federal Rules of Criminal Procedure, charges for any crime punishable by more than a year's imprisonment must be issued by a grand jury unless the defendant waives that right. Thus, the vast majority of federal white collar cases are initiated by grand juries. The grand jury requirement does not apply to the states, however. Slightly over half the states allow the prosecutor to choose whether or not to use a grand jury to bring charges.

Grand juries are usually used as the primary investigative bodies in federal white collar cases. Headed by the prosecutor in charge of the investigation, the actual investigative footwork may be done by law enforcement agencies, such as the Federal Bureau of Investigation, acting at the grand jury's behest. The investigative agents may testify before the grand jury, and present evidence they have gathered. In addition, grand juries have broad subpoena powers. A grand jury may hear live witnesses testify under oath, and review tangible evidence in building its case. The grand jury also has the power to seek immunity for reluctant witnesses. Although ostensibly an independent body, in practice the grand jury "respond[s] favorably to prosecution requests for indictment with few exceptions."[1]

This chapter discusses some of the most frequent issues that arise in connection with white collar grand jury investigations. These include issues relating to grand jury secrecy, and to the scope of the grand jury's powers.[2]

---

[1] John R. Wing & Harris J. Yale, *Grand Jury Practice, in* White Collar Crime: Business and Regulatory Offenses § 8.01 (Otto Obermaier & Robert Morvillo, eds. 2011).

[2] For an overview of the grand jury, see Thaddeus Hoffmeister, *The Grand Jury Legal Advisor: Resurrecting the Grand Jury's Shield*, 98 J. Crim. L. & Criminology 1171 (2008); *Thirty-Ninth Annual Review of Criminal Procedure: Preliminary Proceeding: Grand Jury*, 39 Geo. L.J. Ann. Rev. Crim. Proc. 247, 256–63 (2010).

§ 18.02   COMPOSITION AND DURATION OF THE GRAND JURY

A federal grand jury is a group of citizens who have been called to serve. Courts have held that the grand jury must represent a fair cross-section of the community. The government or the defense may object to a grand jury because jurors were not legally qualified, or because jurors were improperly selected.[3]

The grand jury consists of between 16 and 23 people, at least 12 of whom must agree to bring a formal charge, termed an "indictment." (A charge filed by a prosecutor without using a grand jury is termed an "information.") A grand jury sits for a specified period, usually longer than 18 months, and may investigate one or more matters. By way of contrast, a trial or "petit" jury only sits for the duration of the trial for which the jury has been empanelled. A person upon whom the grand jury has focused for purposes of indictment is called a "target." By contrast, a "subject" is one about whom the grand jury seeks general information but upon whom the grand jury has not focused for purposes of criminal charges.[4]

§ 18.03   PURPOSE OF THE GRAND JURY

As the Supreme Court has stated, a grand jury serves the "'dual function of determining if there is probable cause to believe that a crime has been committed and of protecting citizens against unfounded criminal prosecutions.' It has always been extended extraordinary powers of investigation and great responsibility for directing its own efforts."[5] The grand jury has the power to subpoena witnesses and tangible evidence, and the scope of its inquiry may be quite broad. Further, the federal grand jury is not bound by rules of evidence or by exclusionary rule constraints under the Fourth Amendment. For example, the United States Supreme Court has held that a defendant's constitutional rights are not violated by an indictment based entirely on hearsay that would be inadmissible at trial.[6]

The grand jury system is subject to much criticism. First, there is an inherent conflict in the prosecutor's role both as advocate before the grand jury and as legal advisor to the grand jury. In the end, grand juries do the prosecutors' bidding in the vast majority of cases. Therefore, grand juries may seem superfluous. Second, the prosecutor's power before the grand jury may lead to charges of prosecutorial misconduct.[7] Although the grand jury is nominally under the supervision of the

---

[3] For an overview of grounds for challenging the composition of a grand jury, see Scott Schoettes & Joshua D. Liston, *Grand Jury*, 89 Geo. L.J. 1250, 1250–53 (2001).

[4] United States Attorneys' Manual § 9-11.151 provides:

A "target" is a person as to whom the prosecutor or the grand jury has substantial evidence linking him or her to the commission of a crime and who, in the judgment of the prosecutor, is a putative defendant . . . . A "subject" of an investigation is a person whose conduct is within the scope of the grand jury's investigation.

[5] United States v. Sells Engineering, 463 U.S. 418, 423 (1983), *quoting* Branzburg v. Hayes, 408 U.S. 665, 686–87 (1972) (citations omitted).

[6] Costello v. United States, 350 U.S. 359, 364 (1956).

[7] *See* Wing & Yale, note 1, *supra*, § 8.06[8] (Otto Obermaier & Robert Morvillo, eds. 2011) (discussing at length the types of misconduct allegations that have been raised).

district court in the jurisdiction in which the jury sits, courts rarely interfere with grand jury proceedings.

Nonetheless, grand juries do provide advantages to both prosecutors and defense counsel. For the government, the grand jury's investigative powers may prove useful in a complex and lengthy white collar investigation. For the defense, the grand jury may provide avenues for gaining information about the government's case, through discovery of witness testimony. The defense may also be able to bring legal challenges to the indictment based upon flaws in the grand jury process. As two commentators have written, "[t]he war on white collar crime is frequently waged, and often won or lost, at the grand jury stage of the criminal process."[8] That is so because, once a defendant is indicted and proceeds to trial, there is a strong likelihood that the government will prevail.

§ 18.04   THE GRAND JURY'S INVESTIGATORY POWERS

Grand juries have broad powers to issue *subpoenas duces tecum*, which require the production of documents, and *subpoenas ad testificandum*, which require witness testimony. A subpoena for documents may be quashed under the Fourth Amendment if it is "unreasonable," or under Rule 17(c) of the Federal Rules of Criminal Procedure if it is "unreasonable or oppressive." Because the grand jury's mission is to assess whether a crime has occurred, courts generally have been hesitant to place restrictions on the grand jury's subpoena powers.

[A]   The Scope of the Investigation

The leading case on the scope of the grand jury's investigative powers is *United States v. R. Enterprises*,[9] a 1991 United States Supreme Court decision. In *R. Enterprises*, a federal grand jury sitting in the Eastern District of Virginia was investigating allegations of interstate transportation of obscene materials. The grand jury issued subpoenas to three New York-based companies owned by the same person. The subpoenas sought various corporate books and records and, in one company's case, copies of videotapes shipped to Virginia. The other two companies moved to quash the subpoenas on the grounds that the requested materials were not relevant to the grand jury's investigation.[10] The Fourth Circuit Court of Appeals applied the holding in *United States v. Nixon*.[11] which requires that the government show relevancy, admissibility, and specificity in order to enforce trial subpoenas. Because the government failed to make such a showing, the court granted the motion.

The Supreme Court reversed and reinstated the subpoenas. The Court began by emphasizing that the grand jury

---

[8] *Id.* § 8.01.

[9] 498 U.S. 292 (1991).

[10] The companies also raised First Amendment claims, which the Supreme Court did not address. *Id.*

[11] 418 U.S. 683, 699–700 (1974).

occupies a unique role in our criminal justice system. It is an investigatory body charged with the responsibility of determining whether or not a crime has been committed . . . . [T]he grand jury "can investigate merely on suspicion that the law is being violated, or even just because it wants assurance that it is not. The function of the grand jury is to inquire into all information that might possibly bear on its investigation until it has identified an offense or has satisfied itself that none has occurred."[12] Thus, because of the special role played by grand juries, the *Nixon* rules applicable to trial subpoenas do not apply to grand jury subpoenas.

The Court went on to note, however, that the grand jury does not have unlimited investigatory powers. Grand juries may not engage in arbitrary fishing expeditions, nor select targets based upon malice or an intent to harass. Under Rule 17(c), a court may quash or modify a subpoena if it is "unreasonable or oppressive." Relevance is not the guiding factor; before formal charges are filed it is impossible to know what evidence will be relevant.[13]

The Court then concluded that grand jury subpoenas are presumed to be valid. Specifically, the Court held that the motion to quash or modify on relevancy grounds "must be denied unless the district court determines that there is no reasonable possibility that the category of materials the government seeks will produce information relevant to the general subject of the grand jury's investigation."[14] Under this standard, the Court upheld the subpoenas because one of the companies had shipped sexually explicit materials into the district where the grand jury was sitting, and it was therefore reasonable for the grand jury to seek materials from the other two companies.

The R. *Enterprises* decision does not provide clear standards by which to determine a subpoena duces tecum's validity.[15] It remains difficult for a recipient to obtain an order quashing or modifying a subpoenas duces tecum. Such a motion may succeed, however, in cases where a subpoena demands production of an open-ended number of documents. Thus, where the government has requested production of "all relevant books and records," and where responding to such a demand would be unreasonable, the subpoena may be quashed. Likewise, a broad request for information contained on computer drives and floppy disks may be overbroad. For example, in *In re Grand Jury Subpoena Duces Tecum Dated November 15, 1993*,[16] the grand jury subpoena requested broad categories of information, including all information contained on specified computers' hard drives. The court granted a motion to quash the subpoena on the ground that it was unduly

---

[12] *R. Enterprises*, 498 U.S. at 297, *quoting* United States v. Morton Salt Co., 338 U.S. 632, 642–43 (1950).

[13] *R. Enterprises*, 498 U.S. at 300.

[14] *Id.* at 301.

[15] In his concurring opinion, Justice Stevens suggested that a trial court balance the burden of complying with the subpoena against the government's need for the documents. Once the recipient has established the burden, such as costs or imposition on privacy interests, then the court can evaluate the documents' possible relevancy. *Id.* at 303–04 (Stevens, J., concurring).

[16] 846 F. Supp. 11 (S.D.N.Y. 1994).

burdensome.[17]Finally, a court may find that a subpoena is unreasonable where the subpoena demands the production of privileged information.[18]

[B]   Post-Indictment Investigations

Courts have held that the government may not use the grand jury to gather evidence for trial after the grand jury has issued its indictment.[19] If, however, the grand jury is seeking evidence against additional defendants, or evidence of crimes not yet charged, then a post-indictment investigation is proper. For example, in one high-profile case, the defendant alleged that the government had abused the grand jury process by continuing the investigation after indictment. In *United States v. Arthur Andersen, L.L.P.*,[20] Enron's accounting firm was indicted for obstruction of justice based on evidence that Andersen employees were instructed to shred documents as part of a routine document retention policy. After the indictment was issued, the grand jury subpoenaed the testimony of Andersen employees. Andersen asserted that the government subpoenaed the employees' testimony in order to assist in preparation for the trial and not as part of an ongoing investigation. Andersen asked the trial court to delay any further grand jury proceedings until after the trial, or to prohibit the grand jury from using the additional information at Andersen's trial.

The trial judge rejected Andersen's request. The court noted that a grand jury is not automatically barred from continuing its investigation once an indictment has been issued. The issue was whether the grand jury's investigation was primarily designed to gather evidence for the existing case. In this case, Andersen itself had requested that the indictment be expedited. In addition, Andersen had failed to show that the government was merely seeking additional evidence to use at Andersen's trial.

§ 18.05   PRESENTATION OF EXCULPATORY EVIDENCE

Federal courts also exercise a "hands-off" policy with respect to the evidence that prosecutors present to grand juries. This policy even extends to "exculpatory" evidence, that is, evidence that would tend to show that the defendant is not guilty of the crime or crimes the grand jury is investigating.

This issue arose in *United States v. Williams*,[21] a 1992 United States Supreme Court case. In *Williams*, the defendant was indicted for making materially false

---

[17] *See* Wing & Yale, *supra* note 1, § 8.06[6][a].

[18] *See, e.g.*, United States v. Under Seal (In re Grand Jury Doe No. G.J. 2005-2), 478 F.3d 581 (4th Cir. 2007) (affirming order granting motion to quash subpoena on the grounds that compliance would destroy the confidentiality of a police department internal investigation and would be inconsistent with the interviewed officers' Fifth Amendment rights against self-incrimination).

[19] *See* Schoettes & Liston, *supra* note 1, at 1261 & n.776, and cases cited therein.

[20] Crim. Action No. H-02-0121 (S.D. Texas April 9, 2002), *aff'd*, 374 F.3d 281 (5th Cir. 2004), *rev'd on other grounds*, 125 S. Ct. 2129 (2005). The Supreme Court's decision in this case is discussed in Chapter 12, Obstruction of Justice, *supra*, § 12.06[B].

[21] 504 U.S. 36 (1992).

statements to banks to influence their actions.[22] Williams moved to dismiss the charges, arguing that the government's failure to present "substantial exculpatory evidence" to the grand jury invalidated the indictment. The trial court agreed, dismissing the indictment under its grand jury "supervisory power." The Tenth Circuit affirmed.[23]

In a five-to-four decision, the Supreme Court reversed the dismissal. The Court found that grand juries have traditionally been independent bodies. Thus, they are not subject to strict court supervision.[24] The dissent focused on the dangers of prosecutorial misconduct before grand juries, arguing that courts have power to remedy such misconduct.[25]

Some states, however, do require that prosecutors advise a grand jury that exculpatory evidence exists and, in some instances, that they provide the evidence to the grand jury. This requirement may be the result of obligations imposed by statute or by judicial decision.[26] Further, as a matter of policy, the United States Department of Justice requires that a prosecutor present or disclose substantial exculpatory evidence to a grand jury.[27] Such policy guidelines, however, do not have the force of law and do not provide a basis for dismissing an indictment.

---

[22] *Id.* at 38; case was brought under 18 U.S.C. § 1014.

[23] *Id.* at 39.

[24] *Id.* at 47–55.

[25] *Id.* at 55–69 (Stevens, J., dissenting).

[26] *See, e.g.*, Cal. Penal Code, § 939.71 (Exculpatory evidence; duties of prosecutor). This section provides:

> (a) If the prosecutor is aware of exculpatory evidence, the prosecutor shall inform the grand jury of its nature and existence. Once the prosecutor has informed the grand jury of exculpatory evidence pursuant to this section, the prosecutor shall inform the grand jury of its duties under Section 939.7. If a failure to comply with the provisions of this section results in substantial prejudice, it shall be grounds for dismissal of the portion of the indictment.

Section 939.7 provides: "The grand jury is not required to hear evidence for the defendant, but it shall weigh all the evidence submitted to it, and when it has reason to believe that other evidence within its reach will explain away the charge, it shall order the evidence to be produced, and for that purpose may require the district attorney to issue process for the witnesses." *See also* State v. Hogan, 676 A.2d 533 (N.J. 1996) (holding that the state has a duty to present exculpatory evidence to the grand jury only when the prosecutor was informed of evidence that directly negates guilt and is clearly exculpatory, and finding that the omitted evidence was not clearly exculpatory in this case).

[27] United States Attorneys' Manual, § 9-11.233, provides:

> [T]he Supreme Court held [in *Williams*] that the Federal courts' supervisory powers over the grand jury did not include the power to make a rule allowing the dismissal of an otherwise valid indictment where the prosecutor failed to introduce substantial exculpatory evidence to a grand jury. It is the policy of the Department of Justice, however, that when a prosecutor conducting a grand jury inquiry is personally aware of substantial evidence that directly negates the guilt of a subject of the investigation, the prosecutor must present or otherwise disclose such evidence to the grand jury before seeking an indictment against such a person. While a failure to follow the Department's policy should not result in dismissal of an indictment, appellate courts may refer violations of the policy to the Office of Professional Responsibility for review.

§ 18.06 GRAND JURY SECRECY

The secrecy of grand jury proceedings is historically based, and is formalized in Rule 6(e) of the Federal Rules of Criminal Procedure. Such secrecy serves many purposes. For example, grand jury secrecy protects grand jurors from outside influences. And, at least theoretically, grand jury secrecy protects the rights of innocent persons whose names may arise during the investigation.[28] Under Rule 6(d)(1), those who may be present at a grand jury proceeding are limited to the grand jurors, the prosecutors and their staff members, the witness (if any), and support staff such as stenographers and interpreters.[29] In *United States v. Mechanik*,[30] the Supreme Court held that violations of this rule are subject to harmless error analysis. In that case, two government witnesses testified in tandem, in violation of the rule. The Court found that, because the defendant was convicted, there was necessarily probable cause to charge the defendant and that any Rule 6(d) error was therefore harmless.

Only the witness may reveal the contents of the proceeding to a member of the public.[31] In most instances, such revelation by anyone else may lead to contempt of court proceedings.

[A] Disclosure of Grand Jury Information to Government Officials

Special rules apply to disclosure of grand jury materials to others within the government. Sometimes such disclosure requires a court order, sometimes it does not. Further, even if a court order is required, issues arise as to the showing the government must make in order to gain release of the materials.

These issues arose in *United States v. Sells Engineering*, a 1983 United States Supreme Court case.[32] In that case, the government sought to disclose grand jury materials to attorneys in the Justice Department's civil division to assist them in preparing a civil law suit arising out of the criminal matter.

The Court first considered the issue of when a court order is required for such disclosure. The government argued that such disclosure falls under Rule

---

[28] *See* United States v. Sells Engineering, 463 U.S. 418, 424 (1983). Unfortunately, the identities of those under investigation are all-too-frequently leaked to the press. *See* Wing & Yale, *supra* note 1, § 8.04[4], and cases cited therein.

[29] Fed. R. Crim. P. 6(d)(1) provides: "The following persons may be present while the grand jury is in session: attorneys for the government, the witness being questioned, interpreters when needed, and a court reporter or an operator of a recording device." In United States v. Mechanik, 475 U.S. 66, 67 (1986), the Supreme Court held that violations of this rule are subject to harmless error analysis. In that case, two government witnesses testified in tandem, in violation of the rule. The Court found that, because there was probable cause to charge the defendant, the error was harmless. *Mechanik*, 475 U.S. at 67.

[30] *Mechanik*, 475 U.S. at 67.

[31] One court did hold that a witness may be ordered not to reveal to the target of the investigation the fact that the witness had been subpoenaed. *In re* Grand Jury Subpoena Duces Tecum, 797 F.2d 676 (8th Cir.), *cert. denied*, 479 U.S. 1013 (1986).

[32] 463 U.S. 418 (1983).

6(e)(3)(A)(i) of the Federal Rules of Criminal Procedure, which provides for disclosure without court order.[33] The defendants argued that the government should be required to obtain a court order under Rule 6(e)(3)(C)(i).[34] The Court agreed with the defendants. The Court concluded that, under Rule 6(e)(3)(A)(i), "disclosure is limited to use by those attorneys who conduct the criminal matters to which the materials pertain."[35]

The Court reasoned that Rule 6(e) was never intended to grant free access to grand jury materials to attorneys not working on the criminal matters to which the materials pertain. Such disclosure would increase the number of persons to whom the information is available, thereby increasing the risk of inadvertent or illegal release to others. Also, automatic disclosure to government attorneys for civil use poses a significant threat to the integrity of the grand jury itself. Prosecutors might be tempted to manipulate the grand jury's powerful investigative tools to root out additional evidence useful in the civil suit, or even to start or continue a grand jury inquiry where no criminal prosecution seems likely.[36]

Finally, the Court considered the burden of proof that the government must meet in order to obtain a disclosure order. The Court held that the government must make a "strong showing of particularized need."[37] The Court also stated that parties seeking grand jury transcripts under Rule 6(e) must demonstrate that (a) the transcripts are necessary to avoid injustice in another case, (b) their need for disclosure outweighs the need for continued secrecy, and (c) their request only covers the necessary material.[38]

Four years later, in *United States v. John Doe, Inc. I*,[39] the Court confronted the issue of whether the same government attorneys who are involved in the grand jury proceedings may use grand jury information in a related civil case without first obtaining a court order. The Court held that such use did not violate grand jury secrecy. The Court reasoned that there is literally no "disclosure" in such a situation because the same government attorneys had already obtained lawful access to the information in connections with the criminal investigation.

[B] Disclosure of Grand Jury Materials to Defendants

Grand jury materials may be disclosed to defendants in certain circumstances. For example, a court may order that grand jury materials be disclosed to the defendant where matters that arose before the grand jury might provide grounds

---

[33] Fed. R. Crim. P. 6(e)(3)(A)(i). That section allows for disclosure to be made to "an attorney for the government for use in the performance of such attorney's duty."

[34] Fed. R. Crim. P. 6(e)(3)(C)(i) provided: "Disclosure otherwise prohibited by this rule of matters occurring before the grand jury may also be made when so directed by a court preliminarily or in connection with a judicial proceeding." The rule has since been replaced by Fed. R. Crim. P. 6(e)(3)(E)(i).

[35] *Sells Engineering*, 463 U.S. at 427.

[36] *Id.* at 432–35.

[37] *Id.* at 443.

[38] *Id.*

[39] 481 U.S. 102 (1987).

to dismiss the indictment.[40]

[C] Disclosure to Third Parties

Under Federal Rule of Criminal Procedure 6(e)(3)(E)(i), a court may order disclosure of grand jury materials in connection with a judicial proceeding. For example, a litigant in a civil case may seek such materials as part of the discovery process. As discussed more fully later in this text,[41] the burden is on the party seeking such disclosure.[42]

[D] Disclosure to the Press and Public

Special problems arise when grand jury materials appear to have been leaked to members of the public, such as members of the press. Criminal defendants, and subjects and targets of grand jury proceedings, often claim that government attorneys or others acting at their behest have leaked information in order to prejudice the public or a jury. Violators may be held in contempt of court. However, as the Supreme Court stated in *Bank of Nova Scotia v. United States*,[43] in such circumstances, the indictment will not be dismissed on grounds of prosecutorial misconduct unless the disclosure "influenced substantially the grand jury's decision to indict, or there is grave doubt as to whether the decision to indict was so influenced."

The disclosure issue arose in connection with the grand jury investigation of former President Bill Clinton. In *In re: Sealed Case No. 99-3091*,[44] the District of Columbia Court of Appeals addressed leaks of grand jury materials to the press. The leaks emanated from the Office of Independent Counsel ("OIC"), which was conducting the grand jury investigation. The contents of the leaks were said to have appeared in the *New York Times*, which reported that certain members of the OIC were recommending that criminal charges be filed in the matter. In response, the President filed a motion for an order requiring that the OIC show cause why it should not be held in contempt of court.

The district court granted the motion, and the government appealed. The District of Columbia Circuit reversed. The court agreed with the OIC's position that the contents of the alleged leaks "did not fall within Rule 6(e)'s definition of 'matters occurring before the grand jury.' "[45] The court distinguished a prosecutor's disclosure of the investigation in general, which does not fall within grand jury secrecy rules, from a disclosure of grand jury matters. Where, as in this

---

[40] Fed. R. Crim. P. 6(e)(3)(E)(ii). *See* Wing & Yale, note 1 *supra*, § 8.03[3].

[41] *See* Chapter 20, Civil Actions, Civil Penalties, and Parallel Proceedings, *infra*.

[42] *See* Douglas Oil v. Petrol Stops Northwest, 441 U.S. 211 (1979). In that case, the Court stated that "[p]arties seeking grand jury transcripts under Rule 6(e) must show that the material they seek is needed to avoid a possible injustice in another judicial proceeding, that the need for disclosure is greater than the need for continued secrecy, and that their request is structured to cover only material so needed." *Id.* at 222.

[43] 487 U.S. 250, 259 (1988).

[44] 192 F.3d 995 (D.C. Cir. 1999).

[45] *Id.* at 997.

case, the disclosure appears to be independent of grand jury matters, the secrecy rules do not apply.

Defendants may also raise grand jury secrecy issues during or after trial. For example, in *United States v. Eisen*,[46] the defendants argued that they were entitled to a post-trial hearing to determine whether they were prejudiced by a leak of grand jury testimony. Shortly before the trial began, a local newspaper had published the contents of the testimony of four grand jury witnesses, and had implied that the government was the source of the information. The defendants argued that other witnesses could have read the article and conformed their testimony to that of the witnesses discussed in the newspaper, thus prejudicing the defense. The trial court denied the request, and the Second Circuit affirmed. The appeals court found that the defendants were required to produce evidence that they were actually prejudiced at the trial. Because the defense had failed to adduce such evidence during cross-examination, no hearing was required.

[E]   Disclosure to Grand Jury Witnesses

The circuit courts are split as to whether a grand jury witness has a right to review a transcript of the witness's own grand jury testimony under Rule 6(e)(3)(E)(i).[47] In one leading case, the D.C. Circuit found that witnesses do have a right to view the transcripts.[48] The court reasoned that "grand jury witnesses have a strong interest in reviewing the transcripts of their own grand jury testimony. The government has little reason to prevent witnesses from reviewing their transcripts."[49] In another case, the First Circuit employed a different analysis.[50] Declining to hold that witnesses are automatically entitled to review their transcripts, the court noted that "a less demanding requirement of particularized need applies when a grand jury witness demands access [in order to review] a transcript, rather than a copy of the transcript."[51] The United States Supreme Court has yet to resolve this issue.

---

[46]   974 F.2d 246 (2d Cir. 1992), *cert. denied*, 507 U.S. 1029 (1993).

[47]   *See In re* Grand Jury, 490 F.3d 978, 986–988 (D.C. Cir. 2007) (reviewing circuit split and listing cases).

[48]   *Id.*

[49]   *Id.* at 990.

[50]   *In re* Grand Jury, 566 F.3d 12 (1st Cir. 2009).

[51]   *Id.* at 18.

Chapter 19

THE RIGHT AGAINST COMPELLED SELF-INCRIMINATION

§ 19.01 INTRODUCTION

As in all areas of criminal law, issues concerning the defendant's constitutional rights arise often in white collar cases. The vast majority of these issues are discussed under the general rubric of "criminal procedure," and many study resources on that topic are available.[1] It is also true, however, that certain procedural issues tend frequently to arise in white collar cases. In particular, white collar cases may involve self-incrimination issues in connection with the production of documents to and witness testimony before grand juries.[2]

The Fifth Amendment to the United States Constitution provides that "[n]o person . . . shall be compelled in any criminal case to be a witness against himself." This provision has produced a complex body of case law and doctrine. This chapter provides a brief outline of the most significant United States Supreme Court cases in this area.

§ 19.02 THE FIFTH AMENDMENT PRIVILEGE AGAINST SELF-INCRIMINATION — COMPELLED TESTIMONY

When questioned by the government at a grand jury, at a trial, or in other official settings, an individual has a right not to answer if the response might incriminate the individual in a criminal case. As discussed below,[3] the government can only compel testimony in such a case by obtaining an order that grants the defendant immunity.

The question arises, however, as to when an individual's act is "testimonial" and therefore deserving of Fifth Amendment protection.[4] For example, in *Doe v. United*

---

[1] *See, e.g.*, Joshua Dressler & Alan C. Michaels, Understanding Criminal Procedure (5th ed. 2010). Many procedural issues are also discussed in other chapters in this book, such as Fourth Amendment issues. *See, e.g.*, Chapter 6, Computer Crime, *supra*, § 6.06[A].

[2] Additional Fifth Amendment issues, particularly relating to witness testimony, are discussed in Chapter 20, Civil Actions, Civil Penalties, and Parallel Proceedings, *infra*, § 20.04.

[3] *See infra*, § 19.04.

[4] *See Thirty-Ninth Annual Review of Criminal Procedure: Preliminary Proceeding: Grand Jury*, 39 Geo. L.J. Ann. Rev. Crim. Proc. 247, 256–63 (2010).

States ("*Doe II*"),[5] the defendant contested a court order requiring him to sign a general consent form. The form would allow his banks to provide the government with records relating to the defendant' accounts, if such accounts and records existed. Although the records, if produced, could potentially be incriminating, the Supreme Court held that signing such an order was not testimonial and therefore did not fall within Fifth Amendment protections. The Court reasoned that, for an act to be testimonial, "an accused's communication must itself, explicitly or implicitly, relate a factual assertion or disclose information." The consent form did neither. Rather, it merely allowed the banks to produce the requested information, if any such information existed, without violating bank secrecy laws.[6]

§ 19.03   THE FIFTH AMENDMENT PRIVILEGE AGAINST SELF-INCRIMINATION — THE COMPELLED PRODUCTION OF DOCUMENTS

[A]   The Required Records Rule

Under certain circumstances, the privilege against self-incrimination does not apply to an individual's production of records when the law requires that the individual maintain those records.[7] Specifically, courts have suggested that this "required records rule" applies when (1) the regulations requiring maintenance of the records are regulatory rather than criminal in nature, and (2) the records maintenance requirement is rationally related to the purpose of the regulation.[8]

[B]   The Collective Entity Rule

In a long line of cases extending to the beginning of the twentieth century, the Supreme Court has held that artificial entities, like corporations, do not enjoy Fifth Amendment Self-Incrimination Clause protections.[9] Thus, such entities may not invoke that clause to refuse a government demand for production of documents and other records. These decisions state that corporations and similar entities are

---

[5] 487 U.S. 201, 219 (1988).

[6] *Id.* at 215–19. Other forms of non-testimonial acts include giving writing or body fluid samples. *See* Dressler & Michaels, *supra* note 1, at § 23.04[D].

[7] For an overview of the issues arising from the assertion of the Fifth Amendment privilege in response to grand jury subpoenas, see Sara Sun Beale & James E. Felman, *The Fifth Amendment and the Grand Jury*, 22 Crim. Just. 4 (Spring 2007).

[8] *See* United States v. Hubbell, 530 U.S. 27, 35 (2000) ("the fact that incriminating evidence may be the byproduct of obedience to a regulatory requirement, such as filing an income tax return, maintaining required records, or reporting an accident does not clothe such required conduct with the testimonial privilege"); *Thirty-Ninth Annual Review of Criminal Procedure: Fifth Amendment at Trial*, 39 Geo. L.J. Ann. Rev. Crim. Proc. 635 (2010) (hereinafter "*Fifth Amendment at Trial*").

[9] Braswell v. United States, 487 U.S. 99 (1988); Curcio v. United States, 354 U.S. 118 (1957); Hale v. Henkel, 201 U.S. 43 (1906). The circuit courts have consistently held likewise. *See In re* Grand Jury Subpoena Issued June 18, 2009, 593 F.3d 155, 158 (2d Cir. 2010) (holding that there "simply is no situation in which a corporation can avail itself of the Fifth Amendment privilege"). *See generally* Gregory I. Massing, Note, *The Fifth Amendment, the Attorney-Client Privilege, and the Prosecution of White-Collar Crime*, 75 Va. L. Rev. 1179, 1180–83 (1989).

created by law, and therefore are subject to the law's demands, irrespective of constitutional rights available to individuals. Note that sole proprietorships are not covered by the collective entity doctrine, and may invoke Fifth Amendment protections.[10]

The collective entity rule also extends to individuals who are acting in a corporate capacity. For example, a corporation's "custodian of records," the person officially in charge of maintaining and producing corporate documents to the government, cannot rely on the Self-Incrimination Clause when confronted with a subpoena for corporate records.[11] This is generally true even if the documents themselves would incriminate the custodian in addition to the corporation. Because corporations must rely on individuals to act on their behalf, the Supreme Court has reasoned, allowing a custodian to refuse to produce documents would effectively shield the corporation during a criminal investigation. As the Court explained in *Braswell v. United States*,[12] "recognizing a Fifth Amendment privilege on behalf of the records custodians of collective entities would have a detrimental impact on the Government's effort to prosecute 'white-collar crime.'" Because *Braswell* had organized as a corporation, he could not assert the privilege. The Court subsequently held, however, that the *Braswell* rule does not apply to sole proprietorships.[13]

In *Braswell*, the Court stated that "[w]e leave open the question whether the agency rationale supports compelling a custodian to produce corporate records when the custodian is able to establish, by showing for example that he is the sole employee and officer of the corporation, that the jury would inevitably conclude that he produced the records."[14] In *Amato v. United States*,[15] the First Circuit held that the collective entity doctrine applies even where the custodian of records is the sole shareholder, director, officer, and employee of a corporation. Thus, the court denied the defendant's motion to quash subpoenas served on him as custodian of records.

[C] The Act of Production Doctrine

One of the most complex Fifth Amendment issues is whether, and in what circumstances, the amendment prohibits the compelled production of documents. In *Fisher v. United States*,[16] the Supreme Court held that the content of voluntarily produced documents is not protected because the documents themselves are not testimony. The Court went on to state, however, that "[t]he act

---

[10] United States v. Doe, 465 U.S. 605 (1984).

[11] *See* Fifth Amendment at Trial, *supra* note 10, at 573, *citing* Braswell v. United States, 487 U.S. 99, 109–10 (1988).

[12] 487 U.S. at 100. Note, however, that the identity of the custodian may be kept secret from the jury in certain circumstances.

[13] United States v. Doe, 465 U.S. 605, 620–21 (1984).

[14] 487 U.S. at 118 n.11.

[15] 450 F.3d 46, 51 (1st Cir. 2006) (citing *In re* Grand Jury Proceedings (The John Doe Company, Inc.)), 838 F.2d 624 (1st Cir. 1988)).

[16] 425 U.S. 391 (1976).

of producing evidence in response to a subpoena nevertheless has communicative aspects of its own, wholly aside from the contents of the papers produced."[17] In *Fisher*, the government was investigating an accountant's client. The government subpoenaed work papers that the accountant had created on behalf of the client. The Court held that production of the work papers was not testimonial because it did not require the client to prove the existence or location of the documents.[18]

The *Fisher* decision has produced a great deal of confusion — the Court did not clearly articulate the circumstances in which the act of production is sufficiently testimonial to warrant Fifth Amendment protection. And subsequent cases have not provided a great deal of clarity.

In one case, *United States v. Doe (Doe I)*,[19] the government sought the business records of a sole proprietor. The documents themselves fell under the required records rule, and therefore were not privileged. Nonetheless, the Court found that the *act of producing* the documents was itself incriminating and therefore protected. This was so because a sole proprietor is an individual rather than a corporation and thus can assert the privilege. Further, the Court deferred to the district court's factual determination that producing the documents would be testimonial because it would require Doe to admit that the records existed, that he possessed them, and that they were authentic.[20]

Courts have held that the act of production is incriminating if the person producing the documents is compelled to admit that the documents exist, that they are authentic, and that they are in the producer's possession. This issue arose in *United States v. Hubbell*,[21] a high-profile case arising out of the Whitewater real estate fraud investigation during the Clinton presidency. Hubbell originally pleaded guilty, and agreed to cooperate with the government's investigation. The government believed that Hubbell had not met his obligations under the agreement. The government initiated a new grand jury investigation, and the grand jury subpoenaed Hubbell to produce documents. When Hubbell asserted his Fifth Amendment rights, the government obtained an immunity order and Hubbell produced the documents. Hubbell was subsequently indicted based on information contained in the documents. The district court dismissed the indictment, holding that the government had relied upon the testimonial aspects of Hubbell's immunized act of producing the documents. The court of appeals vacated and remanded. On appeal, the Supreme Court agreed that the Fifth Amendment barred Hubbell's prosecution. The government had made derivative use of the testimonial aspects of the act of production because it needed Hubbell's assistance in identifying and producing potential sources of information.[22]

---

[17] *Id.* at 410.

[18] *Id.* at 412–13.

[19] 465 U.S. 605 (1984).

[20] *Id.* at 620–21.

[21] 530 U.S. 27 (2000).

[22] *Id.* at 42–43. *See* § 19.04, *infra*, for a discussion of use and derivative use immunity. For applications of *Hubbell*, see United States v. Ponds, 454 F.3d 313, 327 (D.C. Cir. 2006) (holding that *Hubbell* did not apply with respect to some subpoenaed documents because the government had prior knowledge of their

What happens after *Hubbell* if the government grants act of production immunity to an individual, and then obtains documents from that person? Are there any circumstances in which the government may use the documents to prosecute the individual? The answer seems to be that the government can bring criminal charges only if the government can prove that it already had a sufficient basis for concluding that the documents were in the individual's possession and that they were authentic. Because the government in *Hubbell* had gone on a fishing expedition to discover documents it did not even know existed, the government could not use the documents against Hubbell.[23]

In the corporate context, there are circumstances when the records custodian's act of production may incriminate the custodian personally. In *Braswell*, the Supreme Court held that the act of production doctrine does not forbid the introduction of such records at trial so long as the jury is not told who produced the documents.[24]

The reach of the act of production privilege remains the subject of litigation. In *In Re three Grand Jury Subpoenas Duces Tecum*,[25] for example, the government served a subpoena on former corporate officers to compel the production of corporate records that the officers possessed. The Second Circuit held that the act of production privilege applies to corporate employees who have terminated employment but still possess corporate records. The court thus affirmed the district court's order denying the government's motion to compel production. Other courts disagree with this result, however.[26]

§ 19.04   IMMUNITY

In federal white collar investigations and prosecutions, prosecutors regularly request that courts issue orders compelling the testimony of witnesses who have asserted the self-incrimination privilege. Such orders are governed by the criminal code's statutory immunity provisions.[27] These provisions apply to testimony in federal courts and specified administrative agency proceedings, and testimony before federal grand juries and congressional committees.

Federal law provides that the witness need only be granted "use or derivative use" immunity. This type of immunity provides that the witness's testimony, and any

---

existence, but that the government did not meet the particularity/prior knowledge requirement for other requested documents); *In re* Grand Jury Subpoena, Dated April 18, 2003, 383 F.3d 905 (9th Cir. 2004) (holding that the existence, location, and authenticity of subpoenaed documents were not a foregone conclusion and that the government therefore failed to show that production of documents by the witness would not be testimonial under *Hubbell*).

[23] *See* Lance Cole, *The Fifth Amendment Privilege and Compelled Production of Personal Documents After* United States v. Hubbell: *New Protection for Private Papers?*, 29 Am. Crim. L. Rev. 123 (2002).

[24] 487 U.S. at 117–18.

[25] 191 F. 3d 173 (2d Cir. 1999).

[26] *See* Park v. Cangen Corp., 7 A.3d 520, 527 (Md. 2010) (describing split in courts and holding that a former employee of a corporation cannot assert the act of production privilege).

[27] 18 U.S.C. §§ 6001–6005.

evidence learned from that testimony, may not be used against the witness in a subsequent prosecution.[28]

Such immunity may be distinguished from the broader "transactional" immunity, used in some states, that forbids any prosecution against the witness concerning the matter at hand, even if the government does not make direct or derivative use of the witness's testimony in that case. According to the United States Supreme Court's decision in *Kastigar v. United States*,[29] use/derivative use immunity is all that the Fifth Amendment requires.

The *Kastigar* decision also held, however, that the government must meet specific requirements to prosecute a previously-immunized witness. In particular, the trial court must hold what is now known as a *"Kastigar* hearing" or a "taint hearing." At such a hearing, the government has the burden of proving by a preponderance of the evidence that its trial evidence came from a "legitimate source wholly independent of the compelled testimony."

Such a showing is often difficult to make.[30] This was demonstrated in the case against Lieutenant Colonel Oliver L. North, who gave immunized testimony before Congress concerning the Iran/Contra affair.[31] North was later charged in connection with that matter, and was convicted in a federal trial. The District of Columbia Circuit Court of Appeals reversed the conviction, finding that the government had not met its burden of proving that its trial evidence against North was untainted.[32] For example, prosecutors and witnesses watched North's congressional testimony on television, potentially tainting the investigation and testimony. Thus, the government was unable to show that it did not make derivative use of North's immunized testimony. This case demonstrates the substantial hurdles that the government must overcome at a *Kastigar* hearing.

---

[28] There is, however, no Fifth Amendment bar to a perjury prosecution based upon immunized testimony that turned out to be false. In that event, the government may prosecute the witness using both the false testimony and any additional truthful testimony necessary to put the false testimony in context. *See* United States v. Apfelbaum, 445 U.S. 115 (1980), discussed in Chapter 11, Perjury, *supra*, § 11.04.

[29] 406 U.S. 441, *reh'g denied*, 408 U.S. 931 (1972).

[30] Recall that immunized testimony can be used in a perjury prosecution. *See* Chapter 11, Perjury, *supra* § 11.04.

[31] For the background of this complex political scandal, see Sandra D. Jordan, *Classified Information and Conflicts in Independent Counsel Prosecutions: Balancing the Scales of Justice After Iran-Contra*, 91 Colum. L. Rev. 1651 (1991).

[32] United States v. North, 910 F.2d 843 (D.C. Cir. 1990), *modified*, 920 F.2d 940 (D.C. Cir. 1991).

Chapter 20

CIVIL ACTIONS, CIVIL PENALTIES, AND PARALLEL PROCEEDINGS[1]

§ 20.01 INTRODUCTION

As noted in a number of earlier chapters,[2] violations of white collar criminal statutes may lead to civil and/or administrative remedies in addition to or instead of criminal penalties. Thus, a person or entity under criminal investigation or indictment may also face civil and/or administrative actions brought by the federal government and civil actions brought by private individuals.[3] In addition, a person or entity may face parallel state and federal administrative, civil, and/or criminal proceedings.

The possibility of parallel civil and criminal proceedings, and parallel state and federal proceedings, raises a number of complex issues for prosecutors and defense attorneys. Issues relating to the attorney-client privilege, the Fifth Amendment right against self-incrimination, double jeopardy, stays of proceedings, and discovery abound in the context of parallel civil/administrative and criminal investigations.

This chapter provides a brief outline of these very complex issues. When reading these materials, it is helpful to keep in mind that the issues overlap substantially with the issues raised in the chapters in this text concerning the Fifth Amendment Privilege and the grand jury.[4]

§ 20.02 PARALLEL STATE AND FEDERAL PROCEEDINGS

In the wake of corporate financial fraud scandals, state attorneys general became much more aggressive in their white collar prosecutions. For example, the WorldCom case spawned high profile prosecutions at both the state and federal

---

[1] Professor Sandra D. Jordan is the co-author of this chapter.

[2] *See, e.g.*, Chapter 5, Securities Fraud, *supra*, § 5.02[A]. For a discussion of issues arising out of parallel proceedings in the securities fraud context, see Charles A. Stillman, Julian W. Friedman & Nathaniel Z. Marmur, *Securities Fraud, in* White Collar Crime: Business and Regulatory Offenses § 12.04 (Otto Obermaier & Robert Morvillo, eds. 2011).

[3] For one high profile example, see United States v. Quattrone, 441 F.3d 153, 160–68 (2d Cir. 2006) (describing parallel investigations brought by the National Association of Securities Dealers, the United States Securities and Exchange Commission, and a federal grand jury). For a fuller discussion of this case, see Chapter 12, Obstruction of Justice, *supra*, § 12.03[C][2].

[4] *See* Chapter 18, Grand Jury Issues, *supra*; Chapter 19, The Fifth Amendment Right Against Compelled Self-Incrimination, *supra*.

level.[5]

In light of the dual sovereignty doctrine, the Double Jeopardy Clause does not bar parallel state and federal prosecutions. Significantly, about half the states have statutes forbidding such parallel proceedings.[6] Even these laws, however, only apply after the defendant has been acquitted or convicted in another jurisdiction. Thus, these laws do not bar parallel criminal investigations.

Such proceedings raise substantial difficulties both for prosecutors and defense counsel. For example, parallel state proceedings may interfere with the parties' ability to arrive at a plea agreement in a federal case because the defendant's guilty plea could negatively affect the defendant in a parallel state proceeding.[7]

§ 20.03   PARALLEL AGENCY PROCEEDINGS

A prospective criminal defendant may face civil or administrative actions initiated in many forums. With respect to federal civil proceedings, the agency with responsibility for that area will typically initiate the civil action. For example, as discussed above with respect to securities fraud,[8] the Securities and Exchange Commission (SEC) is the federal agency principally responsible for enforcing the federal securities laws. The SEC does not have the power to bring a criminal case, however, but can only initiate civil and administrative proceedings.

For most federal agencies, an investigation begins within the Office of Inspector General (OIG).[9] Agencies generally have the power to issues subpoenas or summonses for testimony or documents. As in the grand jury context,[10] courts exercise only limited supervisory powers over the issuance and content of agency subpoenas. Grounds for challenge include arguments that the subpoena (1) does not relate to matters within the agency's authority, (2) is unreasonably broad or imprecise, (3) was not issued pursuant to proper procedures, or (4) was issued for an improper purpose.[11]

Generally, the government is free to conduct parallel civil, administrative, and/or criminal investigations and proceedings. A defendant may argue, however, that such proceedings violate relevant constitutional provisions in certain circumstances. In *United States v. Stringer*,[12] for example, the SEC began an investigation into the

---

[5] *See* Irvin B. Nathan, *Multiple Jeopardy: Concurrent State and Federal Prosecutions for the Same White-Collar Offense*, 13 Bus. Crimes Bull. No. 4 at pp. 1–2 (2005) (describing parallel prosecutions arising out of the WorldCom financial fraud scandal).

[6] *See id.* at 4–5.

[7] *See id.* at 2.

[8] *See* Chapter 5, Securities Fraud, *supra*.

[9] *See* 5 U.S.C. App. 3 § 4(a).

[10] *See* Chapter 18, Grand Jury Issues, *supra*, § 18.04.

[11] *See, e.g.*, CFTC v. Tokheim, 153 F.3d 474, 477 (7th Cir. 1998); EEOC v. Quad/Graphics, Inc., 63 F.3d 642, 645 (7th Cir. 1995).

[12] 521 F.3d 1189 (9th Cir. 2008). *See* Eli Ewing, Comment: *Too Close for Comfort*: United States v. Stringer *and* United States v. Scrushy *Impose a Stricter Standard on SEC/DOJ Parallel Proceedings*, 25 Yale L. & Pol'y Rev. 217 (2006).

defendants' activities. The SEC subsequently referred the matter to the Department of Justice, which later obtained criminal charges against the defendants. The defendants sought dismissal of the criminal charges on the ground that their rights under the Due Process Clause were violated by the conduct of the parallel proceedings. The trial court agreed and dismissed the criminal charges, finding that the SEC had conducted the civil enforcement proceedings to obtain evidence for the criminal case and had misled the defendants about the criminal investigation. On appeal, the Ninth Circuit found that there was no basis for these factual conclusions. The court thus reinstated the charges.

§ 20.04   PARALLEL PROCEEDINGS AND THE FIFTH AMENDMENT

As noted in the introduction, the sequence of parallel proceedings has profound implications for both sides. For the government, a civil case may provide avenues for discovery that can complicate a criminal matter. For the defense, there may be a difficult choice concerning the assertion of the Fifth Amendment privilege in the civil matter.

The latter issue arose in *Keating v. Office of Thrift Supervision*,[13] a case concerning a major savings and loan fraud scandal. In that case, the Ninth Circuit addressed the issue whether a defendant in a civil suit is entitled to a stay of the suit pending the outcome of a parallel criminal case. The Office of Thrift Supervision (OTS) instituted a civil proceeding against Keating. Keating argued that his due process rights were violated by the OTS's refusal to stay the civil proceedings pending the outcome of parallel state and federal criminal proceedings against him. These pending criminal matters forced him to assert his Fifth Amendment privilege in the OTS matter, which took place before the criminal trials.

The Ninth Circuit rejected Keating's claim. The court held that, in the absence of substantial prejudice to the defendant's constitutional rights, the Due Process Clause does not require a stay of civil proceedings pending the outcome of the criminal case. A trial court has the discretion to stay civil proceedings in the interests of justice. In making this determination, the court should weigh factors including (1) the interests of the plaintiffs proceeding expeditiously, (2) the burden on the defendant, (3) the court's convenience and efficiency, (4) the interests of persons who are not parties to the civil case, and (5) the public's interests in the civil and criminal matters.[14] Because Keating had sufficient time to prepare for the OTS proceeding, and because he had no absolute right to a stay, the Ninth Circuit concluded that the trial court did not abuse its discretion in denying a stay.

As the *Keating* case showed, serious Fifth Amendment issues often arise during parallel proceedings. In *Keating*, the issue was whether the lower court abused its discretion in declining to issue a stay of the civil matter — even if that decision effectively forced Keating to assert his Fifth Amendment privilege in the civil matter, allowing the fact-finder to draw an adverse inference. Keating undoubtedly

---

[13]   45 F.3d 322 (9th Cir. 1995).

[14]   *Id.* at 324–25.

asserted the privilege on the advice of counsel, because any testimony in the civil case would constitute a Fifth Amendment waiver and would be admissible in the criminal trial. Defense attorneys generally deem this risk unacceptable because waiving the privilege could hamper the criminal trial strategy in significant ways. For example, such testimony could be used to impeach the defendant.

Although an adverse inference may be drawn against a party who asserts the Fifth Amendment privilege in a civil proceeding, courts have held that such an inference alone is not sufficient to justify a judgment in favor of the other party. In one civil RICO case, for example, the defendants asserted the privilege at the time that a criminal investigation was pending against them.[15] The district court granted summary judgment for the plaintiff, but the Seventh Circuit reversed. The court stated that, "although inferences based on the assertion of the privilege are permissible, the entry of judgment based only on the invocation of the privilege and 'without regard to the other evidence' exceeds constitutional bounds."[16]

A related issue arises when the government seeks discovery in a civil case, and a criminal investigation is also being threatened or is underway. Courts generally read the defendants' rights narrowly in this context. In *United States v. Kordel*,[17] the petitioners were officers of Detroit Vital Foods, Inc. Before petitioners' criminal trial, the United States Food and Drug Administration (FDA) initiated a civil investigation and a civil *in rem* action against the corporation's property. The United States Attorney's office then filed civil interrogatories prepared by an FDA official. Within two weeks, the corporation received notice that the FDA was contemplating recommending that a criminal prosecution be brought in that matter. The corporation moved for a stay of the civil case, which the trial court denied. After the FDA's recommendation for criminal prosecution, the corporation — through respondent Feldten — answered the interrogatories. Respondents were later convicted in the criminal matter.

On appeal, the Sixth Circuit reversed the convictions because the government used interrogatories to obtain evidence from the respondents in a nearly contemporaneous civil action. This, the court held, violated the respondents' Fifth Amendment privilege against compulsory self-incrimination.

The Supreme Court reversed and reinstated the convictions. The Court noted that Feldten was not compelled to answer the interrogatories; he could have invoked his Fifth Amendment privilege even though the corporation had no such privilege of its own. The corporation never asserted that there was no authorized person who could answer the interrogatories on behalf of the corporation without the possibility of compulsory self-incrimination. Thus, the Court did not reach the issue of how to proceed in a situation where no one could answer the interrogatories without a real risk of self-incrimination. The Court also suggested that, in a case where the government initiated parallel proceedings with the intent to unfairly disadvantage the defendant, a constitutional claim might lie.[18]

---

[15]   LaSalle Bank Lake View v. Seguban, 54 F.3d 387 (7th Cir. 1995).

[16]   *Id.* at 391 (citing Baxter v. Palmigiano, 425 U.S. 308, 318 (1976)).

[17]   397 U.S. 1 (1970).

[18]   The Court stated:

Where there is evidence that the government has attempted to obtain an unfair advantage in parallel proceedings, however, a litigant has a better chance at obtaining a stay. In *Afro-Lecon, Inc. v. United States*,[19] for example, the plaintiff company sought payment for costs under a government contract. The General Services Administration Board of Contract Appeals (the "board") requested discovery to substantiate the claim. The company subsequently learned it was the subject of a grand jury investigation involving the same matter, and moved to stay the civil proceedings on Fifth Amendment grounds. Specifically, counsel had advised key witnesses not to participate in the civil litigation because their testimony would waive their Fifth Amendment rights. The board denied the motion, and the company appealed.

The Federal Circuit reversed and remanded. The court stated that a litigant involved in parallel proceedings is not entitled to a stay, but that there are special circumstances when a stay may be appropriate. The court further noted that civil discovery is much broader than criminal discovery. In this case, the government had abused the process by instructing criminal investigators to attend the civil depositions. The court then articulated a common theme in such proceedings: "The broad scope of civil discovery may present to both the prosecution, and at times the criminal defendant, an irresistible temptation to use that discovery to one's advantage in the criminal case."[20] The court reversed the decision and remanded the matter for the board to determine if there were any other sources of information that could provide the accounting it required.

§ 20.05 PARALLEL PROCEEDINGS AND GRAND JURIES

[A] Immunized Testimony

The cases in the previous sections concern issues that arise when the government pursues parallel civil and criminal proceedings. Complex issues also arise when the government institutes a criminal investigation or prosecution and a *private litigant* institutes an action arising out of the same matter. Issues in such a situation may well overlap with grand jury issues.

For example, assume that a witness testifies before a grand jury under a grant of immunity in a criminal antitrust action. May that testimony be the subject of discovery in a parallel civil antitrust action? May the witness be compelled to testify in the civil action? These questions are not easily answered, and require analysis of the scope of the Fifth Amendment privilege.

We do not deal here with a case where the government has brought a civil action solely to obtain evidence for its criminal prosecution or has failed to advise the defendant in its civil proceeding that it contemplates his criminal prosecution; nor with a case where the defendant is without counsel or reasonably fears prejudice from adverse pretrial publicity or other unfair injury; nor with any other special circumstances that might suggest the unconstitutionality or even the impropriety of this criminal prosecution.

Id. at 11–12.

[19] 820 F.2d 1198 (Fed. Cir. 1987).

[20] *Id.* at 1203.

In *Pillsbury Co. v. Conboy*,[21] a grand jury was investigating possible criminal antitrust violations. Conboy was a witness who was granted immunity. He provided interviews to the government and testimony before the grand jury, which issued indictments in the matter. The district court subsequently ordered that portions of the witness's government interview and grand jury testimony be provided to the plaintiffs in a related antitrust civil action. Conboy then was subpoenaed to appear and appeared for a civil deposition at which counsel had copies of his immunized grand jury testimony. During the deposition, questions were read from the transcript and then rephrased to include Conboy's transcript answers. Counsel then asked Conboy whether he had "so testified." Conboy asserted his Fifth Amendment privilege and refused to answer. The district court issued an order to compel, and held Conboy in contempt when he continued to refuse to answer.

The court of appeals reversed, stating that Conboy's fear of prosecution was more than "fanciful," and that he was entitled to assert his Fifth Amendment privilege unless his deposition testimony could not be used against him in a subsequent criminal action.[22] The court reasoned that the answers to such questions "are derived from the deponent's current, independent memory of events" and therefore would "necessarily create a new source of evidence" that could be used in a subsequent criminal prosecution against Conboy.

On appeal, the Supreme Court affirmed. The Court reasoned that, even if Conboy's deposition answers were identical to the immunized answers he gave to the grand jury, he would be under oath to tell the truth as he currently knows it. Use immunity does not prevent the government from prosecuting; it merely limits the sources of evidence. Thus, the trial court could not require Conboy to testify without an effective promise of immunity as to that testimony.[23]

[B] Secrecy

As discussed more fully in the grand jury chapter,[24] Rule 6(e) of the Federal Rules of Criminal Procedure provides for the secrecy of grand jury matters. Such secrecy exists for purposes including the protection of grand jurors from outside influences and the protection of the rights of innocent persons whose names may arise during the investigation. The rule limits disclosure of grand jury matters to the grand jurors, the prosecutors and their staff members, the witness (if any), and support staff such as stenographers and interpreters. Of those parties, only the witness may reveal the contents of the proceeding to a member of the public. Generally, the revelation of grand jury matters by anyone other than a witness subjects that person to sanctions for contempt of court.

---

[21] 459 U.S. 248 (1983).

[22] *Id.* at 251–52.

[23] *Id.* at 263–64. For a fuller discussion of the scope of federal use immunity, see Chapter 19, The Fifth Amendment Right Against Compelled Self-incrimination, *supra*, § 19.04.

[24] *See* Chapter 18, Grand Jury Issues, *supra*, § 18.06. *See generally* John R. Wing & Harris J. Yale, *Grand Jury Practice, in* White Collar Crime: Business and Regulatory Offenses § 8.03[3] (Otto Obermaier & Robert Morvillo, eds. 2011).

One issue that may arise in parallel proceedings is the release of grand jury material in one judicial district for use in another judicial district. The Supreme Court confronted this scenario in *Douglas Oil Co. v. Petrol Stops Northwest*.[25] In that case, respondents were private parties who had filed antitrust actions in the district of Arizona against oil companies, including petitioners. The complaint alleged that the oil companies had engaged in price fixing. At the time these actions were filed, a grand jury was investigating the oil companies in the same matter. The grand jury later returned an indictment, and the companies pleaded nolo contendere. The civil plaintiffs then petitioned the district court in which the grand jury was located, requesting production of the grand jury transcripts. The district court ordered limited production of the documents, subject to protective conditions. The circuit court affirmed.

On appeal, the Supreme Court reversed and remanded. The Court determined that the court in the grand jury's district was the wrong court to decide whether disclosure was proper. That court was not in a position to know whether the disclosure was necessary for the civil proceedings.[26] The civil case plaintiffs were required to show that (1) the material was needed to avoid injustice in the civil case, (2) the need for disclosure was greater than the need for secrecy, and (3) their request was structured to cover only the materials needed. The court in the district where the civil litigation was pending was better situated to make that determination.[27]

Apart from determining the appropriate venue for determining grand jury matters, issues also arise under Rule 6 concerning disclosure of grand jury material "preliminary to or in connection with a judicial proceeding." In *United States v. Baggot*,[28] the Supreme Court considered whether an Internal Revenue Service (IRS) investigation to ascertain an individual's civil tax liability was "preliminary to or in connection with a judicial proceeding" so as to justify disclosure of grand jury materials under Rule 6(e)(3)(C)(i).[29] A federal grand jury investigated Baggot concerning possible violations of the Commodity Exchange Act for his practice of using sham transactions to create tax losses. Baggot pleaded guilty to two misdemeanor counts. The IRS then sought disclosure of the grand jury transcripts so that the IRS could use them when auditing Baggot. The Supreme Court held that disclosures under Rule 6(e)(3)(C)(i) are available only if an actual judicial proceeding is pending or contemplated. Because IRS audits are not judicial proceedings, the IRS was not entitled to disclosure.

[C]   Civil Protective Orders

In the cases in the preceding section, private parties or the government sought disclosure of grand jury materials in connection with parallel judicial or administrative proceedings. The flip side of such issues occurs when a grand jury

---

[25]   441 U.S. 211 (1979).

[26]   *Id.* at 229–30.

[27]   *Id.*

[28]   463 U.S. 476 (1983).

[29]   *Id.* at 481–82.

seeks to obtain materials that are the subject of a protective order in a pending civil suit.

In *In re Grand Jury*,[30] two persons were the plaintiffs in a state court action. As is common in civil litigation, the plaintiffs and defendants agreed to a court order that limited the public disclosure of discovery materials in that action. The grand jury then subpoenaed the civil case discovery materials, and the private plaintiffs filed a motion to quash the subpoenas. The Third Circuit noted that the federal appeals courts are split as to the circumstances in which discovery materials subject to protective orders must be disclosed to a grand jury. Some courts hold that a grand jury subpoena always takes precedence; another circuit gives precedence to civil protective orders; and yet other courts adopt a balancing test.[31]

The Third Circuit adopted a rule that the grand jury subpoena should be enforced absent "exceptional circumstances."[32] Determining such circumstances requires balancing factors including, but not limited to, (1) the government's need for the information, (2) the severity of the possible criminal charges, (3) the harm to society if charges cannot be brought, (4) the interests in confidentiality in the civil case, (5) the value of the protection order in a quick resolution of the civil case, (6) the harm to party seeking the protective order if the information were disclosed, (7) the severity of the harm alleged in the civil case, and (8) the harm to society and the parties due to any disruption of the civil case. Of course, such a test will nearly always result in enforcement of the grand jury subpoena, as was the case here.

[D] Stays

As seen above, parties will often seek to stay civil proceedings in the face of parallel criminal proceedings. In special circumstances, a court may grant such a stay.[33]

Conversely, a party may seek to stay the criminal matter instead of the civil matter. There is an important tactical advantage to this strategy; a criminal conviction may be used as collateral estoppel in the civil matter, but the reverse is not true. This is so principally because the preponderance of the evidence standard applicable in a civil matter does not suffice for proof beyond a reasonable doubt in a criminal matter. A court is nonetheless unlikely to stay a criminal investigation or prosecution.

Given the broad investigative powers of federal grand juries, for example, courts are very hesitant to order stays of grand jury proceedings. In *In re Grand Jury*

---

[30] 286 F.3d 153 (3d Cir. 2002).

[31] *Id.* at 157, citing cases. *See, e.g., In re* Grand Jury Subpoena Served on Meserve, Mumper & Hughes, 62 F.3d 1222, 1226 (9th Cir. 1995) (adopting a per se rule favoring grand jury subpoenas over civil protective orders); Martindell v. International Tel. and Tel. Corp., 594 F.2d 291, 296 (2d Cir. 1979) (adopting a presumption favoring the civil protective order).

[32] 286 F.3d at 159, 162.

[33] *See supra*, § 20.04.

Proceedings (U.S. Steel - Clairton Works),[34] the company had been involved for two years in complex civil environmental standards litigation. When a grand jury was empanelled and subpoenaed witnesses in the same matter, the district court stayed the grand jury proceedings. The Third Circuit reversed, principally on the grounds that grand juries operate independently of the judiciary and are afforded broad latitude in conducting their investigations.[35]

[E]   Deferred Prosecution

Increasingly, the government has employed pretrial diversion agreements, such as deferred and non-prosecution agreements, in corporate white collar prosecutions. This allows corporations to avoid criminal prosecution during a probationary period. During that time, the government has extensive control in determining whether the corporation has complied with the terms of probation. These agreements have affected the attorney-client privilege, the work product protections, restitution, parallel proceedings, fines, compliance, and individual rights within corporations.[36]

§ 20.06   CIVIL FINES

Both individuals and corporations may face civil fines in addition to criminal penalties. The United States Supreme Court has on several occasions addressed the issue of when a civil fine is punitive and thus constitutes "punishment" for purposes of the Double Jeopardy Clause.

The Court's decision in *Hudson v. United States*[37] sets forth the Court's current approach to this issue. In that case, the three petitioners were executives and directors of two banks. In a regulatory investigation, the government discovered that the petitioners had engaged in self-dealing, and issued a "Notice of Assessment of Civil Money Penalty."[38] To resolve the regulatory matter, the petitioners consented to fines of $16,500, $15,000, and $12,500 respectively. In addition, each petitioner agreed not to "participate in any manner" in the affairs of any banking institution without the written authorization of federal regulatory agencies.

Petitioners were later indicted in connection with same matter that had been the subject of the regulatory proceeding. Petitioners moved to dismiss the indictment on double jeopardy grounds, and the district court granted the motion. The court of appeals reversed, following the Supreme Court's earlier decision in *United States v.*

---

[34] 525 F.2d 151 (3d Cir. 1975).

[35] *See* Chapter 18, Grand Jury Issues, *supra*, § 18.04[A], for a further discussion of the scope of the grand jury's powers.

[36] The use of such agreements has increased dramatically, and raises many criminal justice policy issues. *See* Eric Lichtblau, *In Justice Shift, Corporate Deals Replace Trials*, N.Y. Times, April 9, 2008 at A1.

[37] 522 U.S. 93 (1997).

[38] The notice alleged that petitioners had violated 12 U.S.C. §§ 84(a)(1) and 375(b) and 12 C.F.R. §§ 31.2(b) and 215.4(b) by causing the banks with which they were associated to make loans to nominee borrowers in a manner that unlawfully allowed petitioner Hudson to receive the benefit of the loans. 522 U.S. at 96.

Halper.[39] Under that decision, the court concluded that the fines were not so grossly disproportional to the damages to the government as to render the civil sanctions "punishment" for double jeopardy purposes. The Supreme Court affirmed the result, but in so doing largely disavowed the *Halper* analysis.

The Court in *Hudson* stated that, in assessing whether a sanction is criminal or civil, a court should first look to legislative intent. If the statute is a civil statute on its face, then a court should find that the statute imposes punishment only when the "clearest proof" is present showing that the sanction is punishment. The Court's decision in *Kennedy v. Mendoza-Martinez*[40] set forth the following factors to be considered when determining whether a civil sanction is in effect a criminal sanction: (1) whether the sanction involves an affirmative disability or restraint; (2) whether it has historically been regarded as a punishment; (3) whether it comes into play only on a finding of *scienter*; (4) whether its operation will promote the traditional aims of punishment — retribution and deterrence; (5) whether the behavior to which it applies is already a crime; (6) whether an alternative purpose to which it may rationally be connected is assignable for it; and (7) whether it appears excessive in relation to the alternative purpose assigned.

In this case, Congress clearly defined the regulatory fines and debarment as civil penalties. Further, none of the *Mendoza-Martinez* factors transformed the monetary fines and debarment from civil to criminal sanctions. Thus, the Double Jeopardy Clause did not bar subsequent criminal punishment.[41]

The *Hudson* decision has the practical effect of rendering it very difficult to show that a civil sanction should be considered to be punishment for purposes of the Double Jeopardy Clause. For example, as discussed in the forfeitures chapter,[42] the Court has held that civil forfeitures do not constitute punishment under the Double Jeopardy Clause — even though the Court had earlier held that civil forfeitures do constitute punishment for purposes of the Eighth Amendment's Excessive Fines Clause.[43] Fearful of opening the door to a wide range of double jeopardy challenges to civil and administrative sanctions, the Court in *Hudson* made clear that claimants face an especially difficult hurdle under the Double Jeopardy Clause.

---

[39] 490 U.S. 435, 448 (1989).

[40] 522 U.S. at 99–100, *citing* 372 U.S. 144, 168–169 (1963).

[41] 522 U.S. at 103–05.

[42] *See* United States v. Ursery, 518 U.S. 267 (1996), discussed in Chapter 22, Forfeitures, *infra*, § 22.04[D].

[43] *See* United States v. Bajakajian, 524 U.S. 321 (1998), discussed in Chapter 22, Forfeitures, *infra*, § 22.04[C].

§ 20.07 QUI TAM ACTIONS

[A] The False Claims Act

The False Claims Act (FCA)[44] allows for civil suits to be brought on behalf of the United States government. The FCA imposes civil liability upon "[a]ny person" who, *inter alia*, "knowingly presents, or causes to be presented, to an officer or employee of the United States government . . . a false or fraudulent claim for payment or approval."[45] The defendant is liable for up to treble damages, civil penalties of up to $10,000 per claim, and attorney's fees and costs.[46]

The FCA provides that such suits may be brought not only by the government but also by private parties. Like the RICO statute, the FCA thus allows for individuals to serve as "private attorneys general." The FCA thus encourages private parties to uncover fraud against the government.[47]

Private individuals who bring such suits under the FCA are termed "relators," and the suits are termed "qui tam" actions.[48] The FCA provides financial incentives for such suits by allowing the successful relator to receive a percentage of the monetary recovery.[49]

If a relator initiates the action, the government then has 60 days to intervene. If it does so, it assumes primary responsibility for the action. Still, the relator may continue to pursue the claim. If the government does not pursue a claim within 60 days, it may intervene later only on a showing of "good cause." In either case, the relator is entitled to a share of the proceeds and attorney's fees and costs.[50]

[B] Qualifying as a Relator

[1] Direct and Independent Knowledge

Qui tam jurisdiction is limited to cases where the private party is an "original source" of the information, defined as "an individual who has direct and independent knowledge of the information on which the allegations are based and has voluntarily

---

[44] 31 U.S.C. §§ 3729–3733.

[45] 31 U.S.C. § 3729(a).

[46] 31 U.S.C. § 3730(d). The award of such fees is subject to court approval. *See, e.g.*, United States *ex rel.* Taxpayers Against Fraud v. General Electric Co., 41 F.3d 1032 (6th Cir. 1994).

[47] RICO provides for both civil and criminal actions; the FCA only provides for civil actions. One court termed such actions as "one of the least expensive and most effective means of preventing frauds on the Treasury is to make the perpetrators of them liable to actions by private persons acting, if you please, under the strong stimulus of personal ill will or the hope of gain." United States v. Griswold, 24 F. 361, 366 (D. Or. 1885) (quoted, *inter alia*, in U.S. *ex rel.* Springfield Terminal Ry. Co. v. Quinn, 14 F.3d at 649)).

[48] The term "qui tam" is derived from the Latin phrase *"qui tam pro domino rege quam pro seipse,"* which means "he who sues for the king as for himself."

[49] The relator receives 25–30 percent of the recovery if the government does not join, and 15–25 percent if the government does join. 31 U.S.C. § 3730(d).

[50] *See id.*

provided the information to the government before filing an action . . . based on the information."[51] The private party has the burden of proving by a preponderance of the evidence that this provision is met.

This determination requires fact-finding by the trial court. In *United States ex rel. Stone v. Rockwell International Corp.*,[52] for example, the defendant, Rockwell, managed a nuclear power plant for the United States Department of Energy. Stone was a former Rockwell employee who told the government about environmental crimes that Rockwell had committed and then filed an action alleging that Rockwell had defrauded the government when filing claims for reimbursements. After jury verdicts for Stone, Rockwell appealed on the ground that Stone was not an "original source" of the information. The Tenth Circuit found that Stone was an original source, but remanded for a determination of whether he provided the information to the government prior to filing the suit. On remand, the district court found that Stone had not effectively communicated Stone's allegations to the government.

On appeal, the Tenth Circuit reversed, and the Supreme Court granted certiorari.[53] The Court found that Stone did not qualify as an original source as to events at issue. The events occurred at Rockwell in 1987 and 1988. Stone left Rockwell in 1986, and he therefore had no personal knowledge of the events upon which the qui tam action was based.[54]

[2] The "Original Source" Exception to the "Public Disclosure" Rule

The circuits are split on the "original source" exception to the "public disclosure" rule under the FCA. Under § 3730(e)(4)(A), a court lacks subject matter jurisdiction in a qui tam action that is "based upon the public disclosure of allegations or transactions" in certain circumstances unless "the person bringing the action is an original source of the information."[55] Under § 3730(e)(4)(B), the term "original source" means "an individual who has direct and independent knowledge of the information on which the allegations are based and has voluntarily provided the information to the Government before filing an action under this section which is based on the information."

---

[51] 31 U.S.C. § 3730(e)(4)(B).

[52] 282 F.3d 787 (10th Cir. 2002), *rev'd after remand sub nom*, Rockwell International Corp. v. United States, 549 U.S. 457, 466 (2007).

[53] Rockwell Int'l Corp. v. United States, 549 U.S. 457, 466–67 (2007).

[54] *Id.* at 473–74.

[55] 31 U.S.C. § 3130(e)(4) provides:
   (A)   No court shall have jurisdiction over an action under this section based upon the public disclosure of allegations or transactions in a criminal, civil, or administrative hearing, in a congressional, administrative, or [General] Accounting Office report, hearing, audit, or investigation, or from the news media, unless the action is brought by the Attorney General or the person bringing the action is an original source of the information.
   (B)   For purposes of this paragraph, 'original source' means an individual who has direct and independent knowledge of the information on which the allegations are based and has voluntarily provided the information to the Government before filing an action under this section which is based on the information.

The meaning of "provided the information to the Government before filing an action" has divided the circuit courts. The courts have articulated three different approaches.[56] One approach requires only that the relator voluntarily provide the information to the government before filing the qui tam action. Another approach requires that the relator must have been a source of the information provided to the entity that disclosed the allegations on which a suit is based. The third approach requires that an "original source" provide the information to the government before any public disclosure, but not requiring that the relator be the cause of the public disclosure. The Supreme Court has yet to resolve this issue.

[3] Standing

Another common issue in qui tam actions is the relator's standing to sue. The Supreme Court addressed this issue in *Vermont Agency of Natural Resources v. United States ex Rrel. Stevens*.[57] In that case, the relator brought the action against his former employer. The suit alleged that the employer had submitted false claims to the Environmental Protection Agency (EPA) in connection with various federal grant programs administered by the EPA. The United States declined to intervene in the action. The defendant moved to dismiss, and the lower courts denied the motion.

On appeal, the Supreme Court addressed the questions whether the relator had standing under Article III of the Constitution to maintain the action, and whether a state is a "person" subject to liability under the FCA when the federal government has not intervened. As to the first issue, the Court stated that, to have standing under Article III, a plaintiff must (1) demonstrate "injury in fact" — a harm that is both "concrete" and "actual or imminent, not conjectural or hypothetical"; (2) establish causation — a "fairly . . . trace[able]" connection between the alleged injury in fact and the alleged conduct of the defendant; and (3) demonstrate redressability — a "substantial likelihood" that the requested relief will remedy the alleged injury in fact.[58] The Court initially found that the injury the federal government suffered because of a violation of federal law was sufficient to confer standing upon the relator, who stood in the federal government's shoes. That qui tam actions are historically-based supported this conclusion.[59]

As to the second issue, the Court found that the state agency was not a person who could be sued in this case. Under the Eleventh Amendment, states and their agencies are protected from such actions.[60]

---

[56] *See* United States *ex rel.* Duxbury v. Ortho Biotech Prods., L.P., 579 F.3d 13 (1st Cir. 2009) (describing circuit split and listing cases).

[57] 529 U.S. 765 (2000).

[58] *Id.* at 771–72.

[59] *Id.* at 774–75. Qui tam actions have also been upheld in the face of constitutional challenges under separation of powers principles and the appointments clauses, U.S. Const. art II, § 3. *See* Riley v. St. Luke's Episcopal Hospital, 252 F.3d 749 (5th Cir. 2001) (*en banc*).

[60] 529 U.S. at 778–87.

[C]   Claims Made to Private Entities

One issue that has arisen is whether claims not made directly to obtain money from the government are actionable under the FCA. The United States Supreme Court confronted this issue in *Allison Engine Co., Inc. v. U.S. ex rel. Sanders.*[61] In *Allison Engine*, subcontractors falsely stated to government contractors that the subcontractors had adhered to government requirements in completing the work. Although the subcontractors were paid with government funds, there was no evidence that the false statements were made to obtain the funds from the government. Employees of one of the subcontractors brought a *qui tam* action under the FCA seeking damages from the subcontractors.

The Supreme Court held that a FCA action could not be brought in such circumstances. The Court rejected the appeals court's holding that "proof of an intent to cause a false claim to be paid by a private entity using Government funds was sufficient."[62] Instead, the Court stated, "[i]f a subcontractor or another defendant makes a false statement to a private entity and does not intend the government to rely on that false statement as a condition of payment, the statement is not made with the purpose of inducing payment of a false claim 'by the government.'" The Court concluded: "In such a situation, the direct link between the false statement and the government's decision to pay or approve a false claim is too attenuated to establish liability."[63]

Congress responded to the *Allison Engine* decision in the Fraud Enforcement and Recovery Act of 2009 ("FERA").[64] FERA amends the FCA in several important respects, including a provision designed to overturn *Allison Engine*. The definitional section of the statute, among other things, deletes the "by the government" language upon which the *Allison Engine* decision relied. FCA liability now covers requests for funds to a contractor, grantee, or other recipient, if the funds are "to be spent or used on the government's behalf or to advance a government program or interest."[65]

Also, FERA contains a materiality requirement for actions brought under the FCA. The statute defines materiality "having a natural tendency to influence, or be

---

[61] 553 U.S. 662, 665 (2008).

[62] *Id.* at 668.

[63] *Id.* at 672.

[64] New sections 3729(a)(1)(A), (B), (C), and (G) impose liability on one who:
   (A) knowingly presents, or causes to be presented, a false or fraudulent claim for payment or approval;
   (B) knowingly makes, uses, or causes to be made or used, a false record or statement material to a false or fraudulent claim;
   (C) conspires to commit a violation of subparagraph (A), (B), (D), (E), (F), or (G); . . . or
   (G) knowingly makes, uses, or causes to be made or used, a false record or statement material to an obligation to pay or transmit money or property to the government, or knowingly conceals or knowingly and improperly avoids or decreases an obligation to pay or transmit money or property to the government.

31 U.S.C. § 3729.

[65] *Id.*

capable of influencing, the payment or receipt of money or property."[66]

§ 20.08   OTHER SANCTIONS

Many professionals, including lawyers, accountants, doctors, securities brokers, and others fall under state, local, and/or professional regulatory schemes. Under many of these schemes, such a professional may temporarily or fully lose the ability to work in the profession when that professional has committed some wrongdoing. Further, those who have or seek government contracts may be barred from participation in such contracts for a fixed number of years if found guilty of wrongdoing.[67]

In particular, individual states license attorneys. Unfortunately, attorneys all too often are the targets of white collar investigations and are named in white collar indictments. If there is evidence that an attorney has committed a crime, whether or not formal charges are brought, then the attorney could be reprimanded, suspended, or disbarred under the governing ethical rules.[68]

Likewise, in securities fraud cases, the possibility that the individual will lose the ability to act in that profession often looms large. A securities trader convicted of securities laws violations, for example, may be suspended temporarily or barred for life from engaging in trading.[69]

---

[66] *Id.*

[67] *See* Sara N. Welling et al., Federal Criminal Law and Related Actions § 33.1 (1998).

[68] *See, e.g., Lawyer Disciplinary Actions*, 36 Ark. Law. 42 (Spring 2001) (five-year suspension of former President William Clinton).

[69] *See, e.g.,* S.E.C., In the Matter of the Application of New York Stock Exchange, Inc. for an Order Granting the Approval of The Association of Frederick H. Joseph in a Supervisory Capacity with Ing Barings LLC Securities Exchange Act of 1934 Section 6(c)(2) (January 6, 2000) ("The activities of [Michael] Milken . . . led to the institution of numerous civil enforcement actions and criminal proceedings against Milken. . . . As a result of some of these proceedings, Milken was convicted, in 1990, of criminal violations involving securities transactions. . . . Milken also was barred, in 1991, from association with the securities industry.").

Chapter 21

SENTENCING

§ 21.01 INTRODUCTION

Federal sentencing has undergone two profound upheavals in recent decades. First, in 1987 the United States Sentencing Guidelines were enacted. Second, in 2005, the United States Supreme Court decided in *United States v. Booker*[1] that the Sentencing Guidelines, as written, violate a defendant's Sixth Amendment right to a jury trial. The Court further altered the way that federal sentences are imposed under the Guidelines.

Prior to 1987, federal courts had a great deal of sentencing discretion. Trial judges could impose a sentence, in any given case, ranging from parole to the maximum statutory sentence, with little oversight by appellate courts. In addition, most people sentenced to prison were eligible for parole, and the parole board had broad authority to award parole. Not surprisingly, this system produced widely disparate sentences for similar crimes, and also made it difficult to determine the actual amount of prison time that a particular sentence would produce.

In response to criticism over sentencing disparities and wide-spread parole, Congress in 1984 passed the Sentencing Reform Act and created the United States Sentencing Commission.[2] The Sentencing Commission in turn promulgated the Federal Sentences Guidelines in 1987. The Guidelines were designed to ensure uniformity in the sentencing of both individuals and organizations, and required mandatory sentences within fixed ranges. With some narrow exceptions discussed in the next section, the Guidelines as enacted greatly reduced judges' sentencing discretion. Further, parole was abolished.

The Guidelines sentencing scheme has been controversial. Many have argued that a fair system of justice depends upon individual treatment for individual defendants. In this sense, then, some have argued that the Guidelines removed a basis for ensuring fairness within the criminal justice system.[3] Further, some have observed that the Guidelines may have had the effect of simply transferring from judges to prosecutors the key decisions that determine sentencing. The Guidelines, they argued, placed in prosecutors' hands the power to determine the sentence simply by deciding what charges to bring and what pleas to accept.[4]

---

[1] 543 U.S. 220 (2005).

[2] The Sentencing Reform Act is codified at 28 U.S.C. §§ 991–998.

[3] *See* Charles J. Ogletree, Jr., *The Death of Discretion? Reflections on the Federal Sentencing Guidelines*, 101 Harv. L. Rev. 1938 (1988).

[4] *See* Stephen J. Schulhofer & Ilene H. Nagel, *Plea Negotiations Under the Federal Sentencing*

Federal sentencing again underwent dramatic changes in 2005. That year, the United States Supreme Court issued its decision in *United States v. Booker*.[5] In *Booker*, the Court held that Guidelines sentencing — which largely depends on fact-finding by the sentencing judge — violates a defendant's Sixth Amendment right to a jury trial. In a separate opinion, the Court also held that the Guidelines can be constitutionally applied if they are considered merely advisory rather than mandatory.[6] Since *Booker* was decided, the United States Supreme Court has issued a series of decisions interpreting *Booker*. The *Booker* decision and its progeny, including *Rita v. United States*,[7] *Kimbrough v. United States*,[8] and *Gall v. United States*,[9] have the net effect of restoring a substantial amount of sentencing discretion to trial judges.

As a result of *Booker*, then, federal sentencing has undergone and is still undergoing a state of rapid change. To the degree that *Booker* has once again provided trial judges with sentencing discretion, the criticism of the Guidelines as arbitrary has lessened. As judges exercise more individual discretion, however, the debate over sentencing disparities has reemerged. The ultimate impact of the *Booker* decision, and the policy debate over that decision, will continue to evolve in the coming years.[10]

This chapter gives an overview of the complex provisions of the Federal Sentencing Guidelines, focusing on those individual and organizational sentencing provisions most likely to apply in the white collar crime context. Although *Booker* altered the way in which the Guidelines operate, an understanding of the Guidelines remains essential for federal sentencing. The chapter also reviews the *Booker* decision, and the complex issues that the decision raises.[11]

Guidelines: Guideline Circumvention and Its Dynamics in the Post-Mistretta Period, 91 Nw. U. L. Rev. 1284 (1997); Jeffrey Standen, *Plea Bargaining in the Shadow of the Guidelines*, 81 Calif. L. Rev. 1471 (1993).

[5] 543 U.S. 220 (2005).

[6] The *Booker* decision and its aftermath are discussed in detail in § 21.04[B] below.

[7] 551 U.S. 338 (2007) (holding that appeals courts may, but are not required to, presume that Guidelines-range sentences are reasonable).

[8] 552 U.S. 85 (2007) (holding that a district court may rely upon its own disagreement with policies underlying the Guidelines when imposing an outside Guidelines-range sentence).

[9] 552 U.S. 38 (2007) (holding that neither trial nor appellate courts may presume that outside-Guidelines range sentences are unreasonable, and that appellate courts may not require that "extraordinary" circumstances be present to justify non-Guidelines-range sentences).

[10] Because the Federal Sentencing Guidelines (U.S.S.G.) are enormously complex, this chapter necessarily provides only a general overview of the Guidelines. For more comprehensive analyses relating to individual and/or organizational sentencing, see Thomas W. Hutchison et al., Federal Sentencing Law and Practice (2011 ed.). Further, it should be noted that federal sentencing law is evolving at a lightening pace in the wake of *Booker*. The United States Sentencing Commission maintains the most up-to-date information. *See* http://www.ussc.gov/Data_and_Statistics/ Federal_Sentencing_Statistics/index.cfm.

[11] For an overview, see Frank O. Bowman, III, Jennifer C. Woll & Roger W. Haines, Jr., Federal Sentencing Guidelines Handbook (2010); *Thirty-Ninth Annual Review of Criminal Procedure, Sentencing Guidelines*, 39 Geo. L.J. Ann. Rev. Crim. Proc. 699 (2010).

§ 21.02 OVERVIEW OF THE UNITED STATES SENTENCING COMMISSION AND SENTENCING GUIDELINES

[A] The Sentencing Commission

The Sentencing Reform Act established the United States Sentencing Commission as an independent body within the judicial branch of the federal government. The Commission is composed of seven voting members appointed by the President "after consultation with representatives of judges, prosecuting attorneys, defense attorneys, law enforcement officials [and others]" and "with the advice and consent of the Senate."[12] Up to three of the members may be federal judges. The Commission is a standing body, and regularly reevaluates and revises the Guidelines, subject to congressional approval.[13] The Commission is charged with establishing federal sentencing policies that "provide certainty and fairness in meeting the purpose of sentencing, avoiding unwarranted sentencing disparities among defendants with similar records who have been found guilty of similar criminal conduct while maintaining sufficient flexibility to permit individualized sentences when warranted by mitigating or aggravating factors."[14]

[B] The Guidelines[15]

The Guidelines adhere to a "real offense" philosophy. That is, as seen below, the sentence is not primarily determined by the crime or crimes of which the defendant has been found guilty. Rather, and as explained more fully in the next sections, all the facts relating to the particular crimes may affect the sentence imposed.

Based upon these factual determinations, the Guidelines set a range for sentences. The range is determined by the Sentencing Table, which is reproduced at the end of this chapter. The Sentencing Table is a grid, with the "Offense Level" on the vertical axis and the "Criminal History Category" on the horizontal axis. The intersection of the Offense Level and the Criminal History Category produces the range of sentences. The maximum sentence is the statutory maximum, even where the Guidelines range could produce a greater sentence.

With respect to the Offense Level, each federal offense has an associated "base level," which is assigned a number of points. This level can be increased by any of a number of factors specified in the Guidelines. Common factors in white collar cases include the amount of loss, the number of victims, the defendant's use of sophisticated means, the defendant's use of more than minimal planning, the defendant's abuse of a position of trust, and the defendant's role as an organizer in

---

[12] 28 U.S.C. § 991(a).

[13] *See* 28 U.S.C. § 994(p).

[14] 28 U.S.C. § 991(b)(1)(B).

[15] For a succinct overview of Guidelines Sentencing, see Harry I. Subin, Barry Berke & Eric Tirschwell, The Practice of Federal Criminal Law: Prosecution and Defense §§ 7.0–7.3 (2006).

the criminal activity. The Guidelines specify the number of points to be added to the base level for such factors.[16]

Among these factors, the amount of loss is the key disputed factor in many white collar sentences. This is particularly true in fraud cases, where the loss amount for Guidelines purposes is the higher of the intended loss or the actual loss.[17] In these cases, the government and defense often present two very different calculations of the loss involved.[18]

With respect to the Criminal History Category, the Table sets forth points based upon whether the defendant falls within one of the six criminal history categories. The principal factors affecting the points awarded include (a) the number and length of prior sentences, and (b) the commission of the offense while under any criminal justice sentence, including probation, parole, supervised release, imprisonment, work release, or escape status.[19]

In order to find the correct sentencing range, the United States Probation Office completes the sentencing worksheets. The Guidelines as originally adopted allow the sentencing judge to make a "departure" from the prescribed sentence range where the defendant has provided substantial assistance to the government,[20] or where the case is outside the "heartland" of factors considered by the Sentencing Commission.[21]

In 2010, in order to clarify the correct sentencing approach under *Booker*, the Sentencing Commission proposed amendments to the Guidelines that articulate a three-step sentencing approach. Under this approach, discussed more fully in the next section,[22] a defendant may use the same grounds to request both downward departures and downward variances under *Booker*. The commentary defines a "variance" as "a sentence that is outside the Guidelines framework."[23]

§ 21.03 INDIVIDUAL SENTENCING UNDER THE GUIDELINES

The complex instructions for Guidelines sentencing are provided by the Federal Sentencing Guidelines Manual.[24] Not surprisingly, the manual is long and detailed.

---

[16] *See, e.g.*, U.S.S.G. § 2B1.1, Larceny, Embezzlement, and Other Forms of Theft; Offenses Involving Stolen Property; Property Damage or Destruction; Fraud and Deceit; Forgery; Offenses Involving Altered or Counterfeit Instruments Other than Counterfeit Bearer Obligations of the United States.

[17] *See* Alan Ellis & James H. Feldman, Jr., *"Intended Loss" Redefined in Fraud Cases*, 24 Crim. Just. 52 (Spring 2009).

[18] The amount of loss may lead to sentences that appear draconian. *See* Alan Ellis, et al., *At a "Loss" for Justice: Federal Sentencing for Economic Offenses*, 25 Crim. Just. 34, 35 (Winter 2011).

[19] *See* U.S.S.G. § 4A1.1.

[20] *See infra*, § 21.03[J][1].

[21] *See* United States v. Koon, 518 U.S. 81, 98 (1996).

[22] *See* Harlan Protass & Mark D. Harris, *Recent Amendments to the Federal Sentencing Guidelines*, N.Y.L.J. (June 11, 2010). *See* text at note 48 *infra*, for a listing of the § 3553(a) factors.

[23] U.S.S.G. Manual § 1B1.1 commentary. *See* Protass & Harris, *supra* note 22.

[24] United States Sentencing Commission, Guidelines Manual.

According to the Commission, the Guidelines were designed to take into consideration "both the seriousness of the offense, including relevant offense characteristics, and important information about the offender, such as the offender's role in the offense and prior record."[25] Additionally, the Guidelines are based upon the principle that the recidivist should be punished more harshly than the first time offender, and that the "shot caller" in a criminal enterprise should be punished more severely than the underlings.

In a Special Report to Congress,[26] the Sentencing Commission set forth the basic method for fixing a sentence. This method includes: (a) determining the base level offense; (b) examining the specific offense characteristics; (c) applying adjustments; (d) counting multiple counts; (e) assessing the defendant's acceptance of responsibility; and (f) assessing the defendant's criminal history. In addition, the sentencing court must determine "relevant conduct," such as alleged criminal acts for which the defendant has not been charged or convicted, when assessing the base offense level, the specific offense characteristics, and adjustments.

In light of *Booker*'s advisory sentencing scheme, the Sentencing Commission in 2010 set forth an approach requiring three steps: (1) calculation of the applicable Guidelines offense level and criminal history score; (2) consideration of the policy statements and commentary to determine whether a departure is warranted; and (3) consideration of all applicable factors under 18 U.S.C. § 3553(a).[27]

[A]   Base Level Offense

The first step in calculating the Guideline range is determining the base level offense. The Guidelines Manual contains over 2,000 separate criminal offenses that are grouped together by offense type and ranked by severity according to their base level offense. The base level offenses vary from one to forty-three categories, with the higher base level offense indicating the more severe offense and subsequent punishment.[28]

[B]   Specific Offense Characteristics

After determining the base level offense, the court must determine whether aggravating circumstances are present in the case. Like the base level offense, specific offense characteristics are grouped by offense type and severity, generally in subsections under the base level offense. If these characteristics are present, the court must adjust the offense level to account for these factors.

This process can substantially affect the sentences. The United States Sentencing Commission reported that "on average, each offense level increment changes the sentence by about twelve percent. Thus, a four-level enhancement equates to about a 50 percent increase in sentence; an eight-level enhancement

---

[25] United States Sentencing Commission, Special Report to Congress: Mandatory Minimum Penalties in the Federal Criminal Justice System 20-26 (1991).

[26] *See id.*

[27] U.S.S.G. Manual § 1B1.1 commentary. *See* Protass & Harris, *supra* note 22.

[28] U.S.S.G. Sentencing Table, Ch. 5, Pt. A.

effectively doubles the sentence."[29] Further, courts will consider the amount of money involved in the crime and adjust the base level offense accordingly.

[C] Adjustments

After calculating the offense level, the court then examines further aggravating or mitigating circumstances that may increase or decrease the penalty. The first consideration examines the victim with respect to such factors as vulnerability. If the defendant is found to have intentionally selected the victim because of known or perceived vulnerability, the defendant may receive an upward adjustment.[30] Further adjustments may be made based upon the role the defendant played in the offense. An upward adjustment is made if the defendant organized or led criminal activity that involved five or more participants. A downward adjustment is made if the defendant played a minor role.[31]

The Guidelines provide a non-exhaustive list of the types of conduct for which an upward adjustment is warranted. For example, a court may order an upward adjustment if the "defendant willfully obstructed or impeded, or attempted to obstruct or impede, the administration of justice during the course of the investigation, prosecution, or sentencing."[32] Other examples include (1) threatening or intimidating co-defendants, witnesses, or jurors, (2) producing false documentation during an investigation, and (3) destroying or concealing material evidence.

[D] Multiple Counts

The Guidelines provide that if a defendant has been convicted of more than one count, the court shall group together all counts involving substantially the same harm. For example, if the defendant is convicted of two counts of mail fraud and one count of wire fraud, each in furtherance of a single fraudulent scheme, the counts are to be grouped together, even if the mailings and the use of the wires occurred on different days.[33] The product of grouping the counts together is a combined offense level, which determines the appropriate sentence in accordance with other circumstances.

[E] Acceptance of Responsibility

A defendant may lower the offense level by accepting responsibility for the offense. A guilty plea may demonstrate some level of acceptance, but a downward adjustment is not provided as a matter of right.[34] The decrease to the offense level

---

[29] United States Sentencing Commission, Special Report to Congress: Mandatory Minimum Penalties in the Federal Criminal Justice System 20-26 (1991).

[30] U.S.S.G. Ch. 3 — Adjustments, Part A — Victim Related Adjustments.

[31] U.S.S.G. Ch. 3 — Adjustments, Part B — Role in the Offense.

[32] U.S.S.G. § 3C1.1.

[33] U.S.S.G. § 3D1.2, Commentary — Application Notes (4).

[34] See An Introduction to Federal Guideline Sentencing Prepared by Federal Public and Community Defenders (Lucien B. Campbell & Henry J. Bemporad eds., 5th ed. 2001).

is generally two levels and only applies if the defendant "clearly demonstrates acceptance of responsibility." The Guidelines provide for an additional one-level decrease if the offense level is sixteen or greater, and the defendant has assisted authorities in the investigation by "timely notifying authorities of his intention to enter a plea of guilty thereby permitting the government to avoid preparing for trial and permitting the government and the court to allocate their resources efficiently."[35]

[F] Defendant's Criminal History

The Comprehensive Crime Control Act lists a number of purposes in imposing a sentence, and a defendant's prior criminal activity plays an important role in this process. In addition to reflecting the seriousness of the offense and acting as a deterrent to further criminal conduct, the sentencing court shall consider "the history and characteristics of the defendant."[36] To account for this, a criminal history is translated into category points and forms the horizontal reference on the sentencing table. The rationale is that a defendant with a prior criminal record is more culpable than a first-time offender and deserves greater punishment. The Guidelines state:

> General deterrence of criminal conduct dictates that a clear message be sent to society that repeated criminal behavior will aggravate the need for punishment with each recurrence. To protect the public from further crimes of the particular defendant, the likelihood of recidivism and future criminal behavior must be considered. Repeated criminal behavior is an indicator of a limited likelihood of successful rehabilitation.[37]

Points are added for each prior conviction and then calculated to determine the criminal history category that ultimately establishes the range of the sentence. The points are assigned based upon the length of each prior sentence. There are no limits to the number of points that may be counted under the criminal history section. Thus, a defendant with a number of prior sentences will receive a substantially increased sentence for any subsequent conviction.[38]

[G] Relevant Conduct

The Guidelines provide that the trial court may use "relevant conduct" when determining the sentence. Such conduct includes "all acts and omissions . . . that occurred during the commission of the offense, in preparation for that offense, or in the course of attempting to avoid detection or responsibility for that offense." Further, relevant conduct includes "all acts and omissions that were part of the same course of conduct or common scheme or plan as the offense of conviction."[39]

---

[35] U.S.S.G. § 3E1.1(b)(1)–(2).

[36] 18 U.S.C. § 3553(a)(1) (2000).

[37] U.S.S.G. Chapter Four — Criminal History and Criminal Livelihood — Part A — Criminal History — Introductory Commentary.

[38] U.S.S.G. § 4A1.1(a)–(f).

[39] U.S.S.G. § 1B1.3(a).

These provisions have produced a significant amount of litigation. One principal issue was resolved by the Supreme Court in *United States v. Watts*.[40] In that case, the Court held that a sentencing court may consider conduct relating to a criminal charge even when the jury has acquitted the defendant of that charge. Once the prosecution has proven that the conduct occurred by a preponderance of the evidence, the judge may consider the conduct. The Court rejected the defendant's arguments that this use of criminal conduct violated the Sentencing Reform Act and the Double Jeopardy Clause.

In another case, *Witte v. United States*,[41] the Court held that the sentencing court may consider relevant conduct used in a *previous* federal sentence, even when that conduct is the basis of the charges in the second case. In *Witte*, the defendant was found guilty of narcotics charges relating to marijuana. In calculating the sentence, the court took into account an uncharged cocaine transaction as relevant conduct. The defendant was later separately tried, convicted, and sentenced for the same cocaine transaction. The Court held that this did not violate the double jeopardy prohibition. Courts have continued to consider acquitted conduct after *Booker*.[42]

[H]   Sentencing Range

After both the offense level and criminal history are calculated, the court may impose imprisonment or some other form of sanction.[43] In reading the Sentencing Table, the Offense Level (ranging from one to forty-three) makes up the vertical axis, while the Criminal History Category (ranging from I to VI) makes up the horizontal axis. The intersection of the two indicates the appropriate range of the sentence in months of imprisonment.

[I]   Fines

The guidelines also provide detailed instructions for imposing sentences other than imprisonment, including probation, fines, restitution, and forfeitures. Section 5E1.2 provides a "Fine Table" that utilizes the offense level system in conjunction with suggested minimum and maximum impositions. If the defendant establishes that he is unable to pay and is not likely to become able to pay, the court will not impose a fine.[44]

---

[40]   519 U.S. 148, *reh'g denied*, 519 U.S. 1144 (1997).

[41]   515 U.S. 389, 395–99 (1995).

[42]   *See, e.g.*, United States v. Brown, 516 F.3d 1047, 1050 (D.C. Cir. 2008); United States v. Tyndall, 521 F.3d 877, 883 (8th Cir. 2008); United States v. Faust, 456 F.3d 1342, 1348 (11th Cir. 2006).

[43]   The court should impose a sentence sufficient, but not greater than necessary, to comply with the statutory purposes of sentencing. 18 U.S.C. § 3553(a).

[44]   U.S.S.G. § 5E1.2(a).

[J] Departures

Under the 2010 three-step approach, the court first determines the Guidelines range. Then, as a second step, the court should then consider "the [Guidelines] policy statements and commentary to determine whether a departure is warranted." The most common ground for a departure is the defendant's "substantial assistance" to the government. Section 5K1.1 of the Guidelines provides that the government may file a motion (a "5K1.1 motion") for a downward departure when the defendant has provided substantial assistance to a criminal investigation. The decision to file such a motion, however, is within the prosecutor's discretion. In *Wade v. United States*,[45] the Supreme Court held that the defendant is not *entitled* to such a motion. Other courts have also held that the sentencing court is not required to grant such a motion if it is made by the government.

The *Booker* decision has affected courts' ability to adjust sentences based upon the defendant's assistance to the government. First, courts have imposed below-Guidelines sentences based upon the defendant's cooperation even in cases in which the government has not filed a § 5K1.1 motion.[46] Second, where the government has filed such motions, district courts have granted greater substantial assistance departures than the government requested. In both cases, the sentence will then be subject to a reasonableness review.[47]

[K] Section 3553(a) Factors

Under the third step of the sentencing process, courts must comply with the requirements of 18 U.S.C. § 3553(a). That section requires sentencing courts to consider:

(1)   the nature and circumstances of the offense and the history and characteristics of the defendant;

(2)   the need for the sentence imposed –

  (A)   to reflect the seriousness of the offense, to promote respect for the law, and to provide just punishment for the offense;

  (B)   to afford adequate deterrence to criminal conduct;

---

[45] 504 U.S. 181 (1992). *See, e.g.*, United States v. Mariano, 983 F.2d 1150, 1155 (1993) ("[t]he district court is not obliged to depart downward simply because a grateful prosecutor prefers a lighter sentence").

[46] *See* United States v. Fernandez, 443 F.3d 19, 33 (2d Cir. 2006) ("in formulating a reasonable sentence a sentencing judge must consider 'the history and characteristics of the defendant' within the meaning of 18 U.S.C. § 3553(a)(1), as well as the other factors enumerated in § 3553(a), and should take under advisement any related arguments, including the contention that a defendant made efforts to cooperate, even if those efforts did not yield a Government motion for a downward departure pursuant to U.S.S.G. § 5K1.1 ('non-5K cooperation')").

[47] *Compare* United States v. Haack, 403 F.3d 997 (8th Cir. 2005) (the district court granted a greater substantial assistance departure than the government requested; the appeals court reversed the sentence as unreasonable), *with* United States v. Pizano, 403 F.3d 991 (8th Cir. 2005) (the district court granted a greater substantial assistance departure than the government requested; the appeals court affirmed the sentence as reasonable).

(C)   to protect the public from further crimes of the defendant; and

(D)   to provide the defendant with needed educational or vocational training, medical care, or other correctional treatment in the most effective manner;

(3)   the kinds of sentences available;

(4)   the kinds of sentence and the sentencing range established for –

(A)   the applicable category of offense committed by the applicable category of defendant as set forth in the guidelines . . .

(B)   in the case of a violation of probation or supervised release, the applicable guidelines or policy statements issued by the Sentencing Commission . . . ;

(5)   any pertinent policy statement

(A)   issued by the Sentencing Commission . . . ; and

(B)   that . . . is in effect on the date the defendant is sentenced;

(6)   the need to avoid unwarranted sentence disparities among defendants with similar records who have been found guilty of similar conduct; and

(7)   the need to provide restitution to any victims of the offense.[48]

The statute further instructs sentencing courts to impose a sentence that is "sufficient but not greater than necessary" to satisfy the purposes of sentencing — just punishment, deterrence, protection of the public, and rehabilitation of the defendant.[49] The Supreme Court has stated that this "parsimony" clause represents the "overarching provision" of the statute.[50]

---

[48] 18 U.S.C. § 3553(a).

[49] *Id.*

[50] *Kimbrough*, 552 U.S. at 101. In *Booker*'s aftermath, the Department of Justice amended its sentencing policy. In a memorandum dated May 19, 2010, the DOJ announced a policy that requires prosecutors, in their sentencing advocacy, to take into account the § 3553 factors. In addition, the memorandum states:

> [P]rosecutors should generally continue to advocate for a sentence within [the Guidelines] range. The advisory guidelines remain important in furthering the goal of national uniformity throughout the federal system. But . . . given the advisory nature of the guidelines, advocacy at sentencing — like charging decisions and plea agreements — must also follow from an individualized assessment of the facts and circumstances of each particular case.

See May 19, 2010 Memorandum from Eric H. Holder, Jr., To All Federal Prosecutors Re Department Policy on Charging and Sentencing, SS026 ALI-ABA 35 (May 19, 2010).

§ 21.04   CONSTITUTIONALITY OF THE GUIDELINES

[A]   Delegation of Authority and Separation of Powers

The Guidelines adopted by the Commission took effect on November 1, 1987. Almost immediately, the constitutionality of the Guidelines and the Commission itself became a significant issue. Challengers to the Guidelines made two constitutional arguments: that Congress's delegation of authority to the Commission was insufficiently specific and detailed; and that the creation of the Commission violated the separation of powers doctrine. The Supreme Court rejected these arguments and upheld the Guidelines in *Mistretta v. United States*.[51] In that case, the defendant was convicted of narcotics charges. Mistretta moved to have the Guidelines held unconstitutional "on the grounds that the Sentencing Commission was constituted in violation of the established doctrine of separation of powers, and that Congress delegated excessive authority to the Commission to structure the Guidelines."[52]

In response, the Court first found that Congress was not prohibited from assigning to a group of experts within the judicial branch the job of formulating sentencing guidelines. When such a group is guided by a very specific statutory mandate, as here, Congress is not prohibited from obtaining the group's assistance.[53]

As to the separation of powers argument, the Court first found that it was appropriate for the Commission to exist within the judicial branch because that branch is responsible for sentencing in general.[54] Further, because the Commission's judicial members act in an administrative rather than a judicial capacity, their appointment by the President does not violate Article III.[55] Finally, the Court rejected the defendant's argument that the system of presidential appointments to a judicial body violated the separation of powers. The Court found that the system of appointments did not prevent "the Judicial branch from performing its constitutionally assigned function of fairly adjudicating cases and controversies."[56]

[B]   The Sixth Amendment Right to a Jury Trial

This section discusses both the merits and remedial opinions in *Booker*. It then briefly addresses some of the principal issues with which the lower courts are struggling after *Booker*.

---

[51] 488 U.S. 361 (1989).

[52] *Id.* at 370.

[53] *Id.* at 371–72.

[54] *Id.* at 384–97.

[55] *Id.* at 397–408.

[56] *Id.* at 411.

[1] The *Booker* Decision

In a series of decisions, the Supreme Court has held that certain facts must be found by a jury under the Sixth Amendment's right to a jury trial. In *Apprendi v. New Jersey*,[57] the Court held that "other than the fact of a prior conviction, any fact that increases the penalty for a crime beyond the prescribed statutory maximum must be submitted to a jury, and proved beyond a reasonable doubt." In that case, the statute authorized a sentence above the statutory maximum when the judge found that the offense was a "hate crime." The Court held that imposition of a sentence above the statutory maximum, based solely on facts found by the judge, violated the Sixth Amendment.

Then, in *Blakely v. Washington*,[58] the Court held that the sentencing system employed by the state of Washington violated the defendant's Sixth Amendment right to a jury trial because the system allowed the judge to make factual findings that determined a defendant's sentence. In that case, the trial judge found that the defendant's sentence for kidnapping should be longer than the standard sentencing range because the defendant acted with "deliberate cruelty." The United States Supreme Court held that this procedure violated the Sixth Amendment. Even though the sentence did not exceed the statutory maximum, it did exceed a statutorily-defined sentencing range.

In *Booker*, a consolidation of two appeals, the Court extended those holdings to sentencing under the United States Sentencing Guidelines. The *Booker* decision is in effect two separate decisions: (1) the "merits" decision on the substance of the Sixth Amendment issue; and (2) the "remedial" decision on how the Guidelines should be interpreted in light of the merits decision.

In the merits decision, a five-member majority found that the Sixth Amendment's right to a jury trial is violated when a sentence is enhanced based on the sentencing judge's determination of a fact, other than a prior conviction, that was not found by the jury or admitted by the defendant.[59] In Booker's case, the Guidelines sentence based upon the jury verdict was 210–262 months. Based upon additional facts found by the judge at sentencing, the sentence was 360 months to life. Applying *Apprendi* and *Blakely* to Guidelines sentencing, the Court reversed the sentence and held that the Guidelines, as written, were unconstitutional.

The merits dissent argued that there was no Sixth Amendment violation because the law historically has distinguished between facts that are elements of crimes and facts that are relevant only to sentencing.[60] Thus, the dissent argued, federal law has traditionally looked to judges, not to juries, to resolve disputes about sentencing facts. This procedure has long been followed because it is often difficult to obtain relevant sentencing information during the trial. It is therefore more efficient for the judge to determine such information after the trial is over.

---

[57] 530 U.S. 466, 490 (2000).

[58] 542 U.S. 296 (2004).

[59] 543 U.S. at 225.

[60] *Id.* at 326 (Breyer, J., dissenting).

In the separate remedial decision, a different five-member majority (with Justice Ginsburg providing the swing vote) held that the Guidelines could survive constitutional scrutiny if the provisions that make Guidelines sentences mandatory were excised from the Guidelines.[61] This approach, the Court stated, would maintain a strong connection between the sentence imposed and the offender's real conduct — a connection important to the increased sentencing uniformity that Congress intended the Guidelines system to achieve. The Court also found that requiring the jury to determine all facts relevant to sentencing would be contrary to congressional intent, and would prove unduly cumbersome in practice. Thus, courts should consider the Guidelines when imposing sentences, but Guidelines sentences are no longer mandatory. Further, the Court held that appellate courts should evaluate those sentences for "unreasonableness."[62] Finally, the *Booker* remedial decision stated that sentencing judges and courts must still consider the Guidelines range, but must also consider the other directives set forth in § 3553(a) of the Guidelines.

Many predicted that *Booker* would produce the types of sentencing disparities that the Guidelines were adopted to prohibit. The indications are, however, that most courts are continuing to impose Guidelines-range sentences.[63]

[2] Issues Created by *Booker*

The *Booker* decision raises a number of important issues. Not surprisingly, courts are providing varying approaches to these questions.

[a] Plain Error

One issue arising after *Booker* concerns defendants who failed to argue at the trial level that their sentencing violated the Sixth Amendment under *Apprendi*. The circuit courts are split as to whether such defendants may appeal those sentences under the plain error rule. Generally, a federal appeals court will not consider an argument that the defendant did not make at the trial level. One exception to this rule arises when the trial judge committed "plain error." Plain error occurs when the decision was in error, the error was obvious, and the error affected the defendant's substantial rights. Some courts also require the defendant to show that the error seriously affected the fairness of the judicial proceeding. The circuit courts are split as to whether sentencing under a mandatory Guidelines

---

[61] *Id.* at 224.

[62] *Id.* The dissenters from the remedial opinion argued that the majority adopted an approach that Congress had considered and rejected. *Id.* at 272 (Stevens, J., dissenting). Instead, the dissenters would have obliged the government to prove any fact that is required to increase a defendant's sentence under the Guidelines to a jury beyond a reasonable doubt. *Id.*

[63] The United States Sentencing Commission regularly issues reports containing sentencing data. *See* http://www.ussc.gov/Data_and_Statistics/Federal_Sentencing_Statistics/Kimbrough_Gall/ USSC_Kimbrough_Gall_Report_Final_FY2008.pdf. The 2008 report, for example, showed that 61 percent of post-*Booker* sentences were within Guidelines ranges, substantially the same percentage as before *Booker*. The vast majority of departures were government-sponsored departures, most of those substantial assistance departures. Interestingly, courts have been less likely to depart downward in fraud cases than in other areas. *See id.*

system is "plain error."[64]

[b]   Harmless Error

Another issue under the *Apprendi/Blakely/Booker* rulings is whether a violation of the Sixth Amendment in the sentencing context is subject to harmless error analysis. Under *Chapman v. California*,[65] harmless error analysis requires a showing beyond a reasonable doubt that the error did not contribute to the result. The only errors not subject to such analysis are those that, as the Supreme Court has stated, fall within a "limited class of fundamental constitutional errors."[66] In the sentencing context, then, the issue arises when a judge finds a fact that increases the penalty beyond the prescribed range. The question is whether the sentence necessarily must be reversed as a fundamental constitutional error or may be subjected to harmless error analysis. This issue divided the federal circuits and the state courts. The United States Supreme Court resolved this issue, holding that *Booker* violations may be subject to harmless error analysis.[67]

[c]   Reasonableness

The *Booker* remedial opinion states that sentences are now to be reviewed for "reasonableness," but does not define that term.[68] The opinion concludes that this system will "maintain[] a strong connection between the sentence imposed and the offender's real conduct — a connection important to the increased uniformity of sentencing that Congress intended its Guidelines system to achieve."[69] In his dissent, Justice Scalia opined that the reasonableness standard "may lead some courts of appeals to conclude — may indeed be designed to lead courts of appeals to conclude — that little has changed."[70]

The circuit courts sharply split as to whether Guidelines sentences are presumptively reasonable.[71] Some circuits stated that a presumption of reasonableness would implicate a mandatory sentencing scheme, in violation of *Booker*. Other circuits, by contrast, plainly stated that nearly all Guidelines sentences should be considered reasonable.[72]

In *Rita v. United States*,[73] the Supreme Court attempted to resolve this split

---

[64] *Compare* United States v. Hughes, 401 F.3d 540 (4th Cir. 2005) (finding plain error), *with* United States v. Rodriguez, 398 F.3d 1291 (11th Cir. 2005) (finding no plain error because the defendant's rights were not substantially affected).

[65] 386 U.S. 18, 23 (1967).

[66] Neder v. United States, 527 U.S. 1, 7 (1999), *citing* Arizona v. Fulminante, 499 U.S. 279, 309 (1991).

[67] Washington v. Recuenco, 548 U.S. 212 (2006).

[68] 543 U.S. at 246.

[69] *Id.*

[70] *Id.* at 311–12 (Scalia, J., dissenting).

[71] *See* United States v. Fernandez, 443 F.3d 19, 27–28 (2d Cir. 2006) (discussing circuit split and listing cases).

[72] *See id.*

[73] 551 U.S. 338, 347 (2007).

and held that a federal appeals court "may apply a presumption of reasonableness to a district court sentence that reflects a proper application of the Sentencing Guidelines." The Court emphasized that this was an appellate presumption only, and does not apply at the trial level. In his dissent, Justice Souter argued that this result will nonetheless lead district courts to in effect apply a presumption of reasonableness to Guidelines-range sentences, in violation of *Booker*, because a "trial judge will find it far easier to make the appropriate findings and sentence within the appropriate Guideline, than to go through the unorthodox factfinding necessary to justify a sentence outside the Guidelines range."[74]

Another issue related to reasonableness is whether it is proper for a court of appeals to review sentences under a "sliding scale" approach. Under that approach, the court applies a presumption that "the strength of the justification needed to sustain an outside-Guidelines sentence varies in proportion to the degree of the variance."[75]

The Supreme Court rejected the sliding scale approach in *United States v. Gall*.[76] The Court held that an appeals court should review the sentence under a deferential reasonableness standard for (1) procedural error[77] and (2) substantive error. Further, the Court stated that trial courts may not presume that Guidelines-range sentences are reasonable, and that appeals courts may not presume that non-Guidelines sentences are unreasonable. The Court also held that an appeals court may not require "extraordinary" circumstances to justify a non-Guidelines sentence.

Finally, courts of appeal split as to whether a policy disagreement with the Sentencing Guidelines is an appropriate basis for a non-Guidelines sentence. The Supreme Court held in *Kimbrough v. United States*[78] that trial judges may indeed use policy disagreements as the basis for imposing a non-Guidelines sentence.

As one federal appeals court has noted,[79] the decisions in *Booker*, *Rita*, *Gall*, and *Kimbrough* provide some overarching principles for determining a "reasonable" sentence under the Guidelines:

---

[74] *Id.* at 384 (Souter, J., dissenting).

[75] *Rita*, 551 U.S. at 391. *See, e.g.*, United States v. Crisp, 454 F.3d 1285, 1291 (11th Cir. 2006) (holding that "[a]n extraordinary reduction must be supported by extraordinary circumstances").

[76] Gall v. United States, 552 U.S. 38 (2007).

[77] Procedural errors that can render the trial court's sentencing procedure unreasonable include (1) miscalculation of the Guidelines sentence, (2) treating the Guidelines as mandatory, (3) failure to consider the § 3553(a) factors, (4) using clearly erroneous facts, (5) failure to explain the sentence adequately. *Id.* at 51.

[78] 552 U.S. 85 (2007) (sentencing judges can consider the 100-to-1 sentencing disparity in crack-cocaine cases to ensure that a sentence for a cocaine conviction is "sufficient but not greater than necessary" under the Guidelines). In another decision affirming the post-*Booker* discretion afforded to trial judges, the Court held in Pepper v. United States, 131 S. Ct. 1229 (2011), that the sentencing judge has discretion to consider post-sentencing rehabilitation, when resentencing after a remand, and that the statutory subsection stating to the contrary (§ 3742(g)(2)) is invalid under *Booker*.

[79] United States v. Jones, 531 F.3d 163, 170–74 (2d Cir. 2008). *See* http://www.nyfederalcriminalpractice.com/2008/06/second-circuit-issues-notable-5.html.

- Trial courts may not presume that a Guidelines-range sentence is reasonable.

- Trial courts may base sentencing upon disagreements with policies reflected in the Guidelines.

- Policy disagreements are subject to closer review where those policies were based upon empirical study undertaken by the Sentencing Commission.

- Appellate courts may, but are not required to, presume that a Guidelines-range sentence is reasonable.

- Appellate courts may not presume that an outside Guidelines-range sentence is unreasonable.

- Appellate courts should defer to trial courts' sentencing determinations because those courts are more experienced at determining sentences and are in a better position to determine the facts relevant to sentencing.

- Appellate courts may not apply a "sliding scale" approach that requires a proportionately greater justification the farther the sentence is from the Guidelines range.

- Appellate courts may not require "extraordinary" circumstances for a non-Guidelines-range sentence.

- Appellate courts may, however, require that a substantial variance from the Guidelines range be supported by a more substantial justification than a minor variance.

- Appellate courts should apply the abuse of discretion standard, and should not reverse a conviction based merely on disagreement as to the correct sentence.

[d]　The Standard of Review on Appeal

Complex issues arise when an appeals court reviews a federal sentence. In *Koon v. United States*,[80] the United States Supreme Court held that, when reviewing Guidelines sentences, the courts of appeal should apply an abuse of discretion standard.[81] In response to *Koon*, Congress enacted a statute requiring appeals courts to review sentences de novo, with the intention of limiting trial judges' ability to depart from the Guidelines.[82]

In its *Gall* decision, the Court made clear that, after *Booker*, the abuse of discretion standard once again applies.[83] Thus, appellate courts may not engage in de novo review, or apply a heightened standard of review to a non-Guidelines-range sentence. As the Court stated in *Gall*, "the Guidelines are now advisory, and

---

[80] 518 U.S. 81 (1996).

[81] *See supra,* § 21.03[J][2].

[82] The Prosecutorial Remedies and Other Tools to End the Exploitation of Children Today Act of 2003 ("PROTECT Act"), Pub. L. No. 108-21, 117 Stat. 650 (codified as amended at 18 U.S.C. § 3553(b)(2)).

[83] 552 U.S. 38 (2007).

appellate review of sentencing decisions is limited to determining whether they are 'reasonable . . . .' [T]he familiar abuse-of-discretion standard of review now applies to appellate review of sentencing decisions."[84]

[e]   Post-*Booker* Deference to the Guidelines

Courts now must follow the *Booker* scheme, as interpreted by the Court in *Rita, Gall, Kimbrough,* and other cases. Most sentences will likely continue to be within Guidelines ranges, although there are indications that some substantial inconsistencies are also likely, both among trial courts and appellate courts.[85] It does appear that *Gall* and *Kimbrough* have accelerated the post-*Booker* trend towards an increase in non-Guidelines-range sentences.[86] This may especially be true in cases in which the amount of loss — one of the key factors in many white collar sentences — produces lengthy sentences.[87]

[f]   Substantial Assistance

The *Booker* decision has affected courts' ability to order departures from Guidelines-range sentences. First, some courts have expressly stated that, even in the absence of a government motion, a court may now impose a below-Guidelines sentence based upon the defendant's cooperation.[88] Second, where the government has filed a motion, the district court may grant a larger or smaller substantial assistance departure than the government requested. In both cases, the sentence will presumably then be subject to a reasonableness review.[89]

In one high profile case, *United States v. Martin,*[90] the Eleventh Circuit reversed a downward departure as unreasonably lenient. The defendant was Michael Martin, the former HealthSouth Corporation Chief Financial Officer. Martin pled guilty to conspiracy to commit securities fraud and mail fraud and to falsify books and records in connection with a major accounting scandal that

---

[84] *Id.*

[85] Inconsistencies are appearing even among different panels within the same circuits. *Compare, e.g.,* United States v. Jones, 531 F.3d 163 (2d Cir. 2008) (deferring to trial court's sentencing determination), *with* United States v. Cutler, 520 F.3d 136 (2d Cir. 2008) (overturning sentences in white collar case and finding that trial judge abused discretion in making factual determinations underlying the sentence).

[86] In the three years before *Booker* was decided in 2005, within-range sentences averaged from about 65 to 72 percent of all sentences. After *Booker,* but before *Kimbrough and Gall,* 61.3 percent of sentences were within the Guidelines range. After *Gall* and *Kimbrough* were decided 59.2 percent of sentences were within the Guidelines range. *See* http://www.ussc.gov/Data_and_Statistics/ Federal_Sentencing_Statistics/Kimbrough_Gall/USSC_Kimbrough_Gall_Report_Final_FY2008.pdf. These statistics are through 2008.

[87] *See Off the Chart: The U.S. Sentencing Guidelines Become Increasingly Irrelevant in the Wake of the Market Meltdown,* 4 White Collar Crim. R. No. 9 (BNA April 24, 2009).

[88] *See* United States v. Fernandez, 443 F.3d 19, 33 (2d Cir. 2006).

[89] *Compare* United States v. Haack, 403 F.3d 997 (8th Cir. 2005) (the district court granted a greater substantial assistance departure than the government requested; the appeals court reversed the sentence as unreasonable), *with* United States v. Pizano, 403 F.3d 991 (8th Cir. 2005) (the district court granted a greater substantial assistance departure than the government requested; the appeals court affirmed the sentence as reasonable).

[90] 455 F.3d 1227 (11th Cir. 2006).

resulted, among other damages, in a loss of $1.4 billion to HealthSouth shareholders. The parties agreed that the Guidelines range sentence was 108 to 135 months' imprisonment, and that Martin's substantial assistance merited a downward departure pursuant to § 5K1.1.

At the first sentencing, the trial judge sentenced Martin to 60 months' probation. The Eleventh Circuit vacated the sentence for lack of a record capable of meaningful appellate review and remanded for resentencing. At the resentencing, although the government recommended a downward departure to 42 months' imprisonment, the district judge imposed a sentence of seven days' imprisonment based principally on Martin's "extraordinary" assistance to the government in its investigation of the fraud.[91]

The government appealed, and the Eleventh Circuit once again vacated the sentence. Acknowledging the extent of Martin's cooperation, the court nonetheless concluded that the seven-day sentence "was unreasonable where Martin's crimes yielded an advisory guidelines range of 9–11 years' imprisonment and a potential sentence of 15 years. Martin's cooperation, while commendable and extremely valuable, is not a get-out-of-jail-free card."[92] The court found that the sentence failed to consider the seriousness of Martin's crimes and failed to provide the needed deterrence.[93]

In a post-*Gall* case also arising out of the HealthSouth matter, *United States v. Livesay*,[94] the appellate court once again reversed a substantial assistance downward departure. In reversing a sentence of probation, the appeals court found that the trial court had committed procedural error by considering the defendant's withdrawal from the conspiracy when determining the extent of the substantial assistance downward departure. Because the trial judge stated that he would have imposed the same sentence employing the § 3553(a) factors, the appellate court reviewed the reasonableness of the sentence and found that the trial court had failed to adequately explain the basis for the sentence. The court remanded for resentencing.

These cases show that appellate courts continue to exercise the power to overturn trial judges' sentencing determinations. In white collar cases in particular, appeals courts may be wary of allowing substantial downward departures in cases of economic fraud that produced substantial harm.

---

[91] *Id.* at 1234.

[92] *Id.* at 1238.

[93] *Id.* at 1239–40.

[94] 525 F.3d 1081 (11th Cir. 2008). Upon remand, a different district court judge again sentenced Livesay to probation. Again, the court of appeals reversed, this time holding that no sentence of probation would be reasonable. *See* United States v. Livesay, 587 F.3d 1274 (11th Cir. 2009).

§ 21.05 ORGANIZATIONAL SENTENCING UNDER THE GUIDELINES

[A] Overview

When the guidelines originally took effect in 1987, there were no Guidelines or policy statements concerning sentencing of organizations. Four years following adoption of the individual rules, the Organizational Guidelines were adopted.[95] These Guidelines, highlighted in Chapter Eight of the Federal Sentencing Manual, took effect on November 1, 1991. The Organizational Guidelines employ many of the same sentencing methods as the Guidelines for individuals, including determinations of the base offense level, the culpability of the defendant, and the appropriateness of departures.

When the Commission adopted the Organizational Guidelines, it endeavored to follow the general principles reflected in the individual sentencing Guidelines. Thus, the Guidelines provide for determination of base offense levels, culpability, and departures. Although the *Booker* decision did not address the Organizational Guidelines, *Booker* apparently applies in this context and renders the Organizational Guidelines advisory rather than mandatory.[96]

In a major departure from the individual Guidelines, however, a court must impose a restitution order to remedy any harm caused by an organizational defendant. As the introductory notes to the organizational sentencing chapter states, "the resources expended to remedy the harm should not be viewed as punishment, but rather as a means of making victims whole for the harm caused."[97]

The Organizational Guidelines apply to "all organizations for felony and Class A misdemeanor offenses," including fraud, theft, tax violations, antitrust offenses, money laundering, bribery, and kickbacks. According to the Guidelines, the term "organization" includes "corporations, partnerships, associations, joint-stock companies, unions, trusts, pension funds, unincorporated organizations, governments and political subdivisions thereof, and non-profit organizations."[98] As an organization can only act through its individual agents, organizations become vicariously liable for offenses committed by these agents. This has increasingly led to federal prosecution of the organization in addition to, or instead of, individual corporate agents.[99]

---

[95] *See generally* Elkan Abramowitz & Alan P. Williamson, *Corporate Sentencing Under the Federal Guidelines, in* White Collar Crime: Business and Regulatory Offenses §§ 15.01–08 (Otto Obermaier & Robert Morvillo, eds. 2011); Elizabeth A. Plimpton & Danielle Walsh, *Corporate Criminal Liability*, 47 Am. Crim. L. Rev. 331, 342–61 (2010); Thirty-Ninth Annual Review of Criminal Procedure, *Sentencing Guidelines*, 39 Geo. L.J. Ann. Rev. Crim. Proc. 699 (2010); Timothy A. Johnson, *Sentencing Organizations After* Booker, 116 Yale L.J. 632 (2006).

[96] *See* Rebecca Walker, *Impact of* United States v. Booker *and* United States v. Fanfan *on Compliance*, Practicing Law Institute, Corporate Law and Practice Course Handbook Series 170–71 (March–June 2005).

[97] U.S.S.G. Chapter Eight — Sentencing of Organizations — Introductory Commentary.

[98] U.S.S.G. § 8A1.1.

[99] *See* Chapter 2, Corporate and Individual Liability, *supra.*

[B] Effect on Organizational Conduct

The Organizational Guidelines provides incentives that have significantly affected the manner in which organizations operate. Most importantly, the Guidelines provide strong incentives for organizations to adopt effective corporate compliance programs.[100] Under the Organizational Guidelines, four factors can increase the organization's penalty:

(i)   Involvement in or tolerance of criminal activity;

(ii) Prior violations, including civil and administrative dispositions;

(iii) Violation of an earlier court order during the occurrence of the offense which is being prosecuted; and

(iv) Obstruction of justice.

The penalty can be mitigated in two instances:

(i)   When the organization had an effective compliance and ethics program; and

(ii) When the organization engaged in self-reporting, cooperated with the authorities, or accepted responsibility.[101]

[C] Sanctions

[1] Restitution

In the event that the organizational defendant is convicted, it must remedy the harm caused by the offense. When the victim is identifiable, the court must either enter a restitution order for the full amount of the victim's loss or impose a term of probation with a condition requiring restitution in the full amount.[102]

[2] Community Service

A court may order community service where such a remedy "is reasonably designed to repair the harm caused by the offense."[103] The imposition of community service is essentially an indirect monetary sanction because an organization can only perform such service by paying its employees or others to carry out such service.

A court may sentence organizations to probation if such a term is necessary to secure restitution or the completion of community service. The Guidelines provide that "any sentence of probation shall include the condition that the organization not

---

[100] The existence of a corporate compliance program allows for a three-point reduction in a corporation's culpability score if the "offense occurred despite an effective program to prevent and detect violations." U.S.S.G. § 8C2.5(f)(1).

[101] *See* U.S.S.G. Ch. 8 Introduction. For a discussion of compliance programs, see Chapter 17, Internal Investigations and Compliance Programs, *supra*, § 17.03.

[102] U.S.S.G. § 8B1.1(a)(1)–(2).

[103] U.S.S.G. § 8B1.3.

commit another federal, state, or local crime during the term of probation."[104] Other conditions include periodic reports to the court on the organization's financial conditions and business operations, regular submission by the organization to unannounced examinations of its books and records, and notification requirements concerning material adverse changes in the business or financial condition of the organization.[105]

[3] Fines

A court may impose fines to both punish past criminal conduct and to deter future criminal conduct. In calculating fines, courts use a process similar to that used in determining an individual's sentence. The sentence is thus based on the organization's base level offense, any aggravating or mitigating circumstances, and subsequent culpability.

If a court finds that an organization operated primarily for a criminal purpose or primarily by criminal means, then the fine is set so as to divest the organization of all of its net assets.[106] This is referred to as the "corporate death penalty" because the fine imposed is large enough to put the organization out of business. An organization that is merely a front for a scheme designed to commit fraud is an example of the sort of organization that the corporate death penalty is intended to target.

Assuming that an organization is not subject to the corporate death penalty, the fine is calculated after determining the base level offense for each count upon which the conviction was obtained, along with any appropriate adjustments. The next step is calculating the base fine, which takes the largest amount from either an offense level fine table based upon the organization's offense level, or the pecuniary gain to the organization from the offense, or the pecuniary loss caused by the organization to the extent the loss was caused intentionally, knowingly, or recklessly.[107]

After calculating the base fine level, the court determines the organization's culpability using a complex five-point system. This system includes an evaluation of (1) the steps taken by the organization, prior to the offense, to prevent and detect criminal conduct, (2) the level and extent of involvement by certain organizational personnel, and (3) the organization's actions after an offense has been committed.[108]

The organization's culpability score will increase if the organization was involved in or tolerated criminal activity. The organization's score will decrease if it reports the offense to law enforcement, or if it cooperates with a criminal investigation once the offense is reported. Similar downward adjustments are made if the organization

---

[104] U.S.S.G. § 8D1.3(a).

[105] U.S.S.G. § 8D1.4(b)(1)–(3).

[106] U.S.S.G. § 8C1.1.

[107] U.S.S.G. § 8C2.4. The Guidelines were amended in 2001, providing for lower penalties where losses are lower, and higher penalties where losses are higher. The amendments also redefined loss as the greater of actual or intended loss. *See White Collar Crime Institute Focuses on Recent Changes to Sentencing Guidelines*, Crim. L. Rep. (BNA) 561, 561 (March 27, 2002).

[108] *See* Hutchison, *supra* note 10, at 1645.

can demonstrate that it had an effective compliance program in place.[109]

After calculating the scores, the court will determine the amount of the fine within the applicable guideline range. Here, the court considers the "need for the sentence to reflect the seriousness of the offense, promote respect for the law, provide just punishment, afford adequate deterrence, and protect the public from further crimes of the organization."[110]

---

[109] U.S.S.G. § 8C2.5(f).

[110] U.S.S.G. § 8C2.8(a)(1).

SENTENCING TABLE
(in months of imprisonment)

	Offense Level	Criminal History Category (Criminal History Points)					
		I (0 or 1)	II (2 or 3)	III (4, 5, 6)	IV (7, 8, 9)	V (10, 11, 12)	VI (13 or more)
Zone A	1	0-6	0-6	0-6	0-6	0-6	0-6
	2	0-6	0-6	0-6	0-6	0-6	1-7
	3	0-6	0-6	0-6	0-6	2-8	3-9
	4	0-6	0-6	0-6	2-8	4-10	6-12
	5	0-6	0-6	1-7	4-10	6-12	9-15
	6	0-6	1-7	2-8	6-12	9-15	12-18
Zone B	7	0-6	2-8	4-10	8-14	12-18	15-21
	8	0-6	4-10	6-12	10-16	15-21	18-24
	9	4-10	6-12	8-14	12-18	18-24	21-27
Zone C	10	6-12	8-14	10-16	15-21	21-27	24-30
	11	8-14	10-16	12-18	18-24	24-30	27-33
	12	10-16	12-18	15-21	21-27	27-33	30-37
	13	12-18	15-21	18-24	24-30	30-37	33-41
	14	15-21	18-24	21-27	27-33	33-41	37-46
	15	18-24	21-27	24-30	30-37	37-46	41-51
	16	21-27	24-30	27-33	33-41	41-51	46-57
	17	24-30	27-33	30-37	37-46	46-57	51-63
	18	27-33	30-37	33-41	41-51	51-63	57-71
	19	30-37	33-41	37-46	46-57	57-71	63-78
	20	33-41	37-46	41-51	51-63	63-78	70-87
	21	37-46	41-51	46-57	57-71	70-87	77-96
	22	41-51	46-57	51-63	63-78	77-96	84-105
	23	46-57	51-63	57-71	70-87	84-105	92-115
	24	51-63	57-71	63-78	77-96	92-115	100-125
Zone D	25	57-71	63-78	70-87	84-105	100-125	110-137
	26	63-78	70-87	78-97	92-115	110-137	120-150
	27	70-87	78-97	87-108	100-125	120-150	130-162
	28	78-97	87-108	97-121	110-137	130-162	140-175
	29	87-108	97-121	108-135	121-151	140-175	151-188
	30	97-121	108-135	121-151	135-168	151-188	168-210
	31	108-135	121-151	135-168	151-188	168-210	188-235
	32	121-151	135-168	151-188	168-210	188-235	210-262
	33	135-168	151-188	168-210	188-235	210-262	235-293
	34	151-188	168-210	188-235	210-262	235-293	262-327
	35	168-210	188-235	210-262	235-293	262-327	292-365
	36	188-235	210-262	235-293	262-327	292-365	324-405
	37	210-262	235-293	262-327	292-365	324-405	360-life
	38	235-293	262-327	292-365	324-405	360-life	360-life
	39	262-327	292-365	324-405	360-life	360-life	360-life
	40	292-365	324-405	360-life	360-life	360-life	360-life
	41	324-405	360-life	360-life	360-life	360-life	360-life
	42	360-life	360-life	360-life	360-life	360-life	360-life
	43	life	life	life	life	life	life

Chapter 22

FORFEITURES

§ 22.01 INTRODUCTION

Under various forfeiture statutes, the federal government has the power to gain ownership of private property that was used in, or is the fruit of, criminal activity. Further, the government often has the power to take control of the property, or "seize" it, prior to the conclusion of the forfeiture proceeding.[1] Seizures and forfeitures can occur in civil or criminal proceedings. The differences between civil and criminal forfeiture proceedings produce much of the complexity in this area of the law.

Civil forfeitures are long-established in English and American law. These are *in rem* proceedings that are based upon the legal fiction that the property itself is or was the wrongdoer. Thus, jurisdiction in a civil forfeiture proceeding arises once the government assumes control over the property, and the property itself is named as the defendant. The financial crimes laws and the narcotics laws are the most frequent bases for civil forfeiture proceedings.[2]

By contrast, criminal forfeiture is of relatively recent vintage. Criminal forfeitures are *in personam* proceeding against the criminal defendant. Such forfeiture occurs once a criminal defendant has been found guilty and the property has been found forfeitable. The primary statutes used for criminal forfeitures are the financial crimes, RICO, and narcotics forfeiture statutes.[3]

Both civil and criminal forfeiture provisions reach broad categories of property, ranging from materials used to manufacture narcotics to automobiles and homes purchased with laundered money or drug sale proceeds. Further, it is not uncommon for property beyond the defendant's immediate control also to be subject to forfeiture. Thus, property interests of those other than the alleged wrongdoer may be substantially affected by the forfeiture laws.[4]

Government seizures and forfeitures of property have increased dramatically over recent decades. This has occurred both because Congress has expanded the government's power to obtain forfeitures, and because prosecutors have become

---

[1] This chapter follows the general outline of the materials contained in J. Kelly Strader & Diana Parker, *Civil and Criminal Forfeitures, in* White Collar Crime: Business and Regulatory Offenses §§ 6A.01–.05 (Otto Obermaier & Robert Morvillo, eds. 2011). For a more expansive discussion of the topics contained here, please refer to that text.

[2] *See* 31 U.S.C. § 5311 *et seq.;* 18 U.S.C. §§ 1956, 1957; 21 U.S.C. § 841 *et seq.*

[3] 18 U.S.C. §§ 982, 1963; 21 U.S.C. § 853.

[4] *See, e.g.*, United States v. Regan, 858 F.2d 115 (2d Cir. 1988), discussed *infra* § 22.03[D].

more adept at using these laws.[5] Along with this increase has come controversy. For the government, forfeitures are important weapons in preventing crime and in taking away the fruits of the wrongdoing. Critics argue, however, that the laws are draconian and often hurt innocent parties. As discussed more fully below, Congress responded to some of these criticisms by enacting the Civil Asset Forfeiture Reform Act of 2000.[6] Nonetheless, controversy continues to surround the procedures used in securing the seizure and subsequent forfeiture of property.[7]

This chapter provides a brief overview of the main *federal* civil and criminal forfeiture statutes. Note that, as in other areas of white collar crime, many states have statutes that to some degree parallel the federal statutes. The chapter then discusses issues that commonly arise in forfeiture proceedings. These issues include important constitutional questions.[8]

§ 22.02   CIVIL FORFEITURE PROCEEDINGS

[A]   Federal Civil Forfeiture Statutes

Section 981 of the federal criminal code[9] and Section 881 of the federal drug laws[10] provide the statutory basis for most of the federal civil *in rem* forfeitures occurring today.[11]

Section 981 makes subject to forfeiture property involved in or derived from specified financial crimes, including money laundering. Section 881 is technically a drug abuse prevention statute. The statute, however, has significant relevance to white collar practice, most particularly when innocent owner status is claimed by property owners to avoid the forfeiture.

---

[5] Existing statutes have often been expanded by Congress in order to broaden the forfeiture powers of the government. *See, e.g.*, 18 U.S.C. § 1961(1). Section 1961's definition of "racketeering activity" has been expanded to encompass several new crimes which may potentially lead to forfeiture.

[6] In April 2000, the Civil Asset Forfeiture Reform Act went into effect. Pub. L. No. 106-185, 114 Stat. 202 (April 25, 2000). This bill is now codified in various sections of the United States Code, which are cited throughout this chapter. *See infra* § 22.02.

[7] For critical commentary, see Eric Moores, *Reforming the Civil Asset Forfeiture Reform Act*, 51 Ariz. L. Rev. 777 (2009); Heather J. Garretson, *Federal Criminal Forfeiture: A Royal Pain In The Assets*, 18 S. Cal. Rev. L. & Soc. Just. 45 (2008); Michael J. Duffrey, *A Drug War Funded Wwith Drug Money: The Federal Civil Forfeiture Statute and Federalism*, 34 Suffolk L. Rev. 511 (2001); Eric D. Blumenson & Eva Nilsen, *Policing for Profit: The Drug War's Hidden Economic Agenda*, 65 U. Chi. L. Rev. 35, 41 (1998).

[8] More reforms have occurred at the state level than at the federal level. *See* Eric D. Blumenson & Eva Nilsen, *The Next Stage of Forfeiture Reform*, 14 Fed. Sent. R. 76 (2001) (describing state reform efforts to direct that proceeds of state forfeitures be used not for general law enforcement purposes but instead for such p14 Fed. Sent. R. 76urposes as narcotics treatment).

[9] 18 U.S.C. § 981.

[10] 21 U.S.C. § 881. One of Congress's stated goals in enacting Section 881 was to "strengthen existing law enforcement authority in the field of drug abuse, . . . through providing more effective means for law enforcement aspects of drug abuse prevention and control." H.R. Rep. No. 1444, 91st Cong., 2d Sess. 1, *reprinted in* 1970 U.S. Code Cong. & Admin. News 4566, 4566–68.

[11] There are over 100 federal civil forfeiture statutes, but these are by far the most commonly used ones. *See* Strader & Parker, *supra* note 1, § 6A.01.

Under Section 981(a)(1)(A), all property, real or personal, is subject to seizure and forfeiture if such property was or is related to money laundering or currency transaction reporting crimes.[12] The statute also covers property that constitutes, is derived from, or is traceable to the proceeds of dozens of other specified crimes.[13]

Section 881 authorizes the forfeiture of certain specified property when it is sufficiently connected with controlled substances. For example, all proceeds of a controlled substances transaction, whether direct or indirect, as well as "all moneys, negotiable instruments, and securities used or intended [for use]" in the facilitation of such a transaction, are subject to seizure and forfeiture.[14] Subsection 881(a)(7) further subjects all real property interests to seizure and forfeiture if such property was used or intended for use in committing, or facilitating the commission of, a federal drug laws violation.[15] Of course, narcotics themselves, and materials used to manufacture narcotics, are also subject to forfeiture, as are conveyances used in narcotics trafficking.[16]

[B] Property Seizure Procedures

[1] Statutory Provisions

In judicial forfeiture proceedings, the government may seize property prior to a final court ruling in some circumstances. The forfeiture laws incorporate provisions of other laws relating to the seizure proceedings.[17] The rules for such seizures are complex, and are discussed in this chapter only briefly.[18]

Section 981 and § 881 each call for the seizure of property pursuant to a warrant.[19] The warrant is to be secured through the same process required for the issuance of a search warrant under the Federal Rules of Criminal Procedure. There are, however, three exceptions to this warrant requirement. First, a warrantless seizure may be made if a United States District Court has already issued an arrest warrant *in rem* under the Supplemental Rules for Certain Admiralty and Maritime

---

[12] 18 U.S.C. § 981(a)(1)(A). Section 1956, the money laundering statute, is very broad and encompasses a vast range of transactions. Examples include activities based on tax fraud, reporting requirements in currency transactions, and other "specified unlawful activit[ies]." *See* Chapter 15, Money Laundering, *supra*.

[13] 18 U.S.C. §§ 981(a)(1)(C) & (D). There are some forty qualifying crimes, relating either to financial transactions, various financial institutions, or fraud against the United States.

[14] 21 U.S.C. § 881(a)(6). Section 881(a) lists all the categories of forfeitable property.

[15] *See id.* § 881(a)(7). *See also* United States v. 817 N.E. 29th Drive, 175 F.3d 1304, 1308–09 (11th Cir. 1999) (concluding that a case-by-case inquiry must be used to define "property" under 21 U.S.C. § 881(a)(7).

[16] *See* 21 U.S.C. § 881(a).

[17] They are set forth in the Supplemental Rules for Certain Admiralty and Maritime Claims, the Federal Rules of Criminal Procedure, and the customs laws. *See* 18 U.S.C. § 981(b)(2). In addition, the rules allow for summary and administrative forfeitures. *See* Strader & Parker, *supra* note 1, § 6A.02[2].

[18] *See* Strader & Parker, *supra* note 1, § 6A.02[2], for a detailed discussion of these provisions.

[19] 18 U.S.C. § 981(b)(2). Section 881 utilizes the same forfeiture procedures provided for in § 981. 21 U.S.C. § 881(b) ("Any property subject to forfeiture to the United States under this section may be seized . . . in the manner set forth in section 981(b) of Title 18.").

Claims. Second, a warrantless seizure is justified when a lawful arrest or search occurred, and there was probable cause to believe that the property was subject to forfeiture. Third, no warrant is required if a state or local law enforcement agency lawfully made the initial seizure, and then subsequently transferred the property to a federal agency.[20] Additionally, both substantive sections allow the government to seize property without providing notice to the property owner in certain circumstances.[21]

Property that is subject to forfeiture also may be protected through the use of restraining orders and/or injunctions. The requirements and procedures for obtaining either one of these protective devices are set forth in the Civil Asset Forfeiture and Reform Act of 2000. The Act also provides post-seizure hearings in order to prevent the destruction and/or removal of property seized under an *ex parte* order.[22]

[2] The Burden of Proof and Standing

Before seizing property, the government must meet its initial burden of proof by showing that probable cause exists to believe that the property is subject to forfeiture.[23] Probable cause means that there is a "reasonable ground for belief of guilt, supported by less than prima facie proof but more than mere suspicion."[24] This burden may be satisfied through circumstantial evidence.[25]

The formal forfeiture proceeding is initiated upon the filing of the government's complaint. Under the Civil Asset Forfeiture Reform Act, at the forfeiture trial the government has the burden of proving by a preponderance of the evidence that the property is forfeitable. Evidence obtained after the complaint was filed may be used by the government to meet its burden at trial.[26] Standing to contest forfeiture is granted to *bona fide* purchasers and sellers of the contested property. Also, in limited situations, standing is granted to persons using the property as a primary residence.[27]

---

[20] 18 U.S.C. § 981(b)(2).

[21] *See id.* § 981; 21 U.S.C. § 881. The requirements for seizing property without notice are set forth in the Civil Asset Forfeiture and Reform Act of 2000. Pub. L. No. 106-185, 114 Stat. 202 (April 25, 2000).

[22] *See* 18 U.S.C. § 983.

[23] *See* 19 U.S.C. § 1615.

[24] United States v. On Leong Chinese Merchants Ass'n Bldg., 918 F.2d 1289, 1292 (7th Cir. 1990), *quoting* United States v. $364,960, 661 F.2d 319, 322–23 (5th Cir. 1981).

[25] *See* United States v. 4492 South Livonia Road, 889 F.2d 1258, 1267 (2d Cir. 1989).

[26] 18 U.S.C. § 983(c)(2).

[27] 18 U.S.C. § 983(d)(3)(B)(i). *See infra*, § 22.02[D].

[C] The Scope of Property Subject to Seizure and Forfeiture

[1] Introduction

Broad categories of property are subject to forfeiture.[28] Recall that § 981 subjects to forfeiture all real or personal property "involved in" a transaction relating to money laundering or currency transaction reporting violations, and dozens of other crimes. Courts interpret the "involved in" phrase in different ways. Those seeking to avoid forfeiture argue that the phrase "involved in" limits forfeiture to property that "actively participated" in the underlying transaction. On the other hand, the government argues for a broad interpretation under which the phrase embodies any property that is merely used in the facilitation of the underlying transaction.[29] Most courts simply adopted a case-by-case approach.[30]

Section 984 of the federal criminal code,[31]

entitled "Civil forfeiture of fungible property," also has important implications for the scope of civil forfeitures. That section provides that, where property targeted for forfeiture is cash or other fungible property, the government need not "identify the specific property involved in the offense that is the basis for the forfeiture."[32] Furthermore, it is not a valid defense to assert that the property originally involved in the underlying criminal act has since been replaced by identical untainted property.[33] Thus, "identical property found in the same place or account as the property involved in the offense . . . shall be subject to forfeiture."[34]

As discussed more fully below, the Eighth Amendment's Excessive Fines Clause limits the scope of civil forfeitures.[35] In *United States v. Bajakajian*,[36]

the Supreme Court established the "gross disproportionality test," which is to be used in determining whether a forfeiture violates the Excessive Fines Clause. This test has been codified by the Civil Asset Forfeiture Reform Act of 2000 ("CAFRA"),[37]

which presents a significant limitation to the scope of forfeiture.

---

[28] *See* § 22.02(A), *supra.*

[29] United States v. South Side Finance, 755 F. Supp. 791, 797–98 (N.D. Ill. 1991).

[30] *Id.* (dismissing, in part, a complaint brought under § 981(a) because neither of the proposed definitions made the specific property forfeitable).

[31] 18 U.S.C. § 984.

[32] *See id.* § 984(a)(1)(A).

[33] *See id.* § 984(a)(1)(B).

[34] *See id.* § 984(a)(2).

[35] *See* § 22.04[D], *infra.*

[36] 524 U.S. 321 (1998).

[37] 18 U.S.C. § 983(g).

[2]   The Substantial Connection Test

Prior to CAFRA, circuit courts had adopted a number of tests for determining when property is forfeitable. The most often-used such test was the "substantial connection" test. Congress codified that test in CAFRA. Under this test, if the government seeks forfeiture under a civil forfeiture statute, based upon the theory that the property was used in the facilitation of,[38] or was involved in the perpetration of,[39] a criminal act, the government must demonstrate that there is "a substantial connection between the property and the offense."[40]

So far, there have been relatively few published opinions analyzing the substantial connection test under CAFRA. The decision in *United States v. One 1998 Tractor*[41] is instructive because the court there compared and contrasted a number of earlier decisions. In One 1998 *Tractor*, the driver-owner of the defendant property, a tractor-trailer, was stopped in Tennessee by law enforcement agents. The agents discovered nearly 300,000 cigarettes in the tractor cab. The driver had purchased the cigarettes in Virginia, and the cigarettes did not bear Tennessee state tax stamps as required by law. The driver later pleaded guilty to criminal statutes that ban the possession and transportation of contraband cigarettes, that is, cigarettes for which taxes have not been paid in the state where they are being transported.

The government then sought *in rem* forfeiture of the trailer, using two theories. First, the government argued that the tractor-trailer constituted a single "vehicle" and that the trailer was therefore forfeitable under the statute providing for forfeiture of vehicles involved in the transportation of contraband.[42] The district court rejected this theory. First, the court cited a case holding that, because the tugboat and barge at issue were separately titled, they did not constitute a single vessel.[43] By contrast, in another earlier case the court found that two parcels of land lying across the road from each other were a single parcel because they were so titled.[44] Here, claimant's tractor and trailer did not constitute a single vehicle because they were purchased separately and had separate titles and vehicle identification numbers.

Second, the government argued that the trailer was forfeitable because it was "involved in the commission of a criminal offense." Under CAFRA, in order to prove this theory, the government must show, "by a preponderance of the evidence," that there was a "substantial connection between that property and the offense." The government argued that the trailer was substantially connected to the smuggling because it gave the defendant's endeavor an air of legitimacy. The court rejected this argument as well, citing two pre-CAFRA cases that also applied a substantial

---

[38] *See, e.g.,* 21 U.S.C. § 881(a).

[39] *See, e.g.,* 18 U.S.C. § 981(a)(1)(A).

[40] *See id.* § 983(c)(3) ("General rules for civil forfeiture proceedings") (adopted as part of CAFRA).

[41] 288 F. Supp. 2d 710 (W.D. Va. 2003).

[42] 49 U.S.C. § 80303.

[43] 288 F. Supp. 2d at 712–13, *citing* The Dolphin, 3 F.2d 1 (1st Cir. 1925).

[44] 288 F. Supp. 2d at 712–13, *citing* United States v. Santoro, 866 F.2d 1538 (4th Cir. 1989).

connection test. Initially, the court noted that CAFRA only changed prior law in the Fourth Circuit by the increasing the government's burden from probable cause to a preponderance standard; the substantial connection test remained the same.

The court then turned to the early cases. In one case,[45] a boat transported marijuana to a marina, and the contraband was driven across a tract of land to reach a public road. The government sought forfeiture of the land on the theories that it (1) provided access to a public road and (2) shielded the illegal activity from public view. The court in that case found that the land was not substantially connected to the narcotics offense. More must be shown than the property's use to conceal the crime. For example, in another earlier case,[46] a dentist used his office to write some forty illegal prescriptions over a four-month period. The government sought forfeiture of the office property based upon violations of the narcotics laws, and the court ordered forfeiture. There, a substantial connection existed between the offense and the property because the office was actually used to carry out the offense. In this case, on the other hand, the government merely alleged that the trailer shielded the criminal activity by creating the appearance that the claimant was engaged in a legitimate trucking business. Because the government did not show that driver's trucking business was a sham, or that he operated it with the intent of concealing his criminal activity, it did not meet its burden of proof.

The foregoing shows that the substantial connection test will produce results that depend highly on the particular facts of the case. If property merely has a tangential connection to the offense, then the government will not have met its burden. If, however, the property is actually used as the site of the offense, then the test is clearly met. Situations that occur in the gray area between these extremes are likely to produce highly variable results.

[D]   Third-Party Interests — The "Innocent Owner" Defense

Under the Civil Asset Forfeiture Reform Act, "innocent owner" status may provide an affirmative defense to any civil forfeiture claim. To be an innocent owner, the owner must establish, by a preponderance of the evidence, that either (1) the owner did not know of the illegal conduct; or (2) that upon learning of its occurrence, the owner "did all that reasonably could be expected" to end the continued unlawful use of the property.[47]

An innocent owner may contest the forfeiture even if that owner has less than a complete interest in the property. Under CAFRA, when an innocent owner holds an incomplete or partial interest in the property seized, the court may order that the property (1) be severed; (2) be transferred to the government with

---

[45] 288 F. Supp. 2d at 713–14, *citing* United States v. Two Tracts of Real Property, 998 F.2d 204 (4th Cir. 1993).

[46] 288 F. Supp. 2d at 714, *citing* United States v. Schifferli, 895 F.2d 987 (4th Cir. 1990).

[47] 18 U.S.C. § 983(d)(2)(A). Some courts, prior to the enactment of the Civil Asset Forfeiture Reform Act, had required proof that the claimant also took all "reasonable precautions" available in preventing the illegal use of his or her property. *See, e.g.*, United States v. One 1976 Cessna Model 210L Aircraft, 890 F.2d 77, 81 (8th Cir. 1989); United States v. One Parcel of Real Estate, 715 F. Supp. 355, 357–58 (S.D. Fla. 1989).

compensation to the innocent owner; or (3) be retained by the innocent owner, but remain subject to a lien held by the government.[48]

[E] Assistance of Counsel

Under the Civil Asset Forfeiture Reform Act, codified in § 983, a claimant must be appointed counsel in two situations, each at the government's expense. First, the appointment of counsel may be authorized by the court if a *civil* forfeiture claimant is financially unable to obtain independent counsel and is also being represented by appointed counsel in a related *criminal* case.[49] In deciding whether the appointment of counsel is warranted, the court may consider: (1) the claimant's standing to challenge the forfeiture; and (2) whether the claim itself appears to have been made in good faith.[50] Second, the court must insure the appointment of counsel if: (1) the claimant has standing to challenge the forfeiture; (2) the claimant is financially unable to obtain independent counsel; (3) the claimant requests counsel; and (4) the forfeiture concerns *real property* used as the claimant's primary residence.[51]

[F] Post-Judgment Awards of Attorneys' Fees and Fines

In all forfeiture actions brought after August 23, 2000, a prevailing claimant is entitled to collect reasonable attorney's fees, costs incurred, and certain types of interest.[52] Under CAFRA, civil fines may be imposed against a claimant if the government prevails and the court finds the claimant's claim to be frivolous.[53]

[G] The Effect of the Vesting Provision

As provided by § 881(h), title to property that is subject to forfeiture vests in the United States when the illegal act subjecting such property to forfeiture occurs.[54] At first glance it would appear as though this "relation back" provision[55] is directly at odds with the "innocent owner" defense. How can an innocent owner assert a claim if the property already belongs to the government?

This conflict was resolved by the United States Supreme Court in *United States v. 92 Buena Vista Avenue*.[56] In that case, respondent had purchased her home with a cash gift that, unknown to her, constituted illegal proceeds. The government

---

[48] *See* Strader & Parker, *supra* note 1, § 6A.02[5][c].

[49] 18 U.S.C. § 983(b)(1)(A).

[50] *See id.* § 983(b)(1)(B).

[51] *See id.* § 983(b)(2)(A).

[52] 28 U.S.C. § 2465.

[53] 18 U.S.C. § 983(h). The fine may consist of an amount equaling ten percent of the value of the forfeited property, but shall not exceed $5,000 or be less than $250.

[54] 21 U.S.C. § 881(h).

[55] For more analysis on relation-back provisions, see Mark A. Jankowski, *Tempering the Relationship-Back Doctrine: A More Reasonable Approach to Civil Forfeiture in Drug Cases*, 76 Va. L. Rev. 165 (1990).

[56] 507 U.S. 111 (1993).

sought forfeiture of the home, arguing that she was not the owner of the house because ownership vested "in the United States at the moment when the proceeds . . . were used to pay the purchase price."[57] The Court held, however, that the government's title to forfeitable property is not perfected until a forfeiture decree has been entered by the trial court. Thus, an "innocent owner" who successfully meets the burden of proof can avoid the issuance of a forfeiture order and prevent the government from obtaining a perfected title.

In the wake of 92 *Buena Vista Avenue*, persons who had criminal proceeds learned to transfer property to family members to avoid potential forfeiture. Congress responded in CAFRA by restricting "innocent owner" claims when the third party acquired the property interest *after* the criminal conduct. In that instance, the claimant must show that (a) the claimant was a "a bona fide purchaser or seller for value (including a purchaser or seller of goods or services for value)," and (b) the claimant "did not know and was reasonably without cause to believe that the property was subject to forfeiture."[58]

To ameliorate the harshness of this rule, Congress also provided in CAFRA that the third party claim would not be denied where: (a) the property is the primary residence of the claimant; (b) denying the claim would deprive the claimant of the means to maintain reasonable shelter; (c) the property is not traceable to the proceeds of criminal activity; and (d) the claimant acquired the property interest (i) as a result of a marital relationship, or (ii) through inheritance as a spouse or legal dependent of the deceased.[59] Thus, in 92 *Buena Vista Avenue*, the claim would have failed because the property was traceable to the narcotics sales and the claimant was not married to the wrongdoer.

§ 22.03 FEDERAL CRIMINAL STATUTES PROVIDING FOR THE RESTRAINT AND FORFEITURE OF PRIVATE PROPERTY

A criminal forfeiture is an in *personam* proceeding that occurs during the sentencing phase of the defendant's criminal trial. Some constitutional protections governing criminal trials are also applicable to criminal forfeiture proceedings.[60]

---

[57] *Id.* at 124.

[58] 18 U.S.C. § 983(d)(3)(B)(I). For an overview of this provision, see Stefan D. Cassella, *The Uniform Innocent Owner Defense to Civil Asset Forfeiture: The Civil Asset Forfeiture Reform Act of 2000 Creates a Uniform Innocent Owner Defense to Most Civil Forfeiture Cases Filed by the Federal Government*, 89 Ky. L.J. 653 (2001).

[59] 18 U.S.C. § 983(d)(3)(B).

[60] Most courts hold that criminal forfeitures are punitive in nature, and are governed by the same preponderance standard that is used in other criminal sentencing matters. *See, e.g*, United States v. Rogers, 102 F.3d 641, 648 (1st Cir. 1996); United States v. Tanner, 61 F.3d 231, 234 (4th Cir. 1995); United States v. Elgersma, 971 F.2d 690 (11th Cir. 1992). These courts held criminal forfeiture under 21 U.S.C. § 853(a) is not an element of the crime, but rather is part of the sentencing process. Thus, it need not be subjected to a reasonable doubt standard, and may be subjected to a preponderance of the evidence standard. But *see* United States v. Pelullo, 14 F.3d 881, 905–06 (3d Cir. 1994) (government's burden of proof in a forfeiture proceeding under RICO is the reasonable doubt standard; if Congress intended use of preponderance standard for criminal forfeitures under 18 U.S.C. § 1963(a), it would have specifically

These protections, however, are seldom applied in the civil forfeiture context.[61] Finally, it is important to note that a defendant's acquittal in a criminal proceeding does not act as a bar to any subsequent civil forfeiture action instituted by the government.[62]

[A] Statutory Forfeiture Provisions

Since RICO was enacted in 1970, Congress has continually expanded the federal government's ability to obtain forfeiture in criminal cases. Most criminal forfeitures occur under three statutes:

- Section 982 of the federal criminal code provides for forfeiture of property involved in or traceable to financial crimes such as the currency transaction reporting statutes, the money laundering statutes, and other specified crimes.[63]

- Section 1963 of the federal criminal code provides for forfeiture of a broad range of property involved in RICO violations.[64]

- Section 853 of the federal narcotics laws provide for forfeiture of a broad range of property, including real property and tangible and intangible personal property interests involved in narcotics offenses.[65]

Significantly, these forfeiture statutes provide for the forfeiture of "substitute" assets.[66] For example, if the government cannot locate the precise property used in an offense, then it may obtain forfeiture of other assets of an equivalent value.[67] Additionally, courts have held that defendants are jointly and severally liable for RICO forfeitures. These decisions hold that, where more than one defendant is liable, the government need not prove the precise amount attributable to each defendant.[68]

Under a provision enacted as part of CAFRA and amended in 2006, the government may seek criminal forfeiture whenever civil forfeiture is authorized

---

said so, as it did for the Continuing Criminal Enterprise Act). *Cf.* United States v. Houlihan, 92 F.3d 1271, 1299 n.33 (1st Cir. 1996) (the court noted government may have conceded too much when the district court used the reasonable doubt standard under RICO forfeiture statute, but left the question open).

[61] *Cf.* Austin v. United States, 509 U.S. 602 (1993) (applying the Excessive Fines Clause of the Eighth Amendment to civil *in rem* forfeitures).

[62] *See, e.g.*, United States v. Ursery, 518 U.S. 267 (1996) (holding that the double jeopardy clause does not act as a bar to collateral civil and criminal forfeiture proceedings), discussed *infra* § 22.04[D].

[63] *See* 18 U.S.C. § 982.

[64] *See* 18 U.S.C. § 1963. For an overview of RICO's forfeiture provisions, see Corey P. Argust et al., *Racketeer Influenced and Corrupt Organizations*, 47 Am. Crim. L. Rev. 961, 995–98 (2010).

[65] *See* 21 U.S.C. § 853.

[66] *See* 21 U.S.C. § 853(p); 18 U.S.C. § 982(b); 18 U.S.C. § 1963(m). Substitute assets are discussed *infra*, § 22.03[C][4].

[67] *See* Argust et al., *supra* note 64, at 996–97 (discussing RICO's substitute assets provision). The circuit courts are split as to whether the government may obtain pre-trial restraint of substitute assets under RICO and other criminal forfeiture statutes. *See id.* (listing cases).

[68] *See, e.g.*, United States v. Simmons, 154 F.3d 765, 769–70 (8th Cir. 1998).

under the civil forfeiture statutues.[69] Accordingly, the full range of civil forfeiture provisions now may be employed in criminal cases.[70]

[B] Statutory Procedures for Restraining Property

Under §§ 853, 982, and 1963,[71] before the criminal charges are filed, a court may issue a temporary restraining order allowing the government to take control of the property. After a defendant has been indicted, or an information has been filed, the court may: (1) issue a restraining order or an injunction; (2) require the posting of a bond; or (3) take "any other action" necessary to preserve the property.[72] The applicable sections do not indicate the standard of proof to be used in securing an injunction, or whether notice and a hearing must be provided before the court may issue an order.

[C] The Scope of Forfeitable Property

[1] Rule 32.2(b) and the Nexus Requirement

Under Federal Rule of Criminal Procedure 32.2(b), once a defendant's plea of guilty or nolo contendere has been accepted by the court, or once the jury has returned a guilty verdict, the court is required to identify property subject to forfeiture.[73] The court must also determine whether the "requisite nexus between the property and the offense" has been established by the government.[74] Under the rule, in cases where the jury has returned a guilty verdict, a party may request that the jury determine that the "requisite nexus" exists.[75] Once a nexus has been found by either the court or the jury, the court must then promptly issue a preliminary forfeiture order to authorize the seizure of the property. If, however, the indictment or information failed to provide notice to the defendant that forfeiture of property was being sought as part of the sentence, then the court may not enter a forfeiture order.[76] Determining whether the "requisite nexus" exists between the property and the offense raises issues similar to the "substantial connection" test applicable to civil forfeitures. Once again, the determination will be highly fact-specific and will often turn on the precise forfeiture theories that the government has employed.

---

[69] 28 U.S.C. § 2461(c).

[70] *See, e.g.,* United States v. Vampire Nation, 451 F.3d 189 (3d Cir. 2006) (finding that mail fraud may give rise to criminal forfeiture under § 2461(c)).

[71] 21 U.S.C. § 853(e)(2); 18 U.S.C. § 982(b)(1); 18 U.S.C. § 1963(d)(2). Note that the procedures of forfeiture under § 982 are governed by the provisions set forth in § 853.

[72] 21 U.S.C. § 853(e)(1)(A); 18 U.S.C. § 982(b)(1); 18 U.S.C. § 1963(d)(1).

[73] Fed. R. Crim. P. 32.2(b).

[74] This nexus determination is to be based on the evidence of record, unless forfeiture is contested, in which case any additional evidence or information presented during a subsequent hearing may also be considered. Fed. R. Crim. P. 32.2(b)(1).

[75] Fed. R. Crim. P. 32.2(b)(4).

[76] Fed. R. Crim. P. 32.2(a).

[2] The Forfeiture Theory

In the forfeiture phase of a criminal trial, the court or jury will determine whether and to what extent the government has proven that the property is forfeitable. This determination will often turn on the definition of forfeitable property in the applicable statute. Once again, these issues tend to be very complex and require close attention to the facts. The outcome is also likely to turn on the particular forfeiture theory that the government has employed.

For example, in *United States v. Iacaboni,*[77] the government asserted that the property was forfeitable under § 982, the financial crimes forfeiture statute. In support of its argument, the government alleged that the property was (a) used in "concealment" money laundering because the defendant used the property to hide the source of "dirty" money, and (b) used in "promotion" money laundering because the defendant used the "dirty" money to promote his illegal activities.[78]

The defendant pleaded guilty to charges arising from the operation of an illegal gambling business, and the court then held a bench trial on the government's forfeiture allegations. Two of the defendant's employees testified that, in a given week, the business would owe approximately $15,000 to $20,000 to winning bettors or would expect to collect $20,000 to $25,000 from losing bettors. One of the bettors, Landman, testified that when he owed money, he would send "personal checks" made out to the defendant, who then deposited the checks into his personal account. The trial court ordered forfeiture of funds paid to winning bettors and of funds received via the checks from Landman.

With respect to the Landman checks, the district court ordered forfeiture on the theory that the defendant attempted to conceal the source of the funds. On appeal, the defendant argued that this award could not stand because he only pleaded guilty to promotion money laundering. The court agreed, concluding that the difference between the charge and the theory used at the forfeiture trial was error that had prejudiced the defendant. This result demonstrates the importance of carefully pleading the underlying theory supporting forfeiture.

[3] Proceeds

In determining the forfeitable amount, the federal courts of appeal split over the meaning of the term "proceeds" in the money laundering forfeiture provisions. Some courts found that the term refers to net proceeds, reasoning that Congress used the term "proceeds" instead of "profits" to alleviate the heavy burden on the government to prove the amount of net profits in a particular case.[79] Other courts refused to read forfeiture statutes so broadly. As one court concluded when interpreting the money laundering forfeiture provisions, "at least when the crime entails voluntary, business-like operations, 'proceeds' must be net income; otherwise the predicate crime merges into money laundering (for no business can be carried

---

[77] 363 F.3d 1 (1st Cir. 2004).

[78] *See* Chapter 15, Money Laundering, *supra,* for a discussion of these theories of money laundering.

[79] *See, e.g.,* Iacaboni, 363 F.3d at 4; United States v. Simmons, 154 F.3d 765, 771 (8th Cir. 1998).

on without expenses) and the word 'proceeds' loses operational significance."[80]

The United States Supreme Court resolved this conflict in *United States v. Santos*.[81] The Court held that the term "proceeds" in the money laundering statute is ambiguous. Applying the rule of lenity, a five-member majority held that the term "proceeds" refers to "profits," not "receipts." Soon thereafter, however, Congress passed the Fraud Enforcement and Enhancement Act of 2009 (FERA). FERA amends the money laundering statutes to provide that "the term 'proceeds' means any property derived from or obtained or retained, directly or indirectly, through some form of unlawful activity, including the gross receipts of such activity."[82] The statute thus effectively overruled *Santos*.

The bill also includes a provision entitled "Sense of the Congress and Report Concerning Required Approval for Merger Cases." This states that money laundering prosecutions should generally not be undertaken "if the conduct to be charged as 'specified unlawful activity' in connection with the offense under section 1956 or 1957 is so closely connected with the conduct to be charged as the other offense that there is no clear delineation between the two offenses." This non-binding resolution attempts to address the "merger" issue that courts had relied upon when reading "proceeds" to mean "net profits."

[4] Substitute Assets

Various statutes require the defendant to forfeit substitute assets when the otherwise forfeitable assets (1) cannot be found, (2) have been transferred or sold to a third party, (3) are beyond the court's jurisdiction, (4) have been reduced in value, or (5) were commingled with non-forfeitable property and cannot be easily separated.[83] Under any one of these circumstances, the court is required to order the forfeiture of substitute assets (*i.e.*, any other property of the defendant), but only up to the value of the otherwise forfeitable assets.[84]

Section 982, however, includes a safe harbor provision.[85] Thus, where the "defendant acted merely as an intermediary who handled but did not retain the property in the course of the money laundering offense,"[86] that defendant *shall not* be required to forfeit substitute assets *unless* he or she "conducted three or more separate transactions involving a total of $100,000 or more in any twelve month period."[87]

---

[80]   United States v. Scialabba, 282 F.3d 475 (7th Cir. 2002).

[81]   128 S. Ct. 2020 (2008).

[82]   Courts have varied widely in applying *Santos* to pre-FERA cases. For an overview of these cases, see Rachel Zimarowski, *Taking a Gamble: Money Laundering After* United States v. Santos, 112 W. Va. L. Rev. 1139 (2010).

[83]   *See* 21 U.S.C. § 853(p); 18 U.S.C. § 982(b); 18 U.S.C. § 1963(m).

[84]   A related issue arises when the government attempts to base a criminal money laundering case upon "dirty" money that has been "commingled," or mixed in with, "clean money." *See* Chapter 15, Money Laundering, *supra* § 15.04[A][2][b].

[85]   18 U.S.C. § 982(b)(2).

[86]   *Id.*

[87]   *Id.*

Under the substitute assets provision, may the government seek assets that were transferred to third parties? In *United States v. Saccoccia*,[88] the government filed a motion to compel attorneys to turn over assets that they had received as attorneys' fees from a client convicted under the RICO statute. The First Circuit denied the motion, holding that the substitute assets provision only reaches the defendant's substitute assets, and does not reach assets of third parties, such as attorneys, to whom the tainted assets were transferred.[89] The court noted that the government might have other federal or state law remedies, but that the federal forfeiture statutes do not apply in this circumstance.[90]

[5] Money Judgments

At least four circuits have upheld money judgments in criminal forfeiture orders in instances where the defendants do not have sufficient assets for forfeiture. As the First Circuit reasoned in *United States v. Hall*,[91] such judgments are appropriate for two reasons. First, unlike civil forfeiture, criminal forfeiture is a judgment against a person rather than property. Second, "permitting a money judgment, as part of a forfeiture order, prevents a drug dealer from ridding himself of his ill-gotten gains to avoid the forfeiture sanction."[92] The Second Circuit reached a similar result in *United States v. Awad*.[93]

[6] *Apprendi/Booker* Issues

As discussed in the Sentencing Chapter,[94] the Supreme Court held in *Apprendi v. New Jersey*[95] that any fact that produces a sentence beyond the statutory maximum sentence must be submitted to a jury and proven beyond a reasonable doubt. Subsequently, many defendants argued that this rule applies to factual determinations relating to forfeitures. The circuit courts have rejected this argument.[96] The courts have continued to reject such arguments even after the Court in *United States v. Booker*[97] applied *Apprendi* to the United States Sentencing Guidelines.[98]

---

[88] 354 F.3d 9 (1st Cir. 2003).

[89] *Id.* at 13.

[90] *Id.* at 14.

[91] 434 F.3d 42 (1st Cir. 2006).

[92] *Id.* at 59.

[93] 598 F.3d 76 (2d Cir. 2010).

[94] Chapter 21, Sentencing, *supra*.

[95] 530 U.S. 466 (2000).

[96] *See, e.g.,* United States v. Shryock, 342 F.3d 948 (9th Cir. 2003); United States v. Keene, 341 F.3d 78, 85–86 (1st Cir. 2003); United States v. Vera, 278 F.3d 672, 673 (7th Cir. 2002); United States v. Najjar, 300 F.3d 466, 485–86 (4th Cir. 2002); United States v. Cabeza, 258 F.3d 1256, 1257 (11th Cir. 2001) (*per curiam*); United States v. Corrado, 227 F.3d 543, 550–51 (6th Cir. 2000).

[97] 543 U.S. 220 (2005).

[98] *See* United States v. Leahy, 438 F.3d 328, 332–33 (3d Cir. 2006) (listing cases). These courts have held that the Supreme Court's decision in Libretti v. United States, 516 U.S. 29 (1995), compels this result. In *Libretti*, the Court concluded that there is no Sixth Amendment right to a jury determination of forfeiture.

[D] Rights of Innocent Third Parties

Recall that, under Federal Rule of Criminal Procedure 32.2, the court is required to promptly enter a preliminary forfeiture order once the "requisite nexus between the property and the offense" has been established.[99] Once that nexus has been established the order may be entered *regardless* of any existing third party interests.[100] After such order has been entered, however, the Attorney General is authorized "to commence proceedings that comply with any statutes governing third-party rights."[101] The Attorney General may either grant mitigation or remission of forfeiture petitions, restore forfeited property to victims,[102] or "take any other action to protect the rights of innocent persons."[103] After a post-conviction forfeiture order has been entered, any person who claims an interest in the forfeitable property, other than the defendant, may petition the court for a hearing.[104]

Although the rights of innocent third parties appear to be limited by statute, courts have provided additional third-party rights. For example, in *United States v. Regan*,[105] the defendants were partners and executives of Princeton/ Newport Partners, L.P. ("PNP"). The government indicted the defendants under RICO. The indictment alleged that the defendants operated several investment companies, owned and controlled by PNP, through a pattern of racketeering activity.[106] To maintain the assets for forfeiture, the district court entered a pre-trial order restraining PNP from disposing of any of its assets. Although PNP was not a defendant in the action, the court found that PNP's assets were subject to restraint because PNP was essentially "a third party in possession of potentially forfeitable property."[107]

On appeal from the restraining order, the Second Circuit first addressed the validity of restraining the property of an unindicted third party. The court concluded that such action was proper. In making this determination, the court relied on the plain language of § 1963(d)(1), which allows the court to "take any other action to preserve the availability of property."[108] Secondly, the court focused on the appropriateness of the order entered. The court stated that "orders directed at third parties are strong medicine and should not be used where measures that are adequate and less burdensome on the third parties are available."[109]

---

[99] Fed. R. Crim. P. 32.2.

[100] Fed. R. Crim. P. 32.2(b)(2). Under §§ 853, 982, and 1963, any party who claims to have an interest in the property subject to forfeiture is not permitted to intervene in the action or initiate proceedings against the United States. 21 U.S.C. § 853(k); 18 U.S.C. §§ 982(b)(1), 1963(g).

[101] Fed. R. Crim. P. 32.2(b)(3).

[102] 21 U.S.C. § 853(i).

[103] *Id.*; 18 U.S.C. § 1963(g).

[104] 21 U.S.C. § 853(n); 18 U.S.C. § 1963(l).

[105] 858 F.2d 115 (2d Cir. 1988).

[106] 18 U.S.C. § 1961 *et seq.*

[107] *Regan*, 858 F.2d at 117.

[108] *Id.* at 118–19, *citing* 18 U.S.C. § 1963(d)(1)(A).

[109] 858 F.2d at 121.

In considering the availability of alternative measures, the court concluded that a bond equaling the value of the defendants' forfeitable interest would suffice, as would the restraint of a defendant's own substitute assets. Thus, "where the nature of the defendants' forfeitable property makes the imposition of a restraining order burdensome on third parties, the district court should, as an alternative, *restrain assets of the defendant* equal in value to that of the unrestrained forfeitable property."[110]

As noted above, once forfeiture has been ordered, a third party may attempt to assert its property interests. In *United States v. BCCI Holdings*,[111] for example, BCCI pled guilty to RICO and other charges. The court then ordered forfeiture of BCCI's property, including BCCI funds held by American Express Bank. Before the federal case, American Express Bank had exercised its right to claim some of the BCCI funds because of debts BCCI owed to American Express Bank. The court rejected American Express Bank's claim to those funds. First, the government's interest in the funds vested at the time of the illegal acts, which occurred before American Express Bank's right to the funds arose.[112] Second, the claimant did not qualify as a bona fide purchaser for value because it merely had a contractual interest in the funds.[113] In any event, because of widespread publicity, the claimant was on notice, at the time it obtained the funds, that they were potentially forfeitable. The statute provides that a claim will not succeed unless the claimant was "reasonably without cause to believe that the property was subject to forfeiture."[114] This case illustrates the difficult hurdles that third parties must overcome when asserting property interests in criminal forfeiture proceedings.

[E]   The Effect of the Vesting Provision

Section 1963(c) provides that any right, title, or interest held in forfeitable property vests in the United States upon commission of the criminal act, provided the defendant is convicted of the violation.[115] All criminal forfeiture statutes currently contain some variation of this "vesting provision." Vesting provisions are important because they permit the government to seek forfeiture of all forfeitable property within the defendant's control when the underlying crime was committed.

§ 22.04   CONSTITUTIONAL DEFENSES

As shown above, the government has substantial power to seize and obtain forfeiture of property. The government's powers in this regard have been challenged on several constitutional grounds. While the Supreme Court has granted substantial constitutional protections under some constitutional provisions, such as the Due Process and Excessive Fines Clauses, it has declined to do so under other

---

[110] *Id.* (emphasis added).

[111] 961 F. Supp. 287 (D.C.D.C. 1997).

[112] *Id.* at 294–95, *citing* 18 U.S.C. § 1963(L)(6)(A) (RICO forfeiture vesting provision).

[113] 961 F. Supp. at 295, *citing* 18 U.S.C. § 1963(L)(6)(B) (RICO bona fide purchaser provision).

[114] *Id.*

[115] 18 U.S.C. § 1963(c).

provisions, such as the Double Jeopardy Clause.

[A] Procedural Due Process

[1] Civil Forfeitures

Ex parte seizures are permitted under the civil forfeiture statutes summarized above, with certain exceptions.[116] The failure to provide notice and a hearing before seizing or placing a restraint on property raises due process issues under the Fifth and Fourteenth Amendments.

The leading Supreme Court case on this topic is *Calero-Toledo v. Pearson Yacht*, a 1974 case.[117] In *Calero-Toledo*, authorities found marijuana aboard a leased pleasure yacht, and seized the yacht without notice to the owner. The Court held that the government may seize property without providing notice and a hearing when "extraordinary" circumstances exist. The Court concluded that the property in question, a yacht, had been properly seized even though no prior notice or hearing had been provided. A yacht can easily be destroyed, concealed, or moved beyond the jurisdiction of the court if the government is required to give advance warning.[118] Thus, failure to provide notice and a hearing prior to the seizure was not a denial of due process.[119]

In 1993, the Supreme Court's decision in *United States v. James Daniel Good Real Property*[120] addressed due process constraints upon the *ex parte* seizure of *real* property. In that case, the government was seeking forfeiture of the defendant's house, and the land on which it was situated, because the property had been used to facilitate a violation of the federal drug laws. In an *ex parte* proceeding, a federal magistrate found probable cause indicating that the property was subject to forfeiture under § 881(a)(7).[121] A warrant of arrest *in rem* was issued and the property was seized without prior notice or a hearing.

In addressing the owner's due process challenge, the Court noted that the right to prior notice and a hearing is generally required by due process of law. The Court acknowledged that in "extraordinary" situations, *i.e.*, where a valid governmental interest is at stake, exceptions to the rule had been tolerated.[122] Where real property is targeted for seizure, however, there is generally no pressing governmental interest that would justify the postponement of notice and a hearing.[123] For example, in *Calero-Toledo*, the seizure of the yacht was necessary to establish the court's jurisdiction because of the yacht's mobility.[124] Real property, on the other

---

[116] *See* § 22.02[B][1], *supra.*

[117] 416 U.S. 663 (1974).

[118] *Id.* at 678–79.

[119] *Id.* at 681.

[120] 510 U.S. 43, 52 (1993).

[121] 21 U.S.C. § 881(a)(7).

[122] 510 U.S. at 54.

[123] *Id.* at 58–59.

[124] *Id.* at 57.

hand, is incapable of moving, and "the court's jurisdiction can be preserved without prior seizure."[125]

Consequently, the property itself is of great importance in a due process analysis. Absent exigent circumstances, the *ex parte* seizure of real property violates the Due Process Clause. Exigent circumstances can be established by showing that "less restrictive measures, i.e., a *lis pendens*, restraining order, or bond, would not suffice to protect the government's interests in preventing the sale, destruction, or continued unlawful use of the real property."[126] Because no exigency was demonstrated in the *Good* case, the Court ruled in favor of the defendant.[127] The due process requirements set forth in this case have since been codified in § 985 of the Federal Criminal Code.[128]

[2]   Criminal Forfeitures

Both *Calero-Toledo* and *Good* involved *ex parte* seizures in civil forfeiture proceedings. Several distinct issues arise in criminal cases. First, concerning pre-indictment restraints on property, the statute may require that notice be provided to those with ownership interests in the property.[129]

Second, with respect to post-indictment, pre-trial restraining orders issued in criminal forfeiture cases, some courts have recognized constitutional constraints on the pre-trial seizure of property that the defendant may need to use to pay attorneys' fees. As discussed in [E] below, the Supreme Court has held that the government may obtain forfeiture of property needed for attorneys' fees. A different issue arises, however, when the government seeks to obtain control over such property even before forfeiture has been ordered. The Supreme Court in one case specifically declined to decide whether a hearing is required under the Due Process Clause before a court may impose a pre-trial seizure order in such circumstances.[130] On remand in that case, however, the Second Circuit held that a criminal defendant may not be deprived of funds needed to *hire counsel* unless a hearing has already been provided.[131]

Further, a defendant's constitutional rights may compel a pre-trial hearing even when such a hearing requires disclosure of grand jury materials. The D.C. Circuit in *United States v. E-Gold, Ltd.*,[132] for example, stated "while we recognize the weightiness of the government's concern in grand jury secrecy, we find nothing that outweighs the defendant's constitutional rights to due process and to counsel under the Fifth and Sixth Amendments." The court thus found that "defendants have a

---

[125]   *Id.* One way to preserve the court's jurisdiction would be to post notice on the property and leave process with the occupant.

[126]   *Id.* at 62.

[127]   *Id.*

[128]   18 U.S.C. § 985 ("Civil forfeiture of real property").

[129]   *See* 21 U.S.C. § 853(e)(1)(B).

[130]   United States v. Monsanto, 491 U.S. 600, 615 n.10 (1989).

[131]   United States v. Monsanto, 924 F.2d 1186, 1196–98 (2d Cir. 1991) (*en banc*). Other courts have held likewise. *See* Argust, et al., *supra* note 64, at 998 n.275 (listing cases).

[132]   521 F.3d 411, 419 (D.C. Cir. 2008).

right to an adversary post-restraint, pretrial hearing for the purpose of establishing whether there was probable cause 'as to the defendant[s'] guilt and the forfeitability of the specified assets' needed for a meaningful exercise of their rights to counsel."[133]

[B] Substantive Due Process — Innocent Owners

As discussed above,[134] federal civil forfeiture statutes now contain a uniform innocent owner defense. Such a defense is not constitutionally required, however, and the federal government and the states are free to omit such defenses from their forfeiture statutes. In *Bennis v. Michigan*,[135] the petitioner's husband was arrested for engaging in sexual acts with a prostitute in his car. After his conviction, the state sued to have the car abated as a public nuisance. Petitioner claimed that she had been deprived of due process because she was not permitted to contest the abatement by showing that she was unaware of her husband's illegal acts.[136]

In response, the Court noted that "a long and unbroken line of cases holds that an owner's interest in property may be forfeited by reason of the use to which the property is put *even though* the owner did not know that it was to be put to such use."[137] The innocent owner defense is now provided by federal statute, and under many state statutes.[138] The availability of this defense is not, however, constitutionally mandated by the Due Process Clause.

[C] The Eighth Amendment's Excessive Fines Clause

[1] Criminal Forfeitures

In two cases, the Supreme Court has addressed whether the Eighth Amendment's Excessive Fines Clause applies to criminal forfeitures. First, in *Alexander v. United States*,[139] the Court held that the clause applies to RICO forfeitures under § 1963. Later, in *United States v. Bajakajian*,[140] the Supreme Court held that the Eighth Amendment applies to criminal forfeitures under § 982, which applies to financial and other crimes.

In addition, the Court in *Bajakajian* set forth the standard for determining when a criminal forfeiture violates the Excessive Fines Clause. In *Bajakajian*, the respondent had attempted to leave the country without reporting, as required by

---

[133] *Id.* (citing *Monsanto*, 924 F.2d at 1195).

[134] *See* § 22.02[D], *supra*.

[135] 516 U.S. 442 (1996).

[136] *Id.* at 446.

[137] *Id.*

[138] *See* § 22.02[D][4], *supra*.

[139] 509 U.S. 544 (1993).

[140] 524 U.S. 321, 324 (1998).

law, that he was carrying more than $10,000 in cash.[141] Under § 982(a)(1), the government sought criminal forfeiture of the entire $357,144 of cash he was carrying.[142] The district court concluded that full forfeiture would have been "grossly disproportionate" to the underlying offense, and ordered forfeiture of only $15,000.[143] This decision was affirmed by the Court of Appeals.

In its analysis of the Excessive Fines Clause issue, the Supreme Court stated that a "fine" is a "payment to a sovereign as punishment for some offense."[144] Forfeitures, as payments in kind, are "fines" if they are imposed as punishment for an offense.[145] The Court concluded that forfeiture of the currency constituted punishment, and was thus considered to be a fine within the meaning of the Excessive Fines Clause.[146]

Having determined that the Excessive Fines Clause applies, the Court then set forth the standard for applying that clause to forfeitures. The Court began with the principle of proportionality, *i.e.*, the "forfeiture must bear some relationship to the gravity of the offense that it is designed to punish."[147] Ultimately, in accordance with this principle, the Court held that a punitive forfeiture will be deemed constitutionally excessive, and therefore unconstitutional, when that forfeiture "is grossly disproportional to the gravity of a defendant's offense."[148] Proportionality, the Court said, is to be determined by comparing the gravity of the crime to the amount of forfeiture.

Applying this rule to the facts, the Court found that the forfeiture was excessive. The Court looked at a number of factors in reaching this conclusion: Bajakajian's money was not itself derived from wrongdoing; Bajakajian was guilty merely of violating a reporting statute; the sentence for the reporting violation was not severe; and there was no financial loss to the government from the failure to report. Thus, on the facts of the case, $357,144 was an excessive forfeiture.[149] It remains for lower courts to determine exactly how the *Bajakajian* test is to be applied to differing sets of facts.[150]

In an opinion by Justice Kennedy, four justices dissented. They agreed that "gross disproportionality" might well be the appropriate test.[151] The dissent

---

[141] *Id.* at 324. The defendant was charged with violating 31 U.S.C. §§ 5316(a)(1)(A) & 5322(a).

[142] 524 U.S. at 324. *See* 18 U.S.C. § 982(a)(1) ("The court, in imposing sentence on a person convicted of an offense in violation of section . . . 5316 . . . shall order that the person forfeit . . . any property, real or personal, involved in such offense.").

[143] 524 U.S. at 326.

[144] *Id.* at 327, *quoting* Browning-Ferris Industries v. Kelco Disposal, Inc., 492 U.S. 257, 265 (1989).

[145] 424 U.S. at 328.

[146] *Id.*

[147] *Id.* at 334.

[148] *Id.*

[149] *Id.* at 337–40.

[150] In *Bajakajian* itself, the trial court ordered a forfeiture of $15,000, which the Ninth Circuit affirmed. For procedural reasons, the validity of the $15,000 forfeiture was not before the Court. *See id.* at 326–27.

[151] *Id.* at 348 (Kennedy, J., dissenting).

concluded, however, that the Court had misapplied its own test. With regard to the seriousness of the wrongdoing, the dissent stated that "[t]he crime of smuggling or failing to report cash is more serious than the Court is willing to acknowledge. The drug trade, money laundering, and tax evasion all depend in part on smuggled and unreported cash."[152]

Congress responded to the *Bajakajian* decision by enacting the "cash smuggling" statute.[153] This statute makes it criminal to conceal more than $10,000 in cash and to transport or attempt to transport that cash in or out of the country, with the intent to evade the currency reporting requirements. The statute further provides for criminal and civil forfeiture of all property "involved in" or "traceable to" the crime, and contains language intended to reverse the result in *Bajakajian*.[154] In addition, the statutory preamble states that carrying and failing to report the currency "is the equivalent of, and creates the same harm as, the smuggling of goods." Thus, Congress intended that all the cash used in violating this statute be forfeitable, and not subject to excessive fines analysis. District courts, however, have applied the Excessive Fines Clause to forfeitures under this statute.[155]

[2] Civil Forfeiture

In *Austin v. United States*,[156] the Supreme Court held that civil forfeitures are subject to the Eighth Amendment's Excessive Fines Clause. In that case, the defendant pled guilty to one count of possessing cocaine with intent to distribute. The defendant's auto body shop and mobile home had been used to consummate the transaction. The government therefore sought to have those properties forfeited.[157] The Supreme Court granted certiorari to decide whether the Eighth Amendment's Excessive Fines Clause applies to *in rem* forfeitures. The government argued that only *criminal* punishments were subject to that clause. The Court noted that, while some constitutional amendments had been expressly limited to criminal actions, no such limitation had been imposed on the Eighth Amendment.[158] It also stated that the Excessive Fines Clause is directed toward limiting the "Government's power to extract payments, whether in cash or in kind, '*as punishment* for some offense.' "[159]

---

[152] *Id.* at 351.

[153] 31 U.S.C. § 5332, "Bulk Cash Smuggling into or out of the United States." This law was enacted as part of the "USA PATRIOT Act" of 2001.

[154] The statute provides that "any currency or other monetary instrument that is concealed or intended to be concealed in violation of . . . shall be considered property involved in the offense." 31 U.S.C. § 5332.

[155] *See* United States v. $127,856 in United States Currency, 394 F. Supp. 2d 687, 696 (D. Virgin Islands 2005) ("It is clear that the constitutionally appropriate proportional amount of the forfeiture is far, far less than the full $120,856.00 [defendant] attempted to bring in. The appropriate proportional amount would be no more than $7,500"); United States v. $293,316 in United States Currency, 349 F. Supp. 2d 638 (E.D.N.Y. 2004) (Weinstein, J.) (reducing forfeiture under § 5332 from $515,583 to $48,150 on facts similar to those presented in *Bajakajian*, and rejecting the government's argument that § 5332 compels forfeiture of the entire amount).

[156] 509 U.S. 602 (1993).

[157] *Id.* at 604–05.

[158] *Id.* at 607–09.

[159] *Id.* at 609–10, *citing* Browning-Ferris Industries v. Kelco Disposal, Inc., 492 U.S. 257, 265 (1989).

Thus, it is not the civil or criminal nature of the forfeiture that subjects it to the Excessive Fines Clause. Rather, the controlling question is whether the forfeiture itself constitutes punishment.[160] The Court in *Austin* held that civil forfeitures are partly designed to punish. Therefore, civil forfeiture is "payment to a sovereign as punishment for some offense, and, as such, [it] is subject to the limitations of the Eighth Amendment's Excessive Fines Clause."[161]

It is now clear that *Bajakajian*'s gross disproportionality test applies to civil forfeitures as well as criminal forfeitures. That test, as applied to civil forfeitures, has been codified under the Civil Asset Forfeiture Reform Act of 2000.[162]

[D] Double Jeopardy

In *United States v. Ursery*,[163] the Supreme Court held that civil forfeitures are not subject to the Double Jeopardy Clause because they are not punishment for an offense. On its face, this holding is arguably inconsistent with the *Austin* decision. In *Ursery*, however, the Court distinguished the definition of punishment under the Excessive Fines Clause and under the Double Jeopardy Clause.

In the cases before the Court in *Ursery*, the Sixth and Ninth Circuit Courts of Appeals had both held that it would violate the Double Jeopardy Clause to subject a defendant both to (1) punishment at a criminal trial, and (2) civil forfeiture of property arising out of the same matter. In one case, the government sought civil forfeiture of the defendant's house on the grounds that it was used to facilitate drug sales. The government later indicted the home owner for narcotics violations, and he was convicted. The Sixth Circuit reversed the conviction on grounds that the defendant had already been "punished" in the civil forfeiture proceeding against his property, and thus could not be subjected to criminal prosecution arising out of the same offense.[164]

In the second case, two defendants had been convicted for violating drug and money laundering statutes.[165] In a related civil forfeiture proceeding occurring after their conviction, the district court granted summary judgment in favor of the government.[166] The Ninth Circuit reversed the forfeiture action under the Double Jeopardy Clause.[167] For purposes of review, the Supreme Court consolidated the two cases.

The Court in *Ursery* first noted that for many years the government has been permitted to seek both *in rem* civil forfeiture and criminal prosecution, even when

---

[160] 509 U.S. at 610.

[161] *Id.* at 622, *citing* Browning-Ferris, 492 U.S. at 265 (1989).

[162] 18 U.S.C. § 983(g).

[163] 518 U.S. 267 (1996).

[164] *Id.* at 271.

[165] 21 U.S.C. § 846; 18 U.S.C. §§ 371, 1956.

[166] 518 U.S. at 272.

[167] *Id.*

based on the same underlying offense.[168] Furthermore, a long line of cases had conclusively established that the Double Jeopardy Clause is not applicable to civil forfeitures because such actions "do not impose punishment."[169] The Court noted that a sharp distinction was drawn "between *in rem* civil *forfeitures* and in *personam* civil *penalties* such as fines: Though the latter could, in some circumstances, be punitive, the former could not."[170]

The Court devoted considerable analysis to *Austin*, but ultimately stated that "*Austin* was decided solely under the Excessive Fines Clause of the Eighth Amendment, a constitutional provision which we never have understood as parallel to, or even related to, the Double Jeopardy Clause of the Fifth Amendment."[171] The Court further stated that even though civil forfeitures are subject to the Excessive Fines Clause, it "does not mean . . . that those forfeitures are so punitive as to constitute punishment for the purposes of double jeopardy."[172] Thus, civil forfeitures do not constitute punishment for purposes of the Double Jeopardy Clause.

[E] Attorney's Fees

In *United States v. Monsanto*,[173] the Supreme Court held that assets subject to forfeiture under § 853 could be restrained regardless of whether a defendant intended to use them to pay attorney's fees. The indictment in that case alleged that the respondent acquired assets from narcotics transactions, and that such assets were subject to forfeiture under 21 U.S.C. § 853. A restraining order was subsequently issued and the assets were frozen.

On appeal, the defendants argued that assets needed for attorney's fees are not subject to forfeiture because the statute fails to expressly include such property. The Court rejected the argument, noting that § 853 requires forfeiture of "any property" that is derived from the proceeds of the illegal offense.[174] The Court further stated that the statute's plain meaning requires that "all assets falling within its scope . . . be forfeited upon conviction, with no exception existing for the assets used to pay attorney's fees — or anything else, for that matter."[175] According to the Court, the fact that the statute was able to reach many types of assets, including those intended for attorney's fees, was simply evidence of the breadth of the statute.[176] Thus, the Court refused to recognize an exception for property that was to be used to pay attorney's fees.[177]

---

[168] *Id.* at 274.

[169] *Id.*

[170] *Id.* at 275, *citing* Waterloo Distilling Co. v. United States, 282 U.S. 577, 581 (1931).

[171] 518 U.S. at 286.

[172] *Id.* at 287.

[173] 491 U.S. 600 (1989).

[174] *Id.* at 607.

[175] *Id.* at 606.

[176] *Id.* at 609, *citing* Sedima, S.P.R.L. v. Imrex Co., 473 U.S. 479, 499 (1985).

[177] 491 U.S. at 613 ("Permitting a defendant to use assets for his private purposes that, under this

In *Monsanto*, the defendant also argued that § 853 interfered with his Sixth Amendment right to counsel of choice. The crux of this argument was that once the assets had been frozen he would not be able to hire counsel. That issue was resolved in *Caplin & Drysdale v. United States*,[178] a case decided the same day as *Monsanto*. The Court began by emphasizing the purpose of the Sixth Amendment — to guarantee adequate representation for defendants in criminal cases.[179] That provision, however, does not guarantee the defendant the right to hire counsel of choice; state-appointed counsel is sufficient. Thus, forfeitable assets may be restrained without violating a defendant's right to counsel; the Sixth Amendment only requires that the defendant be given adequate representation.

provision, will become the property of the United States if a conviction occurs cannot be sanctioned.").

[178] 491 U.S. 617 (1989).

[179] *Id.* at 624.

TABLE OF CASES

[References are to pages]

[References are to pages]

[References are to pages]

[References are to pages]

M

[References are to pages]

INDEX

[References are to sections.]

[References are to sections.]

[References are to sections.]

[References are to sections.]

[References are to sections.]

[References are to sections.]

[References are to sections.]

[References are to sections.]

[References are to sections.]

[References are to sections.]

[References are to sections.]

[References are to sections.]